ACCOUNTING INSTRUCTIONAL SYSTEM

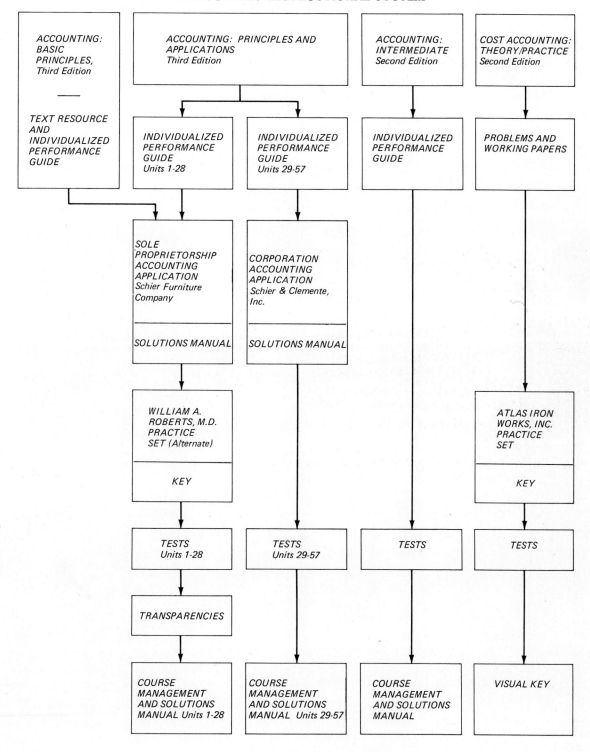

ACCOUNTING: BASIC PRINCIPLES, Third Edition
——
TEXT RESOURCE AND INDIVIDUALIZED PERFORMANCE GUIDE

ACCOUNTING: PRINCIPLES AND APPLICATIONS Third Edition

ACCOUNTING: INTERMEDIATE Second Edition

COST ACCOUNTING: THEORY/PRACTICE Second Edition

INDIVIDUALIZED PERFORMANCE GUIDE Units 1-28

INDIVIDUALIZED PERFORMANCE GUIDE Units 29-57

INDIVIDUALIZED PERFORMANCE GUIDE

PROBLEMS AND WORKING PAPERS

SOLE PROPRIETORSHIP ACCOUNTING APPLICATION Schier Furniture Company
——
SOLUTIONS MANUAL

CORPORATION ACCOUNTING APPLICATION Schier & Clemente, Inc.
——
SOLUTIONS MANUAL

WILLIAM A. ROBERTS, M.D. PRACTICE SET (Alternate)
——
KEY

ATLAS IRON WORKS, INC. PRACTICE SET
——
KEY

TESTS Units 1-28

TESTS Units 29-57

TESTS

TESTS

TRANSPARENCIES

COURSE MANAGEMENT AND SOLUTIONS MANUAL Units 1-28

COURSE MANAGEMENT AND SOLUTIONS MANUAL Units 29-57

COURSE MANAGEMENT AND SOLUTIONS MANUAL

VISUAL KEY

ACCOUNTING: BASIC THIRD EDITION PRINCIPLES

Horace R. Brock, Ph.D., C.P.A.
Professor of Accounting
College of Business Administration
North Texas State University

Charles E. Palmer, D.C.S. (hon.), C.P.A.
Executive Director
State Board for Technical and Comprehensive Education
Columbia, South Carolina

Fred C. Archer, Ph.D.
Professor of Accounting
Shippensburg State College, Pennsylvania

McGraw-Hill Book Company

New York	Kuala Lumpur	Panama
St. Louis	London	Rio de Janeiro
San Francisco	Mexico	Singapore
Düsseldorf	Montreal	Sydney
Johannesburg	New Delhi	Toronto

Library of Congress Cataloging in Publication Data

Brock, Horace R.
    Accounting: basic principles.

    Consists of the first 28 units of the authors' Accounting: principles and
applications, 3d ed.
        1. Accounting.   I. Palmer, Charles Earl, 1919– joint author. II. Archer,
Fred Coleman, 1915– joint author. III. Title.
HF5635. B8542   1974   657   73-19756
ISBN   0-07-008024-0

ACCOUNTING: BASIC PRINCIPLES, THIRD EDITION

Formerly published under the title
College Accounting—Theory/Practice, Parts One and Two

    234567890 MUBP 7987654

The editors for this book were Edward E. Byers, Mary Drouin, and Cynthia
Newby, the designer was Marsha Cohen, and its production was super-
vised by Laurence Charnow. It was set in Melior by York Graphic
Services, Inc.
It was printed by The Murray Printing Company and bound by The Book
Press, Inc.

Preface

A college accounting instructional system should serve the career objectives of all students requiring an understanding of accounting. Its components should satisfy the learning needs of students preparing for professional accounting careers as well as those students preparing for other business and professional pursuits. A complete system should contain performance objectives, reading resources, student application materials (including integrated practice), student self-checks, progress evaluations, and course management guides.

Instructors should be able to customize their accounting offerings by matching instructional components with the abilities of individual students and with the levels of accomplishment which delineate different career objectives. In preparing the third edition of *Accounting: Basic Principles,* the authors have created an instructional system that meets these criteria.

INSTRUCTIONAL SYSTEM

Accounting: Basic Principles. This student resource is intended for use in intensive, self-contained, post-secondary accounting courses which require less than one year to complete. Attention is given to the procedural aspects of accounting. The student is shown how to recognize the accounting elements involved in a transaction before he is expected to record them. The accounting service cycle is presented in the first five units, the service-trading cycle by the end of Unit 16, and the accrual-basis trading cycle by the end of Unit 28. Payroll, internal control, payables, receivables, inventory, and property taxes are also thoroughly explored.

Individualized Performance Guide. The traditional workbook has been superseded by an individualized performance guide that permits each student to pursue a program of independent study at his own pace. Performance objectives tell the student what he should know and be able to do after completing each unit. Reading assignments direct the student to the appropriate section in the resource text. Self-checks of reading comprehension help the student measure his mastery of each reading assignment (a self-check key is provided in the guide). A wide range of problems permit the student to demonstrate his ability to apply accounting principles successfully. Working papers needed to solve the problems are also provided in the guide.

Accounting Application. A realistic accounting application is provided. This application centers on a sole proprietorship for a one-month period and requires the student to maintain a set of ledgers and other records of the transactions that occur. Year-end adjustments, closing entries, and preparation of financial statements are included.

A cash-basis practice set is also available for medical secretaries or paramedical trainees.

Transparencies. A volume of 51 class-tested instructional transparencies has been developed. These transparencies enhance the presentation of accounting concepts relating to the service cycle by making the analysis of transactions more easily understood.

Tests. A set of tests is provided free of charge to instructors who adopt the accounting program. Each test contains a selection of objective exercises that permit valuable measures of student progress.

Course Management and Solution Manual. Extensive guidance and direction are provided for the instructor through the instructional aids and visual solutions contained in this manual. In addition, the instructor's manual contains specific teaching techniques; course enrichment suggestions; unit teaching hints and unit exercises and solutions; testing, grading, and assignment tips; check answers for the problems; course schedules; visual solutions; and transparency masters. These materials are all packaged in a three-ring binder and are provided free of charge to instructors using this accounting instructional system.

SPECIAL FEATURES

A number of teaching-learning features are built into the resource texts for the purpose of improving instructional efficiency.

- The *accounting principles* introduced are those endorsed by the Accounting Principles Board of the American Institute of Certified Public Accountants, Inc. (AICPA).

- *Emphasis* throughout the text is on the accounting process. The unit organization and instructional cycling help the student recognize the significant accounting elements involved in business transactions and how they fit together into the development of complete and realistic systems of accounts. In an effort to ensure a balance of coverage, the authors have provided two special summary sections at the end of each unit: one reviewing the principles and procedures presented in the unit, and the other examining the managerial implications of these principles and procedures.

- A section called "Application of Principles" also appears at the end of each unit. Here the student is given problems correlated with the performance objectives and with the important principles and procedures introduced in the particular unit. The "Managerial Check-Ups" are a new end-of-unit feature that requires the student to relate new learning to management needs and problems. Alternate problems for every unit are provided at the end of the text, and additional short unit exercises are also supplied in the *Course Management and Solutions Manual*. Integrated practical applications follow Units 5, 12, 15, and 28 so that the student can pull together the various skills he or she has developed in the earlier units.

Model accounting papers have been brought together in appendix form for the student's easy reference. Included in this section are models of an income statement, balance sheet, general journal, general ledger account, trial balance, worksheet, postclosing trial balance, cash receipts journal, cash disbursements journal, petty cash analysis sheet, sales journal, accounts receivable and accounts payable ledger accounts.

ADVANCED PROGRAM

Advanced components of this comprehensive accounting instructional system are available and include *Accounting: Intermediate,* Second Edition, and *Cost Accounting: Theory/Practice,* Second Edition. Used consecutively or selectively, this array of instructional materials fits a wide range of curriculum needs and permits a smooth transition from one area of accounting concentration to another.

Horace R. Brock
Charles E. Palmer
Fred C. Archer

Contents

gross pay required by law. Deductions from gross pay not required by law. Determination of gross pay (salaried workers). Deductions from gross pay. Recording gross pay and deductions (hourly workers). Payroll register. The payroll entry. Paying the payroll. Recording gross pay and deductions (salaried workers). Individual earnings records. Completing January payrolls. Proving the individual earnings records. Recording liability for unpaid wages.

Monthly deposit of FICA taxes and income tax withheld. Employer's quarterly federal tax return. Withholding tax statements to employees. Annual reconciliation of tax withheld. Unemployment insurance. State unemployment tax returns (quarterly). Federal unemployment tax return. Workmen's compensation insurance.

General principles of internal control. Internal control over cash receipts. Control of cash receipts at Ashton & Barker. The daily routine. The cash receipts journal. Internal control over cash disbursements. The disbursement voucher. Preparing and approving the voucher. The voucher register. Posting from the voucher register. The check register. Paying an invoice less discount. Posting from the check register. Proving the accounts payable balance. Transactions requiring special treatment. Recording purchases discounts lost. Other cash control procedures.

Notes payable. Noninterest-bearing note given in purchase of an asset. Interest. Interest-bearing note given in purchase of an asset. Partial payment of a note payable. Renewing a note payable. Discounting a note payable at the bank. Notes payable register. Notes payable and interest expense on the statements.

ACCOUNTING AND YOUR FUTURE

Accounting is one of the fastest-growing employment fields in America today, and the job outlook for good accountants seems bright for many years to come. The opportunities are the result of tremendous industrial expansion in all parts of the country. Every time a new business is formed or another expands, the call goes out for accountants to help managers keep track of a firm's operations.

WHAT THE ACCOUNTANT DOES

The duties and responsibilities of an accountant naturally vary somewhat in different firms. Here are some of the things an accountant might do.

Designs the system

The accountant's work begins with the initial planning of a business. A specialist called a *systems accountant* may be asked to design a financial recording and reporting system to meet the special needs of the firm. In designing such a system, the accountant requires a broad knowledge of the activities and problems of the industry as a whole and a detailed understanding of the organization and operations of the individual business.

Records transactions

With the very first business transaction, the accountant assumes the role of business historian. Every transaction must be analyzed, classified, and recorded for future reference. Forms and procedures that have been built into the system make much of this work simply a matter of routine. In addition, a great deal of the work may be done on various accounting machines. However, the judgment and supervision of capable accountants are still necessary to see that the recording system works properly.

Renders periodic reports

Many accountants prepare reports for the purpose of internal management. Some of these are rendered daily; others weekly, monthly, or at longer intervals. Reports may also be furnished to owners, investors, government agencies, and other interested parties. Some reports show results of operations; others show where the firm stands financially on a particular date.

Keeps track of costs

One accounting specialist, the *cost accountant*, devises special records and methods to assemble detailed facts about the costs of doing business, especially in connection with manufacturing and selling operations. Many of the reports prepared by accountants are cost statements that are designed to facilitate control of business operations for maximum efficiency.

Makes special reports

New management problems or proposals for changes in plans usually involve some questions of finance. Often information is needed that is not available in the regular reports. It is the accountant who prepares the special reports that set forth this additional information.

Completes tax returns

Businesses are required to supply tax returns and other reports to government agencies. Of these, the income tax return is perhaps the best known. *Tax accountants* prepare tax returns and give advice about tax matters to businesses.

Audits the books

Business books and records need to be reviewed periodically to verify their accuracy and to obtain an impartial appraisal of the results of the business operation. This work is done for small and large businesses by independent *public accountants*. Larger businesses may also have internal auditors who review and appraise the accounting system and records, and who study operations in order to provide protective advisory service to management.

Advises management

The accountant is in a strategic position to know a great deal about all phases of business and to come into contact with executives at all levels. Because accountants are not directly involved in operations, they can qualify as unbiased observers and are frequently asked for advice and suggestions by top management.

Helps plan the budget

A budget is both a planning device and a control tool. In planning business activities, management forecasts sales and other revenues and then estimates production costs and operating expenses required to carry out the program. The accountant provides valuable facts about past experience that serve as guides to what may be expected in the future. The accountant projects the estimates of future income and expenses and prepares estimated financial statements as they would appear if the plans were carried out successfully. During the following period, the accountant compares actual results against previous estimates. These reports present a picture of performance compared with the plan and thus help management to control operations.

THE FIELDS OF ACCOUNTING

Four broad fields of activity are open to persons who have been trained in accounting and related areas.

Private accounting

Accountants may become salaried employees of a business organization. They perform or supervise the work of recording business transactions and preparing analyses, reports, and statements for management and other interested parties. They also prepare tax returns and reports required by governmental agencies. Similar work is performed by accountants employed by nonprofit and service organizations, such as schools, hospitals, welfare agencies, and clubs. A listing of typical job titles and grades appears at the end of this introduction. Salaries are most attractive and move higher and higher every year.

Public accounting

Accountants may offer their services on a fee basis to the general public. In this capacity, they set up accounting systems, provide management counseling service, audit accounts, express an opinion on financial statements, and prepare tax returns. By passing a strict examination, which is uniform in all states, and by meeting additional requirements set by their own states, they may become *certified public accountants*. As beginners in the field of public accounting, they may work as members of the staff of an established local practitioner or of a large national accounting firm with offices in many cities. They may work up to partnerships in the organization, or decide to go into private practice.

Government accounting

Accountants may work for governmental agencies, keeping the records and preparing the reports required by the agency management or the law under which the agency operates. Agencies of city and state governments and of the federal government employ accountants for these purposes.

The Internal Revenue Service employs many accountants to analyze and investigate the records of persons and businesses subject to income and other taxes. The General Accounting Office, an arm of Congress, audits governmental agencies and operations in much the same way that public accountants audit private business clients.

Teaching

Accounting teachers are employed to provide instruction in public and private high schools, colleges, and universities. In addition to teaching, some serve as consultants or carry on a limited amount of accounting and tax practice. Conversely, many persons employed in full-time public or private accounting positions teach part time in evening schools and adult education centers.

ACCOUNTING AS PREPARATION FOR MANAGEMENT

A thorough knowledge of accounting techniques and processes is essential for every person who aspires to a responsible position in supervision or management of business operations. This background enables the manager to comprehend, interpret, and utilize more effectively the data supplied by accountants who assist and advise the business. The administrator's accounting knowledge also allows anticipation of needs for new information, for system revision, and for more refined devices for financial control. Thus the administrator is able to make recommendations to the accounting specialists, to evaluate their proposals, and to play a vital role in the development and installation of improved procedures. Moreover, the manager's training in accounting provides a special understanding of figures and financial relationships that is vital to sound judgment in decision making.

TYPICAL ACCOUNTING POSITIONS

ACCOUNTANT I

This is a beginning professional-level position distinguished by the variety of assignments; the limited rate and scope of development expected of the employee, and the existence, implicit or explicit, of a planned training program designed to give the beginning accountant practical experience in the operations of an established accounting system. The accountant learns to apply the principles, theories, and concepts of accounting to a particular accounting system. Many of the assignments will include examining standard accounting documents for completeness, internal accuracy, and conformance with specific accounting requirements; tracing and reconciling records of financial transactions; and preparing detailed statements and schedules for reports.

ACCOUNTANT II

At this continuing developmental level the professional accountant makes practical applications of technical accounting practices and concepts beyond the mere application of detailed rules and instructions. Assignments are designed to expand practical experience and to develop professional judgment in the application of basic accounting techniques to simple professional problems. The accountant prepares routine working papers, schedules, exhibits, and summaries that indicate the extent of the examination and develop and support any findings and recommendations.

ACCOUNTANT III

The primary responsibility of most positions at this level is to ensure that the day-to-day operations of the segment or system are carried out in accordance with accounting principles and the policies and objectives of the accounting system. Within limits of delegated responsibility, accountants make daily decisions concerning the accounting treatment of financial transactions. They are expected to recommend solutions of complex problems and propose changes in the accounting system, but they have no authority to effectuate these solutions or changes. Solutions are derived from their own knowledge of the application of well-established principles and practices.

ACCOUNTANT IV

At this level, compared with level III, the technical accounting problems are more difficult and a greater degree of coordination among more numerous types of accounting records and operations is essential. The accountant makes day-to-day decisions concerning the accounting treatment of financial transactions. The accountant is expected to recommend solutions of complex problems beyond the scope of his or her responsibility and to propose changes in the accounting system but has no authority to act independently on these problems.

ACCOUNTANT V

In this case, the accountant performs professional operating or cost accounting work requiring the application of accounting principles and practices to the solution of very difficult problems for which no clear precedents exist, or to the development or extension of theories and practices to problems that have not been previously treated. Also at this level are positions having more than average responsibility because of the nature, magnitude, or impact of the assigned work. In addition to ensuring that the system or segment is operated as intended, the accountant is deeply involved in the fundamental and complex technical and managerial problems.

Salaries for accountants have been rising steadily in the last decade and are expected to continue upward. The following graph shows typical beginning salaries for accounting graduates.*

Trend in beginning jobs for accounting graduates

Monthly salary

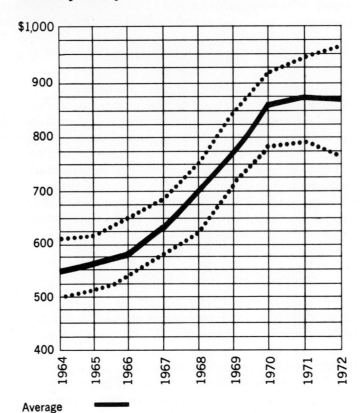

Average ▬▬▬

80% range • • • • • •
(excluding the top 10% and bottom 10% as unusual)

* Reprinted with permission from *We Are Involved,* courtesy of the American Institute of Certified Public Accountants.

ACCOUNTING: BASIC PRINCIPLES

PART 1
ACCOUNTING CYCLE—
SERVICE BUSINESS

1 ANALYZING BUSINESS TRANSACTIONS; THE BASIC FINANCIAL STATEMENTS

The accountant occupies a vital position in today's business. He or she is the one who helps an owner or manager to make countless important decisions, and making right decisions at the right time is the key to successful business operations.

In order for the manager to make these right decisions, full and accurate financial information about the business must be readily available. With an efficient accounting system in operation and an experienced accountant keeping track of the firm's finances, the manager can get prompt answers to such questions as . . .

- What is our cash position today?
- What is the cost of a unit of product?
- What is the amount owed to creditors?
- How much profit have we made?

. . . or any of a thousand other important questions. The accountant provides the facts upon which the manager bases vital decisions.

The manager is not the only person who needs information that is contained in the accounting records. The owners of the business want to know whether they have made profitable investments. Branch managers, department heads, and supervisors need various records and reports to operate their units efficiently. The government wants data for tax and license purposes. Banks and suppliers want figures to help them decide about extending credit. The accountant provides this information by systematically recording business dealings or transactions and preparing financial reports.

However, *recording* and *reporting* financial affairs are only two phases of accounting. In addition, the accountant *interprets* or explains the meaning of the financial reports to management, *gives advice* about technical problems, and *assists in the financial planning* of future operations.

Long before there can be any recording or reporting or interpreting, the accountant has to analyze every business transaction. A business transaction may consist of a purchase, a sale, a receipt or payment of cash, or any other financial happening. The effects of each transaction have to be studied in order to know what to record and where to record it.

Since the accounting process actually begins with an analysis of the transactions of a business, this phase is the natural starting point for a study of accounting. Let us see how the accountant would analyze the transactions of the Carter Cleaning Shop, a dry-cleaning shop owned by A. L. Carter and operated by T. O. Jones, the manager.

STARTING A NEW BUSINESS

Carter obtains the funds to launch the business by withdrawing $6,000 from his personal savings bank account. He deposits the money in a new bank account in the name of the firm, the Carter Cleaning Shop. The new bank account will help Carter keep his financial interest in his business separate from his personal funds. The establishment of this bank account on November 26, 19X1 is the first transaction of the new firm.

The accountant who is helping Carter prepare a set of books for his business explains that there are two important financial facts to be recorded at this time:

(a) The business has $6,000 worth of property in the form of cash, which is on deposit in the bank.
(b) Carter has a $6,000 financial interest in the business, called his *equity* or investment.

The firm's position at this time may be expressed in the form of a simple equation as follows.

CARTER CLEANING SHOP

PROPERTY	=	FINANCIAL INTEREST
(a) Cash $6,000	=	(b) Carter Investment $6,000

The equation *property = financial interest* actually reflects the basic fact that in a free enterprise system all property is owned by someone. In this case, Carter supplied the property (cash); hence, he owns the business.

The manager, Jones, sees that his first problem is to get the shop ready for business operations, which are to begin on December 1, 19X1. He buys $2,000 worth of cleaning equipment, paying for it with money in the form of a check drawn against the firm's bank account. Again, the accountant analyzes the transaction to see what has to be recorded. He quickly identifies the following essential elements:

(c) $2,000 worth of new property in the form of equipment has been acquired.
(d) $2,000 of the firm's cash has been paid out.

Here is the transaction as the accountant sees it.

CARTER CLEANING SHOP

		PROPERTY		=	FINANCIAL INTEREST
		Cash +	Equipment	=	Carter Investment
Initial Investment	(a)	$6,000		=	(b) $6,000
(c) New property acquired			$2,000		
(d) Cash paid out		−2,000			
New balances		$4,000 +	$2,000	=	$6,000

Even though there is a change in the form of some of the firm's property (cash to equipment), the resulting equation shows that the total value of the property remains the same. Carter's financial interest (or equity) also remains unchanged. Again, *property = financial interest* (Carter Investment), because Carter supplied all the funds involved.

Note carefully that the accountant is recording the financial affairs of the *business entity*, the cleaning shop. The personal assets of Carter, such as his personal bank account, home, furniture, or automobile, should be kept separate from business assets and not included in the property of the cleaning shop.

Jones, the manager, also buys a counter and several desks and chairs for the shop, at a cost of $1,000, from Knight, Inc. Knight agrees to allow the Carter Cleaning Shop 30 days in which to pay the bill. This arrangement is sometimes called a *charge account* or *open account* credit. Amounts that

the company is obliged to pay in the future are known as *accounts payable.*
This time the accountant's analysis reveals these basic elements:

(e) $1,000 worth of new property in the form of equipment has been acquired.

(f) The firm owes $1,000 to Knight, Inc.

This increase in equipment is made without an immediate cash payment because the supplier is willing to accept a claim against the Carter Cleaning Shop's property until the bill is paid. There are now two different financial interests or claims against the firm's property—the supplier's claim (Accounts Payable), and the owner's claim (Carter Investment).

Here is how the accountant analyzes the transaction.

CARTER CLEANING SHOP

	PROPERTY			=	FINANCIAL INTERESTS		
	Cash	+	Equipment	=	Accounts Payable	+	Carter Investment
Previous balances	$4,000	+	$2,000	=		+	$6,000
(e) New property acquired		+	1,000				
(f) Owed to Knight, Inc.					+$1,000		
New balances	$4,000	+	$3,000	=	$1,000	+	$6,000

Notice that when property values and financial interests increase or decrease, the sum of the items on one side of the equation still equals that on the other side. This happens because financial interests or claims against business property arise as soon as the property is acquired. The supplier's or creditor's claim lasts until the obligation is settled. The owner's claim lasts as long as he continues to own the business. After the creditors are paid, the owner has sole claim or legal right to all property owned by the business.

PAYING A CREDITOR

If Carter's manager decides to pay $700 to Knight, Inc., to be applied against the firm's bill for $1,000, the effect of the payment on property values and claims may be analyzed as follows:

(g) $700 of the firm's cash is paid out.

(h) Knight's claim against the firm is reduced by $700.

The effect on the firm's property and on the financial interests is shown in equation form.

	Cash	+	Equipment	=	Accounts Payable	+	Carter Investment
			PROPERTY	=	FINANCIAL INTERESTS		
Previous balances	$4,000	+	$3,000	=	$1,000	+	$6,000
(g) Cash paid out	−700						
(h) Knight's claim reduced					−700		
New balances	$3,300	+	$3,000	=	$ 300	+	$6,000

PREPARING THE BALANCE SHEET

Accountants use a formal pattern and special accounting terms in making their reports. For instance, they refer to property owned by the business as the *assets* of the business and the debts or obligations of the business as *liabilities*. The owner's interest (Carter's investment) is called *proprietorship, net worth,* or *owner's equity*. The preference seems to be for the use of the term *owner's equity*. It is the term used throughout this book. The Carter accountant will report the status of the firm's assets, liabilities, and owner's equity on November 30, 19X1 (the day before operations actually commence) in a formal report called a *balance sheet*. Here is how Carter's balance sheet looks at this time.

CARTER CLEANING SHOP
Balance Sheet
November 30, 19X1

ASSETS		LIABILITIES AND OWNER'S EQUITY	
Cash	$3,300	*Liabilities*	
Equipment	3,000	Accounts Payable	$ 300
		Owner's Equity	
		Carter Investment	6,000
Total Assets	$6,300	*Total Liabilities and Owner's Equity*	$6,300

The accountant lists the assets on the left side of the balance sheet in a manner very similar to the previous illustrations, which showed property on the left side of the equation. Liabilities and owner's equity appear on the right side of the balance sheet—the same side as in the previous equations. There are several other important details about the form of the balance sheet:

1. The three-line heading of the balance sheet provides a place for: the firm's name (who), the title of the report (what), and the date on which the report is rendered (when). Every balance sheet heading must contain these three explanatory lines.

2. On this form of balance sheet, the total of the assets always appears on the same horizontal line as the total of the liabilities and owner's equity.
3. In presenting financial statements, dollar signs are generally used at the head of each column and with each total. Dollar signs are placed to the left of the numbers and on the same line.
4. Single lines are used to show that figures above are being added or subtracted. Double lines are used under the final figure in a column or section of a report. Lines should always be drawn with a ruler.

The balance sheet tells how much and what kind of property the business owns. This statement also shows the amount of accounts payable and the amount of the owner's investment in the firm before the Carter Cleaning Shop opens for business. Carter now has a complete picture of the financial position of the Carter Cleaning Shop as it is ready to open. His first balance sheet is a milepost from which all future progress can be measured.

THE FUNDAMENTAL ACCOUNTING EQUATION

The word "balance" in the title "balance sheet" has a very special meaning: it serves to emphasize that the sum of the figures on the left side equals the sum of the figures on the right side. Using accounting terms, the firm's assets, $6,300, are equal to the sum of the liabilities, $300, plus the owner's equity, $6,000. Expressed in equation form, this would be the result.

$$Assets = Liabilities + Owner's\ Equity$$
$$\$6,300 = \$300 + \$6,000$$

This relationship is called the *fundamental equation* in accounting. There are many uses for it in all acounting work. As a matter of fact, the entire process of analyzing, recording, and reporting business transactions is based on this fundamental equation.

EFFECTS OF INCOME AND EXPENSES

Shortly after the Carter Cleaning Shop opens for business on December 1, the first customer comes in with clothes to be dry-cleaned. Soon more customers follow. This begins a stream of income, or revenue, for the business, with a resulting increase in assets. *Income* is the inward flow of money or other assets (including claims to money, such as charge accounts) resulting from sales of goods or services, or from the use of money or property. Of an opposite nature (outward flow) are *expenses*, which include the costs of material, labor, supplies, and services used in an effort to produce income. Any excess of income over expenses will represent profits for Carter—and the chance to make attractive profits is the reason he invested in the Carter Cleaning Shop in the first place. The firm's accounting procedures will show the detailed results of all transactions involving income and expenses.

SELLING SERVICES FOR CASH

The cash receipts for dry-cleaning services rendered by the Carter Cleaning Shop during the month of December amount to $2,200. The accountant analyzes this fact in the following manner:

(i) $2,200 in cash was received by the business.
(j) The owner's equity has been increased by this inflow of assets. (Income always increases the owner's equity.)

Accountants prefer to keep the income figure separate from the owner's investment figure until the financial statements have been prepared. Therefore, the earning of income appears in equation form as follows.

CARTER CLEANING SHOP

	ASSETS			=	LIABILITIES	+		OWNER'S EQUITY		
	Cash	+	Equipment	=	Accounts Payable	+	Carter Investment	+	Income
Previous balances	$3,300	+	$3,000	=	$300	+	$6,000		
(i) Cash received	+2,200								
(j) Owner's equity increased									$2,200
New balances	$5,500	+	$3,000	=	$300	+	$6,000	+	$2,200

Keeping this record of income separate will help the accountant compute total income much more easily at the end of the month, when he will be trying to complete his financial reports in the shortest possible time.

SELLING SERVICES ON CREDIT

The Carter Cleaning Shop also performed $800 worth of cleaning services for charge account customers who were allowed to pay at the end of the month. Amounts owed by these customers are known as *accounts receivable*.

These accounts represent a new form of asset for the firm—claims for future collection from customers. Analysis by the accountant breaks the transaction down into these elements:

(k) A new asset—Accounts Receivable of $800—has been acquired.
(l) The owner's equity has been increased by the income of $800.

The firm's position now looks like this in equation form.

	ASSETS			= LIABILITIES + OWNER'S EQUITY		
	Cash +	Equipment +	Accounts Receivable	= Accounts Payable	+ Carter Invest- ment	+ Income
Previous balances	$5,500 +	$3,000		= $300	+ $6,000	+ $2,200
(k) New asset received			+ $800			
(l) Owner's equity increased by income						800
New balances	$5,500 +	$3,000 +	$800	= $300	+ $6,000	+ $3,000

COLLECTING RECEIVABLES

Near the end of the month, when customers have paid a total of $600 to apply on their accounts, the accountant recognizes the following changes:

(m) $600 in cash has been received.
(n) Accounts Receivable has been reduced by $600.

In turn, the collection affects the equation as follows.

	ASSETS			= LIABILITIES + OWNER'S EQUITY		
	Cash +	Equipment +	Accounts Receivable	= Accounts Payable	+ Carter Invest- ment	+ Income
Previous balances	$5,500 +	$3,000 +	$800	= $300	+ $6,000	+ $3,000
(m) Cash received	+600					
(n) Accounts Receivable reduced			−600			
New balances	$6,100 +	$3,000 +	$200	= $300	+ $6,000	+ $3,000

Observe that no income was recorded at this time. In this transaction there was merely a change in the type of assets (from accounts receivable to cash). Income was recorded when the sales on account were recorded (Entry l). Note also that the fundamental accounting equation, *assets equal liabilities plus owner's equity*, holds true, regardless of the changes in type and amount arising from individual transactions.

So far, Carter has done very well. His equity has been increased by sizable revenues. However, it costs money to keep a business running. When expenses arise, they will have the opposite effect from income—they will reduce Carter's equity.

Employees' Salaries

For example, when the firm pays $1,600 for employees' salaries for the month, the accountant analyzes the transaction as follows:

(o) Cash has been reduced by the payment of $1,600 to cover expenses.
(p) Carter's equity has been reduced by the $1,600 outflow of assets.

The accountant prefers to keep expense figures separate from the owner's investment and from income figures. The effect of the transaction is shown.

	ASSETS			=	LIA-BILITIES	+	OWNER'S EQUITY		
	Cash +	Equipment +	Accounts Receivable	=	Accounts Payable	+	Carter Investment	+ Income	− Expense
Previous balances	$6,100 +	$3,000 +	$200	=	$300	+ $6,000	+ $3,000		
(o) Cash reduced	−1,600								
(p) Owner's equity reduced by expense									− $1,600
New balances	$4,500 +	$3,000 +	$200	=	$300	+ $6,000	+ $3,000	− $1,600

The separate record of expenses is kept for the same reason as the separate record of income—to aid in the analysis of operations for the period.

Rent

Another typical expense is the payment of rent. When the Carter Cleaning Shop pays $700 to the landlord, the accountant analyzes the expenditure in the following terms:

(q) Cash has been reduced by $700.
(r) Carter's equity has been reduced by $700.

In turn, the equation reflects this payment as follows. Note that the expense items are added together to show the total reduction of equity resulting from incurring expenses ($2,300).

	ASSETS			=	LIA-BILITIES	+	OWNER'S EQUITY		
	Cash +	Equipment +	Accounts Receiv-able	=	Accounts Payable	+	Carter Invest-ment	+ Income	− Expense
Previous balances	$4,500 +	$3,000 +	$200	=	$300	+	$6,000	+ $3,000	− $1,600
(q) Cash reduced	−700								
(r) Owner's equity reduced by expense									700
New balances	$3,800 +	$3,000 +	$200	=	$300	+	$6,000	+ $3,000	− $2,300

Supplies Used

At the end of the month, Jones, the shop manager, pays $600 for supplies that were consumed in operations. The use of these supplies represents an additional cost of operation. The accountant analyzes it in this way:

(s) Cash has been reduced by $600.
(t) Carter's equity has been reduced $600 by the additional expense.

These changes are expressed in equation form like this.

	ASSETS			=	LIA-BILITIES	+	OWNER'S EQUITY		
	Cash +	Equipment +	Accounts Receiv-able	=	Accounts Payable	+	Carter Invest-ment	+ Income	− Expense
Previous balances	$3,800 +	$3,000 +	$200	=	$300	+	$6,000	+ $3,000	− $2,300
(s) Cash reduced	−600								
(t) Owner's equity reduced by expense									600
New balances	$3,200 +	$3,000 +	$200	=	$300	+	$6,000	+ $3,000	− $2,900

The balance sheet shows the financial condition of a business at a given time—that is, what it owns and owes, as well as the owner's equity. It does not, however, show the results of business operations, that is, what actually happened to bring about this financial condition. This is the job of another formal accounting report that is called a statement of profit and loss, a statement of income and expense, or simply an income statement. The short title, *income statement*, which is growing in popularity with accountants, is used throughout this book to identify this important report. Here is how the accountant presents the results of the first month of operations of the Carter Cleaning Shop on an income statement.

CARTER CLEANING SHOP
Income Statement
Month Ended December 31, 19X1

Income		
Cleaning Service		$3,000
Less Expenses		
Salaries	$1,600	
Rent	700	
Supplies Used	600	
Total Expenses		2,900
Net Profit for the Month		$ 100

Notice that the heading of the income statement requires three lines to present the "who," "what," and "when." The first line is used for the firm name (who). The second line gives the title of the report (what). The third line tells the period of time covered by the report (when). As to the "when," the exact period of operations must be given. In the illustration, it is clearly indicated that the income statement reports the results of operations for the single month of December.

The third line of a similar statement covering the three months of January, February, and March would properly read: "Three-Month Period Ended March 31, 19X1." The third line of a statement reporting the results of operations for a 12-month period beginning on January 1 and ending on December 31 of the same calendar year would properly read: "Year Ended December 31, 19X1." In those instances where the selected 12-month reporting period ends on a date other than December 31, the third line of the income statement would properly read: "Fiscal Year Ended June 30, 19X1," or "Fiscal Year Ended November 30, 19X1."

Also, note the correct use of ruled lines and the placement of dollar signs. The term *net profit* (or *net income*) for the period identifies what remains after the expenses are deducted from the total income.

Although the income statement by itself is meaningful to the business owner and other interested parties, it is even more meaningful when considered in relation to the assets and the equities utilized in earning the income. Therefore, the balance sheet is once again prepared to give the details of these assets and equities. The final totals in the fundamental accounting equation furnish the figures that are required for preparing the balance sheet on December 31, 19X1. (Profit is equal to income less expenses.)

ASSETS			= LIABILITIES +		OWNER'S EQUITY		
Cash	+ Equipment	+ Accounts Receivable	= Accounts Payable	+ Carter Investment	+ Income	− Expense
$3,200 +	$3,000	+ $200	= $300	+ $6,000	+ $3,000	− $2,900

The resulting balance sheet summarizes the assets, liabilities, and owner's equity as follows.

CARTER CLEANING SHOP
Balance Sheet
December 31,19X1

ASSETS		LIABILITIES AND OWNER'S EQUITY		
Cash	$3,200	*Liabilities*		
Equipment	3,000	Accounts Payable		$ 300
Accounts Receivable	200	*Owner's Equity*		
		Carter Investment,		
		December 1, 19X1	$6,000	
		Profit for December	100	
		Carter Investment,		
		December 31, 19X1		$6,100
Total Assets	$6,400	*Total Liabilities and Owner's Equity*		$6,400

The net profit of $100 that was shown on the income statement for the month appears as an increase in owner's equity on the balance sheet. The owner's equity at December 31 is determined by adding the profit for December to the owner's equity at December 1. Thus, the profit (or loss) figure is a connecting link, explaining the change in owner's equity during the period. Note that the income statement is prepared before the balance sheet so that the amount of the profit or loss for the period will be available to compute the balance of the owner's equity at the statement date. Of course, the balance sheet also shows the types and amounts of property (assets) that the business owns and the amount owed to creditors (liabilities) at the reporting date.

The preparation of financial statements is one of the most important jobs the accountant does, and all figures must be checked and double-checked to make sure that they are accurate. The figures shown on the balance sheet and the income statement are used by the businessman for planning current and future operations. Creditors, prospective investors, governmental agencies, and many others are also vitally interested in the profits of the business and in the asset and equity structure. Each day, literally millions of business decisions are made on the basis of financial reports.

◆ ◆ ◆

PRINCIPLES AND PROCEDURES

The accounting process begins with the analysis of each business transaction. The accountant analyzes each transaction to determine its effect on the fundamental accounting equation: *assets equal liabilities plus owner's equity.* The balance sheet is a statement showing the assets, liabilities, and owner's equity on a given date.

Some changes in owner's equity result from income and from expense. These changes are summarized on the income statement. The difference between the income and expense is the net profit (or loss) of the business for the period. The profit or loss of the period also appears on the balance sheet prepared at the close of the same period, as a connecting link between the owner's equity at the beginning of the period and his equity at the end of the period.

MANAGERIAL IMPLICATIONS

Accurate and informative financial records and statements are necessary for making sound business decisions. Accounting information helps to determine whether a profit has been made, the value of the assets on hand, the amount owed to creditors, and the amount of owner's equity. Any well-run and efficiently managed business will have a good accounting system to provide timely and useful information.

APPLICATION OF PRINCIPLES

PROBLEM 1 · 1

The Sunshine Laundry has just been established and the owner makes a cash deposit of $3,000 in the First State Bank for exclusive use in the business. Analyze and in equation form record changes in property, claims of creditors, and the owner's equity for the following transactions. (Use plus, minus, and equal signs.)

a. Initial investment of $3,000 in cash.
b. Acquired equipment for $1,200 in cash.
c. Obtained equipment costing $2,000 on credit.
d. Paid $600 in cash to creditors.
e. Additional investment by owner, $1,000 in cash.

PROBLEM 1 · 2

◆ Robert Pond is the sole owner of the Pond Jewelry Shop. From the following figures, prepare a balance sheet (use four-column analysis paper) dated Dec. 31, 19X1.

Cash	$2,000
Equipment	2,000
Office Furniture	500
Accounts Payable	1,000
Pond Investment	3,500

- PROBLEM 1 · 3

◆ Peter Hanson owns the County Advertising Research Agency. At the beginning of the month, the books show the following assets, liabilities, and owner's equity:

Cash	$1,600	Accounts Payable	500
Office Furniture	500	Hanson Investment	2,000
Office Machines	600	Income	700
Accounts Receivable	400	Expenses	100

Set up an equation form using the given balances, then record the effects of the following transactions in the equation. (Use plus, minus, and equal signs.) Insert new balances after each transaction has been recorded, and prove the equality of the two sides of the final equation on a separate sheet of paper.

A RA a. Performed services worth $200 on credit.
A P b. Paid $125 in cash for office rent.
A R c. Received $500 in cash for services rendered.
EX d. Paid $50 in cash for supplies used.
A P e. Sent check for $200 to creditors.
EX f. Paid $50 in cash for telephone bill.
IN g. Issued checks to pay salaries, $400.
A R h. Rendered more services for $600 in cash.

Had adding machine repaired for $10; payment due in 30 days. (*Hint:* Transaction has no effect on assets. Firm's liabilities increase; the increase in outsider's claims against the same amount of assets reduces the value of the owner's equity.)

L j. Received $300 from accounts receivable.

PROBLEM 1 · 4

♦ The following equations show the transactions that took place during the month of February 19X1 in the operations of the Ace Tree Service (John Dunn, owner). Analyze each transaction carefully. Then prepare an income statement for the month (list expenses in detail) and a balance sheet at Feb. 28, 19X1. Use two-column analysis paper for the income statement and four-column analysis paper for the balance sheet.

	CASH	+	AUTO	+	EQUIP.	+	ACCTS. REC.	=	ACCTS. PAY.	+	DUNN INVEST.	+	INCOME	−	EXP.
Balances, Feb. 1	500	+	1,500	+	2,000	+	400	=	200	+	4,200		−0−		−0−
Paid rent	− 50														50
New balances	450	+	1,500	+	2,000	+	400	=	200	+	4,200			−	50
Cash from sales	1,500												1,500		
New balances	1,950	+	1,500	+	2,000	+	400	=	200	+	4,200	+	1,500	−	50
Paid creditor	− 50								− 50						
New balances	1,900	+	1,500	+	2,000	+	400	=	150	+	4,200	+	1,500	−	50
Service on credit							500						500		
New balances	1,900	+	1,500	+	2,000	+	900	=	150	+	4,200	+	2,000	−	50
Paid salaries	− 600														600
New balances	1,300	+	1,500	+	2,000	+	900	=	150	+	4,200	+	2,000	−	650
Paid phone bill	− 25														25
New balances	1,275	+	1,500	+	2,000	+	900	=	150	+	4,200	+	2,000	−	675

MANAGERIAL CHECKUPS

♦ How does an accounting system aid management to achieve effective operating control and make sound decisions?

♦ Why should management be concerned about the changes in the amount of creditors' claims against the business?

♦ Is it reasonable to expect that all new businesses will generate profits from the first month's operations? From the first year's operations?

2 SETTING UP ACCOUNTS

The accountant's methods of analyzing transactions and presenting financial information have been discussed. However, the way in which the accountant keeps records of the changes discussed in the previous unit has not yet been explained.

ACCOUNTS FOR ASSETS, LIABILITIES, AND OWNER'S EQUITY

Obviously, he doesn't have time to make up a new equation after every transaction. Instead, a separate written record is kept for each asset and liability, as well as for the owner's equity in the business.

Another look at the affairs of the Carter Cleaning Shop will help explain the accountant's recording procedure. When Carter invested his $6,000 on November 26, 19X1, the accountant analyzed the transaction and identified two important facts to be recorded:

(a) The business had $6,000 worth of property in the form of cash deposited in the bank.

(b) Carter had a $6,000 financial interest in the business.

The firm's position was pictured as follows.

CARTER CLEANING SHOP

PROPERTY	=	FINANCIAL INTEREST
(a) Cash $6,000	=	(b) Carter Investment $6,000

Had a more formal balance sheet been drawn up at that time, it would have looked like this.

CARTER CLEANING SHOP
Balance Sheet
November 26, 19X1

ASSETS		OWNER'S EQUITY	
Cash	$6,000	Carter Investment	$6,000

Accounts for Assets

One record that the accountant uses for analyzing and recording transactions is known as a T account. This skeletal record permits the name of the item to be written on the top line and the increases and decreases to be separated and entered on different sides of the record. The location of the items in the fundamental accounting equation (and the balance sheet) is used as a cue for the recording procedure in the T account. For instance, a separate account is set up for the asset Cash, and the opening balance of $6,000 is entered on the left side of the account because assets always appear on the left side of the balance sheet and on the left side of the accounting equation.

+	CASH	−
(a) 6,000		

Having assigned the left side for recording increases in assets, the accountant must use the right side for recording decreases in assets.

Accounts for Owner's Equity

The accountant sets up another account for Carter's equity. Since the owner's equity always appears on the right side of both the balance sheet and the accounting equation, the opening balance of $6,000 is entered on the right side of the owner's equity account.

−	CARTER INVESTMENT	+
		(b) 6,000

Since the accountant uses the right side of the owner's equity account to record increases in the owner's equity, he must use the left side of the account to record decreases.

Making Entries in Asset Accounts

When the Carter Cleaning Shop bought $2,000 worth of cleaning equipment for cash, the accountant made the following analysis:

(c) $2,000 worth of new assets in the form of equipment was acquired.
(d) $2,000 of the firm's cash was paid out.

To record the first element (c), the accountant opens a new asset account for equipment and records the acquisition on the left, or increase, side.

+	EQUIPMENT	−
(c) 2,000		

The payment of $2,000 in cash (d) is entered on the right side of the Cash account because decreases in assets are recorded on the right side.

+	CASH	−
(a) 6,000		(d) 2,000

Accounts for Liabilities

Later, when additional equipment was bought on credit from Knight, Inc., for $1,000, the accountant's analysis revealed:

(e) $1,000 worth of new assets in the form of equipment was acquired.
(f) The firm owed $1,000 as an account payable to Knight, Inc.

After this transaction, the firm's position was pictured like this.

PROPERTY			=	FINANCIAL INTERESTS		
Cash	+	Equipment	=	Accounts Payable	+	Carter Investment
$4,000	+	$3,000	=	$1,000	+	$6,000

A formal balance sheet prepared at this time (November 28, 19X1) shows the following situation.

CARTER CLEANING SHOP
Balance Sheet
November 28, 19X1

ASSETS		LIABILITIES AND OWNER'S EQUITY	
Cash	$4,000	*Liabilities*	
Equipment	3,000	Accounts Payable	$1,000
		Owner's Equity	
		Carter Investment	6,000
Total Assets	$7,000	*Total Liabilities and Owner's Equity*	$7,000

Again, the accountant uses the location on the balance sheet and in the fundamental equation as his recording guide. The increase in equipment (e) requires an entry on the left side of the Equipment account.

+	EQUIPMENT	−
(c) 2,000		
(e) 1,000		

A liability account covering the account payable to Knight (f) is opened, and the $1,000 is entered on the right side because liabilities appear on the right side of the balance sheet and the accounting equation.

−	ACCOUNTS PAYABLE	+
		(f) 1,000

Since the accountant uses the right side of the liability accounts for increases in liabilities, the left side is used to record decreases in liabilities.

RECORDING PAYMENT TO A CREDITOR

Later, on November 30, 19X1, when a payment of $700 was made to Knight, Inc., to apply against its bill of $1,000, the analysis indicated:

(g) $700 of the firm's cash was paid out.

(h) Knight's claim against the firm was reduced by $700.

The accountant records the decrease in cash (g) as an entry on the right (decrease) side of the Cash account and reduces the liability (h) with an entry on the left (decrease) side of the Accounts Payable account.

+ CASH −	− ACCOUNTS PAYABLE +
(a) 6,000 │ (d) 2,000 │ (g) 700	(h) 700 │ (f) 1,000

After the November transactions necessary to ready the shop for business have been entered in the accounts, the position of the company at the beginning of operations on the morning of December 1, 19X1 is the same as the position shown on the balance sheet of November 30, 19X1 on page 7. Note that this position is represented by account balances to simplify the illustration. (For example, Cash: +$6,000 − $2,000 − $700 = $3,300.)

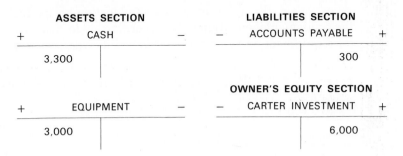

ASSETS SECTION

+ CASH −
3,300

+ EQUIPMENT −
3,000

LIABILITIES SECTION

− ACCOUNTS PAYABLE +
300

OWNER'S EQUITY SECTION

− CARTER INVESTMENT +
6,000

ACCOUNTS FOR INCOME AND EXPENSES

As you saw in Unit 1, many of the transactions of a business involve income and expenses. These items, too, are recorded in accounts. Let's retrace the income and expense transactions of the Carter Cleaning Shop for December to learn how they are recorded in the accounts.

Recording Income

The cash receipts for cleaning services for the month amounted to $2,200. The accountant analyzed the receipt of this income as follows:

(i) $2,200 in cash was received by the business.
(j)   The owner's equity was increased by this inflow of assets.

The accountant records the receipt of cash (i) as an entry on the left (increase) side of the asset account Cash.

+   CASH   −
(bal.) 3,300 │   (i) 2,200 │

But how is the increase in owner's equity recorded? It might be expected that the accountant would record the $2,200 on the right side of the Carter Investment account. However, because the accountant prefers to keep the income figures temporarily separated from the owner's investment until the books are closed, he opens a new account called Income. (It might also be called Cleaning Service Income in Carter's case.) Then he records the $2,200 on the right side of the Income account (j), because income *increases* the owner's equity, and an increase in owner's equity is recorded on the right side of the account.

```
  –          INCOME          +
             |       (j) 2,200
             |
```

Since the accountant uses the right side of the Income account to record increases, he would use the left side of the Income account to record decreases in that account if required by corrections, transfers to other accounts, or refunds (seldom encountered).

Recording Sales on Credit

The next transaction of the Carter Cleaning Shop involved the sale of $800 worth of services to charge account customers. The analysis pointed out the following effects:

(k)   A new asset—Accounts Receivable of $800—was obtained.
(l)   The owner's equity was increased by the income of $800.

First, the accountant opens a new asset account, Accounts Receivable (k), and records the $800 on the left, or increase, side. Then he records the increase in owner's equity (l) as an entry on the right (increase) side of the Income account.

```
 +   ACCOUNTS RECEIVABLE   –        –        INCOME        +
     (k) 800        |                 |     (j) 2,200
                    |                 |     (l)    800
```

Recording Receipts from Customers

When the customers paid a total of $600 to apply on their accounts, the accountant analyzed the recording problem in this way:

(m)   Cash in the amount of $600 was received.
(n)   Accounts Receivable was reduced by $600.

The recording of this information is a routine matter involving two asset accounts. The Cash account is increased (left side) by $600 (m), and the Accounts Receivable account is decreased (right side) by $600 (n). Observe that there is no income from this payment transaction: income was recorded when the sales on account were recorded (entry l).

+	CASH	−		+	ACCOUNTS RECEIVABLE	−
	3,300				(k) 800	(n) 600
(i)	2,200					
(m)	600					

Recording Expenses

Inevitably, the Carter Cleaning Shop encounters expenses in running its business. The first of these expenses was for employees' salaries of $1,600. In the previous analysis in Unit 1, the accountant listed the following effects of this expense:

(o) Cash was reduced by the payment of $1,600.
(p) Carter's equity was reduced by the $1,600 outflow of assets.

The reduction in cash (o) is easily recorded by an entry on the right (decrease) side of the asset account Cash.

+	CASH	−
	3,300	(o) 1,600
(i)	2,200	
(m)	600	

The decrease in Carter's equity resulting from the expense could be entered on the left (decrease) side of the Investment account. However, as with the income figures, the accountant prefers to keep expenses separated from the owner's investment until the books are closed. This recording technique calls for the opening of a new account for the expense involved, namely, Salary Expense. The $1,600 (p) is then entered on the left side, because expenses decrease owner's equity and the owner's equity account is decreased on the left side. Remember that an increase in an expense is a decrease in the owner's equity. The plus and minus signs indicate the effect on the expense account, not the effect on owner's equity.

+	SALARY EXPENSE	−
(p)	1,600	

Recording payment of the rent for December, $700, follows a very similar pattern. The analysis indicated:

(q) Cash was reduced by $700.
(r) Carter's equity was reduced by $700.

The reduction in cash (q) is recorded by another entry on the right side of the Cash account.

+	CASH	−
	3,300	(o) 1,600
(i) 2,200		(q) 700
(m) 600		

The recording of the further decrease in owner's equity (r) calls for the opening of another expense account called Rent Expense. An entry on the left side, of $700, reflects the increase in expense as well as the decrease in Carter's investment.

+	RENT EXPENSE	−
(r) 700		

When the Carter Cleaning Shop paid for the $600 worth of cleaning supplies that had been used in the month's operations, the accountant analyzed the information in this manner:

(s) The asset Cash was reduced by $600.
(t) Carter's equity was reduced $600 by the additional expense.

The reduction of the asset Cash (s) is recorded as an entry on the right (decrease) side of the Cash account shown below.

+	CASH	−
	3,300	(o) 1,600
(i) 2,200		(q) 700
(m) 600		(s) 600

The reduction of Carter's equity (t) is recorded by an entry on the left side of a new account called Supplies Used. An entry on the left side is used to record an expense, which is a decrease in owner's equity.

+	SUPPLIES USED	−
(t) 600		

The pattern for recording expenses is logically the opposite of that for recording income. Increases in expenses are recorded on the left side of the account because they reflect a reduction in owner's equity. Decreases in expenses resulting from corrections, transfers to another expense account, or refunds (seldom encountered) are, logically, recorded on the right side of the expense account.

The balances in the various T accounts after the December, 19X1 transactions have been recorded are the same as were shown in equation form on page 14. This time, the accountant can use the T account balances as a basis for the preparation of the income statement and balance sheet illustrated (income statement first). The account balance is determined by adding the figures on each side of the account and deducting the lesser from the greater. For example, the figures recorded on the left side of the T account for Cash total $6,100. The figures recorded on the right side total $2,900. Then, $6,100 − $2,900 = $3,200, the balance of the Cash account.

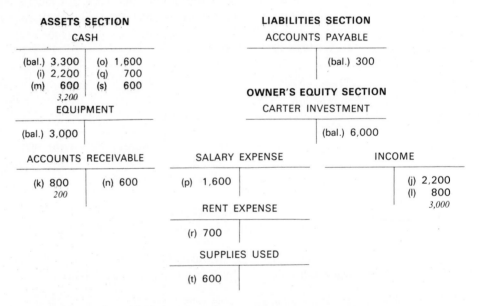

ASSETS SECTION

CASH

(bal.) 3,300	(o) 1,600
(i) 2,200	(q) 700
(m) 600	(s) 600
3,200	

EQUIPMENT

| (bal.) 3,000 | |

ACCOUNTS RECEIVABLE

| (k) 800 | (n) 600 |
| 200 | |

SALARY EXPENSE

| (p) 1,600 | |

RENT EXPENSE

| (r) 700 | |

SUPPLIES USED

| (t) 600 | |

LIABILITIES SECTION

ACCOUNTS PAYABLE

| | (bal.) 300 |

OWNER'S EQUITY SECTION

CARTER INVESTMENT

| | (bal.) 6,000 |

INCOME

	(j) 2,200
	(l) 800
	3,000

Note that items marked "(bal.)" were balances carried forward from November transactions.

CARTER CLEANING SHOP
Income Statement
Month Ended December 31, 19X1

Income		
Cleaning Service		$3,000
Less Expenses		
Salaries	$1,600	
Rent	700	
Supplies Used	600	
Total Expenses		2,900
Net Profit for the Month		$ 100

CARTER CLEANING SHOP
Balance Sheet
December 31, 19X1

ASSETS		LIABILITIES AND OWNER'S EQUITY		
Cash	$3,200	*Liabilities*		
Equipment	3,000	Accounts Payable		$ 300
Accounts Receivable	200	*Owner's Equity*		
		Carter Investment,		
		December 1, 19X1	$6,000	
		Profit for December	**100**	
		Carter Investment,		
		December 31, 19X1		6,100
Total Assets	$6,400	*Total Liabilities and Owner's Equity*		$6,400

THE RULES FOR DEBIT AND CREDIT

The accountant does not say "left side" or "right side" when he talks about making entries in accounts. He uses the term *debit* (or charge) when he refers to an entry on the left side and the term *credit* when he refers to an entry on the right side of an account. For example, the accountant increases assets by debiting asset accounts and decreases assets by crediting asset accounts. However, the accountant increases liabilities by crediting liability accounts and decreases liabilities by debiting liability accounts. The illustration summarizes the rules regarding debits and credits.

GUIDE FOR DEBITING AND CREDITING

ASSET ACCOUNTS

DEBIT	CREDIT
The original amount is entered on this side.	Decreases are entered on this side.
Increases are entered on this side.	

LIABILITY ACCOUNTS

DEBIT	CREDIT
Decreases are entered on this side.	The original amount is entered on this side.
	Increases are entered on this side.

OWNER'S EQUITY ACCOUNT

DEBIT	CREDIT
Decreases are entered on this side (withdrawals, etc.).	The original investment amount is entered on this side. Increases are entered on this side (additional investments, etc.).

INCOME

DEBIT	CREDIT
Decreases in owner's equity through reduction of income are entered on this side (sales returns, allowances, etc.).	Increases in owner's equity are entered on this side (sales of goods and services).

EXPENSES

DEBIT	CREDIT
Decreases in owner's equity through expenses are entered on this side (rent, salaries, purchases, selling expenses, administrative expenses, etc.).	Increases in owner's equity through reduction of expenses are entered on this side (purchases returns and allowances, etc.).

THE DOUBLE-ENTRY SYSTEM

The analysis of every transaction produces at least two counterbalancing effects. The effect of each entry on the left (debit) side is balanced by the effect of an entry on the right (credit) side. This is why the modern system of accounting is sometimes called the *double-entry system*. It is a process of recording both effects of a given transaction in order to present a complete picture. The same relationship also explains why both sides of the equations shown in Unit 1 were always equal.

CHART OF ACCOUNTS

Since there are likely to be many different accounts in a set of business records, it is necessary to establish a plan for identifying each account and locating it quickly. Identification of accounts is easier and the process of location is quicker if numbers as well as names are assigned to all accounts. In developing an index or *chart of accounts*, blocks of numbers are assigned to accounts according to "families"—that is, types of accounts. For example, assets assigned to the block of numbers from 100 to 199; liabilities from 200 to 299; owner's equity from 300 to 399; and so on. These numbers help identify the type of account, no matter where it is in the books.

Carter's accountant sets up a chart of accounts for the business and assigns numbers to them as shown. Notice that the accounts are not numbered in sequence. For example, the numbering under Assets jumps from 101 to 111. These number gaps are ordinarily left in each block so additional accounts may be added in the appropriate sequence, as required.

CHART OF ACCOUNTS

Account Number	Account Name
100–199	ASSETS
101	Cash
111	Accounts Receivable
141	Equipment
200–299	LIABILITIES
201	Accounts Payable
300–399	OWNER'S EQUITY
301	Carter Investment
400–499	INCOME
401	Cleaning Service Income
500–599	EXPENSES
511	Salary Expense
516	Rent Expense
521	Supplies Used

REAL AND NOMINAL ACCOUNTS

As you have noted, the asset, liability, and owner's equity accounts appear on the balance sheet at the end of an accounting period and are carried forward to start the new period. For these reasons, these accounts are sometimes called *real* (in the sense of permanent or continuing) accounts.

The income and expense accounts, which appear on the income statement at the end of an accounting period, are used for convenience in classifying and summarizing changes in owner's equity during the period. They are called *nominal* or *temporary* accounts. As you will learn later, at the end of the accounting period these accounts are transferred to a summary account, which, in turn, is transferred to owner's equity.

PRINCIPLES AND PROCEDURES

Each transaction is analyzed to identify its effect on the elements in the fundamental accounting equation: *assets equal liabilities plus owner's equity.* Then a record of the effects of each transaction is made in the accounts involved. Recording in the accounts is based on the location of the item in the fundamental equation and on the balance sheet. Increases in assets are shown on the left, or debit, side of the account because they are on the left side of the balance sheet and the equation. The right, or credit, side of the asset account is used to record decreases. Since liability items are on the right, or credit, side of the equation and the balance sheet, increases in these elements are recorded on the credit side of the accounts. The opposite side of the accounts is used for recording decreases. In a like manner, increases in owner's equity are shown on the credit side of the account; decreases on the debit side.

Income is shown by entries on the credit side of the Income account because it increases the owner's equity. Expenses are recorded on the debit side of separate expense accounts because they decrease the owner's equity.

The accounts are usually arranged in some predetermined order for handy reference and speedy identification. The list of the accounts used by the business is called the chart of accounts.

MANAGERIAL IMPLICATIONS

The use of a list of accounts provides a simple and efficient means of accumulating data about the financial affairs of the business. From the accounts, the accountant can easily prepare the income statement, which summarizes the income and expenses of the business for the period of time covered, and can prepare the balance sheet, which summarizes the assets, liabilities, and owner's equity at a given time. Business owners, managers, creditors, suppliers, and many others use these summarizing statements as a basis for making decisions concerning the business.

APPLICATION OF PRINCIPLES

PROBLEM 2 · 1

♦ The following transactions are unrelated. Set up T accounts for the accounts indicated in parentheses. Analyze each transaction carefully and record the amounts in the proper positions in the T accounts relating to that transaction. Use plus and minus signs to indicate increases and decreases in each account.

a. Merritt invested $5,000 cash in the business. (Cash and Merritt Investment.)

b. Purchased $300 worth of testing equipment for cash. (Shop Equipment and Cash.)

c. Bought store fixtures for $500; payment due in 30 days. (Store Equipment and Accounts Payable.)

d. Acquired used service truck for $750 in cash. (Truck and Cash.)

e. Merritt turned over to the firm his personal set of tools, valued at $150. (Shop Equipment and Merritt Investment.)

f. Bought used cash register for $100; payment due in 30 days. (Store Equipment and Accounts Payable.)

g. Paid $250 in cash to apply to amount owed on store fixtures. (Cash and Accounts Payable.)

PROBLEM 2 · 2

♦ Analyze each of the following unrelated transactions and record the effects in a pair of T accounts relating to the transaction. Enter the correct heading of each account. Record the increases and decreases by using plus and minus signs before the amounts.

a. A business acquired $1,000 worth of equipment for cash.
b. The owner, Dan Fields, withdrew $500 of the cash he invested.
c. A firm sold a piece of surplus equipment for $250 cash.
d. A firm purchased a delivery truck for $2,000 cash.
e. A business paid $400 cash to apply against account owed.
f. A firm acquired office equipment for $150, to be paid in 60 days.
g. Mr. Black, owner of the Builders Supply Company, made an additional investment of $2,500 cash.
h. A check for $150 was issued in payment for office equipment purchased on credit.

PROBLEM 2 · 3

♦ Analyze each of the following income and expense transactions and record the effects in a pair of T accounts relating to the transaction. Enter the correct heading of each account and indicate the increases and decreases by using plus and minus signs before the amounts.

a. Paid rent for month, $100.
b. Sold services for cash, $500.
c. Paid office salaries, $200.
d. Sold additional services, $300 on credit.
e. Paid monthly telephone bill, $25.
f. Collected $50 from accounts receivable.
g. Received $5 refund for overcharge on telephone bill.
h. Sold services on credit, $600.
i. Paid monthly utilities bill, $20 in cash.

j. Received supplies for immediate use; payment due in 30 days, $75.
k. Received $225 from charge customers.
l. Received payment in cash for services rendered, $900.
m. Received credit for $10 as an adjustment due to damaged packages of supplies previously received.
n. Sent check for $65 in payment for supplies previously purchased on credit.

PROBLEM 2 · 4

◆ Analyze the transactions of the Roper Garage listed here, and record each in appropriate T accounts, using the following accounts (the numbers have been intentionally omitted). Indicate the increases and decreases by using plus and minus signs before the amounts. Key each entry to the alphabetical symbol identifying each transaction.

ASSETS
Cash
Accounts Receivable
Office Equipment
Truck

LIABILITIES
Accounts Payable

OWNER'S EQUITY
Roper Investment

INCOME
Income From Services

EXPENSES
Rent Expense
Utilities Expense
Salaries
Repair Parts
Truck Expense

a. Roper invested $5,000 cash to establish an auto repair shop.
b. Paid rent for one month, $150.
c. Bought used delivery truck for $800 in cash.
d. Received $500 cash for services rendered.
e. Paid $40 for repairs to delivery truck.
f. Sold $150 worth of services on credit.
g. Acquired office desk on credit, $75.
h. Received $50 from credit customers.
i. Paid $25 to reduce amount owed on desk.
j. Issued check to pay for utilities, $25.
k. Purchased office furniture for $400; half cash, balance on 30 days' credit.
l. Issued check to cover salaries, $800.
m. Received $600 cash for services rendered.
n. Performed services on credit, $750.
o. Paid $175 for parts used in repair work.
p. Collected $450 from accounts receivable.
q. Received bill for repair parts used, $225, due in 30 days.
r. Paid $30 in cash for gas and oil consumed by delivery truck.

PROBLEM 2 · 5

Using the figures accumulated in the T accounts for Problem 2 · 4, prepare an income statement (use two-column analysis paper) and a balance sheet (use four-column analysis paper). Assume that the transactions represent the activities for the month ended April 30, 19X1.

MANAGERIAL CHECKUPS

How do the income statement and balance sheet aid management to make sound decisions?

At any given moment, how can management find out whether a firm can pay its bills as they become due?

If a firm's expenses are found to equal or exceed its income, what should management do?

In discussing a firm's latest financial statements, a manager says that it is the "results on the bottom line" that really count. What does this mean?

3 BASIC ACCOUNTING RECORDS

In the last unit, we saw that the accountant's analysis of each transaction was the basis for recording the effects of the transaction in the accounts. Actually, the accountant keeps a written record of each analysis for future reference. Then he can always recheck his work and trace the details of any transaction long after it has happened.

THE GENERAL JOURNAL

The book in which the analysis of each transaction is kept is called the *general journal*. This book is really a diary of business activities used to note every event involving financial affairs as it occurs. A journal of this type is commonly referred to as a *book of original entry*.

When Carter invested his $6,000 and started the Carter Cleaning Shop, the accountant analyzed the transaction and identified these effects:

(a) The business had $6,000 worth of property in the form of cash.
(b) Carter had a $6,000 financial investment in the business.

Then, using the analysis as his guide, the accountant decided to:

(a) Debit Cash to record the increase in the asset Cash.
(b) Credit the Carter Investment account to record the new ownership interest.

The accountant's written record in the general journal of his analysis of the transaction is shown on the next page.

For identification purposes, each journal entry is numbered. Carter's numbering system uses a double number, with the first portion representing

DATE	DESCRIPTION OF ENTRY	ACCT. NO.	√	DEBIT	CREDIT
19 X1	11-1				
Nov. 26	Cash.	101		6,000 00	
	Carter Investment	301			6,000 00
	To record initial cash investment of				
	owner.				

the month and the second portion indicating the sequence of the entry within that month. Thus, the "11-1" shown for this entry designates the first entry in the month of November. (Not all accountants number journal entries, but it is desirable to do so.)

The date of the transaction appears in the left column. The year is entered at the top of the column, and the month and day are recorded on the first line of the entry. After the first entry, the year and month are noted only at the top of a new page or when either changes.

The debit item is always entered first in the Description of Entry section. The account title is written at the margin; the account number is placed in the Account Number column (see the chart of accounts on page 29). The debit amount is then placed in the Debit column.

The credit item is always recorded on the line beneath the debit and is indented about half an inch from the left margin. Its account number is also written in the Account Number column. Next, the credit amount is entered in the Credit column.

A brief explanation always follows the credit entry and should begin at the margin of the Description of Entry section in order to make best use of the limited space available. Entries should be complete but concise.

The accountant writes his transaction analysis in the general journal before making any entry in the accounts, demonstrating that it is indeed a *book of original entry*. The process of recording in a journal is called *journalizing*. By journalizing first, the accountant knows that he will have all the data in one place before any details are forgotten.

General Journal Entries for November

When the Carter Cleaning Shop bought $2,000 worth of cleaning equipment for cash, the accountant made the following analysis:

(c) $2,000 worth of new assets (equipment) was acquired.
(d) $2,000 of the firm's cash was paid out.

The accountant made the following entry in the general journal.

UNIT 3

35

DATE	DESCRIPTION OF ENTRY	ACCT. NO.	✓	DEBIT	CREDIT
19 X1	11-2				
Nov. 27	Equipment	141		2,000 00	
	Cash	101			2,000 00
	To record acquisition of cleaning				
	equipment for cash.				

When additional equipment was bought on credit from Knight, Inc., the accountant's analysis revealed:

(e) $1,000 worth of new assets (equipment) was obtained.
(f) The firm owed $1,000 as an account payable to Knight, Inc.

The required record in the general journal is as shown.

GENERAL JOURNAL   Page 1

DATE	DESCRIPTION OF ENTRY	ACCT. NO.	✓	DEBIT	CREDIT
19 X1	11-3				
Nov. 28	Equipment	141		1,000 00	
	Accounts Payable	201			1,000 00
	To record acquisition of equipment on				
	credit terms from Knight, Inc.				

Finally, an analysis of the payment to Knight, Inc., showed the following results:

(g) $700 of the firm's cash was paid out.
(h) Knight's claim against the firm was reduced by $700.

The accountant's entry in the general journal is as follows.

GENERAL JOURNAL   Page 1

DATE	DESCRIPTION OF ENTRY	ACCT. NO.	✓	DEBIT	CREDIT
19 X1	11-4				
Nov. 30	Accounts Payable	201		700 00	
	Cash	101			700 00
	To record payment to Knight, Inc. on				
	account.				

Note that the accountant always enters the debit item first, even if he happens to consider the credit first in his mental analysis of the event.

General Journal Entries for December

You will recall that the Carter Cleaning Shop officially opened for business on December 1, 19X1, and the following transactions were completed during that month:

1. Collected $2,200 in cash for cleaning services (i & j).
2. Sold $800 worth of cleaning services on account to charge customers (k & l).
3. Received $600 in cash from charge customers to apply on their accounts (m & n).
4. Paid $1,600 for salaries (o & p).
5. Paid $700 for rent (q & r).
6. Paid $600 for supplies used (s & t).

The accountant records the December transactions in the general journal. (In actual practice the transactions would, of course, be spread throughout the month and recorded as they occurred. To complete the record, dates have been assigned for illustrative purposes, as though each type of transaction occurred on the date shown.)

GENERAL JOURNAL
Page 2

DATE		DESCRIPTION OF ENTRY	ACCT. NO.	√	DEBIT		CREDIT	
19	X1	12-1						
Dec	11	Cash	101		2,200	00		
		Cleaning Service Income	401				2,200	00
		To record cash sales.						
		12-2						
	14	Accounts Receivable	111		800	00		
		Cleaning Service Income	401				800	00
		To record credit sales.						
		12-3						
	16	Cash	101		600	00		
		Accounts Receivable	111				600	00
		To record collections to apply on customers' accounts.						
		12-4						
	18	Salary Expense.	511		1,600	00		
		Cash	101				1,600	00
		To record payment of salaries.						
		12-5						
	20	Rent Expense.	516		700	00		
		Cash	101				700	00
		To record payment for December rent.						
		12-6						
	31	Supplies Used	521		600	00		
		Cash	101				600	00
		To record payment for supplies used.						

Note that the entry number is written on an otherwise blank line between entries in the general journal. (Various other systems of numbering journal entries may be used, depending on the preference of the accountant.)

The entries illustrated so far consist of a single debit and a single credit. Some transactions may require a record consisting of several debits or several credits. When journalizing a so-called *compound* entry, list all debits first, then indent and list all credits. Remember, total debits must equal total credits.

For example, a compound entry would be required to record the acquisition of store fixtures worth $400 when the purchaser gives $100 in cash and receives 30 days in which to pay the balance. The transaction is broken down as follows:

1. The asset Store Fixtures is increased by $400.
2. The asset Cash is decreased by $100 paid.
3. The liability Accounts Payable is increased by $300.

The entry is illustrated below.

GENERAL JOURNAL   Page 6

DATE	DESCRIPTION OF ENTRY	ACCT. NO.	√	DEBIT	CREDIT
19 X2 June 2	6-1 Store Fixtures . . . . Cash . . . . Accounts Payable . . . . To record acquisition of store fixtures, paying $100 cash and receiving 30-day credit terms on balance.	146 101 201		400 00	 100 00 300 00

THE GENERAL LEDGER

The entries in the general journal tell the accountant what is to be debited and what is to be credited. With this record as a guide, it is a simple matter for him to enter the information in the individual accounts affected. The accountant actually uses printed forms for his account records. Each account is kept on a separate form called a *ledger sheet*. All the accounts together constitute a *ledger* or *book of final entry*. Thus, the ledger becomes the master reference book of the accounting system and provides a permanent and classified record of every element involved in the business operation. This is how it would be done, step by step, using the general journal entry 11-1 for Carter's $6,000 investment as the first example.

DATE	DESCRIPTION OF ENTRY	ACCT. NO.	√	DEBIT	CREDIT
19 X1 Nov 26	11-1 Cash	101		6,000 00	
	Carter Investment	301			6,000 00
	To record initial cash investment of owner.				

GENERAL LEDGER

Cash   No. 101

DATE	EXPLANATION	POST. REF.	DEBIT	DATE	EXPLANATION	POST. REF.	CREDIT
19 X1 Nov. 26	(Beginning invest.)	11-1	6,000 00				

Carter Investment   No. 301

DATE	EXPLANATION	POST. REF.	DEBIT	DATE	EXPLANATION	POST. REF.	CREDIT
				19 X1 Nov. 26	(Beginning invest.)	11-1	6,000 00

If a question arises later, a look at the ledger account record will reveal a complete running history of the increases and decreases of the item involved, as well as the source of the original data. The ledger accounts may be kept in a post binder or, if they are in card form, in a ledger tray. The accountant uses these records because they permit entering more details than the T accounts.

The Explanation column is used for special notations; routine entries usually require no explanation. The "11-1" in the Posting Reference column refers to November entry number 1 in the general journal.

The process of transferring information from the journal to the ledger is called *posting*. Examine the posting of the remainder of the general journal entries for the Carter Cleaning Shop that follow.

Posting the Remaining Entries

The acquisition of $2,000 worth of cleaning equipment was journalized as follows.

DATE	DESCRIPTION OF ENTRY	ACCT. NO.	√	DEBIT	CREDIT
19 X1	{11-2}				
Nov. 27	Equipment	141		2,000 00	
	Cash	101			2,000 00
	To record acquisition of cleaning equipment for cash.				

This transaction is posted to the proper ledger accounts.

Equipment   **No. 141**

DATE	EXPLANATION	POST. REF.	DEBIT	DATE	EXPLANATION	POST. REF.	CREDIT
19 X1							
Nov. 27		11-2	2,000 00				

Cash   **No. 101**

DATE	EXPLANATION	POST. REF.	DEBIT	DATE	EXPLANATION	POST. REF.	CREDIT
19 X1				19 X1			
Nov. 26		11-1	6,000 00	Nov. 27		11-2	2,000 00

When the posting is completed, a check mark is placed in the Posting Check column beside the Account Number column in the general journal. The check mark shows that the entry has been posted and ensures against posting the same entry twice—or not at all. This is illustrated here. The account numbers provide a handy cross-reference for future use.

DATE	DESCRIPTION OF ENTRY	ACCT. NO.	√	DEBIT	CREDIT
19 X1	{11-2}				
Nov. 27	Equipment	141	√	2,000 00	
	Cash	101	√		2,000 00
	To record acquisition of cleaning equipment for cash.				

The identical procedure is used in posting the other journal entries for November and December, shown on pages 36 and 37. After those entries are posted, the ledger accounts appear as shown here. Refer to the journal entries and trace these postings carefully.

Cash

No. 101

DATE		EXPLANATION	POST. REF.	DEBIT		DATE		EXPLANATION	POST. REF.	CREDIT	
19	X1					19	X1				
Nov.	26		11-1	6,000	00	Nov.	27		11-2	2,000	00
Dec.	11		12-1	2,200	00		30		11-4	700	00
	16		12-3	600	00	Dec.	18		12-4	1,600	00
							20		12-5	700	00
							31		12-6	600	00

Accounts Receivable

No. 111

DATE		EXPLANATION	POST. REF.	DEBIT		DATE		EXPLANATION	POST. REF.	CREDIT	
19	X1					19	X1				
Dec.	14		12-2	800	00	Dec.	16		12-3	600	00

Equipment

No. 141

DATE		EXPLANATION	POST. REF.	DEBIT		DATE		EXPLANATION	POST. REF.	CREDIT	
19	X1										
Nov.	27		11-2	2,000	00						
	28		11-3	1,000	00						

Accounts Payable

No. 201

DATE		EXPLANATION	POST. REF.	DEBIT		DATE		EXPLANATION	POST. REF.	CREDIT	
19	X1					19	X1				
Nov.	30		11-4	700	00	Nov.	28		11-3	1,000	00

Carter Investment

No. 301

DATE		EXPLANATION	POST. REF.	DEBIT		DATE		EXPLANATION	POST. REF.	CREDIT	
						19	X1				
						Nov.	26		11-1	6,000	00

Cleaning Service Income

No. 401

DATE		EXPLANATION	POST. REF.	DEBIT		DATE		EXPLANATION	POST. REF.	CREDIT	
						19	X1				
						Dec.	11		12-1	2,200	00
							14		12-2	800	00

Salary Expense

No. 511

DATE		EXPLANATION	POST. REF.	DEBIT		DATE	EXPLANATION	POST. REF.	CREDIT
19 X1 Dec.	18		12-4	1,600	00				

Rent Expense

No. 516

DATE		EXPLANATION	POST. REF.	DEBIT		DATE	EXPLANATION	POST. REF.	CREDIT
19 X1 Dec.	20		12-5	700	00				

Supplies Used

No. 521

DATE		EXPLANATION	POST. REF.	DEBIT		DATE	EXPLANATION	POST. REF.	CREDIT
19 X1 Dec.	31		12-6	600	00				

The pages in the ledger are generally arranged so that the balance sheet accounts come first—assets, liabilities, and owner's equity. The accounts for the income statement come next, with the income accounts first, followed by the expense accounts. The numbering of the accounts in the chart of accounts also follows this sequence. This arrangement speeds the preparation of the income statement and balance sheet. All figures will be found in the ledger in the order in which they will be listed or presented on the statements.

◆ ◆ ◆

PRINCIPLES AND PROCEDURES

The accountant's entry in the general journal is his permanent record of the analysis of each transaction. The process of recording in a general journal is called journalizing. Each journal entry is dated and numbered. The debit item is always entered first, followed by the credit item on the line below. A brief explanation always follows the credit entry.

Information is transferred from journal entries to ledger accounts. This process is called posting. The ledger accounts together form a ledger. Debits are posted to the left side of the accounts; credits to the right side. Account number columns in journals and posting reference columns in ledger accounts provide a quick cross-reference if a posting needs to be traced or rechecked.

MANAGERIAL IMPLICATIONS

The businessman can always refer back to the journal entries and ledger postings if a question comes up about previous business transactions. These permanent records provide information in an efficient and speedy manner so that management can look back and see what happened or how it was recorded. The records also indicate the effect of a transaction on the assets, liabilities, and owner's equity. The manager obviously wants to make decisions that will increase the equity (create profits) whenever possible.

APPLICATION OF PRINCIPLES

PROBLEM 3 · 1

♦ The following listed transactions relate to the operation of the Scott Launderette Service for July 19X1. Analyze each transaction and record the effects in general journal entry form. Choose your account titles from the following chart of accounts. Be sure to number the journal Page 1 and put the year at the top of the date column.

ASSETS
101 Cash
111 Accounts Receivable
141 Equipment

LIABILITIES
201 Accounts Payable

OWNER'S EQUITY
301 Scott Investment

INCOME
401 Income from Services

EXPENSES
503 Equipment Repairs
504 Telephone Expense
505 Utilities Expense
511 Salary Expense
516 Rent Expense
521 Cleaning Supplies Used
522 Office Supplies Used

JULY
1 Paid July rent on office, $40.
5 Sold services for cash, $250.
5 Sold services on credit, $135.
10 Paid telephone bill, $15.
11 Received bill for repairs to equipment, $22.
12 Collected $100 from credit customers.
15 Paid semimonthly salaries, $150.
18 Sent check for cleaning supplies used, $50.
19 Received invoice for 10 cases of washing powder used, $60; payment due in 30 days.
20 Purchased equipment for cash, $125.
21 Received $130 from credit customers.

UNIT 3

43

JULY

21 Received credit for $48 due to error in quality of cleaning supplies furnished by vendor.
22 Performed services for $170 in cash.
22 Performed services worth $90 for credit customers.
25 Paid bill for $22 previously received on July 11.
26 Paid $16 cash for office stationery.
28 Sent check for monthly electric bill, $18.
31 Paid semimonthly salaries, $150.

PROBLEM 3 · 2

Roberta Boyd has opened an office as a public stenographer in the Palace Hotel. She plans to use the chart of accounts reproduced below. The financial activities of the business during the first month of operations, August 19X1, are also listed.

ASSETS
101   Cash
111   Accounts Receivable
141   Office Equipment

LIABILITIES
201   Accounts Payable

OWNER'S EQUITY
301   Boyd Investment

INCOME
401   Income from Services

EXPENSES
504   Telephone Expense
511   Salary Expense
513   Advertising Expense
516   Rent Expense
517   Equipment Rental Expense
521   Supplies Used

AUG.

1 Miss Boyd invested $1,000 in the business in the form of a cash deposit in the new firm's checking account.
3 Paid office rent, $50 in cash.
5 Bought desk and other furniture for $200 on credit.
6 Paid $5 for rental of typewriter for month.
7 Sold stenographic services for $100 in cash.
10 Paid $7 for advertisement in hotel magazine.
12 Sold services for $150 in cash and $15 on credit. (Use one compound entry.)
15 Paid $40 for supplies used.
17 Paid $50 salary to assistant.
18 Acquired file cabinet, $60 on credit.
20 Paid $100 toward balance due on desk.
22 Received $5 cash refund on supplies due to overcharge.
26 Sold services, $175 in cash.
27 Paid $10 monthly telephone bill.
30 Received $15 in cash from charge customer.

1. Journalize the transactions. Be sure to number the journal Page 1 and put the year at the top of the date column.
2. Post to the ledger accounts. Head the forms by inserting the title and the account number for each account in the order that they are listed in the chart of accounts.

PROBLEM 3 · 3

♦ The accountant for the new Blake Garage has recommended that certain accounts be provided in the firm's books to meet anticipated needs. Selected accounts are as follows:

301	Blake Investment	140	Garage Equipment
541	Truck Operating Expense	401	Service Income
141	Office Equipment	504	Telephone Expense
201	Accounts Payable	516	Rent Expense
527	Janitorial Expense	150	Tow Truck
111	Accounts Receivable	521	Supplies Used
552	Payroll Tax Expense	101	Cash
512	Office Salaries		

INSTRUCTIONS

Arrange the accounts in the form of a chart of accounts similar to the one shown on page 29.

MANAGERIAL CHECKUPS

♦ How do permanent records of previous transactions aid management to achieve effective operating control and to make sound decisions?

♦ How does the general journal make it easier for a newly hired accountant to learn the firm's system of accounts?

♦ If the book of original entry contains a complete record of every transaction, why would a manager need to refer to the general ledger at all?

♦ How can a manager be sure that an accountant is recording a firm's transactions promptly?

THE
TRIAL
BALANCE
AND
WORKSHEET

As you already know, the purpose of having journals and ledgers is to help accumulate data for preparing the financial statements. After all the transactions for the operating period are posted to the ledger accounts, Carter's accountant prepares the financial statements. He knows that these reports should contain no errors, so he tests the arithmetic accuracy of his recording activities for the period before preparing the statements.

THE TRIAL BALANCE

One testing device the accountant uses is the *trial balance*. When the business was started with Carter's cash investment, it was stated that property equaled financial interests. Then, using more technical language, assets were said to equal liabilities plus owner's equity. Later, it was explained that every entry on the left (debit) side is matched by an entry of equal amount on the right (credit) side. Since the books started with equality and continued that equality in the recording process, it follows that the sum of debit balances should equal the sum of credit balances when all transactions have been posted. If the books do not balance—that is, if the debit balances do not equal the credit balances—the accountant knows that an error has been made.

The equality of debits and credits is tested by:

1. Determining the balance of each account.
2. Adding debit and credit balances separately to see if the totals are equal.

The balance of an account is computed by:

1. Adding the figures on each side.
2. Subtracting the smaller total from the larger to obtain the balance.

For example, the Cash account for the Carter Cleaning Shop shows total debits of $8,800 and total credits of $5,600. Subtracting the smaller total, $5,600, from $8,800 reveals a net balance of $3,200. This figure is called a debit balance because there is an excess of debits over credits.

Cash   **No. 101**

DATE		EXPLANATION	POST. REF.	DEBIT		DATE		EXPLANATION	POST. REF.	CREDIT	
19	X1					19	X1				
Nov.	26		11-1	6,000	00	Nov.	27		11-2	2,000	00
Dec.	11		12-1	2,200	00		30		11-4	700	00
	16		12-3	600	00	Dec.	18		12-4	1,600	00
		3,200.00		*8,800*	*00*		20		12-5	700	00
							31		12-6	600	00
										5,600	*00*

Notice that the accountant shows the totals, which are called *footings*, in small pencil figures under the last item on each side. The balance is shown in the Explanation space on the debit side of the Cash account because it is a debit balance. All other asset accounts are handled in the same way.

Accounts Receivable   **No. 111**

DATE		EXPLANATION	POST. REF.	DEBIT		DATE		EXPLANATION	POST. REF.	CREDIT	
19	X1					19	X1				
Dec.	14		12-2	800	00	Dec.	16		12-3	600	00
		200.00									

Note that no footings are required in the Accounts Receivable account because there are only single items entered in the debit and the credit columns. No balance figure is required in the Equipment account because there are no credit figures.

The liability account for Accounts Payable shows an excess of credits over debits. This is called a credit balance and is noted on the credit side of the account.

Equipment   No. 141

DATE	EXPLANATION	POST. REF.	DEBIT		DATE	EXPLANATION	POST. REF.	CREDIT
19 X1 Nov. 27		11-2	2,000	00				
28		11-3	1,000	00				
			3,000	*00*				

Accounts Payable   No. 201

DATE	EXPLANATION	POST. REF.	DEBIT		DATE	EXPLANATION	POST. REF.	CREDIT
19 X1 Nov. 30		11-4	700	00	19 X1 Nov. 28		11-3	1,000 00
						300.00		

The Carter Investment account requires no balancing procedure because there is only a single entry on the credit side. This account has a credit balance of $6,000.

Carter Investment   No. 301

DATE	EXPLANATION	POST. REF.	DEBIT		DATE	EXPLANATION	POST. REF.	CREDIT
					19 X1 Nov. 26		11-1	6,000 00

The Cleaning Service Income account has a credit balance of $3,000. Since there are no amounts on the opposite side, the footing (in this case, the sum of the credit entries) serves to indicate the balance.

Cleaning Service Income   No. 401

DATE	EXPLANATION	POST. REF.	DEBIT		DATE	EXPLANATION	POST. REF.	CREDIT
					19 X1 Dec. 11		12-1	2,200 00
					14		12-2	800 00
								3,000 00

The expense accounts have debit balances as follows.

Salary Expense   No. 511

DATE	EXPLANATION	POST. REF.	DEBIT		DATE	EXPLANATION	POST. REF.	CREDIT
19 X1 Dec. 18		12-4	1,600	00				

Rent Expense

No. 516

DATE	EXPLANATION	POST. REF.	DEBIT	DATE	EXPLANATION	POST. REF.	CREDIT
19 X1 Dec. 20		12-5	700 00				

Supplies Used

No. 521

DATE	EXPLANATION	POST. REF.	DEBIT	DATE	EXPLANATION	POST. REF.	CREDIT
19 X1 Dec. 31		12-6	600 00				

COMPARING BALANCES— THE TRIAL BALANCE

Now that the balances of the accounts are known, the accountant lists them in a trial balance to see if the total of the debit balances equals the total of the credit balances. The accounts are listed in numerical order (the order in which they appear in the general ledger). The balance of each account is placed in the proper column: debit balances are shown in the left column and credit balances are shown in the right column. If an account has a zero balance, its name and number are included in the list, but no figure is entered in the amount columns.

Note that the trial balance illustrated below has a three-line heading showing "who," "what," and "when." The date is the closing date. Observe, too, that dollar signs have been omitted from the trial balance columns. This procedure of omitting dollar signs is usually followed by accountants in preparing financial statements or schedules for their own use.

CARTER CLEANING SHOP
Trial Balance
December 31, 19X1

ACCT. NO.	ACCOUNT NAME	DEBIT	CREDIT
101	Cash	3,200 00	
111	Accounts Receivable	200 00	
141	Equipment	3,000 00	
201	Accounts Payable		300 00
301	Carter Investment		6,000 00
401	Cleaning Service Income		3,000 00
511	Salary Expense	1,600 00	
516	Rent Expense	700 00	
521	Supplies Used	600 00	
	Totals	9,300 00	9,300 00

UNIT 4

49

When the debit and credit columns are equal, or balance, the accountant knows that his books are in balance, and he is sure that he has recorded a debit for every credit.

If the debit and credit columns do not equal one another, the accountant knows that he has made some common type of error, such as:

1. Making errors in addition.
2. Recording only half an entry (the debit without the credit, or vice versa).
3. Recording both halves of the entry on the same side (two debits or two credits, rather than a debit and a credit).
4. Recording one or more amounts incorrectly.
5. Making errors in arithmetic in the journal entry.
6. Making errors in arithmetic in balancing the accounts.

Errors in addition of the trial balance columns can be detected by adding the columns again in the opposite direction. Thus, if the columns were first added from bottom to top, they should be verified by adding from top to bottom.

Even though the books are in balance, the accountant must also consider and eliminate other possibilities for errors such as:

1. A transaction could be omitted.
2. The same transaction could be recorded more than once.
3. A part of an entry could be recorded in the wrong account.
4. There could be offsetting arithmetic errors in the accounts.
5. There could be offsetting arithmetic errors involved in totaling the trial balance columns.

Other sources of arithmetic errors are sometimes suggested by the amount of the difference involved. If the amount is divisible by 9, the discrepancy may be either a transposition ($357 for $375) or a slide ($375 for $37.50). Dividing the difference by 2 may suggest the amount of a debit posted as a credit or a credit posted as a debit.

Fortunately, these types of errors are relatively infrequent. The trial balance, therefore, is regarded as a basic and useful indicator of accuracy.

THE WORKSHEET

When the trial balance indicates that the ledger is in balance, the accountant is ready to prepare the financial statements for the period. To be of maximum use, the financial statements need to be completed as soon as possible. Therefore, anything that the accountant can do to save time is important.

Accountants have learned from experience that they can save time in preparing the reports if they have a way to sort out and organize the figures that are needed. A special form, called a *worksheet,* has been devised for this purpose. Here is how a worksheet looks in its simplest form.

CARTER CLEANING SHOP
Worksheet
Month Ended December 31, 19X1

ACCT. NO.	ACCOUNT NAME	TRIAL BALANCE		INCOME STATEMENT		BALANCE SHEET	
		DR.	CR.	DR.	CR.	DR.	CR.
101	Cash	3,200 00					
111	Accts. Receivable	200 00					
141	Equipment	3,000 00					
201	Accts. Payable		300 00				
301	Carter Investment		6,000 00				
401	Cleaning Service Income		3,000 00				
511	Salary Expense	1,600 00					
516	Rent Expense	700 00					
521	Supplies Used	600 00					
	Totals	9,300 00	9,300 00				

The Trial Balance Section

The starting point in preparing a worksheet is the trial balance data. This is why the first two money columns in the worksheet are headed Trial Balance. The only differences between this form and the one shown on page 49 are: the size of the sheet of paper used, the provision for extra money columns to facilitate the preparation of the statements, and substitution of the period of operation for the closing date on the third line of the heading.

The Income Statement and Balance Sheet Sections

The money columns headed Income Statement and Balance Sheet are used to sort out and organize the figures needed for these financial reports. For instance, the accountant knows that before he can draw up an income statement, he needs to assemble all the income and expense account balances in one place. This is easy for him to do on a worksheet. First, he heads the second pair of money columns Income Statement, designates the following pair of columns Balance Sheet, and subdivides each pair into Debit and Credit columns. Then, starting at the top of the list of accounts in the Trial Balance section, he examines each item in turn. If the item will appear on the balance sheet, the amount is entered in the Balance Sheet columns. If the item will appear on the income statement, it is entered in the Income Statement columns. Accounts with zero balances are ignored.

In carrying each item across the worksheet from the trial balance to the statement columns, debit balances are carried to debit columns in the statement sections, and credit balances are carried to credit columns in the statement sections. An item never changes sides in being extended across the worksheet.

THE BALANCE SHEET COLUMNS. You will recall that the accounts are numbered according to types in the following sequence: assets, liabilities, owner's equity, income, and expense. The first three accounts in the Trial Balance section of the worksheet are assets and are carried over to the Debit column of the Balance Sheet section. Thus the debit items continue to appear as debit items after they have been carried over. The partially completed worksheet is shown as it appears after this has been done.

CARTER CLEANING SHOP
Worksheet
Month Ended December 31, 19X1

ACCT. NO.	ACCOUNT NAME	TRIAL BALANCE		INCOME STATEMENT		BALANCE SHEET	
		DR.	CR.	DR.	CR.	DR.	CR.
101	Cash	3,200 00				3,200 00	
111	Accts. Receivable	200 00				200 00	
141	Equipment	3,000 00				3,000 00	
201	Accts. Payable		300 00				
301	Carter Investment		6,000 00				
401	Cleaning Service Income		3,000 00				
511	Salary Expense	1,600 00					
516	Rent Expense	700 00					
521	Supplies Used	600 00					
	Totals	9,300 00	9,300 00				

The next two items, the credit balances for liabilities and owner's equity, are carried across to the Credit column of the Balance Sheet section.

CARTER CLEANING SHOP
Worksheet
Month Ended December 31, 19X1

ACCT. NO.	ACCOUNT NAME	TRIAL BALANCE		INCOME STATEMENT		BALANCE SHEET	
		DR.	CR.	DR.	CR.	DR.	CR.
101	Cash	3,200 00				3,200 00	
111	Accts. Receivable	200 00				200 00	
141	Equipment	3,000 00				3,000 00	
201	Accts. Payable		300 00				300 00
301	Carter Investment		6,000 00				6,000 00
401	Cleaning Service Income		3,000 00				
511	Salary Expense	1,600 00					
516	Rent Expense	700 00					
521	Supplies Used	600 00					
	Totals	9,300 00	9,300 00				

THE INCOME STATEMENT COLUMNS. The accountant knows that all income and expense items must appear on the income statement. Therefore, he carries the credit balance in the Cleaning Service Income account to the Credit column of the Income Statement section of the worksheet. Then he considers the accounts for Salary Expense, Rent Expense, and Supplies Used and extends their debit balances across to the Debit column of the Income Statement section of the worksheet, as shown.

CARTER CLEANING SHOP
Worksheet
Month Ended December 31, 19X1

ACCT. NO.	ACCOUNT NAME	TRIAL BALANCE DR.	TRIAL BALANCE CR.	INCOME STATEMENT DR.	INCOME STATEMENT CR.	BALANCE SHEET DR.	BALANCE SHEET CR.
101	Cash	3,200 00				3,200 00	
111	Accts. Receivable	200 00				200 00	
141	Equipment	3,000 00				3,000 00	
201	Accts. Payable		300 00				300 00
301	Carter Investment		6,000 00				6,000 00
401	Cleaning Service Income		3,000 00		3,000 00		
511	Salary Expense	1,600 00		1,600 00			
516	Rent Expense	700 00		700 00			
521	Supplies Used	600 00		600 00			
	Totals	9,300 00	9,300 00				

Totaling the Columns

When the accountant has carried each item across the worksheet from the Trial Balance columns to the financial statement columns, the Income Statement columns are totaled. In this case, the debits (expenses) total $2,900 and the credits (income) total $3,000.

CARTER CLEANING SHOP
Worksheet
Month Ended December 31, 19X1

ACCT. NO.	ACCOUNT NAME	TRIAL BALANCE DR.	TRIAL BALANCE CR.	INCOME STATEMENT DR.	INCOME STATEMENT CR.	BALANCE SHEET DR.	BALANCE SHEET CR.
101	Cash	3,200 00				3,200 00	
111	Accts. Receivable	200 00				200 00	
141	Equipment	3,000 00				3,000 00	
201	Accts. Payable		300 00				300 00
301	Carter Investment		6,000 00				6,000 00
401	Cleaning Service Income		3,000 00		3,000 00		
511	Salary Expense	1,600 00		1,600 00			
516	Rent Expense	700 00		700 00			
521	Supplies Used	600 00		600 00			
	Totals	9,300 00	9,300 00	2,900 00	3,000 00	6,400 00	6,300 00

Next, he adds the amounts in the Balance Sheet columns. The debits (assets) total $6,400, and credits (liabilities and owner's equity) total $6,300. These totals are entered as shown.

Since the Income Statement section columns include all expenses and income, the profit or loss can easily be identified. In this instance, the income exceeds the expenses, so a profit of $100 ($3,000 − $2,900) is indicated. (If the expenses had exceeded the income, there would, of course, have been a loss.) Since the profit represents the net increase in owner's equity resulting from operations for the month, it is transferred to the balance sheet section. A record is made on the line below the totals:

1. The difference between income and expense is properly identified on the worksheet as "Profit for the Month."
2. The amount of $100 is entered in the Debit column of the Income Statement section.
3. The same amount is recorded in the Credit column of the Balance Sheet section.

When the transfer is completed, the columns are totaled and all pairs of columns are in balance.

CARTER CLEANING SHOP
Worksheet
Month Ended December 31, 19X1

ACCT. NO.	ACCOUNT NAME	TRIAL BALANCE		INCOME STATEMENT		BALANCE SHEET	
		DR.	CR.	DR.	CR.	DR.	CR.
101	Cash	3,200 00				3,200 00	
111	Accts. Receivable	200 00				200 00	
141	Equipment	3,000 00				3,000 00	
201	Accts. Payable		300 00				300 00
301	Carter Investment		6,000 00				6,000 00
401	Cleaning Serv. Inc.		3,000 00		3,000 00		
511	Salary Expense	1,600 00		1,600 00			
516	Rent Expense	700 00		700 00			
521	Supplies Used	600 00		600 00			
	Totals	9,300 00	9,300 00	2,900 00	3,000 00	6,400 00	6,300 00
	Profit for the Month			100 00			100 00
				3,000 00	3,000 00	6,400 00	6,400 00

If a loss had been incurred, it would have been identified on the worksheet as "Loss for the Month." The amount of the loss would then have been transferred by an entry in the Credit column of the Income Statement section and one in the Debit column of the Balance Sheet section.

All the figures necessary for preparing the financial statements are now properly organized on the worksheet. The accounts are even arranged in the order required for statement presentation. The income statement is prepared directly from the Income Statement columns of the worksheet, and the balance sheet figures are taken directly from the Balance Sheet columns. Notice that the net profit of $100 is added to the investment of Carter at the beginning of the period to arrive at the value of the investment at the end of the month.

CARTER CLEANING SHOP
Income Statement
Month Ended December 31, 19X1

Income		
Cleaning Service		$3,000 00
Less Expenses		
Salary Expense	$1,600 00	
Rent Expense	700 00	
Supplies Used	600 00	
Total Expenses		2,900 00
Net Profit for the Month		$ 100 00

CARTER CLEANING SHOP
Balance Sheet
December 31, 19X1

ASSETS			LIABILITIES AND OWNER'S EQUITY		
Cash	$3,200 00		*Liabilities*		
Accounts Receivable	200 00		Accts. Payable		$ 300 00
Equipment	3,000. 00		*Owner's Equity*		
			Carter Invest. 12/1/X1	$6,000 00	
			Profit for Dec.	100 00	
			Carter Invest. 12/31/X1		6,100 00
Total Assets	$6,400 00		*Total Liabilities and Owner's Equity*		$6,400 00

◆ ◆ ◆

PRINCIPLES AND PROCEDURES

The trial balance is used to verify the equality of debits and credits in the ledger before the accountant prepares the financial reports for the period. Once he knows that the books balance, the accountant prepares a worksheet in columnar form to save time in preparing the statements. First, he records the trial balance information on the worksheet. Then he organizes in the appropriate statement sections the figures needed for the income statement and the balance sheet. Next, he determines the profit or loss for the period. Finally, the amounts in the Income Statement and Balance Sheet sections of the worksheet are presented in the formal financial reports.

MANAGERIAL IMPLICATIONS

Taking a trial balance gives assurance that the books are in balance before the accountant attempts to prepare the periodic statements. This process aids in pinpointing errors and in identifying different types of mistakes that may occur. Repeated errors may signal the need for managerial action to correct careless work habits or to improve the recording procedure. The use of the worksheet speeds statement preparation by the accountant and thus makes vital data more quickly available to management. The more accounts there are in the ledger, the more time can be saved by utilizing a worksheet.

APPLICATION OF PRINCIPLES

PROBLEM 4 · 1

♦ George Berry owns and operates an interior decorating firm known as Creative Decorations. The trial balance at March 31, 19X1, shows the following information.

ACCT. NO.	ACCOUNT NAME	DEBIT	CREDIT
101	Cash	$ 6,089.00	
111	Accounts Receivable	375.00	
141	Office Equipment	1,600.00	
143	Display Equipment	3,760.00	
144	Automobile	–0–	
201	Accounts Payable		$ 140.00
301	Berry Investment		9,878.00
401	Income from Services		4,090.00
504	Telephone Expense	33.00	
511	Salary Expense	825.00	
513	Advertising Expense	160.00	
516	Rent Expense	300.00	
518	Equipment Repairs	40.00	
521	Office Supplies Used	11.00	
522	Utilities Expense	55.00	
523	Materials Used	860.00	
	Totals	$14,108.00	$14,108.00

The firm's transactions for April 19X1 are given on the next page.

1 Paid month's rent, $100.

3 Acquired display equipment costing $900, paying $300 in cash and agreeing to pay the balance in 30 days.

5 Collected $350 cash for professional services rendered.

5 Paid salaries for March, $275.

10 Bought automobile for business use, $2,000 in cash.

17 Paid $50 cash for advertising cards and posters.

19 Received $150 in cash for professional services, and performed additional services on credit, $425. (Use a compound entry.)

22 Paid monthly telephone bill, $9.

23 Collected $150 from credit customers.

26 Paid $200 to apply on balance due for display equipment.

28 Paid utilities bill for month, $18.

30 Paid $15 for office supplies used.

30 Received invoice for materials used on job, $120 to be paid in 30 days.

30 Sold professional services, $200 in cash and $125 on credit.

INSTRUCTIONS

1. Set up a general ledger for the accounts listed in the trial balance at March 31 and enter the amounts as opening balances.

2. Prepare general journal entries to record the April transactions.

3. Post the April general journal entries to the general ledger.

4. Foot each of the accounts and determine the balance of each at April 30. Enter your footing and balance figures in proper form.

5. Take a trial balance at April 30.

PROBLEM 4 · 2

The general ledger accounts and balances of the Casper Insurance Agency at December 31, 19X1, are as follows:

101	Cash	$1,500 Dr.	301	Casper Investment	$5,520 Cr.
111	Accounts Receivable	200 Dr.	403	Inc. from Commis.	6,000 Cr.
130	Office Furniture	250 Dr.	504	Telephone Expense	150 Dr.
131	Automobile	900 Dr.	511	Salaries Expense	3,600 Dr.
132	Building	6,000 Dr.	522	Utilities Expense	120 Dr.
201	Accounts Payable	1,800 Cr.	534	Maintenance Expense	600 Dr.

INSTRUCTIONS

1. Complete the worksheet for the Casper Insurance Agency at the end of six months of operation.

2. Prepare a formal income statement and balance sheet. Use two-column analysis paper for the income statement and four-column analysis paper for the balance sheet.

Jeanne Adams decided to enter the dressmaking business and engaged
♦ in the following transactions during October 19X1, using the listed accounts:

OCT.

1   Invested $4,000 in cash.
3   Paid rent for month, $75.
6   Bought sewing equipment worth $400; $200 in cash, balance on credit.
7   Acquired shop fixtures for $50 in cash.
10 Sold services during first week, $200; $125 in cash and balance on credit.
11 Paid $15 for advertising circulars.
14 Paid $40 for supplies used.
17 Sold additional services, $300; $200 for cash and $100 on credit.
24 Collected $125 from accounts receivable.
25 Paid salaries, $100.
26 Paid for machine repairs, $15.
28 Sold surplus sewing machine for $50 in cash.
29 Paid $10 telephone bill.
30 Paid $16 for additional supplies used.

521	Supplies Used	516	Rent Expense
504	Telephone Expense	201	Accounts Payable
142	Shop Fixtures	111	Accounts Receivable
511	Salary Expense	101	Cash
141	Sewing Equipment	513	Advertising Expense
401	Income from Services	301	Adams Investment
518	Equipment Repairs		

INSTRUCTIONS

1. Classify the account titles (and numbers) shown and prepare a chart of
    accounts.
2. Journalize the October transactions.
3. Set up a general ledger.
4. Post all entries to the general ledger.
5. Foot and balance the accounts.
6. Complete a worksheet as of October 31.
7. Prepare the income statement (use two-column analysis paper) and bal-
    ance sheet (use four-column analysis paper).

MANAGERIAL CHECKUP

♦ How does the preparation of a worksheet make vital data more quickly
available to management?

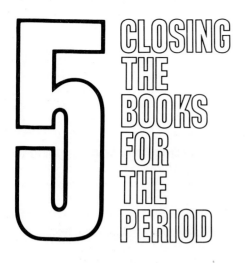

CLOSING THE BOOKS FOR THE PERIOD

Once the worksheet and financial statements are completed, the results of operations must be entered in the ledger as a permanent record for future reference. Since all entries in the ledger are posted from the general journal, it is first necessary to make the journal entries that summarize results.

THE INCOME AND EXPENSE SUMMARY

The procedure of journalizing and posting the results of operations is called *closing the books*. The steps in the closing process parallel those used to organize data on the worksheet. (The accountant used the Income Statement columns in the worksheet to assemble the income and expense amounts in one place.) In the closing procedure, he also uses an assembling or summarizing device for these amounts. Since the summarizing has to take place in the ledger, the assembling device that he uses is a special account called Income and Expense Summary 399. As illustrated, expenses are assembled on the debit side of the summary account and income is assembled on the credit side, just as they are on the worksheet.

INCOME STATEMENT	
DEBIT	CREDIT
(For Expenses)	(For Income)
2,900 00	3,000 00

INCOME AND EXPENSE SUMMARY

Debit Side (For Expenses)	Credit Side (For Income)

A discussion of the process of journalizing and posting the closing entries to transfer the income and expenses to the Income and Expense Summary account follows.

TRANSFERRING INCOME BALANCES

The Cleaning Service Income account of the Carter Cleaning Shop shows a net credit balance of $3,000 as of December 31, 19X1.

Cleaning Service Income   No. 401

DATE	EXPLANATION	POST. REF.	DEBIT	DATE		EXPLANATION	POST. REF.	CREDIT	
				19	X1				
				Dec.	11		12-1	2,200	00
					14		12-2	800	00
								3,000	*00*

Since the Cleaning Service Income account now has a credit balance, it will be necessary to debit the account for the same amount to:

1. Transfer the income account balance to the credit side of the Income and Expense Summary account.
2. Obtain a zero balance as the logical outcome of the closing process.

The following journal entry shows how these goals are achieved. (The C in the entry number indicates that this is a closing entry.)

GENERAL JOURNAL   Page 1

DATE		DESCRIPTION OF ENTRY	ACCT. NO.	✓	DEBIT		CREDIT	
19	X1	12-7C (Closing)						
Dec.	31	Cleaning Service Income	401		3,000	00		
		Income & Expense Summary	399				3,000	00
		To transfer the income account balance						
		to the summary account.						

TRANSFERRING EXPENSE BALANCES

A similar procedure is used to transfer the balances of the expense accounts. On December 31 these accounts appear as follows.

Since each of these accounts has a debit balance, it will be necessary

Salary Expense No. 511

DATE	EXPLANATION	POST. REF.	DEBIT	DATE	EXPLANATION	POST. REF.	CREDIT
19 X1 Dec. 18		12-4	1,600 00				

Rent Expense No. 516

DATE	EXPLANATION	POST. REF.	DEBIT	DATE	EXPLANATION	POST. REF.	CREDIT
19 X1 Dec. 20		12-5	700 00				

Supplies Used No. 521

DATE	EXPLANATION	POST. REF.	DEBIT	DATE	EXPLANATION	POST. REF.	CREDIT
19 X1 Dec. 31		12-6	600 00				

to make an entry to credit each account in order to close it. Usually, the accountant makes a compound journal entry. He closes the expense accounts by crediting each individual account. Then, he debits the total amount of the expenses to the Income and Expense Summary account. In this way, the summary account will reflect the same amount in total that was shown in the individual expense account balances. Here is the journal entry that Carter's accountant makes.

GENERAL JOURNAL Page 2

DATE	DESCRIPTION OF ENTRY	ACCT. NO.	✓	DEBIT	CREDIT
19 X1 Dec. 31	12-8C				
	Income and Expense Summary	399		2,900 00	
	Salary Expense	511			1,600 00
	Rent Expense	516			700 00
	Supplies Used	521			600 00
	To transfer expense account balances to the summary account.				

The next step is for the accountant to post the two closing journal entries to the general ledger accounts. After these two entries have been posted to the accounts, the income and expense accounts have no balances.

The accountant says that they have been *closed* to the Income and Expense Summary account. The ledger sheets look like this.

Income and Expense Summary No. 399

DATE	EXPLANATION	POST. REF.	DEBIT		DATE	EXPLANATION	POST. REF.	CREDIT	
19 X1 Dec. 31		12-8C	2,900	00	19 X1 Dec. 31		12-7C	3,000	00

Cleaning Service Income No. 401

DATE	EXPLANATION	POST. REF.	DEBIT		DATE	EXPLANATION	POST. REF.	CREDIT	
19 X1 Dec. 31	To close	12-7C	3,000	00	19 X1 Dec. 11		12-1	2,200	00
					14		12-2	800	00
								3,000	*00*

Salary Expense No. 511

DATE	EXPLANATION	POST. REF.	DEBIT		DATE	EXPLANATION	POST. REF.	CREDIT	
19 X1 Dec. 18		12-4	1,600	00	19 X1 Dec. 31	To close	12-8C	1,600	00

Rent Expense No. 516

DATE	EXPLANATION	POST. REF.	DEBIT		DATE	EXPLANATION	POST. REF.	CREDIT	
19 X1 Dec. 20		12-5	700	00	19 X1 Dec. 31	To close	12-8C	700	00

Supplies Used No. 521

DATE	EXPLANATION	POST. REF.	DEBIT		DATE	EXPLANATION	POST. REF.	CREDIT	
19 X1 Dec. 31		12-6	600	00	19 X1 Dec. 31	To close	12-8C	600	00

Note that the Income and Expense Summary account now reflects the same information as the first entries in the Income Statement columns of the worksheet on page 53. In other words, the accountant has now formally journalized and posted the information that he had only noted in the Income Statement section of the worksheet before. As a matter of fact, the accountant customarily prepares the closing entries directly from the worksheet. The journal entry to close the income accounts summarizes and transfers the data appearing in the Credit column in the Income Statement section, and the journal entry to close the expense accounts summarizes and transfers the data appearing in the Debit column in the Income Statement section of the worksheet.

TRANSFERRING PROFIT OR LOSS TO OWNER'S EQUITY

The final step for the permanent record is to transfer the $100 credit balance, representing profit, to the owner's equity account. On the worksheet on page 54, this shift was shown by using a pair of counterbalancing figures and making a brief explanatory notation, "Profit for the Month," in the Account Name column.

The accountant now makes a formal journal entry to record the transfer.

GENERAL JOURNAL   **Page 1**

DATE	DESCRIPTION OF ENTRY	ACCT. NO.	✓	DEBIT	CREDIT
19 X1	⌐12-9C⌐				
Dec. 31	Income and Expense Summary	399		100 00	
	Carter Investment	301			100 00
	To transfer profit for the month to the				
	owner's equity account.				

When this entry is posted, the Income and Expense Summary account is closed. (This account is not shown on the worksheet.)

Income and Expense Summary   **No. 399**

DATE	EXPLANATION	POST. REF.	DEBIT	DATE	EXPLANATION	POST. REF.	CREDIT
19 X1				19 X1			
Dec. 31		12-8C	2,900 00	Dec. 31		12-7C	3,000 00
31		12-9C	100 00				
			3,000 00				

The owner's equity account is now increased by the amount of the profit, as follows.

Carter Investment   No. 301

DATE	EXPLANATION	POST. REF.	DEBIT	DATE		EXPLANATION	POST. REF.	CREDIT	
				19	X1				
				Nov.	26		11-1	6,000	00
				Dec.	31		12-9C	100	00
								6,100	*00*

The new balance of the Carter Investment account agrees with the final amount shown in the Owner's Equity section of the balance sheet for December 31, 19X1.

CARTER CLEANING SHOP
Balance Sheet
December 31, 19X1

ASSETS			LIABILITIES AND OWNER'S EQUITY				
Cash		$3,200 00	*Liabilities*				
Accts. Receivable		200 00	Accts. Payable			$ 300	00
Equipment		3,000 00	*Owner's Equity*				
			Carter Invest. 12/1/X1	$6,000	00		
			Profit for Dec.	100	00		
			Carter Invest. 12/31/X1			6,100	00
			Total Liabilities and				
Total Assets		$6,400 00	*Owner's Equity*			$6,400	00

All the changes resulting from operations during the period are now reflected in the ledger account records. (The preceding example shows the closing process at the end of one month for illustrative purposes only. Normally, closing takes place only at the end of the fiscal year.)

RULING THE LEDGER

The ledger is not only a complete record of all the accounts, it is also a continuing record. The same ledger accounts that were used to record the opening transactions and the December transactions are used for the January entries also. If the entries for one fiscal period should become commingled with those of another, the record would be cluttered and confusing. This is why the accountant separates the entries of one period from those of the next by a process called *ruling*.

Ruling Closed Accounts

All income and expense accounts were closed when their balances were transferred to the Income and Expense Summary account. In turn, Income and Expense Summary was closed when its balance was transferred to the owner's equity account. The accounts are considered closed because they have no balances. A closed account is ruled in the following manner:

1. If only one amount appears on each side of the account, a double line is drawn below the entries, across the Date, Posting Reference, and Amount columns.

Salary Expense   **No. 511**

DATE		EXPLANATION	POST. REF.	DEBIT		DATE		EXPLANATION	POST. REF.	CREDIT	
19	X1					19	X1				
Dec.	18		12-4	1,600	00	Dec.	31		12-8C	1,600	00

2. If two or more entries appear on either side of the account, a single line is drawn below the last entry, across the Amount columns on both sides of the account. The total is placed below this line on both sides, and a double line is drawn under all columns except the Explanation spaces.

Cleaning Service Income   **No. 401**

DATE		EXPLANATION	POST. REF.	DEBIT		DATE		EXPLANATION	POST. REF.	CREDIT	
19	X1					19	X1				
Dec.	31		12-7C	3,000	00	Dec.	11		12-1	2,200	00
							14		12-2	800	00
										3,000	*00*
				3,000	00					3,000	00

Ruling Accounts with Balances

Accounts with balances are ruled so that their balances are *carried forward* to the new period of operations. These accounts are assets, liabilities, and owner's equity. The process of ruling and carrying forward works like this:

1. The balance of the account is determined. Often this is the same as

the balance computed when the trial balance was prepared. The balance of the Cash 101 account is $3,200.

Cash   **No. 101**

DATE		EXPLANATION	POST. REF.	DEBIT		DATE		EXPLANATION	POST. REF.	CREDIT	
19	X1					19	X1				
Nov.	26		11-1	6,000	00	Nov.	27		11-2	2,000	00
Dec.	11		12-1	2,200	00		30		11-4	700	00
	16		12-3	600	00	Dec.	18		12-4	1,600	00
		3,200.00		*8,800*	*00*		20		12-5	700	00
							31		12-6	600	00
										5,600	*00*

2. This balance of $3,200 is entered in the account on the side with the *smaller* total and is labeled "Carried Forward."

Cash   **No. 101**

DATE		EXPLANATION	POST. REF.	DEBIT		DATE		EXPLANATION	POST. REF.	CREDIT	
19	X1					19	X1				
Nov.	26		11-1	6,000	00	Nov.	27		11-2	2,000	00
Dec.	11		12-1	2,200	00		30		11-4	700	00
	16		12-3	600	00	Dec.	18		12-4	1,600	00
		3,200.00		*8,800*	*00*		20		12-5	700	00
							31		12-6	600	00
										5,600	*00*
							31	**Carried Forward**		**3,200**	**00**

3. The account is now totaled and ruled as were the closed accounts just studied.

Cash   **No. 101**

DATE		EXPLANATION	POST. REF.	DEBIT		DATE		EXPLANATION	POST. REF.	CREDIT	
19	X1					19	X1				
Nov.	26		11-1	6,000	00	Nov.	27		11-2	2,000	00
Dec.	11		12-1	2,200	00		30		11-4	700	00
	16		12-3	600	00	Dec.	18		12-4	1,600	00
		3,200.00		*8,800*	*00*		20		12-5	700	00
							31		12-6	600	00
										5,600	*00*
							31	Carried Forward		3,200	00
				8,800	00					8,800	00

4. The net balance is then entered on the opposite side, on the first line below the double ruling. This entry bears the date of the beginning of the new period (year, month, and day) and is labeled "Brought Forward." The Brought Forward figure becomes the fresh starting point for recording the transactions of the new period. A check mark (✓) is placed in the Posting Reference column beside both the Carried Forward and Brought Forward figures. This indicates that no journal entry was involved. The other two asset accounts in the ledger so far—Accounts Receivable and Equipment—are handled in the same manner as Cash.

Cash   **No. 101**

DATE		EXPLANATION	POST. REF.	DEBIT		DATE		EXPLANATION	POST. REF.	CREDIT	
19	X1					19	X1				
Nov.	26		11-1	6,000	00	Nov.	27		11-2	2,000	00
Dec.	11		12-1	2,200	00		30		11-4	700	00
	16	*3,200.00*	12-3	600	00	Dec.	18		12-4	1,600	00
							20		12-5	700	00
							31		12-6	600	00
										5,600	*00*
							31	Carried Forward	✓	3,200	00
				8,800							
				8,800	00					8,800	00
19	X2										
Jan.	1	**Brought Forward**	✓	3,200	00						

The liability and owner's equity accounts are balanced, ruled, and carried forward in the same manner. Notice, however, that since the net balance of both these accounts is a credit balance, the amount is entered below the double ruling on the credit side of the account. (It is not necessary to balance and rule an account that contains only one entry.)

Accounts Payable   **No. 201**

DATE		EXPLANATION	POST. REF.	DEBIT		DATE		EXPLANATION	POST. REF.	CREDIT	
19	X1					19	X1				
Nov.	30		11-4	700	00	Nov.	28		11-3	1,000	00
Dec.	31	Carried Forward	✓	300	00						
				1,000	*00*			*300.00*			
				1,000	00					1,000	00
						19	X2				
						Jan.	1	Brought Forward	✓	300	00

DATE	EXPLANATION	POST. REF.	DEBIT		DATE	EXPLANATION	POST. REF.	CREDIT	
19 X1 Dec. 31	Carried Forward	√	6,100	00	19 X1 Nov. 26 Dec. 31		11-1 12-9C	6,000 100	00 00
								6,100 6,100	*00* 00
			6,100	00					
					19 X2 Jan. 1	Brought Forward	√	6,100	00

THE POSTCLOSING TRIAL BALANCE

The accountant wants to avoid mistakes arising from possible errors such as carrying forward the wrong amount or putting the Brought Forward balance on the wrong side of an account. If this should happen, the books would not balance at the end of the next period and it might take hours or days to find the error. For this reason, the accountant takes a *postclosing trial balance* as the last step in his end-of-period routine. Accounts with zero balances are not listed in a postclosing trial balance. This is done to save time. When the postclosing trial balance totals are equal, the accountant knows that he can safely proceed with the recording of the entries for the new period. The postclosing trial balance for the Carter Cleaning Shop is shown.

CARTER CLEANING SHOP
Postclosing Trial Balance
December 31, 19X1

ACCT. NO.	ACCOUNT NAME	DEBIT		CREDIT	
101	Cash	3,200	00		
111	Accounts Receivable	200	00		
141	Equipment	3,000	00		
201	Accounts Payable			300	00
301	Carter Investment			6,100	00
	Totals	6,400	00	6,400	00

The completion of the postclosing trial balance signals the end of the various steps in the accounting cycle that you have learned. These same steps will be repeated in every fiscal period throughout the life of the business.

Although the rules involving the use of dollar signs vary among accountants, the basic rules followed in this text are generally accepted by accountants. Fortunately, there are only two rules to remember.

1. No dollar signs are used in the ledger accounts. Nor are they normally used on financial forms or statements for internal use by the accountant—such as working papers, the postclosing trial balance, and supporting schedules prepared by the accountant to help him in his work.
2. Published statements, or statements prepared for formal use, should always use dollar signs. In this text, dollar signs are placed beside the first number in each column and are always placed beside numbers that follow rulings. For example, the balance sheet illustrated on page 64 contains dollar signs beside the first number of each column and beside the total figures in each column.

DETECTING AND CORRECTING ERRORS

The postclosing trial balance, as well as the trial balance, aids in detecting mathematical errors. But even if an error is detected, the accountant still must determine where it was made and take steps to correct it. Refer to Unit 4 for a discussion of some of the more common errors and how they are detected and corrected.

◆　◆　◆

PRINCIPLES AND PROCEDURES

The closing procedure is devised to complete the records of the period before new business transactions are entered in the books. Here are the steps in the closing procedure:

1. Close the income accounts by transferring their balances to Income and Expense Summary.
2. Close the expense accounts by transferring their balances to Income and Expense Summary.
3. Close the Income and Expense Summary account by transferring its net balance (profit or loss) to the owner's equity account.
4. Rule all accounts.
5. Prepare a postclosing trial balance.

Now, add the following procedures to the steps in the accounting cycle already explained and the complete routine for a cycle results.

1. Analyze and record the daily transactions in the journal.
2. Post the journal entries to the ledger.
3. Prepare a trial balance at the end of the period.
4. Complete the worksheet.
5. Complete the income statement and balance sheet.
6. Record the closing entries in the journal.
7. Post the closing entries to the ledger.
8. Balance, foot, and rule the ledger accounts.
9. Prepare a postclosing trial balance.

MANAGERIAL IMPLICATIONS

Completion of the closing process rounds out the accounting cycle. For management, this means that the accountant has now completed the analysis of each business transaction and has entered it in both a chronological record (journal) and a permanent, classified record (ledger). He has also summarized the ledger account balances in the form of meaningful financial reports. The data in the reports allow those both inside and outside the business to interpret its financial condition and measure its profitability without having to review each business transaction individually. These reports also guide executives and managers in making decisions and formulating policies.

APPLICATION OF PRINCIPLES

PROBLEM 5 · 1

♦ The worksheet of the McFarland Insurance Agency includes the following accounts at Dec. 31, 19X2:

301	McFarland Investment	$5,000	Cr.
401	Commission Income	4,000	Cr.
501	Rent Expense	200	Dr.
505	Salaries	1,000	Dr.
510	Supplies Used	100	Dr.
511	Telephone Expense	50	Dr.

INSTRUCTIONS
1. In general journal form, record the closing entries. Start with Entry 12-11C.
2. Compute balance of owner's equity at the end of the period.

PROBLEM 5 · 2

The E-Z Window Washing Service opened for business on Mar. 1, 19X1.
♦ The accountant who assisted Zarnell in the organization of the business set up the chart of accounts shown on the next page.

101	Cash	401	Income from Services
111	Accounts Receivable	504	Telephone Expense
141	Cleaning Equipment	505	Utilities Expense
143	Automotive Equipment	511	Salary Expense
201	Accounts Payable	513	Advertising Expense
301	Zarnell Investment	519	Automotive Repair Expense
399	Income and Expense Summary	521	Supplies Used

During March 19X1 the following selected transactions took place:

MAR.

1 Earl Zarnell, the owner, made an initial cash investment of $750.

1 Acquired cleaning equipment for $45 in cash.

2 Bought used panel truck for $500; paid half in cash with balance due in 30 days.

3 Sold services for cash, $150.

4 Bought cleaning equipment worth $125 on credit.

6 Paid telephone bill, $5.

9 Paid for supplies used, $6.

11 Sold services totaling $250, of which $100 was collected in cash and $150 was to be carried on credit.

14 Paid for newspaper advertising, $18 in cash.

15 Paid semimonthly salary of part-time helper, $125.

18 Sold services for cash, $65; for credit, $45.

25 Received cash from credit customers, $35.

27 Paid cash to creditors on account, $100.

29 Had truck repaired on credit, $24.

31 Paid utility bill, $8.

31 Paid semimonthly salary of part-time helper, $125.

INSTRUCTIONS

1. Open general ledger accounts, using the chart of accounts as your guide.
2. Journalize the March transactions.
3. Post all entries to the general ledger.
4. Foot and balance the accounts.
5. Complete a worksheet as of Mar. 31.
6. Prepare the income statement (use two-column analysis paper) and balance sheet (use four-column analysis paper).
7. Journalize and post the closing entries.
8. Foot and rule all ledger accounts; carry forward open balances.
9. Prepare a postclosing trial balance.

MANAGERIAL CHECKUP

♦ What kinds of operating and general policy decisions might be influenced by data on financial statements?

INTEGRATED PRACTICAL APPLICATION-- SERVICE BUSINESS ACCOUNTING CYCLE

Now you are given the chance to apply the accounting knowledge you have acquired in this and the preceding units. You will act as the accountant for the Carter Cleaning Shop—analyzing and recording daily transactions, posting to the ledger, and completing the accounting cycle at the end of the month—for the month of January 19X2.

The chart of accounts below will be used. These are the same accounts listed in Unit 2, except that two new accounts, Income and Expense Summary 399 and Miscellaneous Expense 591, have been added.

100–199	ASSETS
101	Cash
111	Accounts Receivable
141	Equipment

200–299	LIABILITIES
201	Accounts Payable

300–399	OWNER'S EQUITY
301	Carter Investment
399	Income and Expense Summary

400–499	INCOME
401	Cleaning Service Income

500–599	EXPENSES
511	Salary Expense
516	Rent Expense
521	Supplies Used
591	Miscellaneous Expense

PREPARING THE LEDGER

Your first task is to prepare the ledger accounts so that the January transactions may be recorded. Enter the December 31, 19X1 postclosing trial balance amounts in their respective accounts. The postclosing trial balance is repeated here for your convenience.

CARTER CLEANING SHOP
Postclosing Trial Balance
December 31, 19X1

ACCT. NO.	ACCOUNT NAME	DEBIT		CREDIT	
101	Cash	3,200	00		
111	Accounts Receivable	200	00		
141	Equipment	3,000	00		
201	Accounts Payable			300	00
301	Carter Investment			6,100	00
	Totals	6,400	00	6,400	00

In entering the postclosing trial balance amounts, use January 1, 19X2 as the entry date, write "Brought Forward" in the Explanation column, and place a check mark in the Posting Reference column as shown in the Cash account illustrated.

DATE	EXPLANATION	POST. REF.	DEBIT		DATE	EXPLANATION	POST. REF.	CREDIT	
19 X2 Jan. 1	Brought Forward	✓	3,200	00					

RECORDING THE DAILY TRANSACTIONS

Analyze each of the following transactions for January 19X2 and then record it in the general journal. If there are any questions, refer to Unit 3, where similar transactions were journalized. Begin the general journal with Page 1.

JAN.

2 Acquired $770 worth of cleaning equipment from the Ajax Company, giving Check 31. (Treat check as cash.)

7 Cash receipts for cleaning services during the first week, $700.

7 Performed $60 worth of cleaning services for R. L. Camp, a charge customer, covered by Sales Slip 1. It is common business practice to prepare an individual sales slip record when a sale is made. The original is given to the customer and carbon copies are retained for bookkeeping and other purposes. Sales Slip 1 is illustrated.

CARTER CLEANING SHOP
365 BROAD STREET   CENTERPORT, STATE 53995
Phone: 555-5678

Sold to   R. L. Camp

Address   14 Oak Lane

Centerport, State

Date Jan. 7, 19X2   Terms 30 Days Net

QUAN.	DESCRIPTION	AMOUNT	
6	Slip Covers		
10	Drapes		
	Clean & Dye	60	00

No. 1   Received by   R. L. Camp

JAN.

9 Collected $200 from December charge customers.

10 Paid $300, by Check 32, to Knight, Inc., to cover balance due them.

11 Bought delivery truck from Ace Motors Co. for $1,000 (debit Equipment 141). Given one month to pay.

14 Cash receipts for cleaning services during the second week, $725.

14 Performed $25 worth of cleaning services for M. F. Coleman, a charge customer (Sales Slip 2).

15 Paid $400, by Check 33, for cleaning supplies used.

16 Collected $30 from R. L. Camp on account.

17 Paid store rent for the month, $700, by Check 34.

19 Sold $30 worth of cleaning services to B. A. Hahn, a charge customer (Sales Slip 3).

21 Cash receipts for sales during the third week, $900.

23 Collected $45 from charge customers ($30 from Camp; $15 from Coleman).

24 Paid $500, by Check 35, to Ace Motors to apply on account.

27 Cash receipts for sales during the fourth week, $800.

28 Bought counter and display fixtures for proposed new Accessories Department giving Check 36, $600. Debit Equipment 141. (This department will begin operations on February 1, with plans to sell a complete line of garment bags, hangers, racks, and mothproofing supplies.)

28 Sold $60 worth of cleaning services to charge customer S. S. Baker (Sales Slip 4).

28 Issued Check 37 for $300 for supplies used.

29 Collected $10 on account from charge customer M. F. Coleman.

30 Paid for miscellaneous expenses, $60, by Check 38.

31 Paid salaries for the month, $1,700, by Check 39.

COMPLETING THE CYCLE

Once the January transactions have been analyzed and journalized, complete the rest of the steps in the accounting cycle.

1. Post the daily transactions to the general ledger.
2. Take a trial balance to prove the accuracy of the posting. (Do as many accountants do in practice: enter the account balances directly in the Trial Balance columns of the worksheet, instead of preparing a separate trial balance and transferring the figures to the worksheet.)
3. Complete the worksheet.
4. Prepare an income statement. (Use two-column analysis paper.)
5. Prepare a balance sheet. (Use four-column analysis paper.)
6. Journalize the closing entries.
7. Post the closing entries to the ledger.
8. Balance, foot, and rule the accounts.
9. Prepare a postclosing trial balance.

(*Note:* After your instructor has checked your work, retain all papers relating to the January transactions for future reference.)

Key figures:

Net profit for the month	$ 140
Total assets	6,740
Carter Investment	6,240
Total assets increase in 2 months	740
Investment increase in 2 months	240

PART 2
SPECIAL JOURNALS
AND LEDGERS

6 ACCOUNTING FOR CASH RECEIPTS

When you journalized the January transactions of the Carter Cleaning Shop certain types of entries were repeated many times. For example, eight of the entries resulted in eight different debits to Cash 101 because cash was received. Some of the journal entries for cash receipts are shown below.

GENERAL JOURNAL Page 1

DATE		DESCRIPTION OF ENTRY	ACCT. NO.	✓	DEBIT		CREDIT	
19	X2	1–2						
Jan.	7	Cash	101	✓	700	00		
		Cleaning Service Income . .	401	✓			700	00
		To record cash sales for week.						
	9	1–4						
		Cash	101	✓	200	00		
		Accounts Receivable . . .	111	✓			200	00
		To record collections from December charge customers.						
	14	1–7						
		Cash	101	✓	725	00		
		Cleaning Service Income . .	401	✓			725	00
		To record cash sales for week.						

Each of these three journal entries, plus the other five not shown, then required posting to the Cash account, as illustrated on page 80.

You will quickly detect the great amount of repetition involved in these journal entries and postings. In the general journal, the eight cash receipts required eight separate journal entries. A look at these entries discloses eight debits to Cash 101, four credits to Cleaning Service Income 401,

DATE	EXPLANATION	POST. REF.	DEBIT		DATE	EXPLANATION	POST. REF.	CREDIT
19 X2								
Jan. 1	Brought Fwd.	✓	3,200	00				
7		1-2	700	00				
9		1-4	200	00				
14		1-7	725	00				
16		1-10	30	00				
21		1-13	900	00				
23		1-14	45	00				
27		1-16	800	00				
29		1-20	10	00				

four credits to Accounts Receivable 111, and eight journal explanations. The posting of 16 items to the ledger accounts represents still further duplication of effort.

The accountant realizes that a more efficient system of recording cash receipts must be developed to save time and manpower. Obviously, if only eight cash receipts required so much space, time, and work, the accountant could never expect to cope with a larger business volume if he continues using the present recording methods.

THE SINGLE-COLUMN CASH RECEIPTS JOURNAL

One way for the accountant to avoid repetition in recording numerous cash transactions is to record receipts in a separate *cash receipts journal* instead of in the general journal, designing the journal column headings to eliminate the repetitive details. The following cash receipts journal, which provides for a simple, one-line entry for each of the January cash receipts, is one form that might be used.

CASH RECEIPTS JOURNAL for Month of January 19X2   Page 1

DATE		ACCOUNT CREDITED	ACCT. NO.	✓	AMOUNT	
Jan.	7	Cleaning Service Income	401		700	00
	9	Accounts Receivable/December customers	111		200	00
	14	Cleaning Service Income	401		725	00
	16	Accounts Receivable/Camp	111		30	00
	21	Cleaning Service Income	401		900	00
	23	Accounts Receivable/Camp $30; Coleman $15	111		45	00
	27	Cleaning Service Income	401		800	00
	29	Accounts Receivable/Coleman	111		10	00

The eight debits to Cash that were necessary in the general journal are eliminated by use of the cash receipts journal. The repetitive and lengthy explanations are also rendered unnecessary, because the title of the journal explains the nature of the transactions entered in it. In other words, the cash receipts journal reduces the recording process for each receipt to the fewest essential elements—the date, account to be credited (title and number), and amount. (The customer's name is recorded for memorandum purposes only, at this time.)

POSTING FROM THE SINGLE-COLUMN CASH RECEIPTS JOURNAL

The single-column cash receipts journal offers an important advantage to the accountant when he posts to the Cash account. All he has to do is add the Amount column and post one summary total ($3,410) as a single debit to Cash instead of posting the eight separate debits. When this summary posting is made, a check mark is entered in the cash receipts journal next to the account number on the total line, as shown.

CASH RECEIPTS JOURNAL for Month of January 19X2   **Page 1**

DATE		ACCOUNT CREDITED	ACCT. NO.	✓	AMOUNT
Jan.	7	Cleaning Service Income	401		700 00
	9	Accounts Receivable/December customers	111		200 00
	14	Cleaning Service Income	401		725 00
	16	Accounts Receivable/Camp	111		30 00
	21	Cleaning Service Income	401		900 00
	23	Accounts Receivable/Camp $30; Coleman $15	111		45 00
	27	Cleaning Service Income	401		800 00
	29	Accounts Receivable/Coleman	111		10 00
	31	**Total Cash Debit**	101	✓	**3,410 00**

Cash   **No. 101**

DATE	EXPLANATION	POST. REF.	DEBIT	DATE	EXPLANATION	POST. REF.	CREDIT
19 X2							
Jan. 1	Brought Fwd.	✓	3,200 00				
31		CRJ-1	3,410 00				

When the above Cash account is compared with the Cash account shown on page 80, it will be seen that eight individual debit postings have been replaced by a single summary posting. (The posting reference CRJ-1 indicates that the amount was posted from Page 1 of the cash receipts journal.) Similarly, if there were 300 cash receipts transactions, use of the single-column cash receipts journal would permit one single debit posting to the

Cash account instead of the 300 individual cash postings that would be required if the general journal were used to record each transaction.

When the single-column cash receipts journal is used, the credits to Cleaning Service Income and Accounts Receivable are posted individually as if posting were being done from the general journal. After these postings have been made, the two accounts now reflect the new method of using a special journal by the posting reference CRJ-1. (The four items in the Cleaning Service Income account without CRJ-1 notations, are credit sale entries that have been posted from the general journal.)

Cleaning Service Income   **No. 401**

DATE	EXPLANATION	POST. REF.	DEBIT	DATE	EXPLANATION	POST. REF.	CREDIT
				19 X2			
				Jan. 7		CRJ-1	700 00
				7		1-3	60 00
				14		CRJ-1	725 00
				14		1-8	25 00
				19		1-12	30 00
				21		CRJ-1	900 00
				27		CRJ-1	800 00
				28		1-18	60 00

Accounts Receivable   **No. 111**

DATE	EXPLANATION	POST. REF.	DEBIT	DATE	EXPLANATION	POST. REF.	CREDIT
19 X2				19 X2			
Jan. 1	Brought Fwd.	✓	200 00	Jan. 9		CRJ-1	200 00
				16		CRJ-1	30 00
				23		CRJ-1	45 00
				29		CRJ-1	10 00

A check mark is entered in the cash receipts journal next to each account number as the posting of the item is completed.

CASH RECEIPTS JOURNAL for Month of January 19X2   **Page 1**

DATE	ACCOUNT CREDITED	ACCT. NO.	✓	AMOUNT
Jan. 7	Cleaning Service Income	401	✓	700 00
9	Accounts Receivable/December customers	111	✓	200 00
14	Cleaning Service Income	401	✓	725 00
16	Accounts Receivable/Camp	111	✓	30 00
21	Cleaning Service Income	401	✓	900 00
23	Accounts Receivable/Camp $30; Coleman $15	111	✓	45 00
27	Cleaning Service Income	401	✓	800 00
29	Accounts Receivable/Coleman	111	✓	10 00
31	Total Cash Debit	101	✓	3,410 00

Although the single-column cash receipts journal eliminates much of the duplication associated with recording cash receipts, it is apparent that not all the repetition has been avoided. For instance, the repetitive posting of credits to Cleaning Service Income and to Accounts Receivable still requires much unnecessary work that may be eliminated by use of a *multicolumn cash receipts journal.*

The accountant very easily eliminates the repeated posting of credits to Cleaning Service Income and to Accounts Receivable by redesigning the cash receipts journal from a single-column to a multicolumn journal. In this journal, he provides three money columns. The first column is used to record all credits to Accounts Receivable 111. The credits to Cleaning Service Income 401 are recorded in the second column. The third column is used to record the amounts to be debited to Cash 101 (as before). The cash receipts of the Carter Cleaning Shop for January 19X2 are recorded in this new journal as shown.

CASH RECEIPTS JOURNAL for Month of January 19X2   Page 1

DATE		EXPLANATION	✓	ACCOUNTS RECEIVABLE CR. 111	CLEANING SVC. INC. CR. 401	CASH DR. 101
Jan.	7	Cash Sales			700 00	700 00
	9	Collections on account/Dec. cust.		200 00		200 00
	14	Cash Sales			725 00	725 00
	16	Collections on account/Camp		30 00		30 00
	21	Cash Sales			900 00	900 00
	23	Collections on account/Camp $30; Coleman $15		45 00		45 00
	27	Cash Sales			800 00	800 00
	29	Collections on account/Coleman		10 00		10 00

At the end of the month, the accountant:

1. Totals the three money columns and checks to see if total debits ($3,410) equal total credits ($285 + $3,125 = $3,410). (This process is known as *crossfooting.*)
2. Posts each column total to the respective ledger account as indicated by the account number in the column heading.

3. Places a check mark below the total amount as each posting is completed. (The Posting Check column (✓) at the left of the Accounts Receivable column is not used at this time.)

The cash receipts journal and related ledger accounts are shown.

CASH RECEIPTS JOURNAL for Month of January 19X2   Page 1

DATE		EXPLANATION	✓	ACCOUNTS RECEIVABLE CR. 111		CLEANING SVC. INC. CR. 401		CASH DR. 101	
Jan.	7	Cash Sales				700	00	700	00
	9	Collections on account/Dec. Cust.		200	00			200	00
	14	Cash Sales				725	00	725	00
	16	Collections on account/Camp		30	00			30	00
	21	Cash Sales				900	00	900	00
	23	Collections on account/Camp $30; Coleman $15		45	00			45	00
	27	Cash Sales				800	00	800	00
	29	Collections on account/Coleman		10	00			10	00
	31	Totals		285	00	3,125	00	3,410	00
				✓		✓		✓	

Cash   No. 101

DATE		EXPLANATION	POST. REF.	DEBIT		DATE	EXPLANATION	POST. REF.	CREDIT
19 X2									
Jan.	1	Brought Fwd.	✓	3,200	00				
	31		CRJ-1	3,410	00				

Accounts Receivable   No. 111

DATE		EXPLANATION	POST. REF.	DEBIT		DATE		EXPLANATION	POST. REF.	CREDIT	
19 X2						19 X2					
Jan.	1	Brought Fwd.	✓	200	00	Jan.	31		CRJ-1	285	00

Cleaning Service Income   No. 401

DATE	EXPLANATION	POST. REF.	DEBIT	DATE		EXPLANATION	POST. REF.	CREDIT	
				19 X2					
				Jan.	7		1-3	60	00
					14		1-8	25	00
					19		1-12	30	00
					28		1-18	60	00
					31		CRJ-1	3,125	00

The multicolumn cash receipts journal permits the accountant to accomplish in three summary postings what would take 16 individual postings if only the general journal were used. Besides saving time, effort, and space, the special journal for cash receipts also permits the accountant to subdivide the work. While he is using the general journal to record other transactions, another member of his staff can be journalizing cash receipts in the cash receipts journal.

RECORDING SALES TAXES

Some states require merchants to collect a tax on the amount of certain retail sales. Thus, each such sale involves at least three elements: the retail price, the tax, and the total amount charged to the customer. For example, a $10 sale subject to a 3% sales tax consists of these elements.

Retail price	$10.00
3% sales tax	30
Total charge to customer	$10.30

When sales taxes must be recorded as part of the cash sales transaction, the accountant makes provision for a special column called Sales Tax Payable in the cash receipts journal. The illustration below shows how a redesigned cash receipts journal looks for a cleaning shop operating in a state that levies a sales tax on such sales.

CASH RECEIPTS JOURNAL for Month of June 19X2 — Page 6

DATE		EXPLANATION	ACCOUNTS RECEIVABLE		SALES TAX PAYABLE CR. 231		CLEANING SERVICE INCOME CR. 401		CASH DR. 101	
			✓	CR. 111						
June	5	Cash Sales				30	10	00	10	30
	30	Totals	1,200	00	10	92	364	00	1,574	92
				✓		✓		✓		✓

The total of the Sales Tax Payable is posted as a credit to Sales Tax Payable 231 because it represents a liability owed to the governmental unit.

Sales Tax Payable   No. 231

DATE	EXPLANATION	POST. REF.	DEBIT	DATE	EXPLANATION	POST. REF.	CREDIT
				19 X2 June 30		CRJ-6	10 92

The merchant is obligated to charge the tax to the customer and to forward the tax to the state, city, or other authority by which the tax levy is imposed. Both cash and credit sales, along with related sales taxes, will be more fully explained in a later unit.

RECORDING CASH DISCOUNTS ON SALES

Like most retail concerns doing business on credit, the Carter Cleaning Shop allows its customers 30 days in which to pay (also expressed as net 30 days, or n/30). However, many manufacturing and wholesaling concerns, and some retailers, allow their credit customers to deduct 1 or 2% (or some other percent) of the invoice amount if the bill is paid within a specified time, often 10 days from the date of sale. (These terms might be indicated on the invoice, for example, as 2%, 10 days, net 30 days; or simply as 2/10, n/30). The purpose of this cash discount is to encourage prompt payment. No discount is, of course, allowed on the sales tax involved.

A cash receipt involving a sales discount calls for the recording of three elements:

1. The amount of the original sale (as a credit to Accounts Receivable).
2. The amount of discount (as a debit to Sales Discount).
3. The net amount of cash received (as a debit to Cash).

In a firm that allows a cash discount, the cash receipts journal would have to be expanded to provide a new column entitled Sales Discount 453, as shown. The sample entry covers the collection of a $150 receivable from Hill Company less 1% cash discount for payment within the discount period.

CASH RECEIPTS JOURNAL for Month of December 19X2   Page 12

DATE	EXPLANATION	ACCOUNTS RECEIVABLE ✓ CR. 111	SALES TAX PAYABLE CR. 231	CLEANING SERVICE INCOME CR. 401	SALES DISCOUNT DR. 453	CASH DR. 101
Dec. 10	Hill Co.	150 00			1 50	148 50

The total of the Sales Discount column is posted as a debit to the Sales Discount account at the end of the period. The Sales Discount account balance is deducted from the Sales account balance on the income statement. (An alternative method for showing Sales Discounts on the income statement will be discussed in Unit 16.)

RECORDING OTHER CASH RECEIPTS

Every receipt of cash must be recorded in the cash receipts journal. You have already seen how the accountant makes special provisions for transactions that occur frequently, such as cash sales and collections on account. He also designs the cash receipts journal so that transactions that do not occur frequently enough to warrant special columns in the journal may be easily recorded. This is accomplished by setting up a new column called Sundry Credits, which also provides a space to enter the number of the account to be credited, along with a space to record a check mark as the item is posted. No end-of-month posting is required for the total of the Sundry Credits section, since the individual items are posted throughout the month. An "X" is placed below the Sundry Credits total to indicate that it is not posted. To illustrate the use of a Sundry Credits column, two fairly common types of cash receipts are shown.

Investment by the Owner

As you learned in Unit 3, an investment of cash by Carter resulted in a debit to Cash and a credit to the Carter Investment account. Assuming that Carter invested an additional $1,000 in the business on August 1, 19X2, the investment would be recorded as shown.

CASH RECEIPTS JOURNAL for Month of August 19X2   Page 8

DATE		EXPLANATION	SUNDRY CREDITS			ACCOUNTS RECEIVABLE		CLEANING SERVICE INCOME	CASH DR. 101	
			ACCT. NO.	✓	AMOUNT	✓	CR. 111	CR. 401		
Aug.	1	Carter Investment	301		1,000 00				1,000	00

The credit to Carter Investment 301 is posted as an individual amount to that account. After the item has been posted, a check mark is placed beside the account number in the journal to indicate that the posting has been made. The Cash debit will, of course, be posted only as a part of the total of the Cash column at the end of the month.

Notes Receivable Collection

A *promissory note* may serve as the basis for credit terms covering certain sales transactions. The buyer's written promise gives the seller greater assurance of payment than a regular charge account; it applies both moral pressure on the buyer and gives legal protection to the seller. The seller may also earn interest in return for the credit accommodation. When the note is paid, a record must be made of the cash received, including interest. The special accounting technique involved can best be understood through a step-by-step study of a typical example.

Suppose that a customer, Arvie Smith, who owes Carter Cleaning Shop $200 on open book account, comes to Jones, the manager, and tells Jones that he is having financial difficulties at the present. Smith offers to give a promissory note payable in 6 months with interest at 8% per year to cover the account. Because of the additional security afforded by the note, Carter agrees to accept the offer and thereby extend the payment date of the debt until October 1. The note, dated April 1, 19X2, is shown below.

$ 200.00		April 1, 19 X2
Six months ——— **AFTER DATE** | **PROMISE TO PAY**		
TO THE ORDER OF Carter Cleaning Shop		
Two hundred and no/100 ——— **DOLLARS**		
PAYABLE AT City National Bank		
VALUE RECEIVED with interest at 8%		*Arvie Smith*
Nº 28 **DUE** October 1, 19X2		

On April 1, an entry for $200 must be made on Carter's books to record the receipt of a new asset, Notes Receivable, for which a new account, Notes Receivable 112, is set up in the ledger. The asset account, Account Receivable 111, is decreased by the same amount. The general journal entry reflecting these changes is illustrated.

19 X2		4–1			
April	1	Notes Receivable	112	200 00	
		Accounts Receivable	111		200 00
		Received a 6-month, 8% note from Arvie Smith for equipment at cost.			

On October 1, Smith pays $208 in cash, representing $200 as the amount of the note plus $8 interest earned during the period. Since this type of transaction is infrequent, the accountant uses the Sundry Credits section in the cash receipts journal to enter the credit to Notes Receivable 112 and the credit to Interest Income 491, as shown.

CASH RECEIPTS JOURNAL for Month of October 19X2   Page 10

DATE		EXPLANATION	SUNDRY CREDITS			ACCOUNTS RECEIVABLE		CLEANING SERVICE INCOME	CASH DR. 101	
			ACCT. NO.	√	AMOUNT	√	CR. 111	CR. 401		
Oct.	1	Notes Receiv./Smith	112		200 00					
		Interest Income	491		8 00				208	00

Again, the individual items in the Sundry Credits section are posted to the proper accounts, and a check mark is entered in the journal beside the account number. The Interest Income 491 account and its appearance on the income statement will be discussed in Unit 16.

SAFEGUARDING RECEIPTS

One of the advantages of having an efficient and speedy procedure for recording cash receipts is that the funds reach the bank sooner, preferably on the date received. The policy of making daily deposits ensures that cash receipts are not kept on the premises. They are not only safer in the bank, but as deposits they become funds available for paying bills owed by the depositor.

INTERNAL CONTROL OVER CASH RECEIPTS

Cash is the most precious and most fluid asset of the average business. Every penny received in payment for goods and services must be protected so that funds will be available to pay bills, salaries, and the many other inevitable obligations. The principles of internal control should be applied to the handling of cash receipts by observing the following precautionary routines:

1. One person should receive the cash, whether it is delivered by mail or in person (over the counter) and, after making a record of the receipt, he should turn the cash over to another person for deposit in the bank.
2. All cash receipts should be deposited in the bank promptly. They should not be used for making cash payments.
3. The recording of cash receipts on the general books of the company should be performed by a person other than the one who receives it and other than the one who deposits it in the bank.
4. At the end of each month, a person other than one of the three above

should obtain the bank statement directly from the bank and should prepare a bank reconciliation statement. Obviously, in a business as small as the Carter Cleaning Shop, there are not enough employees to have each routine handled by a separate person. However, every effort must be made to have as great a division of duties as possible.

♦ ♦ ♦

PRINCIPLES AND PROCEDURES

A special journal is used for cash receipts in order to save time, effort, and recording space. In a small business, the accountant may use a single-column cash receipts journal that provides for one summary debit to the Cash account and for individual postings of credit amounts in the ledger.

However, it is more efficient for the accountant to use a multicolumn cash receipts journal. This journal requires as few as three posting entries to the ledger to record the cash receipts for a whole month. Special columns may be provided in the cash receipts journal to record transactions involving sales tax, cash discounts, and other items.

MANAGERIAL IMPLICATIONS

By deciding upon the use of a cash receipts journal, the knowledgeable manager ensures that the recording work load is reduced. Also, the work can be divided, with one person using the general journal, while another records transactions in the cash receipts journal.

Because cash is extremely easy to lose or steal, the management must exercise special care in safeguarding receipts. The receipts of each day should be deposited intact in the bank so that it will be a simple matter to trace them from the journal to the bank statement. The duties of receiving, recording, and depositing cash should be divided among different persons to allow for greater control.

APPLICATION OF PRINCIPLES

PROBLEM 6 · 1

The ABC Venetian Blind Company sells and installs venetian blinds. Some customers pay cash on installation; others are given extended credit terms. A single-column cash receipts journal is used. The ledger accounts involved in the cash receipts transactions for February 19X1, and their balances at the first of the month are: Cash 101, $4,452.60; Accounts Receivable 111, $2,142.70; and Venetian Blind Sales 404, –0–. The February 19X1 transactions relating to the receipt of cash are as follows:

FEB.

3   Sam Jones paid $78.50 in cash for blinds. (Record as typical cash sale.)

5   Clark Sampson paid $226.70 by check for blinds installed.

7   Received check from Ray Blackwell to apply on his account, $50.

11   Mrs. Chet O'Brien sent in a check for $126.35 to pay her January account in full.

13   Receipts consisted of $229.15 in cash for blinds installed today for Edward Teague and $87.60 in cash for blinds installed today for Cliff Jones.

17   Installed blinds for three customers and received cash payment of $337.55.

21   Received $157.25 from Bruce Parker in payment of his January account and $217.30 for blinds installed today.

22   Blinds installed today for cash, $415.25.

23   Mrs. Mary Boatman sent in check for $100 to apply on account.

25   Collected $302.50 for blinds installed today.

INSTRUCTIONS

1. Open the ledger accounts and enter the Brought Forward balances.
2. Record all transactions in the cash receipts journal.
3. Total the cash receipts journal.
4. Perform the individual and summary postings to the proper ledger accounts. Use CRJ-2 as the posting reference.
5. Foot each account, but do not enter the balance.

PROBLEM 6 · 2

♦   This problem covers the cash receipts procedures for the Sloan Venetian Blind Company for the month of March 19X1. The volume of transactions warrants the use of a multicolumn cash receipts journal, with special columns for Accounts Receivable Cr. 111, Venetian Blind Sales Cr. 404, and Cash Dr. 101. The ledger accounts involved in the cash receipts transactions for March and their balances at the first of the month are: Cash 101, $3,416.85; Accounts Receivable 111, $2,889.68; and Venetian Blind Sales 404, –0–. The March 19X1 transactions involving the receipt of cash are as follows:

MAR.

1   Received check from John Parker to pay his January account, $167.50.

2   Collected cash for blinds installed today, $199.75.

5   Collected $232.60 for blinds installed today, and also received $20 from Calvin Johnson to apply on account.

9   Cash sales of $347.50 for blinds installed.

10   Cash sales of $117.75 for blinds installed.

13   Ms. Blanche Barber sent a check for $75 in part payment of her February account. Collected $98.80 from one customer for blinds installed today.

20   A check for $336.90 was received from Carter Bosworth to pay his February account.

23   Collected cash, $132.75, for blinds installed today.

MAR.

24 Received a check for $97.65 from Margaret Lucas to pay her February account.

27 Received a check from the City Library for $1,017.35 to pay its January account covering blinds installed in the reference rooms.

30 Received cash totaling $180 for blinds installed today and checks from Walker Owens, $110.50, and Mrs. Rita Galvez, $19.50, to pay their February accounts.

INSTRUCTIONS

1. Open the ledger accounts and enter the Brought Forward balances.
2. Record each transaction in the cash receipts journal.
3. Total each column of the journal.
4. Perform the summary postings to the proper ledger accounts using CRJ-3 as the posting reference.
5. Foot the accounts where necessary, but do not enter the balances.

PROBLEM 6 · 3

The Cash Company sells musical instruments for cash and on various credit terms. The specially designed cash receipts journal has columns for Sundry Credits, Accounts Receivable Cr. 111, Sales Tax Payable Cr. 231, Sales Income Cr. 401, Sales Discount Dr. 453, and Cash Dr. 101. During May 19X1, the following selected transactions took place:

MAY

4 Total cash of $444.96 received from cash sales of $432 plus sales tax of $12.96.

7 Received a check from R. O. Miller for $220.50, in payment for $225 invoice dated May 1, less 2% discount.

12 Received a check for $812 from Frank Barnes to pay for his $800 note dated Feb. 12, with interest at 6%.

14 Check for $122.50 received from Sally Davis to pay for $125 invoice dated May 7, less 2% discount.

15 Mr. Allan Case, owner of the Cash Company, made an additional investment of $2,000 cash.

25 F. O. Cades delivered his check for $404 to pay his March 25 note for $400, plus interest of $4.

26 Received $100 in cash from Donald Bunch to apply on his account.

28 Received total cash of $789.39 from cash sales of $766.40, plus sales tax of $22.99.

31 Received a check for $970.20 from Francis Baker to pay for May 1 invoice $980, less 1% discount.

INSTRUCTIONS
1. Record all the transactions in the cash receipts journal.
2. Foot, total, and rule the money columns. Prove the accuracy of your work by adding the credit column totals and the debit column totals and comparing them for equality.

MANAGERIAL CHECKUPS

♦ How can management devise accounting records and procedures to ensure full internal control of cash receipts?

♦ From the viewpoint of an efficiency-minded management, what are the advantages of a cash receipts journal?

♦ Why doesn't management allow the customer to take a cash discount on the sales tax involved in a sales transaction?

♦ How can the management of a small business divide duties in order to achieve internal control over cash receipts?

7
ACCOUNTING FOR CASH DISBURSEMENTS

In Unit 6 you learned how the accountant reduces the amount of effort and time necessary to record repetitive entries for cash receipts by developing a special cash receipts journal. There are also many repetitive entries involving cash payments. For example, nine of the January transactions that you recorded involved credits to Cash 101 because cash was paid out. Some of the general journal entries that you made to record these payments are shown.

19	X2	1–1						
Jan.	2	Equipment	141	✓	770	00		
		Cash	101	✓			770	00
		To record acquisition of cleaning equipment paid by Check 31.						

		1–5						
	10	Accounts Payable	201	✓	300	00		
		Cash	101	✓			300	00
		To record payment in full to Knight, Inc., by Check 32.						

		1–9						
	15	Supplies Used	521	✓	400	00		
		Cash	101	✓			400	00
		To record payment by Check 33 for cleaning supplies.						

		1–11						
	17	Rent Expense	516	✓	700	00		
		Cash	101	✓			700	00
		To record payment of January rent by Check 34.						

Each of these four entries in the general journal, plus the other five not shown, required a credit posting to the Cash account in the general ledger.

Cash   No. 101

DATE		EXPLANATION	POST. REF.	DEBIT		DATE		EXPLANATION	POST. REF.	CREDIT	
19	X2					19	X2				
Jan.	1	Brought Fwd.	✓	3,200	00	Jan.	2		1-1	770	00
	31		CRJ-1	3,410	00		10		1-5	300	00
							15		1-9	400	00
							17		1-11	700	00
							24		1-15	500	00
							28		1-17	600	00
							28		1-19	300	00
							30		1-21	60	00
							31		1-22	1,700	00

It is apparent that the accountant cannot tolerate such a time-consuming system and that he must develop a method to eliminate some of the duplication involved.

THE SINGLE-COLUMN CASH DISBURSEMENTS JOURNAL

One way to avoid so much repetition in handling cash payments is to set up a separate journal for these transactions. One possibility is a *single-column cash disbursements journal*. The journal illustrated here might be used to record the January 19X2 transactions of the Carter Cleaning Shop. Each entry takes only a single line on which to record the date of the check, the check number, the account debited (title and number), and the amount.

CASH DISBURSEMENTS JOURNAL for Month of January 19X2   Page 1

DATE		CHECK NO.	ACCOUNT DEBITED	ACCT. NO.	✓	AMOUNT	
Jan.	2	31	Equipment	141		770	00
	10	32	Accounts Payable/Knight	201		300	00
	15	33	Supplies Used	521		400	00
	17	34	Rent Expense	516		700	00
	24	35	Accounts Payable/Ace Motors	201		500	00
	28	36	Equipment	141		600	00
	28	37	Supplies Used	521		300	00
	30	38	Miscellaneous Expense	591		60	00
	31	39	Salary Expense	511		1,700	00

The nine credits to Cash that are required in the general journal are no longer necessary. The explanations are also left out because the title of the journal is self-explanatory. The purpose of recording the check number is to permit ready reference to the checkbook stub record of payment.

POSTING FROM THE SINGLE-COLUMN CASH DISBURSEMENTS JOURNAL

The time-saving advantage in posting from the single-column cash disbursements journal occurs when the Cash account is to be credited. The accountant does not need to post individual credits. Instead, he adds the Amount column in the cash disbursements journal at the end of the month and posts the total cash payments as a single credit to Cash. When the total has been posted, a check mark is noted in the cash disbursements journal on the total line next to the account number (101). The single credit entry for $5,330, covering all the January cash disbursements, does the job that nine postings were formerly required to do.

Cash   No. 101

DATE		EXPLANATION	POST. REF.	DEBIT		DATE		EXPLANATION	POST. REF.	CREDIT	
19 X2						19 X2					
Jan.	1	Brought Fwd.	✓	3,200	00	Jan.	31		CDJ-1	5,330	00
	31		CRJ-1	3,410	00						

CASH DISBURSEMENTS JOURNAL for Month of January 19X2   Page 1

DATE		CHECK NO.	ACCOUNT DEBITED	ACCT. NO.	✓	AMOUNT	
Jan.	2	31	Equipment	141		770	00
	10	32	Accounts Payable/Knight	201		300	00
	15	33	Supplies Used	521		400	00
	17	34	Rent Expense	516		700	00
	24	35	Accounts Payable/Ace Motors	201		500	00
	28	36	Equipment	141		600	00
	28	37	Supplies Used	521		300	00
	30	38	Miscellaneous Expense	591		60	00
	31	39	Salary Expense	511		1,700	00
	31		Total Cash Credit	101	✓	5,330	00

The single-column cash disbursements journal calls for the posting of individual debits to the asset or expense accounts involved. As each entry is posted, a check mark is placed in the Posting Check (✓) column in the cash disbursements journal. In the Posting Reference column of the ledger accounts involved, the abbreviation "CDJ-1" (cash disbursements journal, page 1) represents the journal and page from which the posting was made.

CASH DISBURSEMENTS JOURNAL for Month of January 19X2   **Page 1**

DATE		CHECK NO.	ACCOUNT DEBITED	ACCT. NO.	✓	AMOUNT	
Jan.	2	31	Equipment	141	✓	770	00
	10	32	Accounts Payable / Knight	201	✓	300	00
	15	33	Supplies Used	521	✓	400	00
	17	34	Rent Expense	516	✓	700	00
	24	35	Accounts Payable / Ace Motors	201	✓	500	00
	28	36	Equipment	141	✓	600	00
	28	37	Supplies Used	521	✓	300	00
	30	38	Miscellaneous Expense	591	✓	60	00
	31	39	Salary Expense	511	✓	1,700	00
	31		Total Cash Credit	101	✓	5,330	00

Equipment   **No. 141**

DATE		EXPLANATION	POST. REF.	DEBIT		DATE	EXPLANATION	POST. REF.	CREDIT	
19	X2									
Jan.	1	Brought Fwd.	✓	3,000	00					
	2		CDJ-1	770	00					
	11		1-6	1,000	00					
	28		CDJ-1	600	00					

Accounts Payable   **No. 201**

DATE		EXPLANATION	POST. REF.	DEBIT		DATE		EXPLANATION	POST. REF.	CREDIT	
19	X2					19	X2				
Jan.	10		CDJ-1	300	00	Jan.	1	Brought Fwd.	✓	300	00
	24		CDJ-1	500	00		11		1-6	1,000	00

Salary Expense   **No. 511**

DATE		EXPLANATION	POST. REF.	DEBIT		DATE	EXPLANATION	POST. REF.	CREDIT	
19	X2									
Jan.	31		CDJ-1	1,700	00					

Rent Expense   **No. 516**

DATE		EXPLANATION	POST. REF.	DEBIT		DATE	EXPLANATION	POST. REF.	CREDIT	
19	X2									
Jan.	17		CDJ-1	700	00					

Supplies Used   No. 521

DATE	EXPLANATION	POST. REF.	DEBIT		DATE	EXPLANATION	POST. REF.	CREDIT
19 X2 Jan. 15		CDJ-1	400	00				
28		CDJ-1	300	00				

Miscellaneous Expense   No. 591

DATE	EXPLANATION	POST. REF.	DEBIT		DATE	EXPLANATION	POST. REF.	CREDIT
19 X2 Jan. 30		CDJ-1	60	00				

THE MULTICOLUMN CASH DISBURSEMENTS JOURNAL

In most businesses there are many repetitive transactions involving cash payments. For example, there are usually many cash payments on accounts payable, many payments for salaries and wages, and many payments for various other expenses. When the single-column cash disbursements journal is used, each payment results in an individual debit being posted to the appropriate account. For example, if there were 200 payments on accounts payable during the month, there would be 200 debit postings to the Accounts Payable account.

Once again, by redesigning the journal, the accountant can avoid posting certain numerous, individual debits. The three-column journal illustrated here is one that might be developed by the accountant of the Carter Cleaning Shop. The first money column (the Sundry Debits column) is used

CASH DISBURSEMENTS JOURNAL for Month of January 19X2   Page 1

DATE	CHECK NO.	EXPLANATION	SUNDRY DEBITS				ACCOUNTS PAYABLE		CASH CR. 101	
			ACCT. NO.	✓	AMOUNT	✓	DR. 201			
Jan. 2	31	Equipment	141		770	00			770	00
10	32	Knight					300	00	300	00
15	33	Supplies Used	521		400	00			400	00
17	34	Rent Expense	516		700	00			700	00
24	35	Ace Motors					500	00	500	00
28	36	Equipment	141		600	00			600	00
28	37	Supplies Used	521		300	00			300	00
30	38	Miscellaneous Expense	591		60	00			60	00
31	39	Salary Expense	511		1,700	00			1,700	00

to record the debits that need to be posted separately; these are the items that do not occur frequently enough to warrant a special column. Note that spaces are also provided for entry of the account number and for entry of a check mark when each item has been posted. In the second money column, the accountant assembles all debits to Accounts Payable. The third money column is used to accumulate the amounts to be included in the total credit to Cash, as in the single-column journal. The January 19X2 transactions of the Carter Cleaning Shop involving cash payments are recorded in the three-column journal illustrated on page 98.

POSTING FROM THE MULTICOLUMN CASH DISBURSEMENTS JOURNAL

Each amount in the Sundry Debits column is posted individually, and a check mark is placed in the Posting Check column of the journal to show that the posting has been made. The postings are made, of course, throughout the month. For example, the payment on January 2 for equipment is posted like this.

Equipment   No. 141

DATE		EXPLANATION	POST. REF.	DEBIT		DATE	EXPLANATION	POST. REF.	CREDIT
19 X2 Jan.	1	Brought Fwd.	✓	3,000 00					
	2		CDJ-1	770 00					

CASH DISBURSEMENTS JOURNAL for Month of January 19X2   Page 1

DATE		CHECK NO.	EXPLANATION	SUNDRY DEBITS			ACCOUNTS PAYABLE		CASH CR. 101
				ACCT. NO.	✓	AMOUNT	✓	DR. 201	
Jan.	2	31	Equipment	141	✓	770 00			770 00

At the end of the month, the accountant:

1. Totals the three money columns and checks to see that total debits ($5,330) equal total credits ($4,530 + $800 = $5,330).
2. Posts the $800 total in the Accounts Payable column as a debit to Accounts Payable 201 in the general ledger.
3. Posts the total of the Cash Credit column, $5,330, as a credit to Cash 101 in the general ledger.

4. Places check marks below the columnar totals as each posting is completed. (The Sundry Debit column total is not posted because it is composed of many different items that have already been individually posted. An X is placed below the Sundry Debits total to indicate that it is not posted.)

The cash disbursements journal and the related accounts to which column totals are posted are shown.

CASH DISBURSEMENTS JOURNAL for Month of January 19X2 Page 1

| DATE | CHECK NO. | EXPLANATION | SUNDRY DEBITS | | | | ACCOUNTS PAYABLE | | CASH CR. 101 | |
			ACCT. NO.	✓	AMOUNT	✓	DR. 201			
Jan. 2	31	Equipment	141	✓	770 00				770 00	
10	32	Knight					300 00		300 00	
15	33	Supplies Used	521	✓	400 00				400 00	
17	34	Rent Expense	516	✓	700 00				700 00	
24	35	Ace Motors					500 00		500 00	
28	36	Equipment	141	✓	600 00				600 00	
28	37	Supplies Used	521	✓	300 00				300 00	
30	38	Miscellaneous Expense	591	✓	60 00				60 00	
31	39	Salary Expense	511	✓	1,700 00				1,700 00	
31		Totals			4,530 00		800 00		5,330 00	
					X		✓		✓	

Accounts Payable No. 201

DATE	EXPLANATION	POST. REF.	DEBIT		DATE	EXPLANATION	POST. REF.	CREDIT	
19 X2					19 X2				
Jan. 31		CDJ-1	800 00		Jan. 1	Brought Fwd.	✓	300 00	
					11		1-6	1,000 00	

Cash No. 101

DATE	EXPLANATION	POST. REF.	DEBIT		DATE	EXPLANATION	POST. REF.	CREDIT	
19 X2					19 X2				
Jan. 1	Brought Fwd.	✓	3,200 00		Jan. 31		CDJ-1	5,330 00	
31		CRJ-1	3,410 00						

ADVANTAGES OF THE CASH DISBURSEMENTS JOURNAL

The advantages of the multicolumn cash disbursements journal may appear somewhat less impressive than those of the cash receipts journal. However, it does save a great deal of time, effort, and recording space. The posting of the January cash payments was completed in only 9 entries, instead of the 18 needed when using only the general journal. Moreover, the saving in posting effort would increase with additional activity involving payments to suppliers. Most businesses actually have many more accounts payable transactions than could be included in the example used here. Also, either form of cash disbursements journal would allow further division of the accounting work load. If the volume of transactions is heavy, it would be possible to have three people recording journal entries at one time. One person could be recording in the general journal, a second could be working with the cash receipts journal, and a third could be assigned to journalize cash payments in the cash disbursements journal.

RECORDING OTHER CASH DISBURSEMENTS

While most of the firm's payments will relate to routine transactions, the accounting system must be versatile enough to handle special types of payments as well. Some indication of the wide range of special situations is suggested by the discussion that follows.

Withdrawals by the Owner

Unit 2 explained how to record a decrease in the owner's equity account by means of a debit. One of the routine decreases in owner's equity encountered in normal operations arises from cash withdrawals. Since the owner does not receive a salary with which to pay his personal living expenses, he draws against profits accumulated as part of his equity or in anticipation of profits to be earned. No withdrawals have been recorded to date for Carter because his capital is so limited and his business is so new. However, when the situation is encountered, the owner's cash withdrawal is made by check and recorded in the cash disbursements journal. The debit account number and amount are entered under Sundry Debits. The accountant usually prefers to debit a special drawing account, such as Carter Drawing 302, instead of making a direct debit to the owner's investment account. He does this as a convenience in accumulating all withdrawals in one place for ready reference and identification. A typical entry appears as shown below.

CASH DISBURSEMENTS JOURNAL for Month of February 19X2   Page 2

| DATE | CHECK NO. | EXPLANATION | SUNDRY DEBITS | | | ACCOUNTS PAYABLE | | CASH CR. 101 | |
			ACCT. NO.	✓	AMOUNT	✓	DR. 201		
Feb. 28	55	Carter Drawing	302		50 00			50	00

Later, at the end of the period, the separate drawing account makes it easy to make a complete presentation in the Owner's Equity section of the balance sheet, as shown.

OWNER'S EQUITY

Carter Investment, February 1, 19X2		$6,240.00
Profit for February	$94.70	
Less Withdrawals	**50.00**	44.70
Carter Investment, February 28, 19X2		$6,284.70

Payment of Sales Taxes

Only one payment of the sales tax collected is ordinarily made to the taxing authority in any given month. Thus, there is no need for a special column in the cash disbursements journal for this item. Payment of the tax collected is made by check and is entered in the cash disbursements journal, with the account number and amount indicated under Sundry Debits.

CASH DISBURSEMENTS JOURNAL for Month of July 19X2   Page 7

DATE	CHECK NO.	EXPLANATION	SUNDRY DEBITS			ACCOUNTS PAYABLE		CASH CR. 101
			ACCT. NO.	✓	AMOUNT	✓	DR. 201	
July 2	549	Sales Tax Payable	231		10 92			10 92

If the firm buys supplies, materials, or other items at retail and pays a sales tax on each transaction, ordinarily no distinction is made between the cost of the material and the tax on it. For example, if office supplies are purchased at a cost of $20 and $.60, which represents a 3% sales tax, is added, the entire amount of $20.60 is ordinarily debited to an expense account such as Supplies Used.

Payment of Notes and Interest

The preceding unit described how a seller might accept a note receivable in settlement of a claim and ultimately collect the amount of the note plus interest. Look at a similar transaction from the opposite side. Suppose that on June 10, 19X2 the Carter Cleaning Shop buys a piece of cleaning equipment costing $300 and gives the seller a 6-month, 6% note in settlement. At the time of the acquisition, the transaction is recorded in the general journal by a debit of $300 to the asset, Equipment 141, and a credit to the liability, Notes Payable 202.

19 X2		6-9				
June 10	Equipment	141	300 00			
	Notes Payable	202			300 00	
	To record a 6-month, 6% note issued for new cleaning equipment.					

Later, on December 10, the payment is recorded in the cash disbursements journal. At that time, Carter pays the $300 note plus $9 interest, writing a check for $309. The credit to Cash is offset by debits to Notes Payable 202 for $300 and to Interest Expense 593 for $9, as follows.

CASH DISBURSEMENTS JOURNAL for Month of December 19X2   Page 12

DATE	CHECK NO.	EXPLANATION	SUNDRY DEBITS			ACCOUNTS PAYABLE		CASH CR. 101
			ACCT. NO.	✓	AMOUNT	✓	DR. 201	
Dec. 10	568	Notes Payable	202		300 00			
		Interest Expense	593		9 00			309 00

The Interest Expense 593 account, will, of course, be shown on the income statement as an expense.

Cash Discount on Purchases

You learned in Unit 6 that some suppliers permit their customers to deduct 1 or 2% for paying a bill within a specified period, frequently 10 days. You also learned that the seller recorded this discount in the Sales Discount account. The purchaser must also record the discount that he takes on such payments. The payment involving a discount calls for the recording of three items in the cash disbursements journal:

1. The total amount of the purchase (as a debit to Accounts Payable).
2. The amount of the discount (as a credit to Purchases Discount 510).
3. The net amount of cash paid out (as a credit to Cash).

In a firm that takes advantage of cash discounts, the accountant will design the cash disbursements journal to facilitate the recording of discounts taken on purchases. The illustration below shows how special columns are provided for recording the three elements just itemized.

CASH DISBURSEMENTS JOURNAL for Month of November 19X2   Page 11

DATE	CHECK NO.	EXPLANATION	SUNDRY DEBITS			ACCOUNTS PAYABLE		PURCHASES DISCOUNT	CASH CR. 101
			ACCT. NO.	✓	AMOUNT	✓	DR. 201	CR. 510	
Nov. 1	984	Howe Wholesale					1,000 00	10 00	990 00

At the end of the month, the Purchases Discount column is totaled, and this amount is credited to the Purchases Discount 510 account in the general ledger. A check mark is placed under the total in the journal to indicate that the posting has been made. Other procedures for recording purchases discounts will be examined in a later unit.

INTERNAL CONTROL OVER CASH DISBURSEMENTS

The importance of internal control over cash receipts was emphasized in Unit 6. A perfect system of control over cash receipts does not provide the total protection that the firm needs if the cash on deposit at the bank can be spent without proper authorization or supervision. Obviously, a company's cash is safe only if there is complete control over both incoming and outgoing funds.

Internal control over cash disbursements may be achieved by the adoption of certain policies and by the planning of records and work assignments to give maximum protection. For example, here are the recommendations that public accountants make to people who are setting out in business.

1. All disbursements should be made by check, except for minor payments from petty cash, discussed more fully later in this unit.
2. No check should be written without proper approval.
3. Bills should be approved only by experienced and responsible personnel.
4. The records covering bills and payments should be kept by someone other than the person approving them for payment.
5. Still another person should sign and mail the checks to creditors.

Again, you can see that in a small business like Carter's, it is impossible to achieve the division of duties and responsibilities desirable.

THE PETTY CASH FUND

Although bills should be paid only by check and only after proper authorization has been given for the payment, it is not practical to make every payment by check. There are times when small expenditures must be made in cash. For example, if 12 cents postage is due on the morning's mail, the postman cannot be expected to sit down and wait until the proper approval has been secured and a check written. Most businesses find it convenient to pay such small expense items from a *petty cash fund*.

Establishing the Fund

To set up a petty cash fund, a check is written to the order of the person in charge of the fund—usually the office manager, the cashier, or a secretary. The check is cashed, and the money is placed in a safe or a cash box to be used for payments as needed. The original entry to record the check establishing the petty cash fund results in a debit to a new asset account, Petty Cash 105. The cash disbursements journal entry made by the Carter Cleaning Shop's accountant to set up a petty cash fund of $25 on May 1, 19X2 is illustrated. (With the opening of this second cash account, the Cash 101 account would ordinarily be referred to as Cash in Bank 101. However, Carter will continue to use Cash 101 during the first year of operations.)

CASH DISBURSEMENTS JOURNAL for Month of May 19X2   **Page 5**

DATE	CHECK NO.	EXPLANATION	SUNDRY DEBITS			ACCOUNTS PAYABLE		CASH CR. 101
			ACCT. NO.	✓	AMOUNT	✓	DR. 201	
May 1	302	Petty Cash	105		25 00			25 00

Making Payments from the Fund

A payment from the petty cash fund is usually limited to some relatively small amount, for example, $5. Each time an expenditure is made from the fund, a receipt, called a *petty cash voucher,* is prepared. The petty cash vouchers are numbered in sequence, and dated as used. When a payment is made, the amount is entered on the voucher, the purpose of the expenditure is noted, and the account to be charged is identified. The person receiving payment is asked to sign the voucher as a receipt, and the petty cash custodian initials the voucher to indicate that he has checked it for completeness.

    A petty cash voucher to record the payment of $4.75 for office supplies is shown on the following page.

The Petty Cash Analysis Sheet

A memorandum record of petty cash transactions is kept on an *analysis sheet,* sometimes called the *petty cash book.* Cash put in the fund is listed in the Receipts column, and cash paid out is listed in the Payments column. Special columns are provided for expenses that occur frequently, such as Supplies Used and Miscellaneous Expense. A Sundry Debits column is provided for other accounts. The petty cash analysis sheet

PETTY CASH VOUCHER #1

NOTE: this form must be filled out in ink or typewritten.

DESCRIPTION OF EXPENDITURE	CHARGE TO ACCOUNT	AMOUNT	
Office Supplies	Supplies Used 521	4	75
	TOTAL	4	75

RECEIVED

THE SUM OF ___Four___ DOLLARS AND ___75/00___ CENTS

SIGNED _A. C. Abbott_ DATE 5/5/X2   APPROVED BY ___T. O. J.___ DATE 5/5/X2

Office Supply Co.

for the Carter Cleaning Shop after petty cash payments for May, 19X2 have been entered is shown.

PETTY CASH ANALYSIS SHEET for Month of May 19X2   Page 1

						DISTRIBUTION OF PAYMENTS				
DATE	VOU. NO.	EXPLANATION	RECEIPTS	PAYMENTS	SUP. USED DR. 521	DEL. EXP. DR. 532	MISC. EXP. DR. 591	SUNDRY DEBITS	
								ACCT. NO.	AMT.
May 1	✓	To estab. fund	25 00						
5	1	Office Sup. Co.		4 75	4 75				
12	2	Ace Exp. Co.		3 00		3 00			
17	3	Roberts Delivery		3 20		3 20			
26	4	H. Tate —							
		windows		1 10			1 10		
27	5	Carter Draw.		5 00				302	5 00

Replenishing the Fund

At the end of each month (or sooner if the fund runs low), the petty cash fund is replenished so that there will be an adequate amount of money available to meet anticipated needs. The total of the vouchers for expenditures from the fund plus the cash on hand should always equal the fixed amount of the fund—$25 in this case.

The first step in replenishing the fund is to total each column in the petty cash analysis sheet. A check is then written for an amount sufficient to restore the petty cash fund to its original balance, and is recorded in the cash disbursements journal. The analysis sheet indicates the accounts to be debited when the check is entered in the cash receipts journal. The column totals for May indicated the following:

521	Supplies Used	$ 4.75
532	Delivery Expense	6.20
591	Miscellaneous Expense	1.10
302	Carter Drawing	5.00
	Total	$17.05

The reimbursement check for $17.05 is issued to the petty cash custodian and recorded in the cash disbursements journal as shown.

CASH DISBURSEMENTS JOURNAL for Month of May 19X2   Page 5

DATE	CHECK NO.	EXPLANATION	SUNDRY DEBITS			ACCOUNTS PAYABLE		CASH CR. 101
			ACCT. NO.	✓	AMOUNT	✓	DR. 201	
May 31	330	Supplies Used	521		4 75			
		Delivery Expense	532		6 20			
		Miscellaneous Expense	591		1 10			
		Carter Drawing	302		5 00			17 05

It is important to note that the petty cash analysis sheet is *not* a book of original entry, and the figures are *not posted* from it to the ledger accounts. The expenditures from the petty cash fund are recorded in the cash disbursements journal only when the fund is replenished. The expenses are posted to the general ledger from the cash disbursements journal.

The reimbursement check is entered on the petty cash analysis sheet, and the sheet is balanced and ruled as shown on page 108.

The balance of $25 will be brought forward on the first line of the petty cash analysis sheet for June. The amount is entered in the Receipts column, a check mark is noted in the Voucher Number column, and "Brought Forward" is used as the explanation.

INTERNAL CONTROL OF PETTY CASH

Whenever and wherever there is valuable property or cash to protect, the accountant must establish safeguards, and petty cash is no exception. This is how the principles of internal control have been applied to petty cash by the Carter Cleaning Shop.

1. The petty cash fund is used only for limited payments of a minor nature that cannot conveniently be made by check.
2. The amount of money set aside for the fund does not exceed an approximate amount needed to cover one month's expenditures from the fund.
3. The check to establish the fund is drawn to the order of the custodian of the fund—never to the order of Cash.
4. The custodian has sole control of the fund, has a locked box or drawer in which to keep it, and is the only one authorized to make payments from it.
5. All payments made from the fund are covered by petty cash receipts signed by those who receive the money. The receipts indicate the details of the expenditure, and thus are valuable for future reference.

PETTY CASH ANALYSIS SHEET for Month of May 19X2 Page 1

DATE		VOU. NO.	EXPLANATION	RECEIPTS	PAYMENTS	DISTRIBUTION OF PAYMENTS				
						SUP. USED DR. 521	DEL. EXP. DR. 532	MISC. EXP. DR. 591	SUNDRY DEBITS	
									ACCT. NO.	AMT.
May	1	√	To estab. fund	25 00						
	5	1	Office Sup. Co.		4 75	4 75				
	12	2	Ace Exp. Co.		3 00		3 00			
	17	3	Roberts Dely.		3 20		3 20			
	26	4	H. Tate — windows		1 10			1 10		
	27	5	Carter Draw.		5 00				302	5 00
	31		Totals	25 00	17 05	4 75	6 20	1 10		5 00
	31		Balance		7 95					
				25 00	25 00					
	31		Balance	7 95						
	31		To replenish fund	17 05						
	31		Carried Fwd.	25 00						

◆ ◆ ◆

PRINCIPLES AND PROCEDURES

The use of a special cash payments journal saves time, effort, and recording space in journalizing and posting transactions involving cash disbursements. The single-column cash disbursements journal requires individual postings of debits to the accounts affected, but only one credit posting to Cash in the general ledger.

The multicolumn journal saves a great deal more time in posting because the Accounts Payable column may be totaled and posted as a single debit. Since Cash is also credited in a total figure from the journal, only the Sundry Debits column items must be posted individually.

Minor payments may be made in cash through a petty cash fund. A petty cash voucher is prepared for each payment and signed by the person receiving the money. A petty cash analysis sheet is kept, with special columns set up for accounts that involve frequent transactions. The fund is replenished periodically, with a check drawn for the amount spent. At that time, an entry is made in the cash disbursements journal to record the debits to the accounts involved.

MANAGERIAL IMPLICATIONS

In addition to saving time and effort, the use of special procedures for recording and handling cash disbursements provides management with added safeguards over cash. Payments to settle larger bills are made only after the proper authorization has been given. Normally, payments are made only by check. Management achieves control over small expenditures through the use of a petty cash system, which requires that written receipts be obtained for all minor expenditures. The responsibility for the petty cash fund can then be delegated to one person.

APPLICATION OF PRINCIPLES

PROBLEM 7 · 1

♦ The ABC Venetian Blind Company uses a single-column cash disbursements journal. The ledger accounts involved in the cash disbursements for February 19X1, and their balances at the first of the month are:

101	Cash	$4,452.60	511	Salary Expense	–0–
141	Equipment	7,227.50	513	Advertising Expense	–0–
201	Accounts Payable	3,476.25	516	Rent Expense	–0–
504	Telephone Expense	–0–	521	Supplies Used	–0–
505	Utilities Expense	–0–			

The February transactions relating to cash disbursements are as follows:

FEB.
2 Paid for new equipment, $612.20, by Check 54.
3 Sent $235 to Boyd & Company to apply on account, by Check 55.
6 Paid rent for the month, $350, by Check 56.
10 Paid $33.85 for utilities bill for January, by Check 57.
12 Paid Baynard Brothers account in full, $888.20, by Check 58.
14 Made payment today for telephone bill for preceding month, $26.50, by Check 59.
15 Issued Check 60 to pay the salaries for first half of the month, $600.
16 Issued Check 61 in payment for supplies used, $56.35.
18 Advertising bill for $75.60 due today; payment made by Check 62.

UNIT 7

22 Palmetto Supply Company invoice of Feb. 12 due today; Check 63 issued for $112.70.

25 Paid for supplies used, $18.15, by Check 64.

27 Sent payment in full to Allen Milling Corp., $1,179.50, by Check 65.

28 Paid for a piece of new equipment, $136.75, by issuing Check 66.

28 Salaries for last half of the month, $625, paid by Check 67.

INSTRUCTIONS

1. Open the ledger accounts and enter the Brought Forward balances.
2. Record each transaction in the cash disbursements journal.
3. Total the journal.
4. Complete the individual and summary postings to the proper ledger accounts, using CDJ-2 as the posting reference.
5. Foot the accounts where necessary, but do not enter the balances.

PROBLEM 7 · 2

This problem covers the cash disbursements procedures for the Gable Venetian Blind Company for the month of March 19X1. For greater efficiency in recording, the company decided to change from a single-column cash disbursements journal to a multicolumn cash disbursements journal with special columns for Sundry Debits, Accounts Payable Dr. 201, and Cash Cr. 101. The ledger accounts involved in the cash disbursements for March and their balances at the first of the month are:

101	Cash	$4,519.84	511	Salary Expense	–0–
141	Equipment	6,876.35	513	Advertising Expense	–0–
201	Accounts Payable	2,425.39	516	Rent Expense	–0–
504	Telephone Expense	–0–	518	Equipment Repairs	–0–
505	Utilities Expense	–0–	521	Supplies Used	–0–
			591	Miscellaneous Expense	–0–

The March 19X1 transactions involving the disbursement of cash are as follows:

MAR.

1 Made payment on account to Pittsburgh Paint Company, $122.70, by Check 68.

2 Paid $465 for new equipment obtained today, by Check 69.

4 Paid Boyd & Company the balance of account, $325, by Check 70.

5 Aluminum Supply Company invoice due today, $297.75; paid by Check 71.

8 Rent for March, $350, paid by Check 72.

9 Issued Check 73 for $43.35 for supplies used.

10 Utilities bill for $30.60, paid by Check 74.

13 Made payment by Check 75 for telephone bill, $26.50.

15 Issued Check 76 for salaries for the first half of the month, $650.
18 Paid Black Brothers account in full, $210, by Check 77.
19 Paid $13.65 to Electrical Repairs, Inc., for repairing equipment, by Check 78.
23 Supplies used amounting to $98.25, paid by Check 79.
24 Paid advertising bill for February, $55.80, by Check 80.
25 Sent Check 81 for $500 to Capital Cord Company to apply on account.
29 Miscellaneous expenses, $22.55, paid by Check 82.
30 Issued Check 83 for $625 for salaries for the last half of the month.

INSTRUCTIONS

1. Open the ledger accounts and enter the Brought Forward balances.
2. Record each transaction in the cash disbursements journal.
3. Total each column of the journal.
4. Complete the individual and summary postings to the proper ledger accounts and use CDJ-3 as the posting reference.
5. Foot the accounts where necessary, but do not enter the balances.

PROBLEM 7 · 3

The Berkeley Company is a retail clothing store owned and operated by James Berkeley. A cash disbursements journal, with columns for Sundry Debits, Accounts Payable Dr. 201, Purchases Discount Cr. 510, and Cash Cr. 101, is used to record all payments by check. The petty cash analysis sheet has special columns for Dr. 513, Dr. 521, Dr. 522, and Dr. 591. During June 19X1, the following accounts were used in the cash disbursements transactions:

101	Cash	510	Purchases Discount
105	Petty Cash Fund	513	Advertising Expense
201	Accounts Payable	516	Rent Expense
202	Notes Payable	521	Office Supplies
231	Sales Tax Payable	522	Postage
302	Berkeley Drawing	591	Miscellaneous Expense
505	Utilities Expense	593	Interest Expense

The cash disbursements for the month were as follows:

JUNE
1 Issued Check 452, $300, to Riley Real Estate Company for June rent.
4 Issued Check 453, $50, to establish a petty cash fund. (Enter in the cash disbursements journal in the usual manner, debiting Account 105. Also record on first line of the petty cash analysis sheet.)
5 Paid Check 454, $237.60, to Miller Brothers for invoice of May 27, $240, less 1% discount.

6   Paid $1.50 from petty cash fund for office supplies (Petty Cash Voucher 1). Disbursements from petty cash are to be recorded in the petty cash analysis sheet.

7   Berkeley issued Check 455 to himself for $100, to be charged to his drawing account.

8   Paid Fashion Frocks invoice dated June 1 for $658 (credit terms 2/10, net/30 days) by Check 456 in the amount of $644.84.

9   Paid $4 from petty cash for postage stamps (Petty Cash Voucher 2).

12   Paid the Commercial Bank $1,015 by Check 457, to cover a note for $1,000, plus interest at 6% for 90 days.

13   Issued Check 458, $355, to the Warren Wholesale Company to pay their invoice of May 15; terms, net cash 30 days.

14   Berkeley issued Check 459, $150, to himself; to be charged to his drawing account.

15   Paid $5 from petty cash to senior high school annual for advertising (Petty Cash Voucher 3).

18   Teen Togs invoice dated June 8, $760, is due today. Deducted 2% discount; paid by Check 460, $744.80.

20   Paid utilities bill for May, $34.65, by Check 461.

21   Paid $10 from petty cash (Petty Cash Voucher 4) to have store windows washed (charge Miscellaneous Expense 591).

22   Paid Alabama Woolen Mills invoice May 25, $390, by Check 462. Deducted $3.90 discount, and made the check payable for $386.10.

25   Issued Check 463, $277.80, to the State Tax Commission for the May sales tax collections.

26   Paid $3.75 from petty cash for office supplies (Petty Cash Voucher 5).

28   Issued Check 464, $606, to Clinton Distributors to pay $600 note plus interest.

29   Reimbursed petty cash fund by issuing Check 465, $24.25. (Get analysis of disbursements from solution of Instruction 2 below.)

INSTRUCTIONS

1. Record all transactions:
    (a) Disbursements from petty cash in the petty cash analysis sheet, Page 6.
    (b) Disbursements by check in the cash disbursements journal, Page 6.
2. Foot and balance the petty cash analysis sheet, enter the totals, rule, and enter the receipt of reimbursement Check 465.
3. Foot the money columns of the cash disbursements journal and prove the accuracy of your work.

MANAGERIAL CHECKUP

♦   Explain how special procedures for recording and handling cash disbursements can ensure management of effective internal control.

8 BANKING PROCEDURES AND RECONCILIATIONS

When Carter was organizing his business back in November 19X1, he consulted his accountant about the books and records that would be required to keep track of his business affairs. The accountant realized at once that there would be a considerable amount of cash received at the counter and that additional amounts would be received by mail from charge customers. In order to protect and control this cash, he knew that provision for adequate records was only part of the story. He also recommended procedures to ensure safety in the physical handling of the funds. Cash coming in by mail should be handled by two persons, one to receive and list it and another to deposit it. Jones, the manager, should receive and prepare a list of mail receipts, and at the end of the day he should give the list to the accountant for entry in the cash receipts journal.

The accountant also suggested that the cash and checks received from customers in person be rung up on the cash register by Jones. Then a detailed list of these across-the-counter receipts for cash sales should be given to the accountant each day for entry in the cash receipts journal and the day's receipts should go to Carter for deposit. At this time, Carter would have both the mail receipts and cash register receipts. The next step would be for him to sort and count all the cash and cash items for listing on the *deposit slip*.

MAKING DEPOSITS

A deposit slip is filled out for each bank deposit that is made. The deposit slip for January 9, 19X2 is shown.

Deposit slips are usually prepared in duplicate or in multicarbon sets or packs. The name of the firm, the Carter Cleaning Shop, is either preprinted or is handwritten on the deposit slip, since the account is in the firm's name. The account number is likewise preprinted or entered by hand. The current

REGULAR CHECKING

CITY NATIONAL BANK $\frac{84-8}{513}$

DATE January 9, 19X2

DEPOSIT TO THE CREDIT OF

Carter Cleaning Shop

ADDRESS 365 Broad St.

Centerport, State 53995

ACCOUNT NUMBER 2 4 2 0 2 7 7 2 0

BILLS		DOLLARS	CENTS
BILLS		45	00
COIN		4	75
Checks as follows, properly endorsed. List place of payment or transit number.			
1	84–11	20	00
2	84–11	15	00
3	84–12	35	00
4	84–12	40	00
5	84–14	30	25
6	84–14	10	00
7			
8			
TOTAL DEPOSIT		200	00

DEPOSITS ACCEPTED SUBJECT TO CONDITIONS ON REVERSE SIDE

date is used (January 9, 19X2 in this case). The total value of the paper money is entered opposite the word "bills" on the deposit slip. Currency to be deposited should be sorted by denomination, with the smallest denomination on top of the pile. The total value of the coins is entered opposite the word "coin." If there is a large number of coins of any one denomination, they should be packaged in coin rolls provided by the bank. The name of the depositor should be written or stamped on each roll of coins to identify the source, in case of possible error.

Checks and any other items presented for deposit should be listed individually and identified. Checks bear an American Bankers Association (ABA) transit number, which identifies the bank and indicates its location. (See illustration on page 117. The ABA number of Carter's bank is 84-8, the numerator of the fraction that appears to the right of the year date.) Many banks like to have the ABA number entered on the deposit slip beside the amount of each check, as is done in the illustration.

Endorsements

Checks to be deposited must be *endorsed.* This is the legal process by which the Carter Cleaning Shop, as the payee (firm to which the checks are made payable), transfers ownership of these checks to the bank. The reason for transferring ownership is to give the bank the legal right to collect payment from the makers or payors (persons who wrote the checks in the first place). In the event that the check cannot be collected, the endorser guarantees payment to all subsequent holders.

There are several forms of endorsement that are in common use. Private individuals frequently use an *endorsement in blank,* which consists of the signature of the payee written on the reverse side of the check and preferably at the left end (the perforated end that was torn away from the stub). A check that has been endorsed in blank can be further negotiated by the bearer (anyone into whose hands it should fall by intentional transfer or through loss).

The *endorsement in full* is a much safer arrangement. The payee indicates, as part of the endorsement, the name of the person, firm, or bank to whom the check is to be payable. Only the person or firm designated in the full endorsement can transfer the title to anyone else.

The most appropriate form of endorsement for business purposes is the *restrictive endorsement,* which limits the further circulation of the check to a stated purpose, usually for deposit to the credit of the firm to which it was made payable. For maximum safety and speedy handling, the Carter Cleaning Shop uses a rubber stamp to affix its restrictive endorsement. All three types of endorsement are illustrated.

In Blank

> Albert L. Carter
> 242-027721

In Full

> PAY TO THE ORDER OF
> CITY NATIONAL BANK
> CARTER CLEANING SHOP
> 242-027720

Restrictive

> PAY TO THE ORDER OF
> CITY NATIONAL BANK
> FOR DEPOSIT ONLY
> CARTER CLEANING SHOP
> 242-027720

Delivery of the Deposit

Once the deposit has been prepared, it should be delivered promptly to the bank. In the Carter Cleaning Shop operation, Carter carries the deposit to the bank after store hours in a locked bag. If the bank is not open at that time, he places the bag in the night depository at the door of the bank. The bag slides down a chute into the bank vault for safekeeping overnight. Then, at his convenience during banking hours the next day, Carter visits the bank, unlocks the bag, makes the deposit, and takes the bag back to the office for reuse.

The Deposit Receipt

The bank may acknowledge receipt of the deposit in a variety of ways. Many banks issue a machine-receipt form indicating the date and amount of money received. In addition, some banks furnish a *passbook* to the depositor with the date and amount of the deposit entered in it, along with the teller's validating initials. However, it is increasingly common for the bank teller to stamp and return the receipt copy of a multicarbon deposit slip. In this way, the depositor obtains a file copy of all the details of the deposit. It can then be retained indefinitely among his financial records as a proof of his deposit, in case it is needed.

MAKING DISBURSEMENTS

You will recall that Carter's accountant recommended that all large payments be made by check. He also advised that Carter be the only person authorized to sign checks for the firm. Carter's signature was supplied to the bank when the Carter Cleaning Shop account was opened in November. The *signature card* illustrated constitutes a contract between the depositor and the bank. It authorizes the bank to make payments against the depositor's account on checks bearing the authorized signature.

TRADESTYLE CHECKING ACCOUNT AGREEMENT   Carter Cleaning Shop

ADDRESS   365 Broad Street
Centerport, State   53995   PHONE   555-5678

The undersigned certifies that he, as sole proprietor, is doing business under the name of............ Carter Cleaning Shop ...., an unincorporated trade name or trade style, that no person other than the undersigned has any interest in said business except as employee, and that the following employees, whose signatures appear below, have authority to, and are hereby authorized to sign checks, drafts or orders for the payment of money; and endorse negotiable instruments in my name and/or in the name of said trade style, such authority to continue until written notice to the contrary from the undersigned shall have been received by you.

Witness my hand and seal this the .... 26th .... day of .... November ...., 19 X1 .

Proprietor Sign Here ...... *Albert L. Carter* ...... (L. S.)
(Signature)

.... Albert L. Carter .... will sign *Albert L. Carter*

(Employee) .... will sign ....

FORMER BANKING CONNECTION Center Savings Bank INITIAL DEPOSIT $ 6,000

OFFICER ACCEPTING   *R.T.*   DATE OPENED   Nov. 26, 19X1

Checkwriting Procedures

A check is a written order prepared by the depositor (called the *drawer*) instructing the bank to pay a specific sum of money to the person designated (the *payee*). As you have already seen, the payee can endorse the check and transfer it to a third party for presentation to the bank.

The Checkbook

Most individuals and many businesses use checkbooks provided by the bank. Ordinarily, checks in this form are written by hand. However, many businesses have their own checks printed so that they may be prepared on a typewriter with a carbon copy that may be kept as a record of the payment and as a basis for the accounting entries involved. Carter decided to use temporarily the bank's standard form of check with the stub attached, like the one illustrated.

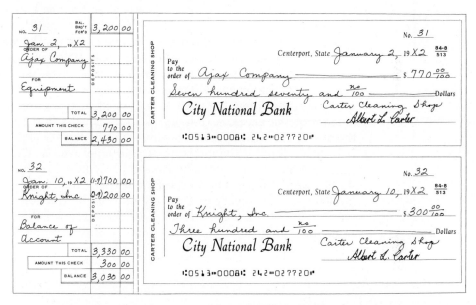

The check number appears on both the check and the check stub, along with other data that are important from an accounting standpoint. The check information is entered more formally than on the stub. The typical check used in business may be signed only by an authorized official.

There are many fine points involved in writing a check. For instance, when using the standard checkbook, the check stub should always be filled out first; otherwise it might be forgotten. The stub contains information that is important for future reference. Notice that the opening balance of $3,200 appears on the first line entitled "Balance Brought Forward." The amount of the first check, $770, is written on the proper line. It is then subtracted from the total to obtain the balance of $2,430. The rest of the details are self explanatory: the date is January 2, 19X2; the name of the payee is Ajax Company; and the purpose of the payment is for equipment.

Once the stub is completed, the check portion is filled out. The date, name of payee, and amount in figures and words are written out very

UNIT 8

carefully. A line is drawn to fill any empty space after the payee's name and amount in words. (A checkwriting machine that imprints the amount in distinctive type and perforates the check paper under the writing to prevent fraudulent alteration may be used.) Then all the details should be reexamined for accuracy before the check is signed and sent out.

On the second stub, two deposits have been entered and the dates noted. On January 7, a deposit of $700 was made, and on January 9, a deposit of $200 was made. When the second check is to be written, the balance of $2,430 (on the first stub) is added to the two deposits, and the total of $3,330 is entered. The amount of the second check of $300 is written on the proper line, where it is immediately deducted from the total to obtain a new balance of $3,030. The remainder of the details are completed as previously explained.

Look again at the checks illustrated and notice how the amounts are expressed. The amount of the check is written in figures in the space provided after the name of the payee. Special care must be taken to write the figures clearly so that they can be read easily. The cents amount is usually indicated as a fraction of a dollar; thus, 15 cents is written as $\frac{15}{100}$. If the check is for an even dollar amount, $\frac{00}{100}$ or $\frac{no}{100}$ is written. (When the check is typewritten, the form $111.22 or $111.00 is often used.) The dollar amount of the check is restated in words on the line below the name of the payee. The writing should begin at the extreme left of the space provided, in order to prevent the insertion of additional words. The cents amount is again written as a fraction and is usually separated from the dollar amount by the word "and." (On a typewritten check, the form used is 22/100 or no/100.) It is customary to draw a line from the fraction to the word "dollars," in order to fill the empty space. (If, through error, the amount expressed in figures is not the same as the amount in words, the bank will pay the amount written in words.)

Carter Cleaning Shop 365 Broad Street Centerport, State 53995		**N°** 301	84-8 / 513

May 1 _____, 19 X2

PAY TO THE ORDER OF Star-Herald Papers ----------------------------------- $ 300.00

Three hundred and no/100--- DOLLARS

CITY NATIONAL BANK
OF CENTERPORT,
STATE

⑈0513⑈0008⑈242⑈027720⑈

Carter Cleaning Shop

By *Albert L. Carter*

AUTHORIZED SIGNATURE

Carter Cleaning Shop, Centerport, State 53995   DETACH BEFORE BANKING

April advertising per Invoice 27641 $300.00

Use of Specially Printed Check Form

When Carter purchases specially prepared checks, the standard bank checks previously described are no longer used. The new check form is in two parts. At the top, there is the check itself, in the usual form. At the bottom, there is a detachable part (called the *voucher*) that is used for writing explanatory information, such as the amount, number, and date of the invoice being paid. The first of the new checks, numbered 301, was issued on May 1, 19X2 to the Star-Herald Papers for $300 in payment of advertising bought by the Carter Cleaning Shop. This *voucher check* is illustrated.

THE BANK STATEMENT

Once a month, a depositor receives from the bank a statement of the deposits received and the checks paid. A typical bank statement is illustrated below. At this time, the bank also returns the checks that were paid during the month, and any charge tickets, credit memorandums, or papers that have a bearing on the account balance.

CITY NATIONAL BANK

CARTER CLEANING SHOP
365 BROAD STREET
CENTERPORT, STATE 53995   242-027720

NOTIFY US OF ANY CHANGE IN YOUR ADDRESS

CHECKS	DEPOSITS	DATE	BALANCE
AMOUNT BROUGHT FORWARD		19X2 JAN 1	3,200.00
770.00–		JAN 3	2,430.00
	700.00+	JAN 8	3,130.00
	200.00+	JAN 10	3,330.00
300.00–		JAN 11	3,030.00
	725.00+	JAN 15	3,755.00
400.00–		JAN 16	3,355.00
	30.00+	JAN 17	3,385.00
700.00–		JAN 18	2,685.00
	900.00+	JAN 22	3,585.00
	45.00+	JAN 24	3,630.00
500.00–		JAN 26	3,130.00
600.00–		JAN 29	2,530.00
300.00–		JAN 30	2,230.00

PLEASE USE YOUR ACCOUNT IDENTIFICATION NUMBER ON ALL CHECKS AND DEPOSITS

LAST AMOUNT IN THIS COLUMN IS YOUR BALANCE

CODE	
DM - DEBIT MEMO	MS - MISCELLANEOUS
DC - DEPOSIT CORRECTION	OD - OVERDRAWN
EC - ERROR CORRECTION	RT - RETURN ITEM
LS - LIST OF CHECKS	SC - SERVICE CHARGE

Immediately after receiving the bank statement (and after balancing the general ledger) the accountant should proceed to *reconcile* the bank statement with the records of the company. The bank statement received by the Carter Cleaning Shop at the close of January 19X2 shows a balance in the company's bank account of $2,230. But the balance reflected in the general ledger Cash 101 account, page 100, and also on the last stub of the checkbook, is only $1,280. The accountant must determine why this difference exists and bring the records into balance. This process of determining the reasons for the difference is known as *reconciling* the bank statement.

An analysis by the accountant of the bank statement and the company's records on January 31 reveals two types of differences between the bank statement and the Cash 101 account. These two types of differences are very common.

1. Two checks, one written on January 30 and one on January 31, were recorded in the cash disbursements journal and in the checkbook. However, the January 31 bank statement does not show that these two checks have "cleared" the bank. The two checks, known as *outstanding checks*, are:

   No. 38, dated January 30, payable to S. S. Baker for miscellaneous expenses, $60.
   No. 39, dated January 31, payable to Carter for salaries, $1,700.

2. A deposit of $810 was made during evening banking hours on January 31, which was too late to be entered on the bank statement that day. This amount represented the receipts of January 27 and January 29 that were entered in the cash receipts journal. Receipts such as these that have been entered on the books but have not been deposited in time to be included on the bank statement, are known as *deposits in transit*.

The accountant proceeds to reconcile the bank balance to the book balance, as shown in the *reconciliation statement* illustrated.

CARTER CLEANING SHOP
Bank Reconciliation Statement
January 31, 19X2

Balance per bank statement		$2,230
Add deposit of Jan. 31, in transit		810
		$3,040
Deduct outstanding checks		
No. 38, January 30	$ 60	
No. 39, January 31	1,700	1,760
Balance per books		$1,280

Many banks have adopted the practice of printing a convenient reconciliation form on the back of the monthly bank statement to assist depositors in reconciling their accounts. The completed reconciliation statement shows how Carter's accountant would have completed a typical form.

THIS FORM IS PROVIDED TO HELP YOU BALANCE YOUR BANK STATEMENT

Date January 31 , 19 X2

Balance Shown on BANK STATEMENT	$ 2,230.00		Balance Shown in Your CHECKBOOK	$ 1,280.00
Add Deposits Not on Statement:	$ 810.00		*Add* any Deposits Not Already Entered in Checkbook:	$
Total . . .	$ 3,040.00			
Subtract Checks Issued but Not on Statement:			*Total* . . .	$ 1,280.00
No. 38 $ 60.00				
39 1,700.00			*Subtract* Service Charges and other Bank Charges Not in Checkbook:	$
Total	$ 1,760.00		*Total*	$
BALANCE	$ 1,280.00		BALANCE	$ 1,280.00

These totals should agree with your checkbook.
Any differences should be reported to the bank within ten days after the receipt of your statement.

No entries are made on Carter's books for the outstanding checks and the deposit in transit. The accountant will examine the next month's bank statement to verify that the deposit is credited and that the checks were charged to the account.

BANK RECONCILIATION —EXTENDED ILLUSTRATION

The accountant of the Carter Cleaning Shop found it a simple task to reconcile the January bank statement because there were very few transactions with the bank during the month. However, as a business grows and transactions become more numerous, the task of reconciling the statement becomes more difficult, and a systematic procedure must be established. To illustrate the steps involved in a larger business, the bank reconciliation procedure for the Baker Sport Store for February, 19X1 is given. This is the first month of operations of the business.

The Bank Statement

On March 1, the Baker Sport Store receives the statement of its checking account for the month of February that is illustrated. The accountant checks at once to see if the balance of $28,501.72 as shown by the bank agrees with the balance on his records.

CITY NATIONAL BANK

BAKER SPORT STORE
180 PARK AVENUE
GREENVILLE, STATE 53970   341-060821

NOTIFY US OF ANY CHANGE IN YOUR ADDRESS

CHECKS		DEPOSITS	DATE	BALANCE
AMOUNT BROUGHT FORWARD				
			19X1	
50.00–	25.00–	27,000.00+	FEB 1	26,925.00
		425.00+	FEB 2	27,350.00
250.00–		575.00+	FEB 3	27,675.00
		500.00+	FEB 4	28,175.00
		1,030.00+	FEB 7	
		1,395.00+	FEB 7	30,600.00
		775.00+	FEB 8	31,375.00
		1,240.00+	FEB 9	32,615.00
1,960.00–		1,080.00+	FEB 10	31,735.00
300.00–		975.00+	FEB 11	32,410.00
200.00–	490.00–	2,050.00+	FEB 14	
719.81–	56.35–	805.00+	FEB 14	33,798.84
82.50–	102.77–	275.00+	FEB 15	33,888.57
101.01–	127.56–	525.00+	FEB 16	34,185.00
		490.00+	FEB 17	34,675.00
		550.00+	FEB 18	35,225.00
		710.00+	FEB 21	35,935.00
		625.00+	FEB 21	36,560.00
		210.00+	FEB 22	36,770.00
5,135.20–		265.00+	FEB 23	31,899.80
4,838.26–		305.00+	FEB 24	27,366.54
25.00–DM		330.00+	FEB 25	27,671.54
102.77–	17.05–	720.00+	FEB 28	28,271.72
400.00–	.00–SC	730.00+	FEB 28	28,601.72
100.00–			FEB 28	28,501.72

PLEASE USE YOUR ACCOUNT IDENTIFICATION NUMBER ON ALL CHECKS AND DEPOSITS

LAST AMOUNT IN THIS COLUMN IS YOUR BALANCE

CODE	
DM - DEBIT MEMO	MS - MISCELLANEOUS
DC - DEPOSIT CORRECTION	OD - OVERDRAWN
EC - ERROR CORRECTION	RT - RETURN ITEM
LS - LIST OF CHECKS	SC - SERVICE CHARGE

Book Balance of Cash

The Cash 101 account in the general ledger has had entries posted to it during the month from two sources—the cash receipts journal and the cash disbursements journal. From the cash receipts journal, the Cash account received a debit posting of $43,805. From the cash disbursements journal, the Cash account received a credit posting of $15,561.85. With the total cash receipts and expenditures posted for the month, the Cash account shows a debit balance of $28,243.15 (called the *book balance*), as shown.

Cash   No. 101

DATE		EXPLANATION	POST. REF.	DEBIT		DATE		EXPLANATION	POST. REF.	CREDIT	
19	X1					19	X1				
Feb.	28		CRJ-1	43,805	00	Feb.	28		CDJ-1	15,561	85
		28,243.15									

Difference between Book Balance and Bank Balance

Since the difference between the book and bank balance may be due to errors made by either the depositor or the bank, the reconciliation process must be undertaken at once. Errors in the firm's records should be corrected immediately. Errors made by the bank should be called to its attention at the earliest possible moment.

Even if no errors have been made in the calculation of the book balance and the bank statement balance, there are four basic reasons why the balances may not agree. You have already encountered the first two in the Carter reconciliation.

1. Outstanding checks may have been written and entered in the firm's cash disbursements journal as cash disbursed, but they may not actually have been paid by the bank and charged to the depositor's account before the end of the month.
2. A deposit recorded in the cash receipts journal of the depositor may have reached the bank too late to be included in the bank statement for the current month—giving rise to a deposit in transit.
3. The bank may have deducted service charges or other items that have not been recorded in the records of Baker.
4. The bank may have credited the firm's account for collections made or for other items that have not yet been recorded in the depositor's records.

As in the Carter situation, differences stemming from the first two causes require no entries. They should be considered in the preparation of the reconciliation statement. Then the next bank statement should be checked to make sure that they have been picked up in the bank records. Differences arising from the last two of these causes should be corrected by adjusting entries in the records of the depositor to reflect the increases or decreases of cash.

In addition, there are other differences that might occur less often: the bank may have made an arithmetic error, may have given credit to the wrong depositor, or may have charged a check against the wrong depositor's account. Similarly, a check may have been recorded in the books at an amount different than that for which it was actually written, or it may not have been entered at all.

Steps in the Bank Reconciliation

There are several steps that should be followed in reconciling a bank statement.

STEP 1. The canceled checks and other charge slips returned by the bank are compared with the deductions listed on the bank statement. Charges other than checks are explained in *debit memos* enclosed with the statement. Two debit memos are included with this bank statement.

The first one covers a check from Thomas Hunt for $25 that the bank could not collect because there were not sufficient funds in Hunt's account. This NSF check, as it is called, is charged back against the Baker bank account because the firm had endorsed it, deposited it, and received credit for it. The debit memorandum is shown here.

DEBIT	Baker Sport Store 180 Park Avenue Greenville, State 53970	**CITY NATIONAL BANK** 341-060821		
	Thomas Hunt — NSF Check		25	00
DATE Feb. 25 19 X1		**APPROVED** *W.E.H.*		

The second debit memorandum covers the calculation of the monthly bank service charges. These charges vary among banks, but they usually include a flat maintenance charge, plus charges for checks paid on the account, for checks deposited or cashed, and for use of the night depository.

Some banks allow a credit against the service charges to reflect the earning power of the minimum balance maintained in the account. Baker's bank allows such a credit. Because of the very large balance in the account during February, the credit exceeds the charges so that no service charge (SC) was made and there is nothing to be deducted from the account.

DEBIT **CITY NATIONAL BANK**	**ADVICE** GREENVILLE, STATE			
15 Checks Paid (over 5) and Debit Items	@ 4c ea.			60
Checks Paid (over 205) and Debit Items	@ 3c ea.			
26 Out of Town Items Deposited and/or Cashed	@ 3c ea.			78
165 Local Items Deposited and/or Cashed	@ 1c ea.		1	65
OTHER CHARGES *Night Depository*			2	00
Maintenance Charge				.50
Total Activity Charge			5	53
Less: Allowance of 15c per $100.00 on Minimum Balance of $ *26,925.00*			40	39
NET CHARGE			*None*	

Baker Sport Store
180 Park Avenue
Greenville, State 53970   341-060821

Your account has been charged for the previous month's activity as indicated by the analysis hereon.

STEP 2. The canceled checks are arranged in numerical sequence, in order to compare them with the entries made in the cash disbursements journal. In making this comparison, the payee, amount of each check, and the check number are verified. (Any differences must be corrected in the general journal.) The endorsement must be examined to make sure that it agrees with the name of the payee.

In making this comparison, the accountant finds that a $100 check was charged by mistake to the account of the Baker Sport Store on February 28, 19X1 and is included in the canceled checks. The check was signed by J. L. Barton and should have been charged to his account. The accountant will, of course, immediately notify the bank of the error, return the check to the bank, and the Baker Sport Store will be given credit for $100.

The numbers and amounts of checks that have been written but have not been returned by the bank (outstanding checks) should be listed for later use. This list for Baker includes No. 117, $127.56; No. 118, $101.01; and No. 120, $375.

STEP 3. The bank record of deposits is compared with the daily receipts listed in the cash receipts journal. In the case of the Baker Sport Store, the bank record agrees with the firm's tally with one exception—a credit for the receipts of February 28. The money had been placed in the night depository on February 28 but had not been deposited in the bank until the following day, March 1. A note is made of the $220, as a deposit in transit.

STEP 4. The final step is to prove that all differences are accounted for by means of a formal bank reconciliation statement, such as the one prepared for the Baker Sport Store on February 28, 19X1.

Note that there are two main sections in the reconciliation statement. The upper section starts with the "Balance per bank statement" ($28,501.72 from the bank's records). To this amount are added any items that increase the bank balance, such as receipts that are entered on the firm's books but have not been recorded by the bank. The deposit in transit of $220 (the

```
                        BAKER SPORT STORE
                     Bank Reconciliation Statement
                          February 28, 19X1

Balance per bank statement                                  $28,501.72
Add: Deposit of Feb. 28, in transit            $220.00
     Check of J. L. Barton incorrectly charged
       by bank to Baker account                 100.00         320.00
                                                            $28,821.72

Deduct outstanding checks
   No. 117 February 27                         $127.56
   No. 118 February 28                          101.01
   No. 120 February 28                          375.00

     Total outstanding checks                                  603.57
Adjusted bank balance                                       $28,218.15


Balance per books                                           $28,243.15
Deduct bank debit memo—Thomas Hunt NSF check                    25.00
Adjusted book balance                                       $28,218.15
```

receipts of February 28) and the $100 check of J. L. Barton that was incorrectly charged to the account of Baker, are the only two items in this category. Addition of the three figures produces a new total of $28,821.72. Then, from this total, items that decrease the bank balance are subtracted, such as the three outstanding checks that had been entered on the firm's books but had not been deducted by the bank. After the subtraction, there is an adjusted bank balance of $28,218.15.

The second section of the reconciliation statement starts with "Balance per books" ($28,243.15 from the Cash account). To this balance, any increases are added, such as special collection items recorded by the bank but not yet entered on the firm's books. There are none of these items involved in this month's business. Next, any items that are deducted by the bank but are not picked up in the firm's records must be subtracted from the previous book balance. There is one of these items this month—the NSF check of Thomas Hunt for $25. Subtracting this check from the $28,243.15 results in an adjusted book balance of $28,218.15. The adjusted bank balance and the adjusted book balance agree, as they always must at this point.

Adjusting the Records

Items in the second section of the reconciliation statement require entries on the books to correct the Cash account balance. The entry (through the general journal) required for the one item in this case is a debit to Accounts Receivable (to charge Hunt's bad check back to him) and an offsetting credit to Cash 101.

After this entry is posted, the Cash account balance will be $28,218.15, the same figure as the adjusted book balance calculated on the reconciliation statement. If checks with stubs are being used, the balance shown on the last stub should be corrected at this point to agree with the adjusted balance shown in the Cash account.

19 X1		3-1				
Mar. 1	Accounts Receivable	111		25 00		
	Cash	101			25 00	
	To record return of NSF check to Thomas Hunt.					

Cash   No. 101

DATE	EXPLANATION	POST. REF.	DEBIT	DATE	EXPLANATION	POST. REF.	CREDIT
19 X1 Feb. 28		CRJ-1	43,805 00	19 X1 Feb. 28		CDJ-1	15,561 85
	28,243.15			28	Carried Fwd.	✓	28,243 15
			43,805 00				43,805 00
Mar. 1	Brought Fwd.	✓	28,243 15	Mar. 1		3-1	25 00
	28,218.15						

♦ ♦ ♦

PRINCIPLES AND PROCEDURES

A bank checking account is absolutely essential to a business firm in order for it to achieve adequate cash control. Once the account is opened, receipts should be deposited daily. Payments can be made conveniently by check. Checkwriting requires careful attention to details. The stub should be completed before the check itself. Some firms use specially printed checks.

As soon as the bank statement is received, it should be promptly reconciled with the Cash account. Frequently, differences arise because of deposits in transit, outstanding checks, and other factors.

MANAGERIAL IMPLICATIONS

The use of banking services and procedures by the business firm completes the list of devices available for safeguarding cash. The formal procedures for receiving, recording, and depositing cash and for making and recording cash payments, provide for authorization, verification, and proof all along the line. In order for management to maintain adequate and necessary cash balances to meet obligations, it must know the true cash position of the company at all times. Hence, business management should insist that reconciliations be made promptly so that errors can be quickly rectified and other differences can be accounted for.

APPLICATION OF PRINCIPLES

PROBLEM 8 · 1

At the end of April 19X1, Larry Fowler received his monthly bank statement for Fowler Florists from the First National Bank. The opening balance shown on the bank statement agrees with the balance of the Cash account at March 31. Since the two figures agree, the Cash account at March 31 has been automatically verified. A list of deposits made and checks issued during April is supplied below. The balance of the Cash account and checkbook at April 30 was $3,972.

APRIL				APRIL		
1	Balance	$6,089		19	Deposit	150
1	Check 244	100		22	Check 249	9
3	Check 245	300		23	Deposit	150
5	Deposit	350		26	Check 250	200
5	Check 246	275		28	Check 251	18
10	Check 247	2,000		30	Check 252	15
17	Check 248	50		30	Deposit	200

FIRST NATIONAL BANK

FOWLER FLORISTS
376 KING AVENUE
CHARLESTON, STATE 29403   454–623016

NOTIFY US OF ANY CHANGE IN YOUR ADDRESS

CHECKS		DEPOSITS	DATE	BALANCE
AMOUNT BROUGHT FORWARD			19X1 MAR 31	6,089.00
		350.00+	APR 6	6,439.00
100.00–			APR 6	6,339.00
275.00–	300.00–		APR 10	5,764.00
2,000.00–			APR 13	3,764.00
1.65–SC			APR 14	3,762.35
		150.00+	APR 20	3,912.35
50.00–			APR 22	3,862.35
		150.00+	APR 25	4,012.35
9.00–			APR 26	4,003.35
200.00–			APR 29	3,803.35

Please Use Your Account Identification Number on All Checks and Deposits

LAST AMOUNT IN THIS
COLUMN IS YOUR BALANCE

Code	
DM–Debit Memo	MS–Miscellaneous
DC–Deposit Correction	OD–Overdrawn
EC–Error Correction	RT–Return Item
LS–List of Checks	SC–Service Charge

1. Verify the Cash account at April 30 by preparing a bank reconciliation statement.
2. Record the entry (4-7) in general journal form to correct the Cash account balance. Charge to Miscellaneous Expense 591.

PROBLEM 8 · 2

♦ On July 31, 19X1, the checkbook balance and the cash account balance of Maria's Dress Shop were $11,549. The records indicate that an $879.60 deposit dated July 30, 19X1, and a $476.80 deposit dated July 31, 19X1, do not appear on the bank statement. A service charge of $4.50 and a debit memo of $80, covering an NSF check, have not been entered on the books. Checks for $110.50, $11.60, $238.20, $576.30, $77.35, and $145 have been issued but have not yet been presented to the bank for payment. The July bank statement balance is $11,267.05.

INSTRUCTIONS

1. Reconcile the book balance with the bank statement balance at July 31, 19X1.
2. Record the entries in general journal form to correct the Cash account. (Start with Entry 7-9.)

MANAGERIAL CHECKUPS

♦ How does the accounting system keep the management informed of its true cash position at all times?

♦ Why must the manager insist that the endorsement on each check be examined by the person reconciling the bank statement?

♦ Would closer supervision of procedures for recording cash receipts and disbursements save time and money by eliminating the need for a monthly bank statement reconciliation?

♦ With banks offering a variety of computer services to clients, why doesn't the typical depositor pay his bank to complete his reconciliation statement at the end of each month?

9
THE SALES JOURNAL

You have already learned that much of the work involved in recording cash receipts and cash disbursements can be reduced by the use of special journals. Naturally, the accountant also devises special journals to handle other types of transactions that occur frequently. Another look at the general journal for the January 19X2 transactions of the Carter Cleaning Shop reveals a third type of repetitive entry—entries recording the sales of cleaning services to customers on account.

19 X2		1–3						
Jan.	7	Accounts Receivable	111	✓	60	00		
		Cleaning Service Income	401	✓			60	00
		To record charge sale to R. L. Camp, Sales Slip 1.						
		1–8						
	14	Accounts Receivable	111	✓	25	00		
		Cleaning Service Income	401	✓			25	00
		To record charge sale to M. F. Coleman, Sales Slip 2.						
		1–12						
	19	Accounts Receivable	111	✓	30	00		
		Cleaning Service Income	401	✓			30	00
		To record charge sale to B. A. Hahn, Sales Slip 3.						
		1–18						
	28	Accounts Receivable	111	✓	60	00		
		Cleaning Service Income	401	✓			60	00
		To record charge sale to S. S. Baker, Sales Slip 4.						

You will quickly detect the great amount of repetition involved in both journalizing and posting. In the general journal, the four credit sales required four separate entries. A closer look at the entries discloses four debits to Accounts Receivable 111, four credits to Cleaning Service Income 401, and four identical explanations. The posting of eight items to the two ledger accounts represents still further duplication of effort. The accountant realizes that a more efficient system of recording credit sales must be developed to save time and effort.

Accounts Receivable   **No. 111**

DATE		EXPLANATION	POST. REF.	DEBIT		DATE	EXPLANATION	POST. REF.	CREDIT	
19	X2									
Jan.	1	Brought Fwd.	✓	200	00					
	7		1-3	60	00					
	14		1-8	25	00					
	19		1-12	30	00					
	28		1-18	60	00					

Cleaning Service Income   **No. 401**

DATE	EXPLANATION	POST. REF.	DEBIT		DATE		EXPLANATION	POST. REF.	CREDIT	
					19	X2				
					Jan.	7		1-2	700	00
						7		1-3	60	00
						14		1-7	725	00
						14		1-8	25	00
						19		1-12	30	00
						21		1-13	900	00
						27		1-16	800	00
						28		1-18	60	00

RECORDING IN THE SALES JOURNAL

A third special journal, this time only for credit sales, provides an efficient system for recording these sales. The January credit sales of the Carter Cleaning Shop are entered in a *sales journal* to illustrate how this special journal works.

SALES JOURNAL for Month of January 19X2   **Page 1**

DATE		SALES SLIP NO.	CUSTOMER'S NAME	✓	AMOUNT	
Jan.	7	1	R. L. Camp		60	00
	14	2	M. F. Coleman		25	00
	19	3	B. A. Hahn		30	00
	28	4	S. S. Baker		60	00

The columns and headings in the sales journal make the recording process much more efficient. Each entry requires only a single line to record the date, sales slip number, customer's name, and amount. All needless repetition is avoided, and all entries for credit sales can now be found grouped together in one place.

Incidentally, the Sales Slip Number column in the sales journal is useful for future reference. For instance, suppose the accountant needs to check some details about the sale to R. L. Camp. He would look for the sales slip number in the proper column in the journal, find a carbon copy of Sales Slip 1 (illustrated on page 71) in the numerical file of sales slips and, in a matter of seconds, have the information he is seeking.

POSTING FROM THE SALES JOURNAL

The sales journal also eliminates repetition in posting to the Accounts Receivable and Cleaning Service income accounts. No posting is made to these accounts until the end of the month, when the accountant adds the Amount column in the sales journal. This total, representing the total sales on account for the month, is posted as a debit to Account 111 (Accounts Receivable) and as a credit to Account 401 (Cleaning Service Income). The two ledger account numbers are noted on the Total Credit Sales line in the sales journal. As they are posted, a check mark is placed beside the account number in the Posting Check (✔) column. When the posting is finished, the sales journal and the related accounts appear as shown. The SJ-1 notation in the Posting Reference column of the accounts indicates that the amount was posted from Page 1 of the sales journal.

SALES JOURNAL for Month of January 19X2 Page 1

DATE		SALES SLIP NO.	CUSTOMER'S NAME		✔	AMOUNT	
Jan.	7	1	R. L. Camp			60	00
	14	2	M. F. Coleman			25	00
	19	3	B. A. Hahn			30	00
	28	4	S. S. Baker			60	00
				Debit 111	✔		
	31		Total Credit Sales	Credit 401	✔✔	175	00

Accounts Receivable No. 111

DATE		EXPLANATION	POST. REF.	DEBIT		DATE	EXPLANATION	POST. REF.	CREDIT
19	X2								
Jan.	1	Brought Fwd.	✔	200	00				
	31		SJ-1	175	00				

				Cleaning Service Income			No. 401	
DATE	EXPLANATION	POST. REF.	DEBIT	DATE	EXPLANATION	POST. REF.	CREDIT	
				19 X2 Jan. 31		SJ-1	175	00

ADVANTAGES OF THE SALES JOURNAL

The previous examples offer clear proof that time, effort, and recording space can be saved by the use of the special sales journal for handling credit sales. Comparing the Accounts Receivable and the Cleaning Service Income accounts with those shown on page 131, it can be seen that four individual postings to each of these accounts have been replaced by a single summary posting to each. Similarly, if there had been 300 credit sales during the month, the 300 postings to each account that would be necessary under the general journal system would be replaced by one summary posting to each account at the end of the month. The use of a special sales journal also permits more division of work. For example, in a large office, the recording of credit sales may be a full-time job for a sales entry clerk.

RECORDING SALES TAX

You have already learned that in some states certain retail sales of goods and services are subject to a sales tax, which the retailer must collect from the purchaser. The retailer is then required to remit the sales tax at specified intervals to the state or other taxing authority.

When a sales tax applies to goods sold on account, the tax must, of course, be charged to the customer and recorded at the time of the sale. Once again, the problem of recording the tax would prompt the accountant to redesign the sales journal. Here is how the redesigned sales journal looks for a cleaning shop operating in a state that has a sales tax on such sales.

SALES JOURNAL for Month of June 19X2   Page 6

DATE	SALES SLIP NO.	CUSTOMER'S NAME	ACCOUNTS RECEIVABLE		SALES TAX PAYABLE CR. 231	CLEANING SERVICE INCOME CR. 401
			✓	DR. 111		
June 1	241	J. T. Roberts		22 66	66	22 00
30		Totals		480 00	13 98	466 02
				✓	✓	✓

Each column is totaled and posted at the end of the month. The check mark beneath each total in the special sales journal indicates that the amount has been posted to the proper general ledger account. The Sales Tax Payable column is posted as a credit to Sales Tax Payable 231 because it represents a liability. (Sales, for both cash and credit, and related sales taxes will be explained more fully in a later unit.)

Sales Tax Payable   **No. 231**

DATE	EXPLANATION	POST. REF.	DEBIT	DATE	EXPLANATION	POST. REF.	CREDIT
				19 X2 June 30		SJ-6	13 98

Accounts Receivable   **No. 111**

DATE	EXPLANATION	POST. REF.	DEBIT	DATE	EXPLANATION	POST. REF.	CREDIT
19 X2 June 1 30	Balance	✓ SJ-6	3,600 00 480 00				

Cleaning Service Income   **No. 401**

DATE	EXPLANATION	POST. REF.	DEBIT	DATE	EXPLANATION	POST. REF.	CREDIT
				19 X2 June 30		SJ-6	466 02

RECORDING SALES RETURNS AND ALLOWANCES

A sale is recorded on the books of the business firm at the time a sale is made or a service is rendered. However, not every sale produces satisfaction, and when something goes wrong, the merchant has to take back the goods (called a *sales return*) and replace them, rectify the error, or make an allowance (called a *sales allowance*). For example, suppose that Ralph Schmidt, one of Carter's customers, complains that a rug was not cleaned properly. After examining the rug, Carter agrees to allow a $6 credit, reducing the bill from $24 to $18. How would the allowance be handled?

This allowance is recorded in the general journal because it does not belong in any of the special journals that you have studied so far. Accounts Receivable 111 is credited to record the reduction in the amount owed by Schmidt. A new account called Sales Returns and Allowances 451 is debited.

19 X2		6-3					
June	2	Sales Returns & Allowances . . .	451		6 00		
		Accounts Receivable	111				6 00
		To allow Ralph Schmidt credit because					
		of improper rug cleaning.					

The use of the Sales Returns and Allowances account is preferred to a direct debit to the Cleaning Service Income account, because this procedure furnishes a complete record of sales adjustments made during the period. Merchants value this record as one of several measures of operating efficiency. The total of Sales Returns and Allowances is later deducted from Cleaning Service Income in the Income section of the income statement.

Income
Cleaning Service Income	$4,725.60
Less Sales Returns and Allowances	39.75
Net Sales Income	$4,685.85

RETURNS AND ALLOWANCES INVOLVING SALES TAX

Sales taxes are levied only on the net amount of the sale to a customer. Thus, if a customer returns goods or is given an allowance on merchandise or services on which he has been charged a sales tax, he is entitled to a credit not only for the amount of the sales price involved, but also for the amount of sales tax he has been charged. Similarly, the merchant is not obligated to pay to the taxing authority the sales tax on returns and allowances. In these cases, the reduction in sales tax liability along with the return or allowance must be recorded. For example, assume that on June 4, 19X2, J. T. Roberts is given an allowance of $3 on the sale of June 1, recorded in the sales journal on page 133. The allowance and the reduction in tax liability are recorded in the general journal as shown.

19 X2		6-6					
June	4	Sales Returns & Allowances . . .	451		3 00		
		Sales Tax Payable	231		09		
		Accounts Receivable	111				3 09
		To record allowance to J. T. Roberts for					
		improper cleaning on sale of June 1.					

If there are numerous sales returns and allowances, a company may set up a special Sales Returns and Allowances journal in which to record such transactions. The Sales Returns and Allowances journal is discussed in Unit 12.

UNIT 9

The operations of the Carter Cleaning Shop are typical of the activities of thousands of firms called *retailers* that sell their goods and services at retail prices to consumers. In turn, retailers purchase goods from wholesalers, manufacturers, and other distributors. The basic accounting procedures used by the various distributors are the same as for retailers. There are, however, two aspects of the sales procedures of wholesalers and manufacturers that are not commonly found in retail businesses. These are *cash discounts* and *trade discounts*.

You have already seen, in Unit 6, how cash discounts on sales are handled, and these cash discounts will be examined again in Unit 16. A wholesale business must offer its goods to trade customers at less than retail price so that they may resell, in turn, at a profit. The price adjustment to the wholesale trade often takes the form of *trade discounts* or reductions from the established retail price. There may be a single trade discount or a series or chain of discounts. The *net price* (list price less all trade discounts) is the amount recorded in the wholesaler's sales journal as the sales price.

Computation of Single Discount

If the list price of an order is $500 and the trade discount is 40%, the discount is $200 and the net sales price to be invoiced and recorded is $300.

List Price	$500.00
Less discount	
(40% of $500)	200.00
Invoice Price	$300.00

Computation of Series of Discounts

If the list price of an order is $500 and the trade discount is quoted in a series such as 25% and 15%, a different net sales price will result.

List price	$500.00
Less first discount	
(25% of $500)	125.00
Difference	$375.00
Less second discount	
(15% of $375)	56.25
Invoice Price	$318.75

The same merchandise or services may be offered to different trade customers at different trade discounts, depending on the size of the order and the costs of selling to various types of outlets.

In a layaway or will-call sale, the customer makes a deposit on a certain item and the store puts it aside for him. The customer must complete payment (usually within a specified time) before he can take possession of the goods. If the customer does not complete his payments within the time allowed, he may legally forfeit the amount that he has already paid. However, in many cases, the store refunds the payments made or credits them against other purchases in an effort to retain customer goodwill. Experience with sales of this type indicates that most customers complete their payments and receive the goods. The accounting procedure calls for the sale to be recorded when the customer makes his deposit and the merchandise is put aside for him. Cash is debited for the amount of the deposit, and Accounts Receivable is debited for the balance. In effect, the sale is recorded as a sale on account, on which a part payment has been made. Subsequent payments are recorded as collections on account. When the price of the goods has been paid in full and the accounts receivable balance has been closed out, the goods are delivered.

COD SALES PROCEDURES

COD (cash on delivery) sales are made to customers without established credit who want goods delivered or shipped to them. The cash is collected from the customer at the time of delivery. If the customer cannot pay, the goods are returned to the seller. The simplest method to account for such sales is to prepare a sales ticket marked COD to accompany the goods for the deliveryperson to collect. No entry is made in the Accounts Receivable account. If the customer pays, the sales ticket is then processed as a cash sale. If the customer does not pay, the sales ticket is voided and the merchandise is returned to stock.

◆ ◆ ◆

PRINCIPLES AND PROCEDURES

The sales journal is a special journal used for recording sales on credit. These sales are recorded in the sales journal as they take place during the period. At the end of the period, the total amount sold on credit is posted in the general ledger as a debit to Accounts Receivable and a credit to Cleaning Service Income.

Sales tax collections may be recorded in a special column in the sales journal. Sales returns and allowances may be entered in the general journal if they occur infrequently; a special journal is used when the returns and

UNIT 9

allowances are numerous. Sales tax liability on sales returns and allowances is adjusted so the customer pays tax only on the net amount. In turn, the seller remits sales tax collections only on net sales during the period.

MANAGERIAL IMPLICATIONS

Management must be certain that all sales are promptly, efficiently, and accurately recorded, since sales represent the source of the income of the business. The use of the sales journal saves time and effort, thus reducing office costs, and permits the division of labor.

The sales journal also provides a convenient record of sales tax collections. An accurate record is necessary, since the seller is required to forward the tax collections to the taxing authority. The complete and systematic tax record in the sales journal expedites the completion of the periodic tax report form and provides proof that would be needed in the event of a tax audit.

APPLICATION OF PRINCIPLES

PROBLEM 9 · 1

The ABC Venetian Blind Company uses a single-column sales journal. The necessary ledger accounts are Accounts Receivable 111, with a balance of $3,242.70 on April 1, 19X1, and Venetian Blind Sales 404, with no balance. The April 19X1 transactions involving sales are as follows:

APR.

2   Sold venetian blind to F. G. Waldrop on credit, $12.50, Sales Slip 32.

3   Installed venetian blinds on credit for H. H. Taylor, $132.15, Sales Slip 33, and for O. W. Lever, $56, Sales Slip 34.

5   Sold $563.70 worth of venetian blinds to Albemarle School on 60 days credit, Sales Slip 35.

6   Sold Mrs. Lila P. Shaw two venetian blinds, $28.70, Sales Slip 36, 30 days credit.

9   Sales Slip 37 for venetian blinds sold to Carlton Arms Apartments on 30 days credit, $215.65.

10   Installed venetian blinds for D. M. DuPree, Sales Slip 38, $88.40, payable half in 30 days and half in 60 days.

11   Sales on credit: Sales Slip 39, $43.20, to Miss Jean Boatwright; Sales Slip 40, $22, to Miss Mary Spell; Sales Slip 41, $67.35, to W. B. Minott.

13   Installed extra-length blinds on credit for Jack O'Reilly, $66.80, Sales Slip 42.

14   Sales Slip 43 for sale on credit to Mrs. Betty Summers, $47.95.

16   Sold venetian blinds on credit to King's College, $332.50, Sales Slip 44.

17   Sold $96.60 of venetian blinds on credit to Sam Solomon, Sales Slip 45.

20   Sales on credit: Sales Slip 46, $9.95, to T. J. Holden; Sales Slip 47, $24.75, to M. D. Goldberg; Sales Slip 48, $95, to S. I. Saxon.

23   Installed venetian blinds for S. Smith, Sales Slip 49, $52.30, 30 days credit.

25   Sales Slip 50, $118.85, for credit sale to R. O. Buckman. Sales Slip 51 covers 30-day credit sale to M. M. Norris, $33.55.

27   Sold blinds on credit to F. C. Black, $37.75, Sales Slip 52.

INSTRUCTIONS

1. Open the ledger accounts and enter the Brought Forward balance of Accounts Receivable 111.
2. Record each transaction in the sales journal. (Page 4.)
3. Total and rule the Amount column of the journal.
4. Perform the required postings to the proper ledger accounts.
5. Foot the Accounts Receivable account, but do not enter the balance, since all postings from other journals have not yet been made.

PROBLEM 9 · 2

This problem covers the cash and credit sales recording procedures for the Sloan Venetian Blind Company for May 19X1. A single-column sales journal is used, since it has proven satisfactory for recording the volume of credit sales. A cash receipts journal is also used, with special columns for Accounts Receivable Cr. 111, Venetian Blind Sales Cr. 404, and Cash Dr. 101. The necessary ledger accounts and their balances at the first of the month are: Cash 101, $2,238.45; Accounts Receivable 111, $783.20; and Venetian Blind Sales 404, –0–. The May 19X1 transactions involving sales are as follows:

MAY

2   Sales Slip 53 for special-width blind sold on credit to Taylor's Haberdashery, $102.25.

3   Sold two venetian blinds for cash, $22.75.

4   Sold venetian blinds on credit to L. L. Tanner, $44.60, Sales Slip 54.

5   Blinds sold on Sales Slip 55, $29.50, to O. R. Sweetman, on credit.

6   Installed blinds in American Can Company office, on credit, $1,335.75, Sales Slip 56.

9   Sales on credit: Sales Slip 57, $111.25, to R. S. Smith; Sales Slip 58, $55, to Susan McNeill; Sales Slip 59, $87.65, to Felder's Drug Store.

10   Sold blinds on 60 days credit to Holly Winters, $152.50, Sales Slip 60.

11   Gave special credit terms on sale to Joe Horner, Sales Slip 61, $195; payable one-third in 30 days, one-third in 60 days, and one-third in 90 days.

12   Collected $34.50 from sale of blinds for cash.

13   Installed three blinds for J. K. Kinmore, $36, Sales Slip 62, on credit.

17   Sales Slip 63 for a credit sale of $11.35 to C. M. Tollman; Sales Slip 64 for a credit sale of $60.35 to J. O. Smalls.

UNIT 9

18   Sold T. K. Wade venetian blinds on credit, Sales Slip 65, $127.55.

19   Sold $99 of venetian blinds to W. T. Byrd, Sales Slip 66, 30 days credit.

20   Mrs. Brenda Harris bought blinds on credit, Sales Slip 67, $53.75.

23   Installed blinds on credit for Smith Boykin, Sales Slip 68, $146.35, and
      for Mrs. Emily Free for $33.95, Sales Slip 69.

25   Installed blinds in Freedom School, $289.95, Sales Slip 70, on credit.

26   Cash sales, $11.25.

27   Sales Slip 71 covers credit sale to John Roberts, $24.25.

30   Sold Ray Warren blinds on credit, $19.50, Sales Slip 72.

31   Sales on credit: Sales Slip 73, $91, Buck Martin; Sales Slip 74, $37.50,
      Mary Whitelaw; Sales Slip 75, $13.65, Helen Pierce.

INSTRUCTIONS

1.   Open the ledger accounts and enter the balances brought forward.
2.   Record each transaction in the appropriate journal. (Page 5.)
3.   Total both journals and rule.
4.   Perform the necessary postings to the ledger accounts.
5.   Foot the three accounts, but do not enter the balances.

PROBLEM 9 · 3

The Wilson Flower Shop sells flowers and floral arrangements, which are
◆ subject to a 3% sales tax. The shop uses a general journal and a
   sales journal with special columns for Accounts Receivable Dr. 111, Sales
Tax Payable Cr. 231, and Sales Income Cr. 401. The following credit transactions
took place during a week in January 19X1:

JAN.

8   Sold wreath to Mrs. J. A. Jonas, Sales Slip 19; $10, plus sales tax of $.30,
      total $10.30.

8   Sold potted plant to Mrs. A. R. Smythe, Sales Slip 20; $4, plus sales tax
      of $.12, total $4.12.

9   Sold blanket arrangement to Adams Mortuary, Sales Slip 21, for $50, plus
      sales tax.

10   Sold corsage to Fred Wright, Sales Slip 22, for $2.50, plus sales tax.

10   Allowed Mrs. J. A. Jonas a credit of $5, plus sales tax, because of withered
      blossoms discovered in wreath. The transaction was covered by Sales Slip
      19, Jan. 8. (Use Sales Returns and Allowances Account 452; the general
      journal entry should be numbered 1-5.)

11   Sold floral arrangement to Angus Baker for $12, plus sales tax, Sales Slip
      23.

11   Sold wreath to Walter Craven for $20, plus sales tax, Sales Slip 24.

12   David Edwards purchased one dozen red roses for $12, plus sales tax, Sales
      Slip 25.

12   Conlon Funeral Home purchased two sprays for $30, plus sales tax, Sales
      Slip 26.

13 City College purchased table arrangements for Parents' Day for $40, plus sales tax, Sales Slip 27.

13 Accepted return of wreath sold to Walter Craven on Jan. 11, Sales Slip 24, and allowed him full credit because of delivery after funeral was over. (The general journal entry should be numbered 1-6.)

INSTRUCTIONS

1. Record all transactions in the sales journal and the general journal. (Number each journal Page 1.)
2. Foot the sales journal columns and prove the accuracy of your work.

MANAGERIAL CHECKUPS

♦ Why should management insist that sales are recorded promptly and efficiently?

♦ How does management utilize the Sales Returns and Allowances account as a measure of operating efficiency? Whose efficiency is involved?

♦ How frequently should special journals, such as the sales journal, be redesigned?

♦ Under what circumstances would an accountant recommend the use of a Sales Returns and Allowances Journal to the management of a business?

10 THE PURCHASES JOURNAL

In the past few units you have seen how the accountant can adjust his accounting procedures to get his work done faster and more efficiently. The accountant must constantly be alert to make sure that the procedures being used are adequate to meet changes in the operations of the business.

STUDYING NEW PLANS

For example, when the accountant hears about Carter's plans to open an Accessories Department on February 1, 19X2, he gives careful thought to the new accounting problems that may arise. He knows that a stock of merchandise must be bought and replenished from time to time. He can reasonably expect that most of the stock will be bought on credit. He can also expect the new department to increase Carter's sales for cash and on credit. With these things in mind, the accountant then considers whether or not his present recording methods are adequate to meet the new conditions.

The new demands from increased sales activities offer no problem. The added volume of credit sales can easily be handled through the sales journal. The income generated by the new department can be readily identified and accumulated through the use of a multicolumn journal arrangement in which separate columns are provided for listing items of Cleaning Service Income 401 and Accessories Sales Income 402. Collections from charge customers can be efficiently recorded in the multicolumn cash receipts journal. Provision can even be made for the possibility of sales returns and allowances arising from both cleaning services and accessories sales by the use of new accounts entitled Sales Returns and Allowances–Cleaning Service 451 and Sales Returns and Allowances–Accessories 452.

However, the new buying activities must be studied carefully. The cash payments made to cover purchases of stock on credit can be readily accommodated in the multicolumn cash disbursements journal. But the accountant soon realizes that the only existing place to record the additional credit purchases is in the general journal. He begins to picture what would happen if the new transactions were recorded by using the present methods. For instance, the following credit purchases might be made during February 19X2.

FEB.

1   Initial stock of merchandise purchased from the Weller Wholesale Company for $1,200. Allowed 30 days to pay. Their Invoice 649, dated February 1, 19X2, is shown.

WELLER WHOLESALE COMPANY
671 Valley Street
Topeka, State 66614

SOLD TO: Carter Cleaning Shop

365 Broad Street

Centerport, State 53995

INV. NO.:   649

INV. DATE: 2/1/X2

TERMS: 30 days net

SHIP VIA: Truck prepaid

QUANTITY	ITEM	UNIT PRICE	AMOUNT
800	Sets, Assorted Hangers, 8 in set	$1.25	$1,000.00
100	Hat racks	2.50	250.00
50	Shoe racks	3.75	187.50
20	Tie racks	3.125	62.50
			$1,500.00
	Less 20%		300.00
			$1,200.00

---

13   Additional stock for Accessories Department purchased on credit from the Beaver Products Company for $300, payable in 30 days. Their Invoice A4973 is dated February 12. (This invoice covered merchandise with a list price of $416.66, but Carter was allowed trade discounts of 20% and 10%.)

17   Purchased more stock for the Accessories Department on 20-day credit terms from Premium Plastics, Inc. Their Invoice 43691 for $100 (net of discounts) is dated February 15.

24   Purchased $210 worth of accessories (net invoice price) from the Weller Wholesale Company to replace items sold. The same 30-day terms apply. Their Invoice 855 bears the date of February 22.

If the February credit purchases were recorded in the general journal, a separate entry would be required for each purchase. When merchandise is bought, a new account, Merchandise Purchases 501, is debited so that a record of stock acquired for the Accessories Department can be kept. The Merchandise Purchases account is placed in the expense group of accounts because the cost of merchandise sold is an expense. The liability, Accounts Payable 201, will be credited for the cost of the goods bought on account. Note that each purchase is recorded at the net invoice price (after discounts have been deducted). The four entries would appear in the general journal as shown.

19 X2		2-2	501	✓	1,200	00		
Feb.	1	Merchandise Purchases.	501	✓	1,200	00		
		Accounts Payable	201	✓			1,200	00
		To record purchase of merchandise from Weller Wholesale Company, terms 30 days, their Invoice 649, dated 2/1/X2.						
		2-20						
	13	Merchandise Purchases	501	✓	300	00		
		Accounts Payable	201	✓			300	00
		To record purchase of merchandise from Beaver Products Company, terms 30 days, their Invoice A4973, 2/12/X2.						
		2-25						
	17	Merchandise Purchases.	501	✓	100	00		
		Accounts Payable	201	✓			100	00
		To record purchase of merchandise from Premium Plastics, Inc., terms 20 days their Invoice 43691, dated 2/15/X2.						
		2-34						
	24	Merchandise Purchases.	501	✓	210	00		
		Accounts Payable	201	✓			210	00
		To record purchase of merchandise from Weller Wholesale Company, terms 30 days, their Invoice 855, dated 2/22/X2.						

These general journal entries would, in turn, require four debit postings to Merchandise Purchases 501 and four credit postings to Accounts Payable 201 as shown on the facing page.

The familiar shortcomings of repetitive journalizing and posting in connection with credit purchases are readily apparent. The accountant avoids this wasted effort by designing a *purchases journal* to be used for recording purchases of merchandise made on credit.

Merchandise Purchases   No. 501

DATE		EXPLANATION	POST. REF.	DEBIT		DATE	EXPLANATION	POST. REF.	CREDIT
19	X2								
Feb.	1		2-2	1,200	00				
	13		2-20	300	00				
	17		2-25	100	00				
	24		2-34	210	00				

Accounts Payable   No. 201

DATE	EXPLANATION	POST. REF.	DEBIT	DATE		EXPLANATION	POST. REF.	CREDIT	
				19	X2				
				Feb.	1	Brought Fwd.	✓	500	00
					1		2-2	1,200	00
					13		2-20	300	00
					17		2-25	100	00
					24		2-34	210	00

RECORDING IN THE PURCHASES JOURNAL

The purchases journal illustrated reflects the same credit purchases that were shown in general journal form.

PURCHASES JOURNAL for Month of February 19X2   Page 1

DATE		PURCHASED FROM	INVOICE NO.	INVOICE DATE	TERMS	✓	AMOUNT	
Feb.	1	Weller Wholesale Company	649	2/1	30 days		1,200	00
	13	Beaver Products Company	A4973	2/12	30 days		300	00
	17	Premium Plastics, Inc.	43691	2/15	20 days		100	00
	24	Weller Wholesale Company	855	2/22	30 days		210	00

The columns organize the vital information about each credit purchase. The record of the supplier's invoice number, invoice date, and terms helps the accountant relate the purchase to a specific invoice. It is especially important that the invoice date and terms be clearly shown so that the bills are paid at the proper time and any cash discounts are taken. The information necessary for each entry comes from invoices, such as the one illustrated on page 143.

UNIT 10

The posting process for the purchases journal is as simple as that used for the sales journal. The accountant waits until he has recorded the last credit purchase for the period. Then he adds the Amount column and enters the total amount purchased. Next, he posts the total figure as a debit to Merchandise Purchases 501 and as a credit to Accounts Payable 201 in the general ledger. The posting reference numbers are noted in the purchases journal on the Total Credit Purchases line and are checked off as they are posted. The following illustrations show how the purchases journal and the related accounts look when the posting is completed. Note that the abbreviation "PJ" is used to identify the purchases journal as the source of the entry.

PURCHASES JOURNAL for Month of February 19X2 Page 1

DATE		PURCHASED FROM	INVOICE NO.	INVOICE DATE	TERMS	✓	AMOUNT	
Feb.	1	Weller Wholesale Company	649	2/1	30 days		1,200	00
	13	Beaver Products Company	A4973	2/12	30 days		300	00
	17	Premium Plastics, Inc.	43691	2/15	20 days		100	00
	24	Weller Wholesale Company	855	2/22	30 days		210	00
					Debit 501	✓/✓		
	28	Total Credit Purchases			Credit 201	✓/✓	1,810	00

Merchandise Purchases No. 501

DATE		EXPLANATION	POST. REF.	DEBIT		DATE	EXPLANATION	POST. REF.	CREDIT
19	X2								
Feb.	28		PJ-1	1,810	00				

Accounts Payable No. 201

DATE	EXPLANATION	POST. REF.	DEBIT		DATE		EXPLANATION	POST. REF.	CREDIT	
					19	X2				
					Feb.	1	Brought Fwd.	✓	500	00
						28		PJ-1	1,810	00

By using the purchases journal, the accountant has greatly simplified the process of recording and posting purchases of merchandise on credit (other purchases, such as equipment, would still be recorded in the general journal).

Instead of requiring 24 lines to record the four purchases in the general journal, only four lines are needed to record the same facts in the purchases journal. The posting process is also simplified, since the accountant makes only two total postings from the purchases journal at the end of the period. Furthermore, only two postings from the purchases journal would be required, regardless of the number of purchases made. In addition to the saving in time and effort, there is still another advantage in using this special journal: there is now additional opportunity to divide the workload among assistants.

RECORDING FREIGHT IN

Some purchases are made with the understanding that the buyer must pay the costs of shipping the goods from the seller's warehouse. If the buyer pays the transportation company directly for the freight, a check is written and the transaction is entered in the cash disbursements journal as a debit to Freight In 506 and a credit to Cash 101. If freight payments are made frequently, a special column may be set up in the cash disbursements journal in which to record them.

Sometimes delivery costs are paid by the seller and then included in the bill sent to the purchaser. In this case, the entire entry is made in the purchases journal. Three elements are recorded, as in this example.

Cost of goods (to be debited to Merchandise Purchases 501)	$126.00
Shipping costs paid by seller (to be debited to Freight In 506)	6.00
Amount of invoice (to be credited to Accounts Payable 201)	$132.00

A multicolumn purchases journal can be easily devised to fit the situation, as shown below. As in the case of other such columns in special journals, all columns are totaled and posted only at the end of the period, in order to eliminate duplication of work.

PURCHASES JOURNAL for Month of June 19X2   Page 6

DATE	PURCHASED FROM	INV. NO.	INVOICE DATE	TERMS	✓	ACCOUNTS PAYABLE CR. 201	MDSE. PURCHASES DR. 501	FREIGHT IN DR. 506
June 3	Dantz Co.	2596	6/1	30 days		132 00	126 00	6 00

Freight In is shown on the income statement as an addition to Purchases, as illustrated in Unit 16, page 247.

After the data from the purchase invoice have been recorded in the purchases journal, the purchased goods may be found to be damaged, defective, or other than those ordered. If this is so, the seller is informed so that an adjustment can be obtained or the goods can be returned for credit. Suppose that on February 27 the inspection of the goods purchased from the Weller Wholesale Company on February 24 disclosed that items with a billed price of $10 were not as ordered. Carter arranges with Weller to return these items and receives a $10 reduction on his bill. How is this return recorded?

Accounts Payable is reduced by $10 and a new account called Purchases Returns and Allowances 509 is credited in a general journal entry.

19	X2	2–2			
Feb.	27	Accounts Payable	201	10 00	
		Purchases Returns & Allowances . .	509		10 00
		Returned accessories purchased from Weller on February 24, Invoice 855, found not as ordered.			

If there are numerous purchases returns and allowances, a special journal may be set up in which to accumulate them.

Although it would be possible to credit Merchandise Purchases 501 for the amounts of purchases returns and allowances, the accountant prefers to keep a separate record of all such items. This separate figure is useful later for studies of purchasing efficiency, suppliers' performance, and for preparing the income statement. (As you will learn later, the total of the Purchases Returns and Allowances account is deducted from Merchandise Purchases in the Cost of Goods Sold section of the income statement.)

**INTERNAL
CONTROL OF
PURCHASES**

Because of the large amounts of money spent for purchases, most companies develop careful procedures for the control of purchases and their payment. In Unit 19 you will learn many of the detailed procedures that are used by most businesses to achieve this internal control. Essentially, however, the control process involves the following safeguards.

1. All purchases are made only after proper authorization has been given in writing.
2. Goods are carefully checked when they are received. Then they are compared with the purchase order and with the detailed listing on the invoice received from the supplier.

3. Authorization for payment is made by someone other than the person ordering and other than the person writing the check. This authorization is given only after all the verifications have been made.
4. Still another person writes the check for payment.

The main object of these procedures is to ensure that several different people are involved in the process of buying and receiving goods, and paying for them. This division of labor constitutes a system of checks and balances.

◆ ◆ ◆

PRINCIPLES AND PROCEDURES

Each credit purchase is recorded in the purchases journal as it occurs during the month. Each purchase requires only one line for recording, because of the design of the journal. At the end of the period, the total amount purchased on credit is posted to the general ledger as a debit to Merchandise Purchases 501 and a credit to Accounts Payable 201.

Freight expense on purchases may be handled in several ways. For example, if the buyer pays the freight bills directly, a simple cash disbursement is involved, debiting Freight In and crediting Cash. On the other hand, if the seller pays the freight in advance for the buyer, the freight cost is added to the seller's invoice. In this case, the invoice total must be analyzed so that the appropriate charges can be made to Merchandise Purchases 501 and Freight In 506 when the invoice is recorded in the purchases journal.

The cost of goods returned or price adjustments allowed is credited to Purchases Returns and Allowances 509. The offsetting debit reduces the liability account, Accounts Payable 201.

MANAGERIAL IMPLICATIONS

The use of the special journal for credit purchases helps provide accurate and up-to-date information to management efficiently and quickly. The special purchases journal also permits a subdivision of work, which reduces costs and saves time. The special column for Freight In in the purchases journal permits the later study of costs of this nature. Internal controls of purchasing operations, attained by a carefully designed system of check and double-check, help to protect the business firm from excessive investment in inventory and from fraud.

APPLICATION OF PRINCIPLES

PROBLEM 10 · 1

The ABC Venetian Blind Company uses a single-column purchases journal
◆ On Apr. 1, 19X1, the necessary ledger accounts and their balances are: Accounts Payable 201, $3,476.25; and Merchandise Purchases 501,

–0–. The April 19X1 transactions involving the purchase of merchandise are as follows:

APR.

2 Purchased slats from the Aluminum Company of Summerville, Invoice 3445, Apr. 1; terms, 30 days net; $995.

8 Bought tapes from Lockhart Milling Company, $247.50, Invoice A11021, Apr. 6, payable in 60 days net.

12 Purchased cords from Dallas Cordage Company, Invoice 2-783, Apr. 11, $126.30, due in 30 days net.

20 Purchased additional slats from the Aluminum Company of Summerville, $1,064.85, Invoice 3558, Apr. 19; terms, 30 days net.

23 Acquired from the Chicago Gear Company, gears for raising and lowering blinds, Invoice G1090, Apr. 20, $469.20, due and payable in 30 days net.

26 Secured special-length slats from Extruded Aluminum Corporation on 60-day credit terms, Invoice 309B, Apr. 25, $115.

28 Purchased 100 gallons of paint from Albright Paint Company; terms, net May 10; Invoice 301-388, Apr. 27, $595.

INSTRUCTIONS
1. Open the ledger accounts and enter the balances brought forward.
2. Record each transaction in the purchases journal. (Page 4.)
3. Total and rule the Amount column of the journal.
4. Perform the required postings to the proper ledger accounts.
5. Foot the Accounts Payable account, but do not enter the balance.

PROBLEM 10 · 2

♦ This problem covers the purchasing procedures of the Sloan Venetian Blind Company for the month of May 19X1. The manager has determined that certain items of merchandise can be acquired for cash more economically than on credit. The company uses a single-column purchases journal and a cash disbursements journal with special columns for Sundry Debits, Accounts Payable Dr. 201, and Cash Cr. 101. The necessary ledger accounts and their balances at the beginning of the month are: Cash 101, $3,612.20; Accounts Payable 201, $2,895.25; and Merchandise Purchases 501, –0–. The May 19X1 transactions involving the purchase of merchandise are as follows:

MAY

4 Purchased slats from the Aluminum Company of Summerville, Invoice 6698, May 2; terms, 30 days net; $1,450.

5 Paid cash for special green tapes, $42.50, by Check 773.

10 Bought cords from the Dallas Cordage Company, Invoice 3-642, May 9, $212.35, due in 30 days net.

15 Bought a set of special ratchet gears for extra-wide blinds from Die Works, Inc., and paid $15.30 by Check 782.

18 Purchased 10 gallons of paint from Sherwin-Williams Paint Company, due in 30 days net, Invoice 2412C, May 16, $69.50.

21 Bought tapes worth $522.50 from the Lockhart Milling Company, their Invoice B23368, payable in 60 days net, invoice dated May 18.

25 Secured a supply of wood bottom slats from the Ashland Lumber Company, Invoice 788, May 23, $249.25, payable net on June 10.

INSTRUCTIONS

1. Open the ledger accounts and enter the Brought Forward balances.
2. Record each transaction in the appropriate journal. (Number each journal Page 5.)
3. Total and rule the columns in both journals.
4. Perform the required individual and summary postings to the proper ledger accounts.
5. Foot the accounts where necessary, but do not enter the balances.

PROBLEM 10 · 3

The College Bookstore purchases textbooks from various publishers and
◆ sells them to students. For recording purposes, the bookstore uses
a purchases journal with special columns for Accounts Payable Cr. 201, Merchandise Purchases Dr. 501, and Freight In Dr. 506; a cash disbursements journal with columns for Sundry Debits, Accounts Payable Dr. 201, and Cash Cr. 101; and a general journal. During a typical week in October 19X1, the following selected transactions took place:

OCT.

16 Bought books from United Publishers, Invoice 835, dated Oct. 12; terms, net cash 30 days; $280, shipped freight collect.

16 Paid freight charges on shipment received from United Publishers, $14.50, by Check 1214.

17 Purchased books from the Scientific Book Company, Invoice 10-213, dated Oct. 13; terms 2/10, net/30; $376, plus prepaid freight $18.75; total invoice, $394.75.

18 Bought books from Tri-State Depository, Invoice 1875, dated Oct. 16; terms, net cash 30 days; $763, shipped freight collect.

18 Paid freight charges on shipment received from Tri-State Depository, $36.15, by Check 1221.

19 Discovered that $155 worth of the books received from Tri-State Depository were the wrong edition and returned them for credit. (Record as general journal entry 10-13, using Account 509 for Purchases Returns and Allowances.)

19 Bought books from Technical Printers, Inc., Invoice 364, dated Oct. 17;

terms, net cash 60 days; $188, plus prepaid freight, $11.70; total invoice, $199.70.

20 Purchased a set of reference books from Almanac Publishing Company, Invoice A534, dated Oct. 16; terms, net 30 days; delivered price $440.

20 Bought books from Boukmann Printing Company, Invoice B832, dated Oct. 17; terms 2/30, net 60 days; $615, plus prepaid freight $43.40; total invoice $658.40.

INSTRUCTIONS

1. Record each transaction in the appropriate journal. (Number each journal Page 10.)
2. Foot all money columns in the purchases journal and the cash disbursements journal, and prove the accuracy of your work.

MANAGERIAL CHECKUPS

♦ How can proper accounting procedures protect a firm from excessive investment in inventory and from frauds?

♦ Why would management insist on absolute completeness and accuracy in recording suppliers' invoice dates and terms in the purchases journal?

♦ How would management benefit from an accounting system that includes separate income accounts for each operating department?

♦ Is the application of division of labor to the recording of purchase transactions in special journals likely to be more or less expensive than the use of general books and general clerks?

THE ACCOUNTS RECEIVABLE LEDGER

In previous units, the ways in which the sales journal and the cash receipts journal simplify the handling of sales on credit were explained. As credit sales at the Carter Cleaning Shop were made, the accountant recorded them in the sales journal. Then, at the end of the month, the Accounts Receivable account in the general ledger was debited for the total and the Cleaning Service Income account was credited for the same amount.

SALES JOURNAL for Month of January 19X2   Page 1

DATE	SALES SLIP NO.	CUSTOMER'S NAME		✓	AMOUNT
Jan. 7	1	R. L. Camp			60 00
14	2	M. F. Coleman			25 00
19	3	B. A. Hahn			30 00
28	4	S. S. Baker			60 00
			Debit 111	✓/✓	
31		Total Credit Sales	Credit 401	/✓	175 00

Accounts Receivable   No. 111

DATE	EXPLANATION	POST. REF.	DEBIT	DATE	EXPLANATION	POST. REF.	CREDIT
19 X2 Jan. 1	Brought Fwd.	✓	200 00				
31		SJ-1	175 00				

Cleaning Service Income   No. 401

DATE	EXPLANATION	POST. REF.	DEBIT	DATE	EXPLANATION	POST. REF.	CREDIT
				19 X2 Jan. 31		SJ-1	175 00

As customers paid their bills, the accountant entered each receipt in the multicolumn cash receipts journal. Then the total of the Accounts Receivable column in the cash receipts journal was posted at the end of the month as a credit to the Accounts Receivable account, as illustrated.

CASH RECEIPTS JOURNAL for Month of January 19X2   Page 1

DATE		EXPLANATION	ACCOUNTS RECEIVABLE			CLEANING SVC. INC. CR. 401	CASH DR. 101	
			✓	CR. 111				
Jan.	7	Cash Sales				700 00	700	00
	9	December customers		200 00			200	00
	14	Cash Sales				725 00	725	00
	16	R. L. Camp		30 00			30	00
	21	Cash Sales				900 00	900	00
	23	R. L. Camp		30 00			30	00
	23	M. F. Coleman		15 00			15	00
	27	Cash Sales				800 00	800	00
	29	M. F. Coleman		10 00			10	00
	31	Totals		285 00		3,125 00	3,410	00
				✓		✓	✓	

Accounts Receivable   No. 111

DATE		EXPLANATION	POST. REF.	DEBIT		DATE		EXPLANATION	POST. REF.	CREDIT	
19	X2					19	X2				
Jan.	1	Brought Fwd.	✓	200	00	Jan.	31		CRJ-1	285	00
	31		SJ-1	175	00						
		90.00		*375*	*00*						

The end-of-month postings to Cleaning Service Income and Cash accounts are not shown to save space at this time.

THE ACCOUNTANT NEEDS MORE INFORMATION

After the sales and cash receipts figures have been posted to the Accounts Receivable account, it is easy to compute the balance of $90 that is owed by credit customers at the end of January. Although this balance of Accounts Receivable is useful to the accountant, it does not give him all the information he needs. For instance, it does not tell him who owes the money or how long each debt has remained unpaid.

To visualize the accountant's problem more clearly, suppose that customer R. L. Camp telephones and asks how much he owes to the Carter Cleaning Shop. Under the present system, the accountant would have to check through all the entries in the sales journal to find the amounts sold to Camp. Next, he would have to look through all the entries in the cash receipts journal to find out how much Camp had paid on his debt. Then he would check the general journal for possible sales returns and allowances. Finally, after matching payments against sales or deducting amounts paid and credits allowed from the total amount sold, the accountant would be able to determine the amount still owed by the customer.

Obviously, the accountant does not have time to waste on such backtracking in order to answer a routine question, nor can the customer be expected to wait so long for an answer. If a few requests like this one were made every day, the accountant would have to neglect his other work; a better system has to be devised.

ACCOUNTS FOR INDIVIDUAL CUSTOMERS

In order to meet requests for information from the customers, the business firm needs an account for each individual customer that shows the balance he owes at any given time. Queries also come from managers and salesmen in the company, and from banks and credit bureaus, making individual customer accounts even more necessary.

Although the record of the customer's account may be kept in the T account form with which you are familiar—with debits on the left side and credits on the right side—this form is not the best available. An account form is needed that will show the balance owed at any time. To meet this need, it is customary to use a three-column sheet, commonly called a *balance form of account,* for customers' accounts. This form is widely used, especially when customers' accounts are to be posted by using bookkeeping machines. It is also convenient when hand bookkeeping methods are used.

The balance owed on January 31, 19X2 by each customer of the Carter Cleaning Shop has been entered in the illustrated balance-form ledger sheets as of February 1, 19X2, the first day of the next accounting period.

Balances in these accounts receivable accounts are presumed to be debit balances. Occasional credit balances, arising because a customer has overpaid his account or because he returned goods for which he has already paid and is given credit, are indicated by a "Cr." notation, red-ink figures, parentheses, or a circle around the balance amount.

Name: **S. S. BAKER**

Address: **1069 Main Street**

                        Centerport, State 53995   Terms: Net 30

DATE		DESCRIPTION	POST. REF.	DEBIT	CREDIT	BALANCE
19 X2 Feb. 1		Balance	✓			60 00

Name: _____ R. L. CAMP _____

Address: _____ 14 Oak Lane _____

Centerport, State 53995   Terms: Net 30

DATE		DESCRIPTION	POST. REF.	DEBIT	CREDIT	BALANCE
19 X2 Feb. 1		Balance	✓			0

Name: _____ M. F. COLEMAN _____

Address: _____ 49 Vista Road _____

Centerport, State 53995   Terms: Net 30

DATE		DESCRIPTION	POST. REF.	DEBIT	CREDIT	BALANCE
19 X2 Feb. 1		Balance	✓			0

Name: _____ B. A. HAHN _____

Address: _____ 611 Tenth Avenue _____

South Centerport, State 53996   Terms: Net 30

DATE		DESCRIPTION	POST. REF.	DEBIT	CREDIT	BALANCE
19 X2 Feb. 1		Balance	✓			30 00

The customers' accounts are kept alphabetically or by account number in a *subsidiary ledger* called the *accounts receivable ledger*. The accounts receivable ledger is known as a subsidiary ledger because it is separate from and subordinate to the general ledger. This is another example of the way in which the accountant designs the accounting system so that similar items are grouped together. The new subsidiary ledger will be used to record the February transactions with credit customers.

REVISING THE SALES JOURNAL

It has been mentioned that the Carter Cleaning Shop plans to open an Accessories Department on February 1, 19X2. Obviously, the owner will want to keep a close watch on the progress made by the new department. To help Carter do this more easily, the accountant arranges to accumulate separate income figures for sales of cleaning services and sales of accessories. A new income account, Accessories Sales Income 402, is opened in the general ledger.

Then separate columns are set up in the sales journal for assembling the information that will ultimately be posted to the separate income accounts. Since sales of both types may be made to a single customer and listed on a single sales slip, the sales journal should also provide a column for entering the charge to the customer's account, as before.

Recording the Sale

The procedure for recording a credit sale remains very much the same. The total of each sale is entered in the Accounts Receivable Debit 111 column and in the appropriate income column (or columns) as a credit (or credits). The latter columns permit classification of the sale according to type. When the Carter Cleaning Shop sells $20 worth of cleaning services to a new customer, J. E. Ayres, on February 1, covered by Sales Slip 5, the entry in the sales journal looks like this.

SALES JOURNAL for Month of February 19X2   **Page 2**

DATE		SALES SLIP NO.	CUSTOMER'S NAME	ACCOUNTS RECEIVABLE		CLEANING SERVICE INCOME	ACCESSORIES SALES INCOME
				✓	DR. 111	CR. 401	CR. 402
Feb.	1	5	J. E. Ayres		20 00	20 00	

Posting the Sale to the Customer's Account

The new part of the procedure is the posting of the amount of the sale immediately to the customer's account in the accounts receivable subsidiary ledger. Here the entry is shown on a balance-form accounts receivable ledger sheet.

Name: **J. E. AYRES**

Address: **216 Main Street**

                         Centerport, State 53995   **Terms: Net 30**

DATE		DESCRIPTION	POST. REF.	DEBIT	CREDIT	BALANCE
19 X2						
Feb.	1	Sales Slip 5	SJ-2	20 00		20 00

After the entry is posted to Ayres' account, the accountant puts a check mark in the Posting Check column of the sales journal, as shown on the next page.

DATE		SALES SLIP NO.	CUSTOMER'S NAME	ACCOUNTS RECEIVABLE			CLEANING SERVICE INCOME CR. 401	ACCESSORIES SALES INCOME CR. 402
				✓	DR. 111			
Feb.	1	5	J. E. Ayres	✓	20	00	20 00	

REVISING THE CASH RECEIPTS JOURNAL

The establishment of the Accessories Department also requires that the cash receipts journal be expanded to include separate columns for the cash sales income of each department. Therefore, a new column is added that is headed Accessories Sales Income Cr. 402.

Recording Customer Collections

The procedure for journalizing a collection from a credit customer remains the same as before. If Ayres pays $5 on his account on February 4, the entry in a multicolumn cash receipts journal would look as shown in the following illustration. Note that only the customer's name is entered in the Explanation column, since the debit to Cash and credit to Accounts Receivable indicates a collection on account.

DATE		EXPLANATION	ACCOUNTS RECEIVABLE			CLEANING SERVICE INCOME CR. 401	ACCESSORIES SALES INCOME CR. 402	CASH DR. 101	
			✓	CR. 111					
Feb.	4	J. E. Ayres		5	00			5	00

Posting the Cash Receipt to the Customer's Account

After the customer's cash payment is recorded, it is posted immediately to the customer's account in the accounts receivable subsidiary ledger as shown on page 159. This again, is a new procedure.

A check mark is then placed in the Posting Check column in the cash receipts journal to show that the entry has been posted to the subsidiary ledger.

| Name: | J. E. AYRES |
| Address: | 216 Main Street |

Centerport, State 53995   Terms: Net 30

DATE		DESCRIPTION	POST. REF.	DEBIT		CREDIT		BALANCE	
19 X2									
Feb.	1	Sales Slip 5	SJ-2	20	00			20	00
	4		CRJ-2			5	00	15	00

RECORDING SALES RETURNS AND ALLOWANCES

As explained in Unit 9, a customer may find that goods purchased are not satisfactory for some reason, and the seller may allow their return for credit (called a *sales return*). In other cases, the customer may keep the goods and accept an allowance or reduction in the amount paid or owed (called a *sales allowance*).

In Carter Cleaning Shop's accounting system, the entry for a sales return or allowance is recorded in the general journal. With the addition of the Accessories Department, separate accounts are kept for the returns and allowances from service and merchandise transactions. Hence, the entry would consist of a debit to either Sales Returns and Allowances—Cleaning Service 451 or Sales Returns and Allowances—Accessories 452. Accounts Receivable 111 is credited, as you already know. However, with an accounts receivable subsidiary ledger now in operation, it is also necessary to credit the individual customer's account.

For example, suppose A. G. Browne, a credit customer, returns defective goods to Carter on February 5. The required entry is shown.

19 X2		2–1					
Feb.	5	Sales Returns & Allowances–Accessories .	452	10	00		
		Accounts Receivable/A. G. Browne .	111/✓			10	00
		Return of accessories sold on February 4, Sales Slip 7.					

Note that the accountant indicates by means of a diagonal line in the Account Number column that two credit postings are to be made. The 111 refers to Accounts Receivable in the general ledger. The check mark refers to Browne's account in the subsidiary ledger.

UNIT 11

159

General journal entries are always posted immediately to the general ledger accounts and to the accounts receivable subsidiary ledger accounts involved. The accounts affected by general journal entry 2-1 are shown after the posting is completed.

Sales Returns and Allowances–Accessories   No. 452

DATE		EXPLANATION	POST. REF.	DEBIT		DATE	EXPLANATION	POST. REF.	CREDIT
19 Feb.	X2 5		2-1	10	00				

Accounts Receivable   No. 111

DATE		EXPLANATION	POST. REF.	DEBIT		DATE		EXPLANATION	POST. REF.	CREDIT	
19 Feb.	X2 1	Brought Fwd.	✓	90	00	19 Feb.	X2 5		2-1	10	00

Name: A. G. BROWNE

Address: 9 Glen Road

     Ridgefield, State 53997   **Terms: Net 30**

DATE		DESCRIPTION	POST. REF.	DEBIT		CREDIT		BALANCE	
19 Feb.	X2 4 5	Sales Slip 7	SJ-2 2-1	25	00	10	00	25 15	00 00

A check mark is placed in the Posting Check column in the general journal as each item in the entry is posted. When a diagonal line is used to signal a double posting, a similar diagonal line is noted in the Posting Check column. A check mark on the left side of the diagonal indicates that the posting was made to Account 111 and a check mark on the right side indicates that the posting was made to Browne's account in the subsidiary ledger.

19 Feb.	X2 5	2–1 Sales Returns & Allowances–Accessories . Accounts Receivable/A. G. Browne . Return of accessories sold on February 4, Sales Slip 7.	452 111/✓	✓ ✓/✓	10	00	10	00

SALES RETURNS AND ALLOWANCES JOURNAL

Carter Cleaning Shop has very few sales returns and allowances; so such transactions are recorded in the general journal. However, in a larger company, these transactions, returns and allowances, may occur frequently enough to justify the use of another special journal, the sales returns and allowances journal. Here is how a sales returns and allowances journal might look in a company whose sales are subject to a sales tax.

SALES RETURNS AND ALLOWANCES JOURNAL for Month of July 19X1

DATE		SALES SLIP NO.	CUSTOMER'S NAME	ACCOUNTS RECEIVABLE		SALES TAX PAYABLE DR. 231	SALES RET. & ALLOW. CLEANING SERVICE DR. 451	SALES RET. & ALLOW. ACCESSORIES DR. 452
				√	CR. 111			
July	2	2346	James Doyle		20 60	60	20 00	
	2	2347	Harry Downs		15 45	45	15 00	
	30	2861	Tom Williams		6 18	18		6 00
	31		Totals		540 00	15 72	518 28	6 00

The credits would be posted daily from the journal to the individual customers' accounts in the subsidiary ledger and a check mark entered in the column after each posting has been made. Column totals would be posted to the general ledger accounts (Accounts Receivable 111 Cr., Sales Tax Payable 231 Dr., Sales Returns and Allowances 451 Dr., and Sales Returns and Allowances 452 Dr.) at the end of the month.

DAILY ROUTINE

Each credit sale made during the month is recorded in the sales journal and is then posted to the account of the customer involved. The February transactions of this type are illustrated.

SALES JOURNAL for Month of February 19X2   Page 2

DATE		SALES SLIP NO.	CUSTOMER'S NAME	ACCOUNTS RECEIVABLE		CLEANING SERVICE INCOME CR. 401	ACCESSORIES SALES INCOME CR. 402
				√	DR. 111		
Feb.	1	5	J. E. Ayres	√	20 00	20 00	
	2	6	R. W. Peters	√	10 00	10 00	
	4	7	A. G. Browne	√	25 00		25 00
	10	8	K. Davies	√	25 00		25 00
	12	9	J. E. Ayres	√	7 00	7 00	
	15	10	R. L. Camp	√	10 00		10 00
	19	11	M. F. Coleman	√	15 00		15 00
	23	12	C. V. Fisher	√	20 00	20 00	
	26	13	A. Dunlap	√	12 00		12 00

Each cash receipt from a credit customer making a payment on his account is entered in the cash receipts journal and then posted at once to the customer's account. The February transactions of this type are illustrated.

CASH RECEIPTS JOURNAL for Month of February 19X2   Page 2

DATE		EXPLANATION	✓	ACCOUNTS RECEIVABLE CR. 111	CLEANING SERVICE INCOME CR. 401	ACCESSORIES SALES INCOME CR. 402	CASH DR. 101
Feb.	4	J. E. Ayres	✓	5 00			5 00
	10	R. W. Peters	✓	10 00			10 00
	11	A. G. Browne	✓	15 00			15 00
	20	K. Davies	✓	20 00			20 00
	21	J. E. Ayres	✓	15 00			15 00
	26	M. F. Coleman	✓	15 00			15 00

Each credit or allowance is entered in the general journal and posted at once to the general ledger and subsidiary ledger accounts involved. The only other credit customer besides A. G. Browne to return defective accessories during February was A. Dunlap. General journal entry 2-3 gives all the details.

19	X2	2–3			
Feb.	28	Sales Returns & Allowances–Accessories .	452	2 00	
		Accounts Receivable/A. Dunlap . .	111/✓		2 00
		Return of accessories sold on February 26, Sales Slip 13.			

SUBSIDIARY LEDGER ACCOUNT BALANCES

After the February transactions have been posted, the customers' accounts in the accounts receivable subsidiary ledger reflect a variety of entries:

Name: **J. E. AYRES**

Address: **216 Main Street**

       Centerport, State 53995   Terms: Net 30

DATE		DESCRIPTION	POST. REF.	DEBIT	CREDIT	BALANCE
19	X2					
Feb.	1	Sales Slip 5	SJ-2	20 00		20 00
	4		CRJ-2		5 00	15 00
	12	Sales Slip 9	SJ-2	7 00		22 00
	21		CRJ-2		15 00	7 00

Name: **S. S. BAKER**

Address: **1069 Main Street**

Centerport, State 53995   **Terms: Net 30**

DATE		DESCRIPTION	POST. REF.	DEBIT		CREDIT		BALANCE	
19	X2								
Feb.	1	Balance	✓					60	00

Name: **A. G. BROWNE**

Address: **9 Glen Road**

Ridgefield, State 53997   **Terms: Net 30**

DATE		DESCRIPTION	POST. REF.	DEBIT		CREDIT		BALANCE	
19	X2								
Feb.	4	Sales Slip 7	SJ-2	25	00			25	00
	5		2-1			10	00	15	00
	11		CRJ-2			15	00	0	

Name: **R. L. CAMP**

Address: **14 Oak Lane**

Centerport, State 53995   **Terms: Net 30**

DATE		DESCRIPTION	POST. REF.	DEBIT		CREDIT		BALANCE	
19	X2								
Feb.	1	Balance	✓					0	
	15	Sales Slip 10	SJ-2	10	00			10	00

Name: **M. F. COLEMAN**

Address: **49 Vista Road**

Centerport, State 53995   **Terms: Net 30**

DATE		DESCRIPTION	POST. REF.	DEBIT		CREDIT		BALANCE	
19	X2								
Feb.	1	Balance	✓					0	
	19	Sales Slip 11	SJ-2	15	00			15	00
	26		CRJ-2			15	00	0	

Name: _____ K. DAVIES _____

Address: _____ 2147 Lake Drive _____

Centerport, State 53995   **Terms: Net 30**

DATE		DESCRIPTION	POST. REF.	DEBIT		CREDIT		BALANCE	
19	X2								
Feb.	10	Sales Slip 8	SJ-2	25	00			25	00
	20		CRJ-2			20	00	5	00

Name: _____ A. DUNLAP _____

Address: _____ 1026 Barr Street _____

Centerport, State 53995   **Terms: Net 30**

DATE		DESCRIPTION	POST. REF.	DEBIT		CREDIT		BALANCE	
19	X2								
Feb.	26	Sales Slip 13	SJ-2	12	00			12	00
	28		2-3			2	00	10	00

Name: _____ C. V. FISHER _____

Address: _____ 147 First Street _____

Centerport, State 53995   **Terms: Net 30**

DATE		DESCRIPTION	POST. REF.	DEBIT		CREDIT		BALANCE	
19	X2								
Feb.	23	Sales Slip 12	SJ-2	20	00			20	00

Name: _____ B. A. HAHN _____

Address: _____ 611 Tenth Avenue _____

South Centerport, State 53996   **Terms: Net 30**

DATE		DESCRIPTION	POST. REF.	DEBIT		CREDIT		BALANCE	
19	X2								
Feb.	1	Balance	✓					30	00

Name:	R. W. PETERS				
Address:	10 Station Plaza				
	Centerport, State 53995				Terms: Net 30

DATE		DESCRIPTION	POST. REF.	DEBIT	CREDIT	BALANCE
19	X2					
Feb.	2	Sales Slip 6	SJ-2	10 00		10 00
	10		CRJ-2		10 00	0

END-OF-MONTH ROUTINE

At the end of the month, column totals in the sales journal are posted to the accounts indicated: $144 to Accounts Receivable, $57 to Cleaning Service Income, and $87 to Accessories Sales Income.

SALES JOURNAL for Month of February 19X2   Page 2

DATE		SALES SLIP NO.	CUSTOMER'S NAME	ACCOUNTS RECEIVABLE		CLEANING SERVICE INCOME	ACCESSORIES SALES INCOME
				✓	DR. 111	CR. 401	CR. 402
Feb.	1	5	J. E. Ayres	✓	20 00	20 00	
	2	6	R W. Peters	✓	10 00	10 00	
	4	7	A. G. Browne	✓	25 00		25 00
	10	8	K. Davies	✓	25 00		25 00
	12	9	J. E. Ayres	✓	7 00	7 00	
	15	10	R. L. Camp	✓	10 00		10 00
	19	11	M. F. Coleman	✓	15 00		15 00
	23	12	C. V. Fisher	✓	20 00	20 00	
	26	13	A. Dunlap	✓	12 00		12 00
	28		Totals		144 00	57 00	87 00
					✓	✓	✓

The procedure for posting totals from the cash receipts journal remains the same. All columns are totaled and then posted as indicated by each column heading. Only the total of the Accounts Receivable Credit column is shown here, in order to simplify the illustration.

CASH RECEIPTS JOURNAL for Month of February 19X2   Page 2

DATE		EXPLANATION	ACCOUNTS RECEIVABLE		CLEANING SERVICE INCOME	ACCESSORIES SALES INCOME	CASH
			✓	CR. 111	CR. 401	CR. 402	DR. 101
Feb.	4	J. E. Ayres	✓	5 00			5 00
	28	Totals		80 00			
				✓			

UNIT 11

165

When the totals from the sales journal and the cash receipts journal are posted to the general ledger, the Accounts Receivable account looks like this.

Accounts Receivable No. 111

DATE		EXPLANATION	POST. REF.	DEBIT		DATE		EXPLANATION	POST. REF.	CREDIT	
19	X2					19	X2				
Feb.	1	Brought Fwd.	✓	90	00	Feb.	5		2-1	10	00
	28		SJ-2	144	00		28		2-3	2	00
		142.00		*234*	*00*		28		CRJ-2	80	00
										92	*00*

**PROVING THE
SUBSIDIARY TO
THE CONTROL**

After all the items and totals are posted from the sales journal, cash receipts journal, and general journal to the subsidiary and general ledger accounts, the accountant checks the accuracy of his work. This is a three-step process:

1. The accountant verifies the balances of all customers' accounts in the accounts receivable subsidiary ledger. (He has figured the balance after each posting during the month.)
2. He prepares a list, or *schedule of accounts receivable,* and adds all balances to determine the total owed by customers. Here are the balances taken from the accounts illustrated on pages 162–165.

CARTER CLEANING SHOP
Schedule of Accounts Receivable
February 28, 19X2

CUSTOMER	BALANCE AMOUNT
J. E. Ayres	$ 7
S. S. Baker	60
R. L. Camp	10
K. Davies	5
A. Dunlap	10
C. V. Fisher	20
B. A. Hahn	30
Total Due From Customers	$142

Notice that in preparing a schedule of accounts receivable, only the accounts that have balances are listed in order to save time and space. A. G. Browne, M. F. Coleman, and R. W. Peters are omitted because their accounts have no balances on February 28.

3. The accountant compares the total due from customers with the

balance of Accounts Receivable 111 in the general ledger. In this case, the total of $142 obtained in Step 2 agrees with the balance of the Accounts Receivable account shown on page 166.

This procedure is called *checking against* or *proving to the control*. Accounts Receivable 111 in the general ledger is known as a *control account* because it summarizes many detailed activities and thereby affords an independent proof of accuracy. The Accounts Receivable account summarizes by assembling four key total figures:

1. What customers owed at the beginning of the month, $90.
2. What customers bought on credit, increasing their debts, $144.
3. What customers received as credits on returns and allowances, $12.
4. What customers paid to reduce their debts, $80.

The balance is the amount still owing. The proof element occurs because the final balance of the control account represents the result of a steady stream of debits and credits posted daily to customers' accounts during the period. From now on, unless otherwise indicated, Accounts Receivable 111 in the general ledger will be called Accounts Receivable Control 111 in accordance with modern accounting practice.

PRINCIPLES AND PROCEDURES

Accounts with individual credit customers are usually kept in a subsidiary ledger called the accounts receivable ledger. This does not change the journalizing procedure. Daily postings are made to the accounts receivable subsidiary ledger from the sales journal, the cash receipts journal, and the general journal. A running balance is calculated after each posting to a customer's account so that the amount owed is known at all times.

When all entries have been posted for the month, the balances in the customers' accounts are added together to compute the total amount owed. The total of the individual accounts in the subsidiary ledger is then checked against the balance of the Accounts Receivable Control account in the general ledger.

When more than one type of sales income is involved, separate income accounts may be used. Provision may be made in the sales journal and cash receipts journal for each type of income.

MANAGERIAL IMPLICATIONS

The use of the subsidiary accounts receivable ledger provides the manager and the credit department with ready and complete information about the balance owed by each customer. This is of special value in setting, reappraising, or carrying out credit and collections policies.

The control feature of the subsidiary accounts receivable ledger system provides an additional proof of the accuracy of the accounting records. When customers' records are maintained efficiently and proved periodically, there will be better customer relations and less chance of misunderstanding.

APPLICATION OF PRINCIPLES

PROBLEM 11 · 1

On July 1, 19X1, a new department of the ABC Venetian Blind Company ♦ was established for the repairing and cleaning of venetian blinds. The income received from services rendered and installations made is to be kept separately. The necessary general ledger accounts and given balances on July 1, 19X1 are:

101	Cash	$4,760.25
111	Accounts Receivable Control	2,409.05
404	Venetian Blind Sales	–0–
405	Repairs and Cleaning Sales	–0–
451	Sales Returns and Allowances	–0–

The company uses a sales journal with special columns for Accounts Receivable Dr. 111, Venetian Blind Sales Cr. 404, and Repairs and Cleaning Sales Cr. 405; and a cash receipts journal with special columns for Accounts Receivable Cr. 111, Venetian Blind Sales Cr. 404, Repairs and Cleaning Sales Cr. 405, and Cash Dr. 101.

Beginning July 1, 19X1, an accounts receivable subsidiary ledger is to be kept, using balance-form ledger sheets. A list of the individual account balances at June 30 follows. (Addresses have been intentionally omitted and will continue to be in future problems containing subsidiary ledgers.)

George Aiken	$ 15.65
Albemarle School	–0–
American Can Company	1,335.75
Carlton Arms Apartments	315.05
Rufus Collins	88.50
Felder's Drug Store	–0–
Freedom School	289.95
Raymond Grooms	115.75
Daniel Likes	23.40
Leon L. Rowland	225.00
Taylor's Haberdashery	–0–
Total Due from Customers	$2,409.05

The July 19X1 transactions involving the sale of merchandise and receipt of cash are as follows:

1 Sold J. W. Spangler venetian blinds on credit, Sales Slip 102, $63.35. Received $1,335.75 from the American Can Company in payment of May 6 sale.

2 Installed blinds on two jobs and received cash payment, $163.80 total. Repaired blinds on credit for Omar Patterson, $43, Sales Slip 103.

3 Received a check from Carlton Arms Apartments, $100 to apply on account. Sold venetian blinds on credit to Taylor's Haberdashery, $136.95, Sales Slip 104. Sold Daniel Likes one venetian blind on credit, $12.50, Sales Slip 105. Received $23.40 from Daniel Likes in payment of his account on June 30.

5 Sold venetian blinds on credit to Albemarle School, $956.65, Sales Slip 106. Received payment of $88.50 on account from Rufus Collins.

6 Installed blinds for Felder's Drug Store on credit, Sales Slip 107, $422.80. Cash sales today: $134 ($114 sale of blinds, $20 cleaning service).

9 Sales of blinds on credit today: Sales Slip 108, $55.95 to Larry Davis on special 60-day net terms; Sales Slip 109, $17.50 to George Aiken. Made one repair for cash, $27.35.

10 Received a check for $289.95 from Freedom School in payment for the June 30 balance. Also received payment in cash for blinds repaired today, $39.25.

11 Sales Slip 110 covers a credit sale of blinds to Carl Langley for $38.45. Sales Slip 111 covers a credit sale of blinds to Edward P. Comary for $76.75.

12 Received $235.70 in cash for blinds installed today.

13 Received a check from George Aiken, $15.65, in payment of his account on June 30. Sold $348 worth of venetian blinds on credit to Zeigler Radio Company, Sales Slip 112.

16 Sold venetian blinds for cash, $97.50. Sold venetian blinds on credit, $122.40, Sales Slip 113, to Carlton Arms Apartments.

17 Blinds cleaned today on credit for Rufus Collins, Sales Slip 114, $24. Leon L. Rowland delivered a check for $112.50 to apply on account and promised to pay the balance on Aug. 15.

18 Cash sales of venetian blinds today, $164.30, to three different customers. Sales Slip 115 covers a special installation for Freedom School, $180.

19 Repaired venetian blinds on credit for J. W. Spangler, $24.65, Sales Slip 116. Received check from Omar Patterson in payment of Sales Slip 103, $43, July 2.

22 Gave credit of $26.65 to Albemarle School for venetian blind returned. Originally charged on Sales Slip 106, June 5. (Use Entry 7-14.)

23 Installed blinds in one home today and received cash payment of $112.

24 Credit sale of blinds today to Carl Langley, Sales Slip 117, $21.55.

25 Credit sales of blinds today to Leon L. Rowland, $46.80, Sales Slip 118, and to Daniel Likes for $39.50, Sales Slip 119.

27 Collected $102.90 for venetian blinds installed today on cash basis. Received a check from Carlton Arms Apartments for $215.05 to complete payment of the June 30 balance of their account.

29 Granted allowance of $4 to J. W. Spangler as an adjustment because wrong color tapes were used in repairs. Originally charged on Sales Slip 116, June 19. (Use Entry 7-19.)

30 Sold venetian blinds for cash, $73.75. Sales Slip 120 was issued for $14.65 to Taylor's Haberdashery for repairs.

31 Sales Slip 121 covers a credit sale of blinds to Zeigler Radio Company, $113.55.

INSTRUCTIONS

1. Open the general ledger accounts and enter the balances brought forward.

2. Open the accounts receivable subsidiary ledger. (A separate ledger account should be used for each customer listed here.) Enter the customer's name, the year, the date of July 1, the word "Balance" in the Description column, a check mark in the Posting Reference column, and the amount in the Balance column. Open accounts for new customers as required. The customary terms are 30 days net.

3. Prove the accuracy of your work in Instruction 2 by listing the balances owed by customers as shown in the accounts receivable subsidiary ledger; then add them, and compare the resulting total with the balance of the general ledger Accounts Receivable Control account and with the total of the schedule of accounts receivable. Use a separate sheet of paper for this step.

4. Record each transaction in the appropriate journal. (Use Page 7 for each journal.)

5. Complete the required daily and summary postings to the general ledger and to the accounts receivable subsidiary ledger.

6. Foot and balance the general ledger accounts, and verify the accuracy of the balances of the accounts receivable subsidiary ledger accounts.

7. Prepare a schedule of accounts receivable at July 31, 19X1 and prove to the control.

MANAGERIAL CHECKUPS

♦ How can accounting records aid management in developing and maintaining sound credit and collection policies?

♦ What are some of the advantages of keeping an accounts receivable subsidiary ledger?

♦ How does a control account aid management?

12 THE ACCOUNTS PAYABLE LEDGER

In Unit 10, you saw how the accountant designed a purchases journal for recording the expected credit purchases of merchandise for the new Accessories Department of the Carter Cleaning Shop. The February 19X2 purchases of merchandise on credit were entered in the new journal as follows.

PURCHASES JOURNAL for Month of February 19X2 — Page 1

DATE		PURCHASED FROM	INVOICE NO.	INVOICE DATE	TERMS	✓	AMOUNT	
Feb.	1	Weller Wholesale Company	649	2/1	30 days		1,200	00
	13	Beaver Products Company	A4973	2/12	30 days		300	00
	17	Premium Plastics, Inc.	43691	2/15	20 days		100	00
	24	Weller Wholesale Company	855	2/22	30 days		210	00
					Debit 501	✓✓		
	28	Total Credit Purchases			Credit 201	✓✓	1,810	00

The total of the Amount column in the purchases journal was posted at the end of the month. The Merchandise Purchases 501 account was debited to record the cost of the new stock of merchandise purchased, and the Accounts Payable 201 account was credited to show the firm's obligation to its suppliers.

Merchandise Purchases — No. 501

DATE		EXPLANATION	POST. REF.	DEBIT		DATE	EXPLANATION	POST. REF.	CREDIT
19	X2								
Feb.	28		PJ-1	1,810	00				

DATE	EXPLANATION	POST. REF.	DEBIT	DATE		EXPLANATION	POST. REF.	CREDIT
				19 X2 Feb.	1	Brought Fwd.	✓	500 00
					28		PJ-1	1,810 00

In the same unit, you also learned that Carter may return defective goods to suppliers for credit or may receive an allowance for unsatisfactory materials purchased or services rendered. In February, the only purchases returns and allowances item was recorded in the general journal as follows.

19 X2 Feb. 27	2–2 Accounts Payable/Weller Wholesale . .	201	10 00	
	Purchases Returns & Allowances . .	509		10 00
	Return of accessories purchased on February 24, Invoice 855, found not as ordered.			

The general ledger accounts involved are shown after the purchases return entry was posted.

Accounts Payable   No. 201

DATE	EXPLANATION	POST. REF.	DEBIT	DATE		EXPLANATION	POST. REF.	CREDIT
19 X2 Feb. 27		2-2	10 00	19 X2 Feb.	1	Brought Fwd.		500 00
					28		PJ-1	1,810 00

Purchases Returns and Allowances   No. 509

DATE	EXPLANATION	POST. REF.	DEBIT	DATE		EXPLANATION	POST. REF.	CREDIT
				19 X2 Feb.	27		2-2	10 00

As payments are made to creditors, the accountant enters the details in the cash disbursements journal. The following illustration shows how a multicolumn cash disbursements journal would be used. To simplify the presentation, only payments to apply on accounts payable have been shown.

CASH DISBURSEMENTS JOURNAL for Month of February 19X2　　　　　Page 2

DATE		CHECK NO.	EXPLANATION	SUNDRY DEBITS			ACCOUNTS PAYABLE		CASH
				ACCT. NO.	✓	AMOUNT	✓	DR. 201	CR. 101
Feb.	3	41	Weller Wholesale Co.					600 00	600 00
	10	44	Ace Motors Company					500 00	500 00
	15	47	Beaver Products Co.					150 00	150 00
	24	51	Premium Plastics, Inc.					100 00	100 00
	28		Totals					1,350 00	

At the end of the month, the total of the Accounts Payable Debit column is then posted to the Accounts Payable 201 account.

Accounts Payable　　　　　No. 201

DATE	EXPLANATION	POST. REF.	DEBIT	DATE	EXPLANATION	POST. REF.	CREDIT
19 X2				19 X2			
Feb. 27		2-2	10 00	Feb. 1	Brought Fwd.	✓	500 00
28		CDJ-2	1,350 00	28		PJ-1	1,810 00
			1,360 00		*950.00*		*2,310 00*

THE ACCOUNTANT NEEDS MORE INFORMATION

The accountant uses the final balance of the Accounts Payable account in the trial balance and the balance sheet, as before. However, when the time comes for him to pay Carter's bills, he quickly realizes that the balance of the Accounts Payable account does not tell him what he needs to know. How can he find out the exact amount that is owed to each creditor and the date that each bill is to be paid?

The accountant might check through all the entries in the purchases journal to find the date and amount of each purchase made from a particular supplier. Then he could check all the entries in the cash disbursements journal to find out how much had already been paid to the same creditor. Next, he could scan the general journal for purchases returns and allowances items. Finally, by deducting the total payments and returns and allowances from total purchases, the accountant could ascertain the amount still due. Obviously, however, this procedure is impractical. It is much simpler to set

UNIT 12

up separate accounts for creditors as individual accounts were provided for the firm's customers. In this way, the amount owed to each creditor is readily available information.

ACCOUNTS WITH INDIVIDUAL CREDITORS

The creditor's record of account could be designed as a two-sided T account, but again the three-column balance form of account is preferred by most accountants. For example, the balance owed to Ace Motors Company on January 31, 19X2 could be shown in an individual record set up on February 1 as follows.

Name: **ACE MOTORS COMPANY**

Address: **204 Drake Avenue**

Centerport, State 53995   Terms: **Net 30**

DATE		DESCRIPTION	POST. REF.	DEBIT	CREDIT	BALANCE
19 X2 Feb. 1		Balance	✓			500 00

All accounts with creditors are kept alphabetically or according to account number in the *accounts payable subsidiary ledger*. Balances are presumed to be credit balances. Occasional debit balances resulting from such transactions as purchases returns and allowances on goods already paid for, are indicated by the use of a "Dr." notation, red-ink figures, parentheses, or a circle around the amount.

RECORDING THE PURCHASE

The procedure for journalizing the credit purchase remains the same as before. The purchase from the Weller Wholesale Company on February 1 is recorded exactly as it appears on page 171.

PURCHASES JOURNAL for Month of February 19X2   **Page 1**

DATE		PURCHASED FROM	INVOICE NO.	INVOICE DATE	TERMS	✓	AMOUNT
Feb.	1	Weller Wholesale Company	649	2/1	30 days		1,200 00

A new procedure is involved, however, in posting purchases to the creditor's account. The amount of the purchase is posted at once as a credit to the supplier's account in the accounts payable subsidiary ledger. The balance of the account is computed after each posting.

Name: **WELLER WHOLESALE COMPANY**

Address: **671 Valley Street**

         Topeka, State 66614   **Terms: Net 30**

DATE	DESCRIPTION	POST. REF.	DEBIT	CREDIT	BALANCE
19 X2 Feb. 1	Invoice 649, 2/1/X2	PJ-1		1,200 00	1,200 00

After the entry is posted to Weller's account, a check mark is noted in the Posting Check column of the purchases journal.

PURCHASES JOURNAL for Month of February 19X2   **Page 1**

DATE	PURCHASED FROM	INVOICE NO.	INVOICE DATE	TERMS	✓	AMOUNT
Feb. 1	Weller Wholesale Company	649	2/1	30 days	✓	1,200 00

RECORDING THE
CASH PAYMENT
TO A CREDITOR

The procedure for journalizing a cash payment to a creditor remains basically the same as before. The payment of $600 to the Weller firm is recorded as shown below.

CASH DISBURSEMENTS JOURNAL for Month of February 19X2   **Page 2**

DATE	CHECK NO.	EXPLANATION	SUNDRY DEBITS ACCT. NO.	✓	AMOUNT	✓	ACCOUNTS PAYABLE DR. 201	CASH CR. 101
Feb. 3	41	Weller Wholesale Co.					600 00	600 00

The procedure for posting payments to the creditor's account is new. The amount paid is posted immediately as a debit to the creditor's account in the accounts payable subsidiary ledger.

Name: **WELLER WHOLESALE COMPANY**

Address: **671 Valley Street**

            Topeka, State 66614   **Terms: Net 30**

DATE		DESCRIPTION	POST. REF.	DEBIT	CREDIT	BALANCE
19 X2 Feb.	1	Invoice 649, 2/1/X2	PJ-1		1,200 00	1,200 00
	3		CDJ-2	600 00		600 00

A check is then placed in the Accounts Payable Posting Check column of the cash disbursements journal to indicate that the posting to the individual subsidiary ledger has been completed.

CASH DISBURSEMENTS JOURNAL for Month of February 19X2   **Page 2**

DATE		CHECK NO.	EXPLANATION	SUNDRY DEBITS			ACCOUNTS PAYABLE		CASH CR. 101
				ACCT. NO.	✓	AMOUNT	✓	DR. 201	
Feb.	3	41	Weller Wholesale Co.				✓	600 00	600 00

Remember that the Posting Check column in the Sundry Debits section relates only to the postings in the general ledger accounts.

The recording of a purchases return or allowance in the general journal remains virtually unchanged. The accountant signals the need for a double posting of the debit by means of a diagonal line in the Account Number column. The general ledger account to be debited (201) is indicated to the left of the diagonal. The check mark on the right of the diagonal indicates the need to post a second debit to the supplier's account in the subsidiary ledger.

19	X2		2–2						
Feb.	27	Accounts Payable/Weller Wholesale .	.	201/√		10	00		
		Purchases Returns & Allowances .	.	509				10	00
		Return of accessories purchased on							
		February 24, Invoice 855, found not as							
		ordered.							

POSTING A PURCHASES RETURN OR ALLOWANCE

Following the cue given in the Account Number column, the accountant double-posts the debit part of the purchases returns and allowances entry. As each posting is completed, he records a check mark in the Posting Check column. A check mark to the left of the diagonal indicates that the debit was posted to Accounts Payable 201 in the general ledger. A check mark to the right of the diagonal signals that the debit was also posted to the Weller account. The credit to Account 509 is posted as before.

19	X2		2–2						
Feb.	27	Accounts Payable/Weller Wholesale .	.	201/√	√/√	10	00		
		Purchases Returns & Allowances .	.	509	√			10	00
		Return of accessories purchased on							
		February 24, Invoice 855, found not as							
		ordered.							

DAILY ROUTINE

Each credit purchase is recorded in the purchases journal and is then posted to the account of the creditor in the accounts payable subsidiary ledger. Credit purchases for February are shown in the purchases journal illustrated.

PURCHASES JOURNAL for Month of February 19X2   Page 1

DATE		PURCHASED FROM	INV. NO.	INVOICE DATE	TERMS	√	AMOUNT	
Feb.	1	Weller Wholesale Company	649	2/1	30 days	√	1,200	00
	13	Beaver Products Company	A4973	2/12	30 days	√	300	00
	17	Premium Plastics, Inc.	43691	2/15	20 days	√	100	00
	24	Weller Wholesale Company	855	2/22	30 days	√	210	00

Each payment to a creditor is recorded in the cash disbursements journal and then posted immediately to the creditor's account. The new balance in each account is calculated after each posting so that the amount owed will be available for quick reference. Here again is how the payments to creditors will appear in the cash disbursements journal after the postings have been made.

| DATE | CHECK NO. | EXPLANATION | SUNDRY DEBITS | | | ACCOUNTS PAYABLE | | CASH CR. 101 |
			ACCT. NO.	✓	AMOUNT	✓	DR. 201	
Feb. 3	41	Weller Wholesale Co.				✓	600 00	600 00
10	44	Ace Motors Company				✓	500 00	500 00
15	47	Beaver Products Co.				✓	150 00	150 00
24	51	Premium Plastics, Inc.				✓	100 00	100 00

Each purchases return or allowance is recorded in the general journal and then posted immediately. The debit is entered in the general ledger Account 201 and in the supplier's account in the subsidiary ledger. The credit is posted to the general ledger in Account 509.

SUBSIDIARY LEDGER ACCOUNT BALANCES

The creditors' accounts in the accounts payable subsidiary ledger of the Carter Cleaning Shop at the end of February 19X2 are shown.

Name: **ACE MOTORS COMPANY**

Address: **204 Drake Avenue**

                          Centerport, State 53995   Terms: Net 30

DATE	DESCRIPTION	POST. REF.	DEBIT	CREDIT	BALANCE
19 X2 Feb. 1	Balance	✓			500 00
10		CDJ-2	500 00		0

Name   **BEAVER PRODUCTS COMPANY**

Address: **Box 164**

                          Beaver Falls, State 13305   Terms: Net 30

DATE	DESCRIPTION	POST. REF.	DEBIT	CREDIT	BALANCE
19 X2 Feb. 13	Invoice A 4973, 2/12/X2	PJ-1		300 00	300 00
15		CDJ-2	150 00		150 00

Name:		PREMIUM PLASTICS, INC.						
Address:		267 Spring Street						
		St. Louis, State 63119					Terms: Net 20	

DATE		DESCRIPTION	POST. REF.	DEBIT		CREDIT		BALANCE	
19	X2								
Feb.	17	Invoice 43691, 2/15/X2	PJ-1			100	00	100	00
	24		CDJ-2	100	00			0	

Name:		WELLER WHOLESALE COMPANY						
Address:		671 Valley Street						
		Topeka, State 66614					Terms: Net 30	

DATE		DESCRIPTION	POST. REF.	DEBIT		CREDIT		BALANCE	
19	X2								
Feb.	1	Invoice 649, 2/1/X2	PJ-1			1,200	00	1,200	00
	3		CDJ-2	600	00			600	00
	24	Invoice 855, 2/22/X2	PJ-1			210	00	810	00
	27		2-2	10	00			800	00

END-OF-MONTH ROUTINE

The procedure for posting totals from the purchases journal at the end of the month is the same as before. The Amount column is totaled as shown. Then the total credit purchases are posted as a debit to Merchandise Purchases 501 and as a credit to Accounts Payable 201 in the general ledger. The posting reference numbers are checked as posting is completed.

PURCHASES JOURNAL for Month of February 19X2   Page 1

DATE		PURCHASED FROM	INVOICE NO.	INVOICE DATE	TERMS	✓	AMOUNT	
Feb.	1	Weller Wholesale Company	649	2/1	30 days	✓	1,200	00
	13	Beaver Products Company	A4973	2/12	30 days	✓	300	00
	17	Premium Plastics, Inc.	43691	2/15	20 days	✓	100	00
	24	Weller Wholesale Company	855	2/22	30 days	✓	210	00
	28	Total Credit Purchases			Debit 501 Credit 201	✓/ /✓	1,810	00

The procedure for posting totals from the cash disbursements journal also remains the same. All columns are totaled, and the Cash and Accounts Payable amounts are posted to the general ledger accounts indicated in the column headings. Check marks are placed below these columnar totals as each posting is completed. Only payments on Accounts Payable are illustrated here to simplify the presentation.

CASH DISBURSEMENTS JOURNAL for Month of February 19X2 Page 2

DATE		CHECK NO.	EXPLANATION	SUNDRY DEBITS			ACCOUNTS PAYABLE			CASH CR. 101
				ACCT. NO.	✓	AMOUNT	✓	DR. 201		
Feb.	3	41	Weller Wholesale Co.				✓	600	00	600 00
	10	44	Ace Motors Company				✓	500	00	500 00
	15	47	Beaver Products Co.				✓	150	00	150 00
	24	51	Premium Plastics, Inc.				✓	100	00	100 00
	28		Totals					1,350	00	
								✓		

When the postings have been made from the purchases journal, the cash disbursements journal, and the general journal, the Accounts Payable account in the general ledger looks exactly as shown on page 173.

Accounts Payable No. 201

DATE	EXPLANATION	POST. REF.	DEBIT		DATE	EXPLANATION	POST. REF.	CREDIT	
19 X2					19 X2				
Feb. 27		2-2	10	00	Feb. 1	Brought Fwd.	✓	500	00
28		CDJ-2	1,350	00	28		PJ-1	1,810	00
			1,360	*00*		*950.00*		*2,310*	*00*

After all items and totals are posted from the purchases journal, cash disbursements journal, and general journal to the subsidiary and general ledger accounts, the accountant checks the work for accuracy. As in the previous unit, it is a three-step process.

1. The accountant verifies the balances of all creditors' accounts in the accounts payable ledger. (The running balances were figured after each posting.)

2. He prepares a list, or *schedule of accounts payable,* and adds all balances to obtain the total owed to creditors. Here are the balances taken from the accounts illustrated on pages 178 and 179 presented formally as a schedule of accounts payable.

CARTER CLEANING SHOP
Schedule of Accounts Payable
February 28, 19X2

CREDITOR	BALANCE AMOUNT
Beaver Products Company	$150
Weller Wholesale Company	800
Total Owed to Creditors	$950

Notice that in preparing the schedule of accounts payable, only accounts that have balances are listed. This is done to save time and space. Ace Motors Company and Premium Plastics, Inc., are omitted because their accounts have no balances on February 28.

3. The accountant compares the total of the schedule of accounts payable with the balance of the Accounts Payable account in the general ledger. In this case, the total of $950 obtained in Step 2 agrees with the balance of Accounts Payable 201 shown previously.

The Accounts Payable account is called a control account for reasons similar to those pointed out in connection with the Accounts Receivable Control account. Accounts Payable Control summarizes many detailed activities and thereby affords an independent proof of accuracy. From now on, unless otherwise indicated, the Accounts Payable account in the general ledger will be called the Accounts Payable Control account, the title commonly used in modern accounting practice.

PRINCIPLES AND PROCEDURES

The accounts payable subsidiary ledger contains an account for each creditor. As soon as a purchase is made and journalized, the amount must be credited to the individual supplier's account in the accounts payable subsidiary ledger. When a payment is made, the amount is posted at once as a debit to the creditor's account in the subsidiary ledger from the cash disbursements journal.

End-of-month postings to the general ledger are made in the usual way. When all entries are posted, the creditor's account balances in the accounts payable subsidiary ledger are added together to determine the total amount owed, and the total is then compared with the Accounts Payable Control 201 account in the general ledger, to be sure that the two balances are equal.

MANAGERIAL IMPLICATIONS

It is important for management to know at all times the total amount owed to creditors. This information helps to ensure that bills are paid promptly, that good relations are kept with suppliers, and that cash can be made available as needed. The process of proving the total of the subsidiary account balances to the control account balance is a valuable check on the accuracy of the records.

The more elaborate accounting system used by the Carter Cleaning Shop in February resembles that used in many medium-sized businesses that have a steady volume of transactions that must be handled quickly and efficiently. If the volume of transactions had warranted, an entry clerk could have been assigned to each journal to speed the recording. Each journal and ledger in the system is interlocked so that resulting records will be accurate and complete.

APPLICATION OF PRINCIPLES

PROBLEM 12 · 1

♦ The ABC Venetian Blind Company uses a cash disbursements journal with special columns for Sundry Debits, Accounts Payable Dr. 201, and Cash Cr. 101; a single-column purchases journal; and a general journal in order to record April 19X1 transactions. The necessary ledger accounts and balances on Apr. 1, 19X1 are:

101	Cash	$4,550.25
201	Accounts Payable Control	3,122.95
501	Merchandise Purchases	3,916.65
509	Purchases Returns and Allowances	–0–

The individual accounts at Mar. 31, 19X1 in the accounts payable subsidiary ledger reveal the following. (Addresses have been intentionally omitted.)

Aluminum Company of Summerville—		
Inv. 6698, Mar. 2, net 30 days		$1,450.00
Lockhart Milling Company—		
Inv. A11021, Feb. 6, net 60 days	$247.50	
Inv. B23368, Mar. 18, net 60 days	522.50	770.00
Dallas Cordage Company		–0–
Chicago Gear Company—		
Inv. G1090, Mar. 5, net 30 days		469.20
Extruded Aluminum Corp—		
Inv. 309-B, Feb. 25, net 60 days		115.00
Albright Paint Company—		–0–
Sherwin-Williams Paint Co.—		
Inv. 2412C, Mar. 16, net 30 days		69.50
Ashland Lumber Company—		
Inv. 788, Mar. 23, net 20 days		249.25
Total Owed to Creditors		$3,122.95

The transactions involving purchases of merchandise on credit and disbursements of cash for April 19X1 are as follows:

APR.

1   Purchased slats from the Aluminum Company of Summerville, Invoice 7211, Apr. 1; terms, net 30 days; $1,023.65.

1   Issued Check 537 for $1,450 to the Aluminum Company of Summerville, in payment for Invoice 6698, dated Mar. 2.

4   Issued Check 538 for $469.20 to Chicago Gear Company for Invoice G1090, dated Mar. 5.

5   Issued Check 539 for purple paint for special job, $15.50. Charge to Merchandise Purchases 501.

6   Issued Check 540 for $247.50 to the Lockhart Milling Company, in payment for Invoice A11021, dated Feb. 6.

8   Bought special trim material from the Lexington Supply Company, Invoice 434, Apr. 6, $33.75, due in 30 days, net.

11 Paid the entire amount owed to the Ashland Lumber Company, $249.25, Check 541.

12 Bought cords from the Dallas Cordage Company, Invoice 4-718, Apr. 10, $255.15, due in 30 days, net.

14 Purchased special gears for extra wide blinds from Die Works, Inc., $198.50, Invoice 976, dated Apr. 12, due in 30 days, net.

15 Paid Sherwin-Williams Paint Company Invoice 2412C, dated Mar. 16, $69.50, by Check 542.

18 Bought special tassels, $5.50, by Check 543.

19 Received $100 allowance from the Aluminum Company of Summerville. Slats purchased on Invoice 7211, Apr. 1, were of inferior quality. (Use Entry 4-16.)

APR.

20   Purchased paint from Sherwin-Williams Paint Company, $433.90, Invoice 2567D, Apr. 15, due in 30 days, net.

21   Obtained a supply of wood bottom slats from the Ashland Lumber Company, payable net on May 10, Invoice 813, Apr. 20, $215.

25   Paid the Extruded Aluminum Corporation $115 by Check 544 to cover Invoice 309B, dated Feb. 25.

28   Purchased tapes from the Lockhart Milling Company, $342.80, payable in 60 days, net, their Invoice C24413, dated Apr. 27.

29   Bought two drums of paint from the Albright Paint Company; terms, net May 10; Invoice 301-493, Apr. 25, $565.75.

30   Received $24.50 credit for gears returned to Die Works, Inc. Original purchase on Invoice 976, Apr. 12. (Use Entry 4-24.)

INSTRUCTIONS

1.   Open the general ledger accounts and enter each Brought Forward balance.

2.   Open the accounts payable subsidiary ledger. Enter the creditor's name (omit address), the year, the date of Apr. 1, the word "Balance" in the Description column; place a check mark in the Posting Reference column; and enter the amount owed to each creditor in the Balance column. Open an account for all listed accounts, even though there may be no balances as of this date. Pertinent information, such as invoice number, date, and terms, has been provided. Open accounts for new creditors as needed.

3.   Prove the accuracy of your work in Instruction 2 by listing the balances owed to creditors as shown in the accounts payable subsidiary ledger; then add them and compare the resulting total with the balance of the general ledger Accounts Payable Control account and with the total of the schedule of accounts payable. Use a separate sheet of paper for this step.

4.   Record each transaction in the appropriate journal. (Number each journal Page 4.)

5.   Complete the required daily and summary postings to the general ledger and to the accounts payable subsidiary ledger.

6.   Foot and balance the general ledger accounts, and verify the accuracy of the balances of the accounts payable subsidiary ledger accounts.

7.   Prepare a schedule of accounts payable at Apr. 30, 19X1 and prove to the control.

MANAGERIAL CHECKUPS

♦   What purpose does the purchases journal serve?

♦   Why is it important for management to know how much is owed to each of its creditors?

♦   How does a control account serve as a check on accuracy?

INTEGRATED PRACTICAL APPLICATION—
SPECIAL JOURNALS AND LEDGERS

Since beginning Unit 6, you have learned how to use five special journals and two subsidiary ledgers. In this unit, these devices will be used for recording the February 19X2 transactions of the Carter Cleaning Shop, some of which have already been studied.

The transactions are presented in chronological order. Each must be analyzed before it is recorded in the appropriate journal. Remember that this month a total of five journals will be used in the accounting system:

Cash Receipts Journal (multicolumn)   (Page 2)
Cash Disbursements Journal (multicolumn)   (Page 2)
Sales Journal   (Page 2)
Purchases Journal   (Page 1)
General Journal   (Page 4)

After the transactions have been journalized, they must be posted to the proper ledger or ledgers, of which there are now three:

General Ledger
Accounts Receivable Subsidiary Ledger
Accounts Payable Subsidiary Ledger

HOW TO GET ORGANIZED

At the end of January, a postclosing trial balance like the one shown was prepared.

CARTER CLEANING SHOP
Postclosing Trial Balance
January 31, 19X2

ACCT. NO.	ACCOUNT NAME	DEBIT		CREDIT	
101	Cash	$1,280	00		
111	Accounts Receivable Control	90	00		
141	Equipment	5,370	00		
201	Accounts Payable Control			$ 500	00
301	Carter Investment			6,240	00
	Totals	$6,740	00	$6,740	00

Review those units from 6 to 10 that relate to the various journals and ledger accounts. Study them carefully, since you will be required to prepare similar journal and ledger forms adapted to fit the February operations of the Carter Cleaning Shop.

CHART OF ACCOUNTS

Carter's entry into the merchandising of accessories calls for the revised chart of accounts that is illustrated. Accounts described in recent units are added. The five accounts to be explained in Unit 14 are included in the list at this time to avoid the necessity of a further revision of the chart within the next few pages. These expanded records make it possible to keep abreast of the expected larger volume of operations more smoothly and efficiently. Again, notice that number gaps are left within each grouping so that accounts may be added when required.

Account Number	Account Name
100–199	ASSETS
101	Cash
111	Accounts Receivable Control
111A	Allowance for Bad Debts (Unit 14)
121	Merchandise Inventory (Unit 14)
141	Equipment
141A	Allowance for Depreciation (Unit 14)
200–299	LIABILITIES
201	Accounts Payable Control
300–399	OWNER'S EQUITY
301	Carter Investment
302	Carter Drawing
399	Income and Expense Summary
400–499	INCOME
401	Cleaning Service Income
402	Accessories Sales Income
451	Sales Returns and Allowances—Cleaning Service
452	Sales Returns and Allowances—Accessories
500–599	EXPENSES
501	Merchandise Purchases
509	Purchases Returns and Allowances
511	Salary Expense
516	Rent Expense
521	Supplies Used
561	Bad Debts Expense (Unit 14)
564	Depreciation Expense (Unit 14)
591	Miscellaneous Expense

PREPARE A NEW GENERAL LEDGER

Head general ledger account forms for all the accounts listed in the chart of accounts. For each account listed on the postclosing trial balance, enter the date of February 1, 19X2 in the Date column, the words "Brought Forward" in the Explanation column, a check mark in the Posting Reference column, and the amount. When all your entries are completed, double-check your work by comparing the ledger balances with the figures shown in the postclosing trial balance from which you worked.

PREPARE NEW JOURNALS

The name of the month and page number (Page 1 for purchases journal; Page 4 for the general journal; Page 2 for others) are to be inserted on the special journal forms. The column headings are the same as appear on the following pages: cash receipts journal, page 162, cash disbursements journal, page 98; sales journal, page 157; purchases journal, page 146.

PREPARE SUBSIDIARY LEDGERS

Open individual balance-form ledger accounts for the two subsidiary ledgers. Omit addresses to save time.

Accounts Receivable

The accounts receivable subsidiary ledger contains the following accounts, with balances at February 1, 19X2:

M. F. Coleman	$ 0
S. S. Baker	60
B. A. Hahn	30
R. L. Camp	0

Accounts Payable

The Accounts Payable balance of $500 is owed to the Ace Motors Company. Complete a balance-form ledger sheet showing this creditor's February 1 balance.

In recording daily transactions, first consider the use of special journals whenever possible; they save much time and effort. For example, all cash received should be entered in the cash receipts journal; all cash payments should be recorded in the cash disbursements journal; sales on credit should be entered in the sales journal; and purchases of merchandise on credit should be recorded in the purchases journal. Remember, an entry is made in the general journal only if it does not belong anywhere else.

Many transactions in the following list for February 19X2 will be familiar, but if there is any difficulty, do not hesitate to review the unit in which the procedure was explained.

FEB.

1   Sold $20 worth of cleaning services on Sales Slip 5 to J. E. Ayres, a new customer; terms, 30 days net. (Open an account in the subsidiary ledger for this new customer. Do the same thing for other new customers or new creditors hereafter.)

1   Purchased initial stock of merchandise from the Weller Wholesale Company for $1,200. Allowed 30 days to pay. Their Invoice 649 is dated February 1.

2   Paid $60 for miscellaneous expenses by Check 40.

2   Sold $10 worth of cleaning services on Sales Slip 6 to R. W. Peters; terms, 30 days net.

3   Issued Check 41 for $600 to the Weller Wholesale Company as partial payment of amount owed to it.

3   Paid the Motor Transport Company $30 by Check 42 for freight on counter and display fixtures purchased January 28. (Debit Equipment because delivery charges are an additional cost of an asset purchased.)

4   Received $5 from customer J. E. Ayres to apply on his account.

4   Sold $25 worth of accessories on Sales Slip 7 to A. G. Browne; terms, 30 days net.

5   A. G. Browne returned $10 worth of the accessories sold to him on February 4 and was given credit for that amount.

5   Cash receipts for cleaning services during the week, $750.

5   Cash receipts for sale of accessories during the week, $225.

8   Paid $250 by Check 43 for supplies used.

10 Sold $25 worth of accessories on Sales Slip 8 to K. Davies; terms, 30 days net.

10 Received check for $10 from customer R. W. Peters to cover his account.

10 Sent Check 44 to Ace Motors Company to pay $500 balance due on delivery truck bought in January.

11 Received payment of $15 from A. G. Browne to settle his account.

12 Sold $7 worth of cleaning services on Sales Slip 9 to J. E. Ayres; terms, 30 days net.

12 Cash receipts for cleaning services during the week, $950.

12 Cash receipts for sale of accessories during the week, $250.

13 Paid $124 for supplies used, by Check 45.

13 Purchased additional stock for Accessories Department on credit from the Beaver Products Company for $300, payable in 30 days. Their Invoice A4973 is dated February 12.

14 Paid $75 for miscellaneous expenses, covered by Check 46.

15 Sold $10 worth of accessories on Sales Slip 10 to R. L. Camp; terms, 30 days net.

15 Paid $150 to Beaver Products Company to apply on account, Check 47.

16 Issued Check 48 to pay store rent for month, $700.

17 Purchased $100 more stock for the Accessories Department on 20-day credit terms from Premium Plastics, Inc. Their Invoice 43691 is dated February 15.

19 Sold $15 worth of accessories on Sales Slip 11 to M. F. Coleman; terms, 30 days net.

19 Cash receipts for cleaning services during the week, $1,000.

19 Cash receipts for accessories sales during the week, $200.

20 Received check for $20 from customer K. Davies to apply on account.

21 Paid $160 by Check 49 for supplies used.

21 Received $15 from J. E. Ayres to apply on his account.

22 Paid $40 by Check 50 for miscellaneous expenses.

23 Sold $20 worth of cleaning services on Sales Slip 12 to C. V. Fisher; terms, 30 days net.

24 Purchased $210 worth of accessories from the Weller Wholesale Company to replace items sold. Same 30-day terms as before. Their Invoice 855 is dated February 22.

24 Paid $100 by Check 51 to Premium Plastics, Inc., to settle account in full.

26 Sold $12 worth of accessories on Sales Slip 13 to A. Dunlap; terms, 30 days net.

26 Customer M. F. Coleman paid $15 to balance her account.

26 Cash receipts for cleaning services during the week, $1,025.

26 Cash receipts for accessories sales during the week, $225.

27 Received credit of $10 for accessories returned from purchase made on February 24 from the Weller Wholesale Company.

27 Paid $400 by Check 52 for supplies used.

28 Paid salaries for the month, $1,950, by Check 53.

28 A. Dunlap returned $2 worth of accessories purchased on February 26 and was given credit for that amount.

28 Refunded $10 by Check 54 to a customer who returned some defective accessories previously sold for cash.

28 Carter withdrew $50 for personal use, by Check 55.

Sales to and cash received from credit customers must be posted daily to individual customers' accounts in the accounts receivable subsidiary ledger.

Purchases and payments made to creditors must be posted daily to individual creditors' accounts in the accounts payable subsidiary ledger.

Entries made in the Sundry Debits column of the cash disbursements journal and all entries in the general journal should be posted daily to the general ledger, and to the customers' accounts in the accounts receivable subsidiary ledger when necessary.

COMPLETE PART OF THE CYCLE

Once the February transactions have been journalized and the required daily postings have been completed, proceed with the following steps in the end-of-month routine.

1. Total all special journals and post, as required, to general ledger accounts.
2. Foot and determine the balance of each general ledger account. (Do not rule the accounts at this time.)
3. Prove the general ledger by preparing a trial balance. List all accounts (except 399), including those with zero balances.
4. Prove subsidiary ledgers to their respective control accounts. Omit accounts with a zero balance from your listings. (Remember that this is actually a three-step process that must be applied to each of the subsidiary ledgers.)

You have now completed the accounting cycle for February through the trial balance and schedule of accounts receivable and payable. After all the journalizing and posting was done, the trial balance should have totaled $11,969 on each side. Completion of the worksheet and preparation of the financial statements will be discussed in the following units.

INTEGRATED PRACTICAL APPLICATION

13 THE COMBINED JOURNAL

In the earlier units, it was shown how a business might record all its transactions in a two-column general journal. Then, as the transactions became more numerous, time and effort were saved through the use of special journals. Cash receipts, cash disbursements, sales, and purchases were each handled more efficiently through the use of specially designed journals. In this unit, the way in which a small business may obtain many of the advantages of special journals while using only a single book of original entry will be discussed. The cornerstone of this simple, yet effective, system is a *combined journal*, sometimes called a *combined cash journal*.

DESIGNING A COMBINED JOURNAL

The combined journal provides a means of journalizing all the transactions of the smaller business in one place faster and easier than by using the general journal. As in the special journals, a single line is usually all that is required to record a particular transaction. Special columns are used to record the transactions that occur most frequently; Sundry columns are provided for handling less frequent types of entries that would normally be made in the general journal.

Selecting the Special Columns

The combined journal of a business should be designed with the firm's specific needs in mind. The first thing the accountant does is to study the company's proposed operations in order to develop an appropriate chart of accounts. Then, each account should be considered individually in planning the journal. Accounts that are likely to be used frequently in recording routine business operations are the ones for which special columns are justified in the new journal. Suppose that the Carter Cleaning Shop had wanted to use a combined journal. Study its chart of accounts on page 188 and follow this step-by-step explanation of what might be done.

The first account in the chart of accounts, Cash, is certainly used often enough to require special columns. Both debit and credit entries are frequently made in the Cash account, so both a Debit column and a Credit column are provided in the journal. The first two money columns in the combined journal are generally used for cash transactions.

The second account, Accounts Receivable, also requires frequent recording of both debits and credits. Therefore, two amount columns are set up in the journal for Accounts Receivable and a check column is provided to indicate that individual debits and credits have been posted to the accounts receivable subsidiary ledger.

On the other hand, the next account in the chart, Equipment, will probably be used in relatively few transactions, thus it does not justify a special column. The few transactions that do occur may be recorded in the Sundry columns of the combined journal.

In the Liabilities section, the Accounts Payable account will usually be debited and credited a number of times during the period. For this reason, two amount columns are provided in the new combined journal for Accounts Payable plus an appropriate column for checking when amounts have been posted to the accounts payable subsidiary ledger. There should be very few transactions affecting the owner's equity account, however, and a special column is not needed for it.

Numerous sales transactions will require many credits to be recorded in the income account during the month. Therefore, one special credit column, called Cleaning Service Income, is used.

Turning to the expense items, Salary Expense might have several debit entries each month and should, therefore, have a special debit column provided in the combined journal. The Rent Expense account normally involves only one payment each month—not enough to warrant a special column. However, the Supplies Used account might be debited in a number of transactions and a special column should be provided for it. In addition to these accounts, the new account, Miscellaneous Expense 591, first encountered in the January transactions, may have frequent debit entries during the month and should have a special column set aside in which to record them.

Sundry Columns

Sundry columns are provided in the combined journal for recording both debit and credit entries in accounts for which no special columns were established. A special Account Number column is included for noting the number of the account in which the record is to be made.

When all designing is done, the combined journal for the Carter Cleaning Shop will appear in the form shown on pages 194 and 195.

As usual, the accountant analyzes a transaction before recording it in the combined journal. Once he has a mental picture of the entry to be made, he enters the date, explanation, and debit and credit figures in their proper columns. If special columns are available, the amounts are entered in them; otherwise, the amounts are recorded in the Sundry columns and the account numbers are noted. Ordinarily, a single line will suffice for each transaction. Of course, the debits recorded in the entry must equal the credits recorded in the same transaction. The operation of the combined journal can be seen by retracing the January 19X2 transactions of the Carter Cleaning Shop that were first encountered in Unit 5.

For example, consider the recording problems involved in the January 2 transaction: *Acquired $770 worth of cleaning equipment from the Ajax Company, giving Check 31.*

As this transaction is analyzed, the accountant realizes that he must debit Equipment 141 and credit Cash 101. Since there is no special column in the combined journal for Equipment, the $770 debit must be entered in the Sundry Debit column and the account number in the Account Number column. The credit to Cash is entered in the special Cash Disbursed column. The first entry in the combined journal for January is shown in the first illustration provided on pages 194 and 195.

OTHER JANUARY TRANSACTIONS

January 7—*Cash receipts for cleaning services for the week, $700.* The entry in the combined journal involves a debit to Cash and a credit to Cleaning Service Income, both in the special columns provided. (See the illustration.) Similar transactions occurred in successive weeks, on January 14, 21, and 27.

January 7—*Sold $60 worth of cleaning services to R. L. Camp on credit.* This transaction is recorded in the combined journal through a debit to Accounts Receivable and a credit to Cleaning Service Income. Again, special columns are available. Similar credit sales took place on January 14, 19, and 28.

January 9—*December accounts receivable, $200, collected in full.* Once more, special columns are used for recording a debit to Cash and a credit to Accounts Receivable. Similar collections on account must be recorded on January 16, 23(2), and 29.

January 10—*Paid $300 to creditor, Knight, Inc., by Check 32.* This payment is recorded as a debit to Accounts Payable and a credit to Cash,

COMBINED JOURNAL for Month of January 19X2

DATE	CHECK NO.	EXPLANATION	CASH			ACCOUNTS RECEIVABLE	
			RECEIVED DR. 101	DISBURSED CR. 101	✓	DR 111	CR. 111
Jan. 2	31	Equipment Purchased		770 00			

both entries being made in special columns. Another payment to a creditor was made on January 24.

January 11—*Bought a delivery truck from Ace Motors on credit, $1,000.* The debit to Equipment 141 is noted in the Sundry Debit column and the credit to Accounts Payable is recorded in the appropriate special column.

January 15—*Paid $400, by Check 33, for supplies used.* The expense account is debited through the special column for Supplies Used and the credit is recorded in the Cash Disbursed column. More supplies were bought and paid for in similar fashion on January 28.

January 17—*Paid rent for January, $700, by Check 34.* A debit to Rent Expense 516 is recorded in the Sundry Debit column and Cash is credited.

January 28—*Paid $600, by Check 36, for counter and fixtures for Accessories Department.* The transaction is recorded by a debit to Equipment 141 in the Sundry Debit column and a credit to Cash.

January 30—*Paid $60 for miscellaneous expenses, by Check 38.* Since

COMBINED JOURNAL for Month of January 19X2

DATE	CHECK NO.	EXPLANATION	CASH			ACCOUNTS RECEIVABLE	
			RECEIVED DR. 101	DISBURSED CR. 101	✓	DR 111	CR. 111
Jan. 2	31	Equipment Purchased		770 00			
7		Cleaning Services	700 00				
7		R. L. Camp			✓	60 00	
9		December Accounts	200 00		✓		200 00
10	32	Knight, Inc.		300 00			
11		Ace Motors Co.					
14		Cleaning Services	725 00				
14		M. F. Coleman			✓	25 00	
15	33	Cleaning Sup. Used		400 00			
16		R. L. Camp	30 00		✓		30 00
17	34	Rent for Month		700 00			
19		B. A. Hahn			✓	30 00	
21		Cleaning Services	900 00				
23		R. L. Camp	30 00		✓		30 00
23		M. F. Coleman	15 00		✓		15 00
24	35	Ace Motors Co.		500 00			
27		Cleaning Services	800 00				
28	36	Fixtures—Acces. Dept.		600 00			
28		S. S. Baker			✓	60 00	
28	37	Supplies Used		300 00			
29		M. F. Coleman	10 00		✓		10 00
30	38	Misc. Expense		60 00			
31	39	Salaries		1,700 00			
31		Totals	3,410 00	5,330 00		175 00	285 00

ACCOUNTS PAYABLE			CLEANING SERVICE INCOME CR. 401	SALARY EXPENSE DR. 511	SUPPLIES USED DR. 521	MISC. EXPENSE DR. 591	SUNDRY			
√	DR. 201	CR. 201					ACCT. NO.	√	DEBIT AMOUNT	CREDIT AMOUNT
							141		770 00	

a special column has been provided for Miscellaneous Expense, the necessary debit can be quickly recorded there. The offsetting credit to Cash is ‚noted in the Cash Disbursed column.

January 31—*Paid salaries, $1,700, by Check 39.* The expense account is debited by using the special column entitled Salary Expense, and Cash is credited. The completed combined journal for January is shown below.

DAILY POSTINGS FROM THE COMBINED JOURNAL

The individual items in the Sundry columns must be posted to the indicated accounts as promptly as possible. In Carter's case, these items include three debits to Equipment 141, for $770, $1,000, and $600, and a debit to Rent

ACCOUNTS PAYABLE			CLEANING SERVICE INCOME CR. 401	SALARY EXPENSE DR. 511	SUPPLIES USED DR. 521	MISC. EXPENSE DR. 591	SUNDRY			
√	DR. 201	CR. 201					ACCT. NO.	√	DEBIT AMOUNT	CREDIT AMOUNT
							141	√	770 00	
			700 00							
			60 00							
√	300 00									
√		1,000 00					141	√	1,000 00	
			725 00							
			25 00							
					400 00					
							516	√	700 00	
			30 00							
			900 00							
√	500 00									
			800 00							
							141	√	600 00	
			60 00							
					300 00					
						60 00				
				1,700 00						
	800 00	1,000 00	3,300 00	1,700 00	700 00	60 00			3,070 00	

Expense 516, for $700. A separate Posting Check column is provided to note the posting of these entries to the ledger accounts.

Daily postings are also made to the accounts receivable and accounts payable subsidiary ledger accounts. After each debit or credit posting has been made, a check is placed in the column which is adjacent to the Accounts Receivable or the Accounts Payable amount column.

PROVING THE COMBINED JOURNAL

When the month's transactions have been entered, the next step is to total each column and verify or prove the equality of debits and credits before posting the column totals. The proof can be shown in a simple schedule like this.

ACCT. NO.	ACCOUNT NAME	DEBIT	CREDIT
101	Cash	$3,410	$5,330
111	Accounts Receivable	175	285
201	Accounts Payable	800	1,000
401	Cleaning Service Income		3,300
511	Salary Expense	1,700	
521	Supplies Used	700	
591	Miscellaneous Expense	60	
	Sundry	3,070	
	Totals	$9,915	$9,915

END-OF-PERIOD POSTINGS FROM THE COMBINED JOURNAL

When the proof of equality is completed, the column totals, except those for the Sundry Debit and Sundry Credit columns, are posted. A check mark is recorded beneath each column total as the posting is made to the account involved. An "X" is noted beneath the Sundry amount columns. Thus, for the Carter operations in January 19X2, the bulk of the posting is disposed of in 10 summary figures.

TYPICAL COMBINED JOURNAL APPLICATIONS

The combined journal is sometimes used in small businesses such as professional offices, service enterprises, and trading businesses.

Professional Offices

The combined journal may be ideal to record the transactions of a professional person, such as a doctor, lawyer, accountant, or architect. However, special journals are more efficient if the transactions become very numerous or are too varied.

Service Enterprises

The application of the combined journal to the January transactions of the Carter Cleaning Shop has already been studied. The combined journal might be advantageous for small service enterprises, such as Carter's, provided that the volume of transactions does not become excessive and provided also that the nature of the transactions does not become too involved.

Trading Businesses

The combined journal might be used by a trading enterprise, but only if the firm is relatively small and has a limited variety of transactions involving a very small number of accounts. In fact, even for a small trading business (such as the Carter Cleaning Shop after the Accessories Department was opened) the use of special journals may prove more advantageous than the use of the combined journal.

If the variety of transactions is so great that many different accounts are required, the combined journal will not work well. The accountant will either have to use so many columns that the journal will become unwieldy, or he will have to record so many transactions in the Sundry columns that little efficiency will result. As a general rule, if the transactions of a business are numerous enough to merit the use of special journals, any attempt to substitute the combined journal is a mistake, since each separate journal can be designed for maximum efficiency in recording.

◆ ◆ ◆

PRINCIPLES AND PROCEDURES

The combined journal unites the functions of the various special journals and the general journal into one book of original entry. In constructing a combined journal, the chart of accounts should be reviewed so that special columns may be set up for accounts that are expected to have numerous entries. Sundry columns are provided to take care of any transactions for which no special column has been established. Items recorded in the Sundry columns are posted daily. At the end of the month, the journal is totaled and the equality of debits and credits is proved. Then column totals are posted for all the special columns.

MANAGERIAL IMPLICATIONS

The combined journal is of special benefit to the small business owner or professional person. It enables him or her to easily keep track of the affairs of the business. Again, it is a time-saving and efficient recording device. However, if the volume of transactions is large and varied, the combined journal becomes unwieldy and does not allow for a division of labor.

APPLICATION OF PRINCIPLES

PROBLEM 13 · 1

Dr. William B. Henderson, upon returning from military service, reestablished his practice of medicine. Based upon his previous experience, he decided to use a simple accounting system consisting of a general ledger and a combined journal with special columns for Cash Received Dr. 101 and Cash Disbursed Cr. 101; Accounts Receivable, Dr. 111 and Cr. 111; Medical Practice Income Cr. 401; Salary Expense Dr. 511; Office Supplies Dr. 521; Medical Supplies Dr. 522; Automobile Expense Dr. 533; and Sundry Debit and Credit. A chart of accounts and the transactions for Henderson's first month of practice (April 19X1) are given below:

ASSETS
101 Cash
111 Accounts Receivable
141 Equipment
143 Automobile

LIABILITIES
201 Accounts Payable

OWNER'S EQUITY
301 Henderson Investment
399 Income and Expense Summary

INCOME
401 Medical Practice Income

EXPENSES
504 Telephone Expense
505 Utilities Expense
511 Salary Expense
516 Rent Expense
521 Office Supplies
522 Medical Supplies
533 Automobile Expense
591 Miscellaneous Expense

APR.

3 Dr. Henderson opened an account in the First National Bank by depositing $4,000 of his accumulated savings.

3 Signed a lease on a suite of offices in the Medical Arts Building and paid $200 for one month's rent in advance by Check 1.

3 Paid $575 for office and examining equipment by Check 2.

4 Paid $16.75 for office supplies by Check 3.

5 Paid $73.50 for medical supplies by Check 4.

7 Bought a new automobile for use in the practice, paying $1,000 by Check 5 and agreeing to pay the balance of $3,100 in 10 monthly installments of $310 each.

APR.

8   Issued Check 6 for $60 for the weekly salary of the receptionist.

8   Income from medical services during the first week amounted to $36 in cash and $144 in accounts receivable.

10   Paid for gasoline and oil for the automobile, $6.50, by Check 7.

10   Bought a new typewriter for $300, paying $150 by Check 8, and promising to make three monthly payments of $50 each. (Use only one line for entry.)

11   Paid $11.65 for medical supplies by Check 9.

14   Bought $7.75 worth of office supplies, paid by Check 10.

15   Paid weekly salary of the receptionist, $60, by Check 11.

15   During this week, received income from medical services amounting to $92 in cash and $263 in accounts receivable.

17   Paid an item of miscellaneous expense, $2.35, by Check 12.

19   Paid for office supplies, $4.95, by Check 13.

21   Paid $9.80 for gasoline and oil for automobile by Check 14.

22   Paid the $60 weekly salary of the receptionist by Check 15.

22   Received $45 in cash from patients to apply on accounts receivable.

22   Income from medical services amounted to $88 in cash and $352 in accounts receivable this week.

25   Paid utilities expense, $21.75, by Check 16.

26   Paid telephone expense for the month, $18.50, by Check 17.

27   Medical supplies amounting to $34.25 paid by Check 18.

28   Received checks totaling $66 to apply on accounts receivable.

29   Paid the receptionist's weekly salary, $60, by Check 19.

29   During this week, received $35 in cash and $190 in accounts receivable from medical services rendered.

INSTRUCTIONS

1.   Record each transaction in the combined journal.
2.   Foot, total, and rule the combined journal at the end of the month.
3.   Prove your work by preparing a simple proof schedule.

MANAGERIAL CHECKUPS

♦   Why is the combined journal of special benefit only to the small business-owner or professional person?

♦   How would a small businessowner, professional person, or accountant design a combined journal?

PART 3
END-OF-CYCLE PROCEDURES—
TRADING BUSINESS

14

DEPRECIATION, BAD DEBTS, AND MERCHANDISE INVENTORY

In the Integrated Practical Application following Unit 12, the transactions for the Carter Cleaning Shop in the month of February 19X2 were recorded and posted, and a trial balance was completed as a proof of accuracy of the debits and credits. Look once more at that trial balance; note again the changes in account titles and the account names that appeared at the end of this month's operations for the first time.

CARTER CLEANING SHOP
Trial Balance
February 28, 19X2

ACCT. NO.	ACCOUNT NAME	DEBIT	CREDIT
101	Cash	$ 786 00	
111	Accounts Receivable Control	142 00	
111A	Allowance for Bad Debts		
121	Merchandise Inventory		
141	Equipment	5,400 00	
141A	Allowance for Depreciation		
201	Accounts Payable Control		$ 950 00
301	Carter Investment		6,240 00
302	Carter Drawing	50 00	
401	Cleaning Service Income		3,782 00
402	Accessories Sales Income		987 00
451	Sales Returns and Allowances—Cleaning Service		
452	Sales Returns and Allowances—Accessories	22 00	
501	Merchandise Purchases	1,810 00	
509	Purchases Returns and Allowances		10 00
511	Salary Expense	1,950 00	
516	Rent Expense	700 00	
521	Supplies Used	934 00	
561	Bad Debts Expense		
564	Depreciation Expense		
591	Miscellaneous Expense	175 00	
	Totals	$11,969 00	$11,969 00

The word "Control" was added to Accounts Receivable 111 and Accounts Payable 201 because subsidiary ledgers were in operation. Certain new accounts warrant special attention. A new income account, Accessories Sales Income 402, reflects the revenue from the first month's activities of the new Accessories Department, and Sales Returns and Allowances—Accessories 452 reflects the returns and allowances for the new department. Merchandise Purchases 501 also appears for the first time. The $1,810 balance in this account represents the cost of the stock of merchandise bought for the new department. Similarly, the Purchases Returns and Allowances 509 account balance of $10 represents the cost of goods returned.

There are also several other less obvious elements that require the accountant's careful consideration after the trial balance is entered on the worksheet. For example, the trained eye quickly discerns that:

1. There is no recognition of any merchandise that remains unsold at the end of the period.
2. The asset Equipment is being carried at the original cost, without regard for the loss in useful life and value due to wear and tear during the month.
3. The balance of $142 in Accounts Receivable Control may include accounts that will not be paid.

Unless such missing elements are recognized and recorded at this time, the financial statements that are to be prepared will not present a complete and true picture of the financial condition of the business and of the profit or loss for the period. The most expedient solution is to give these matters special treatment on the worksheet.

DEPRECIATION EXPENSE

The account entitled Equipment 141 on the trial balance has a balance of $5,400, representing the original cost of the equipment purchased for use in the business. However, the accounting system must reflect the fact that equipment gradually wears out or must be discarded because it no longer serves the purpose intended. The accountant seeks to apportion the cost of the asset over its useful life by recording an expense, called *depreciation expense*, at the end of each period. This process is called *matching*, because the proportionate expense incurred during the period is matched or charged against the income of that period. The apportionment is accomplished by an *adjusting entry* at the end of each period. for example, if an asset costs $5,000 and will be completely worthless at the end of five years, it seems logical that $1,000 of its cost should be charged off as an expense each year. There are several ways of determining how much expense should be charged each period. But in this unit, only one simple and widely used procedure—that of charging to expense an equal amount each period, known as *straight-line depreciation*—will be presented. Other techniques are illustrated in Unit 24.

Schedule of Equipment

The first step in determining the amount of depreciation expense is to prepare a list of the equipment items. The cost, expected useful life, and estimated scrap or salvage value of each item must be known. Estimates of the useful life are based on the experiences of the individual business or of other businesses with similar items of equipment. By checking through the records, this *schedule of equipment* for the Carter Cleaning Shop can be developed.

CARTER CLEANING SHOP
Schedule of Equipment
February 28, 19X2

DATE PURCHASED	DESCRIPTION	COST	ESTIMATED USEFUL LIFE
19X1			
Nov. 27	Cleaning Equipment	$2,000	5 years
28	Counter, Desks, and Chairs	1,000	5 years
19X2			
Jan. 2	Cleaning Equipment	770	5 years
11	Delivery Truck	1,000	5 years
28	Counter and Display Fixtures	600 ⎫	5 years
Feb. 3	Freight on Counter and Display Fixtures	30 ⎭	
	Total per Ledger Account	$5,400	

Note that the useful life of each item is estimated as five years and that it is assumed that there will be no scrap value. In practice, equipment items would probably have different estimated lives, but the assumption of a uniform five-year life simplifies the discussion at this point. It is also assumed that the five-year life starts on February 1 for each item. (Depreciation has been deliberately ignored in previous periods to permit concentration on more urgent matters.) Keeping these assumptions in mind, let us figure out how much depreciation expense should be recorded for the month of February.

Determining Amount of Depreciation Expense

With the aid of the schedule of equipment, the estimated useful life of five years, and the expected salvage value, the depreciation expense for February can be determined by following this formula:

$$\frac{\text{Cost} - \text{Salvage Value}}{\text{Useful Life}} = \text{Depreciation Expense}$$

In using this formula, the useful life must be expressed in months. Five years = 60 months, so, in this case, the resulting depreciation expense for February is determined as follows: $\dfrac{\$5,400 - 0}{60} = \$90$

Recording Depreciation Expense

When Carter's accountant revised the chart of accounts as of February 1, 19X2, he also anticipated the need to record depreciation on the books. The amount of depreciation expense is debited to a new ledger account, Depreciation Expense 564. The offsetting credit is recorded in a new account called Allowance for Depreciation 141A. (An older title, "Reserve for Depreciation," is still is use, but in modern practice "Allowance for Depreciation" is generally preferred, although some accountants use the title "Accumulated Depreciation.") Depreciation expense is first recorded on the worksheet.

Worksheet Adjustment for Depreciation Expense

Having determined the amount of depreciation expense to be recorded, the accountant immediately enters the amount as a debit to Depreciation Expense 564 and a credit to Allowance for Depreciation 141A on the worksheet, in a new pair of columns entitled Adjustments, as shown in the illustration.

CARTER CLEANING SHOP
Worksheet (Partial)
Month Ended February 28, 19X2

ACCT. NO.	ACCOUNT NAME	TRIAL BALANCE		ADJUSTMENTS	
		DR.	CR.	DR.	CR.
101	Cash	786 00			
111	Accounts Receivable Control	142 00			
111A	Allowance for Bad Debts				
121	Merchandise Inventory				
141	Equipment	5,400 00			
141A	Allowance for Depreciation				(A)90 00
201	Accounts Payable Control		950 00		
301	Carter Investment		6,240 00		
302	Carter Drawing	50 00			
401	Cleaning Service Income		3,782 00		
402	Accessories Sales Income		987 00		
451	Sales Ret. & Allow.—Cleaning Serv.				
452	Sales Returns & Allow.—Accessories	22 00			
501	Merchandise Purchases	1,810 00			
509	Purchases Returns & Allow.		10 00		
511	Salary Expense	1,950 00			
516	Rent Expense	700 00			
521	Supplies Used	934 00			
561	Bad Debts Expense				
564	Depreciation Expense			(A)90 00	
591	Miscellaneous Expense	175 00			
	Totals	11,969 00	11,969 00		

Note that both figures are labeled (A) to help identify them for future reference, particularly when journalizing this adjustment later.

Recording the credit in the separate Allowance for Depreciation account permits the accountant to maintain intact a record of the original cost of the asset items in the Equipment 141 account. Account 141A then gives him a cumulative total of the amount of depreciation written off.

BAD DEBTS EXPENSE

A second element calling for attention at this time is the probability that Carter will ultimately be unable to collect some of the amounts owed to him by customers. Most business people who sell goods and services on credit find that there will be some *bad debts expense*. There are two procedures that the accountant might use for recognizing bad debts losses.

Recording a Loss When It Occurs

One procedure used by most small businesses is to wait until they are sure the account of a specific customer definitely is uncollectible and then record the expense. An entry is made debiting an expense account, usually called Bad Debts Expense 561, and crediting the asset accounts, Accounts Receivable Control 111 and the customer's account, for the amount to be charged off as a loss.

Providing for Loss Before it Occurs

Instead of waiting to record a loss until a particular account proves uncollectible, it is possible to anticipate bad debt losses and provide for them ahead of time. This method permits the seller to match the estimated bad debts expense against the sales income from which the account receivable resulted. It also allows the accountant to show the accounts receivable on the balance sheet at the amount that is probably collectible, rather than at the gross amount, even though it is not known which specific customers will not pay their accounts.

Although there are numerous methods for determining the amount of estimated credit losses for the period (discussed in Unit 22), Carter decides to base the estimate on a percentage of credit sales.

DETERMINING THE AMOUNT OF BAD DEBTS EXPENSE. The accountant for the Carter Cleaning Shop realizes that after the firm has been in business for several years and has had more experience with credit losses, it will be possible to estimate fairly accurately what percent of credit sales will be uncollectible. In the meantime, the accountant decides to rely upon data compiled by a trade association in estimating the bad debts. These figures show that for similar businesses, the bad debt losses average approximately 2.5% of *net credit sales* (sales on account less returns and allowances of sales made on account). The estimated bad debts expense for February is thus $3.30, as computed here. (Again, for the sake of simplicity and clarity, estimated bad debt losses from sales made prior to February are being ignored.)

Credit Sales for Month (from sales journal)	$144.00
Less Sales Returns and Allowances on Credit Sales	12.00
Net Credit Sales	$132.00
Estimated Percentage of Loss (2.5%)	x .025
Estimated Bad Debts on February Sales	$ 3.30

RECORDING BAD DEBTS EXPENSE. We find that the revised chart of accounts provides the new ledger accounts required to record the expense arising from bad debts. The amount for the month is debited to Bad Debts Expense 561. The offsetting credit is to Allowance for Bad Debts 111A. Bad Debts Expense is first recorded on the worksheet.

CARTER CLEANING SHOP
Worksheet (Partial)
Month Ended February 28, 19X2

ACCT. NO.	ACCOUNT NAME	TRIAL BALANCE		ADJUSTMENTS	
		DR.	CR.	DR.	CR.
101	Cash	786 00			
111	Accounts Receivable Control	142 00			
111A	Allowance for Bad Debts				(B) 3 30
121	Merchandise Inventory				
141	Equipment	5,400 00			
141A	Allowance for Depreciation				(A)90 00
201	Accounts Payable Control		950 00		
301	Carter Investment		6,240 00		
302	Carter Drawing	50 00			
401	Cleaning Service Income		3,782 00		
402	Accessories Sales Income		987 00		
451	Sales Ret. & Allow.—Cleaning Serv.				
452	Sales Returns & Allow.—Accessories	22 00			
501	Merchandise Purchases	1,810 00			
509	Purchases Returns & Allow.		10 00		
511	Salary Expense	1,950 00			
516	Rent Expense	700 00			
521	Supplies Used	934 00			
561	Bad Debts Expense			(B) 3 30	
564	Depreciation Expense			(A)90 00	
591	Miscellaneous Expense	175 00			
	Totals	11,969 00	11,969 00		

WORKSHEET ADJUSTMENT FOR BAD DEBTS EXPENSE. The amount of the adjustment, $3.30, is entered in the Adjustments section of the worksheet as a debit to Bad Debts Expense and a credit to Allowance for Bad Debts. Note that both figures are keyed (B) in the illustration on page 208 to facilitate the later preparation of the adjusting journal entries.

By recording the credit in the Allowance for Bad Debts account, which is called a *valuation account,* the balance of the Accounts Receivable Control account will show the gross amount owed by customers. It will then remain in balance with the subsidiary ledger. In turn, the balance of the Allowance for Bad Debts account indicates the estimated total of uncollectible debts. The effect of the debit entry is to charge the estimated loss against operations of the period.

CHARGING OFF WORTHLESS ACCOUNTS. Under the system of providing for bad debts before they occur, the Allowance for Bad Debts account is debited and Accounts Receivable Control and the customer's subsidiary account are credited when a particular account becomes uncollectible. Writing off a particular bad account does not affect the bad debts expense for the period because the expense was recorded when bad debt losses were estimated in the period of sale. (This procedure is examined more closely in Unit 22.)

THE ADJUSTED TRIAL BALANCE

The adjustments for depreciation and for bad debts expense are the only adjustments required for the Carter Cleaning Shop. Therefore, the figures in the Adjustments columns may now be added to verify the equality of debits and credits, as illustrated.

Next, another pair of columns, entitled "Adjusted Trial Balance," is set up immediately to the right of the Adjustments columns. The items in the original Trial Balance columns are combined with the items in the Adjustments columns and the results entered in the Adjusted Trial Balance section. Each column of the Adjusted Trial Balance section is added to prove the equality of debits and credits. Thus, the Adjusted Trial Balance section permits the accountant to verify that the debits and credits remain equal after the adjustments have been considered. (See page 210.)

MERCHANDISE ON HAND

Before proceeding to complete the worksheet, the accountant must recognize one other element. Some of the merchandise purchased has not been sold and is still on hand. With this in mind, he reasons as follows:

1. The value of the merchandise remaining unsold should be recorded as an asset called Merchandise Inventory 121.

CARTER CLEANING SHOP
Worksheet (Partial)
Month Ended February 28, 19X2

ACCT. NO.	ACCOUNT NAME	TRIAL BALANCE		ADJUSTMENTS		ADJUSTED TRIAL BALANCE	
		DR.	CR.	DR.	CR.	DR.	CR.
101	Cash	786 00				786 00	
111	Accounts Receivable Control	142 00				142 00	
111A	Allowance for Bad Debts				(B) 3 30		3 30
121	Merchandise Inventory						
141	Equipment	5,400 00				5,400 00	
141A	Allowance for Depreciation				(A)90 00		90 00
201	Accounts Payable Control		950 00				950 00
301	Carter Investment		6,240 00				6,240 00
302	Carter Drawing	50 00				50 00	
401	Cleaning Service Income		3,782 00				3,782 00
402	Accessories Sales Income		987 00				987 00
451	Sales Ret. & Allow.–Cl. Serv.						
452	Sales Returns & Allow.–Acc.	22 00				22 00	
501	Merchandise Purchases	1,810 00				1,810 00	
509	Purch. Returns & Allow.		10 00				10 00
511	Salary Expense	1,950 00				1,950 00	
516	Rent Expense	700 00				700 00	
521	Supplies Used	934 00				934 00	
561	Bad Debts Expense			(B) 3 30		3 30	
564	Depreciation Expense			(A)90 00		90 00	
591	Miscellaneous Expense	175 00				175 00	
	Totals	11,969 00	11,969 00	93 30	93 30	12,062 30	12,062 30

2. The operations of the period should be charged *only* with the cost of goods actually sold—not with the total cost of all merchandise purchased.

Taking an Inventory

The first step for the accountant is to find out how much merchandise remains unsold at this time. The process of checking and counting stock is called *taking an inventory*. A list, called the *inventory sheet,* is prepared. It shows the quantity and description of all items on hand. Later, the quantity is multiplied by the purchase cost of each item. Then these extended amounts are added together to determine the total cost of the stock remaining unsold.

Suppose a count made in the stockroom of the Accessories Department of the Carter Cleaning Shop reveals the inventory at the end of February as shown on the next page.

	CARTER CLEANING SHOP		
	Inventory Sheet		
	Accessories Department		
	February 28, 19X2		
QUANTITY	DESCRIPTION	UNIT COST	TOTAL
600 sets	Assorted hangers, 8 in set	$1.00	$ 600.00
35	Hat racks	2.00	70.00
38	Tie racks	2.50	95.00
20	Shoe racks	3.00	60.00
62	Shoeshine kits	2.25	139.50
18	3-suit garment bags, plastic	.75	13.50
40	2-suit garment bags, plastic	.40	16.00
10	Mothproofing spray bombs	.60	6.00
	Total inventory		$1,000.00
Counted by *J.S.*	Priced by *J.E.A.*		Checked by *C.V.F.*

Having determined the amount of the inventory, the accountant can quickly compute the *cost of goods sold.*

Total Merchandise Purchases (501)	$1,810
Less Purchases Returns and Allowances (509)	10
Net Purchases	$1,800
Less Cost of Goods Remaining (Inventory)	1,000
Cost of Goods Sold	$ 800

Entering Ending Inventory on Worksheet

The accountant records the inventory figure directly on the worksheet to avoid any delay in the preparation of the financial statements. He makes his entries in the Income Statement and Balance Sheet columns provided on the worksheets shown on pages 212 and 213.

MERCHANDISE ASSET. The value of the closing inventory is recorded as an asset on the Merchandise Inventory line in the Debit column of the Balance Sheet section. The $1,000 entry is marked (C) for identification. (Page 212.)

COST OF GOODS SOLD. The other half of the inventory entry is entered on the same line, as a credit in the Income Statement section and the letter (C) is again used for identification (page 213). The effect of this entry is more readily understood by extending the balances of Merchandise Purchases 501 and Purchases Returns and Allowances 509 to the Income Statement section at once.

Observe that the resulting combination of purchases and inventory

UNIT 14

CARTER CLEANING SHOP
Worksheet
Month Ended February 28, 19X2

ACCT. NO.	ACCOUNT NAME	TRIAL BALANCE DR.	TRIAL BALANCE CR.	ADJUSTMENTS DR.	ADJUSTMENTS CR.	ADJUSTED TRIAL BALANCE DR.	ADJUSTED TRIAL BALANCE CR.	INCOME STATEMENT DR.	INCOME STATEMENT CR.	BALANCE SHEET DR.	BALANCE SHEET CR.
101	Cash	786 00				786 00					
111	Accounts Rec. Control	142 00				142 00					
111A	Allow. for Bad Debts				(B) 3 30		3 30				
121	Merchandise Inventory									(C)1,000 00	
141	Equipment	5,400 00				5,400 00					
141A	Allow. for Depreciation				(A) 90 00		90 00				
201	Accts. Payable Control		950 00				950 00				
301	Carter Investment		6,240 00				6,240 00				
302	Carter Drawing	50 00				50 00					
401	Cleaning Serv. Income		3,782 00				3,782 00				
402	Acces. Sales Income		987 00				987 00				
451	Sales Ret. & Allow.—Cl. Serv.										
452	Sales Ret. & Allow.—Acces.	22 00				22 00					
501	Merchandise Purchases	1,810 00				1,810 00					
509	Purch. Ret. & Allow.		10 00				10 00				
511	Salary Expense	1,950 00				1,950 00					
516	Rent Expense	700 00				700 00					
521	Supplies Used	934 00				934 00					
561	Bad Debts Expense			(B) 3 30		3 30					
564	Depreciation Expense			(A) 90 00		90 00					
591	Miscellaneous Expense	175 00				175 00					
	Totals	11,969 00	11,969 00	93 30	93 30	12,062 30	12,062 30				

CARTER CLEANING SHOP
Worksheet
Month Ended February 28, 19X2

ACCT. NO.	ACCOUNT NAME	TRIAL BALANCE DR.	TRIAL BALANCE CR.	ADJUSTMENTS DR.	ADJUSTMENTS CR.	ADJUSTED TRIAL BALANCE DR.	ADJUSTED TRIAL BALANCE CR.	INCOME STATEMENT DR.	INCOME STATEMENT CR.	BALANCE SHEET DR.	BALANCE SHEET CR.
101	Cash	786 00				786 00					
111	Accounts Rec. Control	142 00				142 00					
111A	Allow. for Bad Debts				(B) 3 30		3 30				
121	Merchandise Inventory								(C)1,000 00	(C)1,000 00	
141	Equipment	5,400 00				5,400 00					
141A	Allow. for Depreciation				(A) 90 00		90 00				
201	Accts. Payable Control		950 00				950 00				
301	Carter Investment		6,240 00				6,240 00				
302	Carter Drawing	50 00				50 00					
401	Cleaning Serv. Income		3,782 00				3,782 00				
402	Acces. Sales Income		987 00				987 00				
451	Sales Ret. & Allow.—Cl. Serv.										
452	Sales Ret. & Allow.—Acces.	22 00				22 00					
501	Merchandise Purchases	1,810 00				1,810 00		1,810 00			
509	Purch. Ret. & Allow.		10 00				10 00		10 00		
511	Salary Expense	1,950 00				1,950 00					
516	Rent Expense	700 00				700 00					
521	Supplies Used	934 00				934 00					
561	Bad Debts Expense			(B) 3 30		3 30					
564	Depreciation Expense			(A) 90 00		90 00					
591	Miscellaneous Expense	175 00				175 00					
	Totals	11,969 00	11,969 00	93 30	93 30	12,062 30	12,062 30				

figures in the Income Statement section now reflects the cost of goods sold. Specifically, Merchandise Purchases of $1,810 in the Debit column is offset or reduced by credits for Purchases Returns and Allowances of $10, and for Merchandise Inventory of $1,000. Thus, we get the calculation: $1,810 − $10 − $1,000 = $800, which is the same figure as the cost of goods sold shown on page 211.

COMPLETING THE WORKSHEET

From this point on, the steps for completing the worksheet are as before:

1. Extend the remaining asset, liability, owner's equity, and owner's drawing account balances (Accounts 101-302) to the appropriate columns in the Balance Sheet section. Then extend the remaining income and expense account balances to the columns in the Income Statement section. Total the Income Statement and Balance Sheet section columns. (Page 215.)
2. Transfer the profit for February, the $94.70 credit balance in the Income Statement section, from the Income Statement section to the Balance Sheet section. (Page 216.)
3. Bring down final totals of the Income Statement and Balance Sheet section columns. Debits and credits should be equal for each pair of columns in the entire worksheet. (Page 217.)

♦ ♦ ♦

PRINCIPLES AND PROCEDURES

Before the financial statements can be prepared, the accountant must (1) determine the depreciation expense, (2) estimate the bad debts expense, and (3) take an inventory of the merchandise on hand.

A new pair of columns on the worksheet, entitled Adjustments, is used to record the end-of-period data about depreciation and bad debts. For example, depreciation expense is recorded by a debit to Depreciation Expense and a credit to Allowance for Depreciation. The same columns are used to record the bad debts expense by a debit to Bad Debts Expense and a credit to Allowance for Bad Debts. The items in the Trial Balance columns of the worksheet are combined with those in the Adjustments columns and extended to the Adjusted Trial Balance columns.

The ending inventory is determined by counting and pricing the inventory on hand. The total amount is entered in the Credit column of the Income Statement section of the worksheet and in the Debit column of the Balance Sheet section. The balance of Merchandise Purchases is extended to the Debit column of the Income Statement section. The balance of Purchases Returns and Allowances is extended to the Credit column of the same section. The remainder of the worksheet procedure is the same as before.

CARTER CLEANING SHOP
Worksheet
Month Ended February 28, 19X2

ACCT. NO.	ACCOUNT NAME	TRIAL BALANCE DR.	TRIAL BALANCE CR.	ADJUSTMENTS DR.	ADJUSTMENTS CR.	ADJUSTED TRIAL BALANCE DR.	ADJUSTED TRIAL BALANCE CR.	INCOME STATEMENT DR.	INCOME STATEMENT CR.	BALANCE SHEET DR.	BALANCE SHEET CR.
101	Cash	786 00				786 00				786 00	
111	Accounts Rec. Control	142 00				142 00				142 00	
111A	Allow. for Bad Debts				(B) 3 30		3 30				3 30
121	Merchandise Inventory								(C)1,000 00	(C)1,000 00	
141	Equipment	5,400 00				5,400 00				5,400 00	
141A	Allow. for Depreciation				(A) 90 00		90 00				90 00
201	Accts. Payable Control		950 00				950 00				950 00
301	Carter Investment		6,240 00				6,240 00				6,240 00
302	Carter Drawing	50 00				50 00				50 00	
401	Cleaning Serv. Income		3,782 00				3,782 00		3,782 00		
402	Acces. Sales Income		987 00				987 00		987 00		
451	Sales Ret. & Allow.– Cl. Serv.										
452	Sales Ret. & All.–Acces.	22 00				22 00		22 00			
501	Merchandise Purchases	1,810 00				1,810 00		1,810 00			
509	Purch. Ret. & Allow.		10 00				10 00		10 00		
511	Salary Expense	1,950 00				1,950 00		1,950 00			
516	Rent Expense	700 00				700 00		700 00			
521	Supplies Used	934 00				934 00		934 00			
561	Bad Debts Expense			(B) 3 30		3 30		3 30			
564	Depreciation Expense			(A) 90 00		90 00		90 00			
591	Miscellaneous Expense	175 00				175 00		175 00			
	Totals	11,969 00	11,969 00	93 30	93 30	12,062 30	12,062 30	5,684 30	5,779 00	7,378 00	7,283 30

CARTER CLEANING SHOP
Worksheet
Month Ended February 28, 19X2

ACCT. NO.	ACCOUNT NAME	TRIAL BALANCE DR.	TRIAL BALANCE CR.	ADJUSTMENTS DR.	ADJUSTMENTS CR.	ADJUSTED TRIAL BALANCE DR.	ADJUSTED TRIAL BALANCE CR.	INCOME STATEMENT DR.	INCOME STATEMENT CR.	BALANCE SHEET DR.	BALANCE SHEET CR.
101	Cash	786 00				786 00				786 00	
111	Accounts Rec. Control	142 00				142 00				142 00	
111A	Allow. for Bad Debts				(B) 3 30		3 30				3 30
121	Merchandise Inventory								(C)1,000 00	(C)1,000 00	
141	Equipment	5,400 00				5,400 00				5,400 00	
141A	Allow. for Depreciation				(A) 90 00		90 00				90 00
201	Accts. Payable Control		950 00				950 00				950 00
301	Carter Investment		6,240 00				6,240 00				6,240 00
302	Carter Drawing	50 00				50 00				50 00	
401	Cleaning Serv. Income		3,782 00				3,782 00		3,782 00		
402	Acces. Sales Income		987 00				987 00		987 00		
451	Sales Ret. & Allow.– Cl. Serv.										
452	Sales Ret. & All.–Acces.	22 00				22 00		22 00			
501	Merchandise Purchases	1,810 00				1,810 00		1,810 00			
509	Purch. Ret. & Allow.		10 00				10 00		10 00		
511	Salary Expense	1,950 00				1,950 00		1,950 00			
516	Rent Expense	700 00				700 00		700 00			
521	Supplies Used	934 00				934 00		934 00			
561	Bad Debts Expense			(B) 3 30		3 30		3 30			
564	Depreciation Expense			(A) 90 00		90 00		90 00			
591	Miscellaneous Expense	175 00				175 00		175 00			
	Totals	11,969 00	11,969 00	93 30	93 30	12,062 30	12,062 30	5,684 30	5,779 00	7,378 00	7,283 30
	Net Profit for the Month							94 70			94 70
								5,779 00	5,779 00	7,378 00	7,378 00

CARTER CLEANING SHOP
Worksheet
Month Ended February 28, 19X2

ACCT. NO.	ACCOUNT NAME	TRIAL BALANCE DR.	TRIAL BALANCE CR.	ADJUSTMENTS DR.	ADJUSTMENTS CR.	ADJUSTED TRIAL BALANCE DR.	ADJUSTED TRIAL BALANCE CR.	INCOME STATEMENT DR.	INCOME STATEMENT CR.	BALANCE SHEET DR.	BALANCE SHEET CR.
101	Cash	786 00				786 00				786 00	
111	Accounts Rec. Control	142 00				142 00				142 00	
111A	Allow. for Bad Debts				(B) 3 30		3 30				3 30
121	Merchandise Inventory								(C)1,000 00	(C)1,000 00	
141	Equipment	5,400 00				5,400 00				5,400 00	
141A	Allow. for Depreciation				(A) 90 00		90 00				90 00
201	Accts. Payable Control		950 00				950 00				950 00
301	Carter Investment		6,240 00				6,240 00				6,240 00
302	Carter Drawing	50 00				50 00				50 00	
401	Cleaning Serv. Income		3,782 00				3,782 00		3,782 00		
402	Acces. Sales Income		987 00				987 00		987 00		
451	Sales Ret. & Allow.—Cl. Serv.										
452	Sales Ret. & All.—Acces.	22 00				22 00		22 00			
501	Merchandise Purchases	1,810 00				1,810 00		1,810 00			
509	Purch. Ret. & Allow.		10 00				10 00		10 00		
511	Salary Expense	1,950 00				1,950 00		1,950 00			
516	Rent Expense	700 00				700 00		700 00			
521	Supplies Used	934 00				934 00		934 00			
561	Bad Debts Expense			(B) 3 30		3 30		3 30			
564	Depreciation Expense			(A) 90 00		90 00		90 00			
591	Miscellaneous Expense	175 00				175 00		175 00			
	Totals	11,969 00	11,969 00	93 30	93 30	12,062 30	12,062 30	5,684 30	5,779 00	7,378 00	7,283 30
	Net Profit for the Month							94 70			94 70
								5,779 00	5,779 00	7,378 00	7,378 00

MANAGERIAL IMPLICATIONS

In measuring profit for the period, management must consider the effects of the decrease in the value of equipment, of possible uncollectible accounts, and of the ending merchandise inventory. Matching expenses against revenues of the period is conservative accounting practice. The adjustments are also reflected on the balance sheet where they help to present the most accurate picture of the current position. Recording these data on the worksheet helps the accountant to prepare complete financial statements as quickly as possible. The sooner reliable results are known, the quicker management can make decisions and formulate new plans.

APPLICATION OF PRINCIPLES

PROBLEM 14 · 1

During the fiscal year ended March 31, 19X1, the Northland Trading Company purchased $39,462.50 of merchandise for resale. Purchases returns and allowances for the period were $787.50. The actual inventory of goods on hand unsold at March 31, 19X1 amounted to $6,975.

INSTRUCTIONS
Compute the cost of goods sold for the fiscal year ended March 31, 19X1.

PROBLEM 14 · 2

During the month of April 19X1, the Northland Trading Company sold $3,850 of merchandise, of which $1,142.60 was cash sales. Sales returns and allowances of $157.40 related to credit transactions. The company's experience indicates that 2% of net credit sales will not be collected.

INSTRUCTIONS
Compute the estimated bad debt losses to be anticipated on April sales.

PROBLEM 14 · 3

The Bowen Box Company uses a standard worksheet to record operations at June 30, 19X8. The company began operations on June 1, 19X8.
All of the equipment represented in Account 141 was purchased on June 1 and is estimated to have a useful life of 10 years. Included in the Box Sales Income 401 account is $459.55 of cash sales. Mr. Bowen estimates that 3% of net credit sales will not be collected. All sales returns and allowances relate to credit transactions. The trial balance information is as follows:

ACCT. NO.	ACCOUNT NAME	DEBIT	CREDIT
101	Cash	$ 1,977.50	
111	Accounts Receivable Control	2,944.25	
111A	Allowance for Bad Debts		$ –0–
121	Merchandise Inventory	–0–	
141	Equipment	6,672.25	
141A	Allowance for Depreciation		–0–
201	Accounts Payable Control		3,115.60
301	Bowen Investment		11,960.35
302	Bowen Drawing	100.00	
401	Box Sales Income		4,909.55
451	Sales Returns & Allow.	200.00	
501	Merchandise Purchases	6,779.98	
509	Purchases Returns & Allow.		389.53
511	Salary Expense	725.00	
516	Rent Expense	600.00	
521	Supplies Used	256.70	
561	Bad Debts Expense	–0–	
564	Depreciation Expense	–0–	
591	Miscellaneous Expense	119.35	
	Totals	$20,375.03	$20,375.03

INSTRUCTIONS

1. Enter the trial balance at June 30, 19X8 in a 10-column worksheet.
2. Insert all other column headings in the worksheet. (Use illustration on page 217 as a guide.)
3. Compute the depreciation expense for the month of June, enter it on the worksheet, and identify by the letter (A). Show your computations.
4. Compute the bad debts expense for the month of June, enter it on the worksheet, and identify by the letter (B). Show your computations.
5. Foot, prove, and total the Adjustments columns.
6. Complete the extension of figures into the Adjusted Trial Balance columns; then foot, prove, and total them.
7. Enter Merchandise Inventory of $4,864.30 at June 30, 19X8, and identify by (C).
8. Extend the Adjusted Trial Balance amounts to the appropriate columns and foot.
9. Compute and enter the profit for the period.
10. Bring down final totals of all remaining columns, prove, and then rule all columns.

MANAGERIAL CHECKUPS

♦ How is the measurement of results of the period affected by the application of the matching principle of accounting?

♦ Which of the two procedures for recognizing bad debt losses would be regarded as the probable choice of a conservative management? Explain.

♦ If the useful life of a valuable asset is considerably overestimated, what is the effect of the mistake on the firm's financial statements?

STATEMENTS AND CLOSING ENTRIES FOR A TRADING BUSINESS

When the Carter Cleaning Shop opened its Accessories Department, it changed from a purely service type of business to a service-trading type of enterprise. A trading business is one that buys and sells merchandise in the regular course of operations. So the Carter shop now sells both service and merchandise. The new trading aspect of the business requires certain minor adjustments in the form of the periodic statements.

INCOME STATEMENT

At the end of January 19X2, Carter's income statement looked like this.

CARTER CLEANING SHOP
Income Statement
Month Ended January 31, 19X2

Income		
Cleaning Service		$3,300
Less Operating Expenses		
Salary Expense	$1,700	
Rent Expense	700	
Supplies Used	700	
Miscellaneous Expense	60	
Total Operating Expenses		3,160
Net Profit for the Month		$ 140

Of course Carter wishes to know how much income is being earned from each type of operation. So, beginning with the February statement, the Income section in the illustration shows income from two sources—Cleaning Service (services) and Accessories Sales (goods).

Note that the Cleaning Service Income of $3,782 is handled as before. However, the Accessories Sales figure of $987 is reduced by the Sales Returns and Allowances—Accessories balance of $22, to arrive at the Net Accessories

CARTER CLEANING SHOP
Income Statement
Month Ended February 28, 19X2

Income			
Cleaning Service			$3,782.00
Gross Profit on Accessories Sales			
Accessories Sales		$ 987.00	
Less Sales Returns and Allowances		22.00	
Net Accessories Sales		$ 965.00	
Less Cost of Goods Sold			
Inventory, February 1, 19X2		$ –0–	
Purchases During Period	$1,810.00		
Less Returns and Allowances	10.00		
Net Purchases		1,800.00	
Total Merchandise Available for Sale		$1,800.00	
Less Inventory, February 28, 19X2		1,000.00	
Cost of Goods Sold		800.00	
Gross Profit on Accessories Sales			165.00
Total Gross Profit on Sales			$3,947.00
Less Operating Expenses			
Salary Expense		$1,950.00	
Rent Expense		700.00	
Supplies Used		934.00	
Bad Debts Expense		3.30	
Depreciation Expense		90.00	
Miscellaneous Expense		175.00	
Total Operating Expenses			3,852.30
Net Profit for the Month			$ 94.70

Sales of $965. From this figure is deducted the Cost of Goods Sold ($800) in the determination of the Gross Profit on Accessories Sales of $165. This figure is then added to Cleaning Service Income to arrive at Total Gross Profit on Sales. Next, the various other costs of doing business are subtracted from the Total Gross Profit on Sales in order to arrive at the amount of the Net Profit for the Month.

THE BALANCE SHEET

There are four new elements on the balance sheet for February 28, 19X2. The first new item is the Allowance for Bad Debts, which is subtracted from the Accounts Receivable Control to arrive at the estimated collectible accounts of $138.70. The second is a new asset, Merchandise Inventory; the amount shown for this asset is the result of an inventory taken at the close of business on the last day of the period. The third item is the Allowance for Depreciation, which is subtracted from the related asset, Equipment. These items are shown on the asset side of the balance sheet (page 222).

On the other side of the balance sheet, the fourth item, the owner's drawing account, is subtracted from the profit for February in the Owner's Equity section, to arrive at the net increase in owner's investment during the period.

CARTER CLEANING SHOP
Balance Sheet
February 28, 19X2

ASSETS			LIABILITIES AND OWNER'S EQUITY		
Cash		$ 786.00	*Liabilities*		
Accounts Receivable			Accounts Payable		
Control	$ 142.00		Control		$ 950.00
Less Allowance for					
Bad Debts	3.30	138.70	*Owner's Equity*		
Merchandise Inventory		1,000.00	Carter Investment,		
Equipment	$5,400.00		Feb. 1, 19X2		$6,240.00
Less Allowance for			Profit for February $ 94.70		
Depreciation	90.00	5,310.00	Less Withdrawals 50.00		44.70
			Carter Investment,		
			Feb. 28, 19X2		6,284.70
			Total Liabilities and		
Total Assets		$7,234.70	Owner's Equity		$7,234.70

ADJUSTING ENTRIES

After the periodic statements have been prepared from the worksheet, the accountant turns to the task of making a permanent record of the end-of-period adjustments so that the ledger accounts will agree with the worksheet and the financial statements. The account titles and amounts needed to journalize the adjustments are taken directly from the Adjustments column of the completed worksheet illustrated on page 217. The first adjustment is to record the estimated depreciation expense, $90, for the month. (Note that the letter "A" is placed beside the number of each adjusting entry to identify the item as an adjustment.)

19 X2		2–4A			
Feb. 28	Depreciation Expense	564	90 00		
	Allowance for Depreciation . .	141A		90 00	
	To record depreciation of equipment for February.				

The second adjusting entry records the estimated $3.30 of bad debts from February sales on account.

19 X2		2–5A			
Feb. 28	Bad Debts Expense	561	3 30		
	Allowance for Bad Debts	111A		3 30	
	To record provision for estimated bad debts on credit sales of February.				

The adjustments are then posted to the general ledger accounts affected.

Depreciation Expense   No. 564

DATE	EXPLANATION	POST. REF.	DEBIT	DATE	EXPLANATION	POST. REF.	CREDIT
19 X2 Feb. 28		2-4A	90 00				

Allowance for Depreciation   No. 141A

DATE	EXPLANATION	POST. REF.	DEBIT	DATE	EXPLANATION	POST. REF.	CREDIT
				19 X2 Feb. 28		2-4A	90 00

Bad Debts Expense   No. 561

DATE	EXPLANATION	POST. REF.	DEBIT	DATE	EXPLANATION	POST. REF.	CREDIT
19 X2 Feb. 28		2-5A	3 30				

Allowance for Bad Debts   No. 111A

DATE	EXPLANATION	POST. REF.	DEBIT	DATE	EXPLANATION	POST. REF.	CREDIT
				19 X2 Feb. 28		2-5A	3 30

After the adjusting entries have been posted to the ledger accounts, the accounts will reflect the same balances as shown in the Adjusted Trial Balance columns of the worksheet on page 217.

CLOSING ENTRIES

With the adjustments now recorded on the books, the accountant is ready to begin the closing process. The procedure is very nearly the same as that used in December and January.

1. Transfer the balances that appear in the Credit column of the Income Statement section of the worksheet, including the ending merchandise

inventory, to the Income and Expense Summary account by journalizing and posting the following general journal entry. (The letter "C" after the entry number identifies it as a closing transaction.)

CARTER CLEANING SHOP
Worksheet
Month Ended February 28, 19X2

ACCT. NO.	ACCOUNT NAME	INCOME STATEMENT		BALANCE SHEET	
		DR.	CR.	DR.	CR.
101	Cash			786 00	
111	Accounts Receivable Control			142 00	
111A	Allowance for Bad Debts				3 30
121	Merchandise Inventory		(C)1,000 00	(C)1,000 00	
141	Equipment			5,400 00	
141A	Allowance for Depreciation				90 00
201	Accounts Payable Control				950 00
301	Carter Investment				6,240 00
302	Carter Drawing			50 00	
401	Cleaning Service Income		3,782 00		
402	Accessories Sales Income		987 00		
451	Sales Ret. & Allow.–Cl. Serv.				
452	Sales Returns & Allow.–Acces.	22 00			
501	Merchandise Purchases	1,810 00			
509	Purchases Returns & Allow.		10 00		
511	Salary Expense	1,950 00			
516	Rent Expense	700 00			
521	Supplies Used	934 00			
561	Bad Debts Expense	3 30			
564	Depreciation Expense	90 00			
591	Miscellaneous Expense	175 00			
	Totals	5,684 30	5,779 00	7,378 00	7,283 30
	Net Profit for the Month	94 70			94 70
		5,779 00	5,779 00	7,378 00	7,378 00

19 X2		2–6C					
Feb. 28	Merchandise Inventory	121	✓	1,000 00		
	Cleaning Service Income	401	✓	3,782 00		
	Accessories Sales Income	402	✓	987 00		
	Purchases Returns & Allowances .	509	✓	10 00		
	Income and Expense Summary . .	399	✓		5,779 00
	To record ending inventory and transfer income and other credit items to the summary account.				

2. Transfer balances that appear in the Debit column of the Income Statement section to the Income and Expense Summary by recording and posting the following general journal entry.

19	X2	2-7C						
Feb.	28	Income and Expense Summary	399	✓	5,684	30		
		Sales Returns & Allow.–Acces. . .	452	✓			22	00
		Merchandise Purchases	501	✓			1,810	00
		Salary Expense	511	✓			1,950	00
		Rent Expense	516	✓			700	00
		Supplies Used	521	✓			934	00
		Bad Debts Expense	561	✓			3	30
		Depreciation Expense	564	✓			90	00
		Miscellaneous Expense	591	✓			175	00
		To transfer expense account balances and other debit items to the summary account.						

3. After posting the closing entries to the general ledger, the accounts affected appear as follows.

Merchandise Inventory   **No. 121**

DATE		EXPLANATION	POST. REF.	DEBIT		DATE		EXPLANATION	POST. REF.	CREDIT	
19 Feb.	X2 28		2-6C	1,000	00						

Income and Expense Summary   **No. 399**

DATE		EXPLANATION	POST. REF.	DEBIT		DATE		EXPLANATION	POST. REF.	CREDIT	
19 Feb.	X2 28		2-7C	5,684	30	19 Feb.	X2 28	*94.70*	2-6C	5,779	00

Cleaning Service Income   **No. 401**

DATE		EXPLANATION	POST. REF.	DEBIT		DATE		EXPLANATION	POST. REF.	CREDIT	
19 Feb.	X2 28		2-6C	3,782	00	19 Feb.	X2 28 28		CRJ-2 SJ-2	3,725 57 *3,782*	00 00 *00*

Accessories Sales Income   **No. 402**

DATE		EXPLANATION	POST. REF.	DEBIT		DATE		EXPLANATION	POST. REF.	CREDIT	
19 Feb.	X2 28		2-6C	987	00	19 Feb.	X2 28 28		CRJ-2 SJ-2	900 87 *987*	00 00 *00*

Sales Returns and Allowances—Accessories   No. 452

DATE		EXPLANATION	POST. REF.	DEBIT		DATE		EXPLANATION	POST. REF.	CREDIT	
19	X2					19	X2				
Feb.	5		2-1	10	00	Feb.	28		2-7C	22	00
	28		2-13	2	00						
	28		CDJ-2	10	00						
				22	00						

Merchandise Purchases   No. 501

DATE		EXPLANATION	POST. REF.	DEBIT		DATE		EXPLANATION	POST. REF.	CREDIT	
19	X2					19	X2				
Feb.	28		PJ-1	1,810	00	Feb.	28		2-7C	1,810	00

Purchases Returns and Allowances   No. 509

DATE		EXPLANATION	POST. REF.	DEBIT		DATE		EXPLANATION	POST. REF.	CREDIT	
19	X2					19	X2				
Feb.	28		2-6C	10	00	Feb.	27		2-2	10	00

Salary Expense   No. 511

DATE		EXPLANATION	POST. REF.	DEBIT		DATE		EXPLANATION	POST. REF.	CREDIT	
19	X2					19	X2				
Feb.	28		CDJ-2	1,950	00	Feb.	28		2-7C	1,950	00

Rent Expense   No. 516

DATE		EXPLANATION	POST. REF.	DEBIT		DATE		EXPLANATION	POST. REF.	CREDIT	
19	X2					19	X2				
Feb.	16		CDJ-2	700	00	Feb.	28		2-7C	700	00

Supplies Used   No. 521

DATE		EXPLANATION	POST. REF.	DEBIT		DATE		EXPLANATION	POST. REF.	CREDIT	
19	X2					19	X2				
Feb.	8		CDJ-2	250	00	Feb.	28		2-7C	934	00
	13		CDJ-2	124	00						
	21		CDJ-2	160	00						
	27		CDJ-2	400	00						
				934	00						

Bad Debts Expense No. 561

DATE	EXPLANATION	POST. REF.	DEBIT		DATE	EXPLANATION	POST. REF.	CREDIT	
19 X2 Feb. 28		2-5A	3	30	19 X2 Feb. 28		2-7C	3	30

Depreciation Expense No. 564

DATE	EXPLANATION	POST. REF.	DEBIT		DATE	EXPLANATION	POST. REF.	CREDIT	
19 X2 Feb. 28		2-4A	90	00	19 X2 Feb. 28		2-7C	90	00

Miscellaneous Expense No. 591

DATE	EXPLANATION	POST. REF.	DEBIT		DATE	EXPLANATION	POST. REF.	CREDIT	
19 X2 Feb. 2		CDJ-2	60	00	19 X2 Feb. 28		2-7C	175	00
14		CDJ-2	75	00					
22		CDJ-2	40	00					
			175	*00*					

4. The next step is to transfer the profit (or loss) to the owner's drawing account. In January, when a drawing account was not used, the profit or loss was closed directly from the Income and Expense Summary account to the Carter Investment account. However, when a drawing account is used, it is customary to close the Income and Expense Summary account to the drawing account. (Then, as you will see shortly, the drawing account is closed to the owner's investment account.) The journal entry necessary to close the profit to the Carter Drawing account is shown.

19 X2 Feb. 28	2–8C				
	Income and Expense Summary	399	94	70	
	Carter Drawing	302			94 70
	To close Income and Expense Summary by transferring profit for period to the drawing account.				

After this entry has been posted, the Income and Expense Summary account and the Carter Drawing account will appear as follows.

Income and Expense Summary No. 399

DATE		EXPLANATION	POST. REF.	DEBIT		DATE		EXPLANATION	POST. REF.	CREDIT	
19	X2					19	X2				
Feb.	28		2-7C	5,684	30	Feb.	28		2-6C	5,779	00
	28		2-8C	94	70						
				5,779	*00*						

Carter Drawing No. 302

DATE		EXPLANATION	POST. REF.	DEBIT		DATE		EXPLANATION	POST. REF.	CREDIT	
19	X2					19	X2				
Feb.	28		CDJ-2	50	00	Feb.	28		2-8C	94	70
								44.70			

By this procedure, the Carter Drawing account balance reflects the net increase of $44.70 in the owner's equity for the period (a profit of $94.70 minus the withdrawal of $50), as shown in the February 28 balance sheet on page 222.

5. The final step is to transfer the balance of the Carter Drawing account, reflecting the net increase (or decrease) in owner's equity during the period, to the Carter Investment account. The journal entry to accomplish this is shown.

19	X2		2–9C				
Feb.	28	Carter Drawing	302	44	70		
		Carter Investment	301			44	70
		To close drawing into investment account.					

After this entry is posted, the Carter Drawing account and the Carter Investment account will appear as follows.

Carter Drawing No. 302

DATE		EXPLANATION	POST. REF.	DEBIT		DATE		EXPLANATION	POST. REF.	CREDIT	
19	X2					19	X2				
Feb.	28		CDJ-2	50	00	Feb.	28		2-8C	94	70
	28		2-9C	44	70			*44.70*			
				94	*70*						

DATE		EXPLANATION	POST. REF.	DEBIT		DATE		EXPLANATION	POST. REF.	CREDIT	
19	X1					19	X1				
Dec.	31	Carried Fwd.	✓	6,100	00	Nov.	26		11-1	6,000	00
						Dec.	31		12-9C	100	00
										6,100	*00*
				6,100	00					6,100	00
19	X2					19	X2				
Jan.	31	Carried Fwd.	✓	6,240	00	Jan.	1	Brought Fwd.	✓	6,100	00
							31		1-25C	140	00
										6,240	*00*
				6,240	00					6,240	00
						Feb.	1	Brought Fwd.	✓	6,240	00
							28		2-9C	44	70
										6,284	*70*

BALANCING AND RULING THE LEDGER

After the closing entries have been posted, the accounts must be balanced and ruled to separate the February transactions from those of the next month. The ruling procedure for the books of a trading business is the same as the procedure you have used several times for the service business, so it is not illustrated again here.

POSTCLOSING TRIAL BALANCE

Finally, the accountant prepares the postclosing trial balance at the end of February.

CARTER CLEANING SHOP
Postclosing Trial Balance
February 28, 19X2

ACCT. NO.	ACCOUNT NAME	DEBIT		CREDIT	
101	Cash	$ 786	00		
111	Accounts Receivable Control	142	00		
111A	Allowance for Bad Debts			$ 3	30
121	Merchandise Inventory	1,000	00		
141	Equipment	5,400	00		
141A	Allowance for Depreciation			90	00
201	Accounts Payable Control			950	00
301	Carter Investment			6,284	70
	Totals	$7,328	00	$7,328	00

The ending inventory of $1,000 on February 28, 19X2 becomes the beginning inventory for the new period commencing on March 1. This beginning inventory will also become part of the cost of goods sold during March because it is assumed that the stock in trade carried over from the previous period will be the first consumed or sold in the new period. The treatment of beginning inventory on the worksheet is simple and direct. As a part of the cost of goods sold and, in effect, an expense, the inventory figure is extended to the Debit columns of the Adjusted Trial Balance and Income Statement sections of the worksheet as any other routine expense item. The technique is illustrated in a partial worksheet dated March 31, 19X2, shown on page 231. To complete the inventory data, the March 31 inventory of $1,100, Merchandise Purchases, and Purchases Returns and Allowances figures are also extended, as you learned in Unit 14.

The combination of purchases, returns and allowances, and inventory figures assembled in the Income Statement section reflects the cost of goods sold for March. The effect becomes readily apparent when these data are arranged in the format used in the Cost of Goods Sold section of Carter's income statement for the month ended March 31, 19X2.

Less Cost of Goods Sold		
Inventory, March 1, 19X2		$1,000
Purchases During Period	$1,305	
Less Returns and Allowances	22	
Net Purchases		1,283
Total Merchandise Available for Sale		$2,283
Less Inventory, March 31, 19X2		1,100
Cost of Goods Sold		$1,183

The ending inventory on March 31 is deducted from the Total Merchandise Available for Sale to arrive at the Cost of Goods Sold. Hence, the ending inventory is entered in the Credit column of the Income Statement section as a reduction of the expenses (debits) of the period. The ending inventory also represents an asset on hand on March 31 and must appear on the March 31 Balance Sheet. Therefore, it is entered in the Debit column of the Balance Sheet section of the worksheet.

When the closing entries for March are prepared from the worksheet, the ending inventory is recorded in the usual way along with the other items in the Credit column of the Income Statement section. Next, the total of the Debit column of the Income Statement section is journalized in the usual way as a debit to Income and Expense Summary. This time, however, the total will include the $1,000 beginning inventory figure that has been extended to the Debit column. A credit entry of $1,000 will be made to the Merchandise Inventory account to indicate that this amount has been consumed as part of the cost of goods sold during March.

CARTER CLEANING SHOP
Worksheet
Month Ended March 31, 19X2

ACCT. NO.	ACCOUNT NAME	TRIAL BALANCE DR.	TRIAL BALANCE CR.	ADJUSTMENTS DR.	ADJUSTMENTS CR.	ADJUSTED TRIAL BALANCE DR.	ADJUSTED TRIAL BALANCE CR.	INCOME STATEMENT DR.	INCOME STATEMENT CR.	BALANCE SHEET DR.	BALANCE SHEET CR.
101	Cash	1,839 00									
111	Accounts Rec. Control	492 00									
111A	Allow. for Bad Debts		1 30								
121	Merchandise Inventory	1,000 00				1,000 00		1,000 00	(C)1,100 00	(C)1,100 00	
501	Merchandise Purchases	1,305 00				1,305 00		1,305 00			
509	Purch. Ret. & Allow.		22 00				22 00		22 00		

19	X2	3–6C							
Mar.	31	Merchandise Inventory	121	✓	1,100	00			
		Cleaning Service Income	401	✓	5,455	00			
		Accessories Sales Income	402	✓	1,620	00			
		Purchases Returns & Allowances . .	509	✓	22	00			
		Income and Expense Summary . .	399	✓			8,197	00	
		To close the income accounts and to							
		record the ending inventory.							
		3–7C							
	31	Income and Expense Summary	399	✓	7,976	50			
		Merchandise Inventory	121	✓			1,000	00	
		Sales Returns & Allow.–Accessories .	452	✓			25	00	
		Merchandise Purchases	501	✓			1,305	00	
		Salary Expense	511	✓			3,000	00	
		Rent Expense	516	✓			700	00	
		Supplies Used	521	✓			1,495	00	
		Bad Debts Expense	561	✓			11	50	
		Depreciation Expense	564	✓			90	00	
		Miscellaneous Expense	591	✓			350	00	
		To close the expense accounts and the							
		beginning inventory.							

Merchandise Inventory   **No. 121**

DATE		EXPLANATION	POST. REF.	DEBIT		DATE		EXPLANATION	POST. REF.	CREDIT	
19	X2					19	X2				
Feb.	28		2-6C	1,000	00	Mar.	31		3-7C	1,000	00
Mar.	31		3-6C	1,100	00		31	Carried Fwd.	✓	1,100	00
				2,100	00					2,100	00
				2,100	00					2,100	00
Apr.	1	Brought Fwd.	✓	1,100	00						

There are various methods for handling the inventory in the worksheet and in the adjusting and closing entries. However, the method illustrated above is preferred because it permits the accountant to prepare the adjusting and closing entries directly from the worksheet, using the figures exactly as they are. Most other methods require that alterations be made to the amounts shown on the worksheet before the adjusting or closing entries can be prepared.

◆ ◆ ◆

PRINCIPLES AND PROCEDURES

The income statement for a trading concern indicates the sources and amounts of income and then presents the costs of doing business under two main headings: Cost of Goods Sold and Operating Expenses. The balance sheet normally includes the Merchandise Inventory account among the assets, the Allowance for Bad Debts as a deduction from Accounts Receivable Control, and the Allowance for Depreciation as a deduction from the Equipment account. In the Owner's Equity section, the owner's withdrawals are deducted from the profit.

The trading aspect of the business has little effect on the rest of the end-of-cycle routine. Immediately after the statements are finished, the adjusting entries are journalized and posted. Next, the closing entries are recorded and posted in almost the same manner as for a service operation. Then the accounts are ruled and a postclosing trial balance is taken, as before.

MANAGERIAL IMPLICATIONS

Financial statements are readily adapted to meet the reporting needs of service and service-trading businesses. Management needs to understand the significance of allowance accounts for depreciation and bad debts in order to interpret the balance sheet figures correctly. A knowledge of the techniques for determining the value of the closing inventory and the computation of the cost of goods sold also help management to understand how profit and loss figures were derived. Knowing where these figures came from and where to find more details is extremely important for auditing, comparison, and control purposes.

APPLICATION OF PRINCIPLES

PROBLEM 15 · 1

♦ The adjusted trial balance of the Bowen Box Company for the month ended July 31, 19X8 is given here.

ACCT. NO.	ACCOUNT NAME	DEBIT	CREDIT
101	Cash	$ 2,370.30	
111	Accounts Receivable Control	3,866.40	
111A	Allowance for Bad Debts		$ 301.90
121	Merchandise Inventory	4,864.30	
141	Equipment	7,894.70	
141A	Allowance for Depreciation		121.40
201	Accounts Payable Control		3,694.35
301	Bowen Investment		13,159.60
302	Bowen Drawing	250.00	
401	Box Sales Income		7,133.85
451	Sales Returns & Allowances	225.75	
501	Merchandise Purchases	3,177.25	
509	Purchases Returns & Allow.		151.70
511	Salary Expense	850.00	
516	Rent Expense	600.00	
521	Supplies Used	135.50	
561	Bad Debts Expense	174.40	
564	Depreciation Expense	65.80	
591	Miscellaneous Expense	88.40	
	Totals	$24,562.80	$24,562.80

INSTRUCTIONS

1. Enter the adjusted trial balance data on a ten-column worksheet.
2. Record the Merchandise Inventory of $4,706.35 at July 31, 19X8, on the worksheet and identify by the letter (C).
3. Extend the Adjusted Trial Balance amounts to the appropriate columns and foot.
4. Compute and enter the profit or loss for the period.
5. Complete the worksheet, bringing down final totals of all remaining columns, proving, and then ruling all columns. (Save your worksheet for use in Problems 15 • 2 and 15 • 3.)

PROBLEM 15 • 2

This is a continuation of Problem 15 • 1. Refer to the worksheet of the Bowen Box Company for the month ended July 31, 19X8 that was previously completed.

INSTRUCTIONS

1. Prepare the income statement. (Use three-column analysis paper.)
2. Prepare the balance sheet, using the format shown on page 222. (Use four-column analysis paper.)

PROBLEM 15 • 3

This is a continuation of Problems 15 • 1 and 15 • 2. Refer to the worksheet of the Bowen Box Company for the month ended July 31, 19X8, which you completed.

INSTRUCTIONS

1. Prepare the adjusting entries for depreciation expense and bad debts expense in general journal form, beginning with Entry 7-6A. Assume monthly depreciation of $65.80 and estimated additional bad debts losses of $174.40.
2. Prepare the closing entries for transferring the balances of the Debit and Credit columns of the Income Statement section of the worksheet to Income and Expense Summary 399. Include the beginning and ending merchandise inventory amounts in these entries.
3. Prepare the closing entry to transfer the profit (or loss) for the month to the owner's drawing account.
4. Prepare the closing entry to transfer the balance of the owner's drawing account to the owner's investment account.

PROBLEM 15 • 4

The completed worksheet of the Pelham Paint Store (M. Glaser, owner) for the year ended Dec. 31, 19X3 is given. (See page following.)

PELHAM PAINT STORE
Worksheet
Year Ended December 31, 19X3

ACCT. NO.	ACCOUNT NAME	TRIAL BALANCE DEBIT	TRIAL BALANCE CREDIT	ADJUSTMENTS DEBIT	ADJUSTMENTS CREDIT	ADJUSTED TRIAL BALANCE DEBIT	ADJUSTED TRIAL BALANCE CREDIT	INCOME STATEMENT DEBIT	INCOME STATEMENT CREDIT	BALANCE SHEET DEBIT	BALANCE SHEET CREDIT
101	Cash in Bank	4,756 00				4,756 00				4,756 00	
111	Accounts Receivable Control	14,860 00				14,860 00				14,860 00	
111-A	Allowance for Bad Debts		40 50		D) 300 00		340 50				340 50
121	Merchandise Inventory	35,000 00				35,000 00		35,000 00	E) 36,000 00	E) 36,000 00	
131	Store Furniture & Fixtures	950 00				950 00				950 00	
131-A	Allow. for Depr.-Store F.&F.		180 00		A) 90 00		270 00				270 00
135	Delivery Truck	2,250 00				2,250 00				2,250 00	
135-A	Allow. for Depr.-Del. Truck		750 00		B) 375 00		1,125 00				1,125 00
141	Office Furniture & Equipment	720 00				720 00				720 00	
141-A	Allow. for Depr.-Off. F.&Eq.		130 00		C) 65 00		195 00				195 00
201	Accounts Payable Control		4,235 00				4,235 00				4,235 00
301	Glaser Investment		38,378 50				38,378 50				38,378 50
302	Glaser Drawing										
401	Sales		152,700 00				152,700 00		152,700 00		
501	Merchandise Purchases	108,375 00				108,375 00		108,375 00			
521	Rent Expense	3,600 00				3,600 00		3,600 00			
523	Sales Salaries	16,500 00				16,500 00		16,500 00			
525	Store Supplies & Expense	583 00				583 00		583 00			
527	Depreciation-Store F.&F.			A) 90 00		90 00		90 00			
531	Advertising	2,275 00				2,275 00		2,275 00			
541	Delivery Wages	2,400 00				2,400 00		2,400 00			
543	Delivery Truck Oper. Expense	760 00				760 00		760 00			
545	Depreciation-Del. Truck			B) 375 00		375 00		375 00			
551	Office Salaries	3,000 00				3,000 00		3,000 00			
553	Office Supplies & Expense	385 00				385 00		385 00			
555	Depreciation-Office F.&Eq.			C) 65 00		65 00		65 00			
561	Bad Debts Expense			D) 300 00		300 00		300 00			
	Totals	196,414 00	196,414 00	830 00	830 00	197,244 00	197,244 00	173,708 00	188,700 00	59,536 00	44,544 00
	Net Profit for Year							14,992 00			14,992 00
								188,700 00	188,700 00	59,536 00	59,536 00

1. Prepare an income statement from the completed worksheet.
2. Prepare a balance sheet from the completed worksheet.
3. Journalize the adjusting entries, beginning with Entry 12-1A.
4. Journalize the entries to close all income and expense balances and account for beginning and ending inventory balances.
5. Journalize the entries to transfer the profit or loss from the Income and Expense Summary to the owner's drawing account.
6. Journalize the entry to transfer the balance of the owner's drawing account to the investment account.

MANAGERIAL CHECKUPS

♦ Why does management need to know how the values of the closing inventory and cost of goods sold were computed?

♦ Refer to the income statement on page 230. Is it a good idea for management to allow its investment in inventory to grow by as much as 10% in a month? Explain.

♦ Why should an owner refrain from making sizable and frequent drawings from a business?

INTEGRATED PRACTICAL APPLICATION-- SERVICE-TRADING ACCOUNTING CYCLE

This exercise provides an opportunity for you to handle the accounting duties of the Carter Cleaning Shop for March, the fourth month of the firm's operation. You will learn how to complete the monthly accounting cycle for a service-trading business, using general and special journals and general and subsidiary ledgers.

HOW TO GET ORGANIZED

Use the same system of journals that you used for the February transactions, with Page 2 for the purchases journal, Page 5 for the general journal, and Page 3 for all others.

Cash Receipts Journal (multicolumn, including
    new columns for Sundry Credits)
Cash Disbursements Journal (multicolumn)
Sales Journal
Purchases Journal
General Journal

Use the same three ledgers that were used in February:

General Ledger
Accounts Receivable Subsidiary Ledger
Accounts Payable Subsidiary Ledger

Head general ledger account forms for all the accounts listed in the chart of accounts shown on the next page.

Enter all ledger account balances carried forward from the postclosing trial balance for February 28, 19X2. Use "March 1, 19X2" in the Date column and "Brought Forward" in the Explanation column.

CARTER CLEANING SHOP
Postclosing Trial Balance
February 28, 19X2

ACCT. NO.	ACCOUNT NAME	DEBIT	CREDIT
101	Cash	$ 786 00	
111	Accounts Receivable Control	142 00	
111A	Allowance for Bad Debts		$ 3 30
121	Merchandise Inventory	1,000 00	
141	Equipment	5,400 00	
141A	Allowance for Depreciation		90 00
201	Accounts Payable Control		950 00
301	Carter Investment		6,284 70
	Totals	$7,328 00	$7,328 00

Account Number	Account Name
100–199	ASSETS
101	Cash
111	Accounts Receivable Control
111A	Allowance for Bad Debts
121	Merchandise Inventory
141	Equipment
141A	Allowance for Depreciation
200–299	LIABILITIES
201	Accounts Payable Control
300–399	OWNER'S EQUITY
301	Carter Investment
302	Carter Drawing
399	Income and Expense Summary
400–499	INCOME
401	Cleaning Service Income
402	Accessories Sales Income
451	Sales Returns and Allowances—Cleaning Service
452	Sales Returns and Allowances—Accessories
500–599	EXPENSES
501	Merchandise Purchases
509	Purchases Returns and Allowances
511	Salary Expense
516	Rent Expense
521	Supplies Used
561	Bad Debts Expense
564	Depreciation Expense
591	Miscellaneous Expense

Then enter the individual account names and balances in the accounts receivable subsidiary ledger from the end-of-February schedule of accounts receivable.

CARTER CLEANING SHOP
Schedule of Accounts Receivable
February 28, 19X2

CUSTOMER	BALANCE AMOUNT
J. E. Ayres	$ 7
S. S. Baker	60
R. L. Camp	10
K. Davies	5
A. Dunlap	10
C. V. Fisher	20
B. A. Hahn	30
Total Due from Customers	$142

Finally, enter the individual account names and balances in the accounts payable subsidiary ledger from the end-of-February schedule of accounts payable.

CARTER CLEANING SHOP
Schedule of Accounts Payable
February 28, 19X2

CREDITOR	BALANCE AMOUNT
Beaver Products Company	$150
Weller Wholesale Company	800
Total Owed to Creditors	$950

RECORD THE DAILY TRANSACTIONS

Analyze the following March 19X2 transactions and then record each of them in the proper journal. When an entry involves an account receivable or account payable, remember to post from the journal to the subsidiary ledger account immediately. Entries made in the general journal and in the Sundry section in the cash journals should also be posted daily to the proper general and subsidiary ledger accounts.

MAR.
1 Received $60 from customer S. S. Baker to balance his account.
2 Sent Check 56 for $75 to the Beaver Products Company on account.
2 Carter invested an additional $1,000 cash in the business. (Record the credit in the Sundry Credits column of the cash receipts journal.)
2 Sold $75 worth of accessories to M. F. Coleman, Sales Slip 14; terms, 30 days net.
3 Cash receipts for cleaning services during the week, $1,030.
3 Cash receipts for accessories sales during the week, $250.
5 Paid $100 in cash for miscellaneous expenses (Check 57).

MAR.

5 Bought $50 worth of accessories for stock from Premium Plastics, Inc., on their Invoice 45437, dated March 3; terms, 20 days.

6 Received $10 from customer R. L. Camp to settle his account.

7 Sold $120 worth of accessories to a new customer, C. W. Hayes, on Sales Slip 15; terms, 30 days.

8 Sold $65 worth of cleaning services to S. S. Baker on Sales Slip 16; terms, 30 days.

8 Received $5 in cash from K. Davies to balance his account.

9 Paid $400 to the Weller Wholesale Company on account (Check 58).

9 Sold $25 worth of cleaning services to A. Dunlap on Sales Slip 17; terms, 30 days.

10 Cash receipts for cleaning services during the week, $975.

10 Cash receipts for accessories sales during the week, $240.

11 Issued Check 59 for $125 to cover miscellaneous expenses.

11 Bought $300 worth of accessories from a new supplier, Scott-Blane Corporation. Their Invoice X-1041, dated March 10, carries 30-day terms.

12 Received $10 from customer A. Dunlap to apply on account.

12 Sent Check 60 for $75 to Beaver Products Company to balance account.

13 Paid $500 by Check 61 for supplies used.

14 Sold $15 worth of cleaning services to M. F. Coleman, Sales Slip 18; terms, 30 days.

14 Sold $25 in accessories to R. W. Peters, Sales Slip 19; terms, 30 days.

14 Bought $200 worth of merchandise from the Weller Wholesale Company; their Invoice 1167 is dated March 10; terms, 30 days.

16 Paid store rent for month, $700 (Check 62).

17 Cash receipts for cleaning services during the week, $1,020.

17 Cash receipts for accessories sales during the week, $260.

18 Bought $55 worth of merchandise from the Beaver Products Company; their Invoice A5741, dated March 14; terms, 30 days.

19 Paid $400 to Weller Wholesale Company to apply on account (Check 63).

20 Issued Check 64 for $50 for miscellaneous expenses.

20 Sold $100 worth of cleaning services to A. G. Browne, Sales Slip 20; terms, 30 days.

21 Paid $400 (Check 65) for supplies used.

24 Cash receipts for cleaning services during the week, $1,100.

24 Cash receipts for accessories sales during the week, $280.

25 Sold $60 in accessories to J. B. Pattison, Sales Slip 21; terms, 30 days.

25 Paid $50 to Premium Plastics, Inc., to balance account (Check 66).

26 Bought $100 worth of additional merchandise from the Beaver Products Company; their Invoice A6397, dated March 23; terms, 30 days.

27 Issued credit memorandum to J. B. Pattison for $25 for return of certain accessories sold to him on March 25, Sales Slip 21.

27 Paid $300 by Check 67 for supplies used.

30 Received credit of $22 from the Beaver Products Company, for merchandise returned that was purchased on March 26.

30 Paid $75 for miscellaneous expenses (Check 68).

MAR.

30 Bought $600 worth of merchandise from Premium Plastics, Inc.; their Invoice 47501, dated March 28; terms, 20 days.

31 Paid $295 cash for supplies used (Check 69).

31 Paid salaries for month, $3,000 (Check 70).

31 Cash receipts for cleaning services during the week, $1,125.

31 Cash receipts for accessories sales during week, $310.

31 Received check for $23 from R. W. Peters with a letter stating that he is leaving town. Peters says that he feels he was overcharged $2 on the March 14 sale (Sales Slip 19) and that he does not plan to pay the $2 balance. Since Peters is not entitled to any special allowances, Carter decides to write off the balance of $2 as a bad debt.

31 Carter withdrew $100 for personal use (Check 71).

COMPLETE THE CYCLE

When all the daily transactions have been analyzed and journalized, and then posted to the subsidiary and general ledgers as required, the remaining steps in the accounting cycle must be completed.

1. Total all special journals and post, as required, to the general ledger accounts.
2. Prove the general ledger by taking a trial balance. Use the first two columns of the worksheet.
3. Prove the subsidiary ledgers to their respective control account balances by preparing a schedule of accounts receivable and one of accounts payable.
4. Record the adjustment for Depreciation Expense for March ($90) on the worksheet.
5. Record the adjustment for Bad Debts Expense at 2.5% of the net credit sales.
6. Total the Adjustments columns and complete the Adjusted Trial Balance section of the worksheet.
7. Record the ending merchandise inventory on the worksheet. (The inventory taken on March 31 shows $1,100 in merchandise on hand.)
8. Charge the beginning inventory to the cost of doing business in March by extending the Trial Balance debit amount first to the Adjusted Trial Balance Debit column and then to the Income Statement Debit column, as you learned in Unit 14.
9. Complete the worksheet.
10. Prepare an income statement.
11. Prepare a balance sheet.
12. Journalize and post the adjusting entries.
13. Journalize and post the closing entries.
14. Balance, foot, and rule the accounts.
15. Prepare a postclosing trial balance.

16

CLASSIFIED STATEMENTS

The operations of the Carter Cleaning Shop are typical of those of thousands of small businesses that open every year. When these businesses begin, their accounting records are usually quite simple. Then, as they expand operations, the records are adjusted to meet new demands. To see how this process works, look at the balance sheet of the Carter Cleaning Shop shown on page 243 dated December 31, 19X5, four years after the business was started.

The first thing to be noticed is the more elaborate form of the statement; the second is the many new account titles added to the familiar ones. However, these differences can be readily explained and understood.

THE CLASSIFIED BALANCE SHEET

New accounts are devised from time to time to meet special recording problems, as has been explained in Units 9–14. In turn, as the accounts become more numerous, a more elaborate statement, called a *classified balance sheet*, is commonly used to group and classify the various assets and liabilities for more effective presentation. This balance sheet is shown here prepared in *report form*. As such, it lists assets, liabilities, and owner's equity in vertical order on the page. The report form is usually preferred when there are a great many accounts and when the statement is prepared on the typewriter. Let us examine each section of the classified balance sheet illustrated.

Current Assets

Current assets are those assets that will normally be converted into cash or that will be consumed during the operating cycle of the business or within one year. The items are usually listed in order of liquidity, or ease of conversion. These assets are vital to business survival because they will provide the funds for paying bills and meeting expenses.

A number of current assets, such as cash, accounts receivable, allowance for bad debts, and merchandise inventory have been presented many times before in this book. In the statement of December 31, 19X5, some new

CARTER CLEANING SHOP
Balance Sheet
December 31, 19X5

ASSETS

Current Assets			
Cash in Bank		$ 4,015	
Petty Cash		100	
Change Fund		150	
Investment in U.S. Treasury Securities		500	
Notes Receivable		2,750	
Accounts Receivable Control	$ 6,600		
Less Allowance for Bad Debts	350	6,250	
Prepaid Insurance		120	
Merchandise Inventory		1,625	
Total Current Assets			$15,510
Plant and Equipment			
Buildings and Cleaning Equipment	$20,000		
Less Allowance for Depreciation	1,500	$18,500	
Store Equipment	$ 4,800		
Less Allowance for Depreciation	2,100	2,700	
Delivery Equipment	$ 3,450		
Less Allowance for Depreciation	1,640	1,810	
Office Equipment	$ 3,170		
Less Allowance for Depreciation	1,430	1,740	
Land		5,000	
Total Fixed Assets			29,750
Total Assets			$45,260

LIABILITIES AND OWNER'S EQUITY

Current Liabilities			
Notes Payable		$ 3,000	
Accounts Payable Control		1,100	
Sales Tax Payable		235	
Employee Deductions:			
FICA Tax	$ 198		
Income Tax Withheld	440	638	
Total Current Liabilities			$ 4,973
Long-term Liabilities			
7% Mortgage Payable on Plant, 19Y4			15,000
Total Liabilities			$19,973
Owner's Equity			
Carter Investment, January 1, 19X5		$19,946	
Net Profit for Year 19X5	$12,541		
Less Withdrawals	7,200		
Net Increase in Investment in 19X5		5,341	
Carter Investment, December 31, 19X5			25,287
Total Liabilities and Owner's Equity			$45,260

account titles have been added to the familiar ones. Cash is listed as Cash in Bank and there are two additional cash accounts and three new assets.

- Petty Cash is a small, fixed sum set aside to pay for minor daily cash outlays, such as postage due, carfare, and special supplies, as explained in Unit 7.
- Change Fund is a fixed sum of cash retained in the cash registers to facilitate change making.
- Investments usually represent securities bought as a means of earning interest on funds that are temporarily not required in the business operations. Government bonds and treasury notes are favorite investments for this purpose.
- Notes Receivable might have been obtained as a result of selling operations, such as that described in Unit 6. Notes may be accepted from trade customers in settlement of their overdue accounts. They are usually listed before Accounts Receivable on the balance sheet to reflect the legally preferred character of the claim against the debtors.
- Prepaid Insurance represents insurance premiums paid in advance for protection in future periods. In its first few years, the Carter Cleaning Shop purchased insurance policies that covered only one year or less and charged the premiums to expense when the policies were bought. However, the Carter management later realized that it was more economical to purchase insurance policies covering more than a one-year period. When long-term policies are purchased, it is more appropriate to charge the premiums as an expense over the months to which they apply, rather than charge them as an expense when the policy is purchased. So, beginning January 1, 19X5, the accountant decided to record insurance premiums as an asset called *Prepaid Insurance* when they were paid. Thus, each month (or each year) a portion of the prepaid insurance is transferred to the expense account. On January 1, 19X5, the company paid premiums of $240 for a two-year insurance policy. The effect of this payment is indicated here in general journal form.

19	X5	1–1			
Jan.	2	Prepaid Insurance	126	240 00	
		Cash in Bank	101		240 00
		To record payment of premium on two-year fire insurance policy.			

At the end of each month, a proportionate part ($\frac{1}{24}$th) of the prepaid insurance is transferred to Insurance Expense 536 by an adjusting entry. The monthly expense is $10 ($240 ÷ 24 months).

19 X5		1–26A						
Jan.	31	Insurance Expense	536		10	00		
		Prepaid Insurance	126				10	00
		To record expired insurance for one month ($240 ÷ 24 months).						

Thus, during 19X5, a total of $120, which represented the cost of one year's premiums, was transferred to expense of the period. The $120 balance remaining in the Prepaid Insurance account is the unused premium applicable to the remaining life of the policy (one-half of the original premium of $240).

Similar adjustments may be made for other prepaid expense items, such as office supplies purchased, and prepaid rent. Adjustments of this type are discussed in Unit 26.

Plant and Equipment

Plant and Equipment consists of long-lived property that will be used permanently in the conduct of business operations. Accountants keep a close watch on these assets because they usually represent a very sizable investment and, because of their specialized nature, it is frequently difficult and costly to resell them. All the accounts listed under Plant and Equipment on Carter's statement are new.

- The all-inclusive Equipment account has been replaced by several more specialized accounts: Buildings and Cleaning Equipment, Store Equipment, Delivery Equipment, and Office Equipment. In each of these accounts, the value of the asset is carried at cost.
- An Allowance for Depreciation account is maintained to accumulate the total charges to Depreciation Expense over the life of each asset.
- The firm has also acquired the asset, Land, on which to build a new dry-cleaning plant.

Current Liabilities

Current liabilities are obligations that must be paid within one year or from the current assets of the business realized over a normal operating cycle. Current liabilities are usually listed in order of priority of payment. Since the firm's credit reputation depends upon prompt settlement of its debts, the accountant must make sure that funds are available when the bills become due. The firm's current liabilities include several new items.

- Notes Payable are obligations based on short-term written promises to pay, usually given to suppliers and banks. They are usually listed before Accounts Payable on the balance sheet to reflect the preferred nature of these claims against Carter.
- The Sales Taxes Payable account was devised to record the obligation for paying taxes collected on sales at retail, as described in Unit 6.
- Employee Deductions—FICA Tax represents Carter's liability for payment of payroll taxes deducted from workers' pay for old-age and survivors', and hospital insurance benefits levies. (These will be explained in detail in the next two units.)
- Employee Deductions—Income Taxes Withheld is another liability account that indicates the employer's obligation for amounts deducted from paychecks under federal and other pay-as-you-go income tax regulations.

Long-term Liabilities

Long-term liabilities are debts of the business due more than a year in the future. Although repayment may not be due for several years, the accountant must know where the money for settlement can be found. In the meantime, he must see that periodic interest is paid promptly when due.

There is only one long-term or fixed liability shown for Carter. A long-term loan on the land and plant buildings is secured by a promise in the form of a bond and mortgage. Thus, the account is entitled Mortgage Payable on Plant and identified by year due, 19Y4.

Owner's Equity

The Owner's Equity section of the balance sheet is very much the same as it was in earlier operations. The owner's additional investments (when there are any) and withdrawals of profits during the period are clearly summarized here.

CLASSIFIED INCOME STATEMENT

Carter's income statement for the year ended December 31, 19X5 also reveals a new and more elaborate grouping of items and a number of new accounts. The most significant departmental figures are totaled in the right column. Starting at the top of this income statement, consider the changes within each major segment.

CARTER CLEANING SHOP
Income Statement
Year Ended December 31, 19X5

	ACCESSORIES SALES		CLEANING SUPPLIES SALES		CLEANING SERVICE SALES		TOTAL
Operating Income							
Sales		$20,364		$10,405		$89,189	$119,958
Less: Sales Returns and							
Allowances	$ 286		$ 108		$ 427		
Sales Discounts	230	516	257	365		427	1,308
Net Sales		$19,848		$10,040		$88,762	$118,650
Cost of Goods Sold							
Merchandise Inventory, Jan. 1		$ 1,510		$ -0-			
Merchandise Purchases	$15,960		$12,010				
Freight In	260		190				
Total Purchases Cost		16,220		12,200			
Less: Purchases Returns and							
Allowances	$ 155		$ 45				
Purchases Discounts	285	440	175	220			
Total Merchandise Available for Sale		$17,290		$11,980			
Less Merchandise Inventory, Dec. 31		1,625		3,756			
Cost of Goods Sold		$15,665		$ 8,224		-0-	$ 23,889
Gross Profit on Sales		$ 4,183		$ 1,816		$88,762	$ 94,761
Operating Expenses							
Plant Operating Expenses							
Plant Salaries and Wages					$25,600		
Plant Supplies and Expense					4,780		
Utilities					1,910		
Depreciation on Buildings and Cleaning Equipment					1,500		
Total Plant Operating Expenses						$33,790	
Selling Expenses							
Sales Salaries and Commissions					$15,520		
Store Supplies and Expense					1,160		
Advertising Expense					1,620		
Store Taxes and Licenses					760		
Depreciation on Store Equipment					480		
Delivery Expense					7,450		
Depreciation on Delivery Equipment					690		
Total Selling Expenses						27,680	
Administrative Expenses							
Office Salaries					$ 8,200		
Office Supplies and Expense					1,920		
Depreciation on Office Equipment					400		
Insurance Expense					1,400		
Bad Debts Expense					250		
Donations and Contributions					575		
Payroll Tax Expense					3,024		
Property Tax Expense					780		
Miscellaneous Expense					2,675		
Total Administrative Expenses						19,224	
Total Operating Expenses							80,694
Net Profit From Operations							$ 14,067
Other Income							
Interest Income							368
							$ 14,435
Other Expense							
Interest Expense							1,365
Net Profit for the Year							$ 13,070

Operating Income

A more descriptive title is now used in the first section of the income statement to emphasize the source of the revenue. Only income from operations belongs here; other income (being encountered for the first time) is presented near the bottom of the form.

- There are now three income accounts: Accessories Sales, Cleaning Supplies Sales, and Cleaning Service Sales. (Cleaning Supplies is a new department in 19X5.)
- The total of Sales Returns and Allowances and Sales Discounts is deducted from Sales to determine Net Sales. (All accountants agree that Sales Returns and Allowances should be deducted from Sales. However, some accountants suggest that Sales Discounts should not be offset against Sales, but should be shown as Other Expense because Sales Discount is, in effect, interest paid to the customer to get him to pay promptly.)

COST OF GOODS SOLD. Under the familiar heading, cost of goods sold, there are several new items.

- Merchandise Inventory, January 1, shows no figure for Cleaning Supplies Sales because the department started operations during the current year.
- Freight In is added to the cost of goods purchased, as explained in Unit 10.
- Purchases Returns and Allowances, along with Purchases Discounts, are shown as a reduction of the cost of purchases during the period. The treatment of Purchases Returns and Allowances was discussed in Unit 10. (Some accountants prefer to show Purchases Discounts as Other Income on the basis that these discounts represent interest earned for prompt payment of bills.)

Gross Profit on Sales

The Gross Profit on Sales remains as before.

Operating Expenses

This section is now subdivided to permit grouping of the additional expenses into three classifications: Plant Operating Expenses, Selling Expenses, and Administrative Expenses.

PLANT OPERATING EXPENSES. These are the expenses involved in running the new plant that opened on January 1 of the current year, 19X5.

- Plant Salaries and Wages includes the pay of all plant officials and workers.
- Plant Supplies and Expense includes all the supplies and services required in the plant operations, except utilities.
- Utilities are recorded separately because they represent significant amounts.
- Depreciation on Buildings and Cleaning Equipment represents the proportionate cost for this year of the plant and equipment assets based on their various estimated useful lives.

SELLING EXPENSES. This category includes all costs directly related to the sale and delivery of services and accessories. Several new account titles are used to identify specific costs.

- The Sales Salaries and Commissions account and the Store Supplies and Expense account are adaptations of the familiar Salary Expense account and Supplies Used account.
- The accounts for Advertising Expense, Store Taxes and Licenses, Delivery Expense, and the two depreciation expense accounts are self-explanatory outcomes of expanded operations.

ADMINISTRATIVE EXPENSES. This group of expenses includes costs relating to all other activities of the more complex business. However, there are a number of familiar adaptations.

- The accounts for Office Salaries, Office Supplies and Expense, Depreciation on Office Equipment, Bad Debts Expense, and Miscellaneous Expense have all been encountered before.
- Insurance Expense is a natural outgrowth of the acquisition of plant, equipment, and inventory. The business buys protection against the risks of various forms of loss. Included in the total yearly expense of $1,400 is the expired insurance premium of $120 discussed on page 244.
- Donations and Contributions are another cost of modern business operations. A firm frequently makes contributions to charitable and civic enterprises to build goodwill and improve the social and economic welfare of the community.
- Payroll Tax Expense, explained in Unit 18 represents the employer's costs under various payroll tax laws.
- Property Tax Expense is a result of the ownership of plant, equipment, inventory, and other property. A variety of taxes levied by different taxing authorities must be paid by every business. Property taxes are examined in greater detail in Unit 25.

Net Profit from Operations

Again, as in connection with Operating Income, the caption emphasizes that the profit in question resulted from business operations. Most businesses enjoy a small income from nonoperating sources, but the two incomes must be kept separate to facilitate appraisal of true operating efficiency.

Other Income

This new caption affords a grouping place for such nonoperating items as Interest Income. This might arise from interest-bearing notes receivable (Unit 6) or interest earned on investments.

Other Expenses

Typically, nonoperating expenses relate to costs of financial dealings. Interest Expense represents interest that the firm has to pay on interest-bearing notes payable and on the plant mortgage.

Net Profit for the Period

The final total on the income statement shows the combined results of all types of income and expenses. (A net loss would be shown here in red, in italics, or in parentheses.)

PRINCIPLES AND PROCEDURES

Statements may be more or less elaborate, but they consist of conventional elements combined to tell a familiar story. New accounts quickly fall into familiar patterns and groupings once the basic principles of statement preparation are learned.

Regardless of the size or type of business, the basic accounting principles and procedures discussed so far can be applied and adapted to fit any situation. Individual accountants must do the thinking and the adapting required to devise and operate a workable system.

MANAGERIAL IMPLICATIONS

Classified statements are prepared so that management and others may draw meaningful conclusions from them more readily. The classification aids in analyzing both the financial condition of the business and the results of operations of the period, provided management understands the nature and significance of the grouping. When this method is used consistently from year to year, the classified statements provide an extremely useful means of comparing the current year with prior years to detect trends and patterns. Also, these statements make it possible for the management to compare its business with similar firms in the same industry.

APPLICATION OF PRINCIPLES

PROBLEM 16 · 1

Larry Jackson owns and operates the Jackson Distributing Company, which sells canned food products to retail stores, schools, and churches. The last two sections of the worksheet for the year ended Dec. 31, 19X4 are given here. Note the manner in which numbers have been assigned to accounts. This will give a clue to the classification of the account. For instance, the Jackson Distributing Company classified expenses into three groups:

Warehouse Expenses   "600" series
Selling Expenses   "700" series
Administrative Expenses   "800" series

ACCT. NO.	ACCOUNT NAME	INCOME STATEMENT DR.	INCOME STATEMENT CR.	BALANCE SHEET DR.	BALANCE SHEET CR.
101	Cash in Bank			6,775	
105	Petty Cash Fund			100	
111	Accounts Rec. Control			13,625	
111A	Allow. for Bad Debts				275
112	Notes Receivable			2,700	
113	Invest.—Stocks & Bonds			10,000	
121	Merchandise Inventory	18,500	(A) 16,000	(A)16,000	
126	Prepaid Insurance			1,800	
141	Office Equipment			4,400	
141A	Allow. for Depreciation				1,550
143	Warehouse Buildings			32,000	
143A	Allow. for Depreciation				12,000
144	Warehouse Equipment			8,000	
144A	Allow. for Depreciation				3,000
145	Delivery Equipment			11,500	
145A	Allow. for Depreciation				4,300
151	Land			9,000	
201	Accounts Pay. Control				10,500
202	Notes Payable				4,800
203	Salary & Wages Payable				2,350
221	Employee Ded.—FICA Tax				95
222	Employee Ded.—Inc. Tax WH				235
231	Sales Tax Payable				440
251	Mortgage Pay. on Build.				14,000
301	Jackson Investment				52,865
302	Jackson Drawing			7,200	
405	Sales of Food Prod.		168,400		
451	Sales Returns & Allow.	1,125			
453	Sales Discounts	325			

ACCT. NO.	ACCOUNT NAME	INCOME STATEMENT DR.	INCOME STATEMENT CR.	BALANCE SHEET DR.	BALANCE SHEET CR.
501	Merchandise Purchases	92,600			
506	Freight In	3,200			
509	Purchases Returns & Allow.		830		
510	Purchases Discounts		350		
601	Warehouse Sal. & Wages	7,400			
602	Warehouse Supplies & Equip.	525			
603	Utilities	1,400			
604	Building Repairs	250			
605	Depr.—Build. & Equip.	2,000			
701	Sales Salaries & Comm.	14,800			
702	Sales Supplies & Exp.	975			
703	Advertising Expense	4,150			
704	Travel & Entertain. Exp.	760			
705	Sales Licenses	300			
706	Delivery Expense	1,800			
707	Depr.—Del. Equip.	3,000			
801	Office Salaries	6,200			
802	Office Supplies & Equip.	850			
803	Insurance Expense	1,200			
804	Donations & Contributions	350			
805	Payroll Tax Expense	2,900			
806	Property Tax Expense	1,175			
807	Telephone & Telegraph Exp.	1,200			
808	Depreciation—Office Equip.	225			
809	Bad Debt Expense	1,075			
901	Interest Income		375		
951	Interest Expense	980			
	Totals	$169,265	$ 185,955	$ 123,100	$106,410
	Net Profit for Year	16,690			16,690
		$185,955	$ 185,955	$ 123,100	$123,100

INSTRUCTIONS

1. Prepare a classified income statement (no departmental columns are required).
2. Prepare a classified balance sheet.

MANAGERIAL CHECKUP

♦ Why does management compare its current accounting statements with those of prior years and with those of other firms?

PART 4
PAYROLL AND
CONTROL SYSTEMS

17

PAYROLL COMPUTATIONS, RECORDS, AND PAYMENT

In the discussion of the accounting records of the Carter Cleaning Shop, there was no detailed treatment of salary and wage payments to employees. A consideration of payroll accounting at that time would have interrupted the sequence of the general recordkeeping procedures being described. Also, payroll accounting, including the related payroll taxes and tax returns, is so important that concentrated attention and extended treatment are required. Such coverage is provided in this unit and the next.

OBJECTIVES OF PAYROLL WORK

The primary objective of payroll work is to compute the amount of wages or salary due employees and to pay these amounts promptly. Another objective is to classify payments to employees properly and to charge these amounts to the appropriate expense accounts. Until the mid-1930s, payroll accounting was involved with few other considerations.

In 1935 the federal Social Security Act was passed. Under the terms of this legislation, detailed payroll and employee earnings records became a necessity. The withholding of federal income tax was started a few years later. Several states also enacted plans for income tax withholding that added to payroll recordkeeping problems. The wage and hour provisions of the federal Fair Labor Standards Act of 1938 (as amended) affected the computation of earnings. The various state workmen's compensation insurance laws are a further concern in payroll accounting because they require a careful classification of payrolls according to the type of work done. The provisions of each law are examined in greater detail in the paragraphs that follow. Changes occur in the rates and base figures more frequently than in the methods of computation. Learn the methods and then always be sure to use the latest rates and bases in practice.

The Social Security Program

The federal Social Security Act has been amended several times and is likely to be further amended. The present social security program has two principal parts. The first, discussed in this unit, consists of the old-age, survivors, and disability insurance program and the hospital insurance program (Medicare). This is financed entirely by the federal government through taxes levied under the Federal Insurance Contributions Act (FICA). The second, discussed in Unit 18, is the federal unemployment insurance program. This is financed jointly by the federal government and the several states through taxes levied under the Federal Unemployment Tax Act (FUTA) and the corresponding state unemployment tax laws.

COVERAGE. Most employers and employees are covered by the social security program. Agricultural labor, domestic servants, and most self-employed persons are covered under special provisions. Railroad workers, who have a separate program of their own, are exempt. Employees of state and local governments and of certain religious and nonprofit organizations are exempt but may elect to be covered. Only the cases of ordinary business employers and employees are considered here.

BENEFITS. Retirement benefits may be claimed by insured workers after retirement at age 62 or later. Disability benefits for insured workers over 50 and under 65 are based on average monthly earnings; they are the same as old-age insurance benefits would be if the disabled worker were already 65 and retired. In each case, the amount of benefits depends upon the average monthly earnings of the insured person. In addition to the cash benefits above, hospital insurance benefits are available for people who are 65 or over and are covered by social security. Further details about benefits, including survivors' benefits, may be obtained from the government publication *Your Social Security*, or from district offices of the Social Security Administration (listed in telephone directories under United States Government: Department of Health, Education, and Welfare).

IDENTIFICATION NUMBERS. Each employer and each employee must obtain an identification number, because millions of employers and employees are covered by the social security program. The numbers permit a positive identification and help ensure proper credits for taxes paid in cases in which there may be more than one person or company with the same name. Records are kept by machine and the use of numbers facilitates handling the tremendous volume of entries that must be made each year.

The Fair Labor Standards Act

The Fair Labor Standards Act of 1938 (as amended) applies only to firms engaged directly or indirectly in interstate commerce. Frequently referred to as the Wage and Hour Law, this federal statute fixes a minimum hourly rate of pay ($2.00 scheduled for 1974) and maximum hours of work per week (presently 40) to be performed at the regular rate. Hours worked in excess of 40 per week must be paid for at a premium rate of at least one and a half times the regular hourly rate of pay (called time and a half). Many employers not subject to the federal law pay time and a half for overtime because of union contracts or simply as a good business practice.

The Fair Labor Standards Act requires subject employers to maintain records for each employee to show that the provisions of the law have been followed. No particular form is specified for these records, but they should indicate the name and address of the employee, date of birth, hours worked each day and week, wages paid at the regular rate, and overtime premium wages. Similar information is required for employees subject to the FICA taxes previously discussed. One record for each employee ordinarily serves both purposes.

Workmen's Compensation Insurance

State laws covering workmen's compensation insurance require employers to pay for insurance that will reimburse employees for losses suffered from injuries or compensate their families in the event of death sustained in the course of their employment. Benefits are paid directly to the injured workers or to their survivors.

ILLUSTRATIVE CASE— THE WICKHAM NOVELTY COMPANY

The first step in payroll work is to determine the gross amount of wages or salary earned by each employee. There are a number of common ways of paying employees. Some workers are paid at a stated rate per hour and their gross pay depends on the number of hours they work. This method is called the *hourly rate basis*. Other workers are paid an agreed amount each month or other period. This arrangement is called a *salary basis*.

The Wickham Novelty Company, which produces a variety of novelties and sells them by mail, is used to illustrate typical payroll procedures and records. The firm is owned by Harold Taylor. It is staffed by three production workers and a helper, who are paid on an hourly rate basis, and by one office worker, who is paid a monthly salary. The employees are subject to FICA tax and to federal income tax withholding. Taylor manages the company himself and draws out a portion of the profits from time to time, but receives no regular salary.

The employer is subject to FICA tax and to federal and state unemployment insurance taxes. Since the mail-order business constitutes interstate commerce, the firm is subject to the Fair Labor Standards Act (the Wage and Hour Law). The Wickham Novelty Company is also required by state law to carry workmen's compensation insurance.

DETERMINATION OF GROSS PAY (HOURLY WORKERS)

To determine the gross pay earned by a worker on an hourly rate basis, it is necessary to know the rate of pay and the number of hours worked.

Hours Worked

There are various methods of keeping track of the hours worked by each employee. In the Wickham Novelty Company, the shop foreman keeps a time book in which he enters the number of hours worked each day by each employee who is paid on an hourly basis. At the end of the week, the office clerk uses this record to prepare the payroll.

If the time book system is used in a larger enterprise, each foreman keeps a record of the time worked by the employees under his supervision. More often, however, the larger business uses a time clock. Each worker has a time card that he inserts in the time clock to record the time he arrives and leaves. The payroll clerk collects each card at the end of the week, determines the hours worked, multiplies by the applicable rate, and figures the gross pay.

Gross Pay

Suppose that the time book for the week ended January 7, 19X1 indicates that the first employee, Fred Baker, worked 40 hours. His rate of pay is $4 an hour. His gross pay of $160 is found by multiplying 40 hours by $4.

The second employee, James Dant, has worked 44 hours. Four of these hours are overtime and must be paid for at a premium rate of one half times Dant's regular rate of $2.50 per hour ($2.50 × .50 = $1.25 premium rate). His gross pay is calculated as follows.

Total time x regular rate:	44 hours @ $2.50	$110.00
Overtime premium:	4 hours @ 1.25	5.00
Gross pay		$115.00

This method is the one specified under the Wage and Hour Law and is therefore the one used in the illustrations. Another method, which gives the same gross pay, uses the steps shown on the next page.

Regular time earnings:	40 hours @ $2.50	$100.00
Overtime earnings:	4 hours @ 3.75	15.00
Gross pay		$115.00

The second method quickly answers the employee's question, "How much more did I earn by working overtime than I would have earned for only 40 hours of work?" The employer, however, is more concerned with the amount of premium he had to pay for the overtime hours. This represents the amount he could have saved if all the hours had been paid for at the regular rate. The first method gives this information.

The third worker, Joan King, worked 40 hours. Her hourly rate is $3. Her gross pay is therefore 40 hours times $3, or $120. The fourth employee, Ralph Sanchez, is the foreman. He worked 40 hours and his rate of pay is $5 per hour. Thus, his gross pay is 40 hours times $5, or $200.

DEDUCTIONS FROM GROSS PAY REQUIRED BY LAW

There are two principal deductions from employees' gross earnings that are required by federal law—social security (FICA) tax and income tax withheld.

FICA Tax

The Federal Insurance Contributions Act taxes are levied in an equal amount on both employer and employee. Since, as was previously mentioned, rates and bases are subject to frequent changes, a hypothetical rate and base will be used in this discussion. We shall assume that a tax rate of 6% is applied to a base consisting of the first $12,000 of wages paid to an employee during the calendar year. Wages paid in excess of the base amount are called tax-exempt wages. If an employee works for more than one employer during the year, the FICA tax would be deducted on the current base, such as the first $12,000 he is paid by each employer, and the excess tax will be refunded to him later by the government or applied to payment of his income taxes for the year.

Although the rates technically include two separate rates for (1) old age, survivors, and disability insurance; and (2) hospital insurance benefits, they are generally combined into one rate and referred to simply as "social security" or "FICA." The latter term is used in this textbook.

The FICA tax is deducted from the earnings of each employee of the Wickham Novelty Company at the assumed rate of 6% on the first $12,000 earned. The amount to be deducted can be computed either by multiplying the taxable wages by the rate of 6%, or, by reference to tax tables available from the government and from commercial stationers.

TAX COMPUTED BY THE PERCENTAGE METHOD. When the employee's FICA tax is computed by the percentage method, the employer merely multiplies the taxable wages by the tax rate, 6% in this case, and rounds the answer to the nearest penny. The FICA taxes to be deducted by the Wickham Novelty Company, based on the gross pay previously calculated, are shown below.

EMPLOYEE	GROSS PAY	TAX RATE	FICA TAX
Fred Baker	$160.00	6%	$ 9.60
James Dant	115.00	6%	6.90
Joan King	120.00	6%	7.20
Ralph Sanchez	200.00	6%	12.00
Total			$35.70

TAX DETERMINED FROM TAX TABLE. Taxes on wages (up to certain limits) can be determined from a tax table. For example, the wages of $160 earned by Fred Baker might fall in a bracket of the table ranging from "at least $159.92 but less than $160.09." At the assumed 6% rate, the table might then indicate a tax due of $9.60 on wages paid in this earnings bracket (the same result as with the percentage method).

Federal Income Tax Withholding

Over half the revenue of the federal government is derived from the income tax on individuals. Many rules and regulations are applied in tax determination. Rates, rules, and regulations are subject to frequent changes. The rates used in this text are for illustrative purposes only. In actual practice, a current edition of the Internal Revenue Service's Circular E would be consulted for up-to-date rates and other data.

Most taxpayers are on a pay-as-you-go-basis. The income tax due from a person earning a salary or wages must be withheld by the employer and paid to the government periodically—at the same time the FICA taxes are paid. At the end of the year, the individual employee files his tax return and either pays the balance of tax due or receives a refund for any over-payment.

CLAIMING WITHHOLDING EXEMPTIONS. The amount of income tax a person must pay depends on the amount of his income, the number of his exemptions, and his marital status. The matter of exemptions is a technical subject that cannot be explored fully here. In brief, a person is ordinarily entitled to one exemption for himself or herself, one for a spouse (unless the spouse also works and claims an exemption), and one for each dependent for whom the person furnishes more than half the support during the year. Employees claim the number of exemptions to which they are entitled by filing with their employers an Employee's Withholding Exemption Certificate, Form W-4. Fred Baker's certificate is illustrated.

FORM W-4 U.S. Treasury Department Internal Revenue Service	**EMPLOYEE'S WITHHOLDING EXEMPTION CERTIFICATE**		

Type or print full name ___Fred Baker___   Social Security Number __324-76-1245__

Home address ___24 Oak Street___   City __Wickham__   State __State__   ZIP code __53998__

EMPLOYEE: File this form with your employer. Otherwise, he must withhold U.S. Income tax from your wages without exemption. **EMPLOYER:** Keep this certificate with your records. If the employee is believed to have claimed too many exemptions, the District Director should be so advised.	**HOW TO CLAIM YOUR WITHHOLDING EXEMPTIONS**

1. If SINGLE (or if married and wish withholding as single person), write "1." If you claim no exemptions, write "0" . . .

2. If MARRIED, one exemption each is allowable for husband and wife if not claimed on another certificate.
   (a) If you claim both of these exemptions, write "2"; (b) If you claim one of these exemptions, write "1"; (c) If you claim neither of these exemptions, write "0" **2**

3. Exemptions for age and blindness (applicable only to you and your wife but **not** to dependents):
   (a) If you or your wife will be 65 years of age or older at the end of the year, and you claim this exemption, write "1"; if both will be 65 or older, and you claim both of these exemptions, write "2" . . . .
   (b) If you or your wife are blind, and you claim this exemption, write "1"; if both are blind, and you claim both of these exemptions, write "2" . . . .

4. If you claim exemptions for one or more dependents, write the number of such exemptions. (Do not claim exemption for a dependent unless you are qualified under Instruction 4 on other side.). . . . .

5. If you claim additional withholding allowances for itemized deductions fill out and attach Schedule A (Form W-4), and enter the number of allowances claimed (if claimed file new Form W-4 each year) . . . .

6. Add the exemptions and allowances (if any) which you have claimed above and write total **2**

7. Additional withholding per pay period under agreement with employer. (See Instruction 1.) . . . . $

I CERTIFY that the number of withholding exemptions claimed on this certificate does not exceed the number to which I am entitled.
(Date) ___January 1,___ , 19 _XI_   (Signed) ___Fred Baker___

If a worker fails to file a W-4 certificate, the employer must withhold tax from the wages as though there were no exemptions. If the number of allowable exemptions decreases, the employee must file a new certificate with the employer within ten days. If the number of exemptions increases, the employee *may* file an amended certificate. In this case, the employer may give effect to the amended certificate immediately or wait until the next "status determination" date—January 1 or July 1. If the worker desires, she or he may have the employer withhold a specified amount of income tax each pay period above the amount required by law.

COMPUTING INCOME TAX WITHHOLDING. There are several methods that may be used to compute the amount of income tax to be withheld from an employee's earnings. However, all except one involve cumbersome computations. The exception is the *wage-bracket table method* which permits the use of tables to determine the amount of tax. The simplicity of this method explains why it is used almost universally. The Employer's Tax Guide contains withholding tables for weekly, biweekly, semimonthly, monthly, and daily or miscellaneous payroll periods for married and single people. Sections of the weekly tables for both groups are illustrated.

After the proper table has been chosen, the first step in using the table is to find the line that covers the amount of wages earned. Follow across this line until you reach the column corresponding to the number of withholding exemptions claimed. The amount indicated is the income tax to be withheld. For example, Fred Baker has two withholding exemptions and earned $160 for the week. In the section of the table shown for married people paid weekly, the appropriate line is the one covering wages between $160 and $170. On this line, under the column headed "2," the amount of tax is given as $19.50. Similarly, the amount to be withheld from each of the other hourly employees of the Wickham Novelty Company may be

UNIT 17

WEEKLY Payroll Period—Employee MARRIED—

And the wages are-		And the number of withholding exemptions claimed is—										
At least	But less than	0	1	2	3	4	5	6	7	8	9	10 or more
		The amount of income tax to be withheld shall be—										
$100	$105	$14.10	$11.80	$9.50	$7.20	$4.90	$2.80	$.80	$0	$0	$0	$0
105	110	14.90	12.60	10.30	8.00	5.70	3.50	1.50	0	0	0	0
110	115	15.70	13.40	11.10	8.80	6.50	4.20	2.20	.10	0	0	0
115	120	16.50	14.20	11.90	9.60	7.30	5.00	2.90	.80	0	0	0
120	125	17.30	15.00	12.70	10.40	8.10	5.80	3.60	1.50	0	0	0
125	130	18.10	15.80	13.50	11.20	8.90	6.60	4.30	2.20	.20	0	0
130	135	18.90	16.60	14.30	12.00	9.70	7.40	5.10	2.90	.90	0	0
135	140	19.70	17.40	15.10	12.80	10.50	8.20	5.90	3.60	1.60	0	0
140	145	20.50	18.20	15.90	13.60	11.30	9.00	6.70	4.40	2.30	.30	0
145	150	21.30	19.00	16.70	14.40	12.10	9.80	7.50	5.20	3.00	1.00	0
150	160	22.50	20.20	17.90	15.60	13.30	11.00	8.70	6.40	4.10	2.00	0
160	170	24.10	21.80	19.50	17.20	14.90	12.60	10.30	8.00	5.70	3.40	1.40
170	180	26.00	23.40	21.10	18.80	16.50	14.20	11.90	9.60	7.30	5.00	2.80
180	190	28.00	25.20	22.70	20.40	18.10	15.80	13.50	11.20	8.90	6.60	4.30
190	200	30.00	27.20	24.30	22.00	19.70	17.40	15.10	12.80	10.50	8.20	5.90
200	210	32.00	29.20	26.30	23.60	21.30	19.00	16.70	14.40	12.10	9.80	7.50
210	220	34.40	31.20	28.30	25.40	22.90	20.60	18.30	16.00	13.70	11.40	9.10
220	230	36.80	33.30	30.30	27.40	24.50	22.20	19.90	17.60	15.30	13.00	10.70

WEEKLY Payroll Period—Employee NOT MARRIED—

And the wages are-		And the number of withholding exemptions claimed is—										
At least	But less than	0	1	2	3	4	5	6	7	8	9	10 or more
		The amount of income tax to be withheld shall be—										
$80	$82	$12.00	$9.10	$6.50	$3.90	$1.80	$0	$0	$0	$0	$0	$0
82	84	12.40	9.50	6.90	4.30	2.10	0	0	0	0	0	0
84	86	12.80	9.80	7.20	4.60	2.30	.30	0	0	0	0	0
86	88	13.20	10.20	7.60	5.00	2.60	.60	0	0	0	0	0
88	90	13.60	10.60	8.00	5.40	2.90	.90	0	0	0	0	0
90	92	14.10	11.00	8.30	5.70	3.20	1.20	0	0	0	0	0
92	94	14.50	11.40	8.30	6.10	3.50	1.40	0	0	0	0	0
94	96	14.90	11.90	9.00	6.40	3.90	1.70	0	0	0	0	0
96	98	15.30	12.30	9.40	6.80	4.20	2.00	0	0	0	0	0
98	100	15.70	12.70	9.80	7.20	4.60	2.30	.30	0	0	0	0
100	105	16.50	13.40	10.40	7.80	5.20	2.80	.80	0	0	0	0
105	110	17.50	14.50	11.50	8.70	6.10	3.50	1.50	0	0	0	0
110	115	18.60	15.50	12.50	9.60	7.00	4.40	2.20	.10	0	0	0
115	120	19.60	16.60	13.60	10.50	7.90	5.30	2.90	.80	0	0	0
120	125	20.70	17.60	14.60	11.60	8.80	6.20	3.60	1.50	0	0	0

obtained from the sections of the weekly wage-bracket withholding tables illustrated on the previous page.

The income tax to be withheld from the pay of the four hourly workers is summarized below.

EMPLOYEE	INCOME TAX WITHHELD
Fred Baker	$19.50
James Dant	16.60
Joan King	10.40
Ralph Sanchez	21.30
Total	$67.80

Other Deductions Required by Law

Some states require that state income tax be withheld from employees. The principles and mechanics are similar to those already explained for federal income tax withholding. Of course, the appropriate state withholding tables or tax rates must be used.

In certain states, unemployment tax or disability and sickness taxes must also be deducted from employees' wages. The amounts to be deducted are determined by applying the specified rates to taxable wages as defined in the law. The procedures involved in such deductions are similar to those that have already been illustrated.

At this time, we will assume that no other deductions are required by law as far as the wages of the employees of the Wickham Novelty Company are concerned.

DEDUCTIONS FROM GROSS PAY NOT REQUIRED BY LAW

Many kinds of deductions not required by law may be made from the pay of an employee by agreement or contract between the employee and the employer. For example, a specified deduction from the pay of the employee may be made each month or each payroll period for group life insurance or group hospital insurance. The employer often pays a share of the cost of such programs.

Company retirement plans may be financed entirely by the employer or by the employee and employer jointly. In the latter case, the contributions are usually based on the wages or salary earned and may be deducted each pay period.

In some cases, employees may ask to have amounts deducted from their earnings and deposited in a company credit union or bank, or accumulated and used to buy United States savings bonds, shares of stock, or other investments. The employee signs an authorization for such deductions; he or she may change this authorization or withdraw it at will. Employees who have received advances from their employers or who have bought merchandise from the firm, frequently repay these debts through payroll deductions.

These and other possible payroll deductions increase the payroll record-keeping work but do not involve any new principles or mechanics. They are handled in the same way as the two deductions required by law, which have been illustrated in detail.

DETERMINATION OF GROSS PAY (SALARIED WORKERS)

A salaried employee earns an agreed sum of money each pay period. Salaried workers may be paid by the week but more often are paid semimonthly or monthly. For example, the office clerk at the Wickham Novelty Company is paid monthly.

Hours Worked

Unless not eligible because of the level of their position or the amount of their salary, salaried workers are covered under the maximum hours and overtime premium pay provisions of the Wage and Hour Law. A time record should be kept for each salaried worker to make sure that hourly earnings meet legal requirements.

Gross Pay

Mary West worked her regular 38 hours each week and therefore no overtime premium is involved. Her agreed salary of $500 is her gross pay for the month of January.

DEDUCTIONS FROM GROSS PAY

Regardless of the method of paying an employee, FICA tax is deducted on the base amount ($12,000) of compensation received during the calendar year. For Mary West, this amounts to 6% of $500 for January, or $30.

For federal income tax withholding purposes, Mary West, who is not married, claims only one exemption. The amount of income tax to be withheld is determined by referring to the monthly wage-bracket withholding table. Her gross pay of $500 for the month is included in the line which reads "At least \$500, But less than \$520." Under the column for one exemption, \$72.10 is shown as the amount of income tax to be withheld from her earnings.

MONTHLY Payroll Period—Employee NOT MARRIED—

And the wages are		And the number of withholding exemptions claimed is—										
At least	But less than	0	1	2	3	4	5	6	7	8	9	10 or more
		The amount of income tax to be withheld shall be—										
\$420	\$440	\$68.40	\$55.30	\$42.50	\$31.20	\$20.00	\$10.00	\$1.30	\$0	\$0	\$0	\$0
440	460	72.60	59.50	46.30	34.80	23.60	12.80	4.10	0	0	0	0
460	480	76.80	63.70	50.50	38.40	27.20	15.90	6.90	0	0	0	0
480	500	81.00	67.90	54.70	42.00	30.80	19.50	9.70	.90	0	0	0
500	520	85.20	72.10	58.90	45.80	34.40	23.10	12.50	3.70	0	0	0
520	540	89.40	76.30	63.10	50.00	38.00	26.70	15.50	6.50	0	0	0
540	560	93.60	80.50	67.30	54.20	41.60	30.30	19.10	9.30	.60	0	0
560	580	97.80	84.70	71.50	58.40	45.30	33.90	22.70	12.10	3.40	0	0
580	600	102.00	88.90	75.70	62.60	49.50	37.50	26.30	15.00	6.20	0	0
600	640	108.30	95.20	82.00	68.90	55.80	42.90	31.70	20.40	10.40	1.60	0

RECORDING GROSS PAY AND DEDUCTIONS (HOURLY WORKERS)

Payroll personnel must compute the payroll accurately and promptly so that the net amount can be paid to the workers at scheduled times. The payroll data for each worker are consolidated in a columnar form called a *payroll register* or *payroll journal.*

PAYROLL REGISTER

A payroll register is illustrated on page 266, showing the payroll data for Wickham's four hourly workers.

The information regarding name, withholding exemptions, and regular hourly rate can be entered in the register in advance to save time in payroll preparation. From the completed time records, the hours worked each day are entered in the register, with total and overtime hours noted. Gross pay calculations are made in the manner previously described and are entered in the Earnings section, classified according to Regular and Overtime Premium earnings. The sum of the earnings is entered in the Total column.

The next two columns are used only when an employee has earned wages that are tax exempt (above \$4,200 for FUTA and above the assumed

HOURLY PAYROLL No. 1 Week Beginning Jan. 1, 19X1 and Ending Jan. 7, 19X1   Paid Jan. 9, 19X1

| NAME | INC. TAX EX. | MARITAL STATUS | HOURS BY DAYS | | | | | | | HOURS WORKED | | REG. HRLY. RATE | EARNINGS | | | TAX EXEMPT WAGES | | DEDUCTIONS | | | PAID | |
			S	M	T	W	T	F	S	TOTAL	OVER-TIME		REGULAR	OVERTIME PREMIUM	TOTAL	FICA	FUTA	FICA	INC. TAX WITH-HELD	OTHER	NET AMOUNT	CHECK NO.
Baker, Fred	2	M		8	4	8	8	8	4	40		4 00	160 00		160 00			9 60	19 50		130 90	4725
Dant, James	1	S		8	8	8	8	8	4	44	4	2 50	110 00	5 00	115 00			6 90	16 60		91 50	4726
King, Joan	3	M		8	8	4	8	8	4	40		3 00	120 00		120 00			7 20	10 40		102 40	4727
Sanchez, Ralph	4	M		8	8	8	8	8		40		5 00	200 00		200 00			12 00	21 30		166 70	4728
													590 00	5 00	595 00			35 70	67 80		491 50	

base of $12,000 for FICA). This information comes from the Cumulative Total column on the employee's individual earnings record, illustrated on page 281.

The calculations of FICA tax and the determination of the amount of income tax to be withheld are made as previously described, and the figures are entered in the appropriate columns. Any other deductions are entered with a proper explanation in the Other column. Subtracting the deductions from the gross pay leaves the net amount to be paid.

When the payroll data for all employees in the group have been recorded in the payroll register, the columns are totaled as shown. The accuracy of the register should be proved at this point, before the payroll is paid. This proof is accomplished by adding and subtracting the column totals across the register (called crossfooting) in this manner: Regular Earnings plus Overtime Premium equals Total Earnings; Total Earnings minus Deductions equals the Net Amount Paid.

Once the payroll register has been checked for accuracy, the payroll data are recorded in the general books. The column totals from the payroll register supply all necessary figures. Each item in the entry may be traced back to the register.

THE PAYROLL ENTRY

The gross pay should be charged to the appropriate expense account. For the factory workers at the Wickham Novelty Company, this account might be entitled Shop Labor 601. Separate liability accounts should be set up for each type of deduction made from the employees. A liability should also be recorded for the amount of net pay due, since this entry is made before the actual payment.

The entry for Wickham's January 7 payroll is made in the general journal, as shown.

19 X1		1–5					
Jan.	7	Shop Labor	601	595	00		
		Employee Ded.–FICA Tax . . .	221			35	70
		Employee Ded.–Inc. Tax WH . .	222			67	80
		Wages Payable	203			491	50
		To record gross earnings, deductions, and net wages payable for week ended Jan. 7, 19X1.					

PAYING THE PAYROLL

Some payrolls, particularly those of smaller firms, are paid in cash. However, most firms prefer to pay their employees by check. The canceled check provides a record of payment and the employee's endorsement constitutes a receipt. The use of checks avoids the inconvenience of obtaining the cash and putting it in pay envelopes and eliminates the risks involved in handling large amounts of currency.

Paying in Cash

When the payroll is to be paid in cash, one check is written for the total amount of net pay earned by all the employees. Then this check is cashed and bills and coins of suitable denominations are obtained so that the correct net pay amount may be inserted in the pay envelope of each worker. An information block on the pay envelope usually shows the amount of gross pay, the deductions, and the net pay. The employees may be asked to sign a receipt or to sign on their line of the payroll journal as evidence that his or her pay was received in cash.

Paying by Check

When employees are paid by check, an individual check is written for each employee. The check numbers are entered on the corresponding line in the payroll register in the Check Number column, as shown in the illustration on page 266. Gross pay and deductions are usually shown on a detachable stub of the pay check. The check is written for the net pay. The effect of the payment is to debit (decrease) Wages Payable and to credit (decrease) Cash.

Payroll checks may be drawn on the regular bank account or on a separate payroll bank account that may be established. If a separate payroll bank account is used, one check is usually drawn on the regular bank account for the net amount of wages payable and deposited in the payroll bank account. This check is entered in the cash disbursements journal as a debit to Wages Payable and a credit to Cash. Since individual checks totaling this amount are immediately written on the payroll bank account, this account never has a balance. Thus it does not appear on the financial statements.

RECORDING GROSS PAY AND DEDUCTIONS (SALARIED WORKERS)

If there were several salaried workers, a payroll register similar to the one illustrated for the hourly workers might be used. Since the Wickham Novelty Company has only one salaried employee, her earnings and deductions are recorded in a separate general journal entry, as illustrated.

	19	X1					
	Jan.	31	Office Salaries	501	500	00	
			Employee Ded.–FICA Tax	221			30 00
			Employee Ded.–Inc. Tax Withheld . .	222			72 10
			Wages Payable	203			397 90
			To record gross earnings and deductions and net salary payable to Mary West for the month of January, 19X1.				

Note that the Office Salaries account is debited for the gross earnings of Mary West. Her deductions are recorded in the same liability accounts as those of the hourly rate workers, and the net amount due to her is recorded in the same Wages Payable account. Salaried workers are ordinarily paid by check. The effect of the payment is to debit Wages Payable and credit Cash.

INDIVIDUAL EARNINGS RECORDS

At the beginning of each year, or when a new employee is hired during the year, an *individual earnings record* (sometimes called a compensation record) is set up for each worker. This record contains the employee's name, address, social security number, date of birth, number of withholding exemptions claimed, and any other information that may be needed. The details for each pay period are posted to the worker's individual earnings record from the payroll register. The record for Fred Baker shows the data for the first payroll in January.

NAME Fred Baker   EMPL. NO. 24   SOC. SEC. NO. 324-76-1245
ADDRESS 24 Oak Street, Wickham, State 53998   DATE OF BIRTH Jan. 23, 1928
WITHHOLDING EXEMPTIONS 2   MARITAL STATUS Married

	DATE		HOURS WORKED		RATE PER HOUR	EARNINGS			CUMULATIVE TOTAL	DEDUCTIONS		
	WEEK ENDED	PAID	TOT. HRS.	O.T. HRS.		REGULAR AMOUNT	OVERTIME PREMIUM AMOUNT	TOTAL AMOUNT		FICA	INCOME TAX WITHHELD	OTHER
1	1–7	1–9	40	0	4 00	160 00		160 00		9 60	19 50	

Note the details shown on this record, including the payroll date, the date paid, the hours worked, the hourly rate, the earnings (broken down between regular time and overtime as indicated in the payroll journal), and each deduction. These records may be totaled monthly and at the end of every calendar quarter. In this manner they provide information needed in making tax payments and filing tax returns, as described and illustrated in the next unit.

An individual earnings record is also maintained for each salaried employee. Either the same form of record as the one used for hourly workers or a slightly modified form designed especially for salaried workers may be used. Whatever the form of the record, the details of the earnings and deductions are entered in it for each payment, just as explained for the hourly workers.

COMPLETING JANUARY PAYROLLS

In order to complete the January payrolls, assume that the employees each worked the same number of hours per week during the month as they did the first week. They also earned the same gross pay, had the same deductions, and the same net pay each week.

Journal Entries

The way to record the journal entry covering the payroll of the Wickham Novelty Company for the first week in January has already been explained. Since we are assuming an identical payroll for each week, each of the four weekly payrolls requires an entry similar to the one shown on page 267. The office clerk is paid monthly. Her earnings and deductions for January are recorded in a separate journal entry, shown on page 269.

Ledger Accounts Posted

The entries for the weekly payrolls and for the monthly salaried worker are posted to the indicated ledger accounts. At the end of January, these appear as shown.

Wages Payable   No. 203

DATE	EXPLANATION	POST. REF.	DEBIT		DATE	EXPLANATION	POST. REF.	CREDIT
					19 X1			
					Jan. 7		1-5	491 50
					14		1-9	491 50
					21		1-15	491 50
					28		1-18	491 50
					31		1-21	397 90
								2363 *90*

Employee Deductions—FICA Tax   No. 221

DATE	EXPLANATION	POST. REF.	DEBIT	DATE		EXPLANATION	POST. REF.	CREDIT
				19 Jan.	X1 7		1-5	35 70
					14		1-9	35 70
					21		1-15	35 70
					28		1-18	35 70
					31		1-21	30 00
								172 80

Employee Deductions—Income Tax Withheld   No. 222

DATE	EXPLANATION	POST. REF.	DEBIT	DATE		EXPLANATION	POST. REF.	CREDIT
				19 Jan.	X1 7		1-5	67 80
					14		1-9	67 80
					21		1-15	67 80
					28		1-18	67 80
					31		1-21	72 10
								343 30

Office Salaries   No. 501

DATE		EXPLANATION	POST. REF.	DEBIT	DATE	EXPLANATION	POST. REF.	CREDIT
19 Jan.	X1 31		1-21	500 00				

Shop Labor   No. 601

DATE		EXPLANATION	POST. REF.	DEBIT	DATE	EXPLANATION	POST. REF.	CREDIT
19 Jan.	X1 7		1-5	595 00				
	14		1-9	595 00				
	21		1-15	595 00				
	28		1-18	595 00				
				2,380 00				

As previously mentioned, the earnings and deductions of each employee are posted to an individual earnings record. At the end of each month, the postings to these records for the period can be checked against the amounts posted to the ledger accounts. Each earnings record is totaled for the month; then a list is made of the column totals for gross pay and for each deduction, usually on an adding machine. The adding machine tape totals from the earnings records are compared with the current month's postings to the corresponding ledger accounts, and any differences are found and corrected.

The individual earnings record for Fred Baker at the end of January is shown. The record for each of the other employees would be similar.

NAME Fred Baker   **EMPL. NO.** 24   **SOC. SEC. NO.** 324-76-1245
ADDRESS 24 Oak Street, Wickham, State 53998   **DATE OF BIRTH** Jan. 23, 1928
WITHHOLDING EXEMPTIONS 2   **MARITAL STATUS** Married

| | DATE | | HOURS WORKED | | RATE PER HOUR | EARNINGS | | | CUMULATIVE TOTAL | DEDUCTIONS | | |
	WEEK ENDED	PAID	TOT. HRS.	O.T. HRS.		REGULAR AMOUNT	OVERTIME PREMIUM AMOUNT	TOTAL AMOUNT		FICA	INCOME TAX WITHHELD	OTHER
1	1–7	1–9	40	0	4 00	160 00		160 00		9 60	19 50	
2	1–14	1–16	40	0	4 00	160 00		160 00		9 60	19 50	
3	1–21	1–23	40	0	4 00	160 00		160 00		9 60	19 50	
4	1–28	1–30	40	0	4 00	160 00		160 00		9 60	19 50	
	January					640 00		640 00		38 40	78 00	

Adding machine tapes showing the total earnings and deductions entered on the individual earnings records of the employees of Wickham appear as shown.

Gross Earnings	FICA Withheld	Income Tax Withheld
.00*	.00*	.00*
640.00	38.40	78.00
460.00	27.60	66.40
480.00	28.80	41.60
800.00	48.00	85.20
500.00	30.00	72.10
2,880.00*	172.80*	343.30*

Note that the FICA tax deducted and the income tax withheld totals on the adding machine list taken from the individual earnings records agree with the ledger account balances for these items. The gross earnings total equals the sum of the debits to the Office Salaries and Shop Labor accounts shown on page 271. With this proof completed as shown, the records are ready for the transactions of the next month.

Reconciliation of Ledger Account Balances

Earnings:	Office Salaries	501	$ 500.00	
	Shop Labor	601	2,380.00	$2,880.00 (Dr.)
Deductions:	FICA Tax	221		$ 172.80 (Cr.)
	Income Tax Withheld	222		343.30 (Cr.)
Net Pay:	Wages Payable	203		2,363.90 (Cr.)
				$2,880.00 (Cr.)

RECORDING LIABILITY FOR UNPAID WAGES

In many cases it is not possible for the employer to pay wages in the month in which they are earned. As a result, there are wages owed to employees at the end of the month. These are called *accrued wages payable*. When the amount is large enough to be important, the accountant should make an adjusting entry at the end of the month to record the fact that the expense has been incurred and that a liability exists. The adjusting entry on the worksheet consists of a debit to the appropriate expense account and a credit to Wages Payable.

The accountant of the Wickham Novelty Company did not choose to record the accrued shop wages on January 31 because the amount was insignificant. However, many accountants would have felt that in order to record the expenses of January properly, the earnings of the employees for Monday, January 30, and Tuesday, January 31, should be recorded on January 31. They would then appear on the income statement of January, and the amount owed would appear as a liability on the balance sheet. The total wages earned by the four shop workers on the last two days of January was $216. If an adjusting entry had been made, it would have been recorded on the worksheet and later in the general journal as follows.

19 X1		1–22A					
Jan.	31	Shop Labor	601	216	00		
		Wages Payable	203			216	00
		To record wages accrued for services performed on January 30 and 31.					

Note that only the gross earnings are recorded as an expense and as a liability. No recognition is given to the withholding amounts because the withholdings are not technically made until payment is made to the employee. The accountant is merely interested in recording the total expense and the *total* liability. Adjustments for accrued salaries and wages are discussed further in Unit 26.

♦ ♦ ♦

PRINCIPLES AND PROCEDURES

The main objective of payroll work is to compute the amount due to employees and to pay these amounts promptly. The employer is required to withhold at least two taxes from the employees' paychecks: the employees' FICA tax and the federal income tax withholding. Instructions for computing the amount of each of these taxes are provided by the government to the employer. Other deductions may be made for state and city income taxes or by agreement between the employee and employer. The employer keeps a record of the employees' gross pay and deductions in a payroll register. Information from this register is used to prepare a payroll entry in the general journal.

Details of earnings and deductions for each employee are kept on an individual earnings record. These records may be proved monthly against the entries in the ledger accounts.

MANAGERIAL IMPLICATIONS

Employers must be very careful that their payroll procedures and their wage rates comply with governmental requirements, including the provisions of the federal Wage and Hour Law, which requires additional pay for overtime hours. Similarly, care must be taken to be sure that proper withholdings are made.

Payrolls make up a large part of the operating costs in most business enterprises. Thus, proper and adequate payroll records are also essential to business management as an aid in controlling expenses, knowing how much has been spent for labor, and the use made of the labor so that proper expense accounts may be charged. Payroll records must be kept accurately and must be carefully audited to prevent underpayment, overpayment, or fraud.

APPLICATION OF PRINCIPLES

PROBLEM 17 · 1

♦ White's Repair Shop (James White, owner) pays its employees on an hourly basis and pays one and a half times the regular rate for hours worked in excess of 40 in one week. The following data apply for the week ended Jan. 8, 19X1.

EMPLOYEE	TOTAL HOURS WORKED	HOURLY RATE	WITHHOLDING EXEMPTIONS	MARITAL STATUS
Tim Williams	44	$3.40	4	Married
Glen Wyzanski	42	3.10	3	Married
Lem Taylor	36	2.50	2	Single
Tom Levine	45	4.00	3	Married

INSTRUCTIONS

1. Set up a payroll register containing columns with the following headings: Name, Number of Exemptions, Marital Status, Total Hours Worked, Overtime Hours, Regular Hourly Rate, Regular Earnings, Overtime Premium, Total Earnings, FICA Withheld, Income Tax Withheld, and Net Amount. Enter each employee's name, exemptions, hours worked, and rate.
2. Compute the gross earnings for each worker, including regular time earnings and overtime premium, and enter.
3. Compute the FICA tax to be withheld from each employee's paycheck, using the assumed rate of 6% of gross earnings, and enter this amount in the register.
4. Compute the income tax to be withheld from each worker's paycheck, using the withholding tax wage-bracket tables on page 262. Enter this amount in the proper column of the register.
5. Compute the net pay for each employee and enter this in the register.
6. Total and rule the earnings and deductions columns. Prove by crossfooting.

PROBLEM 17 · 2

Morris Repair Shop is owned and operated by Robert Morris. He pays the workers on an hourly basis with time and a half for hours in excess of 40 worked in one week. Data for the week ended Dec. 24, 19X1 are shown. All three workers are married.

EMPLOYEE	HOURS WORKED	RATE	CUMULATIVE EARNINGS, DEC 17	EXEMPTIONS
Jane Morgan	41	$4.10	$ 7,800	3
Tommy Ness	48	3.50	5,400	4
John Ortiz	24	6.50	11,940	2

INSTRUCTIONS

1. Set up a payroll register containing columns with the following headings: Name, Number of Exemptions, Marital Status, Total Hours Worked, Overtime Hours, Regular Hourly Rate, Regular Earnings, Overtime Premium, Total Earnings, FICA Withheld, Income Tax Withheld, and Net Amount. Enter each employee's name, exemptions, hours worked and rate.
2. Compute the gross earnings for each worker, including regular time earnings and overtime premium, and enter these in the register.
3. Compute the FICA tax to be withheld from each employee's paycheck,

using the assumed rate of 6% of gross earnings, and enter this amount in the register.

4. Compute the income tax to be withheld from each worker's paycheck, using the withholding tax wage-bracket tables on page 262. Enter this amount in the proper column of the register.
5. Compute the net pay for each worker. Total the register.
6. Give the general journal entry (Number 12-4) to record the payroll. Debit Wages Expense 531; for other accounts involved, use account numbers given in the text illustrations.

PROBLEM 17 · 3

◆ A portion of the individual earnings record of J. L. Coker is shown in the *Individualized Performance Guide.* Coker is married and claims five withholding exemptions. He earns $3.50 per hour. During the week ending Mar. 31, he worked 43 hours, for which he was paid on that day. During the week ending Apr. 7, he worked 46 hours, for which he was paid on that date.

INSTRUCTIONS
1. Compute the gross earnings, FICA deduction (assuming a rate of 6%) and the federal income tax withholding (using the table on page 262) for the week ending Mar. 31, and enter the data for that week on Coker's earnings record.
2. Total all money columns for the month of March, and single-rule.
3. Bring down totals in all money columns for the quarter, and double-rule.
4. Compute the gross earnings, FICA deduction and federal income tax withholding for the week ending Apr. 7 and enter the data for that week on Coker's earnings record.

PROBLEM 17 · 4

◆ The two employees of City Delivery Service are paid on Friday of each week. William Smith, who is single, claims one exemption, and earns $3.10 per hour, worked 8 hours on Monday, Feb. 27 and 8 hours on Tuesday, Feb. 28. James Monroe is married, claims 2 exemptions, and earns $4.00 per hour. He worked only 6 hours on Feb. 27 and 8 hours on Feb. 28.

INSTRUCTIONS
Give the journal entry on Feb. 28, 19X1 to record the accrued wages so that an income statement can be properly prepared for the period ended on that date. Use the account numbers given earlier (account 601 for Delivery Wages).

MANAGERIAL CHECKUP

◆ How do proper and adequate payroll records aid management in controlling expenses?

18

PAYROLL TAXES

Under social security legislation and the Internal Revenue Code, the Wickham Novelty Company must act as a collection agent to gather the FICA tax and the income tax due from employees. The firm deducts, accounts for, and transmits these taxes to the government. How the accountant makes tax payments and files the required tax returns will be explained in this unit.

MONTHLY DEPOSIT OF FICA TAXES AND INCOME TAX WITHHELD

If the income tax withheld plus the employee and employer FICA taxes for a month amount to more than $100, the total must be deposited by the employer on or before the fifteenth of the following month in a Federal Reserve bank or in another bank authorized to receive such deposits. (Most commercial banks are so authorized.) Taxes for the third month of a quarter may be either deposited in this manner or paid with the quarterly tax return, which will be described later.

If the income tax withheld plus both FICA taxes total more than $2,500 for any month in the preceding calendar quarter, the employer is required to make semimonthly deposits. These special deposits must be made within three days after the close of the semimonthly period.

Employer's FICA Tax

Since the employer pays the FICA tax at the same rate and on the same taxable wages as his employees, the amount of tax the firm owes should be the same as that deducted from the employees. Hence, when

Wickham applies the assumed 6% rate to the total wages paid for January, $2,880, the same $172.80 tax would result. If any small difference occurred due to rounding off individual tax deductions, the company would probably match the amount deducted from the employees when making the monthly deposit and settle any final difference on the quarterly tax return. Because the Wickham Novelty Company is keeping its records on the cash basis, the employer's tax is not recorded until the cash is actually paid out.

Deposit of January Taxes

The January tax deductions from the employees of the Wickham Novelty Company and the employer's FICA tax are as follows.

Employees' FICA Tax Deducted	$172.80
Employees' Income Tax Withheld	343.30
Employer's FICA Tax Expense	172.80
Total	$688.90

The total exceeds $100 and therefore it must be deposited in an authorized bank by February 15, 19X1. The employer makes this payment by writing a check to the depository bank, which in this case is the Wickham National Bank. This payment is recorded in the cash disbursements journal. The debit amounts are entered in the Sundry Debits section and identified by account numbers. (A new account, Employer's FICA Tax Expense 551, is opened.) The amount of the check, $688.90, is entered in the Cash Credit column. This entry in the cash disbursements journal is illustrated.

CASH DISBURSEMENTS JOURNAL for Month of February 19X1   Page 2

DATE	CHECK NO.	EXPLANATION	SUNDRY DEBITS			ACCOUNTS PAYABLE		CASH CR. 101
			ACCT. NO.	✓	AMOUNT	✓	DR. 201	
Feb. 2	248	Emp. Ded.–FICA Tax	221		172 80			
		Emp. Ded.–Income Tax Withheld	222		343 30			
		Employer's FICA Tax Expense	551		172 80			688 90

The deposit must be accompanied by a properly filled out Tax Deposit, Form 501. This punched card form is processed and the amount paid is credited to the employer by the Internal Revenue Service. The Form 501 filed in February by the Wickham Novelty Company with the payment of its January FICA taxes and income tax withholdings is illustrated.

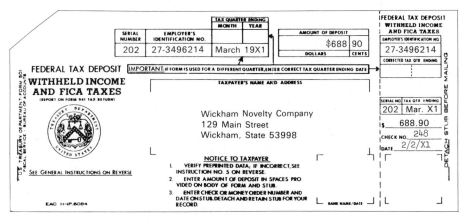

February Payroll Records

There are four payroll weeks in February for the Wickham Novelty Company. To simplify the example, assume that each hourly rate employee worked the same number of hours each week as he did in January and had the same gross pay and deductions. Assume also that the office clerk, Mary West, earned her regular salary and had the same deductions as in January. The individual earnings records would be posted and proved in the manner previously described. Then a tax deposit form would be prepared and the taxes deposited in the bank. Finally, an entry would be made in the cash disbursements journal, showing the same debits and credit to Cash as illustrated on page 278.

March Payroll Records

In March, the Wickham Novelty Company had 5 payroll weeks, making a total of 13 weekly payrolls for the quarter. Assume again that the earnings and deductions of each hourly employee were the same each week as in January and February and that the office clerk's monthly salary and deductions were the same as before.

The ledger accounts for the taxes withheld from employees' earnings with the payroll transactions posted for March are illustrated.

Employee Deductions—FICA Tax   No. 221

DATE	EXPLANATION	POST. REF.	DEBIT	DATE		EXPLANATION	POST. REF.	CREDIT	
				19	X1				
				Mar.	3		3-4	35	70
					10		3-8	35	70
					17		3-14	35	70
					24		3-19	35	70
					31		3-23	35	70
					31		3-26	30	00
								208	*50*

DATE	EXPLANATION	POST. REF.	DEBIT	DATE		EXPLANATION	POST. REF.	CREDIT	
				19	X1				
				Mar.	3		3-4	67	80
					10		3-8	67	80
					17		3-14	67	80
					24		3-19	67	80
					31		3-23	67	80
					31		3-26	72	10
								411	*10*

Quarterly Summary of Earnings Records

At the end of each calendar quarter each individual earnings record is totaled for that quarter. This involves adding the three monthly totals in each column and putting the sum on the line reading First Quarter. The record for Fred Baker, completely posted and summarized, is illustrated. Those for other employees are completed in the same way.

The quarterly columnar totals for each employee, taken from the individual earnings records, are shown.

EMPLOYEE	TOTAL EARNINGS	FICA	INCOME TAX WITHHELD
Fred Baker	$2,080.00	$124.80	$ 253.50
James Dant	1,495.00	89.70	215.80
Joan King	1,560.00	93.60	135.20
Ralph Sanchez	2,600.00	156.00	276.90
Mary West	1,500.00	90.00	216.30
Totals	$9,235.00	$554.10	$1,097.70

EMPLOYER'S QUARTERLY FEDERAL TAX RETURN

During the month following the end of each calendar quarter (April, July, October, and January), the employer must file a quarterly tax return and pay any balance of tax due for the quarter. This quarterly return is designated Form 941.

Listing Wages on Form 941

The first step in preparing the quarterly tax return is to draw up a list of the company's employees showing the social security number, name, and the amount of taxable wages paid to each of them during

NAME Fred Baker
ADDRESS 24 Oak Street, Wickham, State 53998
WITHHOLDING EXEMPTIONS 2

EMPL. NO. 24

SOC. SEC. NO. 324-76-1245
DATE OF BIRTH Jan. 23, 1928
MARITAL STATUS Married

	DATE		HOURS WORKED		RATE PER HOUR	EARNINGS				DEDUCTIONS		
	WEEK ENDED	PAID	TOT. HRS.	O.T. HRS.		REGULAR AMOUNT	OVERTIME PREMIUM AMOUNT	TOTAL AMOUNT	CUMULATIVE TOTAL	FICA	INCOME TAX WITHHELD	OTHER
1	1-7	1-9	40	0	4 00	160 00		160 00	160 00	9 60	19 50	
2	1-14	1-16	40	0	4 00	160 00		160 00	320 00	9 60	19 50	
3	1-21	1-23	40	0	4 00	160 00		160 00	480 00	9 60	19 50	
4	1-28	1-30	40	0	4 00	160 00		160 00	640 00	9 60	19 50	
	January					640 00		640 00		38 40	78 00	
1	2-4	2-6	40	0	4 00	160 00		160 00	800 00	9 60	19 50	
2	2-11	2-13	40	0	4 00	160 00		160 00	960 00	9 60	19 50	
3	2-18	2-20	40	0	4 00	160 00		160 00	1,120 00	9 60	19 50	
4	2-25	2-27	40	0	4 00	160 00		160 00	1,280 00	9 60	19 50	
	February					640 00		640 00		38 40	78 00	
1	3-3	3-5	40	0	4 00	160 00		160 00	1,440 00	9 60	19 50	
2	3-10	3-12	40	0	4 00	160 00		160 00	1,600 00	9 60	19 50	
3	3-17	3-19	40	0	4 00	160 00		160 00	1,760 00	9 60	19 50	
4	3-24	3-26	40	0	4 00	160 00		160 00	1,920 00	9 60	19 50	
5	3-31	3-31	40	0	4 00	160 00		160 00	2,080 00	9 60	19 50	
	March					800 00		800 00		48 00	97 50	
	First Quarter							2,080 00	2,080 00	124 80	253 50	

the quarter. (This information is shown in Items 4, 5, and 6 on the return on the following page.) Continuation sheets are used to list all the employees of a larger business. The taxable wages for the quarter are totaled on Line 8. The information in this listing comes from the individual earnings records that have been summarized and proved for the quarter.

Completing Form 941

The tax deposit forms for the payment of taxes in the earlier months of the period are listed and totaled on the back of Form 941. The front of the form identifies the employer by name and number. The amount of income tax withheld during the quarter is entered, together with any adjustments for preceding quarters. The wages subject to the FICA tax as shown on Line 8 are entered on Line 14. This amount is multiplied by the assumed rate, 12% (6% $\times$ 2), representing the combined rate for both employers and employees, to obtain the amount of FICA taxes due. (When taxable tips are reported, they are entered on Line 15. The tips are subject to the employee's FICA tax, but the employer is not required to pay any FICA tax on these tips.) The sum of the income tax withheld and the FICA taxes is the total tax due. From this total is deducted the sum of the amounts remitted with the monthly federal Tax Deposits, Forms 501 (listed in Schedule B on the reverse side of Form 941) to determine the net amount payable. The balance due must be sent with the return to the District Director of Internal Revenue for the district in which the principal office of the business is situated.

Recording the Payment

At the time the tax return is filed, a check is written to the Internal Revenue Service for the amount due, which in this case is $828.10. The entry to record this payment is given as it appears in the cash disbursements journal on page 284.

If there has been an insufficient collection, the employer must make up any difference, increasing the charge to the tax expense account. Although the employer is supposed to remit excess collections, in actual practice, small overages resulting from rounding off are usually absorbed in the tax expense account.

WITHHOLDING TAX STATEMENTS TO EMPLOYEES

By January 31 (or within 30 days after an employee leaves the service of an employer), the employer must furnish a Withholding Tax Statement, Form W-2, to each employee. This form shows the employer's name, address, and

Employer's Quarterly
Federal Tax Return

SCHEDULE A—Quarterly Report of Wages Taxable under the Federal Insurance Contributions Act—FOR SOCIAL SECURITY

IF WAGES WERE NOT TAXABLE UNDER THE FICA MAKE NO ENTRIES IN ITEMS 1 THROUGH 9 AND 14 THROUGH 18

1. (First quarter only) Number of employees (except household) employed in the pay period including March 12th ▶	5	2. Total pages of this return including this page and any pages of Form 941a ▶	1	3. Total number of employees listed ▶	5

List for each nonagricultural employee the WAGES taxable under the FICA which were paid during the quarter. If you pay an employee more than $12,000 in a calendar year report only the first $12,000 of such wages. In the case of "Tip Income" see instructions on page 4.

Please report each employee's name and number exactly as shown on his Social Security card.

4. EMPLOYEE'S SOCIAL SECURITY NUMBER			5. NAME OF EMPLOYEE (Please type or print)	6. TAXABLE FICA WAGES Paid to Employee in Quarter (Before deductions) Dollars Cents	7. TAXABLE TIPS REPORTED (See page 4) If amount in this column are not tips check here. Dollars Cents
000	00	0000			
324	76	1245	Fred Baker	2,080.00	
416	97	3676	James Dant	1,495.00	
277	46	3128	Joan King	1,560.00	
357	49	5239	Ralph Sanchez	2,600.00	
246	32	1467	Mary West	1,500.00	

If you need more space for listing employees, use Schedule A continuation sheets, Form 941a.

Totals for this page—Wage total in column 6 and tip total in column 7 ▶   9,235.00

8. **TOTAL WAGES** TAXABLE UNDER FICA PAID DURING QUARTER. (Total of column 6 on this page and continuation sheets.) Enter here and in Item 14 below . . . . . $ 9,235.00

9. **TOTAL TAXABLE TIPS** REPORTED UNDER FICA DURING QUARTER. (If no tips reported, write "None.") (Total of column 7 on this page and continuation sheets.) Enter here and in Item 15 below . . . . ▶ $

Employer's name, address, employer identification number, and calendar quarter. (If not correct, please change)

Name (as distinguished from trade name)	Date quarter ended
Harold Taylor	March 31, 19X1

▶ Trade name, if any Wickham Novelty Company

Address and ZIP code 129 Main Street Wickham, State 53998

Employer Identification No. 27-3496214

Entries must be made both above and below this line; if address different from previous return, check here ☐

Name (as distinguished from trade name)	Date quarter ended
Harold Taylor	March 31, 19X1

▶ Trade name, if any Wickham Novelty Company

Address and ZIP code 129 Main Street Wickham, State 53998

Employer Identification No. 27-3496214

T		FP
FF		I
FD		TOT

		Dollars	Cents
10.	TOTAL WAGES AND TIPS SUBJECT TO WITHHOLDING PLUS OTHER COMPENSATION . . . . ▶	9,235	00
11.	AMOUNT OF INCOME TAX WITHHELD FROM WAGES, TIPS, ANNUITIES, etc. (See instructions)	1,097	70
12.	ADJUSTMENT FOR PRECEDING QUARTERS OF CALENDAR YEAR	--	00
13.	ADJUSTED TOTAL OF INCOME TAX WITHHELD . . . . ▶	1,097	70
14.	TAXABLE FICA WAGES PAID (Item 8) . . . . $ 9,235.00 multiplied by 12%=TAX	1,108	20
15.	TAXABLE TIPS REPORTED (Item 9) . . . . $ multiplied by 6%=TAX	--	00
16.	TOTAL FICA TAXES (Item 14 plus Item 15) . . . . ▶	1,108	20
17.	ADJUSTMENT (See instructions) . . . . ▶	--	00
18.	ADJUSTED TOTAL OF FICA TAXES . . . . ▶	1,108	20
19.	TOTAL TAXES (Item 13 plus Item 18)	2,205	90
20.	TOTAL DEPOSITS FOR QUARTER (INCLUDING FINAL DEPOSIT MADE FOR QUARTER) AND OVERPAYMENT FROM PREVIOUS QUARTER LIST IN SCHEDULE B. (See instructions on page 4.)	1,377	80

Note: If undeposited taxes at the end of the quarter are $200 or more, the full amount must be deposited with an authorized commercial bank or a Federal Reserve bank. This deposit must be entered in Schedule B and included in Item 20.

21.	UNDEPOSITED TAXES DUE (ITEM 19 LESS ITEM 20—THIS SHOULD BE LESS THAN $200). PAY TO INTERNAL REVENUE SERVICE AND ENTER HERE	828	10

22. IF ITEM 20 IS MORE THAN ITEM 19, ENTER EXCESS HERE ▶ $ AND CHECK IF YOU WANT IT ☐ APPLIED TO NEXT RETURN, OR ☐ REFUNDED.

23. If not liable for returns in succeeding quarters write "FINAL" here ▶   and enter date of final payment of taxable wages here ▶

Under penalties of perjury, I declare that I have examined this return, including accompanying schedules and statements, and to the best of my knowledge and belief it is true, correct, and complete.

Date April 15, 19X1   Signature *Harold Taylor*   Title (Owner, etc.) Owner

DATE	CHECK NO.	EXPLANATION	SUNDRY DEBITS			ACCOUNTS PAYABLE		CASH CR. 101
			ACCT. NO.	√	AMOUNT	√	DR. 201	
Apr. 5	419	Emp. Ded.–FICA Tax	221		208 50			
		Emp. Ded.–Income Tax Withheld	222		411 10			
		Employer's FICA Tax Expense	551		208 50			828 10

identification number, and the employee's name, address, and social security number. Four amounts are indicated: FICA taxable wages paid, FICA tax deducted, total wages paid, and federal income tax withheld, if any.

The information for Form W-2 is obtained from the individual earnings records, posted and summarized for the year. Earnings and withholding data for the first six months are shown on the front of the card. (Information for the second quarter is identical to that for the first quarter, illustrated on page 281.) The reverse side of the earnings record contains data for the third and fourth quarters and also provides a line for entering yearly totals for each item.

Assume that the records for the employees show the following totals for the year. (Note that none of the Wickham employees earned more than $12,000 during the year. Therefore, all wages paid were subject to FICA tax.)

EMPLOYEE	TOTAL EARNINGS	FICA	INCOME TAX WITHHELD
Fred Baker	$ 8,320.00	$ 499.20	$1,014.00
James Dant	5,980.00	358.80	863.20
Joan King	6,240.00	374.40	540.80
Ralph Sanchez	10,400.00	624.00	1,107.60
Mary West	6,000.00	360.00	865.20
Totals	$36,940.00	$2,216.40	$4,390.80

Withholding Tax Statements (Forms W-2) are prepared from the individual earnings records. The one for Fred Baker is illustrated.

Wickham Novelty Company   27–3496214   **WAGE AND TAX STATEMENT** **19X1**
129 Main Street
Wickham, State 53998
Type or print EMPLOYER'S identification number, name, and address above.   *Copy A—For Internal Revenue Service*

FEDERAL INCOME TAX INFORMATION			SOCIAL SECURITY INFORMATION		
Federal income tax withheld	Wages paid subject to with-holding	Other compensation paid	F.I.C.A. employee tax withheld	Total F.I.C.A. wages paid	
$1,014.00	$8,320.00		$499.20	$8,320.00	

EMPLOYEE'S social security number ▶▶   324–76–1245

Fred Baker
24 Oak Street
Wickham, State 53998

Type or print EMPLOYEE'S name and address (including ZIP code) above.   Uncollected Employee Tax on Tips . . . $............

FORM W-2—U.S. Treasury Department, Internal Revenue Service   EMPLOYER: See instructions on back of copy D.

Four copies of each W-2 form are prepared. Two are furnished to the employee, who must attach one to his federal income tax return and should keep the other for his records. The employer keeps one for his records and must send one to the government with his annual report on Form W-3, described next.

ANNUAL RECONCILIA-TION OF TAX WITHHELD

When filing his last quarterly return for the year on Form 941, the employer must also submit the District Director's copies of all Forms W-2 (Withholding Tax Statement) issued during the year, together with a Reconciliation of Income Tax Withheld from Wages, Form W-3. This reconciliation lists and totals the amount of income tax withheld during the four quarters of the year as shown on the Forms 941 submitted by the employer. The total income tax withheld must be the same as the total of the Forms W-2 submitted. In other words, the government requires the employer at this time to identify the employees from whom he has withheld federal income tax during the year, as shown on their Forms W-2, and to demonstrate that the total withheld agrees with the amount remitted. The illustration shows a completed reconciliation on Form W-3 for the Wickham Novelty Company.

Form W-3 U.S. Treasury Department Internal Revenue Service	RECONCILIATION OF INCOME TAX WITHHELD AND TRANSMITTAL OF WAGE AND TAX STATEMENTS (FORMS W-2)		19X1
Type or Print Employer's Name and Address as it appears on Form 941 or 943	Name (as distinguished from trade name) Harold Taylor	Employer Identification No. (from Form 941 or 943) 27-3496214	
	Trade name (if any) Wickham Novelty Company	COPY FOR INTERNAL REVENUE SERVICE	
	Street address 129 Main Street	1. Number of Forms W-2 (Copy A), Wage and Tax Statements, attached:	
	City, State, and ZIP code Wickham, State 53998	5	

2. Total income tax withheld from wages reported on Forms W-2 .... $ $4,390.80
3. Total "Uncollected Employee Tax on Tips" reported on Forms W-2 .... $
4. Adjusted total of income tax withheld from wages as reported on Form 941 for Quarter ended:
   a. Mar. 31 .. $ 1,097.70   b. June 30 .. 1,097.70
   c. Sept. 30 .. 1,097.70   d. Dec. 31 .. 1,097.70
5. Total of amounts shown on lines 4a through 4d (if different from total on line 2 attach explanation) .... $ $4,390.80

Under penalties of perjury, I declare that I have examined this return, including accompanying schedules and statements, and to the best of my knowledge and belief it is true, correct, and complete.
Date January 20, 19X2   Signature *Harold Taylor*   Title Owner
                                                              (Owner, President, Partner, Member, etc.)

Filing of Form W-3 marks the end of routine procedure in accounting for payrolls and FICA taxes. Protection of workers against the risks of unemployment is the second major part of the social security program. Federal and state provisions for unemployment insurance call for additional taxes, records, and reports by the employer.

You will be able to understand the place and purpose of the accounting procedures involved more readily if you know first how the unemployment insurance legislation works.

Coverage

The basic legislation of 1935 imposes a direct payroll tax on certain employers to provide funds for an unemployment insurance program. For purposes of the Federal Unemployment Tax Act (FUTA), an "employer" includes any person or organization that has one or more employees on at least one day of each of twenty calendar weeks in a calendar year. Employers who qualify as exempt organizations under Section 501(c) (3) of the Internal Revenue Code (such as nonprofit schools and institutions) are not subject to the FUTA tax.

Benefits

When a worker loses his job, he must register with his state employment office and must accept any satisfactory position in his field of work that is offered to him. If, after a waiting period (two weeks in most cases), work cannot be found, the state pays the unemployed person a specified weekly amount designed to help relieve the financial distress resulting from a period of temporary unemployment. The length of time that unemployment benefits are paid varies from state to state, but is normally about 26 weeks.

Taxes

Under the original Act, a gross tax amounting to 3% of the first $3,000 paid each worker during the calendar year was levied on the employer by the federal government. The Act was further designed to encourage the states to provide complementary unemployment insurance programs. Special provisions permitted employers to deduct as much as 90% of the federal tax for payments made to states with approved plans. Each state has taken advantage of these provisions and has established its own unemployment insurance program. The gross federal tax has been changed a number of times, and at this writing it is 3.2%. Since a base rate of 2.7% is levied by the typical state, only the remaining 0.5% of the FUTA tax is actually paid to the federal government (3.2% − 2.7% = 0.5%). Also the base wages subject to the tax was increased to $4,200 beginning in 1972.

In addition to the tax on the employer, a few states also levy a tax on the employee. These taxes are deducted by the employer at the rates and on the bases prescribed by the state law and are remitted by the employer to the appropriate state agency at the time and in the manner required. No difference in principle is involved from that described for the handling of the employee's FICA tax; there is simply another deduction from the employee and a little more recordkeeping for the employer.

Merit Ratings

One of the purposes of the unemployment insurance program is to stabilize employment and to reduce unemployment. Firms that have stabilized their employment are granted a lower state tax rate under a merit-rating system, and the employer may take credit against FUTA as though he paid at the normal state rate (to a maximum of 2.7%). Hence, the employer may pay as little as a fraction of 1% to the state instead of the standard 2.7%. Penalty rates in excess of 2.7% may be levied if the unemployment record is bad.

STATE UNEMPLOYMENT TAX RETURNS (QUARTERLY)

Employers subject to state unemployment insurance (SUI) tax laws must file returns and pay the tax on a quarterly basis. The individual state return forms differ in detail, but generally include a list of employees identified by name and social security number, with the taxable wages paid to each during the quarter listed and totaled. The state limits for taxable wages are usually the same as those of the FUTA (the first $4,200 paid to an employee during the calendar year).

Taxable Wages

The list showing employees and taxable wages paid is prepared from the individual employee earnings records in the same way that the list on Form 941, Schedule A, was prepared for the Wickham Quarterly Federal Tax Return. Except that the limit of taxable wages for the unemployment tax is usually $4,200 (while the limit for FICA is higher), the lists might be identical. For the first quarter, the unemployment tax schedule for the Wickham Novelty Company is actually the same as that filed with federal Form 941.

Merit Rating

Assume that the Wickham Novelty Company has earned a merit rating and that its state unemployment tax rate is 1.3%. At this rate, on the taxable wages of $9,235 paid during the first quarter, the total tax due to the state is $120.06.

Payment of Tax

The SUI tax is usually due in the month following the end of the calendar quarter. The Wickham Novelty Company must pay its tax in April for the first quarter of the year and file the appropriate tax return with a list of employees and their taxable wages.

The accountant draws a check payable to the tax collecting authority, such as the State Division of Employment Security, for the amount of the tax due, $120.06, and submits it with the tax return. The entry that is made to recognize the tax expense and to record the payment is made in the cash disbursements journal, debiting Payroll Tax Expense 552 for that amount.

Payments for Subsequent Quarters

The same procedure is followed in subsequent quarters. Individual earnings records are summarized and taxable wages are listed from them. In the earnings record for Fred Baker, illustrated on page 281, note that there is a Cumulative Total column which is used to indicate when the tax exemption point is reached. Thus, the record would show that Fred Baker reached the $4,200 limit for unemployment insurance with his wages for the week ended July 7. The amount of tax-exempt wages for each employee for each tax would be indicated on the payroll register in the columns provided for that purpose (see page 266).

When preparing the state unemployment tax returns, the accountant examines the individual earnings records at the end of each quarter to determine the amounts of taxable wages and of state unemployment tax paid by the Wickham Novelty Company for each quarter during the year. Here is what he finds.

QUARTER ENDED	TAXABLE WAGES	TAX PAID
March 31	$ 9,235.00	$120.06
June 30	8,235.00	107.06
September 30	3,530.00	45.89
December 31	–0–	–0–
Totals	$21,000.00	$273.01*

*$.01 overage due to rounding off.

Each subject employer must file an Employer's Annual Federal Unemployment Tax Return, Form 940, and pay the tax due for the year by the following January 31. The information for this return comes partly from the individual earnings records and partly from copies of the state unemployment tax returns that the employer has filed during the year.

Computation of Taxable Wages

The computation of taxable wages is shown on Schedule B on the reverse side of Form 940. Total wages paid to employees are listed. From this total are deducted any remuneration in excess of $4,200 paid to an individual employee and any other exemptions. The difference is the total taxable wages, which is carried over to the front of Form 940. As listed on the form illustrated, total remuneration for the year paid by the Wickham Novelty Company was $36,940. Tax-exempt wages amounted to $15,940, leaving $21,000 taxable. (This is easily proved, since the firm had five employees, each of whom earned more than $4,200 for the year.) Schedule B shows these figures.

Schedule B—COMPUTATION OF TAXABLE WAGES
(See Schedule B instructions on page 2)

	Approximate number of employees involved	Amount paid	
1. Total remuneration (including exempt remuneration) PAID during the calendar year for services of employees.			$ 36,940.00
Exempt remuneration: LIST EACH TYPE OF EXEMPTION			
2. Remuneration in excess of $4,200. (Enter only the excess over the first $4,200 paid to individual employees).	5	15,940.00	
3. All other exemptions (Explain each exemption shown, attaching additional sheet if necessary):			
4. Total exempt remuneration.	x x x x x x x	x x x x x x x x	15,940.00
5. Total taxable wages (line 1 minus line 4). Enter this amount in Item 13 on other side.			$ $21,000.00

Computation of Credit

Schedule A of Form 940 is for computation of credit against federal unemployment tax. This credit results from state taxes paid plus those waived because of a merit rating. For each state in which taxable wages were paid, the accountant shows the name of the state, state identification number, taxable payroll, experience (merit) rating, tax payable if the rate had been 2.7%, and tax payable under merit rating. The credit against the federal tax is the sum of the state tax payable plus the amount waived because of the experience rating, or 2.7% of the taxable wages, whichever is smaller. Note the $294 saved because of the merit rating (Item 8 in the report). Schedule A of Form 940 is subject to change to reflect new rates and regulations.

Tax Computation on Form 940

The front of the Employers' Annual Federal Unemployment Tax Return, Form 940, contains, in addition to Schedule A for computing the credit, the employer's name, address, and identification number. Spaces are provided for showing total taxable wages paid (as determined in Schedule B) and the gross federal tax of 3.2% of this amount. From the gross tax, the credit allowable is subtracted (as determined in Schedule A), leaving the remainder of the tax that must be paid with the return, as shown in the illustration.

Payment of Tax

A check for the amount of tax due, $105, is written to the order of the Internal Revenue Service and mailed with the return to the District Director of Internal Revenue for the district in which the principal office of the business is located. This payment is recorded in the cash disbursements journal as a debit to Payroll Tax Expense 552.

WORKMEN'S COMPENSATION INSURANCE

Employers required by state law to carry workmen's compensation insurance generally pay an estimated premium in advance; then, after the end of the year, they pay an additional premium (or receive credit for overpayment) based on an audit of the payroll for the year. The rate of the insurance premium varies with the risk involved in the work performed. Therefore, it is important to have employees classified properly according to the kind of work they do and to summarize labor costs according to the insurance premium classifications.

For the purpose of this insurance rating there are only two different work classifications in the Wickham Novelty Company: office work and shop work. Premium rates are $.20 per $100 for office work and $3.20 per $100 for shop work. Based on the payroll for the previous year, Wickham Novelty paid an estimated premium of $955 on January 15 for the year 19X1. A check was written to the insurance company for this amount and an entry was made in the cash disbursements journal debiting Workmen's Compensation Insurance Expense 555 and crediting Cash.

FORM 940

EMPLOYER'S ANNUAL FEDERAL UNEMPLOYMENT TAX RETURN—19X1
U.S. Treasury Department — Internal Revenue Service
Schedule A — COMPUTATION OF CREDIT AGAINST FEDERAL UNEMPLOYMENT TAX

Name of State (1)	State reporting number as shown on employer's State contribution returns (2)	Taxable Payroll (As defined in State act) (3)	Experience rate period (4) From—	To—	Experience rate (5)	Contributions had rate been 2.7% (col. 3 × 2.7%) (6)	Contributions payable at experience rate (col. 3 × col. 5) (7)	Additional credit (col. 6 minus col. 7) (8)	Contributions actually paid to State (9)
State	26543	$21,000.00	1/1	12/31	1.3	$567.00	$273.01*	$293.99	$273.01

*Adjustment due to rounding off

TOTALS..		$21,000.00	x x x	x x x	x x	x x x x	x x x x x x	$293.99	$273.01

10. Total tentative credit (Column 8 plus column 9) $567.00
11. Enter here 2.7% of amount of wages in Item 13 below. $567.00
12. Credit allowable (Item 10 or 11 whichever is smaller). Enter here and in Item 15 . . . $567.00

EMPLOYERS — DO NOT USE THIS SPACE — CONTINUE BELOW

State reporting number as shown on employer's State contribution returns	Taxable Payroll (As defined in State act)	Experience rate period From—	To—	Experience rate	Dates and amounts of contributions actually paid to State after January 31	Contributions actually paid to State before February 1

TO THE INTERNAL REVENUE SERVICE:

I hereby certify that, except as noted above, the records of this office agree with the entries made by the employer in columns (2), (3), (4), (5), and (9) of Schedule A, and that all contributions were paid before February 1.

Signature of State Officer .... Name of State ....

Employer's name, address, identification number and calendar year.
(If not correct please change.)

Name (as distinguished from trade name) Harold Taylor

Calendar Year **19X1**

Trade name, if any Wickham Novelty Company Identification No. 27–3496214

Address and ZIP code 129 Main Street
Wickham, State 53998

-------- Entries must be made both above and below this line --------

Name (as distinguished from trade name) Harold Taylor

Calendar Year **19X1**

Trade name, if any Wickham Novelty Company Identification No. 27–3496214

Address and ZIP code 129 Main Street
Wickham, State 53998

If no longer in business write "Final."

U.S. TREASURY DEPARTMENT
Internal Revenue Service

OFFICIAL BUSINESS
POSTAGE AND FEES PAID

T
P
I
T

POSTMASTER: If undeliverable treat in accordance with Section 355.56 of Postal Manual.

13. Total taxable wages paid during calendar year (From Schedule B, on other side) . . . . $21,000|00
14. Gross Federal tax (3.2% of wages in Item 13). . . . . 672|00
15. Less: Credit from Item 12 of Schedule A . . . . 567|00
16. Remainder of tax (Item 14 minus Item 15). Pay to "INTERNAL REVENUE SERVICE" ——— 105|00

Under penalties of perjury, I declare that I have examined this return, including accompanying schedules and statements, and to the best of my knowledge and belief it is true, correct, and complete, and that no part of any payment made to a State unemployment fund which is claimed as a credit in Item 15 above was or is to be deducted from the remuneration of employees.

Harold Taylor
(Signature)

Owner
(Title (Owner, president, partner, member, etc.))

Jan. 10, 19X2
(Date)

BE SURE TO ENCLOSE REMITTANCE WITH THIS RETURN (Form 940)
FILE THIS FORM WITH YOUR INTERNAL REVENUE SERVICE OFFICE NOT LATER THAN JANUARY 31, 19X2

At the end of the year, the accountant analyzes the payrolls and applies the proper rates to determine the premium for the year, as follows.

CLASSIFICATION	PAYROLL	RATE	PREMIUM
Office Work	$ 6,000.00	0.2%	$ 12.00
Shop Work	30,940.00	3.2%	990.08
Total	$36,940.00		$1,002.08
Less estimated premium paid			955.00
Balance due			$ 47.08

The final balance due to the insurance company, $47.08, is paid by check and entered in the cash disbursements journal as a debit to Workmen's Compensation Insurance Expense 555.

◆ ◆ ◆

PRINCIPLES AND PROCEDURES

Employers serve as collection agents for FICA taxes and income tax withheld from employees and must remit these amounts, together with the employer's FICA tax, to the government as required by law. These taxes must be deposited in an authorized bank within 15 days following the end of any month in which they amount to more than $100. A Federal Tax Deposit, Form 501 is prepared and submitted with this payment.

At the end of each calendar quarter, the employer must file a quarterly tax return on Form 941 reporting taxable wages paid to employees during the quarter and the income tax withheld. Any balance of tax due must be paid with this return.

By the end of January, each employee must be furnished a Form W-2 statement, showing his earnings for the year and deductions for the FICA tax and the income tax withheld. The employer prepares an annual Reconciliation of Income Tax Withheld from Wages, Form W-3, and files it together with copies of each of the W-2 statements issued to the employees.

Unemployment insurance protects workers against the financial problems of temporary unemployment. It is administered by the separate state governments. The premium, or tax, for this insurance is paid by the employer, although some states levy a tax on employees also. Taxes must be paid to both the state and federal government.

State tax returns differ in detail, but usually call for a list of employees, their social security numbers, and the taxable wages paid. An Employer's Annual Federal Unemployment Tax Return (Form 940) must be filed each January for the preceding calendar year. It shows the amount of total wages paid, the amount of taxable wages, and the gross federal tax, which is currently 3.2% of the first $4,200 paid each employee each year. Credit against the gross tax is allowed for tax paid under state plans or waived because of state merit ratings, up to a total credit of 2.7 percent.

Employers may be required under state law to carry workmen's compensation insurance. Ordinarily, an estimated premium is paid in advance and a final settlement is made with the insurance company on the basis of an audit of the payroll after the end of the year. Premiums vary according to the type of work performed by each employee.

MANAGERIAL IMPLICATIONS

Payroll tax returns and forms must be filed promptly and accurately by the management in order to avoid penalties imposed by law. The accounting records must facilitate the preparation of these reports in an efficient manner. Today's manager must thoroughly understand the various payroll tax laws if he expects to control both direct and related costs of labor in his operations.

APPLICATION OF PRINCIPLES

PROBLEM 18 · 1

During the month following the close of each calendar quarter, an employer is required by law to file Form 941 (Employer's Quarterly Federal Tax Return). Assume that the Shelton Company (Robert Shelton, owner), 3415 Broad Street, Charleston, State, 13507; identification number 57-0202745; received these forms from the Internal Revenue Service for the third quarter of 19X1.

Here is a summary of the payroll for each quarter.

SOCIAL SEC. NUMBER	EMPLOYEE	TOTAL EARNINGS	FICA DEDUCTED	INCOME TAX WITHHELD
251-07-4416	George Brown	$ 2,040.00	$122.40	$ 268.90
586-22-1411	John L. Coker	2,820.00	169.20	336.50
247-15-3319	Thomas Hazel	1,040.00	62.40	94.90
322-08-9935	Walter Morris	4,500.00	180.00	920.00
333-11-8503	John Walker	1,800.00	108.00	184.50
538-13-4976	Dorothy Moore	900.00	54.00	138.12
	Totals	$13,100.00	$696.00	$1,941.92

The owner of the Shelton Company has prepared the Federal Tax Deposit Form 501 and written checks as follows:

	JULY	AUGUST
Employees' FICA Tax Deducted	$ 252.00	$ 252.00
Employees' Income Tax Withheld	647.30	647.31
Employer's FICA Tax Expense	252.00	252.00
Total Payroll Taxes	$1,151.30	$1,151.31

(a) Federal Tax Deposit XX08, paid Aug. 15, 19X1, $1,151.30
(b) Federal Tax Deposit XX09, paid Sept. 12, 19X1, $1,151.31

INSTRUCTIONS
1. Complete Schedule A (Form 941) Quarterly Report of Wages Taxable under the Federal Insurance Contributions Act. (Note that Morris has passed the $12,000 earnings limit and only $3000 of his wages are taxable.)
2. Complete the remainder of Form 941, including Schedule B, using the assumed 12% total FICA rate in computations. Sign the form with your name and use the title "Accountant." Date the report Oct. 25, 19X1.
3. On Oct. 25, 19X1, the owner issues a check in payment of payroll taxes for the amount due as shown on Form 941. In general journal form, record issuance of the check. (Number the entry 10-16.)

PROBLEM 18 · 2

Certain transactions and procedures relating to unemployment taxes and to workmen's compensation insurance for the Wilson Company, 1616 Main Street, Capital City, State, 99999, Identification Number 57-0202746 (Ray Wilson, owner), are given in the following information. Carry out the procedures as instructed in each step.

INSTRUCTIONS
1. Account for the yearly settlement of the workmen's compensation insurance premium. The auditor for the insurance company that issues the policy to the Wilson Company has made an analysis of payrolls for the preceding year (19X0), which disclosed the following:

CLASSIFICATION	AMOUNT OF WAGES PAID	EFFECTIVE INSURANCE RATE	PREMIUM EARNED
Office work	$ 6,300.00	.11%	$ 6.93
Shop labor	27,342.00	2.90%	792.92
Totals	$33,642.00		$799.85
Less estimated premium paid			720.00
Balance of premium due			$ 79.85

The owner issues a check dated Jan. 20, 19X1 for $79.85. Record the payment (Entry 1-15) in general journal form.
2. Account for the payment of the current year's estimated premium for workmen's compensation insurance. An invoice has been received from the insurance company for the estimated premium for the current year. It is based upon the actual premium earned the preceding year, as adjusted in accordance with the owner's estimate of wages to be paid this year, and reads as follows:

CLASSIFICATION	ESTIMATED WAGES	EFFECTIVE RATES	ESTIMATED PREMIUM
Office work	$ 6,600.00	.11%	$ 7.26
Shop labor	34,000.00	2.90%	986.00
Totals	$40,600.00		$993.26

The owner issues a check dated Jan. 31, 19X1 for $993.26. Record the payment in general journal form. (Use Entry 1-17.)

3. Compute the state unemployment insurance taxes required on the employer's quarterly report of employees' wages for the Wilson Company for the quarter ended Mar. 31, 19X1. The Wilson Company has received a merit rating (sometimes known as an "experience rating") and consequently pays only a 2% state unemployment tax rate. (The maximum rate of tax in the state is normally 2.7%.) The other information you need is as follows:

SOCIAL SECURITY NUMBER	NAME OF EMPLOYEE	TOTAL EARNINGS
251-07-4400	Will B. Abbott	$ 1,840.00
586-22-1401	Ken I. Due	1,841.00
247-15-3302	Sam T. Mann	1,840.00
322-08-9903	Thomas T. Todd	2,196.00
333-11-8504	Sally S. Smith	2,007.50
538-13-4905	Mark M. Worth	900.00
Totals		$10,624.50

4. The owner issues a check dated Apr. 29, 19X1, for the amount you computed in Instruction 3. Record the check (Entry 4-22) in general journal form.

5. To complete the problem, assume that all weekly and monthly payrolls have been prepared and paid and that all quarterly reports have been submitted as required. The payroll information for 19X1 is as follows:

QUARTER ENDED	TOTAL WAGES PAID	WAGES PAID IN EXCESS OF $4,200	STATE UNEMPLOYMENT TAX PAID
Mar. 31	$10,724.50	$ –0–	$214.49
June 30	10,816.50	66.50	215.00
Sept. 30	10,400.00	8,400.00	40.00
Dec. 31	10,500.00	10,200.00	6.00
Totals	$42,441.00	$18,666.50	$475.49

Complete the following parts of Form 940 (Employer's Annual Federal Unemployment Tax Return).

a. Schedule A—Computation of Credit Against Federal Unemployment Tax.

b. Schedule B—Computation of Taxable Wages. (Six employees received "excess" wages.)

c. The remainder of Form 940. Sign the form with your name and use the title "Accountant." Date the form Jan. 24, 19X2. (This would be the succeeding year.)

6. The owner issues a check dated Jan. 24, 19X2, for the amount shown on Line 16 of Form 940. Record the check (Entry 1-17) in general journal form.

PROBLEM 18 · 3

The Samuels Company has four employees. Data relating to the July 19X1 payroll are given:

EMPLOYEE	JULY WAGES	CUMULATIVE EARNINGS THROUGH JUNE
H. Adams	$620	$3,720
B. Jones	520	3,120
C. Taylor	600	3,600
D. Davis	450	2,700

INSTRUCTIONS

1. Assuming that the four employees had earnings in August and September equal to their July earnings, compute the amount of state unemployment tax (at a 2.7% rate) that would be paid on the wages by the Samuels Company for the third quarter of the year. (Refer to text illustrations for account numbers to be used throughout this problem.)

2. Give the general journal entry on Oct. 10 to record the payment of the state tax when the quarterly return is filed. (Entry 10-1.)

3. Assuming that the total earnings for the year are as shown below, compute the federal unemployment tax due for the year, and give the general journal entry to record payment of the tax on Jan. 12, 19X2 (Entry 1-12). The federal tax is 3.2%, less a credit for the state tax of 2.7%.

H. Adams	$6,200
B. Jones	6,240
C. Taylor	7,200
D. Davis	5,400

4. On Jan. 4, 19X1, the Samuels Company had paid the estimated workmen's compensation insurance premiums for 19X1. The estimate was based on an expected payroll of $24,000, and a premium rate of $2 per $100 of wages.

a. Give the general journal entry to record payment of the estimated premium on Jan. 4, 19X1 (Entry 1-5).

b. Give the general journal entry to record payment of the balance based on the actual payroll (given in Instruction 3) for the year, payment being made on Jan. 18, 19X2 (Entry 1-6).

MANAGERIAL CHECKUPS

♦ Why is it important for a manager to thoroughly understand the various payroll tax laws and procedures?

♦ What is the significance to the management of the merit rating system of determining the employer's tax under the state unemployment insurance law?

19 INTERNAL CONTROL SYSTEM: VOUCHER REGISTER

Each of the two firms studied so far, the Carter Cleaning Shop and the Wickham Novelty Company, has a single owner. These concerns represent a form of business organization called *sole proprietorship*. In the next several units, you will be studying the operations of another type of business organization, the *partnership*, where there are two or more owners. You will learn the accounting procedures followed by the Ashton & Barker Clothing Store, owned by three partners, George Ashton, Ronald Barker, and William Conrad. The partnership was formed on February 1, 19X1.

At that time Ashton, formerly sole proprietor of the Ashton Clothing Store, transferred the assets and liabilities of his store as his investment in the new business while Barker and Conrad contributed additional capital in the form of cash.

Actually there are very few differences in the routine accounting followed by sole proprietorships and partnerships. At this point, it is sufficient that you know only that a separate investment account and a separate drawing account are opened for each partner. Thus, the chart of accounts for Ashton & Barker Clothing Store contains the following:

    301   Ashton Investment
    302   Ashton Drawing
    311   Barker Investment
    312   Barker Drawing
    321   Conrad Investment
    322   Conrad Drawing

As businesses become larger, it becomes more difficult for a sole owner to personally transact and supervise all the operations of the business. That is why several owners might pool their activities in a partnership such as Ashton & Barker. However, even in a partnership, greater reliance must be placed on the accounting system to help control operations. Losses to American businessmen from employee carelessness, inaccuracy, and dishonesty have been estimated to total almost a billion dollars a year. No business is immune from this hazard, and to ignore it may mean the difference between a profitable operation and a complete failure. This is why the public accountant servicing a firm such as the Ashton & Barker Clothing Store would recommend a strong system of internal control.

GENERAL PRINCIPLES OF INTERNAL CONTROL

Internal control is a system of forms and procedures designed to safeguard the assets of a business and to help ensure the accuracy and reliability of the accounting records. The system should be organized and operated so that the work of one person provides a check on the work of another, with a minimum duplication of effort. If the business has enough employees to permit the necessary separation of duties, a strong system of internal control can be established. If the number of employees is small, internal control will be weaker and will have to be supplemented by more careful attention and supervision from the owner or manager of the enterprise.

The accountant for Ashton & Barker recommends that the partners give careful consideration to the following points when planning the operating routines for their new business. You have already learned some of these principles in Units 7 and 8, but they are repeated here to round out the picture of a total system.

1. No one person should be in complete charge of any important business transaction. Two or more employees should be assigned to every operation, and the work of one should be planned so that it will be checked against the work of the other at some point in the routine.
2. The person or persons who handle cash should not be the same ones who have the accounting responsibility for cash.
3. Every employee should be trained to do his job and should also understand why the job or procedure is to be performed in the prescribed manner.
4. Only capable and experienced personnel of demonstrated reliability should be assigned to key positions in the internal control system. The unannounced rotation of these assignments is also desirable. Annual vacations should be required for each employee, and his regular work should be performed by others during his absence.
5. Management must review and appraise the established system of internal control periodically to make sure that it is operating as planned and will continue to provide adequate safeguards.
6. The modern control system should include mechanical devices as well as forms, records, and routines to provide maximum protection. It is a known fact that cash registers, cashier cages, and locked storerooms, for example, make the misappropriation of assets more difficult.

INTERNAL CONTROL OVER CASH RECEIPTS

Cash is the most precious and most fluid asset of the average business. Every penny received in payment for goods and services must be protected so that funds will be available to pay bills, salaries, and the many other inevitable obligations. The principles of internal control should be applied to the handling of cash receipts by observing the following precautionary routines:

1. One person should receive the cash, whether it is delivered by mail or in person (over the counter) and, after making a record of the receipt, should turn the cash over to another person for deposit in the bank.
2. All cash receipts should be deposited in the bank promptly. They should not be used for making cash payments.
3. The recording of cash receipts on the general books of the company should be performed by a person other than the one who receives it and other than the one who deposits it in the bank.
4. At the end of each month, a person other than one of the three above should obtain the bank statement directly from the bank and should prepare a bank reconciliation statement.

CONTROL OF CASH RECEIPTS AT ASHTON & BARKER

As soon as Ashton & Barker reached an agreement about the terms of their partnership, a bank account for the partnership was opened at the City National Bank on February 1, 19X1. This was only the first step in the development of a complete system of control over cash. The partners agreed from the start that all cash receipts would be deposited daily and that only the partners would be authorized to sign checks drawn against the firm's funds. They completed a signature card similar to the one illustrated in Unit 8.

THE DAILY ROUTINE

The accountant recommended that cash coming in by mail be handled by two persons—one to receive and list it, and another to deposit it. Jean Edwards is assigned to receive and list mail receipts. At the end of the day, she turns the actual receipts over to Ashton for deposit and gives the list to the accountant for entry in the records.

Cash and checks received from customers in person are rung up on the cash register in the store by Harry Gordon, a salesman. Since he needs to make change at the counter, a special *change fund* is established by drawing a check payable to Gordon (who is in charge of and responsible for the fund). After this check is cashed, Gordon has a variety of denominations of coins and bills to speed his operations.

At the end of the day, Gordon separates the change fund from the cash receipts. The change fund is transferred to the company safe for storage overnight. The analysis of receipts is given to the accountant for entry in the records, and the day's receipts go to Ashton for deposit. At this time, Ashton has the receipts from both Edwards and Gordon. He now sorts and counts all cash and cash items for listing on the deposit slip. The banking procedures used by Ashton & Barker are similar to those you learned for the Carter Cleaning Shop in Unit 8.

THE CASH RECEIPTS JOURNAL

The accountant in charge of the general books of the firm occupies a vital spot in the internal control system.

Recording

The accountant enters the cash receipts daily in the cash receipts journal, using the list of mail receipts prepared by Jean Edwards and the analysis of store receipts prepared by Harry Gordon as the basis for his record. Then the accountant compares the amount shown on the day's receipted deposit slip with his records to make sure that all money received has been deposited on the same day, in accordance with company policy.

Cash Short or Over

In making change, some errors are almost certain to result. If such errors are made, the cash available for deposit from cash sales will be either more or less than that listed on the cash register tape. If the amount of cash is greater than that shown on the tape, cash is said to be *over*; if there is less cash than the tape shows, cash is *short*. In practice, cash tends to be short more often than over, perhaps because customers are more likely to notice and complain if they receive too little change than if they receive too much.

For proper control over cash receipts, amounts short or over should be recorded in an expense account (since we expect a net shortage to develop). Ashton & Barker has set up the account Cash Short or Over 529 for this purpose. When the cash register is cleared at the end of each day, the cash is compared with the register tape total. The amount short or over is determined, and this information is passed on with the money to Ashton and to the accountant for his records.

A special column in the cash receipts journal is headed Cash Short or Over. Cash short is entered as a debit in the usual manner; if cash is over, the amount is entered in red or circled or placed in parentheses to show it as a credit. At the end of the month, the net amount short is posted as a debit to Account 529.

Posting

At the end of the month of February, the cash receipts journal, which is very similar to that used by the Carter Cleaning Shop (Unit 6) looks, in part, like this.

CASH RECEIPTS JOURNAL for Month of February 19X1   Page 1

DATE	EXPLANATION	SUNDRY CREDITS			ACCTS. REC.		CASH SALES CR. 401	CASH SHORT OR OVER DR. 529	CASH IN BANK DR. 101
		ACCT. NO.	✓	AMT.	✓	CR. 111			
Feb. 1	Barker Investment	311	✓	27,000 00					27,000 00
1	Adam Cone				✓	29 20			29 20
1	William Drake				✓	73 50			73 50
28	Cash Sales						140 00	(25)	140 25
28	Totals			27,000 00		9,700 00	7,107 75	2 75	43,805 00

From this journal, the total cash received, $43,805, is posted as a debit to Cash in Bank 101. Cash short, $2.75 (the net shortage for the month), is posted as a debit to Cash Short or Over 529. Credits are posted to Accounts Receivable Control, $9,700, and to Sales, $7,107.75. During the month, individual credits have been posted to the accounts receivable subsidiary ledger accounts and to the Barker Investment account. The abbreviation "CR" is often used as the posting reference in the accounts.

INTERNAL CONTROL OVER CASH DISBURSEMENTS

Internal control over cash disbursements may be achieved by the adoption of certain policies and by the planning of records and work assignments to give maximum protection. For example, here are the recommendations that the public accountant made to Ashton and Barker:

1. All disbursements should be made by check, except for minor payments from petty cash, discussed in Unit 7.
2. No check should be written without a properly approved disbursement voucher to authorize payment.

3. Bills should be approved only by experienced and responsible personnel.
4. The records covering bills and payments should be kept by someone other than the person approving them for payment.
5. Still another person should sign and mail the checks to creditors.

THE DISBURSEMENT VOUCHER

As indicated in Recommendation 2, control over disbursements is exercised through the use of a voucher system. A form called a *voucher* is prepared to authorize the payment of contractual obligations, to establish cash funds, and to make cash transfers.

For example, the first cash obligation that Ashton & Barker had to meet was the rent on the store building due on the first of the month. The accountant in charge of the books of the firm prepared Voucher 2-01 on February 1, 19X1, in favor of the Fisher Realty Company for $250, the monthly rental. The next step was to obtain Barker's signature on the voucher (he is the partner in charge of purchasing goods and services) to authorize payment. Then Jean Edwards, as part of her clerical duties, was instructed to write out the check and have Ashton sign and mail it.

Note how the principles of internal control have been applied. One person (the accountant) originated the voucher and a second person (Barker) approved it. Then, a third person (Ashton) signed the check and mailed it. (Barker should not sign the check because he approved the voucher in the first place.)

The same procedure is followed in the issuance of two other vouchers that are required almost at once to facilitate business operations. Voucher 2-02 for $50 provides for the establishment of the change fund for Harry Gordon, salesman for Ashton & Barker. This fund was mentioned earlier in the unit in connection with the receipt of cash over the counter. Another voucher, 2-03, is drawn in favor of Jean Edwards to set up a petty cash fund of $25 in her custody.

Disbursement vouchers are often prenumbered consecutively; however, the Ashton & Barker firm prefers to use a two-part number—the number to the left of the dash representing the month, and the number to the right indicating the sequence within the month. Thus, Voucher 2-01 identifies the first voucher prepared in February.

When a typical bill or invoice is received, the voucher procedure is more elaborate than that required for the rent payment. The first step is to verify the invoice. For example, the first invoice received by Ashton & Barker arrived on the first day from Bright Wholesale Clothiers. Jean Edwards, who opened the mail, passed the vendor's invoice along to Barker, who is responsible for store operations. He inspected the incoming shipment and made sure that it contained everything that was listed on the invoice. Then he passed the invoice to Ashton, who referred to the purchase order files to see that the prices charged on the invoice did not exceed those specified when the order was placed. (A small check mark is frequently placed beside each item verified.)

At this point, the office clerk, Jean Edwards, checked the arithmetic on the invoice. In technical terms, she verified the extensions and the footing. Checking the extensions involves multiplying the quantity of each item by its unit price. Footing involves re-adding the extensions and refiguring the discounts to verify the accuracy of the total. The invoice is illustrated as it appeared after these verifications were made.

BRIGHT WHOLESALE CLOTHIERS
123 PONCE DE LEON AVENUE
ATLANTA, GEORGIA 30308

Date __February 1, 19X1__

Invoice No. __R-47651__

SOLD
TO   Ashton & Barker Clothing Store

Customer's
Order No. __1-34__

246 Main Street

Greenville, State 53970

Terms __2/10, n/30__

QUANTITY	DESCRIPTION OF ITEMS	PER UNIT	AMOUNT
√ 20	Suits D-4786	√ $ 45.00	√ $ 900.00
√ 8	Jackets P-537	√ 12.50	√ 100.00
√ 1 Doz.	Denims R-258	√ 20.14	√ 20.14
			√ $1,020.14
	Less 20%		√ 204.03
			√ $ 816.11
	Less 10%		√ 81.61
			√ $ 734.50

VERIFICATIONS
QUANTITIES RECEIVED — R.B.
PRICES CHARGED — A.A.
EXTENSIONS & FOOTINGS — J.E.

Notice the use of a *verification stamp* on this invoice. As each invoice is received, a rubber stamp is applied to imprint the block of control information shown. Each person making a part of the verification initials it to indicate that he has found the invoice correct in that particular. Jean Edwards entered her initials to show that she had verified the extensions and footing. Barker initialed the invoice to show that he had verified the quantity received and Ashton initialed it to show that he had checked the prices billed.

***PREPARING
AND
APPROVING
THE VOUCHER***

The verified invoice now becomes the basis for the preparation of a *disbursement voucher* (2-04) to authorize the payment when due. When completed, this voucher indicates the amount ($734.50) and the account to be debited (Merchandise Purchases 501). Then the verified invoice of Bright Wholesale Clothiers is attached to the voucher and given to Barker, who is in general charge of purchasing operations. After Barker records his official approval on the voucher form, it is ready for recording in the voucher register.

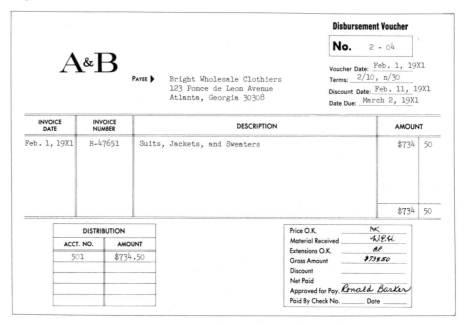

Sometimes it may be necessary to credit accounts other than Accounts Payable 201. In this case, it is customary to enter *all debits and credits* in the Distribution section of the voucher. For example, Voucher 2-14 payable to Jean Edwards is for $182.55. This represents her gross earnings of $225 for the pay period, less $13.50 FICA deducted (at an assumed 6% rate), and less $28.95 income tax withheld. The Distribution section of the voucher would look like this.

DISTRIBUTION

ACCT. NO.	AMOUNT
Dr. 551	$225.00
Cr. 201	182.55
Cr. 221	13.50
Cr. 222	28.95

THE VOUCHER REGISTER

Vouchers are listed in numerical order in a columnar record called a *voucher register*. The voucher register provides space for recording the date and number of each voucher, the payee, the amount to be paid (which is to be credited to Accounts Payable), and the account to be debited. Special columns are set up for accounts having frequent transactions and Sundry Debit and Credit columns are provided for all other accounts with less frequent transactions. Columns are also provided for recording the date paid and the number of the check issued to make the payment. The form of voucher register used by the Ashton & Barker Clothing Store is shown on page 307.

Unpaid vouchers are filed according to the date on which they should be paid. The file of unpaid vouchers thus represents the accounts payable of the firm, and no formal accounts payable subsidiary ledger is required.

Vouchers that have been paid are usually stamped "Paid" and then filed in the paid vouchers file in numerical order. In some cases, paid vouchers may be filed according to the name of the payee to permit more ready reference and avoid the possibility of duplication of payment.

POSTING FROM THE VOUCHER REGISTER

The completed voucher register covering the operations of the Ashton & Barker Clothing Store for the month of February is shown. At the end of January, Ashton Clothing Store, owned by George Ashton, owed the following vouchers: 1-22, $2,000; 1-26, $300; 1-27, $200; 1-28, $500.

Ashton transferred the assets and liabilities of his clothing store to the partnership of Ashton & Barker on February 1, 19X1, and these vouchers payable were assumed as accounts payable by the partnership.

Each item in the Sundry Debits or Credits column is posted shortly after entry, as a debit or credit to the account indicated. At the end of the month, all the columns in the voucher register are totaled and then the equality of debits and credits is proved by crossfooting.

When the proof is completed, the totals of all columns except the Sundry columns are posted to the accounts indicated in their column headings.

THE CHECK REGISTER

In the accounting system of the Carter Cleaning Shop, the cash disbursements journal contained columns for the accounts to be charged as cash was paid out. In the voucher system used by Ashton & Barker, the function of classifying expenditures is performed by use of the voucher register. The actual payment of cash is always made to settle a specific voucher that has previously been recorded in the voucher register as an account payable. Therefore, each check written under the voucher system results in a debit to Accounts Payable and a credit to Cash. Checks are recorded in numerical order in a *check register* that provides space for entering the date, check

VOUCHER REGISTER for Month of February 19X1

DATE	VOU. NO.	PAYABLE TO	PAID DATE	CHECK NO.	ACCOUNTS PAYABLE CR. 201	FICA CR. 221	INC. TAX CR. 222	MERCHANDISE PURCHASES DR. 501	FREIGHT IN DR. 506	STORE SUP. & EXP. 523 DR.	ACCT. NO.	✓	SUNDRY DEBIT	SUNDRY CREDIT
Feb. 1	2-01	Fisher Realty Co.	2-1	101	250 00						542	✓	250 00	
1	2-02	Harry Gordon	2-1	102	50 00						106	✓	50 00	
1	2-03	Jean Edwards	2-1	103	25 00						105	✓	25 00	
1	2-04	Bright Wh. Clothiers	2-10	108	734 50			734 50						
3	2-05	Graham Paper Co.			189 50					189 50				
5	2-06	Office Suppliers			57 75						553	✓	57 75	
9	2-07	Jones & Smith, Atty.			200 00						554	✓	200 00	
10	2-08	C. E. Parker, CPA			75 00						554	✓	75 00	
10	2-09	Burke Clothing Co.	2-11	114	5,240 00			5,240 00						
10	2-10	Railway Express Co.	2-11	109	56 35				56 35					
10	2-11	Fashions, Inc.	2-19	115	4,937 00			4,937 00						
10	2-12	Fast Truckers	2-11	110	82 50				82 50					
12	2-13	Moore Insurance			240 00						536	✓	240 00	
15	2-14	Jean Edwards	2-15	111	182 55	13 50	28 95				551	✓	225 00	
15	2-15	Harry Gordon	2-15	112	209 40	15 00	25 60				521	✓	250 00	
15	2-16	Alfred White	2-15	113	182 00	12 60	15 40				541	✓	210 00	
18	2-17	Better Box Co.			95 00					95 00				
25	2-18	Greenville Water Co.			12 50						543	✓	12 50	
25	2-19	State Utilities Co.			157 25						543	✓	157 25	
27	2-20	Bright Wh. Clothiers			3,465 00			3,465 00						
27	2-21	Bell Telephone Co.			26 75						553	✓	26 75	
28	2-22	Star-Herald Papers			329 75						522	✓	329 75	
28	2-23	Jiffy Delivery Co.			245 00						532	✓	245 00	
28	2-24	Jean Edwards	2-28	116	182 55	13 50	28 95				551	✓	225 00	
28	2-25	Harry Gordon	2-28	117	209 40	15 00	25 60				521	✓	250 00	
28	2-26	Alfred White	2-28	118	182 00	12 60	15 40				541	✓	210 00	
28	2-27	George Ashton	2-28	119	400 00						301	✓	400 00	
28	2-28	Ronald Barker	2-28	120	375 00						311	✓	375 00	
28	2-29	Jean Edwards	2-28	121	17 05				2 55	3 45	522	✓	2 00	
											553	✓	9 05	
28		Totals			18,408 80	82 20	139 90	14,376 50	141 40	287 95			3,825 05	
					✓	✓	✓	✓	✓	✓			X	

number, payee's name, voucher number, and amount of the payment. The following illustration shows how Checks 101 to 103 issued by Ashton & Barker up to this point are entered in the check register.

CHECK REGISTER for Month of February 19X1 Page 1

DATE		CHECK NO.	PAYABLE TO	VOU. NO.	ACCOUNTS PAYABLE DR. 201		PURCHASES DISCOUNT CR. 512		CASH IN BANK CR. 101	
Feb.	1	101	Fisher Realty Company	2-01	250	00			250	00
	1	102	Harry Gordon	2-02	50	00			50	00
	1	103	Jean Edwards	2-03	25	00			25	00

The check form used by Ashton & Barker is a specially printed form similar to that illustrated in Unit 8.

PAYING AN INVOICE LESS DISCOUNT

Ashton & Barker Clothing Store uses the same procedure in accounting for cash discounts on purchases that you learned in Unit 7. Invoices are recorded at gross price. When discounts are taken, they are credited to Purchases Discounts 512 and are shown on the income statement as a reduction of cost of goods sold. (An alternate procedure will be examined later in this unit.)

The invoice of Bright Wholesale Clothiers (Voucher 2-04) was recorded in the voucher register for its full amount, $734.50. The terms are stated on the invoice as 2/10, n/30. This means that a discount of 2% may be taken if payment is made within 10 days; otherwise the face amount is due within 30 days. The discount amounts to $14.69 ($734.50 × .02).

While 2% may not seem like a significant amount, remember that it is offered for paying the invoice only 20 days earlier. On a yearly basis, this saving amounts to slightly more than 36% (365 days ÷ 20 days × .02). A business simply cannot afford to lose such a generous return on its money by not paying within the discount period.

As previously explained, unpaid vouchers are usually filed according to their due dates. If a cash discount is offered, the filing date is the last date on which payment can be made to take the discount. The Bright Wholesale Clothiers invoice must be paid on February 10 in order to claim the discount. Since the amount of the discount is $14.69, the amount of the actual payment should be $719.81 ($734.50 − $14.69). However, if $719.81 is debited to Accounts Payable, the balance of $734.50 payable to Bright Wholesale Clothiers would not be closed.

The recording problem is readily solved by making provision for a special column in the check register for purchases discount. The full amount of the invoice is entered as a debit in the Accounts Payable column; the amount of the discount is entered as a credit in the Purchases Discount column; and the amount of the check is entered as a credit in the Cash column. Here is how the check issued to Bright Wholesale Clothiers is recorded in the check register.

CHECK REGISTER for Month of February 19X1 Page 1

DATE	CHECK NO.	PAYABLE TO	VOU. NO.	ACCOUNTS PAYABLE DR. 201		PURCHASES DISCOUNT CR. 512		CASH IN BANK CR. 101	
Feb. 10	108	Bright Whlse. Clothiers	2-04	734	50	14	69	719	81

POSTING FROM THE CHECK REGISTER

The partial check register for the Ashton & Barker Clothing Store for the month of February is shown. Vouchers 1-26, 1-22, 1-27, and 1-28 represent liabilities of the Ashton Clothing Store assumed by Ashton & Barker in the partnership agreement.

CHECK REGISTER for Month of February 19X1 Page 1

DATE		CHECK NO.	PAYABLE TO		VOU. NO.	ACCOUNTS PAYABLE DR. 201		PURCHASES DISCOUNT CR. 512		CASH IN BANK CR. 101	
Feb.	1	101	Fisher Realty Co.		2-01	250	00			250	00
	1	102	Harry Gordon		2-02	50	00			50	00
	1	103	Jean Edwards		2-03	25	00			25	00
	8	104	Star-Herald Papers	*	1-26	300	00			300	00
	8	105	Essex Wholesalers	*	1-22	2,000	00	40	00	1,960	00
	8	106	Jiffy Delivery Co.	*	1-27	200	00			200	00
	8	107	Burke Clothing Co.	*	1-28	500	00	10	00	490	00
	10	108	Bright Whlse. Clothiers		2-04	734	50	14	69	719	81
	28	119	George Ashton		2-27	400	00			400	00
	28	120	Ronald Barker		2-28	375	00			375	00
	28	121	Jean Edwards		2-29	17	05			17	05
	28		Totals			16,315	30	268	23	16,047	07
						✓		✓		✓	

*Liabilities of Ashton Clothing Store assumed by Ashton & Barker in partnership agreement.

At the end of the month, all the money columns in the check register are totaled and the equality of the debits and credits is proved. Then the totals are posted to the general ledger accounts indicated in each of the column headings (the posting reference CD is commonly used). The postings arising from the totals of the check register may be summarized as follows.

Dr. 201 Accounts Payable	$16,315.30	
Cr. 512 Purchases Discount		$ 268.23
Cr. 101 Cash in Bank		16,047.07
		$16,315.30

After the postings from the voucher register and check register have been made, the balance of Accounts Payable 201 in the general ledger is $5,093.50. The following illustration of this account shows the amount carried over from the Ashton Clothing Store ($3,000) as well as the February transactions of Ashton & Barker.

Accounts Payable   No. 201

DATE		EXPLANATION	POST. REF.	DEBIT		CREDIT		BALANCE		DR. CR.
19	X1									
Feb.	1		2-1			3,000	00	3,000	00	CR.
	28		VR-1			18,408	80	21,408	80	CR.
	28		CD-1	16,315	30			5,093	50	CR.

Note that the Accounts Payable account is shown on a balance-form ledger sheet similar to those used in the Accounts Receivable and Accounts Payable subsidiary ledgers of Carter Cleaning Shop. Balance-form ledger sheets are growing increasingly popular and are used in the remainder of this book instead of the T account forms that have been used in preceding units.

Under the voucher system, no subsidiary ledger of accounts payable is maintained. The unpaid vouchers identify the persons or firms to whom amounts are owed. These unpaid vouchers are listed at the end of the month and their total is checked against the balance of the Accounts Payable 201 account in the general ledger. This list should also be checked against the voucher register to be sure that it includes all items that have not been marked paid. The schedule of unpaid vouchers for February 19X1 taken from the voucher register of Ashton & Barker is shown.

ASHTON & BARKER CLOTHING STORE
Schedule of Vouchers Payable
February 28, 19X1

VOUCHER NUMBER	PAYABLE TO	AMOUNT
2-05	Graham Paper Co.	$ 189.50
2-06	Office Suppliers	57.75
2-07	Jones & Smith Atty.	200.00
2-08	C. E. Parker, CPA	75.00
2-13	Moore Insurance Agency	240.00
2-17	Better Box Co.	95.00
2-18	Greenville Water Co.	12.50
2-19	State Utilities Co.	157.25
2-20	Bright Wholesale Clothiers	3,465.00
2-21	Bell Telephone Co.	26.75
2-22	Star-Herald Papers	329.75
2-23	Jiffy Delivery Co.	245.00
	Total	**$5,093.50**

As long as invoices are received, verified, vouchered, and paid in the normal manner, the voucher system can permit the handling of a great volume of transactions with amazing efficiency. However, the procedures are rather rigid and certain infrequent transactions may be awkward to record. Here are some typical examples.

Partial Payments

After an invoice has been vouchered in its full amount, a firm may decide to pay the bill in two or more installments. For instance, suppose that Ashton & Barker bought furniture and fixtures costing $4,000 on April 4 and prepared Voucher 4-08 to cover this item. Being short of cash at the end of April, the company arranged to pay only half the amount at that time and to pay the other half at the end of May.

In this case, the original voucher is canceled by issuing two new vouchers, each crediting Accounts Payable for half the amount due, with debits to Accounts Payable in the Sundry Debits column to cancel the original voucher. A notation of the cancellation would be made in the Paid Date section on the line on which the original Voucher 4-08 was recorded. The first of the new vouchers is paid at the end of April (right away) and the second is filed for payment at the end of May.

VOUCHER REGISTER for Month of April 19XX   Page 3

| DATE | | VOU. NO. | PAYABLE TO | PAID | | ACCOUNTS PAYABLE CR. 201 | | SUNDRY | | | |
				DATE	CHECK NO.		ACCT. NO.	✓	DEBIT	CREDIT
Apr.	4	4-08	Office Supp., Inc.	Canc.	V4-33 V4-34	4,000 00	131	✓	4,000 00	
	30	4-33	Office Supp., Inc.	4-30	208	2,000 00	201	✓	2,000 00	
	30	4-34	Office Supp., Inc.			2,000 00	201	✓	2,000 00	

Notes Payable

Ashton & Barker owe First National Bank $10,000 on a 6%, 60-day note, dated February 1. Thus, on April 2 when the note falls due, a voucher must be prepared to authorize payment of $10,100 ($10,000 face value plus $100 interest). By means of an entry in the voucher register, Notes Payable-Bank is debited for $10,000, Interest Expense is debited for $100, and Accounts Payable is credited for $10,100. Then a check for $10,100 is issued and entered in the check register to settle the obligation. The entry in the voucher register is shown.

UNIT 19

| DATE | VOU. NO. | PAYABLE TO | PAID | | ACCOUNTS PAYABLE CR. 201 | SUNDRY | | | |
			DATE	CHECK NO.		ACCT. NO.	✓	DEBIT	CREDIT
Apr. 2	4-04	First Nat'l Bank	4-2	204	10,100 00	211 591		10,000 00 100 00	

Another recording problem involving notes payable might arise after a vendor's invoice has been vouchered in the normal manner. Suppose that the debtor decides, instead of writing a check, to issue a note payable to the vendor as a means of postponing payment. The amount owed is no longer an unsecured account payable. Therefore, a general journal entry is made debiting Accounts Payable (thus canceling the original voucher) and crediting Notes Payable-Trade. When the time comes for paying the note, the entries are the same as those previously described for paying the bank note; a new voucher is prepared for the note (plus interest, if any) and it is paid.

Purchases Returns and Allowances

If Ashton & Barker receives goods that are unsuitable for the intended purpose, or if the merchandise delivered is not as ordered, it may be returned to the vendor. At other times, such goods may be kept and an allowance will be made by the vendor to reduce the purchase price. In either case, the amount finally owed to the vendor is less than the amount of the original invoice. If the original invoice has already been vouchered, what can be done to adjust matters?

For example, suppose that on March 2 an invoice for $750 for merchandise purchased from Essex Wholesalers was received and vouchered as 3-05. Then, on March 8, an allowance of $50 was made by the vendor to cover damage in transit. The revised amount is to be paid on March 11, less a 2% cash discount, as computed here.

Voucher 3-05	$750
Allowance, March 8	50
Still owing	$700
Less 2% cash discount	14
To be paid on March 11	$686

METHOD 1. On March 8, when the allowance was made, a new voucher for the revised amount owed, $700, would be issued crediting Accounts Payable. Accounts Payable is debited $750 to cancel the original Voucher 3-05 and Purchases Returns and Allowances 511 is credited $50. Using the Sundry Debit and Credit columns in the voucher register, this entry would appear as shown in the first illustration on the following page.

VOUCHER REGISTER for Month of March 19X1

DATE	VOU. NO.	PAYABLE TO	PAID DATE	PAID CHECK NO.	ACCOUNTS PAYABLE CR. 201	EMPLOYEE DED. FICA CR. 221	EMPLOYEE DED. INC. TAX CR. 222	MERCHANDISE PURCHASES DR. 501	FREIGHT IN DR. 506	STORE SUP. & EXP. DR. 523	ACCT. NO.	✓	SUNDRY DEBIT	SUNDRY CREDIT
Mar. 2	3-05	Essex Wholesalers		Canc. V3-12	750 00			750 00						
8	3-12	Essex Wholesalers			700 00						201		750 00	
											511			50 00

VOUCHER REGISTER for Month of March 19X1

DATE	VOU. NO.	PAYABLE TO	PAID DATE	PAID CHECK NO.	ACCOUNTS PAYABLE CR. 201	EMPLOYEE DED. FICA CR. 221	EMPLOYEE DED. INC. TAX CR. 222	MERCHANDISE PURCHASES DR. 501	FREIGHT IN DR. 506	STORE SUP. & EXP. DR. 523	ACCT. NO.	✓	SUNDRY DEBIT	SUNDRY CREDIT
Mar. 2	3-05	Essex Wholesalers			(50 00)			(50 00)						
					750 00			750 00						
					(50 00)			(50 00)						
					19,980 00	45 00	125 00	15,960 00	440 00	750 00			5,000 00	2,000 00
													750 00	

On the line for Voucher 3-05, a notation would be made in the Paid section, "Canceled by Voucher 3-12." This would pave the way for the issuance on March 11 of a check for $686 ($700 less the discount). This check is entered in the check register, resulting in a debit to Accounts Payable for $700 and offsetting credits to Purchases Discount for $14, and to Cash for $686.

METHOD 2. A simpler method for handling this type of adjustment is used by some accountants. Since the voucher register for March was not closed and posted before the allowance was agreed upon, the original entry can be corrected by making a notation, either circled or in red, for the $50 allowance in the same line space as the original voucher entry. This method is shown in the second illustration on page 313.

The adjustment is recorded on the original voucher and, when approved by Barker, payment is made for the net amount. At the end of the month, the figures that are circled or written in red are totaled separately from the original figures in each column of the voucher register. The $50 item illustrated is posted as a debit to Accounts Payable and a credit to Purchases Returns and Allowances, thereby accomplishing the same result as the first method. Note, however, that the second method can be used only if the revision is made before the voucher register has been summarized for the period.

RECORDING PURCHASES DISCOUNTS LOST

The routine procedures that you have learned for recording purchases and cash discounts are very commonly used. However, this method has one disadvantage that may make it undesirable if a good system of internal control is to be developed. If, due to inefficiency, a discount is not taken because an invoice is not paid promptly, the loss of the discount is not revealed by the accounting records. To overcome this shortcoming, many accountants prefer to record purchase vouchers so that discounts *not taken* will stand out for investigation while discounts taken are not separately stated in the records.

Under this procedure, purchase invoices are recorded in the voucher register *net of discount* (invoice price minus cash discount that may be taken). If the invoice is paid within the discount period, the check is drawn for the exact amount of the voucher. On the other hand, if the invoice is paid too late to take the discount, the gross amount must be paid. This will be larger than the amount of the original voucher. The difference can be recorded in a debit column in the check register to an account entitled Discount Lost 507. This is added to the amount originally debited to Merchandise Purchases for presentation on the income statement under Cost of Goods Sold. To illustrate how this procedure works, assume that Ashton and Barker used the system. On February 1, when they received the invoice for a purchase of $734.50 from Bright Wholesale Company with terms of 2/10, n/30, the invoice would be recorded in the voucher register at net amount ($734.50 − $14.69 = $719.81), as shown.

VOUCHER REGISTER for Month of February 19X1 Page 1

DATE	VOU. NO.	PAYABLE TO	DATE	CHECK NO.	ACCOUNTS PAYABLE CR. 201	MERCHANDISE PURCHASES DR. 501
Feb. 1	2-04	Bright Wholesale Clothiers	2-10	108	719 81	719 81

When payment is made within the discount period, it would be recorded as follows.

CHECK REGISTER for Month of February 19X1 Page 1

DATE	CHECK NO.	PAYABLE TO	VOU. NO.	ACCOUNTS PAYABLE DR. 201	DISCOUNT LOST DR. 507	CASH IN BANK CR. 101
Feb. 10	108	Bright Whlse. Clothiers	2-04	719 81		719 81

If the payment had been made too late to take the discount, the amount of discount lost would be recorded in the check register and management's attention would immediately be directed to this failure. The check register is shown.

CHECK REGISTER for Month of February 19X1 Page 1

DATE	CHECK NO.	PAYABLE TO	VOU. NO.	ACCOUNTS PAYABLE DR. 201	DISCOUNT LOST DR. 507	CASH IN BANK CR. 101
Feb. 20	116	Bright Whlse. Clothiers	2-04	719 81	14 69	734 50

OTHER CASH CONTROL PROCEDURES

As you learned in Unit 7, it is not practical to make each small payment by check, so a petty cash fund should be maintained. The procedures necessary to properly control petty cash funds were discussed and illustrated at that time. Another important aspect of cash control is the prompt and accurate preparation of the bank reconciliation statement each month. Bank reconciliations were explained in Unit 8.

◆ ◆ ◆

PRINCIPLES AND PROCEDURES

Internal control is an important factor in the protection of a business concern. Each step in the accounting routine should be planned to involve more than one person and to provide a basis for double-

UNIT 19

315

checking the work performed. Steps must be taken to insure that cash is deposited each day and entered in the cash receipts journal daily. Cash short or over should be recorded daily.

The voucher system provides a control over cash disbursements. A disbursement voucher is prepared for every expenditure and then approved. An entry is made in the voucher register and a file of approved disbursement vouchers serves in place of an accounts payable subsidiary ledger. When a check is issued to pay the voucher, an entry is made in the check register and the voucher register.

Certain transactions such as purchases returns and allowances, partial payments, and notes payable may require special treatment when they are being recorded under the voucher system.

Purchases may be recorded net of discount. Then, if discounts are not taken, discounts lost will stand out for investigation.

MANAGERIAL IMPLICATIONS

Because of its very nature, cash is easy to lose or steal. Management must make sure that the system of internal control is adequate to prevent misuse of cash funds and other valuable assets. Good control procedures not only guard against loss, but also help improve employee relations because each employee is able to clearly show the amount of cash or property for which he is responsible and how it was handled.

The protection afforded by the voucher system is invaluable to management in safeguarding the outward flow of funds. Every step is recorded, checked, and documented. Responsibility all along the line is clear and definite. The answers to "What," "Why," "Who," "When," etc., are readily available at all times for future reference or for auditing purposes.

APPLICATION OF PRINCIPLES

PROBLEM 19 · 1

Wilbur and Roger Pitts established Pitts Brothers Supply Store on Aug. 1, 19X1, to carry on a retail business. Its chart of accounts is given here:

101	Cash in Bank	401	Sales
111	Accounts Receivable	501	Merchandise Purchases
121	Merchandise Inventory	506	Freight In
131	Store Furniture & Equipment	511	Purchases Returns & Allowances
141	Office Furniture & Equipment		
201	Accounts Payable	512	Purchases Discount
202	Notes Payable	521	Sales Salaries
221	Employee Deductions	522	Advertising
	—FICA	523	Store Supplies & Expense

222	Employee Deductions —Income Tax Withheld	529	Cash Short or Over
301	W. Pitts Investment	542	Rent Expense
311	R. Pitts Investment	551	Office Salaries
		553	Office Supplies & Expense

The business transactions for August 19X1 are as follows:

AUG.

1   W. Pitts invests $10,000 and R. Pitts invests $12,000 in cash in the new business.

1   Acquired $900 worth of office furniture and equipment from Central Supply Co., giving them a noninterest-bearing, 30-day note payable. (In the general journal, debit 141 and credit 202.)

2   Voucher 8-01 to Allrent Co., $100 rent for month; paid by Check 101.

3   Voucher 8-02 to ABC Supply Co., $25 for office supplies used.

4   Voucher 8-03 to York Co., $500 for building fixtures in store. (Dr. 131.)

5   Voucher 8-04 to T & P Railroad, $36.65 for freight on merchandise purchased.

6   Paid Voucher 8-04 by Check 102.

8   Voucher 8-05 to Ace Hardware Co., $1,000 for merchandise; terms 2/10, n/30.

9   Acquired cash register for $500 from Town Supply Co.; terms $200 cash, balance in 30 days. Vouchers 8-06 and 8-07 for the two installments. Paid Voucher 8-06 by Check 103, $200.

10   Voucher 8-08 to Ace Hardware Company, $3,000 for merchandise; terms 2/10, n/30.

12   Voucher 8-09 to TY Supply Co., $100 for store supplies used.

13   Cash sales, $400.

15   Returned $100 worth of merchandise for credit to Ace Hardware Co. (make circled entry in voucher register over Voucher 8-08).

16   Issued Check 104 to pay Voucher 8-05, net of 2% discount.

17   Cash sales, $600, cash short $1.50.

18   Voucher 8-10 to Daily News, $80, for advertising; paid by Check 105.

19   Voucher 8-11 to T & P Railroad, $31.40 for freight on merchandise purchased.

20   Issued Check 106 to pay Voucher 8-11.

20   Issued Check 107 to pay Voucher 8-08, net of return and 2% discount.

23   Cash sales, $470; cash over, $.50.

25   Voucher 8-12 to Ace Hardware Co., $2,150 for merchandise; terms 2/10, n/30.

26   Cash sales, $510, cash short, $1.90.

27   Voucher 8-13 to City Utilities, $86 for store operations; paid by Check 108.

28   Voucher 8-14 to Bell Telephone Co., $54.00 for office telephone service; paid by Check 109.

30   Voucher 8-15 to Central Supply Co., $900 note payable of Aug. 1; paid by Check 110.

31   Cash sales, $610; cash short, $.90.

UNIT 19

31 Voucher 8-16 to Tom Perry for sales salary $700, less $42 FICA tax and $52.00 income tax deducted; paid by Check 111. Voucher 8-17 to Jane Williams, office salary, $500, less $30.00 FICA tax and $33.20 income tax deducted; paid by Check 112.

INSTRUCTIONS

1. Set up a general journal and three special journals: cash receipts journal, voucher register, and check register. (Use the same column headings as the forms illustrated on pages 302, 307 and 308 of the text.)
2. Set up general ledger accounts for Cash in Bank 101 and Accounts Payable 201.
3. Record the given transactions, then foot and crossfoot the special journals.
4. Post from the special journals to Accounts 101 and 201 only.
5. Prepare a schedule of vouchers payable and prove with the balance of Account 201.

PROBLEM 19 · 2

On Mar. 1, 19X1, State Supply Company sold merchandise to City Retailers. The invoice price was $2,000. Terms of the sale were 2/10, n/30.

INSTRUCTIONS

1. Record the purchase on City Retailers' books in general journal form, omitting account numbers and entry numbers throughout, assuming:
    a. Purchases are recorded at gross invoice price.
    b. Purchases are recorded at net invoice price.
2. Assuming that City Retailers paid the invoice on Mar. 9, record the payment on its books if:
    a. City Retailers recorded the purchase at gross price.
    b. City Retailers recorded the purchase at net invoice price.
3. Assuming that City Retailers paid the invoice on Mar. 30 (no discount), record the payment on its books if:
    a. City Retailers recorded the purchase at gross price.
    b. City Retailers recorded the purchase at net invoice price.

MANAGERIAL CHECKUPS

◆ How does the voucher system protect management from the misuse of cash and other valuable assets?

◆ How can management avoid unnecessary red tape as a by-product of its search for adequate internal controls?

◆ In a small business there may be only one or two experienced and reliable employees capable of assuming key positions in an internal control system. Does this mean that it is impractical to introduce internal controls in this type of situation?

PART 5
PAYABLES AND
RECEIVABLES

20 NOTES PAYABLE AND INTEREST

Checks are not the only kind of negotiable instruments that an accountant encounters in the financing and settlement of business transactions. Promissory notes, drafts, and trade acceptances may also be used in the financing of business operations. These instruments are especially popular in connection with larger transactions and with obligations that extend for a longer time than the typical open account credit period. The accountant has to know how all kinds of negotiable instruments work, what to do with them, and how they affect the assets, liabilities, and owner's equity.

The law pertaining to negotiable instruments or commercial paper has been incorporated into the Uniform Commercial Code, adopted by the legislatures of all states. The law states that in order to be negotiable an instrument must conform to the following requirements:

1. It must be in writing and be signed by the maker (or drawer).
2. It must contain an unconditional promise or order to pay a definite sum in money.
3. It must be payable on demand or at a fixed or determinable future time.
4. It must be payable *to the order of someone* or *to bearer.*
5. If the instrument is addressed to a drawee, it must name or indicate him with reasonable certainty.

The checks studied in Unit 8 qualified as negotiable instruments because they were (1) in writing and signed by the depositor-maker, (2) unconditional orders on the bank to pay specified sums of money, (3) payable on demand, and (4-5) payable to a clearly named party in each instance. The promissory note discussed in this unit also meets all the requirements of negotiability. Examine the following note made by the Ashton & Barker Clothing Store in favor of the Columbia Equipment Company.

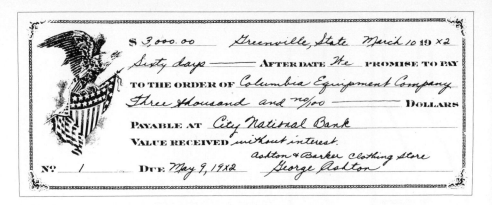

$ 3,000.00   Greenville, State   March 10 19 x2

Sixty days ———— AFTER DATE We PROMISE TO PAY

TO THE ORDER OF Columbia Equipment Company

Three thousand and no/100 ———————— DOLLARS

PAYABLE AT City National Bank

VALUE RECEIVED without interest.

                      Ashton & Barker Clothing Store

N° 1   DUE May 9, 19x2   George Ashton

NOTES PAYABLE

The note illustrated is actually a promise made by the partnership to pay the Columbia Equipment Company the sum of $3,000 in 60 days. It is negotiable because it is (1) in writing and signed by the maker (George Ashton for Ashton & Barker), (2) an unconditional promise for payment of a definite sum, (3) payable on a determinable date, and (4-5) payable to a named party whose identity is unmistakable. Some notes specify that interest at a certain rate must also be paid at maturity. However, this provision for interest is not a factor in negotiability. In the note illustrated, no interest is mentioned and none is due. This is a negotiable *noninterest-bearing* note that arose under the following circumstances.

NONINTEREST-BEARING NOTE GIVEN IN PURCHASE OF AN ASSET

On March 10, the Ashton & Barker Clothing Store purchased furnishings and store fixtures costing $3,000 from the Columbia Equipment Company. The seller agreed to allow the buyer 60 days in which to make payment, on the condition that the buyer execute a noninterest-bearing promissory note. The seller was not seeking extra income through interest. Columbia was primarily concerned with working out an arrangement that would permit it to accommodate Ashton & Barker while enjoying as much legal protection as possible.

Recording the Issuance of the Note

To record this transaction on the books of Ashton & Barker, a general journal entry debiting Furniture and Fixtures and crediting Notes Payable—Trade is made.

19 X2		3–7					
Mar. 10	Furniture and Fixtures	131	3,000	00			
	Notes Payable–Trade . . .	202				3,000	00
	To record 60-day, noninterest-bearing						
	note given for store furnishings bought						
	from Columbia Equipment Company.						

Maturity Date

When the note payable falls due, the Columbia Equipment Company will ask its bank to collect it. Obviously, Ashton & Barker needs to know when to expect such demands for payment so that it will have enough money on deposit to cover the amount due. This is why the maturity date of a credit instrument should be determined immediately. This may be done by counting the number of days from the issue date, but not the issue date itself. For example, a 30-day note issued on January 1 matures 30 days after January 1, or January 31. If the 30-day note were issued on January 15, the determination of its maturity date would involve these steps:

1. Determine the number of days to run in the month of issue—in this case, 31 − 15, or   16
2. Subtract the days to run in the month of issue from the total time for which the note was issued—
   30 − 16 = days to run in February   14
   Proof—total period of note in days   30

Since the note must run 14 days in February, the maturity date is February 14. More than two months may be involved if the time period of the note is longer. For example, the note issued on March 10 to the Columbia Equipment Company was for 60 days. The steps in determining the maturity date would be:

1. Determine the number of days to run in the month of issue—in this case, 31 − 10, or   21
2. Add total days in subsequent months until within one month of the total time period of the note: add days in April   30
   Total days to end of April   51
3. Determine the number of days to run in the month in which the note matures: days to run in May (60—51)   9
   Total period of note in days   60

In this case, the maturity date is May 9. Sometimes the period of the note is described in months instead of days: for example, two months rather than sixty days, as in the Columbia Equipment example. When the period is defined in months, the maturity date is determined by counting ahead to the *same date* in the following month or months. Thus, two months from January 15 would be March 15, regardless of the fact that January has 31 days and February has only 28. No day count is required.

Payment of the Note

On the maturity date, May 9, Ashton & Barker pays the Columbia Equipment Company the $3,000 due. As you learned in Unit 19, a voucher has to be prepared, approved, and entered in the voucher register, where it serves to record a debit to Notes Payable—Trade and a credit to Accounts Payable. Then a check is drawn in settlement. The recording of the check in the check register has the effect of debiting Accounts Payable and crediting Cash in Bank for $3,000.

INTEREST

The extension of credit, as described in the previous transaction, forces the person granting the credit to wait for payment and thus to forego the use of money during the credit period. Conversely, the one receiving the credit postpones payment and has the use of the money during the credit period. Such use of money is a valuable privilege; some creditors feel justified in charging the debtor for it. *Interest* is the name given to the price charged for the use of money or credit.

If interest is specified in a credit transaction, it is accounted for separately and recorded as interest expense or interest income, as the case may be. Let us see how this method works in connection with an *interest-bearing* note payable.

INTEREST-BEARING NOTE GIVEN IN PURCHASE OF AN ASSET

Suppose that the Ashton & Barker Clothing Store purchased office equipment costing $800 from the Greenville Office Supply Company on March 18 and gave a 90-day, 6% note as evidence of its obligation.

Recording the Issuance of the Note

The issuance of the note payable is recorded in the general journal as a debit to Furniture and Fixtures and a credit to Notes Payable—Trade, as illustrated.

19 X2		3–11						
Mar. 18		Furniture and Fixtures	131	800	00			
		Notes Payable–Trade . . .	202			800	00
		To record 90-day, 6% note given for					
		office equipment bought from					
		Greenville Office Supply Company.					

Maturity Date

The maturity date of the note is June 16, determined by the following calculation:

Days to run in March: 31 − 18, or   13
Days in April   30
    Total days to end of April   43
Days in May   31
    Total days to end of May   74
Days to run in June: 90 − 74, or   16

    Total period of note in days   90

On the maturity date, June 16, a voucher is prepared to pay not only the face value, $800, but also the interest on this amount for the 90-day period at the rate of 6% per annum, as specified.

Interest Calculations

The amount of interest for any time period can be determined by using this formula:

Interest = Principal × Interest Rate × Time in Years

Applying this formula, interest on $800 for 90 days at 6% is $12, found as follows:

$$\text{Interest} = \$800 \times .06 \times \frac{90}{360}$$

Interest = $12

In determining the time period, the exact number of days is generally used as the numerator of the fraction and, for convenience, 360 is used in the denominator. The 90-day term of the note used in the example was, therefore, expressed as 90/360 of a year.

SHORTCUT INTEREST CALCULATIONS. If interest is at the rate of 6% and the credit period is 60 days, the 6%, 60-day method of calculation may be used. The method is derived as follows:

$$\text{Interest} = \text{Principal} \times \text{Rate} \times \text{Time}$$

$$\text{Interest} = \text{Principal} \times .06 \times \frac{60}{360}$$

$$\text{Interest} = \text{Principal} \times \frac{6}{100} \times \frac{60}{360}$$

$$\text{Interest} = \text{Principal} \times \frac{\cancel{6}}{100} \times \frac{\cancel{60}}{\cancel{360}}_{\cancel{60}}$$

$$\text{Interest} = \text{Principal} \times \frac{1}{100} \text{ (or .01)}$$

A quick method of multiplying any figure by .01 is to point off two decimal places to the left. Thus, interest at 6% for 60 days is computed by pointing off two decimal places to the left in the principal amount. For example, interest at 6% for 60 days on $800 is $8.

$$\$800 \times .01 = \$8$$

Since interest is in direct proportion to the rate and to the time, the shortcut method can also be used to determine interest where the rate is greater or less than 6%, or where the time is greater or less than 60 days. For example, the interest at 6% for 75 days on $1,200 could be computed as follows:

Interest at 6% for 60 days $(.01 \times \$1,200) = \$12.00$
Interest at 6% for $\underline{15}$ days $(\frac{1}{4}$ of $\$12)$ $\quad\quad = \quad\underline{3.00}$
Interest at 6% for $\underline{\underline{75}}$ days $\quad\quad\quad\quad\quad = \underline{\underline{\$15.00}}$

Similarly, interest at 5% for 60 days on $1,500 would be $12.50:

Interest at 6% for 60 days $(.01 \times \$1,500) = \$15.00$
Interest at 1% for 60 days $(\frac{1}{6} \times \$15.00) = \quad\underline{2.50}$
Interest at $\underline{\underline{5\%}}$ for 60 days $\quad\quad\quad\quad = \underline{\underline{\$12.50}}$

While such calculations may truly be shortcuts in some cases, they may occasionally become so involved that it would be simpler (and perhaps more accurate) to use the regular formula.

Payment of an Interest-bearing Note Payable

The voucher to authorize payment of the note given to the Greenville Office Supply Company must show two elements, the principal and the interest due. These elements are recorded in the voucher register with the following effect.

19X2					
June 16	Notes Payable–Trade	202	800 00		
	Interest Expense	591	12 00		
	Accounts Payable	201			812 00

The next step is the issuance of a check for the $812 and the entry of the payment in the check register. The resulting effect on the ledger accounts is shown.

19X2					
June 16	Accounts Payable	201	812 00		
	Cash in Bank	101			812 00

PARTIAL PAYMENT OF A NOTE PAYABLE

If only partial payment of a note is made at its maturity, the voucher and check are prepared for the amount to be paid. The amount of the payment is endorsed on the note by the payee, or the old note is canceled and a new note prepared for the remaining balance due.

In the absence of an agreement to the contrary, a noninterest-bearing note that is not paid at maturity begins at that time to bear interest at the legal rate (established by law in each state) and continues to do so until it is paid.

RENEWING A NOTE PAYABLE

If, instead of being paid, a note payable is renewed for another 30 days, no new debit or credit entries in the accounts are required. At the time of payment on the deferred maturity date, the usual payment entries are made.

UNIT 20

Business firms often borrow money from a bank, signing a note payable as evidence of the debt. Banks invariably charge interest on loans. Like the interest charged on the note payable to the Greenville Office Supply Company, the interest might be paid at maturity. In many cases, however, the bank deducts the interest in advance and the borrower receives only the difference between the face amount of the note and the interest on it to maturity. Borrowing money under an arrangement in which the interest is deducted in advance is called *discounting*. This is how it works.

Suppose that the Ashton & Barker Clothing Store arranged to borrow $5,000 at 8% from its bank on April 30, discounting a 30-day note payable. Interest on $5,000 at 8% for 30 days is $33.33, calculated according to the formula, as follows:

$$\text{Interest} = \$5,000 \times .08 \times \frac{30}{360}$$

$$\text{Interest} = \$33.33$$

The bank deducts the $33.33 interest from the $5,000 face of the note, and the Ashton & Barker Clothing Store receives the difference, $4,966.67. The company would probably have the bank deposit this amount in its checking account.

Recording the Issuance of the Note

The effect of this transaction is shown. Observe that Notes Payable—Bank is used because the accountant wishes to distinguish notes payable to banks from those payable to businesses.

19	X2						
Apr.	30	Cash in Bank	101	$4,966	67		
		Interest Expense	591	33	33		
		Notes Payable—Bank	211			5,000	00

Since the transaction involves a cash receipt, it should be entered in the cash receipts journal. However, the entry presents an unusual problem because of the debit to Interest Expense, which the typical cash receipts journal is not prepared to handle conveniently. The transaction can, nevertheless, be recorded in the cash receipts journal by entering the Interest Expense in the Sundry Credits column as a red or circled figure to indicate that it is a debit and not a credit. The entry is shown.

DATE		EXPLANATION	SUNDRY CREDITS			ACCTS. REC.		CASH IN BANK DR. 101
			ACCT. NO.	✓	AMT.	✓	CR. 111	
Apr.	30	Notes Payable—Bank	211		5,000 00			
		Interest Expense	591		33 33			4,966 67

Notice that this entry required two lines in the cash receipts journal: one to credit Notes Payable—Bank for the face amount of the note and one to debit Interest Expense for the amount of interest deducted by the bank. Other techniques may also be used for recording the transaction.

Paying the Note

The maturity date of this note is May 30. (Since it was dated April 30, there are no days to run in April.) A voucher is prepared on May 30 for $5,000 to pay the note; Notes Payable—Bank is debited and Accounts Payable is credited in the voucher register entry. A check for $5,000 is written and an entry is made in the check register, debiting Accounts Payable and crediting Cash in Bank. Since the interest was deducted by the bank in advance and recorded at the time the note was issued, no further entry for the interest is required. (The face of the note is paid at maturity.)

NOTES PAYABLE REGISTER

If many notes payable are issued, it may be convenient to keep track of the details by maintaining a *notes payable register,* a columnar record in which the pertinent information on each note payable is contained on one line. This information includes the date of the note, the payee, where payable, the time to run, the maturity date, the face amount of the note, and the interest rate and amount, if any. At the end of an accounting period, a *schedule of notes payable* may be prepared by listing the open (or unpaid) notes that appear in the notes payable register. The total must agree with the total of the Notes Payable account(s) in the general ledger, as though proving to a control account.

The two notes issued in March, used in previous examples, are entered in the notes payable register of the Ashton & Barker Clothing Store as illustrated on pages 330 and 331.

In the form shown, the notes payable register is a memorandum record. It may also be designed for use as a book of original entry, or journal, from which postings are made to the ledger accounts. If the register were used in this way, the issuance of these two notes would have been recorded in the register and postings to the ledger accounts would have been made

UNIT 20

NOTES PAYABLE REGISTER

DATE OF ENTRY		PAYEE	WHERE PAYABLE	DATE OF NOTE		TIME TO RUN
19	X2			19	X2	
Mar.	10	Columbia Equipment Co.	City National Bank	Mar.	10	60 days
	18	Greenville Office Supply Co.	City National Bank	Mar.	18	90 days

from it. In that case, the entries in the general journal previously illustrated would not have been required. (Ashton & Barker does not have enough notes payable to use the register as a book of original entry.)

NOTES PAYABLE AND INTEREST EXPENSE ON THE STATEMENTS

Notes payable represent an obligation of the business and appear on the balance sheet as liabilities. As previously explained, separate accounts have been set up by the Ashton & Barker Clothing Store: Notes Payable—Trade 202 and Notes Payable—Bank 211. Notes due within one year are usually classified as current liabilities; those due in more than one year, as long-term liabilities.

Interest expense is usually classified on the income statement as a nonoperating expense listed under Other Expense, and deducted from the figure for Net Profit from Operations.

Net Profit from Operations	$9,675.25
Less Interest Expense	125.30
Net Income	$9,549.95

◆ ◆ ◆

PRINCIPLES AND PROCEDURES

Notes payable may be noninterest-bearing or interest-bearing. When a note is given for the purchase of an asset, the amount is credited to a notes payable account and debited to an asset account. At maturity, a voucher is prepared for payment of the note and entered in the voucher register as a debit to Notes Payable and a credit to Accounts Payable. When the check is issued, Accounts Payable is debited and Cash in Bank is credited in the check register. If the note given is interest-bearing, only the principal is debited to a notes payable account when the voucher is issued; the interest is debited to an interest expense account and the entire amount to be paid—principal and interest—is credited to Accounts Payable.

YEAR	MATURITY DATE												FACE AMT. OF NOTE		INTEREST				DATE PAID	REMARKS
	J	F	M	A	M	J	J	A	S	O	N	D			RATE		AMT.			
19X2					9								3,000	00	None					
19X2						16							800	00	6%		12	00		

When a note is given to a bank, the bank usually deducts the interest in advance (discounts the note) and the borrower receives only the difference between the face amount of the note and the interest on it. In this case, the Notes Payable account is credited for the face amount, Interest Expense debited for the interest, and Cash in Bank debited for the difference (cash actually received from the bank) when the note is issued.

If many notes are issued, a notes payable register may be kept. Notes Payable appears as a liability on the balance sheet. Interest Expense is usually classified as a nonoperating expense on the income statement.

MANAGERIAL IMPLICATIONS

Management must be aware of opportunities to finance operations through the use of short-term notes payable that provide working capital temporarily. Sources of funds include suppliers (through credit extension) and banks. In securing funds through bank loans, it should be kept in mind that discounting notes payable results in a higher interest rate than the face rate indicates. Since the interest is deducted in advance, the borrower does not have use of funds equal to the entire face of the note.

Managers should be familiar with the Uniform Negotiable Instruments Law so that they fully understand the rights and obligations involved in notes payable commitments.

APPLICATION OF PRINCIPLES

PROBLEM 20 · 1

1. Compute the total interest on each of the following notes, using the interest formula method. Show all computations.
   a. $800 @ 9% for 75 days
   b. $1,400 @ 7% for 4 months
2. Compute the interest on each of the following notes, using the 6%, 60-day method. Show all computations.
   a. $500 @ 6% for 90 days
   b. $812.50 @ 7% for 120 days
   d. $1,450.56 @ 5% for 30 days

3. Compute the discount on the following noninterest-bearing notes. Show all computations.
   a. $7,200 discounted at 9% for 6 months
   b. $3,456 discounted at 7% for 50 days

PROBLEM 20 · 2

♦ North and South is a chain of dry cleaning establishments owned and operated by R. L. Jones and Sam Smith. A program of modernization and expansion has been decided upon to increase efficiency, reduce operating costs, and increase sales. Since the funds for this program will come partly from their own cash reserves but mostly from notes payable, the partners decide to establish a notes payable register as a memorandum record to help them maintain control over the due dates and interest payments. The following selected account titles and numbers are used in recording.

101	Cash in Bank	201	Accounts Payable
131	Cleaning Equipment	202	Notes Payable–Trade
132	Delivery Equipment	211	Notes Payable–Bank
141	Land	591	Interest Expense

Transactions involving notes payable which took place during the month of December 19X1 are listed here.

DEC.

1 Purchased additional cleaning equipment from the Johnson Equipment Company, issuing note for $8,000 for 90 days with interest at 6%. (Enter in the general journal as Entry 12-11. Number all general journal entries consecutively).

8 Purchased three small panel delivery trucks from General Automotive Sales Company on Invoice 857, dated Dec. 8, 19X1. The initial payment of $3,000 was made by Check 316, this date, and was authorized by Voucher 12-10, approved by R. L. Jones on this date. A $3,000 note due in 6 months with interest at 8% was given to cover the balance of the purchase price. (Enter Voucher 12-10 in the Voucher Register.)

10 Issued a 60-day, 6% note for $4,500 to Builders, Inc., in payment for land to be used as a parking area for one of the cleaning establishments.

15 In order to obtain an extension of credit on Cleaner's Supply Company account payable, previously recorded as Voucher 11-26, which is overdue, a 30-day note for $1,250 bearing interest at 8% was given to the company.

16 Renewed $5,000 note dated Nov. 1, which was due today, to Johnson Equipment Company. Gave a new note for 30 days with interest at 6%. (No journal entry is required; make notation in notes payable register.)

18 Borrowed $5,000 from the First National Bank on a 120-day note with interest at 7% and discounted the note at the bank.

20 Purchased two dry-cleaning machines from Automatic Cleaning Equipment company, issuing a $10,000 note payable in 90 days with interest at 9%.

DEC.

30 Borrowed $5,000 from the First National Bank for 60 days with interest at 7% payable at maturity.

31 Paid half of Johnson Equipment Company note due today, including interest, by Check 331 for $5,100, which was authorized by Voucher 12-25, approved by R. L. Jones. Issued a new note for $5,000 payable in 45 days with interest at 6%. (No journal entry is required. Enter Voucher 12-25 in the voucher register. Make notation of cash payment and renewal note opposite the original note in the notes payable register, and enter the new note.)

INSTRUCTIONS

1. Enter the following notes on Dec. 1, 19X1 as a memorandum record in a notes payable register with columns as illustrated in this unit. Compute and enter maturity date and interest, if any, when recording each item.

   a. Note issued to Johnson Equipment Company on Nov. 1, 19X1 for $5,000 due in 45 days without interest. (This note and all others in this problem are payable at the First National Bank.)

   b. Note issued to Johnson Equipment Company on Nov. 1, 19X1 for $10,000 due in 60 days with interest at 6%.

2. Analyze each transaction and enter in the required place, using the following:

   a. A general journal.

   b. The notes payable register listed above.

   c. A cash receipts journal, with columns as illustrated in this unit.

   d. A voucher register, with columns as illustrated on page 307.

MANAGERIAL CHECKUP

♦ Why and how may management use outside sources of funds in the operation of the business?

21

NOTES RECEIVABLE, DRAFTS, ACCEPTANCES

In order for the buyer to use a promissory note to finance his purchases, the seller must be willing to accept the note to facilitate the sales transaction. A note received by a seller that contains his customer's written promise to pay in the future is called a *note receivable*.

NOTES RECEIVABLE

A note receivable may be interest-bearing or noninterest-bearing, according to the wishes of the contracting parties. The maturity date, unexpired term, and the interest due are calculated by using the same techniques that were explained for notes payable in the preceding unit. The entries used to record notes receivable on the seller's books are, of course, different from those used for notes payable.

A note receivable may be received from a customer at the time of a sale, or it may arise in connection with the extension of credit involving a past due account. The procedures for handling notes receivable may be understood from the following typical example.

NONINTEREST-BEARING NOTE RECEIVED

Suppose that Harold Lowndes has an overdue balance of $300 in his account with the Ashton & Barker Clothing Store. He agrees to give the store his 30-day, noninterest-bearing note dated April 8, 19X2 to obtain an extension of time in which to pay. (The note gives Ashton & Barker more positive evidence of the debt in case legal action ultimately becomes necessary.)

Recording Receipt of the Note

The receipt of Lowndes's note is recorded in the general journal. Notes Receivable (a new asset) is debited for $300 and Accounts Receivable is credited for $300.

19	X2		4–6				
Apr.	8	Notes Receivable	112		300	00	
		Accts. Rec./Harold Lowndes . .	111/✓				300	00
		To record 30-day, noninterest-bearing note received in settlement of account.					

Notice in the illustration that the credit entry is recorded as Accounts Receivable/Harold Lowndes. The $300 must now be posted as a credit in two places.

1. The Accounts Receivable Control account is credited in the general ledger.
2. The account with Harold Lowndes is credited in the accounts receivable subsidiary ledger.

As a result of this *dual* or *double posting technique,* the sum of the subsidiary ledger account balances will continue to equal the balance of the Accounts Receivable Control account in the general ledger.

Maturity Date

Lowndes's note matures on May 8.

Days to run in April: 30 − 8, or	22
Days to maturity in May: 30 − 22, or	8
Total period of note in days	30

Collection of the Note

When Lowndes pays the note at maturity, an entry debiting Cash in Bank and crediting Notes Receivable is made in the cash receipts journal. Lowndes's note is marked paid and returned to him.

INTEREST-BEARING NOTE RECEIVED

Most sellers are willing to meet the customer more than halfway to make a sale and to retain goodwill. However, a customer who does not pay his account within the credit period originally agreed upon should reasonably expect to pay interest on the amount owed in consideration for receiving a further extension of credit. Consequently, a note being offered to the seller by a customer whose account is in arrears might properly make provision for the payment of interest. Assume that under such conditions, on April 14, 19X2 Ashton & Barker agrees to accept a 60-day, 8% note for $400 from James Morgan to cover his past due account.

Receipt of the Note

When the note is received, an entry is made in the general journal debiting Notes Receivable and crediting Accounts Receivable/James Morgan for $400.

Maturity Date

The maturity date of the Morgan note is then computed to be June 13.

Days to run in April: 30 − 14, or	16
Days to run in May:	31
Total days to end of May	47
Days in June to maturity: 60 − 47, or	13
Total period of note in days	60

Calculation of Interest

The interest on $400 for 60 days at 8% is computed as follows:

Interest = $400 × 8% × 60/360
Interest = $5.33

Collection of the Note

When Morgan tenders payment on the maturity date, his check should include the $400 face value of the note plus $5.33 interest—a total (maturity value) of $405.33. An entry is recorded in the cash receipts journal debiting Cash in Bank for the total amount, crediting Notes Receivable for $400, and crediting Interest Income for $5.33 as illustrated.

Notice that this entry requires two lines in the cash receipts journal to handle the credits to Notes Receivable and to Interest Income. There is only a single debit (to Cash in Bank).

DATE		EXPLANATION	SUNDRY CREDITS			ACCTS. REC.		CASH IN BANK DR. 101	
			ACCT. NO.	✓	AMT.	✓	CR. 111		
June	13	Notes Receivable	112		400 00				
		Interest Income	491		5 33				405 33

PARTIAL COLLECTION OF A NOTE

Suppose James Morgan had offered to pay half his note if Ashton & Barker would renew the balance for an additional 30 days at 8%. Ordinarily, the payment made is applied first to the interest due and then the balance is applied to reduce the principal. In this case, Morgan is asked to pay the interest to maturity of the original note, $5.33, plus half the face of the note, $200, or $205.33 in all. The $205.33 receipt is recorded in the cash receipts journal by debiting Cash in Bank for the total, crediting Notes Receivable for $200, and crediting Interest Income for $5.33. The effect on the general ledger accounts as shown in general journal form would be as follows.

19	X2				
June	13	Cash in Bank	101	205 33	
		Notes Receivable	112		200 00
		Interest Income	491		5 33

The original note might be endorsed or receipted in part by Ashton & Barker to reflect the partial payment. Or Morgan might prefer to have the first note canceled and to give a new note for the remaining balance due.

NOTE NOT COLLECTED AT MATURITY

If James Morgan had not paid his note at maturity, the accountant would say that he had *dishonored* the note. It is not proper to carry a dishonored note as a note receivable. Therefore, the balance owed by Morgan would be transferred back into his Accounts Receivable account by a general journal entry. In this entry, both the Accounts Receivable Control account in the general ledger and Morgan's individual account in the subsidiary ledger are debited. Since Morgan would now owe the original balance of $400 and the $5.33 interest, these debits total $405.33. This is recorded by crediting the Notes Receivable account for the face amount of the note, $400, and crediting Interest Income for $5.33, as illustrated.

UNIT 21

337

19	X2	6–8					
June	13	Accts. Receivable/James Morgan . . .	111/✓	405	33		
		Notes Receivable	112			400	00
		Interest Income	491			5	33
		To charge back to James Morgan the amount of his dishonored note plus interest due on it to maturity.					

Notice again the double posting required for the debit amount, to the general ledger control account and to Morgan's individual account in the subsidiary ledger.

As with the noninterest-bearing note dishonored at maturity, interest would continue to run on the dishonored interest-bearing note, and at the legal rate (which in most cases is higher than the original contract rate).

NOTES GIVEN AT TIME OF SALE

The Lowndes and Morgan notes arose from the extension of past due open accounts. These transaction situations were used because Ashton & Barker is not engaged in the type of business in which notes are ordinarily received at the time of sale. Should an occasional note be received when a sale is made, the transaction is recorded in the general journal as follows.

19	X2	6–4					
June	5	Notes Receivable	112	250	00		
		Sales	401			250	00
		To record 90-day, 7% note received from Donald Springer on sale of merchandise.					

However, if it were a common practice in the trade to receive notes at the time of sale, a special column would be provided in the sales journal for the debit to Notes Receivable, so that the total could be posted in one amount to the general ledger account at the end of the month.

DISCOUNTING A NOTE RECEIVABLE

One of the advantages of having a note receivable instead of an open book account is that the holder can borrow on the note by discounting it at the bank. The bank will charge interest on the maturity value of the note at a specified rate for the number of days remaining until maturity. This *discount charge* will be deducted in advance by the bank, and the seller will receive the net proceeds (maturity value less the discount). The proceeds are ordinarily credited by the bank as a deposit to the firm's bank account.

NONINTEREST-BEARING NOTE DISCOUNTED

Suppose that Ashton & Barker has to raise additional cash to meet some heavy obligations at the end of April. The store decides to discount a 60-day noninterest-bearing note receivable for $500 received from Peter Kirkwood on April 3 and payable on June 2. The Kirkwood note is turned over to the City National Bank for discounting on April 18, subject to a discount rate of 6%. This transaction should be examined carefully because of the new elements involved.

Review of the Record Prior to Discounting

When the note was received on April 3, the asset, Notes Receivable, was debited through the general journal. The maturity date was determined to be June 2.

Calculating the Discount

The arithmetic involved to determine the discount amount is similar to that used in connection with the discounting of a note payable.

1. Determine the maturity value of the note. Since the note is non-interest-bearing, its value at maturity is the same as its face value—$500.
2. Determine the number of days in the discount period. The number of days from the discount date to the maturity date (discount period) may be determined by working backward from the maturity date to the discount date.

Days to run in June to maturity:	2
Days in May:	31
Days to run in April: 30 − 18, or	12
Total days in discount period	45

3. Determine the amount of the discount. This is found by using the regular interest formula (Interest = Principal × Rate × Time) to calculate the amount to be charged by the bank for the discount period, as follows.

Discount = Maturity Value × Discount Rate × Discount Period
Discount = $500 × .06 × 45/360
Discount = $3.75

4. Determine the proceeds. The amount received from the bank, called the proceeds, is the maturity value of the note less the amount of the discount. In this case the proceeds are $500 − $3.75, or $496.25.

Recording the Discounting of the Note

When the computations are completed, an entry recording the discounting of the note is made in the cash receipts journal as illustrated here.

CASH RECEIPTS JOURNAL for Month of April 19X2   **Page 3**

DATE		EXPLANATION	SUNDRY CREDITS			ACCTS. REC.		CASH IN BANK DR. 101	
			ACCT. NO.	✓	AMOUNT	✓	CR. 111		
Apr.	18	Notes Rec. Discounted	113		500 00			496	25
		Interest Expense	591		(3 75)				

Notice that two debits are involved—one to Cash in Bank for the proceeds, $496.25, and one to Interest Expense for the discount amount, $3.75. The debit to Interest Expense is recorded in Ashton & Barker's cash receipts journal by making a red or circled entry in the Sundry Credits column. Also notice that instead of crediting Notes Receivable, a new account called Notes Receivable Discounted is credited. The effect of this treatment is that the Notes Receivable asset is offset by the credit entry in the Notes Receivable Discounted account.

NOTES RECEIVABLE DISCOUNTED— A CONTINGENT LIABILITY

When a note receivable is discounted, it must be endorsed. If the maker of the endorsed note does not pay it at maturity, the holder (the bank) can then obtain payment from the endorser (Ashton & Barker). Hence, the endorser has a possible, or *contingent*, liability. This fact is recorded on the books by crediting Notes Receivable Discounted. On the balance sheet, the balance of Notes Receivable Discounted is deducted from the total of Notes Receivable, leaving a difference that represents the notes receivable still held, amounting to $750 in this case.

Notes Receivable	$1,250	
Less Notes Receivable Discounted	500	$750

DISCOUNTED NOTE PAID AT MATURITY

At the maturity date, the holder of the discounted note presents it to the maker for payment. If Kirkwood pays the note when the bank presents it to him, the Ashton & Barker Clothing Store has no further contingent liability. At that time, an entry to extinguish the liability is made in the general journal as follows.

19 X2		6–1				
June	2	Notes Receivable Discounted	113	500	00	
		Notes Receivable	112			500	00
		To close out the asset and the contingent liability upon payment by Peter Kirkwood of his note, which we had discounted at the bank.				

DISCOUNTED NOTE DISHONORED AT MATURITY

If Kirkwood dishonors his note by failing to pay it at maturity, the bank may file a formal protest through a notary public. The Ashton & Barker Clothing Store then has to pay the bank for the maturity value of the note plus the protest fee charged by the notary. In fact, the bank often will charge the firm's account with this amount and send a debit memorandum with the note and protest form. If the protest fee is $3 in this case, the resulting entry would be a debit to Accounts Receivable/Peter Kirkwood for $503 and a credit to cash in Bank for $503. Notice that the entire amount of $503 (maturity value and protest fee) is charged back to the account of the delinquent customer in the subsidiary ledger—not merely the amount due on the note that he has dishonored.

Still another entry would be required to complete the record of this transaction. By paying the dishonored note, Ashton & Barker has removed the contingent liability that was set up when the note was discounted. To remove this contingent liability from the books, an entry must be made in the general journal debiting Notes Receivable Discounted and crediting Notes Receivable. (The dishonored note might be turned over to an attorney for collection.)

Another item that Ashton & Barker decides to discount in order to increase its available cash is a note received from Oscar Norman on April 17. The principal is $600 and the note runs for 60 days with interest at 7%.

Review of the Record Prior to Discounting

On April 17, when the note was received, the Notes Receivable account was debited to record the increase of that asset, with a credit to Accounts Receivable/Oscar Norman. The maturity date of the note is June 16.

Calculating the Discount

On May 2, when Ashton & Barker arranges to discount the Norman note at the bank at 8%, the proceeds are computed.

1. Determine the maturity value of the note. Since this is an interest-bearing note, its maturity value is the sum of the face value, $600, and interest on this amount for 60 days at 7% ($7). Thus, the maturity value is $607.

2. Determine the number of days in the discount period. Working back from the maturity date to the discount date, the discount period is found to be 45 days.

Days to run in June to maturity:	16
Days to run in May: 31 − 2, or	29
Total days in discount period:	45

3. Determine the amount of discount. The bank will levy its charge of 8% on the maturity value, $607, for the discount period, 45 days. Putting these figures into the interest formula, the discount is found as follows:

    Discount = $607 × .08 × 45/360
    Discount = $6.07

4. Determine the proceeds. The amount received from the bank is $600.93, the maturity value minus the discount charge.

$$Maturity\ Value = \$607.00$$
$$Discount \qquad = \quad\ \ 6.07$$
$$Proceeds \qquad = \overline{\$600.93}$$

Recording the Discounting of the Note

The discounting of the note receivable is recorded in the cash receipts journal. This time there is one debit to Cash in Bank and two credits —one to Notes Receivable Discounted and the other to Interest Income. Two lines in the cash receipts journal are required to show the credits.

CASH RECEIPTS JOURNAL for Month of May 19X2   **Page 4**

DATE	EXPLANATION	SUNDRY CREDITS			ACCTS. REC.		CASH SALES CR. 401	CASH SHORT OR OVER DR. 529	CASH IN BANK DR. 101
		ACCT. NO.	✓	AMT.	✓	CR. 111			
May 2	Notes Rec. Disc.	113		600 00					
	Interest Income	491		93					600 93

The net Interest Income of $.93 represents the $7 total interest allowed by the bank in computing the maturity value, less the discount of $6.07 charged by the bank. If the proceeds had been less than the face of the note, the difference would have been debited to Interest Expense.

DISCOUNTED NOTE PAID AT MATURITY

If Norman pays the note at the maturity date, an entry is made on the books of Ashton & Barker to cancel the contingent liability that was set up at the time of discounting. A debit of $600 is made to Notes Receivable Discounted and the same amount is credited to Notes Receivable.

NOTES RECEIVABLE REGISTER

If many notes receivable are held, it may be convenient to set up a special *notes receivable register*. This has somewhat the same form as the notes payable register. Information recorded in the register for each note receivable includes the date of the note, the maker, where payable, time to run, maturity date, face amount of note, and the rate and amount of interest, if any. Columns are also provided to record the dates when and the banks at which the notes have been discounted.

UNIT 21

NOTES RECEIVABLE REGISTER

DATE OF ENTRY		MAKER	WHERE PAYABLE	DATE OF NOTE		TIME TO RUN	MATURITY DATE												
							YEAR	J	F	M	A	M	J	J	A	S	O	N	D
19	X2			19	X2														
Apr.	3	Peter Kirkwood	City Nat'l Bank	Apr.	3	60 days	19X2						2						
	8	Harold Lowndes	First Nat'l Bank		8	30 days	19X2					8							
	14	James Morgan	State Trust Co.		14	60 days	19X2						13						
	17	Oscar Norman	City Nat'l Bank		17	60 days	19X2						16						

The four notes received by Ashton & Barker during the month of April and used in the previous examples are entered in the notes receivable register.

NOTES RECEIVABLE AND INTEREST INCOME ON THE STATEMENTS

The notes receivable account is a current asset and appears on the balance sheet, usually just below cash. Interest Income is shown on the income statement as nonoperating income and is listed below and added to Net Profit from Operations. The final sections of a typical income statement might look like this.

Net Profit from Operations	$12,500
Other Income (Add)	
Interest Income	125
	$12,625
Other Expenses (Deduct)	
Interest Expense	200
Net Profit for Year	$12,425

DRAFTS

A *draft* is an order in writing requiring the person addressed to pay a sum of money to the order of someone or to bearer. An ordinary check is one form of draft. Two other examples are bank drafts and commercial drafts.

Bank Drafts

A *bank draft* is a check written by one bank ordering another bank, in which it has funds on deposit, to pay the indicated amount to the order of a specified person. Since bank drafts are more readily ac-

FACE AMT. OF NOTE	INTEREST		DISCOUNTED		DATE PAID		REMARKS
	RATE	AMT.	BANK	DATE			
500 00	None		City National Bank	Apr. 18			
300 00	None				May	8	
400 00	8%	5 33			June	13	
600 00	7%	7 00	City National Bank	May 2			

cepted than individual checks, a person may use a bank draft to pay a debt to an out-of-town creditor.

Another special type of check or draft is the *cashier's check,* which may also be obtained by an individual to pay a bill. The cashier's check is drawn by a bank official ordering his own bank to pay the specified amount. The cashier's check offers greater protection to a creditor than the check of an individual.

The purchase of a bank draft (or cashier's check) is recorded by preparing a voucher debiting the account payable that the draft is to settle, debiting an expense account (perhaps entitled Collection and Exchange) for the bank service charge and crediting an account payable with the bank. A check is drawn to the order of the bank and recorded in the check register. The resulting credit to Cash is offset by a debit to the account payable with the bank.

For example, suppose that a bill for $525, represented by Voucher 5-08, is to be settled by sending the creditor a bank draft instead of a regular check. The bank charges $.65 for drawing its draft. The effect of the entries required for the new voucher (6-12) and the payment (Check 479) is shown in general journal form.

19	X2							
May	15	Accounts Payable (Voucher 5-08) . .	201	525	00			
		Collection and Exchange	559		65			
		Accts. Payable (Voucher 6-12) . .	201			525	65	
	15	Accounts Payable (Voucher 6-12) . .	201	525	65			
		Cash in Bank (Check 479) . . .	101			525	65	

Commercial Drafts

A *commercial draft* is a draft drawn by one person or business firm requesting another to pay a specified sum of money at once or at a determinable later date. This instrument is used to take care of special shipment and collection problems.

A *sight draft* is payable on presentation, or at sight. It is honored by payment. No accounting entry (except possibly a memorandum notation that

UNIT 21

a draft has been issued) is made for the issuance of a sight draft. If the sight draft is honored, the transaction is simply recorded as a cash receipt.

Sight drafts may be used as an aid in collecting accounts receivable. A draft is usually sent for collection to the customer's bank. If the debtor does not honor the draft, his credit standing may be injured in the eyes of his banker. Thus a draft is more likely to be honored than a collection letter.

It is also possible to ship goods with a sight draft attached to an order bill of lading to obtain cash on delivery. In this situation, the bill of lading, with sight draft attached, is sent to a bank near the addressee. The customer must pay the draft to the bank before he can get the bill of lading with which to obtain the goods. The collecting bank sends the money, less its collection fee, to the shipper who drew the draft. Upon receipt of the funds, the seller records a cash receipt and debits an expense account for the collection fee.

A *time draft* differs from a sight draft in that additional time is allowed for payment. The maturity date of a time draft may be:

1. A date specified in the draft.
2. A specified number of days after the date of the draft.
3. A specified number of days after acceptance of the draft.

A time draft requires no entry when it is issued (other than a memorandum notation that it has been issued). If the person upon whom the draft is drawn agrees to honor it at maturity, he indicates his agreement by writing "accepted" on the face of the note, signs it, and dates it. He then records the accepted draft on his books as a note payable and returns it to the drawer who enters it on his books as a note receivable.

TRADE ACCEPTANCES

A trade acceptance is a special form of commercial time draft that arises out of the sale of goods and has this fact noted on its face. The original transaction may be recorded in the same manner as a sale on account. When the draft has been accepted, it is accounted for as a note. Merchants have found that their credit losses on trade acceptances are likely to be lower than on open book accounts. Trade acceptance also can be discounted.

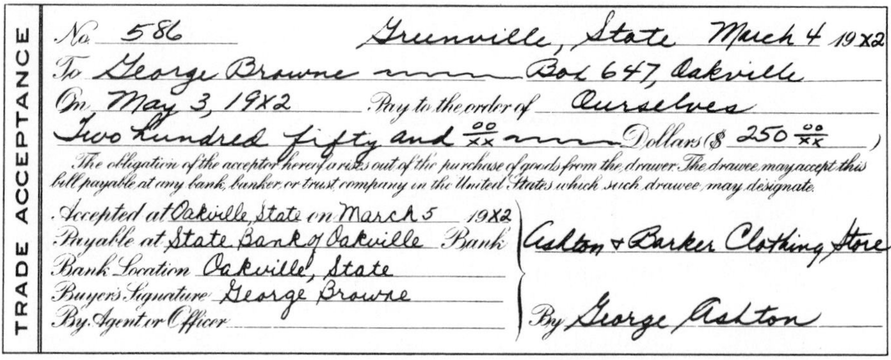
TRADE ACCEPTANCE

No. 586 Greenville, State March 4 19X2

To George Browne Box 647, Oakville

On May 3, 19X2 Pay to the order of Ourselves

Two hundred fifty and 00/xx Dollars ($ 250 00/xx)

The obligation of the acceptor hereof arises out of the purchase of goods from the drawer. The drawee may accept this bill payable at any bank, banker or trust company in the United States which such drawee may designate.

Accepted at Oakville, State on March 5 19X2
Payable at State Bank of Oakville Bank
Bank Location Oakville, State
Buyer's Signature George Browne
By Agent or Officer

Ashton & Barker Clothing Store
By George Ashton

PRINCIPLES AND PROCEDURES

Notes receivable, like notes payable, may be interest-bearing or non-interest-bearing. In a firm such as Ashton & Barker, they may be used to extend past due accounts since they give more legal protection than an open book account. When a note is received, Accounts Receivable is credited and Notes Receivable is debited. When the note is paid, an entry debiting Cash in Bank and crediting Notes Receivable is made in the cash receipts journal. If the note was interest-bearing, the interest received is credited to an Interest Income account. If the note is dishonored (not paid at maturity), the amount becomes an account receivable. Accounts Receivable is debited for the face amount plus interest and Notes Receivable and Interest Income are credited. If it is common practice in a particular trade to receive notes at the time a sale is made, a special column would be provided in the sales journal for debits to Notes Receivable.

A note receivable may be discounted at a bank prior to maturity. In this case, the bank will deduct interest at the discount rate for the time remaining to maturity. Cash in Bank is debited for the proceeds and, since the note remains a contingent liability, a Notes Receivable Discounted account is credited. The interest element may be recorded as a debit to Interest Expense or as a credit to Interest Income, according to the circumstances.

Bank drafts, commercial drafts, and trade acceptances are other types of negotiable instruments occasionally used in business.

MANAGERIAL IMPLICATIONS

Management should be aware of the possibilities of using negotiable instruments in connection with sales and credit policies. Management must be especially cognizant of the possibilities inherent in the instruments when cash is short. Notes due some time in the future may be discounted to raise funds for current operations. In many cases, open book accounts receivable could be converted into notes receivable, both giving more legal protection to the creditor as well as increasing the likelihood of collection.

APPLICATION OF PRINCIPLES

PROBLEM 21 · 1

♦ The notes received by the Brian Equipment Company during 19X1 are summarized on the next page.

DATE	FACE	PERIOD	INTEREST RATE, %
Jan. 18	$2,000	90 days	6
Jan. 30	1,000	1 month	5
May 18	1,300	90 days	6
July 10	825	4 months	7
Oct. 16	425	45 days	7

ADD ACC TO FACE

Two of the notes were discounted by the Brian Equipment Company at the bank. On June 7, the note dated May 18 was discounted at a rate of 7%, and on Aug. 9, the note dated July 10 was discounted at a rate of 6%.

INSTRUCTIONS

1. Compute the total interest and the maturity value of each note.
2. On the two notes discounted, compute the discount charged by the bank and the net proceeds.
3. Record the discounting of the notes in general journal form. (Omit entry numbers.)
4. Give entries in general journal form to record (a) the receipt of the note on Jan. 18 in settlement of Eastern Company's $2,000 account receivable, and (b) receipt of payment from Eastern Company on Apr. 18 for the $2,000 note dated Jan. 18 and interest on the note. (Omit entry numbers.)

PROBLEM 21 · 2

Home Supply Company uses a notes receivable register. Notes outstanding at June 30, 19X1 are as follows:

a. $9,000, 7%, 120-day note of Model Homes Inc., dated Mar. 20. (This note was discounted at First State Bank on Mar. 30.)
b. $1,000, 8%, 8-month note of Parker Construction Company, dated May 8.
c. $4,500, 6%, 60-day note of James Company, dated May 14.
d. $2,000, noninterest-bearing, 30-day note of Hal Parks, dated June 20.

The following note transactions took place during July 19X1.

JULY

2 Accepted a 30-day, 8% note for $1,500, dated today from Broad Street Construction Company, as an extension of credit on their overdue account receivable. (Record in the general journal, using Entry 7-1. All journal entries are to be numbered consecutively. There are no postings to be made to general ledger accounts nor to customers' accounts in the subsidiary ledger. Use account numbers illustrated in text.)

5 Discounted at First State Bank the $2,000 note of Hal Parks received on June 20. Discount rate charged by the Bank was 8%.

JULY

13 Received payment from James Company for their $4,500 note of May 14, plus interest.

19 Received notice that Model Homes Inc. refused to pay First State Bank for their note of Mar. 20 which was discounted at the bank on Mar. 30. The bank charged Home Supply Company's account for $9,215, representing the maturity value of the note plus a protest fee of $5. (Record the charge-back by the bank in the general journal. Also record in the general journal the termination of the contingent liability for the discounted note.)

20 Received notice from First State Bank that Hal Parks had paid his note of June 20, which was discounted on July 5.

22 Discounted at First State Bank the $1,000 note of Parker Construction Company dated May 8. The bank charged a discount rate of 7%.

INSTRUCTIONS

1. Enter the notes outstanding on June 30, 19X1 in a notes receivable register that has the same columns as shown in the illustration on pages 344 and 345. All notes are payable at the First State Bank.

2. Using a general journal and a cash receipts journal, record the given note transactions. The cash receipts journal should have the same column heads as illustrated on page 343. Account numbers and titles needed to complete the solution are:

101	Cash in Bank	491	Interest Income
111	Accounts Receivable	591	Interest Expense
112	Notes Receivable		
113	Notes Receivable Discounted		

Enter data in the notes receivable register where appropriate.

MANAGERIAL CHECKUPS

♦ How do negotiable instruments help management to sell goods on credit while enjoying the protection of important legal safeguards?

♦ Why would the seller be concerned about the contingent liability on a customer's note that has been discounted?

♦ As a manager, would you consider a note received at the time of sale to be as collectible as a note received in exchange for a further extension of credit? Why?

22 RECEIVABLES, BAD DEBTS, AND INSTALLMENT SALES

Whenever there are credit transactions, losses from bad debts may be expected because some people fail to pay their obligations. Although businessmen try to keep bad debt losses to a minimum by exercising care in extending credit and by employing diligence in collecting accounts, such losses are an expense of doing business on credit. Two methods are in general use for recognizing bad debt losses, as you learned in Unit 14. This unit discusses in greater detail the valuation or adjustment of receivables to reflect losses or expected losses resulting from nonpayment by customers. Also, the special problems arising from installment sales are examined.

RECORDING LOSS WHEN IT OCCURS

At the time a merchant extends credit to a customer, he naturally expects to collect the amount in full. If he cannot, he may carry the account on his books until it has definitely become uncollectible and then formally recognize the amount as a bad debt loss. Suppose that customer John Brown has left town without paying his account balance of $75 and that his whereabouts is unknown. After exhausting all possibilities of finding Brown and collecting from him, the firm of Ashton & Barker writes off the account as a bad debt by a general journal entry.

19 X2		9–14			
Sept. 16	Bad Debts Expense	561	75 00	
	Accts. Rec./John Brown . . .	111/✓		75 00
	To write off uncollectible account of John Brown, whose whereabouts is unknown.			

The resulting reduction in the value of Accounts Receivable reflects the current situation, and when the new balance is shown on the balance sheet, it represents the total of receivables believed to be collectible.

PROVIDING FOR LOSS BEFORE IT OCCURS

Instead of waiting until a particular account proves uncollectible and then recording the loss, it is possible to anticipate bad debt losses and provide for them ahead of time. *This method permits the seller to offset the estimated expense against the revenue that the firm has earned during the same accounting period.* This is a logical procedure, because the bad debt loss is related to the sales transaction from which the account receivable resulted.

In order to include the expense from bad debts and the sales income in the same accounting period, the accountant has to estimate the amount of bad debt losses that are likely to result from the accounts receivable that have not yet been collected at the end of the period. There are three common methods of estimating the amount of bad debt losses.

Percentage of Credit Sales

After a business has been operating for a number of years, it may be possible to recognize an average ratio of bad debt losses to credit sales and to use this ratio in estimating future bad debt losses. To be completely correct, this ratio should be based on *net credit sales*—gross sales on account minus the sales returns and allowances of credit sales. However, when sales returns and allowances are very minor, most businesses base the bad debt estimate on gross sales on credit because this figure is more easily computed. In many businesses it may be difficult to determine easily the total sales on credit. In these cases, it may be necessary to express the ratio of credit losses on total sales, including cash sales. However, as a general rule, only the credit sales should be used because there is no bad debt loss on cash sales. Since the sales returns and allowances of Ashton & Barker are relatively minor, the bad debt losses would probably be based on total credit sales.

The experience of other firms in the same line of business may be used in making the estimate for a new firm. Suppose that Ashton & Barker, relying on the experience of its predecessor, the Ashton Clothing Store, estimates that three-tenths of one percent (0.3%) of its credit sales will ultimately be uncollectible bad debts. During the first year of operation of the Ashton & Barker Clothing Store, suppose that $200,000 worth of sales were made on credit. The store's estimated bad debt loss is determined by applying the percentage to the credit sales ($200,000 × .003), giving an estimated Bad Debts Expense of $600. The entry to record this estimate is shown

UNIT 22

in general journal form. (The adjustment is actually entered on the worksheet first and is later included among the adjusting entries in the general journal.)

19	X2		1–19A							
Jan.	31	Bad Debts Expense	561			600	00			
		Allowance for Bad Debts . .	111A					600	00
		To record estimate of bad debt losses based on 0.3% of credit sales of $200,000 for the year.								

The effect of the debit entry is to charge the estimated loss against the operations of the period. As a result of the credit entry, the Allowance for Bad Debts account, called a *valuation account,* reflects the estimated shrinkage in the value of the asset, Accounts Receivable. The valuation account literally revalues or reappraises the asset balance in the light of reasonable expectations. (This account long carried the title Reserve for Bad Debts, but the title Allowance for Bad Debts is now generally preferred.) Note that when bad debts are based on sales, primary emphasis is placed on charging to *expense* the credit losses applicable to the sales of the period. It is through this process that the accounts receivable are valued at their expected realizable value, but valuation is of secondary concern.

Aging Accounts Receivable

An analysis procedure, called *aging the accounts,* may be used as a guide in estimating probable bad debt losses. If this procedure is followed, a special schedule is set up on which each account receivable is listed by name and total amount. Column headings facilitate analysis of the total amount owed in each account. This schedule reveals the length of time for which component items in the account have been outstanding, such as Current (within the net credit terms), Past Due 1–30 days, Past Due 31–60 days, and Past Due Over 60 days. When the total debt of a customer is broken down in this way, a picture of the relative currency of the receivables is obtained.

ASHTON & BARKER CLOTHING STORE
Aging Schedule of Accounts Receivable
January 31, 19X2

ACCOUNT WITH	BALANCE		CURRENT		PAST DUE – DAYS					
					1–30		31–60		OVER 60	
Arthur Adams	125	00	125	00						
Ralph Ames	60	00					45	00	15	00
Samuel Apple	47	50	25	00	22	50				
William Avant	73	00	50	00					23	00
John Zeanah	110	00	80	00	30	00				
Totals	12,500	00	9,500	00	1,575	00	850	00	575	00

The older an account becomes, the less likely it is to be collected. The aging schedule in the illustration might be used in estimating possible bad debt losses. Suppose that past experience indicated that 50% of the accounts more than 60 days past due will be uncollectible and 25% of the 31–60 day group, 10% of the 1–30 day group, and 1% of the current accounts will also be uncollectible. The estimate of doubtful accounts included in accounts receivable will then be $752.50, as follows.

Over 60 days past due	.50	X	$ 575.00	=	$287.50
31-60 days past due	.25	X	850.00	=	212.50
1-30 days past due	.10	X	1,575.00	=	157.50
Current	.01	X	9,500.00	=	95.00
					$752.50

The Allowance for Bad Debts should then be adjusted to this desired balance of $752.50. For example, if the Allowance for Bad Debts account contained a credit balance of $200 on January 31, prior to adjustments, it would be necessary to add $552.50 to bring the balance up to the $752.50 desired. The following entry would be made.

19 X2		1–19A			
Jan. 31	Bad Debts Expense	561	552 50	
	Allowance for Bad Debts . .	111A		552 50
	To adjust allowance account to desired balance of $752.50, based on aging of accounts receivable.			

On the other hand, if the Allowance for Bad Debts account had a debit (deficiency) balance of $50 at the end of the year (resulting from writing off specific accounts, as discussed below), it would be necessary to add $802.50 ($50 + $752.50) to the account to bring it to the desired credit balance of $752.50. Whatever the amount, the debit is to Bad Debts Expense and the credit is to the Allowance for Bad Debts account, as previously illustrated.

Adjusting Allowance to Predetermined Percent of Accounts Receivable

In many cases it is possible to estimate the necessary balance of the Allowance for Bad Debts account by applying a single rate, based on past experience, to the Accounts Receivable balance. For example, it may be estimated that normally one-half of one percent of the gross Accounts Receivable Control account balance will be uncollectible, and the Allowance for Bad Debts account will be adjusted to this resulting figure.

Note that when the provision for bad debts is based on the Accounts Receivable balance, *primary* emphasis is being placed on proper valuation of the accounts receivable on the balance sheet and the amount charged to expense is of *secondary* concern.

As you have seen, under the system of providing for bad debts before they occur, Bad Debts Expense is debited and Allowance for Bad Debts is credited for an estimated amount of loss. Then, when a particular account proves uncollectible, the Allowance for Bad Debts account is debited and Accounts Receivable is credited. For example, suppose that the account of Ralph Ames, with a balance of $60, is determined to be uncollectible and is written off as shown.

19	X2		3–8						
Mar.	10	Allowance for Bad Debts		111A		60	00		
		Accts. Rec./Ralph Ames . . .		111/✓				60	00
		To write off account determined to be uncollectible.							

Notice in this case that the write-off of a particular bad account does not directly affect the Bad Debts Expense account for the period (which is recorded on the basis of the estimate worked out at the end of the year). Normally, the Allowance for Bad Debts account will have a credit (excess) balance. However, if greater losses were written off than were estimated in previous fiscal periods, the Allowance for Bad Debts account may show a debit (deficiency) balance before the current position for estimated losses has been recorded.

It occasionally happens that an account written off as uncollectible is subsequently collected, in whole or in part. Suppose that the John Brown account for $75, written off under the "when it occurs" method by a debit to Bad Debts Expense and a credit to Accounts Receivable/John Brown, is later collected in full. The cash receipt is, of course, recorded in the cash receipts journal, debiting Cash and crediting Accounts Receivable/John Brown. However, since John Brown's account balance has already been written off as a bad debt, it is necessary to make an entry in the general journal reversing the bad debt write-off, as illustrated on page 355.

Some accountants prefer to record the amount to be recovered as a credit to Bad Debts Recovered, especially when the recovery is made in a later year than it was originally charged off. The amount would be restored by debits to Accounts Receivable and John Brown's subsidiary account to make sure that all pertinent facts relating to Brown's debt would be recorded

19 X2		11–8				
Nov. 10	Accounts Receivable/John Brown . .	111/✓	75 00			
	Bad Debts Expense	561			75 00	
	To reverse entry 9-14 dated Sept. 16					
	writing off this account which was					
	collected in full today.					

in the subsidiary ledger account where the information could serve for credit purposes. The collection of cash would be recorded in the cash receipts journal in the usual way as a debit to Cash in Bank and a credit to Accounts Receivable and Brown's account. The Bad Debts Recovered account would be shown on the income statement under Other Income.

The recovery of an accounts receivable balance previously written off when the Allowance for Bad Debts account is used also requires an entry in the cash receipts journal and a second entry in the general journal to reverse the bad debt write-off. The Allowance for Bad Debts account is credited in the reversal process, as illustrated in connection with the recovery of the $60 balance owed by Ralph Ames.

19 X2		6–4				
June 8	Accounts Receivable/Ralph Ames . .	111/✓	60 00			
	Allowance for Bad Debts . . .	111A			60 00	
	To reverse entry 3-8 dated March 10					
	writing off this account, which was					
	collected in full today.					

If in either the Brown or Ames case the amount recovered represented only partial collection of the balance written off, the reversal entry would be used to restore *only the amount actually collected.* For example, if Ames had paid only $40 on his $60 balance, the reversal entry in the general journal would be for the smaller amount.

OTHER RECEIVABLES AND BAD DEBT LOSSES

Just as accounts receivable may result in bad debt losses, so notes receivable and other receivables may prove to be uncollectible. Bad debt losses from notes receivable and other receivables may be recorded as they occur, or they may be estimated and provided for ahead of time in the manner previously described for accounts receivable. The same accounts, Bad Debts Expense and Allowance for Bad Debts, may be used for the valuation of all types of receivables.

The Bad Debts Expense account appears among the expenses on the income statement. If the function of giving credit and collecting accounts rests in the sales department, it would be classified as a selling expense. However, in most businesses, the credit function is separated from the sales function, and bad debts expense is usually shown as a general or administrative expense.

ALLOWANCE FOR BAD DEBTS ON THE BALANCE SHEET

Under the second method of accounting for bad debts, an Allowance for Bad Debts account is first credited for the estimated amount of bad debts and then debited for actual bad accounts written off. The balance in the allowance account at the end of the period represents the amount of accounts receivable estimated to be uncollectible. In presenting the accounts receivable on the balance sheet, the balance of the Allowance for Bad Debts account is deducted from the balance of the Accounts Receivable account, and the difference is considered as the net value of the asset. Using assumed amounts, we might show the items in a balance sheet as follows.

	ASSETS	
Cash in Bank		$10,000.00
Accounts Receivable	$12,500.00	
Less Allowance for Bad Debts	752.50	11,747.50

RECOGNIZING THE EFFECT OF POTENTIAL CASH DISCOUNTS

In some cases, cash discounts are allowed for prompt payment of invoices, as explained earlier. If the accounts receivable listed on the balance sheet are subject to cash discounts, the amount that will be collected may be somewhat less than the invoice amounts recorded. For example, a sale may be recorded as a debit to Accounts Receivable for $150. However, if terms such as 2/10, n/30 are allowed, the debt may be settled with the payment of $147 in cash within 10 days. In some cases, the approximate amount of discounts that may be taken is noted on the balance sheet, so that those studying the statements will have fair notice of this possibility. However, in most cases, people in the trade that are using the financial statements are expected to know the usual terms of sale. Therefore, such a note of possible sales discounts is not considered necessary.

INSTALLMENT SALES PROCEDURES

A special type of receivable is found in businesses that sell on an installment basis. Installment sales are common among retailers of furniture, jewelry, and major household appliances. The usual arrangement calls for the customer to make a down payment and then pay the balance in periodic payments over a length of time.

Although generally accepted accounting principles require installment sales to be recorded exactly like any other sale on account, many smaller dealers use the "installment basis" of accounting for such sales. This procedure is permitted for tax purposes. It allows profit on the sale to be deferred until cash is actually received.

To see how this accounting procedure works, suppose that on September 1, 19X1, customer Burford Williams agrees to buy a color television set on the installment plan for a price of $500. The customer pays $50 down and an additional $150 in periodic payments (3 × $50 per month) during the first year. The remaining $300 balance is collected in six installments during the second year. The set originally cost the dealer $300.

1. At the time of the sale on September 1, 19X1, the total obligation is recorded by an entry debiting an installment accounts receivable account (such as Installment Accounts Receivable—19X1/Burford Williams, as in the illustration that follows), crediting Merchandise Inventory for the cost of merchandise sold, and recording the deferred income arising from the transaction (40% rate of gross profit assumed for all installment sales in 19X1).

19	X1		9–3							
Sept.	1	Installment Accounts Receivable–19X1 /								
		Burford Williams	114/✓	500	00					
		Merchandise Inventory	121					300	00	
		Deferred Installment Sales Income–								
		19X1 Sales	411					200	00	
		To record installment sale and deferred income at 40% rate based on cost of appliance sold. (Assume 40% rate is averaged for all installment sales in year 19X1.)								

2. The cash received in the down payment results in a debit to Cash in Bank and a credit to Installment Accounts Receivable. Subsequent

receipts are handled in the same way (shown here in general journal form).

19 X1		9-4			
Sept.	1	Cash in Bank	101	50 00	
		Installment Accounts Receivable–			
		19X1 /Burford Williams . .	114/√		50 00
		To record down payment at time of sale.			
		10-3			
Oct.	1	Cash in Bank	101	50 00	
		Installment Accounts Receivable–			
		19X1 /Burford Williams . .	114/√		50 00
		To record collections in October.			
		11-4			
Nov.	1	Cash in Bank	101	50 00	
		Installment Accounts Receivable–			
		19X1 /Burford Williams . .	114/√		50 00
		To record collections in November.			
		12-4			
Dec.	1	Cash in Bank	101	50 00	
		Installment Accounts Receivable–			
		19X1 /Burford Williams . .	114/√		50 00
		To record collections in December.			

3. At the end of the year in which the sale is made, a portion of the deferred income must be recognized. A rate of gross profit is determined for the year and is applied to collections on the sales of that year ($50 × 4 = $200 × .40 = $80 in this case).

19 X1		12-18			
Dec.	31	Deferred Installment Sales Income–19X1			
		Sales	411	80 00	
		Realized Installment Sales Income–			
		19X1 Sales	421		80 00
		To record as realized income 40% of $200			
		collections on 19X1 sales.			

4. This rate determines the amount of deferred profit to be recognized at the end of each year during the period of collection, which may actually extend over several years. In this instance, 6 monthly payments of $50 were made to complete the contract in 19X2 (6 × $50 = $300).

19 X2		12-14			
Dec.	31	Deferred Installment Sales Income–19X1			
		Sales	411	120 00	
		Realized Installment Sales Income–			
		19X1 Sales	421		120 00
		To record as realized income 40% of $300			
		collections on 19X1 sales.			

If the customer defaults on his payments, the seller may recover the merchandise and take it back into inventory at its current (wholesale) value. Gain or loss is recognized and recorded at this point, the exact amount being determined by the cost and income figures in the records. The accounts receivable balance and the balance in the deferred income account are, of course, closed out.

Returning once more to customer Burford Williams who agreed to buy the $500 television set on installments, let us suppose that he had made the $50 down payment and the three periodic payments totaling $150 during the first year but had failed to make the further payments required in the second year. Assume further that the television set was repossessed on February 2, 19X2 by the seller and appraised at a value of $125. The repossession entry shows the clearing of the Installment Accounts Receivable account, the recording of the recovery, the closing of the deferred income balance, and the recognition of the loss on the sale. The loss represents the difference between the net cost of the merchandise ($300 − $125 recovery = $175) and the amount collected ($175 − $120 = $55).

19 X2		2–5			
Feb.	2	Deferred Installment Sales Income–19X1			
		Sales	411	120 00	
		Merchandise Inventory	121	125 00	
		Loss From Defaults	461	55 00	
		Installment Accounts Receivable–			
		19X1 /Burford Williams . . .	114/✓		300 00
		To record repossession of appliance and			
		loss on default by Burford Williams.			

If the set had not been recovered, the loss on the default would have been $125 greater, or $180. The other debit and credit involved in the final entry would have been the same ($300 merchandise cost − $120 collected = $180).

19 X2		2–5			
Feb.	2	Deferred Installment Sales Income–19X1	411	120 00	
		Sales	461	180 00	
		Loss From Defaults			
		Installment Accounts Receivable–			
		19X1 /Burford Williams . . .	114/✓		300 00
		To record default on installment contract			
		by Williams–merchandise not repossessed.			

UNIT 22

PRINCIPLES AND PROCEDURES

When credit is extended to customers a certain amount of bad debt losses will inevitably occur. Before receivables can be accurately presented on the balance sheet, the amounts must be studied for possible adjustment to reflect losses from bad debts. Such losses can be recorded as particular accounts become uncollectible, or an estimate of probable losses can be made in advance of the actual occurrence. Such an estimate may be based on past experience that a certain percentage of credit sales will be uncollectible. This amount can be charged off to Bad Debts Expense and credited to Allowance for Bad Debts. Here the emphasis is on the expense charge. The estimate may also be based on examining accounts receivable to determine the estimated balance uncollectible. Then Allowance for Bad Debts is adjusted to the proper balance.

When an account actually becomes worthless under the allowance method, it is removed by a debit to Allowance for Bad Debts and a credit to Accounts Receivable. When accounts that have been charged off are subsequently recovered (as sometimes happens), the account is reinstated by an entry to reverse the one previously made when the account was charged off.

Installment sales usually involve a down payment and the settlement of the balance through additional periodic payments. Special receivables accounts are maintained to keep track of all details. The sales price may be accounted for like other sales on account, or the "installment method" may be used. In the latter case profit is recognized only as the accounts are collected. The gross profit rate, determined in the year of sale, is applied to collections each year to determine the amount of profit recognized.

MANAGERIAL IMPLICATIONS

It is essential that management be kept informed of the losses from bad debts. This will permit an appraisal of the effectiveness of its credit policy, especially with regard to the actual profit of the business. A manager must always weigh the relative advantage to the business of certain bad debts losses against the effects of tighter credit policies on its sales volume. Conservative management will insist that estimated losses be charged against the revenue of the period in which the sale was made.

APPLICATION OF PRINCIPLES

PROBLEM 22 · 1

♦ The Rothman Company records losses on bad debts as specific accounts receivable become worthless. General ledger accounts involved are Accounts Receivable III, Notes Receivable 112, and Bad Debts Expense 561. Selected transactions for 19X1 are described here.

19X1

Feb. 12   Account receivable of Harry Sweeney amounting to $75 is determined to be uncollectible and is to be written off.

Mar. 20   Because of the death of Arnold Baker, his note receivable amounting to $300 is considered uncollectible and is to be written off.

June 4   Received $45 from Harry Sweeney in partial payment of his account written off on Feb. 12.

July 9   Received $30 from Harry Sweeney to complete payment of his account written off on Feb. 12.

Aug. 14   Account receivable of Tom Swift amounting to $80 is determined to be uncollectible and is written off.

Sept. 18   Received $100 from estate of Arnold Baker as part of the settlement of his affairs. This is the pro rata amount applicable to the note receivable written off on Mar. 20.

INSTRUCTIONS

Record each transaction in general journal form, including the entries that would normally be made in the cash receipts journal. You may ignore journal entry numbers in your solution.

PROBLEM 22 · 2

♦ Hainesville Seed Company sells farm supplies at both wholesale and retail. The company has found that there is a higher rate of bad debts from retail credit sales than from wholesale credit sales. At the end of each year the estimated bad debt loss is computed, based on the two rates of estimated losses that have been developed.

At Dec. 31, 19X1 the balance of Accounts Receivable 111 is $186,700, and the Allowance for Bad Debts 111A account has a debit balance of $86.20. The following additional information is given.

CATEGORY	CREDIT SALES AMOUNT	ESTIMATED RATE OF LOSS
Wholesale	$908,000	0.6%
Retail	$274,300	1.1%

INSTRUCTIONS

1. Compute the estimated bad debt loss on each of the two credit sales categories for the calendar year.
2. Prepare the adjusting journal entry (12-18A) to provide for estimated bad debt expense for the year. (Use account titles and numbers illustrated in the text.)
3. Show how the Accounts Receivable and Allowance for Bad Debts accounts would appear on the balance sheet of the Hainesville Company on Dec. 31, 19X1. List only the account titles and the amounts.
4. On Jan. 30, 19X2, the account receivable of Howard Martin, amounting

to $283, is determined to be uncollectible and is to be written off. Use Entry 1-14 to record the transaction in the general journal.

5. On June 13, 19X2, the attorneys for Hainesville Seed Company turned over a check for $283, which they have obtained from Howard Martin in settlement of his account written off on Jan. 30. Record the entire transaction in the general journal (although the cash receipt would normally be recorded in the cash receipts journal). Use Entries 6-12 and 6-13.

PROBLEM 22 · 3

♦ Information from the aging schedule of the Spring Company at the end of the fiscal year December 13, 19X1 is shown:

ACCOUNT WITH	BALANCE	CURRENT	1–30	PAST DUE DAYS 31–60	OVER 60
Andra, James	$ 180	$ 180			
Ardath, Robert	210		$ 150	$ 60	
Aston, Thomas	104				$104
Barley, Joe	80	80			
Barton, Leslie	62	42	20		
Bender, Harold	225	85	100	40	
Benson, Ronald	48			32	16
(All Other Accounts)	10,748	9,075	1,050	360	263
	$11,657	$9,462	$1,320	$492	$383

INSTRUCTIONS

1. Compute the estimated uncollectible accounts at the end of the year using these rates.
   Current   1.2%
   1–30 days past due   4.0%
   31–60 days past due   9.5%
   Over 60 days past due 20.0%

2. At Dec. 31, 19X1, Allowance for Bad Debts 111A has a debit balance of $64.12. Compute the amount of the adjustment for estimated bad debt losses that must be made as part of the adjusting entries.

3. In general journal form, record the entry (12-17A) for the estimated bad debt loss adjustment. (Use account numbers illustrated in the text.)

4. On Feb. 10, 19X2, the account receivable of J. B. Smallwood amounting to $108 was recognized as uncollectible. Record this write-off in the general journal using Entry 2-8.

5. On June 12, 19X2, a check for $50 was received from Elvis Hayes to apply on his account previously written off on Nov. 8, 19X1 as uncollectible. Record the entire transaction in the general journal (Entries 6-8 and 6-9), although the cash receipt would normally be recorded in the cash receipts journal.

6. Suppose that instead of aging the accounts receivable, the uncollectible accounts were estimated to be simply 3% of the accounts receivable on

Dec. 31. Give the journal entry to record the estimated bad debt loss adjustment assuming that the Allowance for Bad Debts 111A had a debit balance of $31.20 before the adjusting entry (Entry 12-17A).

PROBLEM 22 · 4

◆ Ace Appliance has the following partial list of accounts.

101	Cash in Bank	411	Deferred 19X1 Installment Sales Income
114	Installment Accounts Receivable—19X1	421	Realized 19X1 Installment Sales Income
121	Merchandise Inventory	461	Loss from Defaults

The following installment sales transactions for years 19X1 to 19X3 are summarized.

19X1

Aug. 15 Pete Shands bought a $600 hi-fi outfit on the installment plan, paying $75 down in cash. The set cost Ace Appliance $400.

25 Curtis Daniel bought a $420 stereo set on the installment plan, paying $65 down in cash. The outfit cost Ace Appliance $280.

Dec. 31 During the remainder of 19X1, Shands paid an additional $125 on his installment account and Daniel paid an additional $110. (Record as a combined summary entry on Dec. 31.)

31 Recorded the income realized on collections of 19X1 installment sales.

19X2

Dec. 31 During 19X2, Shands paid $70 on his installment account, and Daniel paid $200 on his account.

31 Recorded the income realized in 19X2 on collections of 19X1 installment sales.

19X3

Jan. 25 Shands' contract was declared defaulted and his hi-fi outfit was repossessed. Its wholesale value on this date is $50.

INSTRUCTIONS

Record the given transactions in general journal form. Omit entry numbers. Use account numbers illustrated in the text.

MANAGERIAL CHECKUPS

◆ How does management appraise the effectiveness of its credit policy?

◆ What are the advantages of aging accounts receivable as a guide in estimating bad debt losses as accurately as possible?

UNIT 22

363

PART 6
VALUATION OF OTHER
ASSETS: TAXES

23 INVENTORY VALUATION

The previous unit stated that the Accounts Receivable Control account balance may require adjusting, or valuation, before it can be presented properly on the financial statements. Another important asset that requires valuation is Merchandise Inventory, first discussed in Unit 14.

IMPORTANCE OF INVENTORY VALUATION

Merchandise Inventory is the one account that appears *both* on the balance sheet and on the income statement. Its valuation is important because in many businesses it represents the asset with the largest dollar value. At the same time, the inventory valuation directly affects the amount of profit or loss reported for the accounting period. If other items remain the same, the larger the ending inventory valuation, the lower the cost of goods sold, and the higher the reported profit (or the lower the reported loss). The smaller the ending inventory valuation, the higher the cost of goods sold, and the lower the reported profit (or the higher the reported loss). Thus, the determination of the true value of the inventory is a vital responsibility because the figure that is finally established may have many far-reaching effects.

INVENTORY COSTING METHODS

In Unit 14, the Merchandise Inventory of the Carter Cleaning Shop was valued at purchase cost of the items on hand. In such a small and very new business, the valuation of inventory is a relatively simple matter because there is a limited stock of merchandise and the manager is in direct daily contact with operations. Perhaps the simplest situation for inventory valuation is one that allows for specific identification of merchandise.

Specific Identification

In some trades, it is possible to keep track of the purchase price of each individual item in inventory and thus to determine the exact cost of the specific merchandise sold. Automobile dealers, art dealers, and merchants who deal with items having a large unit cost or with one-of-a-kind items may account for their inventory by the *specific identification* method. However, this method is not practical for a business such as the Ashton & Barker Clothing Store where hundreds of similar items of relatively small unit value, such as socks, shirts, and neckties, are carried in the inventory. Compounding the complications caused by quantity and variety, the purchase cost of many items may change during the period of operations. Fortunately, there are several other costing methods for the accountant to consider in his search for the best method to apply to a specific business situation.

Average Cost

Instead of keeping track of the cost of each item purchased, it is possible to average the cost of all like items available for sale during the period and to use this *average cost* in valuing the ending inventory. To understand how this system works, study the following analysis of purchases of a certain brand and quality of men's shirts during the fiscal year February 1 to January 31.

EXPLANATION	UNITS	UNIT COST	TOTAL COST
Beginning Inventory, Feb. 1, 19X1	100	$3.00	$ 300.00
Purchases:			
Feb. 27, 19X1	50	3.25	162.50
April 20, 19X1	100	3.50	350.00
Oct. 15, 19X1	75	3.75	281.25
Jan. 10, 19X2	75	4.00	300.00
Total Available for Sale	400		$1,393.75
Average Cost ($1,393.75 ÷ 400)		3.4844	
Ending Inventory, Jan. 31, 19X2 (at average cost)	125	3.4844	435.55
Cost of Goods Sold	275	3.4844	$ 958.20

Note that the computation begins with the units, unit cost, and total cost of the beginning inventory. To these figures are added the details of all purchases during the period. The sum of the units in beginning inventory and units purchased represents the total units available for sale. The total cost of the beginning inventory is added to the total cost of each lot purchased to obtain the total cost of the units available for sale. This total cost of $1,393.75 is then divided by the total number of units available to find the average unit cost ($1,393.75 ÷ 400 = $3.4844). The value of the ending inventory is established by multiplying the number of units on hand by the average unit cost (125 × $3.4844 = $435.55). The cost of goods sold may then be readily determined by subtracting the value of the closing inventory from the total value of merchandise available ($1,393.75 − $435.55 = $958.20).

The average cost method of inventory valuation is relatively simple to apply, but it reflects all the limitations of any average figure. The unit cost cannot be related to any tangible unit or lot of merchandise; and it does not reveal price changes as clearly as might be desired. In highly competitive businesses subject to significant price and style changes, a more specific and revealing method of cost determination is desirable. There are two other popular methods of valuation that many such businesses regard as better suited to their circumstances.

First In, First Out Method

In most businesses, merchants naturally try to sell their oldest items first. Thus, at any given time, the merchandise on hand usually reflects the latest goods bought. The *first in, first out method* of inventory valuation (usually referred to as FIFO) parallels this pattern of operation. The cost of the ending inventory is computed by referring to the cost of the latest purchases.

Using the figures from the previous example, the cost of the ending inventory of 125 units would be computed as $487.50 under the first in, first out pricing method.

From Purchase of Jan. 10, 19X2	75 units @ $4.00 =	$300.00
From Purchase of Oct. 15, 19X1	50 units @ $3.75 =	187.50
Ending Inventory, Jan. 31, 19X2	125 units	$487.50

The cost of goods sold would then be found by subtracting the value of the closing inventory from the total value of merchandise available, as previously computed ($1,393.75 − $487.50 = $906.25).

Actually, the FIFO method attempts to approximate the results of the specific identification method even though large and varied stocks are involved. While specific items are not identified, a distinction is made between recent and earlier acquisitions of stock so that the valuation of the inventory will reflect most recent price levels. In a time of rising prices, the difference in the cost of goods sold may have a significant impact on total expenses and profits to be reported. For example, a difference of $51.95 arises between the FIFO and the average cost methods in the costing of the 275 shirts sold during the period.

Cost of Goods Sold (Average Cost Method)	$958.20
Cost of Goods Sold (FIFO)	906.25
Difference	$ 51.95

Last In, First Out Method

While the FIFO method would result in a more favorable profit picture under the circumstances portrayed, many accountants, owners, and managers would hesitate to use it. They believe that the current cost of merchandise should be matched as closely as possible to current sales dollars. They would say that failure to do this would be to ignore the ultimate day of reckoning when inventory has to be replaced at higher costs. The system of valuation that they consider more conservative and realistic is the *last in, first out* (LIFO) *method*.

Under the LIFO method of inventory pricing, it is assumed that the most current costs of merchandise purchased should be charged to cost of goods sold. Thus, the value to be assigned to the inventory still on hand would be the cost of the oldest merchandise available during the period. Using the figures from the preceding example, the value of the 125 shirts on hand at the end of the period would be determined as $381.25, as follows.

From Beginning Inventory, Feb. 1, 19X1	100 units @ $3.00 =	$300.00
From Purchase of Feb. 27, 19X1	25 units @ $3.25 =	81.25
Ending Inventory, Jan. 31, 19X2	125 units	$381.25

The cost of goods sold would be computed by subtracting $381.25 from the previously established value of merchandise available ($1,393.75 − $381.25 = $1,012.50). It is quickly apparent that in a time of rising prices, the relatively lower inventory valuation under the LIFO method tends to increase the cost of goods sold and decrease the reported profit.

Obviously, the LIFO method of determining inventory cost does not match the actual physical flow of merchandise in most businesses. It is merely a procedure developed for charging current costs of goods against current sales prices.

COMPARISON OF RESULTS OF INVENTORY COSTING METHODS

The different results obtained from the use of the average cost, FIFO, and LIFO inventory methods may be seen in the following illustration. (The analysis of purchases is the same as the one shown on page 368.)

Notice that the ending inventory valuation of the same 125 shirts ranges from a low of $381.25, if the LIFO method is used, to a high of $487.50, if the FIFO method is used. The average cost method gives a figure in between (as is almost always the case) of $435.55. Subtracting the ending inventory valuations in each case from the total cost of goods available for

COMPARISON OF RESULTS OF
INVENTORY COSTING METHODS

EXPLANATION	UNITS	UNIT COST	TOTAL COST	INVENTORY VALUATION	COST OF GOODS SOLD
Beginning Inventory, Feb. 1, 19X1	100	$3.00	$ 300.00		
Purchases:					
Feb. 27, 19X1	50	3.25	162.50		
April 20, 19X1	100	3.50	350.00		
Oct. 15, 19X1	75	3.75	281.25		
Jan. 10, 19X2	75	4.00	300.00		
Total Available for Sale	400		$1,393.75		
1. Average Cost					
Average Cost per Unit		$3.4844			
Valuation of Ending Inventory	125	3.4844		$435.55	
Cost of Goods Sold					$ 958.20
2. First In, First Out					
From Purchase Jan. 10	75	$4.00	$ 300.00		
From Purchase Oct. 15	50	3.75	187.50		
Valuation of Ending Inventory				$487.50	
Cost of Goods Sold					$ 906.25
3. Last In, First Out					
From Beginning Inventory, Feb. 1	100	$3.00	$ 300.00		
From Purchase Feb. 27	25	3.25	81.25		
Valuation of Ending Inventory				$381.25	
Cost of Goods Sold					$1,012.50

sale, $1,393.75, gives a high cost of goods sold of $1,012.50 through the use of LIFO and a low of $906.25 through the FIFO method. The average cost method will always give a figure in between ($958.20 in this case).

Since price trends are a vital element in any inventory valuation, remember these basic rules. In a period of rising prices, the LIFO method will result in a lower reported profit than the FIFO method. In a period of falling prices, the LIFO method will result in a higher reported profit than the FIFO method. Whatever the direction prices may take, the average cost method will give a profit result somewhere between that which would be obtained with FIFO and LIFO.

However, a business may not change its inventory valuation method at will from one period to the next in order to report the amount of profit it might prefer. Once a method is adopted it must be used consistently from one period to the next, unless notice of a change of method is clearly stated on the financial statements along with a careful explanation of the approximate dollar effects. Permission of the Director of Internal Revenue must be obtained before making a change in inventory methods for federal income tax purposes.

UNIT 23

All methods of inventory valuation discussed so far have been based on cost. However, accountants generally believe that the asset valuation used on the balance sheet should be conservative and should not overstate the asset values. If the market price of an inventory item has declined, the seller will probably have trouble selling it at his usual increase or markon above original cost. If the price decline is especially severe, he may even have to sell the item at a loss. Consequently, accountants prefer to value inventory according to the rule of *cost or market, whichever is lower.* As the name of this rule suggests, when the price of an item has declined and is below the original purchase cost, the accountant values the item at market price instead of cost, in order to reflect the lower current value on the books.

Market price for the purpose of applying the rule of cost or market, whichever is lower, might be described as the price at which the item could be bought (at the inventory date) through the usual channels and in the usual quantities. In some cases, current market prices are quoted in trade publications. In other cases, a recent purchase may give a price that is reasonably close to the current market price. In still other circumstances, quotations for use in valuation may be obtained from the firm's regular suppliers. There are two principal ways of applying the rule of lower of cost or market. The first is to apply it item by item.

Lower of Cost or Market by Items

For each item in inventory, the cost is determined according to an acceptable method (average cost, FIFO, LIFO). Current market price is also determined for each item. Then the basis of valuation (the lower figure) is identified. Finally, the quantity on hand is multiplied by the valuation figure to obtain total value at lower of cost or market. The lower value figures for all items are added to determine the value of the inventory as a whole. The application of this rule is illustrated here, using two hypothetical stock items, A and B, and assumed figures.

| | | UNIT PRICE | | | LOWER OF COST OR |
DESCRIPTION	QUANTITY	COST	MARKET	VALUATION BASIS	MARKET
Item A	100	$1.00	$1.10	Cost	$100.00
Item B	200	1.50	1.20	Market	240.00
Inventory Valuation—Lower of Cost or Market by Items					$340.00

Lower of Total Cost or Total Market

Under another method of applying the rule of lower of cost or market, the total cost and the total market value of the entire inventory are determined and the lower of these total figures is used as the inventory valuation.

DESCRIPTION	QUANTITY	UNIT PRICE COST	UNIT PRICE MARKET	TOTAL COST	TOTAL MARKET
Item A	100	$1.00	$1.10	$100.00	$110.00
Item B	200	1.50	1.20	300.00	240.00
				$400.00	$350.00

Inventory Valuation—Lower of Total Cost or Total Market $350.00

This procedure gives a somewhat less conservative inventory valuation than the item by item method if the prices of some items have risen while others have declined. However, the method is justified by its advocates on the ground that it is the total inventory figure that should be presented conservatively. If the market value of the inventory as a whole has not declined below cost, then no adjustment is made and the cost valuation is presented in the statements.

A variation on this method involves classifying inventory items by groups or departments and determining the lower of total cost or total market according to these classifications. The lower figure (cost or market) for each group is added to the lower figure for each of the other groups to obtain the total inventory valuation. Assuming that items A and B in the preceding example constitute Group I and that items C and D constitute Group II, the basic computations required for the group total method are shown.

DESCRIPTION	QUANTITY	UNIT PRICE COST	UNIT PRICE MARKET	TOTAL COST	TOTAL MARKET
Group I					
Item A	100	$1.00	$1.10	$100.00	$110.00
Item B	200	1.50	1.20	300.00	240.00
Totals —Group I				$400.00	$350.00*
Group II					
Item C	30	$ .70	$ .60	$ 21.00	$ 18.00
Item D	150	.60	.80	90.00	120.00
Totals —Group II				$111.00*	$138.00

*Lower Figures

Obviously, market ($350) would be the lower basis for valuation of the items in Group I, and cost ($111) would be the lower basis for valuation of the items in Group II. The value of inventory groups I and II combined would be $461 ($350 + $111). Compare this valuation with the figures obtained from the two other methods as shown.

Lower of Cost or Market by Items				Lower of Total Cost or Total Market	
				VALUED AT	
ITEM	BASIS	VALUATION	ITEM	COST	MARKET
A	Cost	$100	A	$100	$110
B	Market	240	B	300	240
C	Market	18	C	21	18
D	Cost	90	D	90	120
		$448		$511	$488*

*Lower Figure

The method of valuation by lower of total cost or total market by groups is a procedure that produces middle-of-the-road figures. While it does not reflect individual fluctuations as the lower of cost or market by items method does, it does not lump together as many value variations as the grand total cost or total market figures do. The final choice by management of one of the three methods will depend upon a consideration of many factors, including size and variety of stock, the margin of profit on which the business operates, the practices in the industry, and future plans for business expansion. Usually, however, the lower of cost or market by items is used.

INVENTORY ESTIMATION PROCEDURES

Sometimes it is desirable to know the approximate cost of an inventory without taking a physical inventory and applying one of the costing procedures that you have learned. For example, in case of a fire it is necessary, for insurance and income tax purposes, to know the cost of goods destroyed. Similarly, a department manager in a retail store may be permitted to have only certain funds tied up in inventory; hence, he must be able at any time to estimate the cost of his inventory. Two common techniques for estimating inventory are (1) the gross profit method and (2) the retail method.

Gross Profit Method

This technique assumes that the rate of gross profit on sales is approximately the same from period to period and, therefore, that the ratio of cost of goods sold to net sales is relatively constant.

To illustrate the procedure, assume that a company's entire merchandise inventory is destroyed by fire on June 26, 19X1, but that its accounting records are preserved. An analysis of the company's income statements for the two preceding years shows that the gross profit rate has been 40% of net sales (or that the cost of goods sold has been 60% of net sales). The records for the current year show the following:

Inventory, at cost, January 1, 19X1	$ 40,000
Net Purchases (January 1 to June 26, 19X1)	120,000
Net Sales (January 1 to June 26, 19X1)	210,000

The first step is to estimate the cost of goods sold for the period January 1 to June 26. Since sales were $210,000 and it is assumed that the ratio of cost of goods sold to net sales is 60%, the estimated cost of goods sold is: 60% $\times$ $210,000 = $126,000.

Next, the cost of goods available for sale is determined.

Beginning Inventory	$ 40,000
Net Purchases	120,000
Cost of Goods Available for Sale	$160,000

Finally, the estimated ending inventory (destroyed) is computed by subtracting the estimated cost of goods sold ($126,000) from the cost of goods available for sale ($160,000).

Cost of Goods Available for Sale	$160,000
Estimated Cost of Goods Sold	126,000
Estimated Ending Inventory	$ 34,000

Retail Method of Inventory Pricing

A method of inventory pricing that is widely used by retailers is called the *retail method.* Under this method, inventory is classified into groups of items that have approximately the same rate of markon. (*Markon* is the difference between cost and the initially established retail price of merchandise.)

The beginning inventory is valued both at cost and at retail. Merchandise purchased is recorded at cost and its retail value is determined simultaneously. The retail value of the merchandise available for sale is obtained by adding the retail value of the beginning inventory and the retail value of the merchandise purchases. Sales are recorded at their retail price in the usual manner. When the total of sales at retail is subtracted from the total retail value of the merchandise available for sale, the difference is the retail value of the ending inventory. This amount is multiplied by the cost ratio (Total Available for Sale at Cost ÷ Total Available for Sale at Retail) to give the approximate cost of the ending inventory. Using assumed figures, the calculations involved in the application of the retail method of inventory pricing are shown on page 376.

In practice, the application of the retail method of inventory pricing is not quite so simple as this example may suggest. Records must be kept to show further price increases—*markups*—above the original markons, as well as markup cancellations. Records must also be kept of *markdowns* below the original markon and of markdown cancellations. When all this

	COST	RETAIL
Beginning Inventory	$ 5,000	$ 7,500
Merchandise Purchases	60,000	90,000
Total Available for Sale	$65,000	$97,500
Less Sales		79,200
Ending Inventory Priced at Retail		$18,300

Cost Ratio $= \dfrac{\$65,000}{\$97,500} = 66\ 2/3\%$

Conversion to Approximate Cost:

Ending Inventory at Retail x Cost Ratio	$18,300
	× .6667
Ending Inventory at Cost	$12,200
Cost of Goods Sold	$52,800

information is assembled, the resulting calculations can yield an inventory valuation that will approximate the lower of cost or market.

When there are many merchandise items of small unit value, as is often the case in retail stores, the retail method of inventory pricing permits the determination of the approximate cost of ending inventory from the book records without taking a physical inventory. In turn, the ease of determining the inventory value makes it possible to prepare financial statements more readily and frequently.

Many retail stores take the periodic physical inventory at retail values, using the sales prices marked on the merchandise. Then, the physical inventory at retail is converted to cost by applying the cost ratio, in the same way that the ending retail inventory computed in the previous example is reduced to cost.

Because of its simplicity and the need to have inventory values available frequently, this method of valuation is the one used by Ashton & Barker.

PRINCIPLES AND PROCEDURES

Several inventory costing methods may be used by businesses. Specific identification uses the actual purchase price of the specific items in inventory. The average cost method uses the average of the cost of all like items available for sale during the period for valuing ending inventory. In the first in, first out method, the cost of the ending inventory is developed from the cost of later purchases. The last in, first out method develops the cost of ending inventory from the cost of earlier purchases. In a period of rising prices, the LIFO method will result in a lower reported profit than the FIFO method. In a period of falling prices, the converse is true. The average cost method will always give a result between the two.

Not all inventory valuation is based on the purchase cost. The rule of cost or market, whichever is lower, is the most conservative method available. The rule can be applied to individual items in the inventory, to groups of items, or to total cost and market of the inventory as a whole.

The gross profit method of estimating inventory involves estimating the cost of goods sold by applying an historical cost ratio to the sales of the current period. This estimated cost of goods sold is then subtracted from the cost of goods available for sale to arrive at the estimated ending inventory.

The retail method of inventory pricing involves the use of the retail selling price of the items remaining. The retail value of the inventory is multiplied by the cost ratio of the current period to reach the approximate cost.

MANAGERIAL IMPLICATIONS

Inventory makes up a large part of the assets of the business and must be carefully controlled. The inventory costing method chosen by management must be one that is practical, reliable, and as simple to apply as possible. Inventory valuation is very important in computing the federal income tax because the value placed on the inventory determines the profit reported. For example, in times of rising prices, the LIFO method should be considered as a means of lowering the income tax by charging off a higher cost of goods sold figure.

The gross profit method of estimating inventory is an especially valuable tool for approximating the cost of an inventory when it is impossible to take a physical count, in preparing budgets, and in verifying the reasonableness of the inventory computed under an actual physical count.

Management should give consideration to the retail method of inventory pricing as a means of estimating the cost of goods on hand at any given time. This is especially important in retail businesses in which the department manager is allowed an inventory budget—the amount that he may have tied up in inventory—and it is necessary to know frequently, often weekly, the amount of inventory on hand.

APPLICATION OF PRINCIPLES

PROBLEM 23 · 1

♦ The following data are given for Superior Company:

Inventory, Jan. 1	800 units @ $2.00	
Purchases, Jan. 8	400 units @ $2.10	
Jan. 16	200 units @ $2.12	
Jan. 24	400 units @ $2.15	
Inventory, Jan. 31	820 units	

INSTRUCTIONS

Determine the cost to be shown for the ending inventory on Jan. 31 under each of the following methods: (1) average cost, (2) first in, first out, (3) last in, first out.

PROBLEM 23 · 2

◆ The following data relating to the inventory of Morris Store are given:

	QUANTITY	UNIT COST	MARKET
Boat Dept.			
Model T	8	$280	$300
Model U	7	420	400
Model W	10	180	190
Motor Dept.			
Model A	6	190	202
Model B	3	390	380
Model C	5	203	194

INSTRUCTIONS

Determine the amount to be reported as the inventory valuation at cost or market, whichever is lower, under each of these methods.

1. Lower of cost or market for each item separately
2. Lower of total cost or total market
3. Lower of total cost or total market by departments

PROBLEM 23 · 3

◆ In 19X1, the rate of gross profit on sales of Parker Company was 39.9%, and in 19X2 the rate was 40.1%. At the end of 19X3, the auditor found the following data in the records of Parker Company.

Sales		$1,000,000
Cost of Goods Sold:		
Inventory, Jan. 1, 19X3	$120,000	
Purchases	600,000	
Cost of Goods Available	$720,000	
Less Ending Inventory		
Dec. 31, 19X3 (est.)	190,000	
Cost of Goods Sold		530,000
Gross Profit		$ 470,000

Inquiry by the auditor revealed that employees of Parker Company had merely "estimated" the inventory on Dec. 31, 19X3 and had not taken a complete physical count.

INSTRUCTIONS

Using the gross profit method of inventory estimation, verify the reasonableness (or lack of reasonableness) of the "estimate" of inventory made by the company's employees.

PROBLEM 23 · 4

◆ The Knome Company uses the retail method of inventory pricing. At Dec. 31, 19X1, the records disclosed the following figures:

	ACTUAL COST	RETAIL SALES PRICE
Beginning Inventory, Jan. 1, 19X1	$ 8,000	$ 11,200
Merchandise Purchases during 19X1	72,640	100,800
Total Merchandise Available for Sale	$80,640	$112,000

Total Sales during 19X1 = $98,000

INSTRUCTIONS
1. Compute the retail value of the ending inventory at Dec. 31, 19X1.
2. Compute the approximate cost of the ending inventory at Dec. 31, 19X1.
3. Compute the cost of goods sold during 19X1.

MANAGERIAL CHECKUPS

◆ Why must management provide for strict control of the firm's inventory?

◆ Why do managers instruct their sales staffs to sell the oldest merchandise first?

◆ Under what special situation are inventory estimation procedures extremely useful?

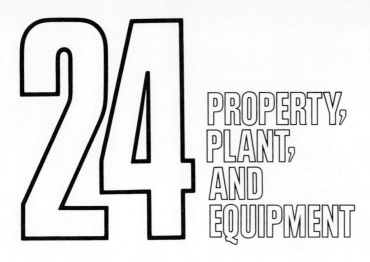

PROPERTY, PLANT, AND EQUIPMENT

Housing a modern business enterprise and equipping it for efficient operation often calls for a large investment in property. In accounting terminology, property that has a useful life of more than one year is known as a *fixed asset*. This unit explains the accounting procedures and records devised to keep track of the acquisition, use, and disposition of fixed assets, usually shown on the balance sheet as property, plant, and equipment. (Both terms are used in this unit.)

CLASSIFICATION OF PROPERTY, PLANT, AND EQUIPMENT

A firm's fixed assets include both tangible and intangible items. Its tangible property consists of real property and personal property. Among the *real property* holdings of a business are the value of land and buildings, and other structures attached to the land. *Tangible personal property* includes machinery, equipment, and furniture and fixtures. Among the *intangible personal properties* of a business are such assets as patents, copyrights, trademarks, and goodwill. A classification of typical property, plant, and equipment is illustrated here in outline form.

  I. Tangible Fixed Assets
      A. Real property
          1. Land
              a. Building sites
              b. Timberland
              c. Mineral land
          2. Buildings and other structures
              attached to the land

B. Personal property
    1. Machinery and equipment
    2. Furniture and fixtures
II. Intangible Fixed Assets
    A. Patents and copyrights
    B. Trademarks and goodwill

ACQUISITION OF PROPERTY, PLANT, AND EQUIPMENT

Items of property, plant, and equipment are usually acquired by purchase. Under the accounting system used by Ashton & Barker, a voucher is prepared to authorize payment for a fixed asset, resulting in a debit to the appropriate asset account and a credit to Accounts Payable. The voucher is paid in the usual manner, at which time Accounts Payable is debited and Cash is credited.

The total purchase cost of a fixed asset may actually be made up of several elements, each of which must be debited to the account covering that asset. For example, suppose that Ashton & Barker decides to purchase an office machine at a price of $367.50 f.o.b. the factory (free on board, the factory meaning that the buyer pays transportation from the factory). The freight bill is $6.25. When the machine arrives, the company decides to have extra features installed on the machine locally, at a net cost of $26.25. At what cost is the machine entered in the Office Equipment account?

The vendor's invoice is the first amount to be debited to the Office Equipment account. The transportation charge paid by Ashton & Barker is part of the cost of the machine and should also be debited to that account. The cost of the changes made in the machine before it is suitable for the intended use is a further charge to the asset. When all these charges have been posted to the Office Equipment account, the amount relating to this machine will be $400.

Net amount paid vendor	$367.50
Freight	6.25
Minor changes in operating features	26.25
Total acquisition cost of machine	$400.00

The general rule is that the acquisition cost of an asset includes the net price paid the vendor, all transportation and installation costs, and the cost of any adjustments or modifications. (A cash discount taken for prompt payment of an invoice for a fixed asset should be credited to the asset account rather than to Purchases Discount. The fixed asset credit can be recorded in the general journal with an offsetting debit to Accounts Payable if a voucher was previously recorded for the gross amount of the invoice.)

UNIT 24

In the case of land purchased for a building site, the acquisition cost of the land should include costs of removing unwanted buildings, grading and draining, the installation of permanent walks or roadways, and landscaping. If the land is bought in advance of the time it is to be used, taxes and other carrying charges should be added to the asset value on the books up to the time the property is utilized for business purposes.

CURRENT COSTS OF USING PROPERTY, PLANT, AND EQUIPMENT

Several obvious costs are incurred in using fixed assets, such as repairs, maintenance, insurance, and taxes. However, there are also hidden costs. Assets such as buildings and machines do not last forever. The inevitable wearing out of these assets through use in connection with the firm's operations must be taken into account as an additional expense of doing business. Other types of assets, such as natural resources and patents, also are consumed in the course of operations. Three technical terms are commonly used by accountants to distinguish the nature of the expense involved.

Depreciation

As explained in Unit 14, the term "depreciation" is used in accounting to describe the gradual or periodic transfer of acquisition cost to expense for assets such as buildings, machinery and equipment, and furniture and fixtures (but not land or goodwill). Four widely used methods of spreading depreciation expense over the useful life of an asset are described later in this unit.

Depletion

Natural resources, such as timber, oil, and minerals, are physically removed from the premises in the process of production. Their cost is part of the expense of carrying on such operations. *Depletion* is the term used to describe this expense. Two methods of determining depletion are discussed later in this unit.

Amortization

Most intangible assets, such as patents and copyrights, have a limited legal or useful life. Their acquisition cost must be spread over the legal life or useful life, whichever is shorter. *Amortization* is the term used in accounting to describe this expense. Methods of accounting for amortization are discussed later in this unit.

RECORDING DEPRECIATION, DEPLETION, AND AMORTIZATION

Assets subject to depreciation or depletion are recorded at acquisition cost and are generally carried at this figure as long as they remain in use. (Of course, subsequent additions or partial dispositions require appropriate adjustment of the acquisition cost figure.)

At the end of an accounting period, the current depreciation or depletion is debited to an appropriate expense account, with a credit to an account entitled Allowance for Depreciation or Allowance for Depletion, as the case may be. For example, suppose a business has plant buildings that cost $100,000 and have an annual depreciation charge of $5,000. It also owns timberlands that cost $200,000 and are depleted at the rate of $15,000 a year. These current-year expenses for depreciation and depletion appear on the worksheet as adjustments and are later recorded in the general journal as illustrated.

19 X1		12–17A			
Dec. 31		Depreciation–Plant Buildings	571	5,000 00	
		Allowance for Depreciation			
		–Plant Buildings	141A		5,000 00
		To record depreciation of plant buildings for the year.			
		12–18A			
	31	Depletion–Timberlands	584	15,000 00	
		Allowance for Depletion–			
		Timberlands	154A		15,000 00
		To record depletion of timberlands for the year.			

Assuming this to be the first year of use for both assets, the balance sheet presentation is as follows.

Plant Buildings	$100,000	
Less Allowance for Depreciation	5,000	$ 95,000
Timberlands	$200,000	
Less Allowance for Depletion	15,000	185,000

The allowance accounts are called *valuation accounts* because they are used to reflect the amount of acquisition cost that has been transferred to expense and thus permit more accurate representation of cost applicable to the remaining life of the asset involved. The difference between acquisition cost and the allowance account balance is called the *book value* or *net book value* of the asset. Thus, the plant buildings show a net book value of $95,000; the timberlands, $185,000.

Assets subject to amortization are also recorded at acquisition cost. However, the periodic amortization, which is debited to an expense account appearing on the income statement, is, by custom, credited directly to the asset account. The balance in the asset account is thus the net book value.

Assume that of an original cost of $34,000 for patents, $2,000 is amortized for the current year. Here is the adjusting entry to record the amortization.

19	X1	12–19A			
Dec.	31	Amortization of Patents	538	2,000 00	
		Patents	158		2,000 00
		To record amortization of patents for the year.			

The balance sheet shows Patents at $32,000 ($34,000 − $2,000). If the same amount of amortization is recorded during the second year, the Patents account appears at the end of that year at a net value of $30,000.

METHODS OF ACCOUNTING FOR DEPRECIATION

As previously explained, the cost of certain tangible fixed assets is spread over their useful life through periodic depreciation charges to an expense account and corresponding credits to a valuation account, commonly entitled Allowance for Depreciation. The total amount charged to expense may not exceed the total cost of the asset less any net salvage value that the asset is expected to have at the end of its useful life. In determining the net salvage value, estimated removal costs are deducted from expected sale proceeds.

Four widely used methods of depreciation are described here. Certain other methods are occasionally used in practice.

Straight-Line

The *straight-line method* (first presented in Unit 14) is perhaps the most widely used method of figuring depreciation. Under it, the same amount of depreciation is recorded for each year or other accounting period over the useful life of the asset. To obtain the annual depreciation, the acquisition cost less the expected net salvage value is divided by the expected life in years. This may be expressed by the following formula.

$$\frac{\text{Acquisition Cost} - \text{Net Salvage Value}}{\text{Useful Life in Years}} = \text{Annual Depreciation}$$

Suppose that the office machine acquired by Ashton & Barker at a total cost of $400 is expected to be used for five years and to have a trade-in or salvage value at the end of that time of $40. The result of substituting these figures in the equation is as follows.

$$\frac{\$400 - \$40}{5} = \frac{\$360}{5} = \$72 \text{ Annual Depreciation}$$

If depreciation were recorded at the end of each year, the $72 would be debited to Depreciation–Office Equipment and credited to Allowance for Depreciation–Office Equipment. (The monthly amount of the depreciation charge would be $\frac{1}{12}$ of $72, or $6.)

Declining-Balance

Under the *declining-balance method,* an appropriate percentage is applied to the net book value at the beginning of the year to obtain the depreciation charge for that year. The maximum percentage allowable for income tax purposes (and therefore widely used by business firms) is twice the rate that the straight-line method uses. When the straight-line method was applied to the Ashton & Barker machine (with an expected useful life of 5 years), the depreciation was $\frac{1}{5}$ or 20% of the cost (minus salvage value) each year. The declining-balance rate allowable on this same item is twice 20%, or 40%. (The tax regulations provide that salvage value is to be ignored.) In the first year, the acquisition cost of $400 would be multiplied by 40% to give $160 depreciation expense for that year. The book value at the beginning of the second year would be $240 ($400 − $160) and the depreciation for the second year $96 (40% of $240). In tabular form, the depreciation under the declining-balance method for the 5 years can be illustrated as follows.

YEAR	BEGINNING BOOK VALUE	RATE	DEPRECIA- TION FOR YEAR	DEPRECIA- TION TO DATE
1	$400.00	40%	$160.00	$160.00
2	240.00	40%	96.00	256.00
3	144.00	40%	57.60	313.60
4	86.40	40%	34.56	348.16
5	51.84	40%	20.74	368.90

Ending Book Value=$31.10

Although no salvage value was used in figuring the annual depreciation, there remains at the end of the 5 years a net book value of $31.10—only slightly less than the $40 estimated salvage value used under the straight-line method.

Sum of the Years-Digits

Under the *sum of the years-digits method,* a fractional part of the depreciable cost of the asset is charged to expense each year. The denominator of the fraction is always the "sum of the years-digits." The sum of the years-digits is found by simply adding the numbers representing the years of the asset's life. For example, the digits of the years of life of a machine expected to last 5 years are: 1, 2, 3, 4, and 5. Thus, the sum of the years-digits is $1 + 2 + 3 + 4 + 5$, or 15. The numerator for any year is the number of years of remaining life of the asset. Thus, for the first year the fraction is $5/15$; the second year it is $4/15$; and so on. The fraction is applied to the acquisition cost minus the salvage value, in this case $400 - 40$, or $360.

In the following table, the results of applying this method are listed and compared with the two methods previously illustrated.

	Sum of the Years-Digits Method			Depreciation by Other Methods	
YEAR	FRACTION	COST MINUS SALVAGE	DEPRECIATION FOR YEAR	DECLINING-BALANCE	STRAIGHT-LINE
1	5/15	$360.00	$120.00	$160.00	$ 72.00
2	4/15	360.00	96.00	96.00	72.00
3	3/15	360.00	72.00	57.60	72.00
4	2/15	360.00	48.00	34.56	72.00
5	1/15	360.00	24.00	20.74	72.00
Total Depreciation —5 years			$360.00	$368.90	$360.00
Net Book Value — End of 5 Years			$ 40.00	$ 31.10	$ 40.00

Note that the declining-balance and sum of the years-digits methods both give higher depreciation charges in the earlier years of the asset life and lower charges in the later years. These two methods are sometimes called accelerated methods. For income tax reporting purposes, a change may be made from the declining-balance method to the straight-line method (for the remaining balance) at any time; but any other change in depreciation method may not be made without the express permission of the tax authorities. A business may use several different depreciation methods simultaneously for different assets or groups of assets.

Units-of-Output

In some situations, asset life may be related more directly to units of work performed by the asset than to the passage of time. In such cases, depreciation may be calculated at so much per unit of output and the expense for any time period may be determined by multiplying the rate per unit by the number of units produced.

For example, suppose that a press is purchased for $10,000 and is expected to have a useful life of 1,000,000 stamping impressions. The rate per stamping is $10,000 divided by 1,000,000, or 1 cent each. If 50,000 stampings are produced during a period, the depreciation charge is 50,000 × $.01, or $500.

DEPLETION METHODS

For accounting purposes, the amount to be charged for depletion of property is based on cost. However, for income tax purposes, the depletion may also be computed as a percentage of gross income (the sale price) of the asset such as oil, a mineral, or metal. These two methods are discussed here.

Cost

Depletion based on cost is determined in a manner very similar to the units-of-output method of determining depreciation. Total cost of the mineral deposit is divided by the estimated number of units of the mineral in the deposit to give the depletion cost per unit of product extracted. For example, suppose a clay pit, which is estimated to contain 500,000 tons of extractable clay suitable for making brick, is purchased for $25,000. The depletion cost per ton of clay is $.05 ($25,000 divided by 500,000 tons). If 60,000 tons of this clay were used in a particular year, the depletion cost would be $3,000 (60,000 × $.05).

Percentage Depletion

For income tax purposes, depletion may be calculated as a percentage of the revenue obtained from the sale of the mineral. The amount of depletion calculated in this manner must not be less than cost depletion would be and not more than 50% of the net income from the property before the deduction of depletion.

Assume that the 60,000 tons of clay sold brought an average price of $2.50 per ton and that *net income* from the operation before the depletion deduction was $40,000. Applying the allowable percentage depletion rate of $7\frac{1}{2}$% (specified by the tax law) to the total sales of $150,000 yields the allowable depletion of $7,500. Since this is well below the 50% limitation on net income before depletion (which is $40,000 × .50, or $20,000), the entire $7,500 could be assigned as the depletion expense for the year.

Over a number of years, total percentage depletion well above the total cost of the property might be taken, and thus the percentage depletion method can provide a considerable tax advantage. The percentage method would be used for income tax purposes, but the cost method would still be used in making entries in the books for financial accounting purposes.

UNIT 24

The choice of methods for calculating the amount of amortization of intangibles is more limited than for calculating depreciation. The straight-line method is most commonly used, although there are situations in which the units-of-output method might be appropriate. The declining-balance or sum of the years-digits methods may not be used.

The *legal life* of a patent is 17 years, that of a copyright is 28 years, with the possibility of renewing the copyright for another 28 years. The *useful* life is usually much shorter. In computing amortization, the shorter life—legal or expected useful—should be used.

Suppose a company paid $6,000 for a patent that it estimates will have a useful life of only 12 years. Annual amortization on the straight-line basis is $500 ($6,000 divided by 12 years). Remember that the entry to record amortization requires a debit to the amortization expense account and a credit to the asset account being amortized.

Other types of intangibles such as the organization costs incurred in forming a corporation will be examined in later units.

DISPOSITION
OF AN ASSET

Assets that are no longer useful to a business are usually retired from use and sold. In other cases, useful assets may be sold to acquire better assets. When an asset is retired or sold, the following steps should be taken to record the facts:

1. Depreciation should be recorded to the date of disposition.
2. The asset account and the related allowance for depreciation account are closed, the proceeds realized are recorded, and the gain or loss, if any, is determined and recorded.

To illustrate the accounting entries necessary to record the sale of an asset under various conditions, suppose that a firm has a $400 office machine like the one owned by Ashton & Barker. Depreciation has been recorded on the straight-line basis for three years at $72 a year, for a total of $216. Six months later ($3\frac{1}{2}$ years after the purchase) the owners decide to sell the machine. The first thing that must be done is to record depreciation to the date of sale. This amounts to $36 for the 6 months following the last year for which depreciation was recorded. This amount is debited to Depreciation—Office Equipment and credited to Allowance for Depreciation—Office Equipment.

The Office Equipment account has a debit balance of $400 representing the acquisition cost; the allowance account now has a credit balance of $252 ($216 + $36). The net book value is $148 ($400 − $252).

Sale at Net Book Value

Suppose first that the sale is made on account for the net book value, $148. The following recording elements are involved:

1. The new account receivable of $148 must be recorded on the books.
2. The allowance account balance of $252 must be closed out.
3. The cost of $400 in the asset account must be closed out.

In the general journal, all these details could be handled in one compound entry, as follows.

19 X1	7–12			
July 31	Accounts Receivable 111		148 00	
	Allowance for Depr.–Off. Equip. 132A		252 00	
	Office Equipment 132			400 00
	To record sale of machine at net book value.			

Since the sale was for the net book value, there is no gain or loss to be recorded.

Sale above Book Value

Suppose that the agreed sales price was $175, or $27 above net book value. Accounts Receivable is debited for $175; the allowance account is debited $252 and the asset account is credited $400, as before. Then a new account called Gain on Sale of Equipment is credited for $27 to complete the entry, as shown.

19 X1	7–12			
July 31	Accounts Receivable 111		175 00	
	Allowance for Depr.–Off. Equip. 132A		252 00	
	Office Equipment 132			400 00
	Gain on Sale of Equipment 495			27 00
	To record sale of machine above book value.			

The gain of $27 represents, of course, the excess of the sales price of $175 over the net book value of the asset, $148.

Sale below Book Value

Suppose this time that the sales price is $125. Compared with the book value of $148, this price represents a loss of $23. Accounts Receivable is debited for the agreed price of $125 and the allowance account is debited for its balance of $252, as previously explained. Then a new account called Loss on Sale of Equipment is debited for $23 and the asset credited for $400. This general journal entry appears as shown here.

19 X1		7–12			
July	31	Accounts Receivable	111	125 00	
		Allowance for Depr.–Off. Equip.	132A	252 00	
		Loss on Sale of Equipment	595	23 00	
		Office Equipment.	132		400 00
		To record sale of machine below book value.			

TRADE-IN OF AN ASSET

Businesses often trade in existing equipment on the purchase of new equipment. There are two widely used methods for recording the trade-in and acquisition of the new item: the *income tax method,* and the *fair market value method.* In either method, the *first step* is to record the depreciation on the old asset up to the date of the trade. Then the proper entries to record the transaction may be made.

The Income Tax Method

Under federal tax laws, when an asset used in trade or business is traded in on a similar asset, no gain or loss is recognized on the transaction. The cost of the new asset acquired is assumed to be the book value (cost minus accumulated depreciation) of the old asset, plus the cash amount paid. The following elements must be recorded under this procedure after depreciation has been brought up to date.

1. The asset account must be credited for the cost of the old asset traded.
2. The allowance account balance covering the old asset must be closed.
3. The cash payment to be made must be recorded (as a credit to accounts payable if the voucher system is used).
4. The new asset is recorded at the sum of the cash to be paid plus the book value of the old asset.

To illustrate this procedure, assume that a desk calculator that cost $750 has had depreciation of $500 recorded to the date of trade-in, leaving a net book value of $250. The calculator is traded in for a new model having a list price of $900. The vendor offers an allowance of $300 on the old calculator in trade against the purchase of the new $900 model. In accordance with the procedure outlined above, the following facts are recorded:

1. The cost of the old asset, $750, is removed from the asset account.
2. The allowance account balance of $500 is removed.
3. The amount of cash to be paid, $600 ($900 cost minus $300 allowance on new model) is credited to Accounts Payable.
4. The new calculator is recorded in the books at $850, the sum of the $600 cash to be paid and the $250 book value of the old calculator traded in ($750 cost minus $500 depreciation to date). The entry, in general journal form, would be as shown.

19 X1					
Oct. 31	Office Equipment	132	850 00		
	Allowance for Depr.–Off. Equip. . . .	132A	500 00		
	Office Equipment	132		750 00	
	Accounts Payable	201		600 00	
	To record trade-in of old calculator on new model (tax method used showing no gain or loss on the exchange).				

If the vendor of the new equipment had made an allowance of only $150 on the trade, the difference to be paid in cash would be $750, and the trade would have been recorded as follows.

19 X1					
Oct. 31	Office Equipment	132	1,000 00		
	Allowance for Depr.–Off. Equip. . . .	132A	500 00		
	Office Equipment	132		750 00	
	Accounts Payable	201		750 00	
	To record trade-in of old calculator on new model (tax method used, showing no gain or loss on the exchange).				

The Fair Market Value Method

Although the income tax method is used by most businesses to record trade-ins because it is required for income tax purposes, many accountants argue that the new asset should be recorded at its fair market value and that a gain or loss should be recorded on the trade-in allowance received for the old asset. If this procedure is followed, the following steps are necessary:

1. The asset account is credited for the cost of the old asset traded in.
2. The allowance account balance covering the old asset must be closed.
3. The cash payment to be made is recorded.
4. The new asset is recorded at its fair market value (its cash purchase price).

5. Gain or loss, equal to the difference between the trade-in allowance received and the book value of the old asset, is recorded. If this procedure were followed in the first example given under the income-tax method and a trade-in allowance of $300 is offered for the old asset with a book value of $250, a gain of $50 is indicated. The facts are recorded as follows.

19	X1							
Oct.	31	Office Equipment	132	900	00			
		Allowance for Depr.—Office Equip. . .	132A	500	00			
		Office Equipment	132			750	00	
		Accounts Payable	201			600	00	
		Gain on Sale of Equipment . .	495			50	00	
		To record trade-in of old calculator on a new model —allowance greater than book value of old machine.						

In the second illustration, in which only a $150 trade-in allowance was received on the old asset, a loss of $100 would be involved ($250 book value minus the trade-in allowance of $150). The trade-in would be recorded as follows.

19	X1							
Oct.	31	Office Equipment	132	900	00			
		Allowance for Depr. —Office Equip. . .	132A	500	00			
		Loss on Sale of Equipment	595	100	00			
		Office Equipment	132			750	00	
		Accounts Payable	201			750	00	
		To record trade-in of old calculator on a new model —allowance below book value of old machine.						

◆ ◆ ◆

PRINCIPLES AND PROCEDURES

Fixed assets, usually referred to as *property, plant, and equipment,* may be classified as tangible, including real and personal property, or as intangible, including patents, copyrights, trademarks, and goodwill. Depending on the nature of the asset, depreciation, depletion, or amortization must be included as a current cost. Through these charges, the cost of the asset is spread over its useful (or legal) life. Four widely used methods of accounting for depreciation are the straight-line method, declining-balance method, sum of the years-digits method, and units-of-output method. Depletion may be based on cost or, for tax purposes, on a percentage of revenue obtained. Amortization may be calculated by the straight-line method, or in some cases, by the units-of-output method.

Fixed assets may be disposed of by sale or they may be traded in for other assets. At the time of sale or trade-in, the depreciation to date and the actual proceeds must be recorded and the asset and allowance accounts must be closed or adjusted. The gain or loss must also be determined and recorded.

MANAGERIAL IMPLICATIONS

Fixed assets involve large sums of money, thus management must keep close watch over them and the records used in accounting for them.

Management must also understand the wide variety of methods of depreciation used and those methods that are permissible for income tax purposes. Knowing how the methods work will help to evaluate possible effects and aid in selection of the one that is most advantageous to the firm. Methods to be used for recording sales or trade-ins of assets must also be studied, because the results affect reported profits and taxes.

APPLICATION OF PRINCIPLES

PROBLEM 24 · 1

Macomb Company has purchased an automobile at a cost of $4,400. Its estimated life is 5 years and the estimated salvage value is $600.

INSTRUCTIONS
1. Compute the annual depreciation charge under the straight-line method.
2. Using the declining-balance method, compute the depreciation charge for each year and determine both the depreciation to date (the balance in the allowance account at the end of each year) and the ending book value.
3. Using the sum of the years-digits method, compute the depreciation charge for each year and determine both the depreciation to date (the balance in the allowance account at the end of each year) and the ending book value.
4. Compare the results obtained under the three methods in a table providing columns for Year, Depreciation for Year (one column for each: Straight-Line, Declining-Balance, Sum of the Years-Digits), and Depreciation to Date (one column for each: Straight-line, Declining-Balance, Sum of the Years-Digits). Also compute book value at the end of 5 years.

PROBLEM 24 · 2

Klennor Company purchased four identical machines on Jan. 2, 19X1 for $600 each, paying cash. The useful life of each machine is expected to be 5 years and salvage value at the end of that time is estimated to be $100 each. The Company uses the straight-line method of depreciation and has the following accounts on its books:

UNIT 24

101	Cash in Bank	495	Gain on Sale of Machinery
141	Machinery	541	Depreciation of Machinery
141A	Allowance for Depreciation —Machinery	595	Loss on Sale of Machinery
		597	Fire Loss on Machinery

The following selected transactions took place from 19X1 through 19X4.

19X1

Jan. 2   Purchased four machines for cash, $600 each. (Entry 1-1.)

Dec. 31   Recorded depreciation for the year on the four machines. (Entry 12-1A.)

19X2

Apr. 1   Machine 1 was destroyed by fire. No insurance was carried. (Entries 4-1 and 4-2.)

Dec. 31   Recorded depreciation for the year on the three remaining machines. (Entry 12-1A.)

19X3

Aug. 31   Machine 2 was sold for $400. (Entries 8-1 and 8-2.)

Dec. 31   Recorded depreciation for the year on two remaining machines. (Entry 12-1A.)

19X4

June 4   Machine 3 was traded in on a similar machine with a list price of $700. A trade-in of $300 was received. The balance was paid in cash. (Use the income tax method to record the trade-in.) (Entries 6-1 and 6-2.)

Aug. 29   Machine 4 was traded in on a similar machine with a list price of $720. A trade-in of $250 was received. The balance was paid in cash. (Use the income tax method.) (Entries 8-1 and 8-2.)

INSTRUCTIONS

1. Record the transactions in general journal form.
2. Assuming that the trade-ins of machines 3 and 4 had been recorded under the fair market value method, give the journal entries to record the trade-ins on June 4 and Aug. 29.

PROBLEM 24 · 3

♦ The accounts of Caruth Development Company on Jan. 1, 19X1 included the following:

153	Patents	536	Amortization of Patents
155	Oil Deposits	584	Depletion—Oil Deposits
155A	Allowance for Depletion —Oil Deposits		

An analysis of account balances revealed:

1. The Patents account contained a debit balance of $13,600. This represents the unamortized cost of a patent purchased on Jan. 2, 19X0 for $17,000. Because of rapid technological changes, management had decided to amortize the cost over a period of 5 years. Consequently, $3,400 was charged to expense in 19X0 and was credited to Patents.
2. Oil Deposits contained a balance of $600,000 and the Allowance for Depletion—Oil Deposits account contained a credit balance of $200,000. It was estimated that on Jan. 1, 19X1 the remaining mineral content of the deposit was 2,000,000 barrels. In 19X1, 200,000 barrels were produced and sold for $3.50 per barrel.

INSTRUCTIONS

1. Give general journal entries to record the patent amortization and the depletion expense for 19X1. (Entries 12-1A and 12-2A.)
2. Assuming that expenses (other than depletion) related to the oil production totaled $150,000 during the year, what amount of depletion could the company claim on its federal income tax return during 19X1? (Statutory depletion for oil production is at a rate of 22%.)

MANAGERIAL CHECKUPS

♦ Explain how management's choice of one method of depreciation might be more advantageous to a firm than another.

♦ Why would a firm use percentage depletion for tax purposes while using cost depletion methods for its financial records? Why not use percentage depletion for both purposes?

♦ Why should management insist that a firm's intangible assets, such as patents, be amortized over their useful lives rather than over their legal lives?

25

BUSINESS TAXES

Previous units have explained how a business deducts social security and income taxes from salaries of employees and accounts for the payroll taxes that it must pay. You have also learned how a business adapts its accounting records to keep track of retail sales taxes collected from customers. There are many other accounting problems arising from taxes on business operations, profits, and property. For example, there are taxes on real and personal property, excise taxes, retail licenses, use taxes, and income taxes. Even in the case of retail sales tax, the accounting work does not end with the mere collection of the tax—proper information must be accumulated and tax returns completed and submitted, accompanied by the proper amount of money.

This unit discusses some of these additional problems in complying with tax requirements, with special emphasis on retail licenses, property taxes, and procedures for completing and submitting sales tax returns to a state or local governmental unit.

RETAIL LICENSE

The typical state law requires every person or firm doing business as a retailer to obtain a retail license from the state tax commission. In Ashton & Barker's state, the license must be obtained prior to June 30 for the following fiscal year starting July 1 (or before the opening of any new business). The license fee is $5 for the first retail store, with higher fees for second and additional outlets, rising to a maximum of $150 for each outlet over 30.

Property taxes are often called *ad valorem* taxes because they are levied on the value of the property taxed. The actual amount of tax to be paid under this type of levy depends upon two basic factors: the *value* of the property for tax purposes and the *rate* of tax applied to this value.

Taxable Property

Some jurisdictions may tax only real property, others may tax both real and personal property. Real property includes land and buildings or other structures attached to the land. All other property is personal property, including such items as machinery and equipment, furniture and fixtures, and intangible assets.

The valuation of property for tax purposes is rarely the amount recorded in the accounting records (which is typically cost or cost less depreciation or amortization). Rather, the assessed value of property for tax purposes is usually supposed to bear some relation to current market value on the assessment date. Total market value (or 100%) might be the basis, but more often some percentage of market value (for example, 40%) is established as the basis for assessed value of the property for tax purposes.

Assessment and Collection of Property Taxes

In some jurisdictions, real property is appraised by public officials to determine the assessed value for tax purposes. In other cases, the property owner places a value on his own property, subject to review and change by a public official or board before the tax rate is applied. Personal property values are frequently assessed by the owner himself. (The property owner who is required to set the value of his own property should investigate local customs in establishing the final figures. It is possible for substantial inequities to occur in the assessment of property value for tax purposes.)

Tax Rate

The tax rate is often established by the taxing body after the total assessed value of the property subject to tax has been determined. The amount of revenue needed from property taxes is estimated and a tax rate is then set which, when applied to the total assessed valuation, will yield the desired amount of tax revenue.

The same property may be subject to tax by a number of governmental units (for example, a city, a county, a school district, and a lighting district)

UNIT 25

simultaneously. Each taxing authority may determine the rate of tax required to raise the revenue it needs. The sum of these rates is the total rate of tax for the property. A tax notice or bill is illustrated for a situation in which real property is taxed by several taxing authorities. (A mill is one thousandth part of a dollar or $.001.)

TAX NOTICE 19xx — N⁰ 7940

COUNTY OF BEAUREGARD
CITY OF GREENVILLE

RECEIPT for your taxes for **19XX**, as itemized below. In accordance with law.

BRYAN CLEMMONS, Sheriff and Ex-Officio Tax Collector.

Per_____Deputy.

	Ward THREE	ITEMIZED TAXES	
	Page No. 742	TAXPAYERS COLUMN TAXES PAYABLE	HOMESTEAD EXEMPTION COLUMN
	ASSESSED VALUATION	$5,250.00	
	State Tax 5.75 Mills	$ 30.19	
	*County Tax 28.50 Mills	149.63	
	Sewer CS1 1.70 Mills	8.93	
	Rural Lighting 3.00 Mills	15.75	
	Garbage		
	Acreage 2¢ per Acre		
	PAY LAST AMOUNT IN	THIS COLUMN	
	TOTAL	$204.50	
	INTEREST		
	PENALTY		
	TOTAL		

NAME AND ADDRESS OF TAXPAYER

Vanderbilt Garage Company
620 Magnolia Avenue
Greenville, State 53970

DESCRIPTION OF PROPERTY

Lot 94
Magnolia Subdivision

Collection is sometimes made by one governmental unit, often the county. The collecting agency then divides and distributes the revenue among the taxing authorities that are entitled to it.

Assessment and Payment Dates

The assessed value of property is established at a certain date for each tax jurisdiction. As noted previously, this is often done before the rate of tax can be established. Thus, some time must ordinarily elapse between the assessment date and the date on which tax bills are sent out or made available to the taxpayer. Taxes due must then be paid by some specified date; late payments involve penalties and interest, in addition to the assessed tax. (In a few cases, a discount may be allowed for early payment of tax.)

Accounting for Property Taxes

The accountant in charge of records and procedures for property tax (or any other tax) must know how to:

1. Determine the correct amount of tax due and pay it in time to avoid penalties and interest charges.
2. Charge the tax in the appropriate accounting period or periods as an

expense on the income statement and show the correct amount of tax payable or of prepaid tax expense on the balance sheet.

Computing the tax liability and completing the appropriate tax returns requires a thorough knowledge of the various tax laws and regulations to which the business is subject. Payment of taxes due is handled within the usual disbursement routines used by the business.

As might be supposed, there is a variety of procedures for accounting for taxes, for assigning them as expenses in different accounting periods, and for presenting them on the firm's balance sheet. However, the American Institute of Certified Public Accountants makes the following recommendation in its 1953 *Restatement and Revision of Accounting Research Bulletins,* which is generally followed today:

> Generally, the most acceptable basis of providing for property taxes is monthly accrual on the taxpayer's books during the fiscal period of the taxing authority for which the taxes are levied. The books will then show, at any closing date, the appropriate accrual or prepayment.

The discussion of property tax accounting in the remainder of this unit follows the treatment preferred by the Institute.

ASHTON & BARKER TAX SITUATION

The Ashton & Barker Clothing Store is subject to three taxes, which are accounted for in the Taxes and Licenses 555 account. The first of these is the retail license previously described. The second is the merchant's stock tax, a form of property tax levied on the value of the merchandise inventory. The third is the property tax levied on items not covered by the stock tax.

So that complete information about each of these taxes can be provided without having a different ledger account for each tax, an *analysis ledger sheet* is used. Under this system, one Taxes and Licenses account is carried in the ledger with separate *analysis columns* used in the account to record the details of each type of tax. Note in the illustration on the following page that the three columns on the right (Debit, Credit, and Balance) provide space for the regular postings and the resulting total balance. The columns on the left provide for the recording of each of the individual taxes. Subcode numbers are provided for each type of tax to be recorded in the separate analysis columns, as follows:

555.6   Retail License
555.7   Stock Tax
555.8   Property Taxes

The entry for payment of the retail store license has already been recorded to illustrate how the columns are used.

RETAIL LIC. DR. 555.6	STOCK TAX DR. 555.7	PROP. TAX DR. 555.8	DATE	EXPLANATION	POST. REF.	DEBIT	CREDIT	BALANCE	DR. CR.
5 00			19 X1 June 30		VR-1	5 00		5 00	Dr.

Stock Tax on Merchandise Inventory

Assume that the tax year for the stock tax is July 1 to the following June 30 and that the tax is levied on the assessed value of merchandise inventory on hand on June 30, the last day of the tax year. In the discussion that follows, many technical tax provisions have been omitted to make it easier to understand the basic procedural steps involved. (Procedures vary widely from state to state; those described below for Ashton & Barker are merely illustrative of one situation.)

An information return reporting the value of the inventory on June 30 must be filed by each merchant on or before August 31. Then the state tax commission, which administers this tax, makes whatever adjustment in assessed valuation it deems necessary, applies the tax rate, and renders a tax bill in December, which is payable without penalty on or before December 31.

In the first year of partnership operations, Ashton & Barker will submit the required information for the stock tax as of June 30. The store should start recording the proportionate amount of this tax each month beginning July 1 (the start of the state's fiscal year for this tax). However, it will not know the exact amount of the tax due until its bill is received in December. To make the monthly accruals prior to the receipt of the actual tax bill, Ashton & Barker must estimate the amount of tax due for the year and convert this to a monthly provision.

Assume that Ashton & Barker estimates that its stock tax for the year will amount to $960, or $80 per month. The latter amount is recorded each month (beginning with July) in a journal entry debiting Taxes and Licenses 555.7 and crediting Property Taxes Payable 235.7, as follows.

19 X1	7–16A			
July 31	Taxes and Licenses	555.7	80 00	
	Property Taxes Payable . . .	235.7		80 00
	To record estimated stock tax for month of July.			

Note that the tax payable credit entry also bears the subcode .7, identifying the stock tax. This will make it possible to use an analysis ledger sheet for the liability account also, and to keep the amount of stock tax payable separate from the other property taxes payable that may be credited to this same account later.

A similar entry for the estimated stock tax payable is made each month from July through November, by which time the total amount in the Property Taxes Payable account will have increased to $400 (5 months at $80). In December, suppose that the actual tax bill shows a total tax due of $995 ($35 more than the estimate of $960). At this point, the actual tax liability is known and may be recorded. The Property Taxes Payable account will be credited for $595 to increase it from its present balance of $400 to the actual liability of $995. Since this $595 applies to December and future months, it is debited to a new account, Prepaid Taxes, by the following entry. (Note that the term *prepaid* does not, in this case, mean literally "paid in advance." It means that the recorded cost applies to future months. Some accountants prefer to use the title *Deferred Property Tax Expense*, rather than Prepaid Taxes.)

19 X1		12–7				
Dec. 10	Prepaid Taxes	128	595 00		
	Property Taxes Payable . . .	235.7		595 00
	To record balance of Stock Tax Payable			
	as determined on receipt of tax bill.			

At the end of each month, beginning in December and continuing through June, $85 ($595 ÷ 7) is transferred to the expense account Taxes and Licenses, so that by June 30 all the prepaid property tax cost will have been charged to expense. The journal entry to be made each month is shown:

19 X1		12–19A				
Dec. 31	Taxes and Licenses	555.7	85 00		
	Prepaid Taxes	128		85 00
	To transfer to expense the December			
	portion of the prepaid stock tax.			

The new asset will, of course, be shown on the balance sheet on December 31 as $510, representing the costs applicable to the future months of January through June (6 months × $85 = $510). When the tax bill is actually paid in January, the payment is debited to Property Taxes Payable.

In July the same cycle of entries starts over again—monthly estimates through November, then actual figures for December through June.

Property Tax on Other Property

Suppose that the real and personal properties are appraised at December 31 for the following year in the state in which the Ashton & Barker Clothing Store is situated. Tax returns used as the basis for assessments must be filed by property owners before the end of February. Tax bills are sent out toward the end of the year, payable without penalty on or before December 31.

Since it was not in business and therefore owned no property on December 31 of the year preceding the beginning of its operations on February 1, 19X1, the Ashton & Barker Clothing Store pays no property tax for the first eleven months of its business life, February 1 to December 31, 19X1. However, the store must file its first tax return before February 28 of its second year of operation and is subject to tax for that and each succeeding year.

The yearly procedure for the Ashton & Barker Clothing Store requires making a monthly record of the estimated tax starting in January and continuing the monthly entries at the estimated amount until the tax bill is received, usually in December. At that time, since this is the last month of the tax year, a general journal entry can be made correcting both the tax expense and tax liability accounts.

Assume that in January the property tax for the year is estimated to be $240, or $20 a month. This amount is recorded each month by an entry as follows.

19	X2	1–18A			
Jan.	31	Taxes and Licenses	555.8	20 00	
		Property Taxes Payable	235.8		20 00
		To record estimated property taxes for month of January.			

If the tax bill received the following December shows only $210 due, it is necessary to reduce both the tax expense and the tax payable balances by $10, since in 11 months a total of $220 estimated tax has been recorded ($20 × 11). The general journal entry to make this adjustment debits Property Taxes Payable 235.8 and credits Taxes and Licenses 555.8, both for $10, as illustrated.

19	X2	12–21A			
Dec.	31	Property Taxes Payable	235.8	10 00	
		Taxes and Licenses	555.8		10 00
		To correct estimate for prior eleven months for property tax, in order to show actual amount for year per tax bill received.			

Payment of the tax bill in December results in a debit of $210 to Property Taxes Payable and a credit to Cash in Bank. The following January, the cycle of entries for this tax begins again with the recording of the estimated amount of tax for that month.

Let us see how the various tax items that have been discussed appear on the books of the Ashton & Barker Clothing Store at the end of the first year of operations, January 31, 19X2. The three ledger accounts involved are Prepaid Taxes, Property Taxes Payable, and Taxes and Licenses. These are shown here with all entries posted and balances determined at January 31.

Prepaid Taxes   No. 128

DATE	EXPLANATION	POST. REF.	DEBIT	CREDIT	BALANCE	DR. CR.
19 X1 Dec. 10		12-7	595 00		595 00	Dr.
31		12-19A		85 00	510 00	Dr.
19 X2 Jan. 31		1-17A		85 00	425 00	Dr.

Property Taxes Payable   No. 235

STOCK TAX CR. 235.7	PROP. TAX CR. 235.8	DATE	EXPLANATION	POST. REF.	DEBIT	CREDIT	BALANCE	DR. CR.
		19 X1						
80 00		July 31		7-16A		80 00	80 00	Cr.
80 00		Aug. 31		8-15A		80 00	160 00	Cr.
80 00		Sept. 30		9-17A		80 00	240 00	Cr.
80 00		Oct. 31		10-14A		80 00	320 00	Cr.
80 00		Nov. 30		11-16A		80 00	400 00	Cr.
595 00		Dec. 10		12-7		595 00	995 00	Cr.
(995 00)		31		VR-1	995 00		–0–	
		19 X2						
	20 00	Jan. 31		1-18A		20 00	20 00	Cr.

Taxes and Licenses   No. 555

RETAIL LIC. DR. 555.6	STOCK TAX DR. 555.7	PROP. TAX DR. 555.8	DATE	EXPLANATION	POST. REF.	DEBIT	CREDIT	BALANCE	DR. CR.
			19 X1						
5 00			June 30		VR-1	5 00		5 00	Dr.
	80 00		July 31		7-16A	80 00		85 00	Dr.
	80 00		Aug. 31		8-15A	80 00		165 00	Dr.
	80 00		Sept. 30		9-17A	80 00		245 00	Dr.
	80 00		Oct. 31		10-14A	80 00		325 00	Dr.
	80 00		Nov. 30		11-16A	80 00		405 00	Dr.
	85 00		Dec. 31		12-19A	85 00		490 00	Dr.
			19 X2						
	85 00		Jan. 31		1-17A	85 00		575 00	Dr.
		20 00	31		1-18A	20 00		595 00	Dr.
5 00	570 00	20 00							

Balance Sheet

The two tax accounts that appear on the balance sheet at January 31, 19X2 are Prepaid Taxes (stock tax), $425 (5 months × $85 = $425), which is classified as a current asset, and Property Taxes Payable, $20, which is classified as a current liability.

Income Statement

The tax account that appears on the income statement is Taxes and Licenses, an operating expense of $595 consisting of:

Retail Licenses	$ 5
Stock Tax Estimated, 5 months × $80	400
Stock Tax Adjusted, 2 months × $85	170
Property Tax Estimated, 1 month × $20	20
	$595

Since this is the first year of operations for Ashton & Barker, taxes shown are for only a part of the year. In subsequent years, the income statement will contain tax amounts for a full 12 months.

SALES AND EXCISE TAXES

Although sales and excise taxes imposed by city and state governments vary, there is sufficient similarity in accounting for them that a study of the most typical provisions will be a very informative point of departure.

State and City

Many states and cities impose a tax on sales at the retail price, specifying that the tax is to be collected by the merchant making the sale. The tax may be levied on all retail sales, but frequently certain items are exempt. In most cases, the amount of the sales tax is stated separately and then added to the sales price of the merchandise. In previous units you have learned how to record routine sales and sales returns and allowances subject to a sales tax. The merchant is required to make periodic reports (usually monthly) to the taxing authority and to remit the tax due at the same time. In some cases, the government allows the merchant to retain part of the tax as compensation for his services in collecting it.

Federal

The federal government levies an excise tax (which is simply another sales tax) on certain kinds of merchandise, such as automobile tires and petroleum products. These taxes are passed on to the consumer by the retailer. Normally, the retailer pays the tax to the manufacturer, who assumes responsibility for preparing quarterly tax returns and remitting the taxes to the federal government.

The procedures to be followed at the time a typical sales tax return must be filed are similar to those used in Ashton & Barker at the end of July 19X1, when the monthly sales tax return is filed with the tax commissioner of the state. Ashton & Barker's sales are subject to a 3% state sales tax.

PREPARING THE STATE SALES TAX RETURN

At the end of each month, after the accounts have all been posted, the state sales tax return form is usually prepared. The information required for this return comes from the accounting data of the current month. Three accounts are involved: Sales Tax Payable, Sales, and Sales Returns and Allowances. To highlight the data needed, only the July postings are shown in the ledger accounts.

Sales Tax Payable   Page 231

DATE	EXPLANATION	POST. REF.	DEBIT	DATE	EXPLANATION	POST. REF.	CREDIT
19 X1 July 31		SR-6	16 50	19 X1 July 31 31	*802.50*	CR-6 SJ-6	282 00 537 00 *819 00*

Sales   No. 401

DATE	EXPLANATION	POST. REF.	DEBIT	DATE	EXPLANATION	POST. REF.	CREDIT
				19 X1 July 31 31		CR-6 SJ-6	9,400 00 17,900 00 *27,300 00*

Sales Returns and Allowances   No. 452

DATE	EXPLANATION	POST. REF.	DEBIT	DATE	EXPLANATION	POST. REF.	CREDIT
19 X1 July 31		SR-6	550 00				

Using these account figures as a basis, the amount of the taxable gross sales for July is determined as follows.

July Sales — Cash	$ 9,400
Credit	17,900
Total Sales	$27,300
Deduct Sales Returns and Allowances	550
Taxable Gross Sales for July	$26,750

The 3% sales tax on the gross sales of $26,750 amounts to $802.50. In the state in which the Ashton & Barker Clothing Store is located, the retailer who files his sales tax return on time and who pays his tax when due is entitled to a discount intended to compensate him, at least in part, for acting as a collection agent for this tax. The rate of discount depends on the amount of tax to be paid. On amounts between $100 and $1,000, the rate is 2%, which amounts to $16.05 in this case (.02 × $802.50). With this discount deducted, the net tax due is $786.45 ($802.50 − $16.05) as shown. A voucher is prepared and a check is sent with the sales tax return form.

The voucher authorizing payment of the net tax calls for a debit to Sales Tax Payable (for $786.45 in this case). After posting the amount of the payment, the balance in the account should be equal to or very nearly equal to the discount.

Sales Tax Payable   No. 231

DATE	EXPLANATION	POST. REF.	DEBIT		DATE	EXPLANATION	POST. REF.	CREDIT	
19 X1					19 X1				
July 31		SR-6	16	50	July 31		CR-6	282	00
Aug. 5		VR-6	786	45	31		SJ-6	537	00
			802	*95*		*16.05*		*819*	*00*

Slight differences may arise because the tax collected at the time of the sale is determined by a bracket method that may give results slightly more or less than the final computations on the tax return. (In this case there is no difference.) The remaining balance in the Sales Tax Payable account, $16.05, is transferred to Miscellaneous Income 493 by a general journal entry debiting Sales Tax Payable and crediting the Miscellaneous Income account. The effect of this entry is shown in general journal form.

19 X1						
Aug. 5	Sales Tax Payable	231		16	05	
	Miscellaneous Income	493				16 05
	To transfer remaining balance in Sales Tax Payable account to the special income account.					

SALES TAX RETURN

ALWAYS REFER TO THIS NUMBER WHEN WRITING THE DIVISION	LICENSE NUMBER
	217539

—IMPORTANT—
ANY CHANGE IN OWNERSHIP REQUIRES A NEW LICENSE: NOTIFY THIS DIVISION IMMEDIATELY.

This return DUE on the 1st day of month following period covered by the return, and becomes DELINQUENT on 21st day.

FED. E. I. NO. OR S. S. NO. 37-9462315

JULY 31, 19X1

—Sales For Period Ended—

OWNER NAME AND LOCATION

MAKE ALL REMITTANCES
PAYABLE TO
STATE TAX COMMISSION
DO NOT SEND CASH
STAMPS NOT ACCEPTED

ASHTON & BARKER CLOTHING STORE
246 MAIN STREET
GREENVILLE, STATE 53970

COMPUTATION OF SALES TAX	For Taxpayer's Use	Do Not Use This Column
1. TOTAL Gross proceeds of sales or Gross Receipts (to include rentals)	$26,750.00	
2. Add cost of personal property Purchased on a RETAIL LICENSE FOR RESALE, but USED BY YOU or YOUR EMPLOYEES, including GIFTS and PREMIUMS	-0-	
3. USE TAX—Add cost of personal property purchased outside of STATE for your use, storage or consumption	-0-	
4. Total (Lines 1, 2 and 3)	$26,750.00	
5. LESS ALLOWABLE DEDUCTIONS (Must be itemized on reverse side)	-0-	
6. Net taxable total (Line 4 minus Line 5)	$26,750.00	
7. Sales and Use Tax Due (3% of Line 6)	$ 802.50	
8. LESS TAXPAYER'S DISCOUNT—(Deductible only when amount of Tax due is not delinquent at time of payment) IF LINE 7 IS LESS THAN $100.00 —DEDUCT 3% IF LINE 7 IS $100.00 BUT LESS THAN $1,000.00 —DEDUCT 2% IF LINE 7 IS $1,000.00 OR MORE —DEDUCT 1%	$ 16.05	
9. NET AMOUNT OF TAX PAYABLE (Line 7 minus Line 8)	$ 786.45	
Add the following penalty and interest if return or remittance is late 10. Specific Penalty: 25% of tax _ _ _ _ _ _ _ _ _ $		
11. Interest: ½ of 1% per month from due date until paid. $ TOTAL PENALTY AND INTEREST		
12. TOTAL TAX, PENALTY AND INTEREST	$ 786.45	
13. Subtract credit memo No.		
14. TOTAL AMOUNT DUE (IF NO SALES MADE SO STATE)	$ 786.45	

I certify that this return, including the accompanying schedules or statements, has been examined by me and is to best of my knowledge and belief, a true and complete return, made in good faith, for the period stated, pursuant to the provisions of the Code of Laws 19X1, and Acts Amendatory Thereto.

URGENT—SEE THAT LICENSE NUMBER IS ON RETURN

George Ashton
Signature

Partner
Owner, partner or title

August 5, 19X1
Date

Division Use Only

Return must be signed by owner, partner, or if corporation, authorized person.

Recording Tax in Sales Account

In some states, the retailer may credit the entire sales price plus tax to the Sales account. Then, at the end of the period, it will be necessary to remove from the Sales account the amount of tax included and transfer that amount to the Sales Tax Payable account.

For example, assume that during January 19X5 a retailer whose sales were all taxable sold merchandise for a total invoice price of $10,815, including the 3% tax. The entry made to record these sales may be summarized in general journal form as follows.

19	X5				
Jan.	31	Accounts Receivable	111	10,815 00	
		Sales	401		10,815 00
		To record total sales, including sales tax collected during period.			

At the end of the month, it is necessary to transfer the sales tax out of the Sales account to the Sales Tax Payable account. The first step will be to determine the amount of tax involved. The sales tax payable may be computed as follows.

Sales + Tax $\qquad$ = $10,815
100% of Sales + 3% of Sales $\quad$ = $10,815
103% of Sales $\qquad$ = $10,815

$$\text{Sales} = \frac{\$10,815}{1.03}$$

Sales $\qquad$ = $10,500

Tax = $10,500 x .03 $\qquad$ = $ 315

The following entry is then made to transfer the liability from the Sales account.

19	X5				
Jan.	31	Sales	401	315 00	
		Sales Tax Payable	231		315 00
		To transfer sales tax payable from Sales account to liability account.			

FEDERAL EXCISE TAX

As previously observed, some retailers may be subject to the federal excise tax. In this event, the excise tax is accounted for in much the same manner as the state sales tax. A separate column is set up in the cash receipts journal and in the sales journal to record the excise tax liability on sales. A separate liability account, Excise Tax Payable, is opened in the ledger.

A firm that owes more than $100 of federal excise tax in any month must deposit the amount of such tax due in an authorized bank on or before the last day of the following month. In this case, a voucher would be prepared, debiting the tax liability account and crediting Accounts Payable for the amount due. Finally, a check would be issued and sent to the bank with a Tax Deposit Form 504, similar to that used for social security taxes.

If the tax for the month is $100 or less, it is remitted with the Quarterly Federal Excise Tax Return, Form 720, that must be filed within the month following the close of each calendar quarter. Because excise taxes are now infrequently applicable to the retailer, details of the quarterly return are not examined here.

INCOME TAX RETURN FOR PARTNERSHIP

A partnership is required to file an information return for the federal government on Form 1065. This return indicates the income and expense of the partnership for its tax year and the distribution of the resulting net profit or loss among the partners. The partnership information return must be filed on or before the fifteenth day of the fourth month following the end of the firm's fiscal year. Since the fiscal year of the Ashton & Barker Clothing Store ends on January 31, its information return must be filed by May 15. A similar information return must be filed for the state. Ultimately, each partner reports on his own individual tax return and pays tax on his share of the partnership profit whether this has actually been distributed to him or not.

TAX CALENDAR

By now, it has been shown that there are a considerable number of tax returns to be filed and tax payments to be made. You have studied payroll taxes, sales and excise taxes, and property taxes, and have also seen that in some cases firms must file income tax returns. The accountant must keep up with all these tax responsibilities and must make sure that they are taken care of promptly and correctly. He uses a tax calendar to remind himself of important tax dates throughout the year.

A tax calendar should be prepared for each particular business. It should indicate the dates before which individual tax items must receive attention. It should be checked periodically so that the required tax information can be assembled carefully without any last-minute rush. Form numbers are also indicated where appropriate.

A portion of the tax calendar for Ashton & Barker Clothing Store (for January and February only) is shown.

ASHTON AND BARKER CLOTHING STORE
Tax Calendar

JANUARY

20	State Sales Tax Return for December; Form ST-3
31	State Unemployment Tax Return, quarter ended Dec. 31; Form UCE-101
31	Employer's Annual Federal Unemployment Tax Return (previous year); Form 940
31	Employer's Quarterly Federal Tax Return, quarter ended Dec. 31; Form 941
31	Withholding Tax Statements to each employee for previous year; Form W-2
31	Reconciliation of Income Tax Withheld from Wages (previous year); Form W-3

15   Deposit FICA Taxes and Income Tax Withheld for January; Form 501
20   State Sales Tax Return for January; Form ST-3
28   Property Tax Return; values as of December 31 (previous year)

◆ ◆ ◆

PRINCIPLES AND PROCEDURES

Property taxes are levied by various taxing authorities, including cities, counties, school districts, lighting districts, and some states. The same property may be subject to several taxing authorities. Usually, one agency collects the entire tax and distributes it to the participating agencies. The accountant's job in connection with property taxes is twofold. First, he must know how to determine the amount of tax due and get it paid on time. Second, he must record the tax as an expense in the appropriate accounting period and show prepayments or accrued tax liabilities properly on the balance sheet.

Since tax bills are often presented many months after the valuation of the property on which they are based, an estimate of the tax for the year is made. The monthly portion of this estimate is debited to a tax expense account and credited to a tax liability account. When the actual bill is received, the liability and expense accounts must be adjusted to reflect the correct figure, if it is different from the estimate.

Many states and cities impose sales taxes that must be collected by the retail merchant from his customers. Although these taxes vary from place to place, typical regulations require that the merchant collect a certain percent tax on each sale at the retail price of the item sold. This amount is remitted to the taxing authority, usually monthly or quarterly. In some localities, the merchant may be permitted to retain a portion of the tax as commission for acting as a collection agent.

MANAGERIAL IMPLICATIONS

Management must investigate the property tax structure before locating the business. It must also watch developments and changes in the tax structure and rates, in order to be able to gauge effects on the firm's costs and profits. It is especially important that management be familiar with local property valuation customs to make sure that its property taxes are equitable.

Management must make sure that sales taxes are properly charged to customers and collected. Taxes must also be accurately recorded in the records and promptly remitted to the taxing authority, along with the required reports. The seller is, of course, liable for any undercollection of taxes. Such an unnecessary expense can be avoided with an efficient control system. The tax calendar provides a ready means to make sure that all tax returns and reports are filed properly on time.

UNIT 25

APPLICATION OF PRINCIPLES

The Riley Appliance Shop operates on a calendar-year basis. The taxing
♦ authority of the city and county in which Riley is located operates on a
fiscal year basis from July 1 to June 30. On Jan. 1, 19X2, the Prepaid
Taxes account of Riley contains a balance of $360, representing the prepaid
property taxes through June 30, 19X2. The following occurred during 19X2.

19X2

Jan. 31   January tax expense recorded. (Entry 1-1A).

June 30   June tax expense recorded. (Assume that the tax expense was
recorded monthly from January through May.) (Entry 6-1A.)

July 31   Estimated July tax expense recorded. The estimate of tax for the
taxing authority's fiscal year beginning July 1, 19X2 is based on
a proposed assessed value of $20,000 and an assumed tax rate of
36 mills. (Entry 7-1A.)

Aug. 31   Recorded estimated tax expense. (Entry 8-1A.)

Sept. 10   Recorded tax bill received for July 1, 19X1, to June 30, 19X2, in
amount of $800. (Entry 9-1.)

Sept. 30   Recorded tax expense for September. (Entry 9-2A.)

Oct. 16   Recorded payment of tax bill of $800. (Entry 10-1.)

Oct. 31   Recorded tax expense for October. (Entry 10-2A.)

INSTRUCTIONS

In general journal form, record the necessary entries, using these accounts:
Cash in Bank 101, Prepaid Taxes 128, Property Taxes Payable 235, and Tax
Expense 555.

PROBLEM 25 · 2

The following sales data are given for a small company on June 30,
♦ 19X1:

1. Sales on account for the month of June were $208,790.20, plus a 5%
state sales tax on all sales.

2. Cash sales for June totaled $31,820, plus a 5% state sales tax on all
sales.

3. Goods sold for cash were returned, and the customers were given a cash
refund of $109, plus the 5% sales tax.

4. Goods sold for $385.70, plus the 5% sales tax, were returned, and
customers were given credit.

INSTRUCTIONS

Record each of the above transactions in general journal form. (Start with
Entry 6-1).

PROBLEM 25 · 3

◆ During January 19X1, the Samson Company had total sales of $364,610.80 and sales returns and allowances of $3,217.40. At the end of January, the Sales Tax Payable account showed a balance of $18,052.13. The sales tax rate is 5%, and the commission is $2\frac{1}{2}\%$ of the gross amount of sales tax due.

INSTRUCTIONS

1. Make the calculations that are required in preparing the sales tax return:
   a. Taxable gross sales for January
   b. Total sales tax due
   c. Amount of commission earned by Samson
   d. Amount of sales tax to be paid to the collecting agency
2. Show the following in general journal form (omit entry and account numbers and explanation):
   a. The entry required to record payment to the collecting agency of the sales tax due
   b. The entry required to transfer the commission to Miscellaneous Income and close the Sales Tax Payable account for January

PROBLEM 25 · 4

◆ Winfield Company must collect a tax on all its sales. The tax of 5% is added to the retail selling price and the entire amount (sales plus tax) is credited to the Sales account. Similarly, when merchandise is returned by customers, the entire return and allowance, both retail sales price and the tax, is debited to Sales Returns and Allowances.

On Mar. 31, 19X1, at the time the quarterly sales tax return is filed, the company's accounts include the following balances:

Sales	$485,467.28 (Credit)
Sales Returns and Allowances	2,855.68 (Debit)

The company is entitled to retain 2% of the sales tax due as a commission to help cover its expenses of collection.

INSTRUCTIONS

1. Compute the amount of sales tax on net sales.
2. Prepare a general journal entry to transfer the gross amount of sales tax from the Sales account to the Sales Tax Payable account, and from the Sales Returns and Allowances account to the Sales Tax Payable account. (Ignore entry and account numbers.)

3. Give the journal entry to transfer the commission earned from the Sales Tax Payable account to the Miscellaneous Income account.
4. Give the journal entry to record payment of the net sales tax due.

MANAGERIAL CHECKUPS

♦ How do various common business taxes affect a firm's costs and profits? What can management do about these taxes?

♦ Why can't a taxing body set the property tax rate at the time it determines the appraised value of the property under its jurisdiction?

PART 7
COMPLETION OF CYCLE— ACCRUAL BASIS

26 ACCRUALS AND DEFERRALS

In the previous units you have learned that an accountant must make certain adjustments to the accounts at the end of the fiscal period in order to make sure that all items of income and expense applicable to the current period are included in the income statement. In this way, the expenses of the period are matched against the revenues that they helped to produce. This is really the only way that a meaningful net profit figure can be reached.

THE ACCRUAL BASIS

The procedure that most nearly attains the objective of precisely matching revenues and expenses of specific fiscal periods is called the *accrual basis* of accounting. Under this system, all income and all expenses are recorded and shown on the income statement for the period in which the income was realized or the cost consumed, regardless of when cash was received or paid. Matching revenues and expenses with the period to which they apply is referred to as the *matching principle*.

For example, revenue is recognized when the sale is completed, which is usually when title to the goods passes to the buyer or the service is rendered. The revenue is recognized at the time of sale even though accounts receivable resulting from sales on credit may not be collected immediately. Purchases are also recorded when made, that is, when title to the goods passes to the buyer, regardless of the actual time of payment for the goods.

Transactions involving income and expense items often occur and are recorded before the period to which the income or expense actually relates. For example, insurance premiums are frequently paid in advance, and supplies may be purchased but remain unused at the end of the period.

In other cases, the actual transaction involving an income or expense item may not take place until after the period to which the item relates. For example, you have learned how to estimate bad debt expense on sales of the particular fiscal period even though the specific worthless accounts receivable may not be known until future years. As another example, employees may work during January but not be paid for their January work until February.

In view of the lag between the time that an item is recorded in the accounts and the time that it is actually used or consumed, it is necessary to examine each account balance at the end of an accounting period to see if it contains amounts of income or expenses allocable to other periods. It is impossible to present an accurate picture of where the business stands or what it has accomplished until the missing information is recorded and until the *mixed* accounts (accounts that may contain elements of both assets and expenses) have been analyzed. An adjusting entry may be necessary so that the income and expense accounts will contain amounts relating only to the current period, and the asset and liability accounts will reflect amounts properly classified as assets and liabilities.

PREPARATION OF THE WORKSHEET

In this unit you will study various typical adjustments necessary at the end of the fiscal period so that the accounts will reflect the true and complete financial facts of a business. As a basis for this discussion, look at the trial balance of Ashton & Barker Clothing Store as it has been entered in the first two columns of the worksheet at the end of the company's second year of operation, January 31, 19X3. (Remember that the company's fiscal year runs from February 1 through January 31.) Note that some accounts have no balances in the trial balance.

The accountant provides additional pairs (debit and credit) of columns on the worksheet with the following headings:

- Adjustments
- Adjusted Trial Balance
- Income Statement
- Balance Sheet

RECORDING BAD DEBTS

Unit 14 explained how to make an estimate of bad debts at the end of an accounting period so that the expense involved could be matched against the revenues of the same period. The Bad Debts Expense account is debited and the Allowance for Bad Debts account is credited for the estimated bad debts resulting from the current year's sales. Trade experience indicated that 0.3% of credit sales would probably become uncollectible in a business of the type, size, and circumstances of Ashton & Barker. This percentage was then applied to the amount of the first year's total credit sales of $200,000,

ASHTON & BARKER CLOTHING STORE
Worksheet (Partial)
Year Ended January 31, 19X3

Acct. No.	Account Name	TRIAL BALANCE Debit		TRIAL BALANCE Credit	
101	Cash in Bank	$ 14,305	89		
105	Petty Cash	25	00		
106	Change Funds	100	00		
111	Accounts Receivable	23,067	35		
111A	Allowance for Bad Debts			$ 7	06
112	Notes Receivable	800	00		
113	Notes Receivable Discounted				
116	Interest Receivable				
121	Merchandise Inventory (Feb. 1)	65,000	00		
126	Prepaid Insurance				
127	Prepaid Interest Expense				
128	Prepaid Taxes	600	00		
129	Store Supplies on Hand				
131	Furniture & Fixtures	4,600	00		
131A	Allow. for Depreciation–Furniture & Fixtures			360	00
132	Office Equipment	2,750	00		
132A	Allow. for Depreciation–Office Equipment			215	00
201	Accounts Payable			5,190	25
202	Notes Payable–Trade			2,000	00
211	Notes Payable–Bank			12,000	00
216	Interest Payable				
221	Employee Deductions—FICA Taxes			109	20
222	Empl. Deductions–Income Tax Withheld			216	00
225	Salaries & Wages Payable				
226	Payroll Taxes Payable				
231	Sales Tax Payable			825	28
235	Property Taxes Payable				
301	Ashton Investment			29,000	00
302	Ashton Drawing	4,800	00		
311	Barker Investment			28,000	00
312	Barker Drawing	4,800	00		
321	Conrad Investment			28,500	00
322	Conrad Drawing	4,800	00		
401	Sales			327,550	90
452	Sales Returns & Allowances	6,041	25		
491	Interest Income			226	00
493	Miscellaneous Income			218	60
501	Merchandise Purchases	255,350	00		
506	Freight In	3,590	00		
511	Purchases Returns & Allowances			1,065	00
512	Purchases Discount			5,048	30
521	Sales Salaries	11,400	00		
522	Advertising	7,370	00		
523	Store Supplies & Expense	4,363	75		
529	Cash Short or Over	72	00		
532	Delivery Expense	3,860	00		
536	Insurance	3,390	00		
541	Janitorial Wages	5,040	00		
542	Rent	3,000	00		
543	Utilities	981	35		
551	Office Salaries	5,400	00		
552	Payroll Tax Expense	1,477	50		
553	Office Supplies & Expense	804	50		
554	Professional Services	775	00		
555	Taxes & Licenses	1,206	00		
561	Bad Debts Expense				
562	Depreciation–Furniture & Fixtures				
563	Depreciation–Office Equipment				
591	Interest Expense	762	00		
	Totals	$440,531	59	$440,531	59

resulting in a provision of $600 among the adjusting entries (debit Bad Debts Expense and credit Allowance for Bad Debts) to reflect the expected losses. Since that time (during the second year of operations), the actual uncollectible accounts have been debited to the Allowance for Bad Debts account as they have been charged off. On January 31, 19X3, the end of the second year, there is a credit balance remaining in the Allowance for Bad Debts account of only $7.06. The accountant for Ashton & Barker now has to compute the estimated losses arising from the second year's business.

Assume that an analysis of the Sales account shows that credit sales totaled $223,050. At the 0.3% rate of estimated loss, the bad debts arising from this year's sales are estimated to be $669.15. The adjustment is recorded on the worksheet in the Adjustments column as a debit to Bad Debts Expense 561 and a credit to Allowance for Bad Debts 111A and marked "A," as illustrated.

ACCT. NO.	ACCOUNT NAME	TRIAL BALANCE		ADJUSTMENTS	
		DEBIT	CREDIT	DEBIT	CREDIT
111A	Allowance for Bad Debts		7 06		A) 669 15
561	Bad Debts Expense			A) 669 15	

RECORDING DEPRECIATION

Another familiar, important adjustment to be made at the end of the accounting period is that for depreciation (see Unit 14). The Ashton & Barker Clothing Store owns several types of assets, such as furniture and fixtures and office equipment, for which there must be a gradual, periodic transfer of acquisition cost to expense. Depreciation is recorded on the worksheet at the end of the accounting period by a debit to Depreciation Expense and a credit to Allowance for Depreciation. Ashton & Barker use the straight-line method of computing depreciation.

Depreciation of Furniture and Fixtures

Account 131 indicates that furniture and fixtures cost $4,600. The estimated useful life of these assets is 10 years, and there is no estimated salvage. Depreciation for the year is computed to be $460:

$$\frac{\$4,600 \text{ (cost)} - \$0 \text{ (salvage)}}{10 \text{ years}} = \$460 \text{ per year}$$

This adjustment is shown on the worksheet as entry "B," illustrated below.

ACCT. NO.	ACCOUNT NAME	TRIAL BALANCE		ADJUSTMENTS	
		DEBIT	CREDIT	DEBIT	CREDIT
131A	Allow. for Dep.–F. & F.		360 00		B) 460 00
132A	Allow. for Dep.–Off. Equip.		215 00		C) 215 00
562	Depreciation–Furn. & Fix.			B) 460 00	
563	Depreciation–Off. Equip.			C) 215 00	

Depreciation of Office Equipment

The office equipment, which costs $2,750, is estimated to have a useful life of 10 years and an estimated salvage value of $600 at that time. Based on these data, the annual depreciation is computed to be $215:

$$\frac{\$2,750 \text{ (Cost)} - \$600 \text{ (Salvage)}}{10 \text{ Years}} = \$215 \text{ per year}$$

Depreciation of the office equipment is entered on the worksheet as shown in entry "C."

RECORDING ACCRUED AND DEFERRED EXPENSES

As noted earlier, some expense items that are recorded in the current period may not be fully used until a later period and some expense items that pertain to the current period may not have been recorded at all in the day-to-day entry procedure. Therefore, adjustments may be necessary so that the records of the period will show all expenses related to the firm's current operations—no more and no less—before the final statements are prepared.

Accrued Expenses

Accrued expenses are those representing items that have been consumed or used in the current period, but which have not yet been paid for. As a result, it is necessary to record both the expense item and the liability. Ashton & Barker has four accrued expense items that require adjustment at January 31. You are already familiar with the first of these.

PROPERTY TAX EXPENSE. In Unit 25, it was stated that Ashton & Barker pays its property taxes for the calendar year in December of that year. In January, the store estimates its property tax for the coming year and accrues one-twelfth of the yearly tax as an expense for January. This is accomplished by debiting Taxes and Licenses 555.8 and crediting Property Taxes Payable 235.8.

     The current estimate of a $240 tax for the calendar year 19X3 means that $20 must be accrued at the end of January. Therefore, an entry is made in the Adjustments columns of the worksheet debiting Taxes and Licenses 555.8 for $20, and crediting Property Taxes Payable 235.8 for the same amount. The elements of the transaction are identified with the letter "D" and the code ".8" to indicate property tax, as illustrated.

ACCT. NO.	ACCOUNT NAME	TRIAL BALANCE		ADJUSTMENTS	
		DEBIT	CREDIT	DEBIT	CREDIT
235	Property Taxes Payable				D).8–20 00
555	Taxes & Licenses	1,206 00		D).8–20 00	

ACCRUED SALARIES AND WAGES. All employees except the janitor are paid on the 15th and last day of each month. Hence, at the trial balance date, the semimonthly wages for January have been properly charged to expense. However, the janitor is paid weekly—on Friday. Since January 31, 19X3 is a Thursday, janitorial wages for four days (Monday, January 28, through Thursday, January 31) are unpaid and have not yet been recorded on the books. Thus the accountant must debit Janitorial Wages 541 and credit Salaries and Wages Payable 225 for the $80 (the janitor earns $20 per day × 4 days), so that both the expense and liability will be properly shown. Entry "E" on the worksheet accomplishes this.

PAYROLL TAX EXPENSE. The Ashton & Barker trial balance figure of $1,477.50 on January 31 for Payroll Tax Expense 552 includes all taxes that

ACCT. NO.	ACCOUNT NAME	TRIAL BALANCE		ADJUSTMENTS	
		DEBIT	CREDIT	DEBIT	CREDIT
225	Salaries & Wages Payable				E) 80 00
541	Janitorial Wages			E) 80 00	

apply to salaries for the months of February through December 19X2, including the:

1. FICA tax (recorded when the Employer's Quarterly Federal Tax Return was filed in January 19X3 for the last quarter of 19X2)
2. Federal unemployment tax for 19X2 (recorded when the federal unemployment tax return was filed in January 19X3)
3. State unemployment tax (recorded when the quarterly state return was filed in January 19X3 for the last quarter of 19X2)

However, payroll tax expense related to January 19X3 earnings has not yet been recorded because the various tax returns covering these earnings have not yet been filed.

In order to properly match expenses and revenue, the payroll taxes applicable to salaries earned in January should be recorded as an expense of January and as a liability on January 31. The January earnings of the four employees totaled $1,900, including the $80 janitorial wages accrued above. The applicable tax rates are 6% for FICA (assumed), 1.3% for state unemployment, and 0.5% for federal unemployment. Applying these rates to the taxable payroll, the total tax chargeable to January operations is $148.20, as follows:

FICA	$1,900 × .06 =	$114.00
SUI	1,900 × .013 =	24.70
FUI	1,900 × .005 =	9.50
Total Payroll Tax Accrued		$148.20

The accrued expense is entered in the Adjustments columns on the worksheet as a debit to Payroll Tax Expense 552, and a credit to Payroll Taxes Payable 226, as illustrated by adjustment "F" on the partial worksheet shown here. Note that Ashton & Barker uses a single tax expense account for both FICA and unemployment insurance taxes.

ACCT. NO.	ACCOUNT NAME	TRIAL BALANCE		ADJUSTMENTS	
		DEBIT	CREDIT	DEBIT	CREDIT
226	Payroll Taxes Payable				F) 148 20
552	Payroll Tax Expense	1,477 50		F) 148 20	

INTEREST EXPENSE ON NOTES PAYABLE—TRADE. The January 31 trial balance (see page 419) shows $2,000 owed on trade notes payable. The files contain a copy of a note dated December 2 for $2,000, payable in 90 days, with interest at 8%. In the normal routine, the interest is paid at the maturity of the note. However, the interest expense is actually incurred from day to day and should be apportioned to each accounting period involved, if a complete and accurate picture of expenses is to be obtained. The amount accrued from December 2 to January 31 must be set up on the books as an expense and as a liability through an adjusting entry. The period is 60 days (31 − 2 = 29 in December plus 31 in January). Applying the interest formula, principal × rate × time, the accrued interest amounts to $26.67.

$$\$2,000 \times \frac{8}{100} \times \frac{60}{360} = \$26.67$$

An entry is then recorded in the Adjustments columns of the worksheet debiting Interest Expense 591 and crediting Interest Payable 216. The entry is identified with the letter "G," as illustrated.

ACCT. NO.	ACCOUNT NAME	TRIAL BALANCE		ADJUSTMENTS	
		DEBIT	CREDIT	DEBIT	CREDIT
216	Interest Payable				G) 26 67
591	Interest Expense	762 00		G) 26 67	

An adjustment for accrued interest expense is made on the worksheet at the end of any month for which financial statements are to be prepared. However, the adjustment is entered in the accounts only at the end of the fiscal year. Hence, the amount of accrued interest expense in the adjustment illustrated is for the entire period from the date of the note to the current date, January 31.

Deferred (Prepaid) Expenses

An item of expense that has been recorded in the current period but that pertains in part to a later accounting period should be analyzed so that the unused element may be identified and carried over to the period in which it belongs.

In the initial recording of the expense, a debit may have been made directly to the expense account. Thus, if the expense is not all used during the current period, the expense account balance is overstated when the period closes. An adjustment should be made to reduce the expense account for the value of the unused portion and to set up the deferred expense as an asset. The first three deferred expense items in the Ashton & Barker accounts fall into this category.

STORE SUPPLIES ON HAND. Ashton & Barker charge office supplies and store supplies to expense as purchased. If any considerable amount of these supplies remains unused at the end of an accounting period, their value should be determined and removed from the expense of the current period. Assume that the amount of office supplies on hand was too small to justify an adjustment. However, an inventory discloses that there are $110 worth of store supplies on hand.

The $110 cost of supplies on hand is recorded by debiting the asset account Store Supplies on Hand 129. Since the cost of all store supplies purchased has been charged to the Store Supplies and Expense 523 account, the cost of items on hand must be removed from that account by a credit of $110 to avoid overstatement of the expense for the year. This procedure is indicated by adjustment "H" on the partial worksheet shown here.

ACCT. NO.	ACCOUNT NAME	TRIAL BALANCE		ADJUSTMENTS	
		DEBIT	CREDIT	DEBIT	CREDIT
129	Store Supplies on Hand			H) 110 00	
523	Store Supplies & Expense	4,363 75			H) 110 00

UNEXPIRED INSURANCE. Insurance premiums are usually paid in advance. Ashton & Barker has charged all its payments for insurance to the Insurance expense account during the year. An analysis of the insurance policies indicates that several contracts run into the following period. The appropriate portion of the cost of this protection (prorated on a time basis) should be deferred by an adjustment. It is found that $300 worth of insurance presently charged to expense should be deferred. The adjusting entry crediting the expense account, Insurance 536, and setting up the appropriate asset, Prepaid Insurance 126, is shown on the partial worksheet as entry "I."

ACCT. NO.	ACCOUNT NAME	TRIAL BALANCE		ADJUSTMENTS	
		DEBIT	CREDIT	DEBIT	CREDIT
126	Prepaid Insurance			I) 300 00	
536	Insurance	3,390 00			I) 300 00

PREPAID INTEREST ON NOTES PAYABLE—BANK. In borrowing at the bank, Ashton & Barker gave its $12,000 note dated December 22, payable in 60 days and bearing interest at 6%. The bank deducted $120 interest for the entire period in advance and this was debited to Interest Expense at the time. On January 31, the note still had 20 days to run until maturity on February 20. Interest expense for these 20 days has already been recorded, although it should properly appear as an expense of the next period. An adjusting entry is necessary to get all the facts on the records. First, the usual interest formula would be applied to determine the amount of interest prepaid for 20 days.

$$\$12{,}000 \times \frac{6}{100} \times \frac{20}{360} = \$40$$

Then, in the Adjustments columns on the worksheet, Prepaid Interest Expense 127 is debited for $40 and Interest Expense 591 is credited. The entry is marked "J" as illustrated on the partial worksheet.

ACCT. NO.	ACCOUNT NAME	TRIAL BALANCE		ADJUSTMENTS	
		DEBIT	CREDIT	DEBIT	CREDIT
127	Prepaid Interest Expense			J) 40 00	
591	Interest Expense	762 00		G) 26 67	J) 40 00

ALTERNATE METHOD. In the initial recording procedure of deferred expenses, a transaction could have been entered as a debit to a prepaid expense account (asset). Under this arrangement, any amount that has become a proper charge to expense at the end of the period is transferred out of the prepaid (or deferred) expense account and debited to the appropriate expense. Ashton & Barker has one such item.

Ashton & Barker is subject to a stock tax on its merchandise inventory for the period July 1, 19X2 to June 30, 19X3, payable in December of 19X2. At the time of payment in December, the tax for 6 months (January 1 to June 30, 19X3) is prepaid and is accordingly debited to the Prepaid Taxes account. At the end of January, one-sixth of this amount is transferred to the Taxes and Licenses expense account. At January 31, the Prepaid Taxes account has a balance of $600, representing the prepayment for 6 months. An adjustment must now be made for one-sixth of this amount, or $100, to record January's share of the prepayment.

The entry required in the Adjustments columns on the worksheet is a debit to Taxes and Licenses 555 for $100 and a credit to Prepaid Taxes 128. The debit is labeled ".7" to identify it as stock tax. All parts of the entry are keyed with the letter "K," as illustrated.

ACCT. NO.	ACCOUNT NAME	TRIAL BALANCE		ADJUSTMENTS	
		DEBIT	CREDIT	DEBIT	CREDIT
128	Prepaid Taxes	600 00			K) 100 00
555	Taxes & Licenses	1,206 00		D) .8– 20 00 K) .7–100 00	

ACCRUED INCOME

All income that has been earned in the current period should be included in the proper income account before the books are closed. If, at the time the trial balance is taken, an item of earned income has not yet been entered on the records, an adjustment is necessary to recognize it. The individual income account balance should be increased even though the amount involved has not been actually received or collected. The offsetting debit may represent an increase in assets or a reduction in liabilities. There are two accrued income items in the Ashton & Barker operations.

Interest on Notes Receivable

Interest-bearing notes receivable are ordinarily recorded at face value when received and carried in the records at that value until collected or written off as uncollectible. The interest income is recorded when it is received, which is usually when the note is settled at maturity. However, the interest is actually earned day by day throughout the period that the note is held. Therefore, at the end of an accounting period, any accrued interest income earned but not recorded should be included in the records by means of an adjusting entry.

The Ashton & Barker trial balance at January 31, 19X3 shows a balance of $800 in the Notes Receivable account, representing a 60-day, 6% note dated December 17 and signed by Robert Jones. Interest of $6 has therefore accrued on the note as of January 31.

$$\$800 \times \frac{6}{100} \times \frac{45}{360} = \$6$$

If financial statements had been prepared sometime during the fiscal year, such as on December 31, an adjustment for accrued interest on this note would have been made on the worksheet and the appropriate amount would have appeared in the statements. However, except at the end of the fiscal year, such an adjustment would *not have been recorded* in the journal and would therefore *not appear* in the ledger account. Consequently, at the end of January in this case, accrued interest must be determined and recorded from the date of the note to the current date.

The facts are entered in the Adjustments columns of the worksheet by a debit to Interest Receivable 116 for $6 to show that this amount has been earned but not yet received. This adjustment is identified by the letter "L" on the worksheet.

ACCT. NO.	ACCOUNT NAME	TRIAL BALANCE		ADJUSTMENTS	
		DEBIT	CREDIT	DEBIT	CREDIT
116	Interest Receivable			L) 6 00	
491	Interest Income		226 00		L) 6 00

The Interest Receivable 116 account is shown on the balance sheet as a current asset.

Commission on Sales Tax

In Unit 25, it was stated that Ashton & Barker is entitled to retain a commission on the 3% sales tax collected if it files its sales tax return and pays the net amount due promptly. The commission is 2% of the gross sales tax due. At the end of January, the balance shown in the Sales Tax Payable 231 account, $825.28, includes both the amount that will have to be paid to the state tax authorities and the amount of the commission to be retained by Ashton & Barker.

January sales	$27,550.90
Sales returns and allowances	41.25
Taxable sales for January	$27,509.65
Gross tax (.03 × $27,509.65)	$825.29
Commission to be retained (.02 × $825.29)	16.51
Net tax liability	$808.78
Balance of Sales Tax Payable account	$825.28
Net tax liability	808.78
Adjustment necessary (commission)	$ 16.50

The commission is treated as miscellaneous income. An adjustment is needed to transfer the amount of the commission from the liability account to the income account.

Note that there is a difference of $.01 between the trial balance figure of $825.28 and the amount ($825.29) to be shown as tax due on the return. Such slight differences frequently occur because the sales tax is collected by tax brackets or is computed to the nearest penny on each transaction; the resulting total will rarely agree exactly with the amount calculated as due when the tax rate is applied to the taxable sales. The procedure is to adjust the Sales Tax Payable account to show the actual correct liability to the taxing authority.

The commission is recorded in the Adjustments columns of the work-sheet, debiting Sales Tax Payable 231, for $16.50 and crediting Miscellaneous Income 493 for the same amount. Each entry in the illustration is labeled "M."

ACCT. NO.	ACCOUNT NAME	TRIAL BALANCE		ADJUSTMENTS	
		DEBIT	CREDIT	DEBIT	CREDIT
231	Sales Tax Payable		825 28	M) 16 50	
493	Miscellaneous Income		218 60		M) 16 50

OTHER ACCRUED INCOME ITEMS

Ashton & Barker has no other accrued income items. However, a question is sometimes raised about the treatment of Purchases Discount 512. Specifically, should the amount of discount available if payment is made on time (but in the next accounting period) be accrued at the end of this period in those cases where purchases have been recorded at gross invoice price—the procedure followed by Ashton & Barker? Most accountants would not make an accrual, because earning the discount is not yet certain—the invoice must be paid before the discount period expires in order to earn it. Accountants generally prefer to wait until a discount has definitely been earned before they record it. The discount is not earned day by day like the interest on a note receivable—either it is all earned or none of it is earned when the invoice is paid. Therefore, no adjustment is made for purchases discount.

DEFERRED INCOME

Any portion of a firm's income that has been received but that has not yet been fully earned at the end of the period should be deferred and not reported on the income statement until it is earned in the succeeding accounting period. Since there are no deferred income items in the Ashton & Barker operations, a hypothetical example is presented.

UNIT 26

Subscriptions Income for a Publisher

Magazine publishers obtain subscriptions in advance, often several years in advance. The entire subscription may be credited to income when received. Then, at the end of the year, the publisher must analyze his subscriptions to determine how much that has been credited to income has not yet been earned because it applies to future periods. When the amount to be deferred has been determined, an adjustment is made debiting Subscriptions Income and crediting Unearned Subscriptions Income. The latter account appears on the balance sheet in the Liabilities section.

Using assumed amounts for an imaginary publisher, suppose that in the first year a total of $125,000 in subscriptions was received and credited to Subscriptions Income 441. Of this total, $80,000 was for current-year subscriptions and $45,000 was for services beyond the first year.

The balance in the Subscriptions Income account at the end of the first year is $125,000. Since only $80,000 has actually been earned in the first year, the amount of the adjustment required to reduce this account to the proper balance is $45,000, as a debit to Subscriptions Income. The credit to record the amount applicable to future periods is to the Unearned Subscriptions Income account, as shown on the partial worksheet illustrated here.

ACCT. NO.	ACCOUNT NAME	TRIAL BALANCE		ADJUSTMENTS	
		DEBIT	CREDIT	DEBIT	CREDIT
241	Unearned Sub. Income				A)45,000 00
441	Subscriptions Income		125,000 00	A)45,000 00	

The Unearned Subscriptions Income account would be classified as a current liability on the balance sheet.

Alternative Method

In the above example, the Subscriptions Income account was credited when payment was received in advance. However, it is possible to make the initial credit to the Unearned Subscriptions Income account when the cash is received. Indeed, this might be considered a more logical and accurate procedure because, at the time of receipt, most subscription revenue is entirely unearned. If the company in the preceding example had used this method of recording subscription receipts, the trial balance of the firm at the end of the first year would show Unearned Subscriptions Income with a credit balance of $125,000 while the Subscriptions Income account would show no balance. An adjustment would then be needed to transfer the amount earned during the first year, $80,000, to an income account. The amount still unearned, $45,000, would remain in the Unearned Subscriptions Income account. The required entry is illustrated here with the two ledger accounts involved. The account balances reflect the posting of the adjustment.

19 XX		12–9A						
Dec. 31	Unearned Subscriptions Income . . .		241	✓	80,000 00			
	Subscriptions Income		441	✓			80,000 00	
	To transfer to income the subscriptions earned during the year.							

Unearned Subscriptions Income   No. 241

DATE		EXPLANATION	POST. REF.	DEBIT	CREDIT	BALANCE	DR. CR.
19 XX Dec.	31		✓			125,000 00	Cr.
	31		12-9A	80,000 00		45,000 00	Cr.

Subscriptions Income   No. 441

DATE		EXPLANATION	POST. REF.	DEBIT	CREDIT	BALANCE	DR. CR.
19 XX Dec.	31		12-9A		80,000 00	80,000 00	Cr.

Results of the Two Methods Compared

The ledger account balances in the two preceding groups of illustrations will show the same results after the adjusting entries have been posted. Since the facts are the same, the final outcome must be identical regardless of which method is used. In each case, the Subscriptions Income account shows an adjusted balance of $80,000, while the Unearned Subscriptions Income account contains an adjusted balance of $45,000.

RECORDING THE ENDING MERCHANDISE INVENTORY

In Unit 15 you learned that, at the end of the period, the accountant must close the beginning merchandise inventory into the Income and Expense Summary account and must set up the ending merchandise inventory as an asset. The accountant normally has the merchandise inventory information available at the time he makes the previously described adjustments on the worksheet. Therefore, he often finds it convenient to note the entries for the merchandise inventory on the worksheet at the same time as he records the adjusting entries. However, since entries for merchandise inventory are not entered in the Adjustments column of the worksheet, they are considered in the next unit, along with other closing procedures.

◆ ◆ ◆

PRINCIPLES AND PROCEDURES

The accrual basis of accounting requires that all income and expenses of a period be matched and reported on the income statement of that period to determine the net profit. Typically, certain adjustments must be made to income and expense accounts at the end of the period in order to make sure that only those items properly reflected in income of the period are included. The provision for bad debts and the depreciation expense charge are common examples. In addition, certain other expense accounts must be adjusted.

Accrued expenses that have been incurred or used but not yet paid or recorded, and *deferred,* or *prepaid, expenses* (those recorded but not yet incurred or used) are other typical adjustments of expense accounts. In addition, *accrued income* that has been earned but not yet recorded, and *deferred,* or *unearned, income* that has not yet been earned but has been received and recorded, must be adjusted.

MANAGERIAL IMPLICATIONS

The matching process is necessary in order that management may know the true income, expenses, and net profit of the period. If deferred and accrued items were not adjusted, the financial statements would be incomplete and misleading. Such statements would be of no help in evaluating operations. Since adjustments tend to increase or decrease the net profit, managers should be familiar with the procedure and the underlying assumptions used by the firm's accountant.

APPLICATIONS OF PRINCIPLES

PROBLEM 26 · 1

Examination of the account balances that appear in the trial balance of
◆ the Hart Company at the end of its fiscal year on Sept. 30, 19X8 indicates the need for the adjustments given here.

A. Anticipated bad debt losses are to be calculated at 0.5% of net credit sales of $150,000 for the fiscal year.

B. Depreciation on the equipment for the fiscal year is to be computed using the straight-line method. The total cost of equipment amounts to $44,000 at Sept. 30, 19X8. The equipment is estimated to have a useful life of 10 years and a net salvage value of $2,000.

C. Property taxes for the calendar year 19X8 are estimated at $600, to be accrued at the rate of $50 per month.

D. Salaries and Wages earned and recorded in September that were subject to payroll taxes amounted to $3,000. Applicable tax rates are 6% (assumed rate) for FICA, 1.2% for state unemployment, and 0.5% for federal unemployment. All payroll taxes through Aug. 31 have been recorded.

E. Notes Payable—Trade consists of a $10,000 note dated Aug. 31, 19X8, payable in 60 days with interest at 8%.

F. The inventory of supplies on hand unused at Sept. 30 is valued at $150.

G. Insurance unexpired at Sept. 30 amounts to $860.

H. Notes Payable—Bank consists of a $25,000 note dated Aug. 1, 19X8, payable in 180 days. The interest at 6% was deducted from the proceeds in advance and was debited to Interest Expense.

The following selected accounts and balances are to be used in making the required adjustments.

111A	Allowance for Bad Debts	$ 14.50 Dr.
126	Prepaid Insurance	–0–
127	Prepaid Interest Expense	–0–
129	Supplies Inventory	–0–
131A	Allow. for Depr.—Equipment	13,300.00 Cr.
216	Interest Payable	–0–
226	Payroll Taxes Payable	–0–
235	Property Taxes Payable	–0–
523	Supplies Expense	1,320.00 Dr.
536	Insurance Expense	2,870.00 Dr.
552	Payroll Tax Expense	2,126.00 Dr.
555	Property Tax Expense	160.00 Dr.
561	Bad Debts Expense	–0–
563	Depreciation—Equipment	–0–
591	Interest Expense	1,485.00 Dr.

INSTRUCTIONS

1. Prepare a partial worksheet that has the same columns as shown in the illustration on page 441.
2. Enter on the worksheet the given accounts and balances.
3. Enter on the worksheet the given adjustments, identifying each with its appropriate letter. (No adjustments have been entered on the books this year.)
4. Combine the Trial Balance amounts with the Adjustments figures and enter in the Adjusted Trial Balance columns.

PROBLEM 26 · 2

♦ Art Supply Store had the following accounts and trial balance data at the close of the year's business on Dec. 31, 19X2.

ACCT. NO.	ACCOUNT NAME	DEBIT	CREDIT
101	Cash in Bank	$ 1,883.46	
111	Accounts Receivable	8,425.00	
111A	Allowance for Bad Debts		$ 31.00
121	Merchandise Inventory	25,000.00	
131	Prepaid Insurance	385.00	
141	Furniture & Equipment	1,200.00	
141A	Allow. for Depr.—F.&E.		310.00
201	Accounts Payable		388.00
226	Payroll Taxes Payable		81.00
301	Laney Investment		15,000.00
302	Laney Drawing	3,600.00	
311	Simms Investment		18,000.00
312	Simms Drawing	4,200.00	
401	Sales		124,750.00
501	Merchandise Purchases	84,650.00	
521	Rent Expense	1,650.00	
531	Salaries & Wages	8,125.00	
533	Payroll Tax Expense	696.54	
535	Insurance Expense	525.00	
537	Depreciation—Furn. & Equip.		
539	General Operating Expenses	18,220.00	
	Totals	$158,560.00	$158,560.00

Following are listed the adjustments for the Art Supply Store.

A. An analysis of accounts receivable results in an estimate that $249.50 worth of the accounts are uncollectible. Adjust the Allowance for Bad Debts account for this amount. (Debit account 539.)
B. Prepaid insurance was $270 at Dec. 31.
C. Depreciation is 8% of cost of furniture and equipment.
D. Rent expense for December of $150 has not been recorded or paid; it was due Dec. 1. (Credit Accounts Payable 201.)
E. Payroll taxes on $600 of December salaries and wages have not been recorded. Payroll tax rates are: FICA 6%; state unemployment 2.7%; and federal unemployment 0.5%.

INSTRUCTIONS

1. Set up a typical ten-column worksheet, listing the given accounts and recording the amounts in the first pair of money columns, headed Trial Balance. Total the columns.
2. Record the adjustments in the second pair of money columns, identifying each by letter. Show computations on a separate sheet. Total the adjustments columns.
3. Save your worksheet for use in Problem 27 · 1.

PROBLEM 26 · 3

A. Olds Company follows a policy of charging directly to prepaid expense (asset) accounts certain expenditures made during the year. At Dec. 31, 19X2, these asset accounts had the balances shown below, before adjustment.

Prepaid Insurance	$1,650
Prepaid Interest Expense	850
Supplies Inventory	2,084

Analysis at Dec. 31, 19X2 indicates $450 of insurance unexpired, $180 of interest prepaid on notes payable outstanding, and $356 of supplies on hand unused.

INSTRUCTIONS
Show in general journal entry form the adjustment required in each of the accounts at Dec. 31, 19X2. (Omit entry and account numbers and explanations.)

B. Assume, instead, that Olds Company (Part A) charges expenditures directly to the expense accounts involved, so that at Dec. 31, 19X2 the expense accounts have the balances shown below, before adjustment.

Insurance Expense	$1,650
Interest Expense	850
Supplies Expense	2,084

Analysis at Dec. 31, 19X2 indicates $450 of insurance unexpired, $180 of interest prepaid on notes payable outstanding, and $356 of supplies on hand unused.

INSTRUCTIONS
Show in general journal entry form the adjustment required in each of the accounts at Dec. 31, 19X2. (Omit entry and account numbers and explanations.)

PROBLEM 26 · 4

◆ During the year 19X1, Gala Publishers received revenue from magazine subscriptions totaling $840,000. Analysis at Dec. 31, 19X1 indicates that $500,000 is applicable to the current year and that the remainder is applicable to 19X2 and future years.

INSTRUCTIONS
1. Assuming that the $840,000 was credited to Unearned Subscriptions

Income when it was received, show in general journal form the entry necessary to adjust the books on Dec. 31, 19X1. (You may omit entry number, account number, and explanation.)

2. Assuming, instead, that the $840,000 was credited to Subscriptions Income when it was received, give the necessary adjusting journal entry on Dec. 31, 19X1.

MANAGERIAL CHECKUPS

♦ Why should management understand the underlying assumptions used by the firm's accountant in the completion of its financial statements?

♦ How can the owner of a business be sure that the firm's accountant has recognized all accrued and deferred expenses?

♦ Why is the outlay for insurance premiums frequently recorded as prepaid insurance instead of as insurance expense? Does the first method produce any different final results than the alternate method would produce?

27 COMPLETING THE WORKSHEET; FINANCIAL STATEMENTS

In the preceding unit you learned how the end-of-period adjustments for Ashton & Barker are made on January 31, 19X3, so that expenses and revenues of the year are properly matched and that the net income is correctly stated. The twelve adjustments are restated below using the letters corresponding to those on the worksheet. The partial worksheet on pages 420–429 shows how the adjustments are entered in the Adjustments columns, and how these columns are then totaled to make sure that the debits and credits are equal. The page number on which each adjustment is discussed and illustrated is indicated in parentheses.

A. Estimated bad debts expense for the year (page 420).
B. Depreciation of furniture and fixtures (page 421).
C. Depreciation of office equipment (page 421).
D. Estimated property taxes payable (page 422).
E. Accrued salaries and wages (page 423).
F. Payroll taxes payable (page 423).
G. Interest payable (page 424).
H. Store supplies on hand (page 425).
I. Prepaid insurance (page 425).
J. Prepaid interest expense (page 426).
K. Prepaid taxes transferred to expense (page 427).
L. Interest receivable (page 428).
M. Commission earned on sales taxes (page 429).

COMPLETING THE ADJUSTED TRIAL BALANCE

The next step in completing the worksheet is to determine the amount to be extended to the adjusted trial balance columns for each account. This is done by combining the adjustment figure (if any) with the original trial balance figure in each account. Each item on the worksheet illustrated on pages 441–442 will now be traced. You should closely examine each item as it is discussed.

101–111   There are no adjustments related to any of the first four accounts in the original Trial Balance section. The amounts shown are simply moved across the worksheet into the corresponding Adjusted Trial Balance column. Each of the first four items is a debit in the Trial Balance section and remains a debit in the Adjusted Trial Balance section.

111A   Allowance for Bad Debts, has a credit balance of $7.06 in the Trial Balance columns and a credit under Adjustments (A) of $669.15. The amount shown as a credit in the Adjusted Trial Balance section is the sum of the two credits, $676.21.

112   Notes Receivable is extended unchanged as a debit of $800 to the Adjusted Trial Balance.

113   There are no amounts for Notes Receivable Discounted, either in the Trial Balance or in the Adjustments columns. Hence, no amount is shown in the Adjusted Trial Balance section on this line. (It is customary to enter all ledger accounts except Income and Expense Summary on the worksheet even though they have no balances.)

116   The next account listed, Interest Receivable, has no amount in the Trial Balance columns but has a debit of $6 under Adjustments. Thus, the amount shown in the Adjusted Trial Balance section for this item is a debit of $6.

121   The Trial Balance section amount for Merchandise Inventory (beginning), a debit of $65,000, is carried over as a debit in the Adjusted Trial Balance columns.

126,127   Prepaid Insurance and Prepaid Interest Expense have no amounts in the Trial Balance section. Their respective debit adjustment figures of $300 and $40 are carried over to the Adjusted Trial Balance Debit column.

128   The original Trial Balance Debit column figure of $600 for Prepaid Taxes is combined with the credit adjustment of $100 to arrive at a $500 amount in the Adjusted Trial Balance Debit column.

129   Since there was no Trial Balance section amount shown for Store Supplies on Hand, the $110 debit adjustment is extended to the Adjusted Trial Balance Debit column.

131   The debit balance of Furniture and Fixtures, $4,600, is extended unchanged to the Adjusted Trial Balance section.

131A   The $360 Trial Balance section credit of Allowance for Depreciation—Furniture and Fixtures is combined with the credit adjustment of $460 to make an $820 credit in the Adjusted Trial Balance section.

132   The debit balance of Office Equipment is moved across without adjustment.

132A   Allowance for Depreciation—Office Equipment involves combining the two credits to make a total of $430 in the Adjusted Trial Balance Credit column.

201   Accounts Payable was not adjusted. Its credit balance is extended to the Adjusted Trial Balance Credit column. The same procedure is applied to Notes Payable—Trade and Notes Payable—Bank.

216   The credit adjustment of $26.67 for Interest Payable is extended to the credit column in the Adjusted Trial Balance section, since there is no balance in the Trial Balance.

221,222   The credit balances of Employee Deductions—FICA and Employee Deductions—Income Tax Withholding are carried across from the Trial Balance to the Adjusted Trial Balance section.

225   The only item for Salaries and Wages Payable is the adjustment of $80 for accrued janitorial wages. The $80 credit is carried to the credit column of the Adjusted Trial Balance section.

226   The adjustment entered for Payroll Taxes Payable, a credit of $148.20, is moved across to the credit side of the Adjusted Trial Balance section.

231   Next, Sales Tax Payable appears in the Trial Balance section as a credit of $825.28 and the adjusting entry is a debit of $16.50. The difference of $808.78 is carried over as a credit in the Adjusted Trial Balance section.

235   The $20 credit adjustment to Property Taxes Payable is extended to the credit side of the Adjusted Trial Balance section.

301–322   All three investment accounts are extended to the Adjusted Trial Balance Debit column.

401,452   The credit balance in the Sales account is moved unadjusted to the Adjusted Trial Balance. The Sales Returns and Allowances balance is extended directly to the Adjusted Trial Balance Debit column.

491   Interest Income calls for the combination of two credit balances for a credit entry in the Adjusted Trial Balance section of $232.

493   Two credits are combined to arrive at the Adjusted Trial Balance section figure for Miscellaneous Income.

501,506   Merchandise Purchases and Freight In are moved across to the Adjusted Trial Balance Debit column unchanged.

511,512   Purchases Returns and Allowances involves a simple extension of an unadjusted credit. The same is true of Purchases Discount.

521,522   Sales Salaries and Advertising are moved across without change to their new debit positions.

523   Store Supplies and Expense shows a debit of $4,363.75 in the Trial Balance section and a credit adjustment of $110 for supplies on hand. Subtracting the credit leaves a debit of $4,253.75 that is carried into the Adjusted Trial Balance section.

529,532   The debit balances of Cash Short or Over and Delivery Expense are moved across without adjustment.

536   The credit adjustments shown for Insurance 536 must be subtracted from the original debit balance to obtain a net debit figure of $3,090.

541   Janitorial Wages shows an original balance of $5,040 in the Trial

Balance. This, combined with the adjustment of $80 for accrued janitorial wages on January 31, gives a final balance of $5,120 in the Adjusted Trial Balance section.

542-551 Rent, Utilities, and Office Salaries can be moved directly to the Debit column of the Adjusted Trial Balance section unchanged.

552 Payroll Tax Expense involves the combining of debits to produce an adjusted balance of $1,625.70.

553,554 Office Supplies and Expense and Professional Services are two more unchanged debits that are extended.

555 Taxes and Licenses has a debit of $1,206 in the Trial Balance section and two debit adjustments—one for $20 and one for $100. Adding these three debit items together gives $1,326 carried over as a debit in the Adjusted Trial Balance section.

561 The Bad Debts Expense adjustment debit of $669.15 is moved to the Debit column of the Adjusted Trial Balance section.

562 The Depreciation—Furniture and Fixtures account has a debit adjustment of $460, which is carried over as a debit in the Adjusted Trial Balance section.

563 The adjustment figure listed for Depreciation—Office Equipment is moved to the Debit column in the Adjusted Trial Balance section.

591 The last item, Interest Expense, has a debit of $762 in the Trial Balance section and two adjustments—a debit of $26.67 and a credit of $40. The two debits are added to give a subtotal of $788.67 and the credit is subtracted, leaving $748.67, which is carried over as a debit in the Adjusted Trial Balance section.

With all the items in the Trial Balance section combined with the related adjustments to complete the Adjusted Trial Balance section, the next step is to add the debit items and the credit items in the Adjusted Trial Balance columns and prove equality of total debits and total credits.

EXTENDING BALANCE SHEET ITEMS

With the Adjusted Trial Balance completed, the accountant's next step is to extend each item into the appropriate statement columns. This is where the account numbering system is helpful.

In setting up the chart of accounts for the Ashton & Barker Clothing Store, blocks of numbers were assigned to assets, liabilities, and owners' equity with the numbers 100-199 for assets, 200-299 for liabilities, and 300-399 for owners' equity accounts. With this information, it is known in advance that all accounts through 399 will appear on the balance sheet.

Starting with the first item, Cash in Bank, the debit balance of $14,305.89 shown in the Adjusted Trial Balance section is carried over, or extended, into the Balance Sheet Debit column. The next three items are also debits in the Adjusted Trial Balance section and are carried over to

ASHTON & BARKER CLOTHING STORE
Worksheet (Partial)
Year Ended January 31, 19X3

	ACCT. NO.	ACCOUNT NAME	TRIAL BALANCE DEBIT	TRIAL BALANCE CREDIT	ADJUSTMENTS DEBIT	ADJUSTMENTS CREDIT	ADJUSTED TRIAL BALANCE DEBIT	ADJUSTED TRIAL BALANCE CREDIT
1	101	Cash in Bank	14,305 89				14,305 89	
2	105	Petty Cash	25 00				25 00	
3	106	Change Funds	100 00				100 00	
4	111	Accounts Receivable	23,067 35				23,067 35	
5	111A	Allowance for Bad Debts		7 06		A) 669 15		676 21
6	112	Notes Receivable	800 00				800 00	
7	113	Notes Receivable Discounted						
8	116	Interest Receivable			L) 6 00		6 00	
9	121	Merchandise Inventory	65,000 00				65,000 00	
10	126	Prepaid Insurance			I) 300 00		300 00	
11	127	Prepaid Interest Expense			J) 40 00		40 00	
12	128	Prepaid Taxes	600 00			K) 100 00	500 00	
13	129	Store Supplies on Hand			H) 110 00		110 00	
14	131	Furniture & Fixtures	4,600 00				4,600 00	
15	131A	Allow. for Depreciation—Furniture & Fixtures		360 00		B) 460 00		820 00
16	132	Office Equipment	2,750 00				2,750 00	
17	132A	Allow. for Depreciation—Office Equipment		215 00		C) 215 00		430 00
18	201	Accounts Payable		5,190 25				5,190 25
19	202	Notes Payable—Trade		2,000 00				2,000 00
20	211	Notes Payable—Bank		12,000 00				12,000 00
21	216	Interest Payable				G) 26 67		26 67
22	221	Employee Deductions—FICA Taxes		109 20				109 20
23	222	Empl. Deductions—Income Tax Withheld		216 00				216 00
24	225	Salaries & Wages Payable				E) 80 00		80 00
25	226	Payroll Taxes Payable				F) 148 20		148 20
26	231	Sales Tax Payable		825 28	M) 16 50			808 78
27	235	Property Taxes Payable				D) 8 20 00		20 00
28	301	Ashton Investment		29,000 00				29,000 00
29	302	Ashton Drawing	4,800 00				4,800 00	
30	311	Barker Investment		28,000 00				28,000 00
31	312	Barker Drawing	4,800 00				4,800 00	
32	321	Conrad Investment		28,500 00				28,500 00
33	322	Conrad Drawing	4,800 00				4,800 00	
34	401	Sales		327,550 90				327,550 90
35	452	Sales Returns & Allowances	6,041 25				6,041 25	
36	491	Interest Income		226 00		L) 6 00		232 00
37	493	Miscellaneous Income		218 60		M) 16 50		235 10
38	501	Merchandise Purchases	255,350 00				255,350 00	
39	506	Freight In	3,590 00				3,590 00	
40	511	Purchases Returns & Allowances		1,065 00				1,065 00
41	512	Purchases Discount		5,048 30				5,048 30
42	521	Sales Salaries	11,400 00				11,400 00	
43	522	Advertising	7,370 00				7,370 00	
44	523	Store Supplies & Expense	4,363 75			H) 110 00	4,253 75	
45	529	Cash Short or Over	72 00				72 00	
46	532	Delivery Expense	3,860 00				3,860 00	
47	536	Insurance	3,390 00			I) 300 00	3,090 00	
48	541	Janitorial Wages	5,040 00		E) 80 00		5,120 00	
49	542	Rent	3,000 00				3,000 00	
50	543	Utilities	981 35				981 35	
51	551	Office Salaries	5,400 00				5,400 00	
52	552	Payroll Tax Expense	1,477 50		F) 148 20		1,625 70	
53	553	Office Supplies & Expense	804 50				804 50	
54	554	Professional Services	775 00				775 00	
55	555	Taxes & Licenses	1,206 00		D) 8 20 00 / K) 7 100 00		1,326 00	
56	561	Bad Debts Expense			A) 669 15		669 15	
57	562	Depreciation—Furniture & Fixtures			B) 460 00		460 00	
58	563	Depreciation—Office Equipment			C) 215 00		215 00	
59	591	Interest Expense	762 00		G) 26 67	J) 40 00	748 67	
60		Totals	440,531 59	440,531 59	2,191 52	2,191 52	442,156 61	442,156 61

appear as debits in the Balance Sheet columns. The first credit balance in the Adjusted Trial Balance section is $676.21 for Allowance for Bad Debts. This is carried across and entered as a credit in the Balance Sheet columns. (Note the basic rule that debit balances are always extended into debit columns and credit balances are always extended into credit columns.)

ASHTON & BARKER CLOTHING STORE
Partial Worksheet
Year Ended January 31, 19X3

ACCT NO	ACCOUNT NAME	ADJUSTED TRIAL BALANCE		BALANCE SHEET	
		DEBIT	CREDIT	DEBIT	CREDIT
101	Cash in Bank	14,305 89		14,305 89	
105	Petty Cash	25 00		25 00	
106	Change Funds	100 00		100 00	
111	Accounts Receivable	23,067 35		23,067 35	
111A	Allowance for Bad Debts		676 21		676 21
112	Notes Receivable	800 00		800 00	
113	Notes Receivable Discounted				
116	Interest Receivable	6 00		6 00	
121	Merchandise Inventory	65,000 00		66,000 00	
126	Prepaid Insurance	300 00		300 00	
127	Prepaid Interest Expense	40 00		40 00	
128	Prepaid Taxes	500 00		500 00	
129	Store Supplies on Hand	110 00		110 00	
131	Furniture & Fixtures	4,600 00		4,600 00	
131A	Allow. for Depreciation—Furniture & Fixtures		820 00		820 00
132	Office Equipment	2,750 00		2,750 00	
132A	Allow. for Depreciation—Office Equipment		430 00		430 00
201	Accounts Payable		5,190 25		5,190 25
202	Notes Payable—Trade		2,000 00		2,000 00
211	Notes Payable—Bank		12,000 00		12,000 00
216	Interest Payable		26 67		26 67
221	Employee Deductions—FICA Taxes		109 20		109 20
222	Empl. Deductions—Income Tax Withheld		216 00		216 00
225	Salaries & Wages Payable		80 00		80 00
226	Payroll Taxes Payable		148 20		148 20
231	Sales Tax Payable		808 78		808 78
235	Property Taxes Payable		20 00		20 00
301	Ashton Investment		29,000 00		29,000 00
302	Ashton Drawing	4,800 00		4,800 00	
311	Barker Investment		28,000 00		28,000 00
312	Barker Drawing	4,800 00		4,800 00	
321	Conrad Investment		28,500 00		28,500 00
322	Conrad Drawing	4,800 00		4,800 00	

Notes Receivable is an asset and is extended to the debit column in the Balance Sheet section. There is no balance in Notes Receivable Discounted at this time. Interest Receivable is another asset and is handled the same as Notes Receivable.

Next, the Adjusted Trial Balance shows a debit of $65,000 for Merchandise Inventory, representing the beginning inventory. Also, at this time in the end-of-period activities (if not before), the accountant is informed that merchandise valued at $66,000 ($56,000 Clothing, $10,000 Shoes) is on hand at the close of business, January 31, 19X3.

As you already know:

(a) The beginning inventory is to be charged to the cost of goods sold because it is presumed to be the first merchandise consumed or sold during the period.
(b) The ending inventory must be recorded as an asset.
(c) The ending inventory must also be recorded as a reduction in the cost of goods sold.

The accountant proceeds to achieve these three objectives by considering the closing inventory elements first (b and c).
1. The ending inventory amount ($66,000) is extended to the Balance Sheet Debit column as an asset (and identified with the letter "N").
2. The ending inventory amount ($66,000) is also extended on the Income Statement Credit column where it too represents a reduction in the cost of goods sold during the period (also identified by the letter "N").
3. The beginning inventory figure is disregarded for the moment. As will be explained shortly, this amount will be extended to the Income Statement Debit column when you extend other accounts representing expenses of doing business.

The remaining asset balances are carried over from the Adjusted Trial Balance Debit column to the Balance Sheet Debit column. The two allowance for depreciation accounts have their credit balances carried over from the Adjusted Trial Balance section to the Credit column of the Balance Sheet section. (See the illustration on page 447.)

Each liability account (200–299) has a credit balance in the Adjusted Trial Balance section. The individual balances are carried over to appear as credits in the Balance Sheet section.

The three investment accounts in the owners' equity group (300–399) have credit balances in the Adjusted Trial Balance section; each is carried over to appear in the Credit column in the Balance Sheet section. The three drawing accounts have debit balances in the Adjusted Trial Balance section; each is carried over to appear in the Debit column in the Balance Sheet section.

The Balance Sheet columns of the worksheet now contain all the amounts that should be extended to them from the Adjusted Trial Balance section. Note that all the amounts in both sets of columns are the same, with one exception—the ending inventory appears in the Balance Sheet columns, whereas the beginning inventory is shown in the Adjusted Trial Balance columns.

On the 10-column worksheet being used, a pair of Income Statement columns is provided for entering all items that will appear on the income statement.

First, the beginning inventory figure of $65,000 in account 121 is extended from the Adjusted Trial Balance to the Income Statement section Debit column since it represents one of the major expenses of doing business. Record the letter N next to this figure to identify it as a merchandise inventory item. (As previously pointed out, the accountant may actually have already entered this figure at the time he was entering the adjusting entries on the worksheet.)

Then, the accountant extends the balances of the income and expense accounts (numbered from 400 through 599) from the Adjusted Trial Balance section, making sure that each debit balance and credit balance is properly entered in the Debit and Credit columns of the Income Statement section.

ASHTON & BARKER CLOTHING STORE
Worksheet (Partial)
Year Ended January 31, 19X3

ACCT NO	ACCOUNT NAME	ADJUSTED TRIAL BALANCE DEBIT	ADJUSTED TRIAL BALANCE CREDIT	INCOME STATEMENT DEBIT	INCOME STATEMENT CREDIT
121	Merchandise Inventory	65,000 00		M) 65,000 00	N) 66,000 00
401	Sales		327,550 90		327,550 90
452	Sales Returns & Allowances	6,041 25		6,041 25	
491	Interest Income		232 00		232 00
493	Miscellaneous Income		235 10		235 10
501	Merchandise Purchases	255,350 00		255,350 00	
506	Freight In	3,590 00		3,590 00	
511	Purchases Returns & Allowances		1,065 00		1,065 00
512	Purchases Discount		5,048 30		5,048 30
521	Sales Salaries	11,400 00		11,400 00	
522	Advertising	7,370 00		7,370 00	
523	Store Supplies & Expense	4,253 75		4,253 75	
529	Cash Short or Over	72 00		72 00	
532	Delivery Expense	3,860 00		3,860 00	
536	Insurance	3,090 00		3,090 00	
541	Janitorial Wages	5,120 00		5,120 00	
542	Rent	3,000 00		3,000 00	
543	Utilities	981 35		981 35	
551	Office Salaries	5,400 00		5,400 00	
552	Payroll Tax Expense	1,625 70		1,625 70	
553	Office Supplies & Expense	804 50		804 50	
554	Professional Services	775 00		775 00	
555	Taxes & Licenses	1,326 00		1,326 00	
561	Bad Debts Expense	669 15		669 15	
562	Depreciation—Furniture & Fixtures	460 00		460 00	
563	Depreciation—Office Equipment	215 00		215 00	
591	Interest Expense	748 67		748 67	

The beginning and ending merchandise inventories, the sales, purchases, and other income and expense items have now been carried over to the Income Statement columns. It is time to total the debits and credits in the Income Statement columns to determine the net profit or loss for the year.

The items in the Income Statement Debit column are added and found to total $381,152.37, as shown on the worksheet on page 447. The credits are likewise added and found to total $400,131.30, as shown. Since the credits exceed the debits, the difference of $18,978.93 represents a net profit for the period. The profit of $18,978.93 is entered in the Debit column so that the two columns will balance.

Since the profit belongs to the owners and represents an increase in equity, it is also entered in the Credit column of the Balance Sheet section, as you learned in Unit 4.

Next, the Balance Sheet Debit and Credit columns are added and the totals are entered above the net profit line (to make it easier to find any possible errors). The total of the Debit column is $127,004.24 and the total of the Credit column is $108,025.31. Of course the difference should equal the net profit (or loss) for the period, $18,978.93 in this case.

Finally, the Balance Sheet column totals, including net profit, are determined to be $127,004.24, and are entered to complete the worksheet. The completed worksheet for Ashton & Barker for the year ending January 31, 19X3, is shown on pages 446–447.

PREPARATION OF FINANCIAL STATEMENTS

The next accounting task is to prepare financial statements from the information assembled on the worksheet. The figures needed for the income statement are contained in the Income Statement columns in the worksheet. All the figures needed for the balance sheet are in the Balance Sheet columns. A separate statement of partners' equities can also be prepared, using part of the information in the Balance Sheet columns.

Income Statement

The income statement for Ashton & Barker, illustrated on page 448, is very much like that for Carter Cleaning Shop. Note, however, that at the bottom of the statement the distribution of profit to the partners is shown. In this case, each partner got one-third of the net profit by agreement when the partnership was established.

UNIT 27

ASHTON & BARKER CLOTHING STORE
Worksheet
Year Ended January 31, 19X3

	ACCT. NO.	ACCOUNT NAME	TRIAL BALANCE DEBIT	TRIAL BALANCE CREDIT	ADJUSTMENTS DEBIT	ADJUSTMENTS CREDIT
1	101	Cash in Bank	14,305 89			
2	105	Petty Cash	25 00			
3	106	Change Funds	100 00			
4	111	Accounts Receivable	23,067 35			
5	111A	Allowance for Bad Debts		7 06		A) 669 15
6	112	Notes Receivable	800 00			
7	113	Notes Receivable Discounted				
8	116	Interest Receivable			L) 6 00	
9	121	Merchandise Inventory	65,000 00			
10	126	Prepaid Insurance			I) 300 00	
11	127	Prepaid Interest Expense			J) 40 00	
12	128	Prepaid Taxes	600 00			K) 100 00
13	129	Store Supplies on Hand			H) 110 00	
14	131	Furniture & Fixtures	4,600 00			
15	131A	Allow. for Depreciation—Furniture & Fixtures		360 00		B) 460 00
16	132	Office Equipment	2,750 00			
17	132A	Allow. for Depreciation—Office Equipment		215 00		C) 215 00
18	201	Accounts Payable		5,190 25		
19	202	Notes Payable—Trade		2,000 00		
20	211	Notes Payable—Bank		12,000 00		
21	216	Interest Payable				G) 26 67
22	221	Employee Deductions—FICA Taxes		109 20		
23	222	Empl. Deductions—Income Tax Withheld		216 00		
24	225	Salaries & Wages Payable				E) 80 00
25	226	Payroll Taxes Payable				F) 148 20
26	231	Sales Tax Payable		825 28	M) 16 50	
27	235	Property Taxes Payable				D) 8 20 00
28	301	Ashton Investment		29,000 00		
29	302	Ashton Drawing	4,800 00			
30	311	Barker Investment		28,000 00		
31	312	Barker Drawing	4,800 00			
32	321	Conrad Investment		28,500 00		
33	322	Conrad Drawing	4,800 00			
34	401	Sales		327,550 90		
35	452	Sales Returns & Allowances	6,041 25			
36	491	Interest Income		226 00		L) 6 00
37	493	Miscellaneous Income		218 60		M) 16 50
38	501	Merchandise Purchases	255,350 00			
39	506	Freight In	3,590 00			
40	511	Purchases Returns & Allowances		1,065 00		
41	512	Purchases Discount		5,048 30		
42	521	Sales Salaries	11,400 00			
43	522	Advertising	7,370 00			
44	523	Store Supplies & Expense	4,363 75			H) 110 00
45	529	Cash Short or Over	72 00			
46	532	Delivery Expense	3,860 00			
47	536	Insurance	3,390 00			I) 300 00
48	541	Janitorial Wages	5,040 00		E) 80 00	
49	542	Rent	3,000 00			
50	543	Utilities	981 35			
51	551	Office Salaries	5,400 00			
52	552	Payroll Tax Expense	1,477 50		F) 148 20	
53	553	Office Supplies & Expense	804 50			
54	554	Professional Services	775 00			
55	555	Taxes & Licenses	1,206 00		D) 8 20 00 / K) 7 100 00	
56	561	Bad Debts Expense			A) 669 15	
57	562	Depreciation—Furniture & Fixtures			B) 460 00	
58	563	Depreciation—Office Equipment			C) 215 00	
59	591	Interest Expense	762 00		G) 26 67	J) 40 00
60		Totals	440,531 59	440,531 59	2,191 52	2,191 52
61		Total Net Profit				
62		Totals				

ADJUSTED TRIAL BALANCE		INCOME STATEMENT		BALANCE SHEET		
DEBIT	CREDIT	DEBIT	CREDIT	DEBIT	CREDIT	
14,305 89				14,305 89		1
25 00				25 00		2
100 00				100 00		3
23,067 35				23,067 35		4
	676 21				676 21	5
800 00				800 00		6
						7
6 00				6 00		8
65,000 00		N) 65,000 00	N) 66,000 00	66,000 00		9
300 00				300 00		10
40 00				40 00		11
500 00				500 00		12
110 00				110 00		13
4,600 00				4,600 00		14
	820 00				820 00	15
2,750 00				2,750 00		16
	430 00				430 00	17
	5,190 25				5,190 25	18
	2,000 00				2,000 00	19
	12,000 00				12,000 00	20
	26 67				26 67	21
	109 20				109 20	22
	216 00				216 00	23
	80 00				80 00	24
	148 20				148 20	25
	808 78				808 78	26
	20 00				20 00	27
	29,000 00				29,000 00	28
4,800 00				4,800 00		29
	28,000 00				28,000 00	30
4,800 00				4,800 00		31
	28,500 00				28,500 00	32
4,800 00				4,800 00		33
	327,550 90		327,550 90			34
6,041 25		6,041 25				35
	232 00		232 00			36
	235 10		235 10			37
255,350 00		255,350 00				38
3,590 00		3,590 00				39
	1,065 00		1,065 00			40
	5,048 30		5,048 30			41
11,400 00		11,400 00				42
7,370 00		7,370 00				43
4,253 75		4,253 75				44
72 00		72 00				45
3,860 00		3,860 00				46
3,090 00		3,090 00				47
5,120 00		5,120 00				48
3,000 00		3,000 00				49
981 35		981 35				50
5,400 00		5,400 00				51
1,625 70		1,625 70				52
804 50		804 50				53
775 00		775 00				54
1,326 00		1,326 00				55
669 15		669 15				56
460 00		460 00				57
215 00		215 00				58
748 67		748 67				59
442,156 61	442,156 61	381,152 37	400,131 30	127,004 24	108,025 31	60
		18,978 93			18,978 93	61
		400,131 30	400,131 30	127,004 24	127,004 24	62

ASHTON & BARKER CLOTHING STORE
Income Statement
Year Ended January 31, 19X3

Operating Income			
Sales			$327,550.90
Less Sales Returns and Allowances			6,041.25
Net Sales			$321,509.65
Cost of Goods Sold			
Merchandise Inventory, Feb. 1, 19X2		$65,000.00	
Purchases	$255,350.00		
Freight In	3,590.00		
Delivered Cost	$258,940.00		
Less Purchase Ret. & Allowances	$1,065.00		
Purchases Discounts	5,048.30	6,113.30	
Net Delivered Cost of Purchases		252,826.70	
Total Mdse. Available for Sale		$317,826.70	
Less Mdse. Inventory, Jan. 31, 19X3		66,000.00	
Cost of Goods Sold			251,826.70
Gross Profit			$ 69,682.95
Operating Expenses			
Selling Expenses			
Sales Salaries	$ 11,400.00		
Advertising	7,370.00		
Store Supplies & Exp.	4,253.75		
Cash Short	72.00		
Delivery Expense	3,860.00		
Depreciation of Furn. & Fixt.	460.00		
Total Selling Expenses		$ 27,415.75	
General Administrative Expenses			
Insurance	$ 3,090.00		
Janitorial Wages	5,120.00		
Rent	3,000.00		
Utilities	981.35		
Office Salaries	5,400.00		
Payroll Tax Expense	1,625.70		
Office Supplies & Exp.	804.50		
Professional Services	775.00		
Taxes & Licenses	1,326.00		
Bad Debts Expense	669.15		
Depreciation of Off. Eqpt.	215.00		
Total Gen. Administrative Expenses		23,006.70	
Total Operating Expenses			50,422.45
Net Profit from Operations			$ 19,260.50
Add: Other Income			
Interest Income	$ 232.00		
Miscellaneous Income	235.10		
Total Other Income		$ 467.10	
Deduct Other Expense			
Interest Expense		748.67	
Net Nonoperating Expense			$ 281.57
Net Profit for Year			$ 18,978.93

Distribution of Net Profit

Ashton (⅓)	$ 6,326.31
Barker (⅓)	6,326.31
Conrad (⅓)	6,326.31
Total	$ 18,978.93

Statement of Partners' Equities

The statement of partners' equities is prepared to show the changes that have taken place in the partners' equities during the period. There were no new investments during the year; the balances shown in the trial balance and now appearing in the Balance Sheet Credit column on the worksheet are the balances at the beginning of the period. The profit distribution presented on the income statement shows the amount to be added to each partner's equity. The drawing account balances in the ledger (and in the Balance Sheet Debit column on the worksheet) show the amounts to be deducted. The statement of partners' equities is illustrated. Note that this contains the same information that was shown in the Owner's Equity section of the balance sheet for Carter in the Carter Cleaning Shop. However, where there is more than one owner, as in a partnership, showing these details in the balance sheet takes too much space in the Owner's Equity section, so a separate statement is normally prepared.

ASHTON & BARKER CLOTHING STORE
Statement of Partners' Equities
Year Ended January 31, 19X3

	ASHTON INVESTMENT	BARKER INVESTMENT	CONRAD INVESTMENT	TOTAL INVESTMENT
Investment Balances, Feb. 1, 19X2	$29,000.00	$28,000.00	$28,500.00	$ 85,500.00
Profit for Year	6,326.31	6,326.31	6,326.31	18,978.93
Totals	$35,326.31	$34,326.31	$34,826.31	$104,478.93
Less Withdrawals	4,800.00	4,800.00	4,800.00	14,400.00
Investment Balances, Jan. 31, 19X3	$30,526.31	$29,526.31	$30,026.31	$ 90,078.93

Balance Sheet

The balance sheet is prepared in the usual form, using the information in the Balance Sheet columns of the worksheet. Assets are classified as current and fixed. The counterbalancing portion of the statement is usually subdivided into current liabilities, long-term liabilities, and owners' equity. The completed balance sheet for Ashton & Barker is shown on page 450. There are no long-term liabilities involved in this instance. Note that the figures shown as final balances of the partners' investment accounts agree with the balance amounts that appear on the last line of the statement of partners' equities.

♦ ♦ ♦

PRINCIPLES AND PROCEDURES

As soon as all the adjustments have been entered on the worksheet, the accountant proceeds to complete it and prepare the financial statements. The first step is to combine original Trial Balance figures and adjusting entries to make an Adjusted Trial Balance. Each item is carried

ASHTON & BARKER CLOTHING STORE
Balance Sheet
January 31, 19X3

ASSETS

Current Assets

Cash in Bank			$ 14,305.89
Petty Cash			25.00
Change Funds			100.00
Accounts Receivable		$23,067.35	
Less Allowance for Bad Debts		676.21	22,391.14
Notes Receivable			800.00
Interest Receivable			6.00
Merchandise Inventory			66,000.00
Prepaid Expenses			
Prepaid Insurance		$ 300.00	
Prepaid Interest Expense		40.00	
Prepaid Taxes		500.00	
Store Supplies on Hand		110.00	950.00
Total Current Assets			$104,578.03

Fixed Assets

Furniture & Fixtures	$4,600.00		
Less Allowance for Depreciation	820.00	$ 3,780.00	
Office Equipment	$2,750.00		
Less Allowance for Depreciation	430.00	2,320.00	
Total Fixed Assets			6,100.00
Total Assets			$110,678.03

LIABILITIES AND OWNERS' EQUITY

Current Liabilities

Accounts Payable			$ 5,190.25
Notes Payable–Trade			2,000.00
Notes Payable–Bank			12,000.00
Interest Payable			26.67
Employee Deductions–FICA Taxes			109.20
Employee Deductions–Income Tax WH			216.00
Salaries and Wages Payable			80.00
Payroll Taxes Payable			148.20
Sales Tax Payable			808.78
Property Taxes Payable			20.00
Total Current Liabilities			$ 20,599.10

Owners' Equity

Ashton Investment		$30,526.31	
Barker Investment		29,526.31	
Conrad Investment		30,026.31	
Total Owners' Equity			90,078.93
Total Liabilities and Owners' Equity			$110,678.03

across the worksheet in turn to the appropriate debit or credit column corresponding to the statement in which it is to appear.

When all items in the Adjusted Trial Balance columns have been carried across to the columns for the statement on which they are to appear, Income Statement columns are totaled and net profit or loss is determined. The resulting net profit or loss for the business is carried into the Balance Sheet section. At this point, total debits must equal total credits in the Balance Sheet columns.

Next, statements are prepared from the information contained in the respective columns on the worksheet. An income statement, a statement of partners' equities, and a balance sheet were prepared for the Ashton & Barker Clothing Store.

MANAGERIAL IMPLICATIONS

Management is keenly interested in receiving timely financial statements, especially periodic income statements showing the results of operations. The worksheet is a very useful device for facilitating the accumulation of adjustment data and the preparation of the income statement. Similarly, management is very much interested in prompt preparation of the balance sheet, showing the financial condition of the business. Current statements and supporting schedules provide up-to-date information needed by management in running the business.

APPLICATION OF PRINCIPLES

PROBLEM 27 · 1

♦ (This problem is a continuation of Prob. 26 · 2)

INSTRUCTIONS
1. Prepare an adjusted trial balance in the third pair of money columns on the worksheet begun for Art Supply Store in Problem 26 · 2. Total the columns to prove the equality of debits and credits.
2. Record the ending merchandise inventory of $25,400 and complete the worksheet. Save your worksheet for use in Problem 28 · 3.
3. Prepare the income statement for the year 19X2, including the Distribution of Net Profit section at the bottom. Laney and Simms share profits and losses equally.
4. Prepare a statement of partners' equities for the year. There were no additional investments during the year.
5. Prepare a classified balance sheet at Dec. 31, 19X2, in report form.

♦ Following are listed the adjustments for the Varsity Men's Shop.

A. Bad Debts are estimated at 0.3% of sales. (Debit Account 539.)
B. Prepaid Insurance, $65.
C. Depreciation is 10% of office equipment cost.
D. Rent expense for December of $100, payable Dec. 1, has not yet been paid or recorded. (Credit Account 201.)
E. Payroll taxes on $500 of December salaries and wages have not been recorded. Payroll tax rates are: FICA 6%; state unemployment 2.7%; and federal unemployment 0.5%.

The Varsity Men's Shop has the following accounts and trial balance at Dec. 31, 19X1.

ACCT. NO.	ACCOUNT NAME	DEBIT	CREDIT
101	Cash in Bank	$ 2,199.24	
111	Accounts Receivable	5,675.00	
111A	Allowance for Bad Debts		$ 23.00
121	Merchandise Inventory	20,000.00	
131	Prepaid Insurance		
141	Office Equipment	825.00	
141A	Allow. for Depr.—Off. Equip.		220.00
201	Accounts Payable		200.00
226	Payroll Taxes Payable		75.00
301	Fox Investment		12,500.00
302	Fox Drawing	3,000.00	
311	Jacobs Investment		15,500.00
312	Jacobs Drawing	3,600.00	
401	Sales		85,225.00
501	Merchandise Purchases	52,500.00	
521	Rent Expense	1,100.00	
531	Salaries & Wages	6,750.00	
533	Payroll Tax Expense	575.00	
535	Insurance Expense	425.00	
537	Depreciation—Off. Equip.		
539	General Operating Expenses	17,093.76	
	Totals	$113,743.00	$113,743.00

INSTRUCTIONS

1. Set up a typical ten-column worksheet, listing the given accounts and recording the amounts in the first pair of money columns, headed Trial Balance.
2. Record the adjustments in the second pair of money columns, identifying each by letter. On a separate sheet, show the computations of each adjustment.
3. Prepare an adjusted trial balance in the third pair of money columns and total the columns to prove the equality of debits and credits.

4. Record the ending merchandise inventory of $21,000 and complete the worksheet.
5. Prepare the income statement for the year 19X1, including the Distribution of Net Profit section at the bottom. Profits or losses are shared 40% to Fox and 60% to Jacobs.
6. Prepare a statement of partners' equities for the year. (There were no additional investments during the year.)
7. Prepare a balance sheet at Dec. 31, 19X1.

MANAGERIAL CHECKUP

♦ What specific information do financial statements provide that helps management to run the business with better chances for success?

28 ADJUSTING AND CLOSING THE BOOKS

After the worksheet and the financial statements have been completed, the accountant journalizes and posts the adjusting entries and then proceeds to close the books for the period.

JOURNALIZING THE ADJUSTING ENTRIES

In the preparation of the worksheet, the accounts to be adjusted and the amounts involved have already been determined. This information must now be entered in the general journal to complete the written record of events. An entry is required for each of the worksheet adjustments.

For example, the Adjusting Entry A for bad debts now appearing on the worksheet (debit Bad Debts Expense 561, and credit Allowance for Bad Debts 111A) is formally recorded in the general journal as follows.

19	X3	1–3A (Adjustment A)			
Jan.	31	Bad Debts Expense	561	669 15	
		Allowance for Bad Debts . . .	111A		669 15
		To set up estimated bad debt loss for year, based on 0.3% of credit sales of $223,050.			

It is particularly important in recording adjusting entries in the general journal to make complete explanations. The computations made in arriving at the amounts to be debited and credited should be set forth in enough detail so that another person, such as the auditor, can readily understand what was done and why.

The next two adjustments (worksheet Adjustments B and C) were for depreciation, with separate computations for furniture and fixtures and for office equipment. In each case, the adjusting journal entry explanation should refer the reader to the schedule on which the computations were based.

19 X3						
Jan. 31	1–4A (Adjustment B)					
	Depr.–Furn. & Fix.	562	460	00		
	Allow. for Depr.–Furn. & Fix. . .	131A			460	00
	To set up depreciation for year as shown in detail on schedule in file.					
	1–5A (Adjustment C)					
31	Depreciation–Office Equipment . . .	563	215	00		
	Allow. for Depr.–Off. Equip. . . .	132A			215	00
	To set up depreciation for year as shown in detail on schedule in file.					

Each of the remaining worksheet adjustments is journalized in typical fashion as illustrated. The identifying letter used on the worksheet is indicated in each case. (The ending inventory is set up in the closing entries, as explained in Unit 14.)

19 X3						
Jan. 31	1–6A (Adjustment D)					
	Taxes and Licenses	555.8	20	00		
	Property Taxes Payable	235			20	00
	To set up estimated property tax for January.					
	1–7A (Adjustment E)					
31	Janitorial Wages	541	80	00		
	Salaries & Wages Payable	225			80	00
	To record janitorial wages accrued for four days, January 28–31.					
	1–8A (Adjustment F)					
31	Payroll Tax Expense	552	148	20		
	Payroll Taxes Payable	226			148	20
	To accrue payroll taxes on January payroll:					

FICA   6% of $1,900 = $114.00
SUI   1.3% of 1,900 =   24.70
FUTA   .5% of 1,900 =   9.50
Total $148.20

	1–9A (Adjustment G)					
31	Interest Expense	591	26	67		
	Interest Payable	216			26	67
	To accrue interest on trade note payable dated Dec. 2:					

$$\$2,000.00 \times \frac{8}{100} \times \frac{60}{360} = \$26.67$$

	1–10A (Adjustment H)					
31	Store Supplies on Hand	129	110	00		
	Store Suppl. & Exp.	523			110	00
	To record ending inventory of store supplies on hand.					

19 X3		1–11A (Adjustment I)					
Jan. 31		Prepaid Insurance	126	300	00		
		Insurance	536			300	00
		To record unexpired insurance at January 31.					
		1–12A (Adjustment J)					
31		Prepaid Interest Expense	127	40	00		
		Interest Expense	591			40	00
		To record interest prepaid on note payable to bank:					

$$\$12{,}000 \times \frac{6}{100} \times \frac{20}{360} = \$40$$

19 X3		1–13A (Adjustment K)					
Jan. 31		Taxes and Licenses—Stock Tax	555.7	100	00		
		Prepaid Taxes	128			100	00
		To transfer to expense the amount of prepaid stock tax expired in Januray.					
		1–14A (Adjustment L)					
31		Interest Receivable	116	6	00		
		Interest Income	491			6	00
		To accrue interest earned on Robert Jone's note dated Dec. 17 for 45 days to Jan. 31:					

$$\$800 \times \frac{6}{100} \times \frac{45}{360} = \$6$$

		1–15A (Adjustment M)					
31		Sales Tax Payable	231	16	50		
		Miscellaneous Income	493			16	50
		To set up commissions earned on sales tax for January, computed as follows:					

Sales	$27,550.90	
Returns & Allow.	41.25	
Net Sales	$27,509.65	
Balance of Account 231 =	$825.28	$825 28
Gross tax,		
3% × $27,509.65 =	$825.20	
Commission, 2%	16.51	
Net tax due	808.78	
Balance to Account 231	$ 16.50	

POSTING THE ADJUSTING ENTRIES

Next, the adjusting entries must be posted from the general journal to the general ledger accounts. The procedures to be followed are exactly like those described in Unit 15. However, when adjustments are posted to expense analysis accounts, the amounts are recorded in *both* the related individual subdigit expense column and the usual debit or credit column. For example, the postings to the Taxes and Licenses 555 account to record the adjustments for stock taxes and property taxes would be entered on the expense analysis sheet as shown on the next page.

RETAIL LIC. DR. 555.6	STOCK TAX DR. 555.7	PROP. TAX DR. 555.8	DATE	EXPLANATION	POST. REF.	DEBIT	CREDIT	BALANCE	DR. CR.
5 00	1,000 00	201 00	19 X3 Jan 31	Brought Forward	✓			1,206 00	dr.
		20 00	31		1–6A		20 00	1,226 00	dr.
	100 00		31		1–13A		100 00	1,326 00	dr.

When the adjustments have been posted, the ledger account balances should be the same as the amounts shown in the Adjusted Trial Balance section of the worksheet, $1,326.00 in the case of Taxes and Licenses 555.

JOURNALIZING THE CLOSING ENTRIES

The worksheet is also the source of information for the general journal entries required to close the income and expense accounts. Each account balance appearing in the Income Statement columns on the worksheet is closed into the Income and Expense Summary account.

The four-step closing procedure was explained in Unit 15. The steps are as follows:

1. Set up the ending merchandise inventory; debit the income accounts and other credit items to close their balances; and credit the Income and Expense Summary account for the total.
2. Debit the Income and Expense Summary account for the total of the beginning inventory, the expense account balances, and other debit items, crediting each account individually.
3. Transfer the resulting balance in the Income and Expense Summary account to the owners' drawing accounts.
4. Transfer the balance of each owner's drawing account to his equity account as the final step in the closing process.

The information for the first two steps comes directly from the worksheet. The division of profit or loss is shown at the bottom of the income statement. The balances in the drawing accounts are shown on the worksheet also. The process will be traced step by step.

Step 1: Setting Up Inventory and Closing Income Accounts

Refer to the Credit column in the Income Statement section of the completed worksheet on page 447. Six items appear in the column. Each account is debited for the amount shown. This sets up the ending inventory of $66,000 and closes each of the other accounts. Income and Expense Summary 399 is credited for the total being transferred, $400,131.30. This entry is illustrated below.

19	X3	1–16C					
Jan.	31	Merchandise Inventory	121	66,000	00		
		Sales	401	327,550	90		
		Interest Income	491	232	00		
		Miscellaneous Income	493	235	10		
		Purchases Returns &					
		Allow.	511	1,065	00		
		Purchases Discount	512	5,048	30		
		Income and Expense Summary	399			400,131	30
		To close income accounts and set up					
		the ending merchandise inventory.					

Step 2: Closing Expense Accounts

Next, refer to the Debit column under the Income Statement section of the worksheet on page 447. Income and Expense Summary is debited for the column subtotal, $381,152.37. Each listed account is credited for the amount shown in the Debit column. This charges the beginning inventory to the current period's cost of operations and closes all the expense accounts. The entry is illustrated.

19	X3	1–17C					
Jan.	31	Income and Expense Summary . . .	399	381,152	37		
		Merchandise Inventory	121			65,000	00
		Sales Ret. & Allow.	452			6,041	25
		Merchandise Purchases	501			255,350	00
		Freight In	506			3,590	00
		Sales Salaries	521			11,400	00
		Advertising	522			7,370	00
		Store Suppl. & Exp.	523			4,253	75
		Cash Short or Over–	529			72	00
		Delivery Expense	532			3,860	00
		Insurance	536			3,090	00
		Janitorial Wages	541			5,120	00
		Rent	542			3,000	00
		Utilities	543			981	35
		Office Salaries	551			5,400	00
		Payroll Tax Expense	552			1,625	70
		Office Supplies & Expense . . .	553			804	50
		Professional Services	554			775	00
		Taxes & Licenses	555			1,326	00
		Bad Debts Expense	561			669	15
		Depreciation–Furn. & Fix	562			460	00
		Depreciation–Office Equip. . . .	563			215	00
		Interest Expense	591			748	67
		To close the beginning merchandise					
		inventory and expense accounts to					
		Income and Expense Summary.					

Step 3: Closing Income and Expense Summary

The next step is to close the Income and Expense Summary account and divide the net profit according to the profit-sharing agreement of the partners (equal shares in this case). The information for this entry is shown at the bottom of the income statement. Since the business has a net profit of $18,978.93, the Income and Expense Summary account is debited for this amount and the partners' drawing accounts are credited to distribute the profit in the agreed manner. The following entry is required.

19	X3	1–18C			
Jan.	31	Income and Expense Summary . . .	399	18,978 93	
		Ashton Drawing	302		6,326 31
		Barker Drawing	312		6,326 31
		Conrad Drawing	322		6,326 31
		To divide net profit for the year equally among the partners.			

Step 4: Transferring Drawing Accounts

The final step in the closing process is to transfer the balance in each partner's drawing account to his investment account. This may be accomplished in separate entries for each partner or in a single compound entry as in the following illustration.

19	X3	1–19C			
Jan.	31	Ashton Drawing	302	1,526 31	
		Barker Drawing	312	1,526 31	
		Conrad Drawing	322	1,526 31	
		Ashton Investment	301		1,526 31
		Barker Investment	311		1,526 31
		Conrad Investment	321		1,526 31
		To close partners' drawing accounts.			

POSTING THE CLOSING ENTRIES

When the closing entries have been journalized, they are posted to the ledger accounts in the usual manner. Entries are also made in the individual item columns (as circled figures) of expense analysis accounts. The Taxes and Licenses expense analysis ledger sheet illustrates this posting technique.

RETAIL LIC. DR. 555.6	STOCK TAX DR. 555.7	PROP. TAX DR. 555.8	DATE	EXPLANATION	POST. REF.	DEBIT	CREDIT	BALANCE	DR. CR.
			19 X3						
5 00	1,000 00	201 00	Jan. 1	Brought Forward	✓			1,206 00	Dr.
		20 00	31		1–6A	20 00		1,226 00	Dr.
	100 00		31		1–13A	100 00		1,326 00	Dr.
5 00	1,100 00	221 00	31		1–17C		1,326 00	–0–	

TAKING A POSTCLOSING TRIAL BALANCE

When the adjusting and closing entries have all been posted, a postclosing trial balance is taken of the general ledger to prove the accuracy of the books at the end of the period. This trial balance should contain the same asset and liability account balances as are shown in the Balance Sheet section of the worksheet. The owners' equity account balances should be the same as those shown on the balance sheet at the end of the period. The postclosing trial balance of the Ashton & Barker Clothing Store at January 31, 19X3, is illustrated on the next page.

RULING THE ACCOUNTS

When the equality of debits and credits has been demonstrated by the postclosing trial balance, the accounts may be ruled to indicate the point at which the year has ended. In order to use the balance-form ledger sheet for a succeeding year, the income and expense accounts should be ruled with double lines across all columns (including the analysis columns, when these are used) except the Explanation column. This procedure is illustrated.

Taxes and Licenses   No. 555

RETAIL LIC. DR. 555.6	STOCK TAX DR. 555.7	PROP. TAX DR. 555.8	DATE	EXPLANATION	POST. REF.	DEBIT	CREDIT	BALANCE	DR. CR.
			19 X3						
5 00	1,000 00	201 00	Jan. 31	Brought Forward	✓			1,206 00	Dr.
		20 00	31		1–6A	20 00		1,226 00	Dr.
	100 00		31		1–13A	100 00		1,326 00	Dr.
5 00	1,100 00	221 00	31		1–17C		1,326 00	–0–	

Many accountants prefer to set up new ledger account sheets for each income and expense item each year, filing the prior year's ledger sheets in a permanent file.

ASHTON & BARKER CLOTHING STORE
Postclosing Trial Balance
January 31, 19X3

ACCT. NO.	ACCOUNT TITLE	DEBIT	CREDIT
101	Cash in Bank	$ 14,305.89	
105	Petty Cash	25.00	
106	Change Funds	100.00	
111	Accounts Receivable	23,067.35	
111A	Allowance for Bad Debts		$ 676.21
112	Notes Receivable	800.00	
116	Interest Receivable	6.00	
121	Merchandise Inventory	66,000.00	
126	Prepaid Insurance	300.00	
127	Prepaid Interest Expense	40.00	
128	Prepaid Taxes	500.00	
129	Store Supplies on Hand	110.00	
131	Furniture & Fixtures	4,600.00	
131A	Allowance for Depr.–Furn. & Fix.		820.00
132	Office Equipment	2,750.00	
132A	Allowance for Depr.–Office Equip.		430.00
201	Accounts Payable		5,190.25
202	Notes Payable–Trade		2,000.00
211	Notes Payable–Bank		12,000.00
216	Interest Payable		26.67
221	Employee Deductions–FICA Taxes		109.20
222	Employee Deductions–Income Tax WH		216.00
225	Salaries & Wages Payable		80.00
226	Payroll Taxes Payable		148.20
231	Sales Tax Payable		808.78
235	Property Taxes Payable		20.00
301	Ashton Investment		30,526.31
311	Barker Investment		29,526.31
321	Conrad Investment		30,026.31
	Totals	$112,604.24	$112,604.24

No end-of-period ruling is necessary for balance sheet accounts. However, if the balance sheet accounts are to be ruled, this procedure should be followed. Enter the date and "Carried Forward" on the next line. On the same line, enter the ending balance in the opposite money column (debit balance in Credit column, credit balance in Debit column). Draw single lines across Debit and Credit columns and total to prove equality. Draw double lines across the Date column, Posting Reference column, and all three amount columns. Bring the balance down, entering the new period date and "Brought Forward" on the next line and the balance amount in the appropriate column, Debit or Credit, and in the Balance column. Put a check mark in the Posting Reference column on both lines—Carried Forward and Brought Forward—to show this is not a posted amount. The Cash in Bank account illustrates this treatment. (This procedure is obviously rather cumbersome and is not normally used.)

When the accounts have been ruled, the accounting cycle for the current period is essentially completed. However, the experienced accountant knows that certain adjustments made at the end of the previous period

DATE		EXPLANATION	POST. REF.	DEBIT		CREDIT		BALANCE		DR. CR.
19	X3									
Jan.	1	Brought Forward	√	13,977	29			13,977	29	Dr.
	31		CR-2	34,218	12			48,195	41	Dr.
	31		CD-2			33,889	52	14,305	89	Dr.
	31	Carried Forward	√			14,305	89	–0–		
				48,195	41	48,195	41			
19	X3									
Feb.	1	Brought Forward	√	14,305	89			14,305	89	Dr.

may lead to recording difficulties in the new cycle. Adjusting Entry L (page 456) provides a good illustration of a potentially time-consuming problem ahead.

THE NEED FOR REVERSALS

On the worksheet and later in the general journal, Interest Receivable was debited for $6 and Interest Income was credited to record 45 days' interest earned but not yet collected on Robert Jones's 60-day, 6% note receivable for $800 due February 15.

When this note is collected at maturity, a total of $808 ($800 principal plus $8 interest) will be received. A busy cashier might accidentally overlook the fact that $6 of the interest was accrued as revenue of the prior period by an adjusting entry. Even if the cashier recognizes the item as related to Adjusting Entry L, he may not know how to prorate or subdivide the $8 between the two periods without tracing the transaction back into the previous year's records. After determining the proper split, he would have to make a compound entry so that the debit to Cash for $808 is offset by three credits—$800 to Notes Receivable; $6 to Interest Receivable; and $2 to Interest Income.

Fortunately, there is a much simpler technique for handling this type of situation. Potential complications never occur, because a *readjusting* or *reversing* entry is made before the transactions of the new period are recorded.

An entry made on February 1 debiting Interest Income and crediting Interest Receivable for $6 guards against any cashier's oversight, eliminates the need for checking old records, and makes the subdivision of the interest amount unnecessary when note and interest are collected.

19	X3	2-1R (Reversing)					
Feb.	1	Interest Income	491	6	00		
		Interest Receivable	116			6	00
		To reverse Adjusting Entry L made January 31.					

After the reversing entry has been posted, the asset, Interest Receivable, is closed out and the debit of $6 in the Interest Income account will be waiting to offset the credit of $8 to be posted on February 15 when the note and interest are collected. At that time, the cashier will simply record the entire $8 amount as a credit to Interest Income. Then the debit offset of $6 already in the account will have the effect of a necessary partial counterbalance. The net difference of $2 represents the amount of interest income actually earned during February. Study the two accounts illustrated, showing the reversing entry posted and the collection of interest on February 15 recorded.

Interest Receivable   **No. 116**

DATE	EXPLANATION	POST. REF.	DEBIT	CREDIT	BALANCE	DR. CR.
19 X3						
Jan. 31		1-13A	6 00		6 00	Dr.
Feb. 1		2-1R		6 00	−0−	

Interest Income   **No. 491**

DATE	EXPLANATION	POST. REF.	DEBIT	CREDIT	BALANCE	DR. CR.
19 X3						
Feb. 1		2-1R	6 00		6 00	Dr.
15	On collection of note	CR-1		8 00	2 00	Cr.

Notice that the readjustment entry (2-1R) was simply a reversal of the related adjusting entry (1-13A). This is why readjustment or readjusting entries are commonly called *reversing entries*.

ITEMS REQUIRING REVERSALS

Items to be reversed can be determined by following a few simple rules.

1. *Only adjusting entries can possibly be involved,* so that only the adjusting entries made at the end of the last period need be considered. (Ending inventory is immediately excluded as a possibility because it is set up as part of a closing entry.)
2. Not all adjusting entries require reversal. *Only those adjusting entries that put balances in new asset or new liability accounts need to be reversed.* ("New" in this situation, refers to an asset or liability account that does not contain a balance when the trial balance is taken and does not normally have a balance during the year.)

Refer to the completed worksheet (pages 446–447) or, better still, to the adjusting journal entries for the period just ended (see pages 454–456).

Entry A

Entry A involved a debit to Bad Debts Expense and a credit to Allowance for Bad Debts. Neither of these items is a new asset or a new liability. Hence, under Rule 2, this entry requires no readjustment.

Entries B and C

The two entries, B and C, called for debits to depreciation expense accounts and credits to allowance for depreciation accounts. No "new" assets or liabilities are involved; hence, no readjustment is necessary.

Entry D

Adjustment D debited Taxes and Licenses and credited Property Taxes Payable. Property Taxes Payable is a liability and since no balance was shown for this account in the trial balance, a readjustment seems to be needed. However, checking the ledger account indicates that no reversal is actually necessary because of an unusual timing element. Property Taxes Payable is actually an old and continuing liability. For eleven months of the year, this account has an end-of-month balance in a trial balance listing as the amount of tax payable builds up. However, in December, the annual tax is paid and for a brief interval the account is clear. An experienced accountant recognizes the exceptional condition of this account in January and, therefore, does not make a reversing entry.

Entry E

Adjustment E debited Janitorial Wages and credited Salaries and Wages Payable for $80 to recognize the unpaid Monday through Thursday wages. On Friday, when the janitor's paycheck is issued, the $100 payment would normally require analysis and proration between the liability ($80) account at January 31 and the expense account for February ($20). Again, a reversing entry such as Entry 2-2R will eliminate the need to analyze and prorate.

19 X3		2–2R				
Feb. 1	Salaries and Wages Payable		225	80 00		
	Janitorial Wages		541		80 00	
	To reverse Adjusting Entry (E) made January 31.					

The debit posting of $80 to the Salaries and Wages account cancels the liability. The $80 credit set up in the Janitorial Wages expense account will offset the $100 debit that will be posted when the full week's wages are paid on February 1. The net effect in the expense account is then $100 − $80, or a net charge of $20 to the operations of the new period. This amount correctly represents the one day's wages earned by the janitor in February.

Salaries and Wages Payable — No. 225

DATE	EXPLANATION	POST. REF.	DEBIT	CREDIT	BALANCE	DR. CR.
19 X3 Jan. 31		1-7A		80 00	80 00	Cr.
Feb. 1		2-2R	80 00		–0–	

Janitorial Wages — No. 541

DATE	EXPLANATION	POST. REF.	DEBIT	CREDIT	BALANCE	DR. CR.
19 X3 Jan. 18		VR-XX	100 00		4,940 00	Dr.
25		VR-XX	100 00		5,040 00	Dr.
31		1-7A	80 00		5,120 00	Dr.
31		1-17C		5,120 00	–0–	
Feb. 1		2-2R		80 00	80 00	Cr.
1		VR-XX	100 00		20 00	Dr.

Entry F

Payroll Tax Expense was debited and Payroll Taxes Payable was credited in adjusting entry F. The latter account is a new liability (no amount shown on the trial balance or in the ledger account during the year) and the adjustment is reversed as follows.

19 X3		2–3R				
Feb. 1	Payroll Taxes Payable		226	148 20		
	Payroll Tax Expense		552		148 20	
	To reverse Adjusting Entry F made January 31.					

Entry G

Interest expense on the trade note payable for 60 days was recorded by a debit to Interest Expense and a credit to Interest Payable. The Interest Payable account represents a new liability and, therefore, the entry is reversed as indicated in the illustration.

19	X3								
Feb.	1	Interest Payable	2–4R	216		26	67		
		Interest Expense		591				26	67
		To reverse Adjusting Entry G made							
		January 31.							

Entry H

The Store Supplies on Hand account was debited and the Store Supplies and Expense account was credited in entry H. The asset account is new, and for this reason the adjusting entry that was used to set it up is reversed as illustrated.

19	X3								
Feb.	1	Store Supplies & Expense	2–5R	523		110	00		
		Store Supplies on Hand		129				110	00
		To reverse Adjusting Entry H made							
		January 31.							

Entry I

Unexpired insurance was recognized in Adjustment I by a debit to a new asset account, Prepaid Insurance, with an offsetting credit to the insurance expense account. The adjusting entry is reversed as shown below.

19	X3								
Feb.	1	Insurance	2–6R	536		300	00		
		Prepaid Insurance		126				300	00
		To reverse Adjusting Entry I made							
		January 31.							

Entry J

Interest prepaid on the note payable to the bank was set up in a new asset account called Prepaid Interest Expense and Interest Expense was credited. Here again, because a new asset account is involved, the adjusting entry is reversed as follows.

19	X3	2-7R			40	00		
Feb.	1	Interest Expense	591		40	00		
		Prepaid Interest Expense	127				40	00
		To reverse Adjusting Entry J made						
		January 31.						

Entry K

Taxes and Licenses was debited and Prepaid Taxes was credited for the January share of the prepaid stock tax. No new asset or new liability account is involved here and no readjustment is made.

Entry L

Entry L, debiting Interest Receivable and crediting Interest Income, was used as the opening example of the readjustment process. The entry clearly qualifies for reversing because it is an adjusting entry, and it involves a new asset—Interest Receivable (Entry 2-1R, page 462).

Entry M

Sales Tax Payable was debited and Miscellaneous Income was credited. Sales Tax Payable is a liability account, but it is one that already had a balance (see original trial balance), which this entry reduces. Since no new liability is set up, no readjustment is required.

POSTING THE READJUSTING ENTRIES

The readjusting entries should be posted as soon as they have been journalized, in order to clear the way for recording the transactions of the new period. The postings will be carried out like those for accrued interest on notes receivable and accrued janitorial wages previously illustrated.

After the reversing entries have been posted, the following two types of changes will have taken place:

1. The balances of the new assets and new liabilities that were created by adjusting entries have now been closed.
2. Expense and income accounts involved in the readjustment process now contain offset figures set up in advance so that certain later postings will not have to be analyzed and subdivided.

The illustration previously given for posting reversing entries involved balance-type ledger accounts. If standard T accounts are used, the reversing entries will be entered after the accounts have been balanced and ruled as shown in the illustration below for reversing the adjustment made for accrued janitorial wages on January 31.

Salaries and Wages Payable　　　　　　　　　　　　　　**No. 225**

DATE		EXPLANATION	POST. REF.	DEBIT		DATE		EXPLANATION	POST. REF.	CREDIT	
19	X3					19	X3				
Feb.	1		2-2R	80	00	Jan.	31		1-7A	80	00

Janitorial Wages　　　　　　　　　　　　　　**No. 541**

DATE		EXPLANATION	POST. REF.	DEBIT		DATE		EXPLANATION	POST. REF.	CREDIT	
19	X3					19	X3				
Jan.	18	Brought Forward	√	4,840	00	Jan.	31		1-17C	5,120	00
	18		VR-XX	100	00						
	25		VR-XX	100	00						
				5,040	*00*						
	31		1-7A	80	00						
				5,120	*00*						
				5,120	00					5,120	00
Feb.	1		VR-XX	100	00	Feb.	1		2-2R	80	00
		20.00									

◆　◆　◆

PRINCIPLES AND PROCEDURES

When the year-end worksheet and financial statements have been completed, adjusting and closing entries are made in the general journal and posted to the general ledger. These entries come from the appropriate columns on the worksheet.

With the adjusting entries journalized and posted, the closing entries are prepared from the Income Statement columns of the worksheet. When the closing entries have been posted, the accuracy of the work is verified by taking a postclosing trial balance of the general ledger.

Ledger accounts may be ruled at the end of the year and used in succeeding years. However, some accountants prefer to start the new year's income and expense records on new sheets and file the old account sheets for future reference.

At the beginning of each new accounting period, certain of the adjusting entries of the preceding period must be reversed or readjusted, in order to avoid the necessity of analyzing future entries involving carry-over items.

Only adjusting entries need be considered in the readjusting process. Furthermore, only those adjusting entries that set up new asset or new liability accounts should be readjusted. The accountant refers to the Adjustments columns in the worksheet or to the adjusting entries in the general journal, checking the entries one at a time to spot the items that require readjustments.

MANAGERIAL IMPLICATIONS

Proper adjusting and closing entries are necessary so that all items of income and expense are recorded or matched in the proper period.

Management must be concerned with the adjusting and closing process to ensure that the records are adequate and correct. Explanations must be sufficiently informative to facilitate future reference. For example, future audits and reviews of the records are greatly expedited by good adjusting and closing procedures. Also, the sooner the books are closed for the old period, the sooner the recording for the new period can begin. Any significant lag between a transaction and the recording of it may lead to serious consequences.

The reversing process has two managerial implications. First, it saves time and promotes efficiency by eliminating the necessity of analyzing future income and expense transactions to see which portion applies to past periods and which portion to the period in which the transaction occurred. Second, it helps to make sure that income and expenses are properly matched in the period to which they apply, thus improving the accuracy and meaningfulness of financial statements when rendered.

APPLICATION OF PRINCIPLES

PROBLEM 28 · 1

The following information for Corner Clothing Store is given as of Dec. 31, 19X1.

a. Unpaid wages on Dec. 31 total $700. These wages have not yet been recorded.
b. The balance of the Prepaid Insurance account is $600. This represents the unexpired insurance premium as of Jan. 1, 19X1, on a 3-year insurance policy purchased for $720 on July 1, 19X0.
c. Interest accrued on notes payable totals $85.

d. The Supplies Expense account shows a balance of $1,560. However, an actual physical count shows part of these supplies, costing $156.50, are still on hand on Dec. 31.

e. Depreciation on buildings totals $1,000 for the year.

f. The Rent Expense account balance is $1,300. This includes $100 rent paid in advance for January 19X2.

g. Employer's FICA taxes of 6% on $500 of the accrued wages must be recorded. None of the unpaid wages is subject to unemployment taxes.

INSTRUCTIONS

1. Give the adjusting entry required on Dec. 31, 19X1, for each of the given cases. (Begin with Entry 12-10A. Omit account numbers.)

2. In general journal form, give the reversing or readjusting entries necessary on Jan. 1, 19X2.

PROBLEM 28 · 2

♦ The completed worksheet for Berry Service Company for the year ended Dec. 31, 19X1, is shown on the following page.

INSTRUCTIONS

1. Journalize the adjusting journal entries for Dec. 31. (Begin with Entry No. 12-15A.) Omit explanations.

2. Journalize the closing entries on Dec. 31. (Income and Expense Summary account is No. 399.) Omit explanations.

3. Journalize the necessary reversing entries on Jan. 1, 19X2. Omit explanations.

PROBLEM 28 · 3

♦ (This problem is a continuation of Prob. 27 · 1.)

INSTRUCTIONS

Refer to the worksheet for Art Supply Store prepared in Prob. 27 · 1 and carry out the following steps.

1. Open a general ledger and enter the Dec. 31, 19X1, balance for each account given in the trial balance. Write the word ''balance'' in the Explanation column and place a check mark in the Posting Reference column in each case to show that the amount was not posted from a journal. Also set up an account for Income and Expense Summary 399.

2. Journalize the adjusting and closing entries. (Begin with Entry 12-14A.) Omit explanations.

3. Post the adjusting and closing entries to the ledger accounts.

4. Prepare a postclosing trial balance of the general ledger.

BERRY SERVICE COMPANY
Worksheet
Year Ended December 31, 19X1

ACCT. NO.	ACCOUNT NAME	TRIAL BALANCE DR.	TRIAL BALANCE CR.	ADJUSTMENTS DR.	ADJUSTMENTS CR.	ADJUSTED TRIAL BALANCE DR.	ADJUSTED TRIAL BALANCE CR.	INCOME STATEMENT DR.	INCOME STATEMENT CR.	BALANCE SHEET DR.	BALANCE SHEET CR.
101	Cash	4,800 00				4,800 00				4,800 00	
111	Accts. Rec.	6,600 00				6,600 00				6,600 00	
111A	Allow. for Bad Debts		150 00		(F) 800 00		950 00				950 00
121	Mdse. Inv.	15,500 00				15,500 00		15,500 00	17,000 00	17,000 00	
131	Prepaid Insur.	380 00			(A) 130 00	250 00				250 00	
132	Supplies	1,550 00			(B) 980 00	570 00				570 00	
141	Equipment	17,000 00				17,000 00				17,000 00	
141A	Allow. for Depr.—Equipment		6,900 00		(C) 1,700 00		8,600 00				8,600 00
201	Accts. Payable		3,400 00				3,400 00				3,400 00
202	Salaries & Wages Payable				(D) 800 00		800 00				800 00
203	Payroll Taxes Payable		190 00		(E) 72 00		262 00				262 00
301	Berry Investment		29,000 00				29,000 00				29,000 00
302	Berry Drawing	9,600 00				9,600 00				9,600 00	
401	Sales		159,000 00				159,000 00		159,000 00		
501	Purchases	102,300 00				102,300 00		102,300 00			
531	Salaries & Wages	22,600 00		(D) 800 00		23,400 00		23,400 00			
532	Payroll Tax Exp.	1,810 00		(E) 72 00		1,882 00		1,882 00			
533	Bad Debts Exp.			(F) 800 00		800 00		800 00			
534	Supplies Used			(B) 980 00		980 00		980 00			
535	Ins. Expense			(A) 130 00		130 00		130 00			
537	Depr.—Equipment			(C) 1,700 00		1,700 00		1,700 00			
538	Other Expenses	16,500 00				16,500 00		16,500 00			
		198,640 00	198,640 00	4,482 00	4,482 00	202,012 00	202,012 00	163,192 00	176,000 00	55,820 00	43,012 00
	Net Profit							12,808 00			12,808 00
								176,000 00	176,000 00	55,820 00	55,820 00

5. Rule the income and expense accounts. Do not rule the balance sheet accounts.
6. Record in general journal form the readjusting or reversing entries necessary on Jan. 1, 19X2. (Reverse the Rent Expense adjustment, since Accounts Payable was credited only to simplify Prob. 26 • 2.) Omit explanations.
7. Post these reversing entries to the ledger accounts.

MANAGERIAL CHECKUPS

◆   Why must management be concerned about the possibility of a lag between the completion of a transaction and the recording of it?

◆   Why should management insist that a firm's accountant include a complete explanation with each adjusting entry?

◆   How do reversing entries minimize confusion and save recording time and effort in a new accounting period?

INTEGRATED PRACTICAL APPLICATION— THE ACCRUAL BASIS OF ACCOUNTING

In the past several units you learned how to make adjustments so that the books will reflect the accrual basis of accounting. You also learned how the worksheet for Ashton & Barker was completed, adjusting entries and closing entries prepared, financial statements drawn up, and readjusting entries made. This activity is designed to give you practical experience in carrying out the procedures that you have learned in these units.

THE TRIAL BALANCE

The trial balance of the Ashton & Barker Clothing Store on January 31, 19X4, at the end of the third year of operations of the business, is illustrated on the following page.

Enter this trial balance in the first set of columns of a 10-column worksheet with headings identical to those on the worksheet shown on pages 448 and 449.

ENTERING ADJUSTMENTS

Enter the adjustments on the worksheet and extend the amounts to the Adjusted Trial Balance section. Data needed for the adjustments are as follows:

- Entry A—Bad Debts Expense is estimated at 0.3% of credit sales. The credit sales are shown by the records to be $253,200.
- Entry B—Depreciation of Furniture and Fixtures is $460.
- Entry C—Depreciation of Office Equipment is $215.
- Entry D—Estimated property taxes for the calendar year 19X4 are $264. One-twelfth of this amount should be accrued as January 19X4 taxes.
- Entry E—Accrued janitorial wages to be recorded total $60.
- Entry F—Employer's payroll taxes to be accrued for January total $153.97.
- Entry G—Interest must be accrued on a trade note payable with a face value of $2,000. This 6% note is dated Dec. 20, 19X3, and has accrued interest for 42 days. The other trade notes payable are noninterest bearing.
- Entry H—An inventory of store supplies on hand shows $122 unused.

ASHTON & BARKER CLOTHING STORE
Trial Balance
January 31, 19X4

ACCT. NO.	ACCOUNT NAME	DEBIT	CREDIT
101	Cash in Bank	$ 14,110.39	
105	Petty Cash	25.00	
106	Change Funds	100.00	
111	Accounts Receivable	24,520.00	
111A	Allowance for Bad Debts		24.00
112	Notes Receivable	1,900.00	
113	Notes Receivable Discounted		
116	Interest Receivable		
121	Merchandise Inventory	66,000.00	
126	Prepaid Insurance		
127	Prepaid Interest		
128	Prepaid Taxes	600.00	
129	Store Supplies on Hand		
131	Furniture & Fixtures	4,600.00	
131A	Allowance for Depr.–Furn. & Fix.		$ 820.00
132	Office Equipment	2,750.00	
132A	Allowance for Depr.–Office Equip.		430.00
201	Accounts Payable		5,205.00
202	Notes Payable–Trade		2,150.00
211	Notes Payable–Bank		9,600.00
216	Interest Payable		
221	Employee Deductions–FICA Taxes		114.66
222	Employee Deductions–Income Tax WH		286.65
225	Salaries and Wages Payable		
226	Payroll Taxes Payable		
231	Sales Tax Payable		867.50
235	Property Taxes Payable		
301	Ashton Investment		30,526.31
302	Ashton Drawing	5,000.00	
311	Barker Investment		29,526.31
312	Barker Drawing	5,000.00	
321	Conrad Investment		30,026.31
322	Conrad Drawing	5,000.00	
401	Sales		353,754.97
452	Sales Returns & Allowances	6,721.35	
491	Interest Income		200.00
493	Miscellaneous Income		30.00
501	Merchandise Purchases	275,060.90	
506	Freight In	3,775.00	
511	Purchases Returns & Allowances		1,150.00
512	Purchases Discount		5,195.00
521	Sales Salaries	11,970.00	
522	Advertising	7,650.00	
523	Store Supplies & Expense	6,456.00	
529	Cash Short or Over	51.00	
532	Delivery Expense	4,162.27	
536	Insurance Expense	3,960.00	
541	Janitorial Wages	5,292.00	
542	Rent	3,000.00	
543	Utilities	1,169.85	
551	Office Salaries	5,670.00	
552	Employer's Payroll Tax Expense	1,527.95	
553	Office Supplies & Expense	955.00	
554	Professional Services	875.00	
555	Taxes & Licenses	1,208.00	
561	Bad Debts Expense		
562	Depreciation–Furn. & Fix.		
563	Depreciation–Office Equip.		
591	Interest Expense	749.00	
	Totals	$469,882.71	$469,882.71

- Entry I—An analysis of insurance policies reveals that there is prepaid insurance totaling $305.
- Entry J—Prepaid interest on the bank note payable must be recorded. This 60-day $9,600 note is due on Feb. 25, 19X4. It was discounted at 6% on Dec. 27, 19X3, and the discount of $96 was charged to interest expense. Record the prepaid interest for 25 days.
- Entry K—The Prepaid Taxes 128 account represents the $600 stock taxes for the period Jan. 1, 19X4, through June 30, 19X4, paid in advance in December 19X3. The amount to be transferred to expense in January is $100.
- Entry L—Interest must be accrued on one 6%, $1,600 note receivable dated Jan. 1, 19X4. The other notes receivable are noninterest bearing.
- Entry M—An analysis reveals net taxable sales for January of $28,916.70, subject to the 3% state sales tax. Ashton & Barker is entitled to a commission of 2% on the tax due. Record this commission by debiting Sales Tax Payable 231 and crediting Miscellaneous Income 493.

COMPLETING THE WORKSHEET

Complete the worksheet. The January 31, 19X4 merchandise inventory is $67,500. The January 31, 19X3 inventory was $66,000.

PREPARING THE FINANCIAL STATEMENTS

Prepare the following financial statements:

1. Classified income statement for the year, similar to that on page 448 with the distribution of net profit or loss at the bottom. (Partners share profits and losses equally.)
2. Statement of partners' equities.
3. Balance sheet at January 31, 19X4.

COMPLETING THE CYCLE

Then complete the remaining steps in the accounting cycle:

1. Journalize the adjusting entries (start with Entry 1-21A).
2. Journalize the closing entries.
3. Journalize the readjusting or reversing entries that would be necessary on February 1, 19X4.

(Note: You are not required by these instructions to open ledger accounts and post to them. Your instructor may, however, require that you do so.)

APPLICATION OF PRINCIPLES: ALTERNATE PROBLEMS

The problems in this unit are supplementary to those at the end of Units 1–28. They are numbered to correspond with individual units. In working these problems, the following will be needed: two-column, four-column, and fourteen-column paper with item space, and paper with ledger ruling. Headings and account names and numbers should be entered on these forms as needed, to conform as nearly as possible with examples given in the textbook units.

PROBLEM 1 · 1A

♦ The Fleet Messenger Service has just been established, and the owner makes a cash deposit of $5,000 in the Valley State Bank for exclusive use in the business. Analyze and in equation form record changes in property, claims of creditors, and the owner's equity for the following transactions. (Use plus, minus, and equal signs.)

a. Initial investment of $5,000 in cash.
b. Acquired equipment for $3,000 in cash.
c. Obtained additional equipment costing $1,000 on credit.
d. Paid $500 in cash to creditors.
e. Additional investment by owner, $1,500.

PROBLEM 1 · 2A

♦ Henry Marks is the sole owner of the Appliance Repair Shop. From the following figures, prepare a balance sheet (use four-column analysis paper) dated December 31, 19X1.

Cash	$4,000
Equipment	3,500
Truck	3,000
Accounts Payable	1,500
Marks Investment	9,000

PROBLEM 1 · 3A

♦ Jill Simpson owns the Towne Decorating Service, an interior decorating business. At the beginning of the month, the books showed the following assets, liabilities, and owner's equity:

Cash	$2,000
Accounts Receivable	1,000
Furniture and Fixtures	1,000
Auto	2,000
Accounts Payable	700
Simpson Investment	4,300
Income	3,000
Expense	2,000

Set up an equation form using the given balances, then record the effects of the following transactions in the equation. (Use plus, minus, and equal signs.) Insert new balances after each transaction has been recorded, and prove the equality of the two sides of the final equation on a separate sheet of paper.

a. Performed services worth $700 for cash.
b. Paid $50 in cash for supplies used.
c. Received $500 in cash from credit customers.
d. Paid $100 in cash for telephone services.
e. Sent $400 check in part payment of amount due creditors.
f. Paid salaries $1,000, in cash.
g. Paid utilities bill $40 by check.
h. Rendered services on credit, $2,000.
i. Paid $60 in cash for auto repairs expense.
j. Received $500 in cash for services performed.

PROBLEM 1 · 4A

♦ The following equations show the transactions that took place during the month of March 19X2 in the operations of the Sparkle Window Cleaning Service, owned by Mary Haldie. Analyze each transaction carefully. Then prepare an income statement for the month (list expenses in detail) and a balance sheet at Mar. 31, 19X2. Use two-column analysis paper for the income statement and four-column paper for the balance sheet.

	ASSETS				=	LIABILITIES			+	OWNER'S EQUITY		
	CASH	+ TRUCK	+ EQUIP.	+ ACCTS. REC.	=	ACCTS. PAY.	+ HALDIE INVEST.	+		INC.	−	EXP.
Balances, Mar. 1	700	+ 2,000	+ 300	+ 500	=	300	+ 3,200	+		−0−	−	−0−
Paid rent	− 70										−	70
New balances	630	+ 2,000	+ 300	+ 500	=	300	+ 3,200	+		−0−	−	70
Services on credit				+ 700				+		700		
New balances	630	+ 2,000	+ 300	+ 1,200	=	300	+ 3,200	+		700	−	70
Paid for supplies used	− 50										−	50
New balances	580	+ 2,000	+ 300	+ 1,200	=	300	+ 3,200	+		700	−	120
Services for cash	1,000							+		1,000		
New balances	1,580	+ 2,000	+ 300	+ 1,200	=	300	+ 3,200	+		1,700	−	120
Paid salaries	− 1,000										−	1,000
New balances	580	+ 2,000	+ 300	+ 1,200	=	300	+ 3,200	+		1,700	−	1,120
Paid auto repair	− 75										−	75
New balances	505	+ 2,000	+ 300	+ 1,200	=	300	+ 3,200	+		1,700	−	1,195

PROBLEM 2 · 1A

◆ The following transactions are unrelated. Set up T accounts for the accounts indicated in parentheses. Analyze each transaction carefully and record the amounts in the proper positions in the T accounts relating to that transaction. Use plus and minus signs to indicate increases and decreases in each account.

a. Dale invested $7,500 cash in the business. (Cash and Dale Investment.)
b. Purchased office furniture for $2,000 cash. (Office Furniture and Cash.)
c. Bought electronic calculator for $450; payment due in 30 days. (Office Equipment and Accounts Payable.)
d. Acquired used car for business purposes, $1,000 cash. (Automobile and Cash.)
e. Dale turned over his personal library of technical accounting and tax books, valued at $300. (Library Books and Dale Investment.)
f. Bought new typewriter for $400; payment due in 60 days. (Office Equipment and Accounts Payable.)
g. Paid $450 to cover amount owed on calculator. (Accounts Payable and Cash.)

Analyze each of the following unrelated transactions and record the
♦ effects in a pair of T accounts relating to the transaction. Enter the correct heading of each account. Record the increases and decreases by using plus and minus signs before the amounts.

a. An owner, L. Fiber, made an additional investment of $5,000 in cash.
b. A business acquired $2,500 worth of equipment for cash.
c. A firm sold some surplus office furniture for $200 cash.
d. A firm purchased a large outdoor sign for $750, to be paid in 60 days.
e. A company pays $1,000 to creditors who previously supplied equipment on credit.
f. A business owner withdraws $1,000 of his original investment in cash.
g. A firm buys a delivery truck for $4,000 cash.
h. A check for $250 is sent to a supplier in partial payment of open account balance.

PROBLEM 2 · 3A

Analyze each of the following unrelated income and expense transactions
♦ and record the effects in a pair of T accounts relating to the transaction.
Enter the correct heading of each account and indicate the increases and decreases by using plus and minus signs before the amounts.

a. Sold services for cash, $600.
b. Paid rent for month, $200.
c. Sold additional services on credit, $1,000, on credit.
d. Paid monthly utility bill $50, cash.
e. Received $100 worth of supplies for immediate use; payment due in 30 days.
f. Paid office salaries $1,000.
g. Sold services for cash, $1,500.
h. Collected $400 from credit customers.
i. Received $5 cash refund for overcharge on utility bill.
j. Paid monthly telephone bill, $25 in cash.
k. Collected $100 from accounts receivable.
l. Received $15 credit as an adjustment due to damaged supplies previously received.
m. Paid balance due on supplies previously purchased for credit.
n. Sold additional services on credit, $500.

PROBLEM 2 · 4A

Analyze the transactions of Richard Miller, architect, listed here, and
♦ record each in appropriate T accounts, using the following accounts
(the numbers have been intentionally omitted). Indicate the increases and

ALTERNATE PROBLEMS

479

decreases by using plus and minus signs before the amounts. Key each entry to the alphabetical symbol identifying each transaction.

ASSETS
Cash
Accounts Receivable
Office Furniture
Office Equipment

LIABILITIES
Accounts Payable

OWNER'S EQUITY
Miller Investment

INCOME
Income from Services

EXPENSES
Rent Expense
Utilities Expense
Salaries
Telephone Expense
Miscellaneous Expense

a. Miller invested $7,000 cash to establish his architect practice.
b. Paid rent on office for one month, $200.
c. Bought office furniture for $1,500 in cash.
d. Received $400 in cash for services rendered.
e. Paid monthly telephone bill, $35.
f. Sold $300 worth of services on credit.
g. Purchased typewriter for $250, terms $100 cash; balance due in 30 days.
h. Received bill for $65 for cleaning office windows and polishing floors and woodwork, payment due in 30 days.
i. Received $100 from accounts receivable.
j. Acquired additional chairs for office $150, terms 30 days.
k. Paid salaries for month, $400.
l. Issued check for $75 in partial payment of amount owing for office chairs.
m. Received $700 cash for services rendered.
n. Paid utility bill by check, $20.
o. Performed $900 worth of services on credit.
p. Collected $500 from accounts receivable.
q. Paid bill for office cleaning service previously recorded, $65.
r. Received and paid bill from Eddy's Duplicating Service for photocopy work performed during month, $30.

PROBLEM 2 · 5A

♦ Using the figures accumulated in the T accounts for Prob. 2 · 4A, prepare an income statement (use two-column analysis paper) and a balance sheet (use four-column analysis paper). Assume that the transactions represent the activities for the month ended June 30, 19XX.

PROBLEM 3 · 1A

♦ The following listed transactions relate to the operation of City Building Maintenance for October 19X1. Analyze each transaction and record the effects in general journal form. Choose your account titles from the following chart of accounts. Be sure to number the journal Page 1 and put the year at the top of the date column.

ASSETS
101   Cash
111   Accounts Receivable
141   Truck

LIABILITIES
201   Accounts Payable

OWNER'S EQUITY
301   Jamison Investment

EXPENSES
503   Cleaning Supplies Used
504   Equipment Rental Expense
505   Telephone Expense
506   Truck Expense
511   Salary Expense
516   Office Rental Expense
522   Utilities Expense

OCT.
 1   Paid October office rent, $100.
 3   Paid equipment rental expense, $250.
 5   Sold services for cash, $500.
 6   Paid telephone bill, $30.
 9   Sold services on credit, $1,400.
14   Received bill for repairs to truck, $50; paid in cash.
15   Paid semimonthly salaries, $1,000.
18   Collected $300 from credit customers.
21   Paid for supplies used, $100 cash.
24   Sold services on credit, $300.
25   Received invoice for cleaning supplies used, $10, terms 30 days.
26   Received $200 in cash from accounts receivable.
27   Performed $600 worth of services for cash.
28   Received $10 cash refund due to overcharge on telephone bill.
29   Paid utilities bill for October, $50.
30   Paid semimonthly salaries, $1,000.
31   Performed $800 worth of services on credit.
31   Received bill for additional truck repairs, $100, due in 30 days.

PROBLEM 3 · 2A

Eddy Gaertner has opened a duplicating and mailing service in the Union Bank Building. She plans to use the chart of accounts reproduced below. The financial activities of the business during the first month of operations, July 19X1, are also listed.

ASSETS
101   Cash
111   Accounts Receivable
141   Office Equipment

LIABILITIES
201   Accounts Payable

OWNER'S EQUITY
301   Gaertner Investment

INCOME
401   Income from Services

EXPENSES

504	Telephone Expense	516	Rent Expense
506	Advertising Expense	517	Equipment Expense
507	Salary Expense	521	Supplies Used

JULY

1   Ms. Gaertner invested $3,000 in the business, depositing the money in new checking account in the name of Handy Duplicating and Mailing Company.

2   Paid $100 office rent by check.

3   Bought duplicating equipment $3,000, paying $1,000 at once; balance payable in 30 days.

4   Paid advertising bill, $100, in cash.

5   Performed services for cash, $350.

5   Paid $100 for supplies used.

8   Paid salaries $200 by check.

11 Sold services $1,000 on credit.

15 Collected $150 from accounts receivable.

17 Acquired supply cabinet, $200, cash.

20 Paid monthly telephone bill, $45.

22 Sold services for $500 cash.

24 Received bill for $200 worth of supplies used; terms 30 days.

25 Paid $100 for equipment repair expenses.

26 Received $50 credit to correct overcharge on June 24 invoice for supplies used.

INSTRUCTIONS

1. Journalize the transactions. Be sure to number the journal Page 1 and put the year at the top of the date column.

2. Post to the ledger accounts. Head the forms by inserting the title and the account number for each account in the order in which they are listed in the chart of accounts.

PROBLEM 3 · 3A

The accountant for Central Air Conditioning Service Agency has recommended that certain accounts be provided in the firm's books to meet anticipated needs. Selected accounts are as follows.

301	Harold Burkhart Investment	514	Insurance Expense
140	Office Equipment	401	Service Income
111	Accounts Receivable	531	Supplies Used
101	Cash	141	Repair Equipment
145	Truck	201	Accounts Payable
547	Truck Expense	504	Telephone Expense
512	Salaries	552	Payroll Tax Expense
501	Advertising Expense		

INSTRUCTIONS

Arrange the accounts in the form of a chart of accounts similar to the one shown on page 29 of the text.

PROBLEM 4 · 1A

Ronald Wells owns and operates an employment service known as the
◆ Wells Personnel Agency. The trial balance at Feb. 28, 19X1 is as
follows:

ACCT. NO.	ACCOUNT NAME	DEBIT		CREDIT	
101	Cash	7,810	00		
111	Accounts Receivable	2,590	00		
141	Office Equipment	3,000	00		
143	Office Furniture and Fixtures	3,500	00		
144	Automobile	4,000	00		
201	Accounts Payable			12,000	00
301	Wells Investment			8,510	00
401	Income from Fees			2,000	00
504	Telephone Expense	150	00		
511	Salary Expense	700	00		
513	Advertising Expense	200	00		
516	Rent Expense	300	00		
518	Office Equipment Repairs	15	00		
521	Office Supplies Used	140	00		
522	Utilities Expense	60	00		
523	Auto Repairs Expense	45	00		
	Totals	22,510	00	22,510	00

The firm had the following transactions for March 19X1:

MAR.

1 Paid month's rent, $300.

3 Acquired office furniture costing $1,000, paying $300 in cash, balance due in 30 days.

5 Collected fees for professional services, $700 cash.

6 Paid salaries, $700, cash.

9 Bought new typewriter, $600, cash.

12 Paid $150 cash for newspaper advertising.

13 Received $600 in cash as fees for professional services; also performed $400 of services on credit. (Use a compound entry.)

17 Collected $1,500 in cash from accounts receivable.

18 Paid utilities bill for month, $55.00.

21 Paid $170 for supplies used.

24 Paid monthly telephone bill, $160.

26 Sold additional professional services, $500 in cash and $300 on credit.

27 Paid $6,000 to apply on accounts payable arising from equipment and furniture previously acquired.

31 Received bill for office supplies used, $100, payable in 30 days.

INSTRUCTIONS

1. Set up a general ledger for the accounts listed in the trial balance at Feb. 28 and enter the amounts as opening balances.
2. Prepare general journal entries to record the March transactions shown on page 483.
3. Post the March general journal entries to the general ledger.
4. Foot each of the accounts and determine the balance of each at Mar. 31. Enter your footing and balance figures in proper form.
5. Take a trial balance at Mar. 31.

PROBLEM 4 · 2A

The general ledger accounts and balances of Paul Mower, Attorney, at Dec. 31, 19X2 are as follows:

101	Cash	$3,000 Dr.	301	Mower Investment	$ 5,000 Cr.
111	Accounts Receivable	4,200 Dr.	401	Income from Fees	17,850 Cr.
130	Office Furniture	2,000 Dr.	504	Telephone Expense	1,500 Dr.
131	Professional Library	750 Dr.	511	Salaries Expense	6,000 Dr.
132	Building	7,000 Dr.	522	Utilities Expense	500 Dr.
201	Accounts Payable	2,500 Cr.	534	Supplies Used	400 Dr.

INSTRUCTIONS

1. Complete the worksheet for Paul Mower, Attorney, at the end of 6 months of operation.
2. Prepare a formal income statement and balance sheet. Use two-column analysis paper for the income statement and four-column analysis paper for the balance sheet.

PROBLEM 4 · 3A

Edgar Burkholder decided to enter the house painting and decorating business and engaged in the following transactions during November 19X2, using the listed accounts:

NOV.

1 Invested $5,000 in cash.
3 Paid rent for month, $100.
7 Purchased equipment, $1,000 in cash.
9 Acquired truck for $3,000; $500 in cash, balance payable in 30 days.
12 Paid $25 cash for newspaper advertising.
14 Sold services totaling $700; $200 for cash, and $500 on credit.
15 Paid $25 cash for minor truck repairs.
18 Paid $125 for supplies used.
20 Collected $400 from accounts receivable.

NOV.

22 Sold additional services for $1,200; $350 in cash and balance payable in 30 days.

24 Paid salaries, $700.

28 Paid $40 for additional supplies used.

29 Sold surplus equipment for $100 in cash.

30 Paid monthly telephone bill, $40.

521	Supplies Used	515	Rent Expense
142	Equipment	201	Accounts Payable
511	Salary Expense	111	Accounts Receivable
504	Telephone Expense	101	Cash
144	Truck	301	Burkholder Investment
401	Income from Services	512	Advertising Expense
518	Truck Repair Expense		

INSTRUCTIONS

1. Classify the account titles (and numbers) shown and prepare a chart of accounts.
2. Journalize the November transactions.
3. Set up a general ledger.
4. Post all entries to the general ledger.
5. Foot and balance the accounts.
6. Complete a worksheet as of Nov. 30.
7. Prepare the income statement (use two-column analysis paper) and balance sheet (use four-column analysis paper).

PROBLEM 5 · 1A

The worksheet of the Chambers Secretarial Service includes the following accounts at Dec. 31, 19X1.

301	Chambers Investment	$3,000 Cr.
401	Income from Services	7,000 Cr.
501	Rent Expense	1,000 Dr.
505	Salaries	6,000 Dr.
510	Supplies Used	100 Dr.
512	Telephone Expense	150 Dr.

INSTRUCTIONS

1. In general journal form, record the closing entries. Start with Entry 12-5C.
2. Compute the balance of the owner's equity at the end of the period.

PROBLEM 5 · 2A

The Cooley Investment Counseling Service opened for business on July 1, 19X4. The accountant who assisted Mr. Cooley in the organization of the business set up the following chart of accounts:

101	Cash	401	Income from Fees
111	Accounts Receivable	503	Telephone Expense
141	Office Equipment	505	Utilities Expense
143	Office Furniture	511	Salary Expense
201	Accounts Payable	513	Advertising Expense
301	Cooley Investment	521	Supplies Used
399	Income and Expense Summary	525	Miscellaneous Expense

During July, 19X4, the following selected transactions took place:

JULY

1 Mr. Cooley, the owner, made an initial investment of $4,000 in cash.

2 Acquired office equipment, $2,000; paying $1,000 cash, balance due in 30 days.

3 Bought used office furniture for $750, cash.

4 Performed services for $1,500, cash.

7 Bought additional office furniture on 30-day credit, $250.

10 Paid $25 cash for supplies used.

12 Paid $20 for newspaper advertising.

15 Performed additional professional services, $2,500. Collected $1,500 in cash and allowed 30-day credit on balance.

17 Paid $50 telephone bill for month.

18 Paid salaries of office staff, $1,200.

19 Received cash from accounts receivable, $500.

21 Paid utility bill for the month, $24.

22 Paid $500 toward amount owing on office equipment.

25 Issued check for $100 to cover miscellaneous expenses.

27 Sold services for cash, $500.

28 Paid $100 toward amount owing on office furniture.

31 Paid $20 to have office cleaned. (Miscellaneous Expense.)

INSTRUCTIONS

1. Open general ledger accounts, using the chart of accounts as your guide.
2. Journalize the July transactions.
3. Post all entries to the general ledger.
4. Foot and balance the accounts.
5. Complete a worksheet as of July 31.
6. Prepare the income statement (use two-column analysis paper) and balance sheet (use four-column analysis paper).
7. Journalize and post the closing entries.
8. Foot and rule all ledger accounts; carry forward open balances.
9. Prepare a postclosing trial balance.

PROBLEM 6 · 1A

The Jones Hardware Company sells building hardware and paints at retail. Some customers pay cash for their purchases; others are given 30-day credit terms. The firm's books include a single-column cash receipts journal. The ledger accounts involved in the cash receipts for January 19X2, and their balances at the first of the month are: Cash 101, $2,455.85; Accounts Receivable 111, $4,528.55; and Sales Income 401, –0–. The January transactions relating to the receipt of cash are follows:

JAN.

2   Received $20 for cash sales.
7   A customer, H. Wall, pays $100 on account.
9   Received $1,400 for cash sales.
11   Collected $200 on accounts receivable.
12   Checks totaling $425 were received from T. Long and L. Browne to balance their accounts.
15   Collected $1,150 for cash sales.
18   Received an additional $300 in cash from accounts receivable.
22   Received $500 in cash; $250 represents cash sales; the balance is to be applied on accounts receivable.
28   Customer's check for $50 is received to balance his account.
31   Today's receipts from additional cash sales amounted to $500.

INSTRUCTIONS

1. Open the ledger accounts and enter the balances brought forward.
2. Record all transactions in the cash receipts journal.
3. Total the cash receipts journal.
4. Perform the individual and summary postings to the proper ledger accounts. Use CRJ-1 as the posting reference.
5. Foot each account, but do not enter the balance.

PROBLEM 6 · 2A

This problem covers the cash receipts procedures for Bob's Sporting
♦   Goods Store for the month of February 19X1. The volume of transactions warrants the use of a multicolumn cash receipts journal with special columns for Accounts Receivable Cr. 111, Sporting Goods Sales 401, and Cash Dr. 101. The ledger accounts involved in the cash receipts transactions for February and their balances at the first of the month are: Cash 101, $3,509.00; Accounts Receivable 111, $3,120; and Sporting Goods Sales 401, –0–. The February 19X1 transactions involving the receipt of cash are as follows:

FEB.

1   Received check from T. Cameron, a customer, to pay his account, $125.
2   Received $275 for cash sales.
3   Received $750 from customers to apply on their accounts.
4   Collected $300 for goods sold today.
5   Checks totaling $850 received from credit customers.
9   Gordon Garnett, customer, sends check for $150 to balance his account.
13   Today's receipts from additional cash sales total $182.
17   Collected $300 on accounts receivable.
24   Received cash, $1,000: $450 represents cash sales; balance is from accounts receivable.

27 Check received from credit customer, W. Segal, $100.
28 Cash received from cash sales today, $610.

INSTRUCTIONS
1. Open the ledger accounts and enter the balances brought forward.
2. Record each transaction in the cash receipts journal.
3. Total each column of the journal.
4. Perform the summary postings to the proper ledger accounts, using CRJ-2 as the posting reference.
5. Foot the accounts where necessary, but do not enter the balances.

PROBLEM 6 · 3A

The Deroy Company sells radio, television, and hi-fi equipment for cash
♦ and on various credit terms. The specially designed cash receipts journal
has columns for Sundry Credits, Accounts Receivable Cr. 111, Sales Tax
Payable Cr. 231; Sales Income Cr. 401; Sales Discount Dr. 453, and Cash Dr.
101. During July 19X2, the following selected transactions took place.

JULY
1 Total cash of $546 received, resulting from cash sales of $525 plus 4% sales tax of $21.
5 Paul Pactor, a customer, sends check for $441 in payment for $450 invoice dated June 25, less 2% discount.
11 Received $137.20 from R. Armstrong to pay for invoice of May 2, $140, less 2% discount.
14 Collected $606 from R. Rollins to cover his $600 note due, plus interest, $6.
17 Collected total of $832 for cash sales: $800 represents total actual selling price of goods, $32 a 4% sales tax.
21 Received additional investment of $2,000 from owner, B. Deroy.
24 Received $160 check from M. Miller, customer, to apply on his account.
27 Collected $392 from customer, J. Leister, to cover $400 invoice of May 21, less 2% discount.
31 D. Van Horn pays June 1 note for $500 plus interest, $5, by check for $505.

INSTRUCTIONS
1. Record all the transactions in the cash receipts journal.
2. Foot, total, and rule the money columns. Prove the accuracy of your work by adding the credit column totals and the debit column totals and comparing them for equality.

PROBLEM 7 · 1A

The Dunlap Company uses a single-column cash disbursements journal.
♦ The ledger accounts involved in the cash disbursements for March 19X1 and their balances at the first of the month are:

101	Cash	$5,050	511	Salary Expense	–0–
141	Store Equipment	9,000	513	Advertising Expense	–0–
201	Accounts Payable	2,600	516	Rent Expense	–0–
504	Telephone Expense	–0–	521	Supplies Used	–0–
505	Utilities Expense	–0–			

The March 19X1 transactions relating to the disbursement of cash are as follows:

MAR.

1 Paid rent for the month, $200, by Check 750.

3 Paid telephone bill for the month, $50, by Check 751.

6 Paid William Gott $100, by Check 752, to apply on account.

7 Issued Check 753 in payment for supplies used, $50.

10 Purchased additional store equipment, $1,000, by Check 754.

12 Paid semimonthly salaries, $1,100, by Check 755.

14 Paid $200 by Check 756 to cover advertising bill due today.

17 Sent Check 757 to Kenneth Oyler in payment of accounts, $200.

18 Check 758 for $100 sent to John Carmody to cover balance due.

23 Made payment for additional supplies used, $60, by Check 759.

24 Issued Check 760 to cover account payable to M. Remp due today, $125.

25 Paid $100 to cover special advertising expense, by Check 761.

27 Sent Check 762 for $200 to Ralph Stanburg to settle account payable.

31 Issued Check 763 for semimonthly salaries $1,100.

INSTRUCTIONS

1. Open the ledger accounts and enter the balances brought forward.
2. Record each transaction in the cash disbursements journal.
3. Total the journal.
4. Complete the individual and summary postings to the proper ledger accounts, using CDJ-2 as the posting reference.
5. Foot the accounts where necessary, but do not enter the balances.

PROBLEM 7 · 2A

This problem covers the cash disbursements procedures for the Reese Research Laboratory for the month of April 19X1. The firm uses a multi-column cash disbursements journal with special columns for Sundry Debits, Accounts Payable Dr. 201, and Cash Cr. 101. The ledger accounts involved in the cash disbursements for April and their balances at the first of the month are:

101	Cash	$5,100	513	Advertising Expense	–0–
141	Laboratory Equipment	8,000	516	Rent Expense	–0–
201	Accounts Payable	2,500	518	Equipment Repairs	–0–
504	Telephone Expense	–0–	521	Supplies Used	–0–
505	Utilities Expense	–0–	591	Miscellaneous Expense	–0–
511	Salary Expense	–0–			

The April 19X1 transactions involving the disbursement of cash are as follows.

1 Paid $300 rent for Mar. by Check 171.
2 Issued Check 172 to pay for equipment purchased last month on credit, $500.
3 Made payment to E. Goodhart, $100, by Check 173 to cover balance due on account.
4 Paid monthly utility bill, $35, by Check 174.
7 Issued Check 175 for $200, payable to Gunder Equipment Company, in payment of their invoice for equipment, terms net cash.
10 Sent Check 176 for $100 to Jerry Weigle for legal advice (Miscellaneous Expense).
12 Made payment of telephone bill, $25, by Check 177.
15 Issued Check 178 to pay salaries for first half of month, $1,200.
18 Paid advertising bill by Check 179 for $100.
20 Check 180 for $200 sent to Mills Supply for supplies used.
22 Issued Check 181 to Cleary and Kelly for equipment repairs performed today, $40.
23 Paid for new laboratory equipment, $100, by Check 182 issued to Modern Laboratory Machinery Company.
25 Supplies used amounting to $25 paid by Check 183.
27 Paid Rosenberg Brothers $750 on account by Check 184.
28 Issued Check 185 to cover miscellaneous expenses totaling $35.
30 Issued Check 186 to pay salaries for second half of month, $1,200.

INSTRUCTIONS

1. Open the ledger accounts and enter the balances brought forward.
2. Record each transaction in the cash disbursements journal.
3. Total each column of the journal.
4. Complete the individual and summary postings to the proper ledger accounts and use CDJ-3 as the posting reference.
5. Foot the accounts where necessary, but do not enter the balances.

PROBLEM 7 · 3A

The Ludwig Company is a retail jewelry store owned and operated by
♦   William Ludwig. A cash disbursements journal, with columns for Sundry
Debits, Accounts Payable Dr. 201, Purchases Discount Cr. 510, and Cash
Cr. 101, is used to record payments by check. The petty cash analysis sheet
has special columns for Dr. 513, Dr. 521, Dr. 522, and Dr. 591. During July
19X1, the following accounts were used in the cash disbursements transactions:

101	Cash	302	Ludwig Drawing
105	Petty Cash Fund	505	Utility Expense
201	Accounts Payable	510	Purchases Discount
202	Notes Payable	513	Advertising Expense
231	Sales Tax Payable	516	Rent Expense

521	Office Supplies	591	Miscellaneous Expense
522	Postage	593	Interest Expense

The cash disbursements for the month were as follows:

JULY

1 Issued Check 101 to Reese Realtors for July rent, $250.

2 Established a petty cash fund of $100, issuing Check 102 for required amount. (Enter in cash disbursements journal in the usual manner, debiting Account 105. Also record on first line of the petty cash analysis sheet.)

3 Issued Check 103, $147.50, to the Hamilton Watch Co., to pay their invoice of June 10, terms 30 days net.

4 Sent Check 104 for $147 to Jeweler's Exchange to cover their invoice of June 27, $150 less 2% cash discount.

7 Paid $2.50 from petty cash fund for postage (Petty Cash Voucher 1). Record disbursements from petty cash in the petty cash analysis sheet.

8 Made payment to the Peoples National Bank of $202 by Check 105 to cover $200 note due today plus $2 interest expense.

10 Issued Check 106 to Ludwig, the owner, for $250, to be charged to his drawing account.

12 Paid July 7 invoice of $650 from Gem Imports, Inc. (terms 1% 10 days, net 30 days) by issuance of Check 107 for $643.50.

14 Paid $4 from petty cash fund for office supplies (Petty Cash Voucher 2).

15 Issued Check 108 for $245 to Harris Supply Co. to cover their July 7 invoice for $250 less 2%.

18 Ludwig issued Check 109 payable to himself for $250 to be charged to his drawing account.

20 Paid $7 from petty cash fund for delivery service (Miscellaneous Expense).

21 Paid Check 110 to Rapid Service Co. for advertising leaflets, $40.

25 Paid utilities bill for the month by Check 111 for $60.

27 Paid $10 from petty cash for advertising poster.

30 Sent Check 112 to State Tax Commission to pay sales taxes due today, $160.40.

31 Reimbursed petty cash fund by issuing Check 113, $23.50. (Get analysis of disbursements from solution of Instruction 2 below.)

31 Issued Check 114 to Art Metal Creations Corp. for $505 to pay note, $500, and interest, $5.

31 Paid Parker Tools for their $200 invoice dated July 22, taking 1% cash discount allowed, issuing Check 115 to cover.

INSTRUCTIONS

1. Record all transactions:
   a. Disbursements from petty cash in the petty cash analysis sheet, Page 7.
   b. Disbursements by check in the cash disbursements journal, Page 7.
2. Foot and balance the petty cash analysis sheet, enter the totals, rule, and enter the receipt of reimbursement Check 113.

3. Foot the money columns of the cash disbursements journal, and prove the accuracy of your work.

PROBLEM 8 · 1A

At the end of February 19X1, William Moran received his monthly bank statement for the Moran Towing Service from the Peoples National Bank.

◆ The opening balance shown on the bank statement agrees with the balance of the Cash account at Jan. 31. Since the two figures agree, the Cash account at Jan. 31 has been automatically verified. A list of deposits made and checks issued during February is supplied below. The balance of the Cash account and the checkbook at Feb. 28 was $8,311.

February	1	Balance	$6,500
	1	Check 421	100
	3	Check 422	10
	5	Deposit	500
	6	Check 423	225
	11	Check 424	200
	15	Check 425	75
	19	Deposit	410
	21	Check 426	60
	24	Deposit	730
	25	Check 427	4
	26	Check 428	20
	27	Check 429	35
	28	Deposit	900

PEOPLES NATIONAL BANK

Moran Towing Service
401 King Street
Mayville, State 14404   110-624-0

Notify us of any change in your address.

CHECKS		DEPOSITS	DATE	BALANCE
AMOUNT BROUGHT FORWARD			19 X1 JAN. 31	6,500.00
		500.00+	FEB. 4	7,000.00
100.00−			FEB. 6	6,900.00
200.00−	10.00−	410.00+	FEB. 11	7,100.00
225.00−			FEB. 15	6,875.00
60.00−			FEB. 19	6,815.00
		730.00+	FEB. 23	7,545.00
20.00−	4.00−		FEB. 25	7,521.00
3.75-SC			FEB. 28	7,517.25

INSTRUCTIONS

1. Verify the Cash account at Feb. 28 by preparing a bank reconciliation statement.
2. Record the entry (2-7) in general journal form to correct the Cash account balance. Charge to Miscellaneous Expense 591.

PROBLEM 8 · 2A

The balance in the Marshall Company's checkbook and ledger account
♦ Cash 101 was $6,418.59 at June 30, 19X1. The balance on the bank statement on the same date was $7,542.03. The records also indicate that the June 30 night deposit of $944.07 does not appear on the bank statement. A service charge of $14.34 and a debit memo of $120 covering an NSF check have not been entered on the firm's books. Checks 533 for $148.95, 535 for $97.50, and 536 for $425.40 have not yet been paid by the bank. On the last day of the month the bank collected a $1,500 note receivable plus $30 interest.

INSTRUCTIONS

1. Reconcile the book balance with the bank balance at June 30, 19X1.
2. Record the entries in general journal form to correct the Cash account. (Start with Entry 7-9.)

PROBLEM 9 · 1A

The Capital Refrigeration Company uses a single-column sales journal.
♦ The necessary ledger accounts are Accounts Receivable 111, with a balance of $18,500 on June 1, 19X1, and Refrigeration Sales 401, with no balance. The June 19X1 transactions involving sales are as follows:

JUNE

1 Sold air conditioner to R. Cleary on 30-day credit, $250, Sales Slip 59.
2 Sold refrigerator on 30-day credit to E. G. Casler, $175, Sales Slip 60.
5 Delivered and installed cooling system at The Shopping Mart, $1,000, on credit, Sales Slip 61.
7 Sold dehumidifier to Mrs. J. Weller on credit, Sales Slip 62, $100.
9 Installed refrigerator for H. Keller, Sales Slip 63, $500, payable half in 15 days and balance in 30 days.
12 Delivered and installed air conditioner for R. Hise, on credit, $300, Sales Slip 64.
14 Sold portable fans to Mrs. R. Bell, on credit, Sales Slip 65, $75 and B. A. Aster, also on credit, Sales Slip 66, $95.
16 Sold exhaust fan to Corner Sweet Shoppe on credit, $125, Sales Slip 67. Also sold another fan to Mrs. R. Bell on credit, Sales Slip 68, $75.
19 Sold air filter to R. Yancey on credit, Sales Slip 69, for $60.

20 E. Seuss purchased refrigerator on credit, $200, covered by Sales Slip 70.

22 Delivered and installed air conditioner for R. Esterbrook, Sales Slip 71, $300 on credit terms.

23 Sales on credit: to F. Beardsley, $100, Sales Slip 72; to Mrs. H. Gillies, $140, Sales Slip 73; to L. Mahoney, $175, Sales Slip 74.

24 Recorded sale to W. Goetz on Sales Slip 75, $210, regular credit terms.

26 Installed attic fan in home of L. Smith, Sales Slip 76, $145, payable in 30 days.

28 Sold automobile air conditioner to L. Bates, $400, Sales Slip 77, on credit.

30 Sales on credit: to G. Lesher, $200, Sales Slip 78; to D. Helm, $315, Sales Slip 79.

INSTRUCTIONS

1. Open the ledger accounts and enter the Brought Forward balance of Accounts Receivable 111.

2. Record each transaction in the sales journal.

3. Total and rule the Amount column of the journal.

4. Perform the required postings to the proper ledger accounts.

5. Foot the Accounts Receivable account, but do not enter the balance, since all postings from other journals have not yet been made.

PROBLEM 9 · 2A

This problem covers the cash and credit sales recording procedures for the City Supply Company. The company's books include a single-column sales journal; a cash receipts journal with columns for Accounts Receivable Cr. 111, Sales Cr. 401, and Cash Dr. 101; and the general ledger showing the following accounts and balances at the opening of business on Mar. 1, 19X1: 101 Cash, $1,880 Dr.; 111 Accounts Receivable, $3,600 Dr.; 401 Sales, –0– Cr. The March 19X1 transactions involving sales are as follows:

MAR.

1 Sold merchandise for cash, $150.

3 Received $258.50 from accounts receivable.

5 Sold merchandise on account to F. Cannon, $175, Sales Slip 601.

6 Cash received from credit customers, $250.

8 Sale on account to T. Ulrich, Sales Slip 602, $240.

10 Received $100 to cover cash sales.

12 Sales on credit: To W. Neal, $55, on Sales Slip 603; to L. Duffield, $35, on Sales Slip 604.

13 Sold merchandise totaling $1,500; on credit to H. Haddin, $300, covered by Sales Slip 605; on credit to F. Feamster, $900, covered by Sales Slip 606; for cash, $300.

15 R. Brooks purchased merchandise on credit, Sales Slip 607, $215.

17 Credit sales to: N. Williams, $25, Sales Slip 608; R. Link, $10, Sales Slip 609; E. Westerman, $22, Sales Slip 610.

20 Sales Slip 611 issued to cover credit sale to R. Werth, $25.

21 Sold merchandise on credit to E. Dallow, $15, on Sales Slip 612.

22 Sold on credit, $85, to W. Bassin, Sales Slip 613.

23 Merchandise sold on account to: L. Brendel, $15, Sales Slip 614; P. Gross, $40, Sales Slip 615; D. Stoner, $17, Sales Slip 616.

24 Sales Slip 617 covers credit sale to L. Valentine, $85.

25 Collected cash from accounts receivable, $2,500.

26 Sales on credit: M. Banks, $16, Sales Slip 618.

27 Merchandise sold on account: Sales Slip 619 to T. Nasissi, $75; Sales Slip 620 to J. Becker, $45.

29 Sold merchandise to H. Reynolds, $110, on account, Sales Slip 621.

31 Sales Slip 622 covers credit sale to P. Lomax, $90.

INSTRUCTIONS

1. Open the ledger accounts and enter the balances brought forward.
2. Record each transaction in the appropriate journal.
3. Total both journals and rule.
4. Perform the necessary postings to the ledger accounts.
5. Foot the three accounts, but do not enter the balances.

PROBLEM 9 · 3A

The Albright Gift Shop sells china, glassware, and other gift items which
♦ are subject to a 6% state sales tax. The shop uses a general journal and a sales journal with special columns for Accounts Receivable Dr. 111, Sales Tax Payable Cr. 231, and Sales Income Cr. 401. The following credit transactions took place during a week in November 19X1:

NOV.

1 Sold chinaware to Mrs. N. King, on Sales Slip 141; $100, plus $6 sales tax, total $106.

1 Sold brass serving tray to Ms. R. Cooley, Sales Slip 142: sales tag price $50, sales tax, $3.

2 W. Knerr buys wedding gift on credit, Sales Slip 143; total $42.40, $40 plus $2.40 tax.

3 M. Gable purchases punch bowl and glasses for $80 plus tax on Sales Slip 144, terms 30 days.

3 Sold set of mahogany serving bowls to F. Plasterer on credit. Sales Slip 145 includes price of bowls, $20 plus 6% tax.

3 Allow, $5 credit, plus sales tax, to Mrs. N. King because of broken cup discovered when unpacking chinaware covered by Sales Slip 141. (Use Sales Returns and Allowances Account 452; the general journal entry should be numbered 11-5.)

4 Sold coffee table on credit to R. Oravetz for $60 plus sales tax. Transaction covered by Sales Slip 146.

4 E. Gunder buys a two-place setting of sterling silverware, $110, plus tax, covered by Sales Slip 147.

5 Accepted return of gift serving tray from Ms. R. Cooley. It was a duplicate

of one already owned by the person for whom it was intended. Item in perfect condition. Full credit allowed (Entry 11-6).

5   K. Davies purchases table linen as wedding present on credit. Sales Slip 148, $175 plus sales tax.

5   Sales Slip 149 for credit sale to V. Costello, total $106: merchandise $100 plus $6 tax.

INSTRUCTIONS

1.   Record all transactions in the sales journal and the general journal. (Number each journal Page 1.)
2.   Foot the sales journal columns and prove the accuracy of your work.

PROBLEM 10 · 1A

The Winfield Glass Company uses a single-column purchases journal.
♦   On Jan. 1, 19X2, the necessary ledger accounts and their balances are: Accounts Payable 201, $5,964.20; Merchandise Purchases 501, –0–.
The January 19X2 transactions involving the purchase of merchandise are as follows:

JAN.

3   Purchased window glass from the I-O-F Glass Works, their Invoice 1694, Jan. 2; terms, 30 days net; $995.69.

4   Bought mirror glass from the Allied Products Company, their Invoice A 491-64, $290; dated Jan. 2; terms 2% 10 days, net 30 days.

8   Obtained plate glass from Klearview Manufacturing Company for $150 on their Invoice 69,201, dated Jan. 5, payable in 30 days.

11   Bought safety glass from the Plastic Specialties Corp. Their Invoice 44-98-A-1, for $175.50, is dated Jan. 9 and is due in 30 days.

18   Secured a special order of tinted glass from Charles and Company for $60 covered by their Invoice 648 dated Jan. 17; terms, 2% 10 days, net 30 days.

24   Acquired reserve stock of window glass from Bell Glass Distributors, $250.14. Their Invoice 301-296 is dated Jan. 20, with net payment due in 30 days.

28   Purchased frame mouldings from Boyle's Mill Products, $200. The invoice is numbered 4,596 and dated Jan. 25; terms, 1% 10 days, net 30 days.

INSTRUCTIONS

1.   Open the ledger accounts and enter the balances brought forward.
2.   Record each transaction in the purchases journal.
3.   Total and rule the Amount column of the journal.
4.   Perform the required postings to the proper ledger accounts.
5.   Foot the Accounts Payable account, but do not enter the balance.

PROBLEM 10 · 2A

♦ The Russell Stores Corp. purchases its merchandise from various suppliers for cash or on credit terms. The firm uses a single-column purchases journal and a cash disbursements journal with special columns for Sundry Debits, Accounts Payable Dr. 201, and Cash Cr. 101. The necessary ledger accounts and their balances at the beginning of the month of June 19X1 are Cash 101, $7,421.60; Accounts Payable 201, $4,709.40; and Merchandise Purchases 501, –0–. The June 19X1 transactions involving the purchases of merchandise are as follows:

JUNE

4   Purchased women's wear from Bartlett Products for cash (Check 116), $449.80.

6   Bought swim suits from Central Wholesale Co.; their Invoice 11,098 for $785.15, dated June 3, is due in 30 days.

11   Obtained new stock of curtains and drapes on credit from the County Distributors Co., $740.10. Their invoice is dated June 8; terms 2/10, net 30.

14   Bought hardware and house furnishings from East Point Fixtures Co., for cash. Issued Check 136 for $362.20.

22   Bought boy's clothing for $279.20 in cash from Waynesboro Mills, Check 152.

23   Purchased rugs from McCormick Fabrics Co., terms 30 days net. Their Invoice 869 is dated June 21 and totals $1,187.15.

27   Secured stock of new appliances from Acme Electric Supply. The invoice for $690.40 is dated June 25 and numbered 45,269. Terms are 10% 10 days, net 60 days.

30   Bought women's shoes from Hanover Shoe Manufacturing Co., terms net 30 days. Their Invoice 60-4091 is dated June 29 and totals $586.00.

INSTRUCTIONS

1.   Open the ledger accounts and enter the balances brought forward.
2.   Record each transaction in the appropriate journal. (Number each journal Page 5.)
3.   Total and rule the columns in both journals.
4.   Perform the required individual and summary postings to the proper ledger accounts.
5.   Foot the accounts where necessary, but do not enter the balances.

PROBLEM 10 · 3A

♦ The Office Suppliers Company obtains its merchandise from various suppliers. Their accounting records include a purchases journal with special columns for Accounts Payable Cr. 201, Merchandise Purchases Dr. 501, and Freight In Dr. 506; a cash disbursements journal with columns for Sundry Debits, Accounts Payable Dr. 201, and Cash Cr. 101; and a general journal. During a typical week in July 19X1, the following selected transactions took place:

JULY

2 Bought stock of stationery from Fulton Paper Co. on credit, $450.00. Their Invoice A 431, dated July 1, is due in 30 days, with no charge for delivery.

3 Obtained filing equipment for stock from Smead Manufacturing Co., terms 2% 10 days, 30 days net. Their Invoice J2-41-7 of July 3 amounts to $1,469.40.

3 Paid freight charges on shipment of filing equipment received from the Smead Company, $46.10. Issued Check 981.

5 Purchased stock of office desks and other furniture from Superior Products Co., $1,980.00 on 30-days credit; their Invoice A 4,290 is dated July 3.

5 Replenished stock of duplicator supplies by purchase from Sharpe Visual Products Co. totaling $860.15. Their invoice of July 2, 80,681, allows terms of 2% 10 days, net 60 days, with free delivery.

5 Issued Check 1012 for $80.50 to pay freight charges on shipment received from Superior Products Co. on July 3.

6 Purchased additional stock of electric typewriters, $2,469.60. The supplier, Modern Equipment Wholesalers, allows 60-day terms. Their Invoice T91-648-K is dated July 3, and includes freight prepaid by seller of $69.60.

7 Returned chair obtained from Superior Products Co., in their shipment of July 3. When this item was unpacked it was found to be badly damaged. The amount of $37.50 should be credited to Purchases Returns and Allowances 509 (Entry 7-4).

7 Bought stock of clocks and timekeeping equipment, $1,200, from the Timex Corp., covered by their Invoice 9,816, dated July 5; terms, net 60 days, with free delivery.

INSTRUCTIONS
1. Record each transaction in the appropriate journal. (Number each journal Page 7).
2. Foot all money columns in the purchases journal and the cash disbursements journal, and prove the accuracy of your work.

PROBLEM 11 · 1A

On Oct. 1, 19X1 the Barker Radio Service opened a new department for the sale of table and portable radios and television sets. Its repair service operations will continue as before. The income received from the sale of merchandise is to be recorded separately from the income arising from service rendered. The necessary general ledger accounts and given balances on Oct. 1, 19X1 are:

| 101 | Cash | $4,021.00 |
| 111 | Accounts Receivable Control | 439.24 |

401	Repair Service Income	–0–
402	Merchandise Sales Income	–0–
451	Sales Returns and Allowances	–0–

The company uses a sales journal with special columns for Accounts Receivable Dr. 111, Repair Service Income Cr. 401, and Merchandise Sales Income Cr. 402. The cash receipts journal has special columns for Accounts Receivable Cr. 111, Repair Service Income Cr. 401, Merchandise Sales Cr. 402, and Cash Dr. 101.

Beginning Oct. 1, 19X1, an accounts receivable subsidiary ledger is to be kept using balance-form ledger sheets. A list of the individual account balances at Sept. 30 follows. (Addresses have been intentionally omitted and will continue to be in future problems containing subsidiary ledgers.)

Ruth Armstrong Secretarial Service	$ 55.40
Cannon High School	25.60
Dr. Myron Gable	9.26
Susan Harvey	40.00
Henry Heller	5.25
Kelly's Garden Apartments	10.50
Moore's Motel	110.69
Newville Community Center	67.29
Charles L. Seale and Co.	45.15
Star Nursing Home	70.10
Total Due From Customers	$439.24

The October 19X1 transactions involving the sale of merchandise and services as well as the receipt of cash are as follows:

OCT.

1 Received $110.69 from Moore's Motel in payment of Sept. 5 sale. Rendered repair services on credit to James Carpenter, $48.50, Sales Slip 101.

3 Sold portable television set for cash, $149.75. Performed repair service for Arthur Whitford, $25.00, Sales Slip 102, payable in 30 days.

3 Received check for $35.40 from Ruth Armstrong Secretarial Service to apply on account. Sold table radio to Susan Harvey on credit, $46.85 Sales Slip 103. Check for $35.10 received from Star Nursing Home to apply on their account.

5 Payment received from Henry Heller to balance his account, $5.25. Sold portable AM-FM radio to Dr. Myron Gable, $79.50, Sales Slip 104, due in 30 days.

6 Sold and delivered two portable television sets to Cannon High School, Sales Slip 105, for $185, terms net 30 days. Cash sales for the day: services, $50.50; merchandise, $65.90.

9 Merchandise sold on credit today: on Sales Slip 106 to Williams College,

$18.75; and on Sales Slip 107 to Robert C. Miller, $25.00. Also received $10 cash for small repair job.

10   Received check for $25.60 from Cannon High School in payment of September balance. Received $22.50 cash for repair services rendered today.

11   Sales Slip 108 covers a credit sale of merchandise to Ronald Nelson for $15.95. Sales Slip 109 covers credit sale of radio to Harold Geiger for $49.10.

12   Sold merchandise for cash: $130.50.

13   Check received from Susan Harvey, $40.00, in payment of her September account. Sold merchandise on credit to Union Bus Depot Shop, Sales Slip 110, $47.25.

16   Cash sales of merchandise today, $117.50; credit sales of merchandise, $45.56, on Sales Slip 111 to Star Nursing Home.

17   Check received from Newville Community Center, $50, to apply on September account. Rendered repair services on credit for Moore's Motel, Sales Slip 112, $30.

18   Cash sales of merchandise today total $85.60. Also sold Williams College $75 worth of merchandise on credit, Sales Slip 113.

19   Sold merchandise to James Carpenter, $35, on Sales Slip 114. Received check from Arthur Whitford in payment of Sales Slip 102, $25.

22   Gave credit of $92.50 to Cannon High School for return of one of the portable television sets originally charged on Sales Slip 105, dated Oct. 6. (Use Entry 10–7.)

23   Sold merchandise for cash, $57.95.

24   Sold table radio to Ronald Nelson, Sales Slip 115, $61.55.

25   Henry Heller, a charge customer, bought a portable radio for $15.95 on Sales Slip 116; Robert Comfort purchased a clock radio for $10.50, Sales Slip 117, also on credit.

27   Merchandise sold for cash today totaled $50.25. Received check from Kelly's Garden Apartments in payment of September account, $10.50.

29   Gave allowance of $5 to James Carpenter due to slight scratch on cabinet of radio purchased on Oct. 19, Sales Slip 114. (Use Entry 10-12.)

30   Sold merchandise for cash, $35.15. Issued Sales Slip 118 to cover sale of $10 of repair services to Charles L. Seale and Co. on credit.

31   Sold $129.49 worth of merchandise to Union Bus Depot Shop on credit, Sales Slip 119.

INSTRUCTIONS

1.   Open the general ledger accounts and enter the balances brought forward.

2.   Open the accounts receivable subsidiary ledger. (A separate ledger account should be used for each customer listed here.) Enter the customer's name, the year, the date of Oct. 1, the word "Balance" in the Description column, a check mark in the Posting Reference column, and the amount in the Balance column. Open accounts for new customers as required. The customary terms are 30 days net.

3. Prove the accuracy of your work in Instruction 2 by listing the balances owed by customers as shown in the accounts receivable subsidiary ledger; then add them, and compare the resulting total with the balance of the general ledger Accounts Receivable Control account and with the total of the schedule of accounts receivable. Use a separate sheet of paper for this step.
4. Record each transaction in the appropriate journal. Use Page 10 for each journal.
5. Complete the required daily and summary postings to the general ledger and to the accounts receivable subsidiary ledger.
6. Foot and balance the general ledger accounts, and verify the accuracy of the balance of the accounts receivable subsidiary ledger accounts.
7. Prepare a schedule of accounts receivable at July 31, 19X1, and prove to the control.

PROBLEM 12 · 1A

◆ The Barker Radio Service uses a cash disbursements journal with special columns for Sundry Debits, Accounts Payable Dr. 201, and Cash Cr. 101; a single-column purchases journal; and a general journal in order to record December 19X1 transactions. The necessary ledger accounts and balances on Dec. 1, 19X1 are:

101	Cash	$4,506.21
201	Accounts Payable Control	2,736.84
501	Merchandise Purchases	–0–
509	Purchases Returns and Allowances	–0–

The individual accounts at Dec. 1, 19X1 in the accounts payable subsidiary ledger reveal the following. (Addresses have been intentionally omitted.)

BARKER RADIO SERVICE
Schedule of Accounts Payable
December 1, 19X1

CREDITOR	BALANCE AMOUNT
Colonial Radio Corp.	$ 150.00
General Electronics, Inc.	735.00
Repair Parts and Supply Co.	125.00
Central Radio/TV Distributors	1,005.00
Bryan Laboratories	75.00
ABC Communications Systems	275.10
Lincoln Television Sales Corp.	0
Apollo Sound Systems	371.74
Total Owed to Creditors	$2,736.84

The transactions involving purchases of merchandise on credit and disbursements of cash for December 19X1 are as follows:

DEC.

2   Purchased merchandise from Colonial Radio Corp., Inv. 4964, Dec. 1; terms net 30 days, $1,205.60.

3   Issued Check 741 for $125 to Repair Parts and Supply Co., for Inv. 10,469, dated Nov. 4.

4   Check 742 issued to General Electronics, Inc. to pay for Inv. 694 J 6, dated Oct. 6, $510.

6   Paid Colonial Radio Corp. Inv. 4721, dated Nov. 8, by Check 743, $150.

8   Purchased merchandise for cash, $34.10. Issued Check 744. (Charge to Merchandise Purchases 501.)

11   Bought stock of clock-radios from Emerson Radio Corp., $208.40, their Inv. 941, dated Dec. 9, terms 30 days net.

12   Purchased color TV sets from Central Radio/Television Distributors, Inv. B 10-941, dated Dec. 10, terms net 30 days, $1,180.

14   Bought $125 worth of merchandise from Repair Parts and Supply Co., Inv. 12,631, Dec. 12, terms 30 days net.

14   Paid the balance of account owed to Apollo Sound Systems, $371.74, by Check 745.

15   Issued Check 746 to pay ABC Communications Systems, $275.10.

18   Bought merchandise for cash, $100, Check 747.

19   Purchased additional merchandise from Bryan Laboratories, Inv. 207-B, dated Dec. 15, terms 60 days, $40.

20   Received $85 allowance from Central Radio/Television Distributors for damaged merchandise received on their invoice of Nov. 25. (Use Entry 12-15).

22   Obtained new merchandise from Apollo Sound Systems, Inv. 509731, Dec. 20, net 30 days, $415.

24   Paid Central Radio/Television Distributors net balance due on purchase of Nov. 25, their Inv. A 14-680, Check 748, $920.00.

26   Bought portable radios from General Electronics, Inc., Inv. 97849, dated Dec. 23, terms net 60 days, $605.

27   Allowed credit of $18.40 by Emerson Radio Corp. to cover shortage in shipment of Dec. 9, their Inv. 941. (Entry 12-21).

31   Purchased $65.20 worth of pocket radios from ABC Communications Systems, Inv. 41,276, Dec. 29, terms net 30 days.

INSTRUCTIONS

1.   Open the general ledger accounts and enter each balance brought forward.

2.   Open the accounts payable subsidiary ledger. Enter the creditor's name (omit address), the year, the date of Dec. 1, the word "Balance" in the Description column; place a check mark in the Posting Reference column; and enter the amount owed to each creditor in the Balance column. Open an account for all listed accounts, even though there may be no balances as of this date. Pertinent information, such as invoice number, date, and terms has been provided. Open accounts for new creditors as needed.

3.   Prove the accuracy of your work in Instruction 2 by listing the balances

owed to creditors as shown in the accounts payable subsidiary ledger; then add them and compare the resulting total with the balance of the general ledger Accounts Payable Control account and with the total of the schedule of accounts payable. Use a separate sheet of paper for this step.

4. Record each transaction in the appropriate journal. (Number each journal Page 4.)

5. Complete the required daily and summary postings to the general ledger and to the accounts payable subsidiary ledger.

6. Foot and balance the general ledger accounts, and verify the accuracy of the balances of the accounts payable subsidiary ledger accounts.

7. Prepare a schedule of accounts payable at Dec. 31, 19X1 and prove to the control.

PROBLEM 13 · 1A

R. P. Cavalier opens an office for the conduct of a managerial consult-
◆ ing service. His accountant designs a simple accounting system consist-
ing of a general ledger and a combined journal with special columns for Cash Received Dr. 101 and Cash Disbursed Cr. 101; Accounts Receivable Dr. 111 and Cr. 111; Professional Fees Income Cr. 401; Salary Expense Dr. 511; Office Supplies Dr. 521; Traveling Expenses Dr. 522; Duplicating and Printing Expense Dr. 533; and Sundry Debit and Credit. A chart of accounts and the transactions for Cavalier's first month of consulting work (May 19X1) are given below:

ASSETS

101	Cash
111	Accounts Receivable
141	Office Furniture
143	Automobile

LIABILITIES

| 201 | Accounts Payable |

OWNER'S EQUITY

| 301 | Cavalier Investment |
| 399 | Income and Expense Summary |

INCOME

| 401 | Professional Fees Income |

EXPENSES

504	Telephone Expense
505	Utilities Expense
511	Salary Expense
516	Rent Expense
521	Office Supplies
522	Traveling Expense
533	Duplicating and Printing Expenses
591	Miscellaneous Expense

MAY

1 Cavalier deposited $7,500 of his personal savings in the City National Bank to open a checking account for the Cavalier Consulting Service.

1 Paid office rent for May, $200, by Check 1.

3 Issued Check 2 to pay for duplicating and printing services, $200.

4 Purchased office furniture by Check 3, $550.

5   Paid $50 for office supplies, Check 4.

5   Bought automobile for use in business, $4,000; terms $1,000 cash down, balance payable in 30 days. Check 5 issued for down payment.

7   Check 6 issued to pay weekly salary of office assistant, $120.

7   Received fees for professional services to clients, $400 cash; also professional services on credit, $250.

9   Paid by Check 7 for gasoline, oil, and routine servicing of automobile, $20. (Charge Traveling Expense 522).

10 Paid telephone bill by Check 8, $24.

10 Bought bookcases for the office, $100. Paid $50 by Check 9, balance due in 30 days.

12 Purchased additional office supplies, $60; terms 30 days net.

14 Issued Check 10 to pay weekly salary of office assistant, $120.

14 Sold professional services during the week: $200 cash, $300 on account.

16 Paid for airline tickets and hotel accommodations in connection with a regional convention, $260, Check 11.

17 Paid utility bill for the month, $20, Check 12.

18 Paid for trash removal services for the month, $20, Check 13. (Charge Miscellaneous Expense 591.)

19 Issued Check 14 to pay for additional duplicating and printing service, $50.

21 Paid salary of office assistant by Check 15, $120.

21 Sold professional services during the week: $100 cash, $600 on credit.

21 Received $250 cash from clients on account.

23 Paid for gasoline and minor servicing of automobile, $10, Check 16.

25 Bought railroad tickets for business trip to client's plant, $65, covered by Check 17.

25 Received checks from clients to apply on their accounts, $300.

28 Paid weekly salary of office assistant by Check 18.

28 Performed professional services during the week: $150 for cash, $300 on credit.

29 Issued Check 19 for additional office supplies, $15.

INSTRUCTIONS

1. Record each transaction in the combined journal.
2. Foot, total, and rule the combined journal at the end of the month.
3. Prove your work by preparing a simple proof schedule.

PROBLEM 14 · 1A

♦   The Carson Wholesale Supply Company purchased $64,246.18 of merchandise for resale during the calendar year ended Dec. 31, 19X1. Purchases returns and allowances for the period were $1,106.41. The actual inventory of merchandise on hand at Dec. 31, 19X1, amounted to $21,269.12.

INSTRUCTIONS

Compute the cost of goods sold for the fiscal year ended Dec. 31, 19X1.

PROBLEM 14 · 2A

During the month of January 19X2, the Carson Wholesale Supply
♦ Company sold $60,618.21 of merchandise, of which $5,460.08 was
cash sales. Sales returns and allowances of $746.88 related to credit
transactions. The company's experience indicates that 3% of net credit sales will
not be collected.

INSTRUCTIONS
Compute the estimated bad debt losses to be anticipated on January sales.

PROBLEM 14 · 3A

The Campbell Products Company uses a 10-column worksheet to record
♦ its trial balance taken at Dec. 31, 19X1, the end of its first year of
operations. All equipment was purchased on Jan. 2, 19X1 and is estimated to have a useful life of 10 years. Included in the balance of the Sales
Income account is $748.17 of cash sales. All sales returns and allowances relate
to credit transactions. The firm estimates that 2% of net credit sales will not
be collected. The trial balance is as follows.

CAMPBELL PRODUCTS COMPANY
Trial Balance
December 31, 19X1

ACCT. NO.	ACCOUNT NAME	DEBIT	CREDIT
101	Cash	2,396 04	
111	Accounts Receivable Control	3,519 08	
111A	Allowance for Bad Debts		–0–
121	Merchandise Inventory	–0–	
141	Equipment	7,526 50	
141A	Allowance for Depreciation		–0–
201	Accounts Payable Control		3,210 81
301	Campbell Investment		8,000 00
302	Campbell Drawing	200 00	
401	Sales Income		27,531 41
451	Sales Returns and Allow.	300 00	
501	Merchandise Purchases	5,007 46	
509	Purchase Returns and Allow.		375 00
511	Salary Expense	10,000 00	
519	Rent Expense	9,000 00	
522	Supplies Used	1,000 00	
562	Bad Debts Expense	–0–	
565	Depreciation Expense	–0–	
591	Miscellaneous Expense	168 14	
	Totals	39,117 22	39,117 22

INSTRUCTIONS
1. Enter the trial balance at Dec. 31, 19X1, in a 10-column worksheet.
2. Insert all other column headings in the worksheet. (Use illustration on page 215 as a guide.)

3. Compute the bad debts expense for the year, enter on the worksheet, and identify by the letter (A). Show your computations.
4. Compute the depreciation for the year, enter it on the worksheet, and identify by the letter (B). Show your computations.
5. Foot, prove, and total the Adjustments column.
6. Complete the extension of figures into the Adjusted Trial Balance columns; then foot, prove, and total them.
7. Enter merchandise inventory of $1,941.86 at Dec. 31, 19X1, and identify by the letter (C).
8. Extend the Adjusted Trial Balance amounts to the appropriate columns and foot.
9. Compute and enter the profit for the period.
10. Bring down final totals of the remaining columns, prove, and then rule all columns.

PROBLEM 15 · 1A

♦ The adjusted trial balance data for Johnson Hardware Store for the year ended Dec. 31, 19X2 is given on page 507.

INSTRUCTIONS
1. Copy the adjusted trial balance on your worksheet.
2. Record the Merchandise Inventory at Dec. 31, 19X2 on the worksheet, $37,000, and identify by the letter (E).
3. Extend the Adjusted Trial Balance amounts to appropriate columns and foot.
4. Compute and enter the profit or loss for the period.
5. Complete the worksheet, bringing down final totals of all remaining columns, proving, and then ruling all accounts.

PROBLEM 15 · 2A

♦ This is a continuation of Prob. 15 · 1A. Refer to the partial worksheet of the Johnson Hardware Store for the year ended Dec. 31, 19X2 that was completed in Prob. 15 · 1A.

INSTRUCTIONS
1. Prepare the income statement. (Use three-column analysis paper.)
2. Prepare the balance sheet, using the format shown on page 222. (Use four-column analysis paper.)

PROBLEM 15 · 3A

♦ This is a continuation of Probs. 15 · 1A and 15 · 2A. Refer to the partial worksheet of Johnson Hardware Store for the year ended Dec. 31, 19X2 that was completed in Prob. 15 · 1A.

JOHNSON HARDWARE STORE
Worksheet (Partial)
Year Ended December 31, 19X2

ACCT. NO.	ACCOUNT NAME	ADJUSTED TRIAL BALANCE DR.	ADJUSTED TRIAL BALANCE CR.
101	Cash	4,626 00	
111	Accounts Rec. Control	14,680 00	
111A	Allow. for Bad Debts		588 50
121	Merchandise Inventory	10,000 00	
131	Store Furniture and Fixtures	950 00	
131A	Allow. for Deprec.—Store Furn. & Fix.		95 00
135	Delivery Truck	2,250 00	
135A	Allow. for Deprec.—Delivery Truck		400 00
142	Office Furniture and Fixtures	720 00	
142A	Allow. for Deprec.—Office Furn. & Fix.		65 00
201	Accts. Payable Control		4,985 00
301	Johnson Investment		38,378 50
401	Sales		117,700 00
501	Merchandise Purchases	98,375 00	
509	Purch. Ret. & Allow.		500 00
512	Office Salaries	3,000 00	
516	Rent Expense	4,100 00	
523	Sales Salaries	16,500 00	
525	Store Supplies & Expense	542 50	
527	Depreciation—Store Furn. & Fix.	95 00	
531	Advertising	2,275 00	
541	Delivery Wages	2,400 00	
543	Delivery Truck Operating Expense	760 00	
545	Depreciation—Delivery Truck	400 00	
553	Office Supplies & Expense	385 00	
555	Depreciation—Office Furniture & Fix.	65 00	
561	Bad Debts Expense	588 50	
	Totals	162,712 00	162,712 00
	Net Profit for the Year		

INSTRUCTIONS

1. Prepare the adjusting entries for depreciation expense and bad debts expense in general journal form, beginning with Entry 12-1. Assume depreciation of $95 on Store Furniture; $400 on Delivery Trucks; $65 on Office Furniture and Fixtures; and bad debt losses of $588.50.

2. Prepare the closing entries for transferring the balances of the Debit and Credit columns of the Income Statement section of the worksheet to Income and Expense Summary 399. Include the beginning and ending inventory amounts in these entries.

3. Prepare the closing entry to transfer the profit (or loss) for the month to the owner's investment account.

PROBLEM 15 · 4A

◆ The completed worksheet of the Point Auto Parts Company (Thomas Point, owner) for the year ended Dec. 31, 19X4 is given.

POINT AUTO PARTS COMPANY
Worksheet
Year Ended December 31, 19X4

ACCT. NO.	ACCOUNT NAME	TRIAL BALANCE		ADJUSTMENTS		ADJUSTED TRIAL BALANCE		INCOME STATEMENT		BALANCE SHEET	
		DEBIT	CREDIT	DEBIT	CREDIT	DEBIT	CREDIT	DEBIT	CREDIT	DEBIT	CREDIT
101	Cash in Bank	7,602 63				7,602 63				7,602 63	
111	Accounts Receivable Control	5,194 45				5,194 45				5,194 45	
121	Merchandise Inventory	15,000 00				15,000 00		15,000 00	C) 16,500 00	C) 16,500 00	
131	Furniture & Equipment	3,000 00				3,000 00				3,000 00	
131A	Allow. for Depr.—Furn. & Equipment		900 00		A) 300 00		1,200 00				1,200 00
141	Delivery Truck	2,775 00				2,775 00				2,775 00	
141A	Allow. for Depr.—Del. Truck		1,200 00		B) 600 00		1,800 00				1,800 00
201	Accounts Payable Control		3,511 20				3,511 20				3,511 20
301	Point Investment		14,372 50				14,372 50				14,372 50
401	Sales		123,101 45				123,101 45		123,101 45		
451	Sales Discount	2,266 73				2,266 73		2,266 73			
492	Purchases Discount		822 26				822 26		822 26		
501	Merchandise Purchases	83,237 70				83,237 70		83,237 70			
511	Rent Expense	1,800 00				1,800 00		1,800 00			
521	Sales Salaries	6,960 00				6,960 00		6,960 00			
523	Store Supplies & Expense	3,546 25				3,546 25		3,546 25			
525	Depreciation—Furn. & Equip.			A) 300 00		300 00		300 00			
531	Advertising	1,738 90				1,738 90		1,738 90			
541	Delivery Salary	3,295 00				3,295 00		3,295 00			
543	Delivery Truck Expense	1,081 40				1,081 40		1,081 40			
545	Depreciation—Del. Truck			B) 600 00		600 00		600 00			
551	Office Salaries	3,360 00				3,360 00		3,360 00			
553	Office Supplies & Expense	3,049 35				3,049 35		3,049 35			
	Totals	143,907 41	143,907 41	900 00	900 00	144,807 41	144,807 41	126,235 33	140,423 71	35,072 08	20,883 70
	Net Profit for Year							14,188 38			14,188 38
								140,423 71	140,423 71	35,072 08	35,072 08

INSTRUCTIONS

1. Prepare an income statement from the completed worksheet.
2. Prepare a balance sheet from the completed worksheet.
3. Journalize the adjusting entries beginning with Entry 12-3 A.
4. Journalize the entries to close all income and expense balances and account for beginning and ending inventory balances.
5. Journalize the entries to transfer profit or loss from the Income and Expense Summary to the owner's investment account.

PROBLEM 16 · 1A

The adjusted trial balance data for the Miller Wholesale Company prepared at the end of the year's operations on Dec. 31, 19X2 is shown on the next page.

INSTRUCTIONS

Prepare a classified income statement for the year 19X2 and a classified balance sheet at Dec. 31, 19X2, using the data given. (No departmental columns are required in the income statement.)

PROBLEM 17 · 1A

Wilton Electric Shop (Max Wilton, owner) pays its workers on an hourly basis, and pays one and a half times the regular rate for hours worked in excess of 40 in one week. Data for the week ended Jan. 22, 19X1, are shown:

EMPLOYEE	TOTAL HOURS WORKED	HOURLY RATE	WITHHOLDING EXEMPTIONS	MARITAL STATUS
Thomas Wilton	43	$4.00	3	Married
Harry Hill	36	3.00	5	Married
Nolan Nees	39	2.50	5	Single
Tim Tyler	45	4.50	3	Married

INSTRUCTIONS

1. Set up a payroll register containing columns with the following headings: Name, Number of Exemptions, Marital Status, Total Hours Worked, Overtime Hours, Regular Hourly Rate, Regular Earnings, Overtime Premium, Total Earnings, FICA Withheld, Income Tax Withheld, and Net Amount. Enter each employee's name, exemptions, hours worked, and rate.
2. Compute the gross earnings for each worker, including regular time earnings and overtime premium earnings, and enter these data in the register.
3. Compute the FICA tax to be withheld from each employee's paycheck,

ACCOUNT NAME	DEBIT	CREDIT
Cash in Bank	$ 43,060.20	
Petty Cash	200.00	
Change Fund	800.00	
Invest. in U.S. Treasury Bonds	5,390.00	
Notes Receivable	5,000.00	
Accounts Receivable Control	50,375.15	
Allowance for Bad Debts		$ 982.71
Interest Receivable	50.00	
Merchandise Inventory, Jan. 1	65,200.00	
Prepaid Insurance	1,820.00	
Supplies on Hand	800.00	
Building	30,500.00	
Allow. for Depr.–Building		2,750.00
Furniture and Equipment	38,500.00	
Allow. for Deprec.–Furn. and Equip.		7,700.00
Land	7,500.00	
Deposits with Utility Companies	100.00	
Notes Payable		9,200.00
Accounts Payable Control		29,505.45
Sales Taxes Payable		1,235.20
Wages Payable		990.00
Employee Ded.–FICA		115.35
Employee Ded.–Income Taxes With.		673.20
Miller Investment		161,072.70
Sales		495,138.35
Sales Returns & Allowances	3,782.15	
Interest Income		240.00
Merchandise Purchases	269,795.10	
Depreciation of Building	750.00	
Depreciation of Furn. & Equip.	2,400.00	
Insurance Expense	4,530.20	
Property Taxes Expense	6,217.30	
Sales Salaries	26,225.00	
Payroll Tax Exp.–Sales Salaries	2,210.30	
Delivery Expense	18,240.60	
Sales Supplies & Expense	31,248.75	
Advertising	11,710.20	
Officers' Salaries	55,000.00	
Office Salaries	17,325.00	
Payroll Tax Exp.–Officers' & Office Sal.	3,615.10	
Office Supplies & Expense	6,310.20	
Miscellaneous General Expense	100.00	
Bad Debts Expense	847.71	
Totals	$709,602.96	$709,602.92

The merchandise inventory on December 31 was $62,500.

using the assumed rate of 6% of gross earnings, and enter the amounts in the register.

4. Compute the income tax to be withheld from each worker's paycheck using the withholding tax wage-bracket tables given on pages 262 and 265. Enter these amounts in the register.

5. Compute the net pay for each employee and enter in the register.

6. Total and rule the earnings and deductions columns. Prove by crossfooting.

Thomas operates a woodworking shop. He pays employees an hourly
♦ wage, with time and a half for hours over 40 worked in one week.
Data for the week ended Dec. 31, 19X1 are shown. All four employees
are married.

EMPLOYEE	HOURS WORKED	RATE	CUMULATIVE EARNINGS DEC. 24	EXEMPTIONS
Kevin King	40	$3.20	$ 5,640	2
Larry Luling	48	4.00	6,400	3
Toby Thomas	26	7.50	11,910	3
Warren Wade	40	4.50	7,000	4

INSTRUCTIONS

1. Set up a payroll register with column headings for: Name, Number of
   Exemptions, Marital Status, Total Hours Worked, Overtime Hours, Regular
   Hourly Rate, Regular Earnings, Overtime Premium, Total Earnings, FICA
   Withheld, Income Tax Withheld, and Net Amount. Enter each employee's
   name, exemptions, hours worked, and rate.
2. Compute the gross earnings, including regular time earnings and overtime
   premium, and enter these in the register.
3. Compute the FICA tax to be withheld from each employee's earnings,
   using the assumed rate of 6%, and enter this amount in the register.
4. Compute the income tax to be withheld from each worker's earnings, using
   the withholding tax tables on pages 262–265. Enter this amount in the
   proper column of the register.
5. Compute the net pay for each worker. Total the register.
6. Give the general journal entry (Number 12-7) to record the payroll. Debit
   Wages Expense 531; for other accounts involved, use account numbers
   given in the text illustrations.

PROBLEM 17 · 3A

A portion of the individual earnings record of J. L. Coker is shown in
♦ the Individualized Performance Guide. Coker is married and claims five
withholding exemptions. He earned $3.50 per hour through the month
of March. During the week ending Mar. 31, he worked 38 hours, for which he
was paid on that day. Beginning Apr. 1, Coker's wages were increased to $4.00
per hour, and during the week ending Apr. 7, he worked 42 hours, for which
he was paid on that date.

INSTRUCTIONS

1. Compute the gross earnings, FICA deduction (assuming a rate of 6%),
   and the federal income tax withholding (using the table on page 262) for
   the week ending Mar. 31, and enter the data for that week on Coker's
   earnings record.

2. Total all money columns for the month of March, and single-rule.
3. Bring down totals in all money columns for the quarter, and double-rule.
4. Compute the gross earnings (don't forget the pay increase), the FICA deduction, and federal income tax withholding for the week ending Apr. 7, and enter the data for that week in Coker's earnings record.

PROBLEM 17 · 4A

Carson Milling Company has three employees. Employees are paid on Friday of each week. On Wednesday, Apr. 30, 19X1, the accountant wishes to accrue earnings for the last three days of April, which will be paid on Friday, May 2. Data concerning wage rates, hours worked, etc., for the three employees are shown below.

- Abel Adams, age 28, single, one exemption, hourly wage rate, $4. Worked 8 hours on each of the three days.
- Homer Henson, age 45, married, three exemptions, hourly wage rate, $4. Worked 8 hours on Monday, did not work on Tuesday, worked 8 hours on Wednesday.
- Konrad Kinard, age 40, single, one exemption, hourly wage rate, $3.50. Worked 10 hours on Monday, 8 hours on Tuesday, and 9 hours on Wednesday.

INSTRUCTIONS

Give the journal entry on Apr. 30 to record the accrued wages so that an income statement can be properly prepared for the period ended on that date. Use the account numbers given on page 267 (account 601 for Mill Labor).

PROBLEM 18 · 1A

During the month following the close of each calendar quarter, an employer is required to file Form 941 (Employer's Quarterly Federal Tax Return). Assume that the Street Company (Keith Street, owner), 1111 Main Street, Capital City, State, 10000, identification number 57-0202222, received these forms from the Internal Revenue Service for the fourth quarter of 19X1.

Here is a summary of the payroll for the quarter.

SOCIAL SEC. NUMBER	EMPLOYEE	TOTAL EARNINGS	FICA DEDUCTED	INCOME TAX WITHHELD
111-08-1100	Arnold Arp	$2,080.00	$124.80	$300.10
112-08-0011	Betty Brown	1,600.00	96.00	138.10
113-07-1010	Clarence Cates	3,200.00	144.00	685.00
114-06-0110	Donald Daws	2,100.00	126.00	330.00
	Totals	$8,980.00	$490.80	$1,453.20

The owner of the Street Company has prepared the Federal Tax Deposit form 501 and written checks as follows:

	OCTOBER	NOVEMBER
Employees' FICA Tax Deducted	$180.00	$180.00
Employees' Income Tax Withheld	484.00	484.80
Employer's FICA Tax Expense	180.00	180.00
Total Payroll Taxes	$844.00	$844.80

a. Federal Tax Deposit, paid Nov. 15, $844.00 (Form 501 No. 111111).
b. Federal Tax Deposit, paid Dec. 15., $844.80 (Form 501 No. 211111).

INSTRUCTIONS
1. Complete Schedule A (Form 941) Quarterly Report of Wages Taxable under the Federal Insurance Contributions Act. (Note that only $2,400 of Cates' earnings were subject to the tax because his total earnings for the year exceeded $12,000.)
2. Complete the remainder of Form 941, including Schedule B, using the assumed 12% total FICA rate in computations. Sign the form with your name and use the title "Accountant." Date the report Jan. 30, 19X2.
3. On Jan. 30, 19X2, the owner issues a check in payment of payroll taxes for the amount due as shown on Form 941. In general journal form, record issuance of the check. (Number the entry 1-30.)

PROBLEM 18 · 2A

Certain transactions and procedures relating to unemployment taxes and to workmen's compensation insurance for the Krantz Company, 1111 University Drive, Capital City, State, 99999, identification number 57-6161611 (Claude Krantz, owner), are given in the following information. Carry out the procedures as instructed in each step.

INSTRUCTIONS
1. Account for the yearly settlement of the workmen's compensation insurance premium. The following analysis of payrolls for the preceding year (19X0) has been made by the insurance company auditor.

CLASSIFICATION	AMOUNT OF WAGES PAID	INSURANCE RATE	PREMIUM EARNED
Construction work	$61,000	3.10%	$1,891.00
Office work	8,000	.15%	12.00
Totals	$69,000		$1,903.00
Less estimated premium paid			1,800.00
Balance of premium due			$ 103.00

The owner issues a check dated Jan. 25, 19X1 for $103.00. In general journal form, record the payment of the premium due. (Entry 1-30.)

2. Account for the payment of the current year's estimated premium for workmen's compensation insurance. Estimated premiums and wages are as follows:

CLASSIFICATION	AMOUNT OF ESTIMATED WAGES	EFFECTIVE RATES	ESTIMATED PREMIUM
Construction work	$65,000	3.10%	$2,015.00
Office work	8,000	.15%	12.00
Totals	$73,000		$2,027.00

The owner issues a check dated Jan. 28, 19X1 for $2,027.00. In general journal form, record the payment. (Use entry 1-33.)

3. Compute the state unemployment insurance taxes required on the employer's quarterly report of employee's wages for the Krantz Company for the quarter ending March 31, 19X1. Krantz Company has received a merit rating and consequently pays only 1.5% on a state unemployment tax rate of 2.7%. The wages for the first quarter are given below.

SOCIAL SECURITY NUMBER	NAME OF EMPLOYEE	TOTAL EARNINGS
444-00-1234	Fred Fox	$1,625.00
444-09-4325	Gerald Franklin	2,400.00
333-01-3456	Glenn Grandy	1,800.00
333-09-5431	William Harrison	2,800.00
222-02-4567	Homer Henson	2,130.00
222-09-7531	James Hundley	2,800.00
111-03-5678	Irene Ivers	2,050.00
	Total	$15,605.00

4. The owner issues a check dated April 28, 19X1, for the amount you computed in Instruction 3. Record the check (Entry 4-25) in general journal form.

5. To complete the problem, assume that all weekly and monthly payrolls have been prepared and paid and that all quarterly reports have been submitted as required. The payroll information for 19X1 is as follows:

QUARTER ENDED	TOTAL WAGES PAID	WAGES PAID IN EXCESS OF $4,200	STATE UNEMPLOYMENT TAX PAID
Mar. 31	$15,605.00	–0–	$234.08
June 30	17,200.00	$ 3,400.00	207.00
Sept. 30	17,500.00	13,300.00	63.00
Dec. 31	19,100.00	15,100.00	60.00
Totals	$69,405.00	$31,800.00	$564.08

Complete the following parts of Form 940 (Employer's Annual Federal Unemployment Tax Return).

a. Schedule A—Computation of Credit against Federal Unemployment Tax.

b. Schedule B—Computation of Taxable Wages.

c. The remainder of Form 940. Sign the form with your name and use the title "Accountant." Date the form Jan. 28, 19X2, the succeeding year.

6. The owner issues a check dated Jan. 28, 19X2, for the amount shown on Line 16 of Form 940. In general journal form record issuance of the check. (Entry 1-21.)

PROBLEM 18 · 3A

Cumulative earnings of the four employees of Noles Company at the
◆ end of June, September, and December, 19X1 are shown:

EMPLOYEE	CUMULATIVE EARNINGS THROUGH JUNE	CUMULATIVE EARNINGS THROUGH SEPT.	CUMULATIVE EARNINGS THROUGH DEC.
Elmer Estes	$2,400	$3,600	$4,800
Frances Fagan	3,240	4,860	6,480
Gene Goodman	4,260	6,390	8,520
Harry Hanson	–0–	1,400	3,100

INSTRUCTIONS

1. Compute the amount of state unemployment tax (at a 2.7% rate) that would be paid on the wages by Noles Company for the third quarter of the year.

2. Give the general journal entry on Oct. 12 to record payment of the state tax when the quarterly return is filed. (Entry 10-5.) (Refer to text illustrations for account numbers to be used throughout this problem.)

3. Compute the federal unemployment tax due for the year, and give the general journal entry to record payment of the tax on Jan. 15, 19X2. (Entry 1-10) The federal tax is 3.2%, less a credit for the state tax of 2.7%.

4. On Jan. 5, 19X1, the Noles Company had paid the estimated workmen's compensation insurance premiums for 19X1. The estimate was based on an expected payroll of $19,000 and a premium rate of $1.75 per $100 of wages.

    a. Give the general journal entry to record payment of the estimated premium on Jan. 5, 19X1. (Entry 1-8.)

    b. Give the general journal entry to record payment of the balance based on the actual payroll for the year, payment being made on Jan. 20, 19X2. (Entry 1-11)

PROBLEM 19 · 1A

Rose Brothers Accessories Store is established on Aug. 1, 19X1 by
◆ James and Roy Rose to carry on a retail accessories business. Its chart of accounts is given here.

101	Cash in Bank	401	Sales
111	Accounts Receivable	501	Merchandise Purchases
121	Merchandise Inventory	506	Freight In
131	Store Furniture & Equipment	511	Purchases Returns &
141	Office Furniture & Equipment		Allowances
201	Accounts Payable	512	Purchases Discount
202	Notes Payable	521	Sales Salaries
221	Employee Ded.—FICA	522	Advertising
222	Employee Ded.—Income Tax WH	523	Store Supplies & Expense
301	J. Rose Investment	529	Cash Short or Over
311	R. Rose Investment	542	Rent Expense
		551	Office Salaries
		553	Office Supplies & Expense

The business transactions for August 19X1 are as follows:

AUG.

1   J. Rose invests $6,000 and R. Rose invests $5,000 in cash in the new business.

1   Acquired $800 worth of office furniture and equipment from City Office Supply Co., giving them a noninterest-bearing, 30-day note payable. (In the general journal, debit 141 and credit 202.)

2   Voucher 8-01 to Office Rental Co., $100 rent for month; paid by Check 101.

3   Voucher 8-02 to City Office Supply Co., $25 for office supplies used.

4   Voucher 8-03 to Town Builders, $500 for building fixtures in store. (Dr. 131.)

5   Voucher 8-04 to T & O Railroad, $36.65 for freight on merchandise purchased.

6   Paid Voucher 8-04 by Check 102.

8   Voucher 8-05 to American Hardware Co., $2,500 for merchandise; terms 2/10, n/30.

9   Acquired cash register for $500 from Machine Supply Co.; terms $250 cash, balance in 30 days. Vouchers 8-06 and 8-07 for the two installments. Paid Voucher 8-06 by Check 103, $250.

10   Voucher 8-08 to Tester Hardware Company, $3,000 for merchandise; terms 2/10, n/30.

12   Voucher 8-09 to Kell Supply Co., $100 for store supplies used.

13   Cash sales, $400.

15   Returned $100 worth of merchandise for credit to Tester Hardware Co. (make circled entry in voucher register over Voucher 8-08).

16   Issued Check 104 to pay Voucher 8-05, net of 2% discount.

17   Cash sales, $525; cash short $1.50.

18   Voucher 8-10 to Daily Herald, $45 for advertising; paid by Check 105.

19   Voucher 8-11 to T & O Railroad, $31.40 for freight on merchandise purchased.

20   Issued Check 106 to pay Voucher 8-11.

AUG.

20 Issued Check 107 to pay Voucher 8-08, net of return and 2% discount.

23 Cash sales, $470; cash over, $.50.

25 Voucher 8-12 to American Hardware Co., $2,150 for merchandise; terms 2/10, n/30.

26 Cash sales, $460; cash short, $1.

27 Voucher 8-13 to City Utilities, $33 for store operations; paid by Check 108.

28 Voucher 8-14 to Bell Telephone Co., $11.60 for office telephone service; paid by Check 109.

30 Voucher 8-15 to City Office Supply Co., $800 note payable of Aug. 1; paid by Check 110.

31 Cash sales, $475; cash short, $.80.

31 Voucher 8-16 to Frank Sims, sales salary $400, less $36 FICA tax and $40.70 income tax deducted; paid by Check 111. Voucher 8-17 to Mary Hill, office salary, $450, less $27.00 FICA tax and $31.40 income tax deducted; paid by check 112.

INSTRUCTIONS

1. Set up a general journal and three special journals: cash receipts journal, voucher register, and check register. (Use the same column headings as the forms illustrated on pages 302, 307 and 308).
2. Set up general ledger accounts for Cash in Bank 101 and Accounts Payable 201.
3. Record the given transactions, then foot and crossfoot the special journals.
4. Post from the special journals to Accounts 101 and 201 only.
5. Prepare a schedule of vouchers payable and prove with the balance of Account 201.

PROBLEM 19 · 2A

On Apr. 10, 19X1, Ames Department Store purchased merchandise from
♦ Gross Manufacturing Company. The invoice price was $1,600. Terms of the sale were 3/20, n/60.

INSTRUCTIONS

1. Record the purchase on Ames' books in general journal form, omitting account numbers and entry numbers throughout, assuming:
   a. Purchases are recorded by Ames at gross price.
   b. Purchases are recorded by Ames at net invoice price.
2. Assuming that Ames Department Store paid the invoice on Apr. 28, record the payment on its books if:
   a. Ames recorded the purchase at gross price.
   b. Ames recorded the purchase at net invoice price.
3. Assuming that Ames Department Store paid the invoice on June 7 (no discount), record the payment on its books if:
   a. Ames recorded the purchase at gross price.
   b. Ames recorded the purchase at net invoice price.

1. Compute the total interest on each of the following notes, using the interest formula method. Show all computations.
   a. $580 at 7% for 90 days.
   b. $1,856.80 at 5% for 6 months.
2. Compute the interest on each of the following notes, using the 6%, 60-day method. Show all computations.
   a. $800 at 6% for 120 days.
   b. $1,857.25 at 6% for 60 days.
   c. $9,850.00 at 5% for 120 days.
3. Compute the discount on the following noninterest-bearing notes. Show all computations.
   a. $8,000, discounted at 8% for 60 days.
   b. $4,500, discounted at 6% for 40 days.

PROBLEM 20 · 2A

Andrew Miguel operates a business involving substantial purchases of equipment. As a result, there are numerous transactions involving notes payable. A notes payable register is maintained. Selected account titles and numbers are given below:

101	Cash in Bank	201	Accounts Payable
131	Factory Equipment	202	Notes Payable—Trade
132	Delivery Equipment	211	Notes Payable—Bank
141	Land	591	Interest Expense

Transactions involving notes payable which took place during the month of July 19X1 are listed below.

JULY

9   Purchased factory equipment from Peterson Company, issuing notes for $12,000 for 3 months with interest at 7%. (Enter in the general journal as Entry 7-11.)

16 Purchased delivery equipment from Main Auto Co. on Invoice 888, dated July 16, 19X1. The initial payment of $4,000 was authorized by Voucher 7-10 and was made by Check 701. A $4,000 note due in 6 months with interest at 7% was given to cover the balance of the purchase price. (Enter Voucher 7-10 in the Voucher Register. General journal entry to record note is 7-14.)

18 Issued a 90-day, 8% note for $5,000 to Blue Realty in payment of land to be used by the company. (General journal Entry 7-16.)

23 A 50-day note for $1,500, bearing interest at 9%, was given to Apex Manufacturing Company for factory equipment that had been previously purchased on account and recorded as Voucher 6-3. (General journal Entry 7-20.)

JULY

24 Renewed $7,000 note dated May 24, in favor of Peterson Equipment Company which was due today. Gave a new note for 60 days with interest at 8%. (No journal entry is required; make notation in notes payable register.)

26 Discounted $8,000 note at First State Bank. The bank deducted an 8% discount charge for the 120-day loan.

28 Paid half of the Mallard Distributors note due today, including all interest due, by Check 745 for $4,620, authorized by Voucher 7-34. Issued a new note for $4,500 payable in 60 days with interest at 8%. (Enter Voucher 7-34 in the voucher register. No journal entry is required in the general journal. Make notation of cash payment and renewal note opposite the original note in the notes payable register, and enter the new note.)

INSTRUCTIONS

1. Enter the following notes on July 1, 19X1, as a memorandum record in a notes payable register with columns as indicated in Unit 20, pages 330 and 331. Compute and enter maturity date and interest, if any, when recording each item.

   a. Note issued to Peterson Equipment Company on May 24, 19X1 for $7,000, payable in 2 months without interest. (This note and all others in this problem are payable at First State Bank.)

   b. Note issued to Mallard Distributors on May 29, 19X1 for $9,000, due in 60 days with interest at 8%.

2. Analyze each transaction and enter in the required journal using:

   a. A general journal.

   b. The notes payable register listed above.

   c. A cash receipts journal with columns as illustrated on page 329.

   d. A voucher register, with columns as illustrated on page 307.

PROBLEM 21 · 1A

The notes received by Barns Manufacturing Company during 19X1 are summarized here.

DATE	FACE	PERIOD	INTEREST RATE
Jan. 22	$ 700	3 months	9%
Mar. 5	3,400	60 days	7
July 8	1,000	45 days	8
Sept. 15	2,400	3 months	6

Two of the notes were discounted by Barns at the First State Bank. On Feb. 1, the note dated Jan. 22 was discounted at a rate of 7½%, and on October 1, the note dated Sept. 15 was discounted at 7%.

INSTRUCTIONS

1. Compute the total interest and the maturity value of each note.

2. On the two notes discounted, compute the discount charged by the bank and the net proceeds.
3. Record the discounting of the two notes in general journal form. (Omit entry numbers.)
4. Give entries in general journal form to record (a) the receipt of the note on Mar. 5 in settlement of Adair Company's account receivable of $3,400, and (b) receipt of payment from Adair Company on May 4 for the $3,400 note dated Mar. 5 and interest on the note. (Omit entry numbers.)

PROBLEM 21 · 2A

The Lucas Lumber Company uses a notes receivable register as a mem-
◆ orandum record to maintain control over the numerous notes which it handles. Notes outstanding at Mar. 31, 19X1 are as follows:

$2,400, 8%, 6-month note of Ralph Smith, dated Jan. 10.
$2,000, 6%, 90-day note of William Parker, dated Jan. 15. (This note was discounted at First National Bank on Feb. 1, 19X1.)
$3,000, 8%, 90-day note of Black Construction Co., dated Jan. 18, discounted Feb. 1.
$1,350, noninterest-bearing, 60-day note of John Savage, dated Feb. 7.
$2,200, 6%, 45-day note of Thompson Contractors, dated Feb. 25.
$4,800, 7%, 120-day note of Blalock Home Bldg., dated Mar. 20, payable at Commercial Bank.

The following note transactions took place during April 19X1. (In solving this problem, you are not required to post to the general ledger or subsidiary ledger accounts, nor to make any disbursement vouchers or any entries in the voucher register or check register.)

APRIL
2 Accepted a 60-day noninterest-bearing note for $1,800, dated today, from Winston Builders, as an extension of credit on their overdue account receivable. (Record in the general journal, using Entry 4-1, and in the notes receivable register. All journal entries are to be numbered consecutively.)
5 Discounted Ralph Smith's 6-month note for $2,400 dated Jan. 10 and due July 10. (When the term of the note is specified in months, the maturity date is determined by counting forward in "round" months.) The discount rate set by Commercial Bank was 9%. (Record in the cash receipts journal.)
8 John Savage's 60-day note dated Feb. 7, 19X1 was due today. He gave a check for $650 and a new note for $700 due in 90 days with interest at 8%. (Record the receipt of cash in the cash receipts journal. Make appropriate comments in the Remarks section of the notes receivable register opposite the entry of the original note, and enter the new note on the next open line.)
11 Thompson Contractor's note for $2,200 dated Feb. 25, 19X1, with interest

at 6%, was due today and was dishonored. (Charge the note plus interest to accounts receivable.)

15 Received notice that William Parker's 90-day $2,000 note dated Jan. 15, 19X1, which was discounted at the First National Bank on Feb. 1, 19X1, was dishonored today. The bank charged the Lucas Lumber Company account for $2,035, representing the maturity value of the note plus a protest fee. (Record the charge-back by the bank in the general journal. Also record in the general journal the termination of the contingent liability for the discounted note.)

16 Accepted a 90-day 8% note for $2,600 from Sam Gibson as an extension of credit on his past due account receivable.

18 Received payment including interest from Black Construction Company for their note dated Jan. 18, 19X1, due today.

19 Discounted Blalock Home Builders note for $4,800 dated Mar. 20, 19X1, at the First National Bank. The discount rate was 9%.

INSTRUCTIONS

1. Enter the notes outstanding on March 31, in a notes receivable register that has the same columns as shown in the illustration in this unit. All notes are payable at the First National Bank unless otherwise indicated.

2. Using a general journal and a cash receipts journal, record the given note transactions. The cash receipts journal should have the same column heads as the illustration on page 340. The required account titles and numbers are provided here.

101 Cash in Bank
111 Accounts Receivable
112 Notes Receivable
113 Notes Receivable Discounted

491 Interest Income
591 Interest Expense

3. Enter data in the notes receivable register where appropriate.

PROBLEM 22 · 1A

The T. R. Roof Company records losses on bad debts as they occur. The accounts involved are Accounts Receivable 111, Notes Receivable 112, and Bad Debts Expense 561. Selected transactions for 19X1 are described here.

19X1

Jan. 15 Account receivable of Edwin Tate amounting to $75 is determined to be uncollectible and is to be written off. (Entry 1-4.)

Mar. 20 Because of the death of Henry Booker, his note receivable amounting to $250 is considered uncollectible and is to be written off. (Entry 3-9.)

June 4 Received $40 from Edwin Tate in partial payment of his account written off on Jan. 15. (Entry 6-3.) The receipt of cash has already been recorded in the cash receipts journal.

July 17 Received $35 from Edwin Tate to complete payment of his account written off on Jan. 15. (Entry 7-8.) The receipt of cash has already been recorded in the cash receipts journal.

Sept. 24 Received $105 from the estate of Henry Booker as a part of the settlement of his affairs. This is the pro rata amount applicable to the note receivable written off on Mar. 20. (Entry 9-17.) The receipt of cash has already been recorded in the cash receipts journal.

INSTRUCTIONS
Record each transaction in general journal form.

PROBLEM 22 · 2A

The Ackerman Supply Company sells building materials on credit and

♦ records sales in three separate income accounts. Experience indicates that each sales category has a different rate of bad debt losses, and the total charged off each accounting period is based on three computations under the percentage of credit sales method (one computation for each income account). At Dec. 31, 19X1, the balance of Accounts Receivable 111 is $234,550 and the credit balance of Allowance for Bad Debts 111A is $2,860. The following information is given.

CATEGORY	CREDIT SALES AMOUNT	ESTIMATED RATE OF LOSS
Masonry	$625,000	0.9%
Lumber and Millwork	470,000	1.4
Hardware	138,000	2.0

INSTRUCTIONS
1. Compute the estimated bad debt loss on each of the three credit sales categories for the calendar year.
2. Prepare the adjusting entry (12-22A) in general journal form to provide for the bad debt losses before they occur. (Use Bad Debts Expense 561.)
3. Show how the Accounts Receivable and Allowance for Bad Debts accounts would appear on the balance sheet of the Ackerman Supply Company at Dec. 31, 19X1. List only the account titles and the amounts.
4. On Feb. 17, 19X2, the account receivable of Robert Woodson, amounting to $344, is determined to be uncollectible and is to be written off. Use Entry 2-11 to record this transaction in the general journal.
5. On May 15, 19X2, the attorneys for the Ackerman Supply Company turn over a check for $344, which they have obtained from Robert Woodson in settlement of his account written off on Feb. 17. Receipt of the money has been recorded in the cash receipts journal, and it is only necessary to make Entry 5-9 in the general journal to cancel the original bad debt entry.

PROBLEM 22 · 3A

An aging schedule of the accounts receivable of the Mart Furniture Company at the end of the fiscal year is reproduced here.

MART FURNITURE COMPANY
Aging Schedule of Accounts Receivable
June 30, 19X2

ACCOUNT WITH	BALANCE	CURRENT	PAST DUE—DAYS 1–30	31–60	OVER 60
Akard, J. T.	$ 127	$ 63	$ 64		
Ball, B. C.	236	111	90	$ 35	
Cline, J. D.	98	98			
Derr, A. R.	19	19			
Everett, M. W.	316			208	$108
Faison, N. O.	74	29	45		
Gaines, C. R.	197	68	92		37
Hayes, W. A.	252	114	138		
Ivan, T. S.	132			132	
Jones, J. S.	59		59		
(All other accounts)	5,637	2,932	1,874	453	378
Totals	$7,147	$3,434	$2,362	$828	$523

INSTRUCTIONS

1. Compute the estimated uncollectible accounts at the end of the fiscal year using these rates:

Current	1%
1–30 days past due	5%
31–60 days past due	10%
Over 60 days past due	25%

2. At June 30, 19X2, Allowance for Bad Debts 111A has a debit balance of $113.50. Compute the amount of the adjustment for estimated bad debt losses that must be made as part of the adjusting entries.
3. In general journal form, record the entry (6-18A) for the estimated bad debt loss adjustment. (Charge it to Bad Debts Expense 561.)
4. On July 18, 19X2, the account receivable of T. S. Ivan amounting to $132 was recognized as uncollectible because of his serious illness. Record this write-off in the general journal, using Entry 7-11. (Use Accounts Receivable 111.)
5. On Aug. 2, 19X2, a check for $100 was received from James Scott to apply on his account previously written off (Entry 4-12, Apr. 19, 19X1) as uncollectible. Record the cancellation of the previous bad debt write-off by Entry 8-1.
6. Suppose that instead of aging the accounts receivable, the uncollectible accounts were estimated to be simply 5% of the accounts receivable on June 30. Give the journal entry to record the estimated bad debt loss adjustment, assuming that the Allowance for Bad Debts 111A account had a credit balance of $62.50 before the adjusting entry. (Entry 6-18A.)

PROBLEM 22 · 4A

♦ Vane's Appliances is a retail store for the sale of household appliances and equipment. Small items are sold for cash or on open account to approved credit customers. Major appliances are sometimes sold for cash but are usually sold on the installment plan. On July 2, 19X4, Vane's sells to Ernest Alward a refrigerator for $1,000 on the installment plan. The refrigerator cost Vane's $600. Alward agrees to make a down payment of $75 and to pay $25 on the first day of each month thereafter, beginning Aug. 1, 19X4.

INSTRUCTIONS

Prepare in general journal form the entries required to record the following. Use the same account numbers and titles used in the textbook. Omit entry numbers.

1. The sale on July 2, 19X4 of the refrigerator on the installment plan.
2. The receipt of the agreed cash down payment on the sale date.
3. The receipt on Aug. 2, 19X4 of the agreed monthly cash payment.
4. Recognition on Dec. 31, 19X4 of that portion of the deferred income that has been earned, assuming all monthly payments have been received as agreed.
5. Recognition on Dec. 31, 19X5 of that portion of the deferred income that has been earned during the year, assuming all monthly payments have been received as agreed.
6. The repossession of the refrigerator by Vane's on Mar. 15, 19X6, and the return to inventory at its appraised value of $200, since Alward failed to make any 19X6 payments.

PROBLEM 23 · 1A

The following data are given:

Inventory, June 1	150 units @ $4.00
Purchases, June 6	200 units @ $4.05
June 14	150 units @ $4.20
June 24	100 units @ $4.25
Inventory, June 30	162 units

INSTRUCTIONS

Determine the cost to be shown for the ending inventory on June 30 under each of the following methods:

1. Average cost.
2. First in, first out.
3. Last in, first out.

PROBLEM 23 · 2A

The following data are given:

	QUANTITY	UNIT COST	MARKET
ACCESSORIES DEPARTMENT: Type 1	250	$3.00	$3.20
2	400	4.40	4.20
3	370	2.00	2.10
APPLIANCES DEPARTMENT: 4	4	$170.00	$182.00
5	2	410.00	400.00
6	5	153.00	144.00

INSTRUCTIONS

Determine the amount to be reported as the inventory valuation at cost or market, whichever is lower, under each of these methods:

1. Lower of cost or market for each item separately.
2. Lower of total cost or total market.
3. Lower of total cost or total market by departments.

PROBLEM 23 · 3A

In 19X0, the gross profit rate on sales of Wise Company was 24.8%, and in 19X1 the rate was 25.2%. At the end of 19X2 the income statement of the company included the following.

Sales		$820,000
Cost of Goods Sold		
Inventory, Jan. 1, 19X2	$ 60,000	
Purchases	604,000	
Cost of goods available	$664,000	
Less Inventory, Dec. 31, 19X2	94,000	
Cost of Goods Sold		570,000
Gross Profit on Sales		$250,000

Investigation revealed that employees of the company had not taken an actual physical count of the inventory on Dec. 31, 19X2, but had merely estimated the inventory.

INSTRUCTIONS

Using the gross profit method of inventory estimation, verify the reasonableness (or lack of reasonableness) of the ending inventory shown in the financial statement.

PROBLEM 23 · 4A

The July 1 inventory of the McClellan Company cost $18,000 and had a retail value of $24,500. During July, merchandise was purchased for $8,840 and marked to sell for $11,500. Freight In on purchases during July totaled $160. July sales totaled $10,600.

INSTRUCTIONS

1. Estimate the July 31 inventory using the retail method.
2. Compute the cost of goods sold.

PROBLEM 24 · 1A

The Salty Chemical Company has purchased a machine, net cost of
♦ $3,200. The estimated useful life is 5 years and the estimated salvage
value is $200.

INSTRUCTIONS
1. Using the straight-line method, compute the annual depreciation charge.
2. Using the declining-balance method, compute the annual depreciation
    charge for each year, and determine both the depreciation to date (the
    balance in the allowance account at the end of each year) and the ending
    book value.
3. Using the sum of the years-digits method, compute the annual depreci-
    ation charge for each year and determine both the depreciation to date
    (the balance in the allowance account at the end of each year) and the
    ending book value.
4. Show a comparison of the results obtained under these various methods
    in a table providing columns for Year, Depreciation for Year (Straight-Line,
    Declining-Balance, Sum of the Years-Digits), and Depreciation to Date
    (Straight-Line, Declining-Balance, Sum of the Years-Digits). Also compute
    book values at the end of 5 years.

PROBLEM 24 · 2A

The Contour Company purchased four identical machines on Jan. 2,
♦ 19X1, for $555 each, paying cash. The useful life of each machine is
expected to be 6 years and salvage value at the end of that time is
estimated to be $75 each. The company uses the straight-line method of depre-
ciation and has the following accounts on its books.

101	Cash in Bank	495	Gain on Sale of Machinery
141	Machinery	541	Depreciation—Machinery
141A	Allow. for Depr.—Mach.	595	Loss on Sale of Machinery
		596	Loss on Machinery Stolen

The following selected transactions took place from 19X1 through 19X4.

19X1

Jan. 2   Bought four machines for cash, $555 each. (Entry 1-1.)

Dec. 31   Recorded depreciation for the year on the four machines. (Entry
12-1A.)

19X2

Mar. 31   Machine 1 was stolen. No insurance was carried. (Entries 3-1 and
3-2.)

Dec. 31   Recorded depreciation for the year on the three remaining machines.
(Entry 12-1A.)

19X3

Sept. 30   Machine 2 was sold for $356 cash. (Entries 9-1 and 9-2.)

Dec. 31   Recorded depreciation for the year on two remaining machines. (Entry 12-1A.)

19X4

Apr. 30   Machine 3 was traded in on a similar machine with a list price of $610; paid in cash, less a trade-in allowance of $310. (Use the income tax method of recording the trade-in.) (Entries 4-1 and 4-2.)

July 31   Machine 4 was traded in on a similar machine with a list price of $620; paid in cash, less a trade-in allowance of $285. (Use the income tax method.)

INSTRUCTIONS

1. Record the given transactions in general journal form.
2. Assuming that the trade-ins of Machines 3 and 4 were recorded under the "fair market value" method, give the general journal entries to record the trade-in of Machine 3 on Apr. 30, 19X4 and the trade-in of Machine 4 on July 31, 19X4.

PROBLEM 24 · 3A

The accounts of Eastex Company on Jan. 1, 19X1 included the following:

154	Copyrights	536	Amortization of Copyrights
156	Ore Deposits	583	Depletion—Ore Deposits
156A	Allowance for Depletion— Ore Deposits		

An analysis of account balances revealed:

1. The Copyright account contains a debit balance of $20,000. This represents the unamortized cost of a copyright purchased on Jan. 1, 19X0 for $25,000. Management had estimated the useful life of the copyright to be 5 years and had charged $5,000 to expense in 19X0, crediting that amount to the Copyright account.
2. Ore deposits, $180,000. Allowance for Depletion of Ore Deposits, $30,000. It was estimated that the deposits contained 1,000,000 tons of ore. In 19X1, 160,000 tons of ore were produced and sold for $1.20 per ton.

INSTRUCTIONS

1. Give general journal entries to record the copyright amortization and the depletion expense for 19X1. (Entries 12-6A and 12-7A.)
2. Assuming that expenses, other than depletion, related to the ore produc-

tion totaled $175,000 in 19X1, what amount of depletion could the company claim on its federal income tax return during 19X1? Statutory depletion for this type ore is 10%.

PROBLEM 25 · 1A

County Farm Supply Company estimates its 19X1 property tax based on a proposed assessed value of property of $8,000 and a tax rate of 60 mills. The taxing authority is on a calendar-year basis. The tax bill is usually received in September and must be paid by Nov. 30 to avoid penalty. The following occurred during 19X1.

19X1

Jan. 31	Estimated January tax expense recorded. (Entry 1-1A.)
Feb. 28	Estimated February tax expense recorded. (Entry 2-1A.)
Sept. 15	Recorded the tax bill received, $524. (Assume that estimated property taxes were recorded monthly, from January through August.) (Entry 9-1.)
Sept. 30	Recorded September tax expense. (Entry 9-2A.)
Nov. 25	Recorded payment of the tax bill, $524. (Entry 11-1.)
Nov. 30	November tax expense recorded. (Entry 11-2A.)
Dec. 31	December tax expense recorded. (Entry 12-1A.)

INSTRUCTIONS

In general journal form, record the entries required, using these accounts: Cash in Bank 101, Prepaid Taxes 128, Property Taxes Payable 235, and Tax Expense 555.

PROBLEM 25 · 2A

The following sales data are given for a retail business on May 31, 19X1.

1. Sales on account for the month of May were $155,609.10, plus a 4% state sales tax on all sales.
2. Cash sales for May totaled $3,455.40, plus the 4% state sales tax on all sales.
3. Goods sold for cash were returned and the customer was given a cash refund for the amount of the sale, $45.40, plus the 4% tax.
4. Goods sold for $890.80 on account were returned and customers were given credit for the sales price plus the 4% tax.

INSTRUCTIONS

Record each of the given facts in general journal form. (Start with Entry 5-1.)

PROBLEM 25 · 3A

♦ During April 19X9 the Wagner Building Materials Company had total sales of $565,400 and sales returns and allowances of $4,600. At the end of April, the Sales Tax Payable account showed a balance of $16,822.18. The sales tax rate is 3%, and the commission is 3% of the gross amount of sales tax due.

INSTRUCTIONS

1. Make the calculations that are required in preparing the sales tax return:
   a. Taxable gross sales for April.
   b. Total sales tax due.
   c. Amount of commission earned by Wagner.
   d. Amount of sales tax to be paid to collecting agency.
2. Show in general journal form (omit entry and account numbers and explanation), the following:
   a. The entry required to record payment to the collecting agency of the sales tax due.
   b. The entry required to transfer the commission to Miscellaneous Income and close the Sales Tax Payable account for April.

PROBLEM 25 · 4A

♦ Level Company must collect a tax on all its sales. The tax is 4% of retail selling price and is credited to the Sales account along with the actual amount of the sale. Similarly, when merchandise is returned by customers, the entire return and allowance, both retail sales price and the tax, is debited to the Sales Returns and Allowances account.

On Mar. 31, 19X1, at the time the quarterly sales tax return is filed, the company's accounts include the following balances:

Sales	$114,240.50
Sales Returns and Allowances	1,354.60

The company is entitled to retain 3% of the sales tax due as a commission to help cover its expenses of collecting the tax.

INSTRUCTIONS

1. Compute the amount of sales tax on net sales.
2. Prepare a general journal entry to transfer the gross amount of sales tax from the Sales account to the Sales Tax Payable account, and from the Sales Returns and Allowances account to the Sales Tax Payable account. (Ignore journal entry numbers and account numbers.)
3. Give the journal entry to transfer the commission earned from the Sales Tax Payable account to the Miscellaneous Income account.
4. Give the journal entry to record payment of the net sales tax due.

PROBLEM 26 · 1A

♦ Examination of the account balances in the trial balance of Foot Company at the end of its fiscal year on July 31, 19X2 indicates the need for the adjustments given here.

(A) Anticipated bad debt losses are to be calculated at 0.2% of net credit sales of $784,000 for the fiscal year.

(B) Depreciation on equipment is to be computed using the straight-line method. Total cost of equipment is $82,000, and it is estimated to have a net salvage value of $4,000, with a useful life of 12 years.

(C) Property taxes for the calendar year 19X2 are estimated to be $1,200, to be accrued at the rate of $100 per month.

(D) Salaries and Wages earned recorded in July subject to payroll taxes were $6,000. Applicable tax rates are 6% (assumed) for FICA, 2% for state unemployment, and 0.5% for federal unemployment. All payroll taxes through June 30 have been recorded.

(E) Notes Payable—Trade consists of a $12,000 note dated May 31, 19X2 and bearing interest at 7%.

(F) The inventory of supplies on hand at July 31 is valued at $285.

(G) Insurance unexpired on July 31 amounts to $750.

The following selected accounts and balances are to be used in making the required adjustments.

111A	Allowance for Bad Debts	$	134.00 Cr.
125	Prepaid Insurance		–0–
127	Supplies Inventory		–0–
131A	Allow. for Depr.—Equipment		13,950.00 Cr.
216	Interest Payable		–0–
226	Payroll Taxes Payable		–0–
235	Property Taxes Payable		–0–
523	Supplies Expense		2,340.00 Dr.
536	Insurance Expense		4,354.00 Dr.
552	Payroll Tax Expense		3,250.00 Dr.
555	Property Tax Expense		324.00 Dr.
561	Bad Debts Expense		–0–
563	Depreciation—Equipment		–0–
591	Interest Expense		–0–

INSTRUCTIONS

1. Prepare a partial worksheet that has the same columns as shown in the illustration on page 210.
2. Enter on the worksheet the given accounts and balances.
3. Enter on the worksheet the given adjustments, identifying each with its appropriate letter. (No adjustments have been entered on the books this year.)

4. Combine the Trial Balance amounts with the Adjustments figures and enter in the Adjusted Trial Balance columns.

PROBLEM 26 · 2A

In this problem, you are to use the Dec. 31, 19X2 trial balance of Art
♦ Supply Store, given in Prob. 26-2, page 434.
Following are listed the adjustments for the Art Supply Store on Dec. 31.

(A) An analysis of accounts receivable results in an estimate that $286.10 of the accounts are uncollectible. Adjust the Allowance for Bad Debts account to this balance. (Debit Account 539.)
(B) Prepaid insurance at Dec. 31 was $187.
(C) Depreciation is 10% of cost of furniture and equipment.
(D) Rent expense for December of $150 has not been recorded or paid; it was due Dec. 27. (Credit Accounts Payable 201.)
(E) Payroll taxes on $700 of December salaries and wages have not been recorded. Payroll tax rates are: FICA 6%, state unemployment 2.5%, and federal unemployment 0.5%.

INSTRUCTIONS

1. Set up a typical 10-column worksheet listing the given accounts and recording the amounts in the first pair of money columns, headed Trial Balance. Total the columns.
2. Record the adjustments in the second pair of money columns, identifying each by letter. Show computations on a separate sheet. Total the adjustments.
3. Save your worksheet for use in Prob. 27-1A.

♦ ## PROBLEM 26 · 3A

1. New Supply Co. follows a policy of charging directly to prepaid expense (asset) accounts certain expenditures made during the year. At Dec. 31, 19X6, these asset accounts had the balances shown, before adjustment.

Prepaid Insurance	$3,800
Prepaid Interest Expense	1,850
Supplies Inventory	1,420

Analysis at Dec. 31, 19X6 indicates $1,150 of insurance unexpired, $400 of interest prepaid on notes payable outstanding, and $240 of supplies on hand unused.

INSTRUCTIONS

Show in general journal entry form, the adjustment required in each of the accounts at December 31, 19X6. (Omit entry and account numbers and explanation.)

2. Assume instead that New Supply Co. charges expenditures directly to the expense accounts involved, so that at Dec. 31, 19X6 the expense accounts have the balances shown, before adjustment.

Insurance Expense	$3,800
Interest Expense	1,850
Supplies Expense	1,420

Analysis at Dec. 31, 19X6, indicates $1,150 of insurance unexpired, $400 of interest prepaid on notes payable outstanding, and $240 of supplies on hand unused.

INSTRUCTIONS

Show in general journal entry form, the adjustment required in each of the accounts at Dec. 31, 19X6. (Omit entry and account numbers and explanation.)

PROBLEM 26 · 4A

♦ During its first year of existence, 19X1, Magazine Publishing Company received subscriptions in cash totaling $548,600. Analysis at Dec. 31, 19X1 indicates that $234,500 is applicable to the current year and that the remainder is applicable to 19X2 and future years.

INSTRUCTIONS

1. Assuming that the $548,600 was credited to Unearned Subscriptions Income when it was received, show in general journal form the entry necessary to adjust the books on Dec. 31, 19X1. (You may omit entry number, account number, and explanation.)

2. Assuming, instead, that the $548,600 was credited to Subscriptions Income when it was received, give the necessary adjusting journal entry on Dec. 31, 19X1.

♦ **PROBLEM 27 · 1A** This problem is a continuation of Prob. 26 · 2A.

INSTRUCTIONS

1. Prepare an adjusted trial balance in the third pair of money columns on the worksheet for Art Supply Store that you completed in Prob. 26 · 2A. Total the columns to prove the equality of debits and credits.

2. Record the ending merchandise inventory of $24,850 and complete the worksheet. (Save the worksheet for use with Problem 28 · 3A.)

3. Prepare the income statement for the year 19X2, including the Distribution

of Net Profit section at the bottom. Laney receives 60% of the profit; Simms receives 40%.

4. Prepare a statement of partners' equities for the year. There were no additional investments during the year.

5. Prepare a classified balance sheet at Dec. 31, 19X2 in report form.

PROBLEM 27 · 2A

The trial balance of Varsity Men's Shop at Dec. 31, 19X1 is given in
◆ Prob. 27 · 2, page 452. Information regarding the adjustments for the business on Dec. 31 is given below.

(A) Bad debts are estimated at 0.2% of sales. (Debit Account 539.)
(B) Prepaid insurance, $85.
(C) Depreciation is 8% of office equipment cost.
(D) Rent expense for December of $100, which is past due, has not yet been paid or recorded. (Credit Account 201.)
(E) Payroll taxes on $600 of December salaries have not been recorded. Payroll tax rates are FICA 6%, state unemployment 2.7%, and federal unemployment 0.5%.

INSTRUCTIONS

1. Set up a typical 10-column worksheet, listing the given accounts and recording the amounts in the first pair of money columns, headed Trial Balance. (Use Accounts and balances given in Prob. 27 · 2.)

2. Record the adjustments in the second pair of money columns, identifying each by letter. On a separate sheet, show the computations of each adjustment.

3. Prepare an adjusted trial balance in the third pair of money columns and total the columns to prove the equality of debits and credits.

4. Record the ending merchandise inventory of $20,750 and complete the worksheet.

5. Prepare the income statement for the year 19X1, including the Distribution of Net Profit section at the bottom. Profits and losses are shared equally by Fox and Jacobs.

6. Prepare a statement of partners' equities for the year. (There were no additional investments during the year.)

7. Prepare a balance sheet at Dec. 31, 19X1.

PROBLEM 28 · 1A

The following information for Apex Retail Company is given as of Dec.
◆ 31, 19X1.

(A) Unpaid wages on Dec. 31 total $1,850. These wages have not been recorded.

(B) The balance of the Prepaid Insurance account is $2,000. This represents the unexpired insurance premium as of Jan. 1, 19X1 on a 2-year insurance policy purchased for $2,400 on Aug. 31, 19X0.

(C) Interest accrued on notes payable totals $88.

(D) The Supplies Expense account shows a balance of $2,245. However, a physical count shows that supplies costing $281.50 are still on hand on Dec. 31.

(E) Depreciation on equipment totals $1,760 for the year.

(F) The Rent Expense account balance is $3,000. This includes $500 paid in advance for the month of January 19X2.

(G) Employer's FICA taxes of 6% on $600 of the accrued wages must be recorded. None of the unpaid wages is subject to unemployment taxes.

INSTRUCTIONS

1. Give the adjusting entry required on Dec. 31, 19X1 for each of the items given. (Begin with Entry 12-13A. Omit account numbers.)

2. In general journal form, give the reversing or readjusting entries necessary on Jan. 1, 19X2.

PROBLEM 28 · 2A

The completed worksheet for Margin Service Company for the year
♦ ended Dec. 31, 19X1 is shown on the following page.

INSTRUCTIONS

1. Journalize the adjusting journal entries for Dec. 31. (Begin with Entry 12-12A.) Omit explanations.

2. Journalize the closing entries on Dec. 31. Omit explanations. (Income and Expense Summary account 399.)

3. Journalize the necessary reversing entries on Jan. 1, 19X2. Omit explanations.

PROBLEM 28 · 3A

♦ This problem is a continuation of Prob. 27 · 1A.

INSTRUCTIONS

Refer to the worksheet for Art Supply Company prepared in Prob.
27 · 1A, and carry out the following steps.

1. Open a general ledger and enter the Dec. 31, 19X2 balance for each account given in the trial balance. Write the word "balance" in the Explanation column and place a check mark in the Posting Reference column in each case to show that the amount was not posted from a journal. Also set up an account for Income and Expense Summary 399.

MARGIN SERVICE COMPANY
Worksheet
Year Ended December 31, 19X1

ACCT. NO.	ACCOUNT NAME	TRIAL BALANCE DEBIT	TRIAL BALANCE CREDIT	ADJUSTMENTS DEBIT	ADJUSTMENTS CREDIT	ADJUSTED TRIAL BALANCE DEBIT	ADJUSTED TRIAL BALANCE CREDIT	INCOME STATEMENT DEBIT	INCOME STATEMENT CREDIT	BALANCE SHEET DEBIT	BALANCE SHEET CREDIT
101	Cash	4,800.00				4,800.00				4,800.00	
111	Accounts Receivable	4,200.00				4,200.00				4,200.00	
111A	Allowance for Bad Debts		20.00		A) 305.00		325.00				325.00
121	Merchandise Inventory	9,000.00				9,000.00		9,000.00	10,200.00	10,200.00	
131	Prepaid Insurance	420.00			B) 270.00	150.00				150.00	
132	Supplies	1,280.00			C) 930.00	350.00				350.00	
141	Equipment	9,000.00				9,000.00				9,000.00	
141A	Allow. for Depreciation–Equipment		1,800.00		D) 900.00		2,700.00				2,700.00
201	Accounts Payable		1,020.00				1,020.00				1,020.00
202	Salaries & Wages Payable				E) 200.00		200.00				200.00
203	Payroll Taxes Payable				F) 16.00		16.00				16.00
301	Fox Investment		12,460.00				12,460.00				12,460.00
302	Fox Drawing	3,400.00				3,400.00				3,400.00	
401	Sales		94,060.00				94,060.00		94,060.00		
501	Purchases	60,000.00				60,000.00		60,000.00			
531	Salaries & Wages	6,500.00		E) 200.00		6,700.00		6,700.00			
532	Payroll Tax Expense	410.00		F) 16.00		426.00		426.00			
533	Bad Debts Expense			A) 305.00		305.00		305.00			
534	Supplies Used			C) 930.00		930.00		930.00			
535	Insurance Expense			B) 270.00		270.00		270.00			
537	Depreciation–Equipment			D) 900.00		900.00		900.00			
538	Other Expenses	10,350.00				10,350.00		10,350.00			
	Totals	109,360.00	109,360.00	2,621.00	2,621.00	110,781.00	110,781.00	88,881.00	104,260.00	32,100.00	16,721.00
	Net Profit for Year							15,379.00			15,379.00
								104,260.00	104,260.00	32,100.00	32,100.00

2. Journalize the adjusting and closing entries. (Begin with Entry 12-14A). Omit explanations.
3. Post the adjusting and closing entries to the ledger accounts.
4. Prepare a postclosing trial balance of the general ledger.
5. Rule the income and expense accounts. Do not rule the balance sheet accounts.
6. Record in general journal form the readjusting or reversing entries necessary on Jan. 1, 19X3. (Reverse the Rent Expense adjustment, since Accounts Payable was credited only to simplify Prob. 26 • 2A.) Omit explanations.
7. Post these reversing entries to the ledger accounts.

APPENDIX: MODEL ACCOUNTING PAPERS

Carter Cleaning Shop
Income Statement
Month Ended December 31, 19X1

Income			
Cleaning Service			$300000
Less Expenses			
Salary Expense	$160000		
Rent Expense	70000		
Supplies Used	60000		
Total Expenses			290000
Net Profit for the Month			$10000

Carter Cleaning Shop
Balance Sheet
December 31, 19X1

Assets		Liabilities and Owner's Equity		
Cash	$320000	Liabilities		
Accts. Receivable	20000	Accts. Payable		$30000
Equipment	300000	Owner's Equity		
		Carter Invest. 12/1/X1	$600000	
		Profit for Dec.	10000	
		Carter Invest. 12/31/X1		610000
		Total Liabilities and		
Total Assets	$640000	Owner's Equity		$640000

GENERAL JOURNAL

DATE	DESCRIPTION OF ENTRY	ACCT. NO.	✓	DEBIT	CREDIT
19 X1	12-1				
Dec. 11	Cash	101		220000	
	Cleaning Service Income	401			220000
	To record cash sales.				
	12-2				
14	Accounts Receivable	111		80000	
	Cleaning Service Income	401			80000
	To record credit sales.				
	12-3				
16	Cash	101		60000	
	Accounts Receivable	111			60000
	To record collections to apply on				
	customers' accounts.				

GENERAL LEDGER

Cash
NO. 101

DATE	EXPLANATION	POST. REF.	DEBIT	DATE	EXPLANATION	POST. REF.	CREDIT
19 X1 Nov. 26		11-1	6000 00	19 X1 Nov. 27		11-2	2000 00
Dec. 11		12-1	2200 00	30		11-4	700 00
16		12-3	600 00	Dec. 18		12-4	1600 00
	3,200.00		8800 00	20		12-5	700 00
				31		12-6	600 00
							5600 00

Carter Cleaning Shop
Trial Balance
December 31, 19 X 1

ACCT. NO.	ACCOUNT NAME	DEBIT	CREDIT
101	Cash	3200 00	
111	Accounts Receivable	200 00	
141	Equipment	3000 00	
201	Accounts Payable		300 00
301	Carter Investment		6000 00
401	Cleaning Service Income		3000 00
511	Salary Expense	1600 00	
516	Rent Expense	700 00	
521	Supplies Used	600 00	
	Totals	9300 00	9300 00

Carter Cleaning Shop
Worksheet
Month Ended December 31, 19X1

ACCT. NO.	ACCOUNT NAME	TRIAL BALANCE DR.	TRIAL BALANCE CR.	INCOME STATEMENT DR.	INCOME STATEMENT CR.	BALANCE SHEET DR.	BALANCE SHEET CR.
101	Cash	3200 00				3200 00	
111	Accounts Receivable	200 00				200 00	
141	Equipment	3000 00				3000 00	
201	Accounts Payable		300 00				300 00
301	Carter Investment		6000 00				6000 00
401	Cleaning Service Income		3000 00		3000 00		
511	Salary Expense	1600 00		1600 00			
516	Rent Expense	700 00		700 00			
521	Supplies Used	600 00		600 00			
	Totals	9300 00	9300 00	2900 00	3000 00	6400 00	6300 00
	Profit for the Month			100 00			100 00
				3000 00	3000 00	6400 00	6400 00

Carter Cleaning Shop
Postclosing Trial Balance
December 31, 19X1

ACCT. NO.	ACCOUNT NAME	DEBIT	CREDIT
101	Cash	3 2 0 0 00	
111	Accounts Receivable	2 0 0 00	
141	Equipment	3 0 0 0 00	
201	Accounts Payable		3 0 0 00
301	Carter Investment		6 1 0 0 00
	Totals	6 4 0 0 00	6 4 0 0 00

CASH RECEIPTS JOURNAL FOR MONTH OF *January* 19X2 PAGE 1

DATE	EXPLANATION	ACCOUNTS RECEIVABLE ✓ CR. 111	CLEANING SVC. INC. CR. 401	CASH DR. 101
Jan. 7	Cash Sales		7 0 0 00	7 0 0 00
9	Collections on account / Dec. customers	2 0 0 00		2 0 0 00
14	Cash Sales		7 2 5 00	7 2 5 00
16	Collection on account / Camp	3 0 00		3 0 00

CASH DISBURSEMENTS JOURNAL FOR MONTH OF *January* 19X2 PAGE 1

DATE	CHECK NO.	EXPLANATION	SUNDRY DEBITS ACCT. NO.	✓	AMOUNT	✓	ACCOUNTS PAYABLE DR. 201	CASH CR. 101
Jan. 2	31	Equipment	141		7 7 0 00			7 7 0 00
10	32	Knight					3 0 0 00	3 0 0 00
15	33	Supplies Used	521		4 0 0 00			4 0 0 00
17	34	Rent Expense	516		7 0 0 00			7 0 0 00

PETTY CASH ANALYSIS SHEET FOR MONTH OF *May* 19X2 PAGE 1

DATE	VOU. NO.	EXPLANATION	RECEIPTS	PAYMENTS	DISTRIBUTION OF PAYMENTS SUP. USED DR. 521	DEL. EXP. DR. 532	MISC. EXP. DR. 591	SUNDRY DEBITS ACCT. NO.	AMOUNT
May 1	✓	To establish fund	25 00						
5	1	Office Supply Company		4 75	4 75				
12	2	Ace Express Company		3 00		3 00			
17	3	Roberts Delivery		3 20		3 20			
26	4	H. Tate — windows		1 10			1 10		
27	5	Carter Drawing		5 00				302	5 00
31		Totals	25 00	17 05	4 75	6 20	1 10		5 00
31		Balance		7 95					
			25 00	25 00					
31		Balance	7 95						
31		To replenish fund	17 05						
31		Carried Forward	25 00						

SALES JOURNAL FOR MONTH OF January 19X2   PAGE 1

DATE	SALES SLIP NO.	CUSTOMER'S NAME	✓	AMOUNT
Jan. 7	1	R. L. Camp		60 00
14	2	M. F. Coleman		25 00
19	3	B. A. Hahn		30 00
28	4	S. S. Baker		60 00
31		Total Credit Sales	Debit 111 ✓ Credit 401 ✓	175 00

PURCHASES JOURNAL FOR MONTH OF February 19X2   PAGE 1

DATE	PURCHASED FROM	INV. NO.	INVOICE DATE	TERMS	✓	AMOUNT
Feb. 1	Weller Wholesale Company	649	2/1	30 days		1200 00
13	Beaver Products Company	A4973	2/12	30 days		500 00
17	Premium Plastics, Inc.	43691	2/15	20 days		100 00
24	Weller Wholesale Company	855	2/22	30 days		210 00
28	Total Credit Purchases				Debit 501 ✓ Credit 201 ✓	1810 00

ACCOUNTS RECEIVABLE LEDGER

NAME: J. E. Ayres
ADDRESS: 216 Main Street
Centerport, State 53995   TERMS: Net 30

DATE	DESCRIPTION	POST. REF.	DEBIT	CREDIT	BALANCE
Feb. 1 19X2	Sales Slip 5	SJ-2	20 00		20 00
4		CRJ-2		5 00	15 00

ACCOUNTS PAYABLE LEDGER

NAME: Weller Wholesale Company
ADDRESS: 671 Valley Street
Topeka, State 66614   TERMS: Net 30

DATE	DESCRIPTION	POST. REF.	DEBIT	CREDIT	BALANCE
Feb. 1 19X2	Invoice 649, 2/1/X2	PJ-1		1200 00	1200 00
3		CPJ-2	600 00		600 00

INDEX

A

Accountant:
  duties of, 3–4
  new plans, 42–43
Accounting:
  for cash disbursements, 94–109
  for cash receipts, 79–90
  equation, fundamental, 8, 10, 15, 30
  financial statements and, 15
Accounts:
  for assets, liabilities, and owner's equity,
      18–21
  balances of, determining, 46–49
  balancing voucher register and check
      register, 310
  chart of, 28–29, 186
  combined journal, 191–192
  drawing, transferrable, 459
  expense, 22
    journalizing, 458
    recording, 24–27
  for income and expenses, 22–27
  for individual creditors, 174
  for individual customers, 155–156
  ledger sheet, analysis, 399
  liability, 20
  mixed, 418
  nominal, 29
  owner's equity, 19
  real, 29
  ruling, 460–462
    with balances, 65–68
  standard T, 468
  valuation, 209
  (See also Bad debts)
Accounts payable, 171–182
  cash disbursements journal, 172–173
  in purchase journal, 171–172
Accounts payable ledger, 171–182
  control account, 180–181
  individual creditors' accounts, 174–175
  preparing, 187
  (See also Voucher register)
Accounts receivable, 153–168
  aging, 352–353
  and bank reconciliation statement, 126–127

  bill payment and, 153–154
  in combined journal, 192
  layaway or will-call sales, 137
  schedule, 166
  (See also Bad debts)
Accounts receivable ledger, 153–168
  control account, 166–167
  defined, 156
  posting to, 160
  preparing, 187
  sales returns and allowances, 159–160
Accrual basis, 417–418
Accrued expenses, 421–424
Accrued income, 427–429
Accrued wages payable, 273–274
Adjusted trial balance, 209
Adjustments:
  bad debt, 353
  journalizing, 454–456
  posting, 456–457
Administrative expenses, 249
Aging accounts receivable, 352–353
Allowance for bad debt (see Bad debts)
Allowances (see Sales returns and allowances,
      Purchases returns and allowances)
American Institute of Certified Public
      Accountants, statement on property
      taxes, 399
Amortization:
  defined, 382–383
  of intangibles, 388
  recording, 383–384
Analysis, 4
Analysis ledger sheet, 399
Asset(s):
  accounts, 18–21
  on balance sheet, 7–8
  current, 242–245
  disposition of, 388–390
  fundamental accounting equation, 8, 10
  intangible, amortization of, 388
  trade-in of, 390–392

B

Bad debts, 350–360
  adjustments for, 353